SAINT-SAËNS

By the same author

A Musical Peacemaker: The Life and Work of
Sir Edward German

History and Idealism: Essays, Addresses and Letters.
Robert Birley. (*Edited*)

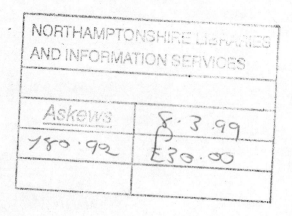

CAMILLE
SAINT-SAËNS
A Life

Brian Rees

Chatto & Windus
LONDON

Published by Chatto & Windus 1999

2 4 6 8 10 9 7 5 3 1

Copyright © Brian Rees 1999

Brian Rees has asserted his right under the Copyright,
Designs and Patents Act 1988 to be identified as
the author of this work

This edition published in Great Britain in 1999 by
Chatto & Windus
Random House, 20 Vauxhall Bridge Road
London SW1V 2SA

Random House Australia (Pty) Limited
20 Alfred Street, Milsons Point, Sydney
New South Wales 2061, Australia

Random House New Zealand Limited
18 Poland Road, Glenfield
Auckland 10, New Zealand

Random House South Africa (Pty) Limited
Endulini, 5A Jubilee Road, Parktown 2193, South Africa

Random House UK Limited Reg. No. 954009

A CIP catalogue record for this book is available from the British Library

ISBN 1 85619 773 5

Papers used by Random House UK Limited are natural,
recyclable products made from wood grown in sustainable forests.
The manufacturing processes conform to the environmental
regulations of the country of origin.

Typeset by Deltatype Ltd, Birkenhead, Merseyside

Printed and bound in Great Britain by
Creative Print and Design (Wales), Ebbw Vale

Contents

List of Illustrations

The author and the publishers are grateful to the following for permission to reproduce illustrations: Henri-Claude Boniface,

Camara, Dieppe Photo, Dieppe Bibliothèque Nationale de France, Service Reproduction.

Acknowledgements

A great deal of the music of Saint-Saëns has appeared in recent years on compact discs and tape recordings, not only by distinguished soloists and orchestras, but by groups (often young) of instrumentalists, singers and organists. But a large proportion of the pages of his operas and official cantatas must still conceal striking musical ideas and felicities of orchestration. The same is true of his life; much new material has been made available, but the base of the iceberg, hidden in correspondence and countless witty and perceptive articles has disappeared from view.

I am most grateful for the permission of Professor Jean-Michel Nectoux and the Société Francaise de Musicologie to include material from the detailed and fascinating Saint-Saëns-Fauré Correspondence, *Sixty Years of Friendship* (Heugel et Cie, 1973). Dr Barrie Jones has allowed me to quote from his very helpful *Gabriel Fauré; A Life in Letters* (Batsford, 1989) which enlarges the picture, mostly from Fauré's letters to his wife, Marie. I am equally grateful to Jeremy Nicholas for the account of the strange friendship with Godowsky related in his *Godowsky: The Pianists' Pianist* (Appian Publications, 1989). Edward Blakeman has allowed me to quote the letters from his article on Paul Taffanel in *Life and Letters* No 63, 1982. Gerald Norris's *Stanford: The Cambridge Jubilee and Tchaikowsky* (David and Charles, 1980) is a mine of information on Saint-Saëns' Honorary Doctorate, into which he has permitted me to delve freely.

No-one could fail to be indebted to Rollin Smith's *Saint-Saëns and the Organ* (Pendragon Press, New York) with its detail and anecdotes. Also to Dr Michael Stegemann's pioneering *Saint-Saëns and the Solo French Concerto* (Scolar Press, translated by A. Sherwin, 1991), Michel Faure's *Music and Society: The Second Empire to the 20th*

Century (Harmoniques Flammarion, 1985) and Gerard Gefen's *Augusta Holmes: L'Outranciere* (Pierre Belfond, 1987).

Individual thanks are owing to Jaques and Monique Lay of Louveciennes, Priscilla Thomas of Christie's Rare Books Dept, Professor Robert Orledge, and Dr Gerald Gifford. Help for embarking on the project was given by Alan Duncan, M.P., Rodolphe d'Erlanger of the D'Erlanger Trust and Maurice de Bunsen. For hospitality I should like especially to thank Mme Francoise Seignier of Meudon, Paris, and Mr and Mrs Robert Pelly of Fulbourn, Cambridge.

Professor Yves Gerard, a great Saint-Saëns scholar, was unfailingly encouraging from the outset. To Mme Catherine Massip of the Bibliothèque Nationale, Dept of Music, Mlle Blavette and her colleagues in the Institut Gustave Mahler, Mr Pierre Ickiewicz and the staff of the Musée Saint-Saëns, Dieppe, and the Renoir Insitut of Dieppe, which also provided valuable information, I am most grateful.

For help with the kind of French demanded by the more exalted institutions of France, the assistance of Denis Ogan was essential. For help in puzzling out Saint-Saëns' often invented words and expressions, two of my kind neighbours in Flore, John Levell and Wendy Pitman, spent much time. In helping to type the early chapters, Miss Tracy Gunner of Lewis Silkin spent many hours. By his expertise with word-processing, Len Gully achieved great things in collating my text and comments. Penelope Hoare bravely commissioned the work. Thanks to her and all others who have worked on it at Chatto and Windus especially Ilsa Yardley and Stuart Williams.

My wife, Juliet, has shared many hours with the music of Saint-Saëns and the fascinations of his career. Her responses to my comments have greatly enhanced the writing of this work.

Brian Rees,
Flore,
November 1998

Cypresses and Laurels

Late in the night of 16 December 1921 Camille Saint-Saëns, patriarch of French music, died in the arms of a faithful manservant at the Hôtel de l'Oasis in Algiers. He was eighty-six years of age, but his vitality had remained astonishing; his talents appeared to draw upon some unfailing elixir. The end had now come and it may safely be said that no composer has ever been laid to rest with greater pomp or solemnity. Algiers at this time, far from being a Moslem stronghold, bore the stamp of a French provincial city. As a holder of the Grand Cross of the Legion of Honour, Saint-Saëns was entitled to full military honours and, throughout the night, while musicians from the Opéra were roused from their sleep, troops were assembled from the barracks and formed into detachments to escort the body to the Cathedral. In the presence of the Governor-General, the Archbishop of Algiers conducted the service. Players and singers from the Opéra performed Saint-Saëns's *Marche Héroïque* and 'Ave Verum'; the leading cellist paid tribute with a rendering of 'The Swan', the only published fragment of *Carnival of the Animals*.

Then, to the sounds of Beethoven's *Eroica*, the cortège, escorted by squadrons of cavalry, Chasseurs d'Afrique, Zouaves, Senegalese and companies of infantry, moved towards the Port, where the coffin was placed upon the *Lamoricière* for the overseas return to France. The vessel reached Marseilles on 21 December. Civic dignitaries were massed by the quayside, supported by hussars, colonial troops and a great concourse of the public, which followed the procession from the harbour to the Gare St Charles. On the 22nd the coffin was taken from the Gare de Lyon in Paris to the Madeleine, where in earlier days Saint-Saëns had been famed as greatest among the great organists of France. The Chamber of Deputies swiftly voted a sum of 40,000 francs to ensure the splendour of the State Funeral. The imposing façade of the Madeleine was hung with black draperies fringed with silver, and two battalions of infantry and a squadron of the Republican Guard were stationed in the boulevards and across the place de la Concorde to hold back the populace. From earliest dawn on Christmas Eve the iron gates of the church were besieged and, despite a stringent issue of invitations, every gallery and recess in the huge building overflowed with spectators. The composer's own wishes on his funeral had been brief and caustic: 'If my obsequies are religious, I desire that the Office should be short and *I forbid* anyone to play "Pie Jesus" [known under the name of "Air of Stradella"]' – a final lunge at the fitting of pious words to popular melodies. The ceremony, in fact, was far from short. Cardinal Dubois, Archbishop of Paris, led the worship before representatives of the President, the Chamber, the Diplomatic Corps, the Institut, the Préfectures and all things musical and artistic in the capital. Saint-Saëns's pupil Eugène Gigout was at the organ and the Chorus and Orchestra of the Société des Concerts of the Conservatoire performed pieces by Charles Gounod, the 'Adagio' of Saint-Saëns's Organ Symphony, extracts from his *Requiem*, works by another pupil, Gabriel Fauré, and his own (indisputably authentic) 'Pie Jesus'. The church was lit by flares and torches, and once again the *Marche Héroïque* was invoked as the procession moved to the lofty silver hearse drawn by six black horses, and the several carriages needed to contain his orders and decorations. Among the clusters of operatic stars and concert artists we may be sure that many eyes rested upon one figure, chief mourner, a veiled lady in black, the widow whom the composer had banished from his life for forty years and who incarnated certain mysteries of the personality that was no more.

In the gathering winter darkness at the cemetery of Montparnasse a series of tributes were declaimed. No powers of invention were needed to recall Saint-Saëns's brilliance and overflowing talents. In the name of dramatic composers, Alfred Bruneau[1] described the deceased as last of the great line of classical composers: one who had moved among all genres with the consummate ease of Mozart or Beethoven. Those who had heard him interpret the giants of the past on pianoforte and organ could alone understand the passion with

---

[1] Bruneau, in harness with Emile Zola, wrote operas with a social and political message. George Bernard Shaw thought him a finer composer than Saint-Saëns.

which he fought to preserve his classic inheritance. When he sat down at the keyboard, one had the impression that the composer of the sonata or concerto had come back to life and substituted himself for the artist. Embarking on a theme that appealed to many of the orators, Bruneau observed that the music of Saint-Saëns best expressed the character of France: the clarity, the finesse, the loyalty, the vigour and the impeccable sense of form and style.

A M. Joubert, President of the Society of Authors and Publishers, and a M. M. Harcourt, President of the Society of Men of Letters, both dwelt upon the vast erudition of the departed Master, his discoursing upon all manner of subjects with the authority of the Encyclopaedists, and his enormous and witty correspondence. The former also mentioned unexpectedly Saint-Saëns's friendship with the Royal House of Belgium, 'an alliance realised in the realms of art long before it was forged in the necessities of war'. He remembered himself hearing the *Danse Macabre* played upon the famous Carillon at Bruges.

Photographs of the gathering show us the group around the family vault; bearded and black-coated men from official institutions. The subject of their eloquence would not have wished them to endure prolonged oratory in extreme temperatures. He had, long before, complained to his piano-duet partner, Caroline de Serres, that he had seen Ambroise Thomas, Director of the Conservatoire, enduring the summer heat at the burial of Victor Massé. 'He appeared greatly afflicted and I suffered to see him in this horrible heat climbing the slopes which led to the cemetery. It is absurd for the demands of etiquette to expose the health of a man of his age and importance.' Heat was not a problem on 24 December; the speeches continued bravely in the biting cold. Charles-Marie Widor, Secretary of the Academy of Fine Arts, lamented the occasion as a 'national bereavement'. Each work by Saint-Saëns, said Widor, had its own character and *raison d'être*. Together they formed a building in which elegance was achieved by simplicity of means and proportion of line. One of Saint-Saëns's final joys, as a lover of classical art, had been to conduct his Symphonic Poem, *The Youth of Hercules*, at the base of the Acropolis, enunciating its theme of duty triumphing over excess. As a member of the Institut, the composer had been ever conscious of his duties, punctual at meetings, examinations and competitions. 'The man is no more, but living and glorious; his thought hovers above the world and will continue to do so as long as orchestras and instrumentalists endure.'

Gigout, Professor of Organ at the Conservatoire, had wished to speak on behalf of ex-pupils of the Niedermeyer School, but he was too overcome with emotion and was unable to proceed. The final oration was made by the Minister of Education and Fine Arts on behalf of the government and people. He expressed his admiration for the long career and the achievements which drew strength from the national heritage. The profoundest explanation of Saint-Saëns's genius was that he was a French artist. 'In his works there breathes something of the grace, the charm, the smiling beauty of our country. And thus by music, which is an international language, Saint-Saëns was one of the great forces of light which spread and made loved the French soul by the whole world.' Despite its political assumptions, the Minister's speech was eloquent. He spoke of the composer's long life, which surpassed in years of creativity 'the span normally accorded by Fate to Genius'.[1] Within the last month Saint-Saëns had been supervising rehearsals of his *Ascanio* at the Opéra, full of energy, sometimes impatient, but accompanying the singers at the piano with a delicacy of touch and a sureness of rhythm that many a young virtuoso might envy. Yet in a different age he had played in the salon of King Louis Philippe. His fame rested upon all forms of music, from that which was severe and noble to the lightest of fantasies. 'Even in a ceremony where we are face to face with the mystery of death, it would be to trace an unfaithful portrait and diminish him, not to speak of his wit and fantasy in music.' In a suite which he did not wish to publish, as it was only a fantastic jest, we find a page penetrated with emotion and reverie: 'It evokes a countryside uncertain, indistinct in the mist, where there glides on the pale softness of the silvery water a swan which is about to die and breathes its swan-song'. Having paid tribute to the diversity of Saint-Saëns's talents, his love of science and history, his tireless travels which enriched his music with impressions of countries still scarcely known, his meditations on lost civilisations glimpsed in Egypt, Greece and the Indies, and on the philosophies, myths and religions to which the spirit of Man had responded throughout the ages, the Minister praised the writer, the polemicist,

[1] 'The childhood of Mozart: the old age of Titian' was the graphic phrase of a colleague at the Institut.

'gifted as Voltaire had been with unexpectedness and diversity'. When his letters were published they would complement his writings; the lively conversations he held on paper would reverberate through time as they had done through space in those periods when he sought the tranquillity of far-off solitudes. 'He will continue to be one of the greatest advocates of Graeco-Latin and French culture.'

In his magisterial survey, *French Music from the Death of Berlioz to the Death of Fauré* (1951), Martin Cooper recorded the death of Saint-Saëns with the dismissive epitaph: 'In 1921, Saint-Saëns died, full of years and malice.' After the praise and prophecies quoted above, the phrase comes as an alerting shock. Few composers have suffered so swift a passage from acclaim to neglect as this 'incarnation of the French genius', whose craftsmanship was ignored in the search for the sublime and the solemn. In the 1940s Sir Thomas Beecham was castigated in the *Musical Times* for including such 'meretricious pieces' as the *Rouet d'Omphale* in his programmes. In Saint-Saëns's centenary year, 1935, the same publication regretted that the talents of the organist Marcel Dupré had been 'squandered' on the Organ Symphony 'in the general din'. The characteristics which the funeral tributes praised were regarded by Mr Cooper as deficiencies of French music in general: 'To seek in French music primarily for a revelation of the composer's soul or for marks of the sublime is to look for something which the French consider a by-product ... Music has remained in France longer than elsewhere the art of arranging sounds in agreeable and intellectually satisfying patterns ...'

Once, visiting the ruins of Pompeii, Saint-Saëns had sought a quiet corner and, as he said, 'wept' over the erasing tides of time that obliterate civilisations and human achievements. He might well have been reflecting upon the destiny of his own work which, only fifty years after his death, bore comparison with the defunct relics of the once bustling Pompeii. In 1971 a successor of Widor at the Secretariat of the Academy of Fine Arts, Emmanuel Bondeville, announced a lecture on 'Saint-Saëns, a little-known great composer'. He asked why the impression was one of an old curmudgeon, repulsing all novelty, a musician gifted with technical facility but lacking in deep feeling. He had, said Bondeville, contributed to this image by advertising himself as a man of fixed views and by rejecting the kinds of music which he had once admired, a sure method of creating enemies. For in the first part of his life he had been a courageous defender of 'modern' music, music disdained by the public and attacked by the critics. He had allied himself with adventurous composers such as Berlioz and Liszt who were the subjects of bitter onslaughts. He had imposed the unfamiliar Piano Concerto of Alexis de Castillon upon an audience which barracked him with hoots and whistles. His own works had been scorned. The critic Escudier had joked: 'It is necessary to have a sixth sense to understand it.' Yet he was now remembered only as the implacable enemy of Debussy, Stravinsky and all the champions of experiment, whom he had compared to political anarchists who were throwing bombs indiscriminately around Paris. Even later, when it was suggested to the musicologist Michel Faure that he might include Saint-Saëns in a survey of significant French composers, Faure admitted that (mistakenly) he had regarded Saint-Saëns as a 'sunken vessel from which only two or three masts protruded above the water-line'.

Paris, now, has its place Igor Stravinsky adjacent to the church of St Merri, where Saint-Saëns was once organist. He would not have enjoyed the juxtaposition. A place Leonard Bernstein is under consideration, but there is no place Saint-Saëns. He is not named in the cramped but prestigious network of streets that surround the Opéra, although minor composers such as Nicolas Dalayrac have their names recorded. There is a rue Saint-Saëns, but it is not sited to attract the notice of foreign visitors, as, for example, is the place Colette adjoining the Comédie-Française. The publication of his brilliant correspondence to which the mourners looked forward never took place, although this was partly because of restrictions he himself imposed.[1] Some of it now rests in the Institut Gustav Mahler, of all composers perhaps the one whose aesthetics are remotest from his own.[2] A recent study of repertoires of provincial opera houses in France shows that Saint-Saëns comes between thirtieth and fortieth in

---

[1] At the Musée Saint-Saëns at Dieppe, publication of the letters from other composers is currently being prepared. Professor Yves Gérard had already catalogued over 2000 letters out of the 15,000 held at the Museum and the current Director, M. Pierre Ickowicz, is keen that modern technology should be employed to hasten the progress of making the documents available.

[2] The Princess Metternich, earlier a champion of Richard Wagner, tried in her old age to convert Saint-Saëns to Mahler but did not succeed. He declared himself bored by Anton Bruckner.

the tables of performances given, and that solely by the enduring popularity of *Samson and Delilah*. Of *Ascanio, Proserpine* or *Etienne Marcel* there is no trace. A glance through a week's programme for radio's 'France Musique' – perhaps an unlucky week – failed to uncover the name of Saint-Saëns at all.

Leaving aside the abuse thrown at him in his early years, Saint-Saëns was no stranger to criticism even at his most eminent. Together with the normal jealousies of fellow composers (in 1877 Edouard Lalo wrote to a friend: 'As for the Durand firm[1] it is always the same thing; they make me no proposal since at the place de la Madeleine there is only Saint-Saëns whose least trifles are immediately published') he endured the persistent dislike of the partisans of César Franck, perpetuated by Franck's biographers. In England, George Bernard Shaw was a particularly virulent critic, making the familiar accusations of plagiarism and saying that, if one subtracted Bach, Meyerbeer and Gounod from the scores, one would find 'nothing but graceful knick-knacks, barcarolles, serenades, ballets and the like'. Shaw praised a lady pianist, Beatrice Langley, who, by including Nils Gade in her programme, 'showed some spirit and common sense by giving the eternal Saint-Saëns a rest'.

There were reservations concerning his supremacy in French music even as he was laid to rest. Pierre Lalo, son of the composer, while praising his facility, felt obliged to add:

If he is truly the descendant of the Great Masters he is not, however, their equal, and above all not that of a Mozart. Craft and technique have taken too great a place with him: there was lacking to him that which makes the genius of Mozart, the 'shining forth' of the idea, the ardour and beauty of emotion. His melodic ideas are ordinarily neither very personal, very prominent, nor very significant, and emotion is rare in his elegant and brilliant music; he always appears to attach less importance to what is said than the manner of saying it.

With much of this Saint-Saëns would not have disagreed. His

[1] Publishers. The Durand great-grandfather had walked from the Auvergne to Paris to make his fortune. Auguste Durand, founder of the publishing firm, was himself an organist, composer and a friend of Saint-Saëns at the Conservatoire.

veneration for Mozart was lifelong. He remembered as a boy defending *The Marriage of Figaro* against Rossini's *Barber of Seville*, which was thought superior at the time. The composer Paul Dukas declared that no one had ever heard the piano works of Mozart to perfection unless they had heard them played by Saint-Saëns. As for 'emotion in music', he theorised, in contrast to his own practice, that it was undesirable and could be pernicious.

Camille Mauclair in the *Courrier Musical*, while thanking 'the clement Gods' for granting Saint-Saëns the 'two supreme benefits: a lucid old age and a sudden death' and having admitted that he had brought honour to France in other lands for seventy years ('If the foreigner asks us to name our most glorious musician we reply: "Saint-Saëns'"), gave as his opinion: 'Genius accepts other laws. Genius dares at certain times the risk of making a basic mistake or of joining together at a single leap the sublime and the banal. Genius sees the end: intelligence prevents the fall. The mind of Saint-Saëns was so made that he had a horror of the immoderate, of the obscure, even if it harbours a prestigious light, of the tentative, of the adventure counselled by the demon within ... No lyric transport, in his eyes, ought to escape from the rules, from craftsmanship, from the prerequisite supremacy of beautiful form.' In *Le Ménestrel* Jean Chantavoine, Secretary of the Conservatoire, later Saint-Saëns's biographer, who as a young man had heard him play extracts from his *Proserpine* at the home of some friends and draw the most beautiful sounds from a most ordinary piano, divined a reticence and absence of striving:

[He] is not perhaps of all our musicians the one who has most loved music. He has not sought it out like Rameau with the dogged persistence of the inventor. It has not snatched from him cries nor inflicted tortures, as on Berlioz, nor ecstasies as on Gounod. Perhaps Debussy has tasted it with keener refinement. But it is he who has lived it the most. The thought of Saint-Saëns propelled itself in music as does that of ordinary folk in their native language – a tongue sometimes made for poetry, for drama, for speculation, for eloquence, but also made for the most ordinary discussions and does not demean itself in knowing and satisfying these needs.

By the time that the centenary of his birth was reached in 1935, although the President, Albert Lebrun, attended an anniversary concert, these reservations had become more positive charges. In *La Revue Musicale*[1] a Robert Bernard deplored recent comparisons with Racine. 'This artist without passion, incapable of raising himself to truly pathetic grandeur – who lacks the access of vigour as of serenity and who is incapable of choosing among his too numerous ideas –' would never share a throne with the great dramatist. As for being the representative of his native genius, this could never be justified by sentimental tepidness, academic elegance, search for the well-fashioned, the preoccupation with style. Saint-Saëns possessed the gift of chatting amiably in company, 'discourses spangled with familiar phrases, with polished scales and glittering arpeggios, all vain sound which obeys no interior laws'. One could not deny that the orchestration was infallible, just as were the polyphonic techniques. 'If the absence of faults constitutes the touchstone of genius, Bach himself could only bow before Saint-Saëns.' Having declared himself willing to surrender all Saint-Saëns's works for a 'single page' of the *St Matthew Passion, Don Giovanni*, or even *Boris Godunov* ('Can one assess the worth of music by its power to synthesise aspects of the people's culture? Must "Jacques Bonhomme" be accounted greater than the exception – the Villon, Stendhal, or Baudelaire?'), Bernard finds in Saint-Saëns only that which satisfies the bourgeoisie: 'The art of a nation comes from the great exceptions rather than the middle-class ideals and that of Saint-Saëns is based not upon a balance of opposites but rather on the principle – honest enough – of the "just mean".' By the same token Felix Mendelssohn could be regarded as the 'guardian of the inner light of the Germanic musical soul'.

Jean Chantavoine's biography in 1947 dwelt principally upon the major works – *Samson and Delilah* and the Third Symphony – both the fruits of long meditation and hence superior to much that was, by inference, rapidly conceived. Fecundity, admired in J. S. Bach, Haydn, or Schubert, seemed to be at variance with excellence in the case of Saint-Saëns. In Britain, James Harding's *Saint-Saëns and his Circle*, written with all the author's extensive knowledge of French culture, re-created the milieu in which the composer worked but was not a plea for a revaluation of musical currency.

[1] This journal gave special attention to the death of Vincenzo Bellini in the year of Saint-Saëns's birth, 1835, a feature which would not have pleased him, as he despised the cult of mere 'melody' in the Italian tradition.

In recent years knowledge of his output has at least begun to move from its rigid permanence in the area of the *Carnival of the Animals*, the *Danse Macabre* and the Second Piano Concerto. There have been recordings of two previously unheard and un-numbered symphonies. Enterprising young instrumentalists have recorded a quantity of smaller-scale works and distinguished soloists the piano and violin concertos. The performance of the opera *Henry VIII* at Compiègne, even upon a stage that did not permit grandiose effects, proved that the image of Saint-Saëns's stage works as undramatic was incorrect. Many years before, Reynaldo Hahn had defended him against the charge that he lacked a theatrical sense. 'That comes from the fact that, perhaps wrongly – but one may sometimes be right in being wrong – he brought to his theatrical works the same care for Form, the same intellectual control and – it is his greatest crime in the eyes of the multitude – the same finesse of taste as to his chamber or concert music.' While regretting Saint-Saëns's attraction towards historical subjects, he asserted that *Ascanio* – 'very stupidly described as a Meyerbeerian opera since it is the single French opera, alone with those of M. d'Indy, constructed after the Wagnerian system – is truly marvellous, similar in character, colour and ornamentation to an art-work of the Renaissance. It offers an incomparable model of lyric declamation, so just the accents, so completely is the psychology perfectly traced.' Across the Atlantic there have been many academic studies of his output. In France, Professors Jean-Michel Nectoux and Yves Gérard have restored a share of his lost esteem. Nectoux, while admitting that Saint-Saëns made a speciality of mixing styles, epochs and civilisations and that he produced fewer great works as his reputation advanced, has noted his affinities with the developing style of Fauré and the favour with which Maurice Ravel looked even upon some of Saint-Saëns's more popular compositions. 'Saint-Saëns', he concludes, 'is so diverse a musician that one does not know how to grasp him in one synthetic view.' Michel Faure, who had regarded the composer as a 'sunken vessel', declares that on closer study of the Master, he moved with astonishment from amusement to 'marvelling'.

If, as a young man, Saint-Saëns was condemned as a supporter of 'modern' music, as an old man he was depicted as an arch-reactionary, a latter-day Luigi Cherubini frozen in retrograde classicism, prophesying the doom of serious music. In certain respects his opinions have been proved correct and much of twentieth-century composition represents a wasteland, which the average listener shrinks from exploring. In criticising the immoderate adulation of Wagner in France, however, in scorning the well-marshalled cohorts under the command of Vincent d'Indy, who extolled the greatness of César Franck, and by seeking to deflate the reputation of Claude Debussy he invited a great deal of reciprocal condemnation. He remarked that he 'produced music as an apple tree produces apples' but it has to be said that, by his combats in print, he also produced irritation as a thorn bush produces thorns. The heat engendered by these controversies lingered. Francis Poulenc even blamed Saint-Saëns for the poor official attendance at Franck's funeral, where the Ministry of Fine Arts and the Conservatoire were unrepresented. 'Probably Saint-Saëns was responsible for much of this indescribable attitude,' he declares, although Saint-Saëns himself took part in the ceremony as one of the pallbearers. Poulenc recalled that, as a youth of eighteen, he had written to various musicians asking their opinions on Franck. From Saint-Saëns he received the following reply:

Dear Sir,

Perhaps the same will happen to César Franck as happened to Richard Wagner about whose music people have been asking my opinion for the last forty years. Franck had great talent and I myself gave him a chance to display it by persuading Jules Simon, then Minister of Fine Arts, to give him the organ classes at the Conservatoire, which had been offered to me. This meant that Franck no longer had to waste his time giving piano lessons to earn his living and was able to concentrate on composition. It was made out that his great talent amounted to genius. I entertained no such notion. But in spite of questionnaires, César Franck by now belongs to posterity. In the last resort it will be posterity which judges whether he deserves a crown of gold or silver.

With my sincere good wishes.
    CSS.

Saint-Saëns and Franck shared a dislike of much that was superficial in French music and sentimental in religious music. But Saint-Saëns did not approve of a 'school' of music, where too many people wrote under similar influences, or of the teaching in the Schola Cantorum, a

religious rival to the Conservatoire, where a serious Jansenist spirit
prevailed, and where adherence to certain rules of composition was
stressed by d'Indy and others. He did not approve of Franck's desire to
see music leading people to religion. At the Schola Cantorum, d'Indy
taught an intimate connection between art and religion, not as a
vaguely mystical thing but as full-blooded Catholicism, which was
asserting itself in political groups such as the Action Française against
the Republic. Saint-Saëns also admired the work of Giacomo
Meyerbeer and therefore could not but dislike the anti-Semitism that
was a feature of d'Indy's outlook. The Schola Cantorum gravely
established provincial academies to try and break down the division
between artistic coteries and the people. Yet Saint-Saëns in his
innumerable concert tours, his piano and organ recitals in every region
of France, his many compositions for choral societies and his labours
on behalf of popular festivals had been singled-handedly carrying on
such a campaign for decades.

He also carried a torch for Charles Gounod, for whom the
Franckists had small affection. As a rationalist and much travelled man
of the world he had a suspicion of Franck's unworldliness, which the
Franckists contrasted with the worldly and sensual predilections of
Gounod. Writing to his friend Camille Bellaigue from Algeria in
December 1912, he said of Gounod: 'Formerly, the critics were hostile
to him. They reproached him with not being a melodist and preferred
Donizetti; now they reproach him with being too much so and prefer
Franck, to whom lacks the charm, the spirit, the grace more beautiful
than beauty ... In truth, Franck was not naïve but he established a
reputation for naïveté and made it believable.' He would not have
been pleased to read in Martin Cooper that 'César Franck is probably
still the most highly rated French composer among the ordinary
concert-going public in England', for this was a position he cherished
with pride himself. After 1871 he came to London almost every year,
wrote his Third Symphony for the Philharmonic Society, his cantata
La Lyre et la Harpe for the Birmingham Festival and the oratorio *The
Promised Land* for the Three Choirs Festival. His Honorary Doctor-
ates from Cambridge and Oxford, and the testimony he received from
a phalanx of famous British musicians, were matters of high importance to him. Among his numerous encounters with European royalty
he recalled with particular pleasure his meetings with Queen Victoria,
who requested Covent Garden (unsuccessfully as it transpired) to

mount his opera *Etienne Marcel*, and with Queen Alexandra, who had poured out his tea with her own hand and rushed forward to open the piano lid for his performance. When Watson Lyle produced an English biography of Saint-Saëns in the 1920s he could observe that the themes of the B minor Violin Concerto were so well known that they did not need to be quoted.

If he limited the fervour with which he approached the music of Franck, he also invited rebuffs from the dazzled admirers of Debussy and called into play an opponent as acerbic as himself. It was Debussy, in reviews which appeared in the *Revue Blanche* and *Gil Blas*, who sneered at the prolixity of Saint-Saëns and the apparent stagnation of his style. Of Saint-Saëns's opera *Les Barbares* Debussy, alias 'Monsieur Croche', declared: 'I am sorry to see how difficult it is to keep one's respect for an artist who was once filled with enthusiasm and a thirst for pure glory. I hate sentimentality! But I wish I could forget his name is Camille Saint-Saëns.' It should be remembered, however, that only five years before, when Debussy was much depressed by set-backs, he met Saint-Saëns on a Channel ferry. Although they had already had disagreements, Saint-Saëns greeted the younger man cordially and presented him to Sir Hubert Parry at the Royal College of Music in the hope that some practical results for Debussy's career would ensue.

The rift went back to the days Debussy spent at the Villa Medici in Rome after winning the Prix de Rome for composition. The recipients were expected to send back to Paris some fruits of their studies. Debussy's appeared to show a disregard for the teaching he had received at the Conservatoire. In 1886 the *Journal Officiel*, having praised the pieces sent back by two colleagues, Paul Vidal and Gabriel Pierné, expressed its disappointment that the winner of the 1884 competition, M. Debussy, had not developed the melodic and dramatic gifts which had gained him the prize. 'The Academy regrets to have to state a totally contrary result. M. Debussy seems tormented by a desire to do the bizarre, the incomprehensible, the unplayable. In spite of some passages which do not lack a certain character, the vocal part of this work offers no interest either from a melodic point of view or that of declamation. The Academy wishes to hope that time and experience will bring in the ideas and works of M. Debussy salutary modifications.' It is believed that Saint-Saëns had collaborated in drawing up these censures, for several months before he had delivered a paper to the combined Academies on the 'Past, Present and Future of Music', which had expressed his misgivings about the deliberate rejection of the characteristics of form and notation as practised in Europe for over a century and sanctified by the usage of the Great Masters. Debussy, by contrast, represented a move against the 'oratorical' elements in music, the repetitions, the balancing of phrases, the deliberate contrasts of mood. Significantly, he also seems to have disliked government through rhetoric and the vocabulary of socialist demagogues. He believed that certain chords, like certain words and phrases, had become hackneyed through over-use. Saint-Saëns, however, could still draw new impressions from the same material (as in the common chords which open the Fifth Piano Concerto).

The fact that there was much in the sensuous elements in Saint-Saëns that pointed forward to Debussy did not diminish the contrast of opinions. Yet while he was in Rome, Debussy had visited the home of Giovanni Sgambati, the pupil of Liszt, who arrived also on a surprise visit with the Cardinal de Hohenloe. The Cardinal requested some French music and the two pianists obliged with the *Beethoven* Variations of Saint-Saëns. The fact that this work was one with which he had no affinities did not prevent Debussy from retaining thirty years later a vivid memory of the performance and the impression it made upon him.[1] Debussy's second envoi from Rome in 1887 met with muted criticism, though the hand of Saint-Saëns might be noted in the comment that F sharp major is an unsuitable key for orchestral writing. (He had already made the point with regard to a passage in Franck's *Rédemption* in 1873.) It was in this year that Debussy came to London to try to interest the publishers in his work. He was unsuccessful and could only note in *Le Ménestrel* a comment by his friend Franz Hueffer that French music was ignored in England save for the works of Hector Berlioz, Gounod and Saint-Saëns, 'who anyway has more affinity with the German genius'.

Despite the great difference in their backgrounds and personalities the two men shared many views. Both had a great admiration for Rameau (although Debussy did not share Saint-Saëns's fondness for

[1] In his young days Debussy had made piano arrangements of extracts from Saint-Saëns's opera *Etienne Marcel* (whom he described as a 'former municipal councillor'). He also arranged the *Rondo Capriccioso* and Second Symphony for two pianos.

the declamatory style of Gluck), both came to have a powerful dislike of Wagner's propagandist methods, if not his genius, and Debussy was also suspicious of d'Indy and the Franckists: 'To my mind the enthusiasm of a "Circle" spoils an artist for I dread his becoming eventually the mere expression of his circle.'

But Debussy contended that Saint-Saëns had wasted the opportunities to lead young musicians into more adventurous paths. He wrote in *Gil Blas*: 'Saint-Saëns knows more about music than any other man in the whole world. His profound knowledge of music has moreover prevented him from ever subjecting it to his own personal desires. He must be defined as the musician of tradition. [He] lost the respect of all those young people who counted ardently on him to open new paths, to satisfy their longing for freedom and the open air.' He could not understand Saint-Saëns's fascination with historical opera. 'Surely the Almighty in his liberality has placed innumerable opera makers on earth! Saint-Saëns was not needed to swell their number. Moreover, his example could only encourage their odious trade. It is a pity.' In the unkindest cut of all Debussy suggested that, as Saint-Saëns was so famously addicted to travel, he should abandon composition and take up the profession of explorer.

It was Saint-Saëns's determination to prevent Debussy's election to the Institut which has enraged the Debussyists most profoundly. The move of Widor to the post of Perpetual Secretary to the Institut in 1914 left a vacancy in the Academy of Fine Arts, and several voices were raised in favour of overlooking the 'unrespectful' offerings made to the Academy by the former Prix de Rome winner and welcoming him into their midst. Léon Vallas, Debussy's biographer, describes Saint-Saëns's opposition as 'deaf and tenacious ... a reactionary without mercy and the implacable enemy of his illustrious colleague', and records how proceedings were delayed until death removed Debussy from the contest. Marcel Dupré relates an anecdote of how Saint-Saëns one day swept into Widor's office, drew him towards the piano and ordered him to turn the pages. He unfurled a roll of music and proceeded to play with all the virtuosity at his command. From time to time he nudged Widor scornfully: 'You like that, do you? You could vote for it?' Widor's magnificently diplomatic reply was: 'You have played it in such a fashion that you have obliged me to fall in love with it.' These were the Studies of Debussy. Such episodes, according

to Vallas, did not detract from the glory of Debussy, but robbed the
Institut of the glory it might have enjoyed.[1]

One is bound to admit that it would have been more generous of
Saint-Saëns to have stood aside. Yet it must be remembered that,
despite the popular perceptions, few composers were more generous
to colleagues than he. He provided Widor himself with an opening as
an organist-composer at a Lisbon Festival, he used his success with
Henry VIII at the Paris Opéra to gain a commission for the unhappy
André Messager: the ballet *The Two Pigeons*. Thanks to his advocacy,
two young winners of the Prix Rossini had their works played at the
Conservatoire. His guidance and generous assistance to Fauré saved
the handsome, dreamy young man from drifting into obscurity as a
provincial choirmaster and raised him to be the Director of the
Conservatoire. Alone among those on whom Liszt lavished time and
wealth, he tried to repay the debt by giving at his own expense a
concert of Liszt's orchestral works in Paris. One could extend the list.
His opposition to Debussy in the Institut was based upon principles,
even if history has proved these mistaken. Although the laws of art and
music cannot claim divine origin and must be susceptible to change
and the flow of ideas, they do not benefit from revolution as opposed
to evolution any more than laws in the State.

Saint-Saëns also saw the dangers that lurked in Debussy's proposi-
tion that music came mysteriously out of the ether, the 'longing for
freedom and the open air' referred to above. In speaking of
Beethoven, Debussy had remarked that the Master does not demand
that we follow in his footsteps slavishly: 'Rather would he invite us to
look through open windows to the clear sky.' Saint-Saëns might well
doubt the integrity of Debussy, especially urban and Parisian, extolling
the merits of nature. He had himself revelled in nature since
childhood visits to Champagne and he knew well the scenic beauties of
France. He had infused the rhythms and sounds of Arab cities from
Algeria to Egypt into his work. He had traversed the Atlantic,
Mediterranean and Indian Oceans, and knew more of the phonic
properties of the sea than any other musician before his time. Yet he

---

[1] It seems unlikely that Saint-Saëns alone could have influenced the
procedures of so large and eminent a body. Some years earlier he had failed
to exclude Gustave Charpentier and it required huge efforts to secure Fauré's
admission.

did not believe that these impressions could be conveyed without a rigorous translation into forms that were accessible.

Debussy was openly élitist. 'Are we not correct in affirming', says Michel Faure, 'that Saint-Saëns has been the victim of "music lovers" to whom music serves only as a means of distinguishing themselves from the herd?'

There must be a case for Saint-Saëns, who could at the same time write fastidious chamber music, serious opera and organ works, which rival in architectural splendour the preludes and fugues of Bach, and also make music open and enjoyed by the ordinary citizen. At the performances of his *Déjanire* in the arena at Béziers, Saint-Saëns was cheered to the skies by crowds whose numbers many a modern football club might envy. In the days of the silent cinema, whatever the nature of the film, his music accounted for twenty per cent of the background scores. In the cafés and the restaurants where orchestras played, in France and America, his share of the programmes was similarly high. He gave concerts up and down France, often in industrial towns to audiences that had no experience of fashionable salons. By contrast, Debussy had expensive private tastes which coloured his views on musical appreciation. 'One can no more order the crowd to love beauty than one could decently demand that they should walk on their hands,' declared 'Monsieur Croche'. Though Saint-Saëns was always interested in new inventions, Debussy was fearful of the newly created 'phonograph' lest it should make art 'too democratic'.[1]

It is more important to view Saint-Saëns in relation to his own abilities and achievements than simply as an adversary of other creative artists: Franck, Debussy, or Jules Massenet. He was founder, along with fellow composer Alexis de Castillon and Romain Bussine, Professor of Singing at the Conservatoire, of the Société Nationale, the group which encouraged native-born French composers and, more than any other institution, inspired the great efflorescence of French music around the turn of the century. At this society he not only encouraged composition, but acted indefatigably as accompanist to songs, participated in the chamber pieces and joined in the two-piano renderings of orchestral works. He was a brilliant sight-reader, who, as

[1] Debussy was also opposed to programme notes (which Saint-Saëns had helped to introduce from England, for the Third Symphony) and thought they would be useless to the masses.

a young man, had amazed Wagner by playing the scores of *Lohengrin* and *Tristan* so as to give an impression of orchestral effects. When Louis Diémer was prevented from joining him in a two-piano version of Liszt's *Les Préludes*, Saint-Saëns simply put both scores on the piano and gave a combined version. Hans von Bülow was startled by his mastery of Schumann's symphonies, scarcely known in France at the time. His memory was without rival. Pierre Lalo told the tale of how Saint-Saëns once arrived at the home of his father and asked how progress was going on the latter's symphony. Edouard protested that he was not writing a symphony, whereupon Saint-Saëns sat down at the piano and played long stretches of a work which Lalo had long since discarded. At his first concert, at the age of eleven, he not only surprised the audience by playing from memory – the practice was not common at the time – but offered to give as an encore any of the Beethoven sonata. At over sixty he repeated the offer at a concert to the musical elect of Madrid. When the cellist Hollmann left the complex piano part of a cello sonata in a taxi just before the first performance, he wrote it out again from memory without any apparent difficulty.

His talents, unlike those of many child prodigies, never faded and he maintained a regime of practice to the end. Although he expressed a wish to retire many times, his last concert was at eighty-five in Dieppe and, to the end, he could still give a wonderful performance of Liszt's *Fountains at the Villa d'Este*. Professor Gérard places him as a pianist among the greatest of the nineteenth century, along with Liszt and Anton Rubinstein. In an age of great French organists he was the acknowledged master. Liszt himself declared that Saint-Saëns's organ transcription of his *St Francis Preaching to the Birds* was the greatest feat he had ever heard. He was able to maximise the organ's power of simulating orchestral sounds, more by natural inspiration than careful planning, for his organ works contain comparatively few instructions upon registration. 'The organ is more than an instrument; it is an orchestra,' he claimed. 'A combination of Pan's pipes of every calibre, some as tiny as a children's plaything; others as gigantic as the pillars of a temple.'

As a composer he developed in France a new approach to the concerto form in which the aim was not an empty virtuosity but symphonic development shared by orchestra and soloist in partnership. He salvaged the classical traditions of chamber music and symphony at a time when contemporaries sought success only on the operatic stage. In assessing the originality of Saint-Saëns we have to remember that, as late as the 1890s, Ambroise Thomas would not have purely instrumental composition taught at the Conservatoire. Romain Rolland praised his independence of mind:

> . . . very rare in our own day, when the power of public opinion is tyrannical, and rarest of all in France, where artists are perhaps more sociable than in other countries!
>
> He stands for something exceptional in French music, which was almost unique until lately: that is a great classical spirit and a fine breadth of musical culture – German culture we must say, since the foundation of all modern art rests on the German classics. French music of the nineteenth century is rich in clever artists, imaginative writers of melody and skilful dramatists, but it is poor in true musicians and in good and solid workmanship.

We may add to this that he was one of the first to extend his gaze overseas and in this reflected the growing colonisation of the planet by Western Europe. Wherever he travelled he collected sounds, themes and impressions and, although he transmuted these into Western musical language, the result was a much greater richness of material, which later composers exploited. The Russians have been greatly praised for bringing Slavonic and Oriental ideas into music, but even Nikolay Rimsky-Korsakov admitted that he used North African themes on occasion. Saint-Saëns was, in fact, one of the first major composers also to utilise folk-song, in Brittany, in the Auvergne, Spain and Italy.

He has been accused of being too eclectic and, largely because of his own over-emphatic views, of lacking emotion. Camille Bellaigue refuted the composer directly on this latter charge by telling him of the emotional impact on audiences of both the hushed opening organ chords at the start of the Adagio of the Third Symphony and the caressing phrases of Delilah. Fauré thought that it was too summary to dismiss the emotional appeal of Saint-Saëns, as if the brain had a larger share than the heart. He spoke of listening to the orchestral works: 'To follow the curve, the progression of the ample developments, where the lines keep such neatness, acquiring such "visibility" that one could believe that one was reading them – this pleasure, could it be exempt from emotion, and would the public acclaim such works, if it were not profoundly touched?' Messager made a similar point: 'It is enough to run through his operas, even in the most deliberately historical, in order to discover each time that he is able to pour forth the outbursts of a passionate soul.' It is true that some of Saint-Saëns's themes give the feeling of being artefacts rather than bursts of untrammelled inspiration. True also that he was, from the start, deeply interested in questions of form and made many experiments with the architectural traditions of music: concertos in single or double movements in which one section might be interwoven with another, the introduction of purely fugal passages into developments or codas, the substitution of sonata form for a Scherzo, the separation of Scherzo and Trio etc. As Gounod remarked: 'Most musicians do what they can with notes; Saint-Saëns alone does what he wishes.' It is true also that he was able to emulate the styles of any of his predecessors, although one can never find instances of direct plagiarism. 'One seems to be passing through scenery that one has seen before and one loves, but one can never find resemblances,' said Romain Rolland. 'Nowhere are reminiscences more rare than with this master, who carries in his memory all the ancient masters. It is in spirit itself that he resembles them.' Gounod once remarked that 'one might as well expect a son not to have a father as a composer not to have predecessors'. His biographer, Augé de Lassus, described him as 'the twin brother of all the great composers who have been'. Another biographer, Georges Servières, asserted that from the age of twenty 'he had no need of a programme to recognise a piece by Saint-Saëns, its essence existing under the most varied forms. . . . Imitative he may sometimes have been but no one has been able to write a pastiche of Saint-Saëns.'

His cultivation of older styles was always deliberate. The nineteenth century believed that it stood at the end of a great chain of progress. Scientists built upon the discoveries of their predecessors, the diverse passions for Gothic and Renaissance influenced public architecture, previous inventiveness in the arts was there to be used by the moderns. The musical historian Louis Bourgault-Ducoudray, in a speech at the Paris Exhibition of 1878, referred to his collecting folk-songs in Greece and added: 'No element of expression to be found at any time, however ancient or remote in origin, should be banished from our musical idiom – The question is not one of giving up any previous conquests but, on the contrary, of adding to them.' When Saint-Saëns wrote preludes and fugues in the form in which Bach had established them, it was his aim to make known the greatness and potentialities of this particular vehicle of expression. When he re-created the old dance forms and suites of the eighteenth century, it was a kind of homage to the refining graces of that period, in which music had become sophisticated. He developed the idea of the song-cycle. He enjoyed recalling the excitement generated by the great virtuosi of his youth in his Finales.

To the forms of older times he undoubtedly brought an unmistakable individuality, which would be clearer if his music were more widely known: the building up of themes from two or more component parts, his dislike of abruptly finishing a melody, preferring to allow it to dissolve into its elements as a snake sheds its layers of skin, the long, extended cantilenas by which he takes a theme and broadens it through a series of progressions. His mastery of the orchestra came to him early in life and certain fingerprints remained: the soft and muffled use of the kettledrums, the reliance upon the effects of the harp and the sparing use of the full orchestra. Servières wondered whether his facility for crafting musical ideas came from his maternal grandfather, who was a carpenter, accustomed to composite materials and the fashioning of objects out of inanimate matter. 'He uses the chisel rather than the mallet.' Oddly enough, Saint-Saëns wrote to Durand in 1892, when working on his Second Piano Trio: 'I write two pages of music a day. I scrape, file and chisel; it is true happiness. This is the way I began and this is the way I want to finish.' It is worth remembering also that few composers have written so frequently with a particular performer or soloist in mind, which has left us a gallery of musical portraits without equivalent in the works of the great composers.

A Child of the Bourgeois Monarchy

lthough Saint-Saëns wrote a great deal about certain episodes in his life he omitted others entirely and biographers have been left to leap from one stepping stone to another across the swirling waters. We know nothing, for example, of his experiences in the 1848 revolution, when stormy demonstrations swept the streets near his home, and he never made public his views on the Dreyfus affair which preoccupied France for a decade. He was, however, generous with information about his childhood in his memoirs of old age, *Ecole Buissonnière* (*Playing Truant*), and the picture is familiar.

He was born in Paris on 9 October 1835, in the third storey of the third house in the rue de Jardinet on the Left Bank. The name of the little closed street reminds us that the Royal Abbey of St Germain des Prés was fed and adorned by gardens and groves. He regarded himself, rightly, as a true Parisian, but he was conscious of his family roots in Normandy and Champagne. When he had occasion to point out that César Franck was actually Belgian, he used the expression that Franck 'did not come from the *soil* of France'. He accused the Germans of 'trespassing on the *soil* in France' rather than attacking the French armies. The ancient cradle of his father's family was the small town of Saint-Saens in the valley of the Varenne in Normandy, a region of farms, orchards and forests. In the Dark Ages, while Merovingian kings and queens fought one another, a monastery had been founded under the aegis of a young Irish priest who took the name of Sidonius at his baptism. Sanctified after his death, the memory of Sanctus Sidonius was kept alive by legends and relics, and by the arrival of successive waves of Benedictine and Cicerstian monks. His name, by the slow process of unwritten speech, turned into Saint-Saëns, was acquired by many families throughout the social scale and moved with them to other parts of Normandy. Devoted to the soil many of these families may have been, but from even remoter times Saint-Saëns seems to have inherited the roving instincts of the first Normans, the urge to seek out new horizons across the oceans and to blend a deep feeling for his homeland with the habits of the nomad. Even piratical figures have been suggested. The name the town gave him, alliterative and memorable, was a providential gift for an artist. A young admirer and poet, Pierre Aguétant, tell us that he had fallen in love with the name Saint-Saëns long before he heard a note of the music. 'I did not know his works, but the fascinating design of his name ... seemed predestined to have some aureole of glory. People with heavy unprepossessing names have to struggle to reach immortality.'[1] The trema on the 'e' was apparently adopted by the composer's father as a means of distinguishing his tribe from lesser breeds without it.

Victor, the composer's father, was born into a family that hovered between small farming and labouring on the land. The grandfather, Jean-Baptiste Nicholas, passed on a basic sturdiness of physique, which enabled his grandson to survive periods of serious illness. Jean-Baptiste lived to be eighty and to learn of the birth of his grandson before his own death in 1837. Relatively literate (he had a florid signature somewhat like Saint-Saëns's own), he became Mayor of the little village of Rouxmesnil, close to Dieppe. He was chosen to draft a local contribution from Arques to the famous '*cahiers*' of grievances, which accompanied the calling of the States-General and the beginnings of the French Revolution in 1789. In the dangerous times which followed, with coastal raids by the British against both the Revolution and Napoleon, and forays by government agents to seize provisions and recruits, he had to guard his tiny commune. He even had to make stalwart efforts to reserve his milk supplies for faithful customers in times of shortage, fending off attacks upon his pitchers. He survived to retire in old age to the district of Arques.

He had married Marguerite-Marie Vallet, daughter of a labourer, and they had three sons and five daughters. The boys, their experience broadened by the turmoil of the times, sought careers in wider fields. The eldest, Nicholas, became a grocer in Paris. The second, Jean-Baptiste Camille, whose name was given to the composer, entered the Church and became the curé of Neuville, Dieppe. He was highly

---

[1] Saint-Saëns somewhat scornfully attributed part of Debussy's celebrity to his euphonious name, seemingly unaware of his own advantage in this respect.

respected in the rough seafaring community, especially for his work in the cholera outbreak of 1832, and declined preferment, possibly because of a premonition of his early death at thirty-nine. Victor, like his elder brother, was drawn to Paris and entered the Ministry of the Interior as a 'copyist'. He was a young man with a talent for accountancy and he rose from the humble duties on which he was first employed to oversee the secret accounts of the Ministry. In view of his son's success with elderly patrons (Albert Libon, Postmaster General at Paris, left Saint-Saëns a substantial legacy), it is noteworthy that Victor appears to have had similar gifts. Antoine Miot, a civil servant at the head of the Ministry of Commerce, regarded Victor 'as his son' and recommended him for promotion. His own chief, a Monsieur Rougeois, shared this opinion and reported Victor as being the sole person capable of acting as deputy in his absence. Victor became Assistant Head of the Bureau, a post created for him. He had the same unstoppable facility in writing verse that his son showed in music. He wrote letters in verse to his brother Camille and other Dieppois relatives on all manner of incidents, such as the grandfather's retirement to Arques, and attempted many light comedies and poems, often on the back of official Ministry receipts. He was not a great musician (he described himself as a 'mediocre violinist' whose only gift on the instrument was to frighten people), but two of his poems had been set to music and published. In collaboration with a writer from Le Havre, Jacques Arsène Ancelot (sufficiently distinguished later to be a defeated rival of Victor Hugo in the election to the Institut), he wrote a comedy, *La Petite Maison*, which was given at the Palais-Royal after his death and he dreamed of being a stage writer.

In 1834 he married Françoise-Clémence Collin, daughter of a carpenter in Wassy in the Haute-Marne. Jean Bonnerot, the composer's secretary, who wrote the nearest thing to an 'official' biography, describes her as 'a young girl', but she was twenty-five at the time of her marriage and living in Paris as the adopted daughter of a childless uncle and aunt, M. and Mme Masson. One can only register astonishment at the haphazard circumstances that produced the only musical child prodigy who can be compared with Mozart and Mendelssohn. Both these young geniuses came from cultured and performing families, where music was a constant presence. Saint-Saëns's situation was not comparable. Charlotte Masson, his 'second mama', was herself adopted by a legal family, the Gayards, and one wonders which unknown parents parted with a girl who was the composer's first musical educator. Moreover, what circumstances obliged the Collin family in Wassy to hand over a daughter whose determination to mother and mould a genius was so strong? There was ambition in the mother's family as well as the father's. A cousin of hers, a General Delambre, had availed himself of the opportunities in Napoleon's army to rise to the top and had displayed heroism during the retreat from Moscow. General Delambre was a witness at the wedding of Saint-Saëns's parents and proudly noted as a Grand Officer of the Legion of Honour. He made a gift of Beethoven's death-mask to his young musical relative.

During the revolution the Gayards were plunged into poverty and Charlotte was forced to give lessons in reading, music, embroidery and many such accomplishments, which in turn she had to teach herself. The secrets of child education were already familiar to her when her great-nephew was born. She and her husband, Esprit Masson, owned a bookseller's establishment in the Latin quarter, but they suffered a collapse of business and, with the remnants of their capital, moved in with Victor and Clémence. The influence of the Massons may be seen in Saint-Saëns's taste for fine bindings and handsome collections of French and classical literature in his library.

The year of Saint-Saëns's birth was marked with bereavements. The Abbé Camille, a figure held in high respect in the family, died in January. Esprit Masson did not survive the shock of financial misfortune and died in March. Victor himself was dying of consumption. He announced the birth of a son to a Dieppois cousin in flippant verse, but relapsed into what he termed 'vile prose' when furnishing the details: 'Clémence has made me the father of a *"gros garçon"* on Friday at 6.45 in the morning. Mother and child are well – there were fourteen hours of suffering but the birth took place as naturally as possible. [The child] shows every determination to live. He will be baptised as soon as the mother is back to health.'

Victor had just two months in which to enjoy the joys of fatherhood and died in the last hours of the expiring year. The baptism had duly taken place at St Sulpice, but, as the doctors suspected that the child might have inherited the seeds of consumption, he was immediately removed to fresher country air and, for two years, was looked after by a foster-mother at Corbeil, then a village on the road to Fontainebleau. When he returned to Paris it was to a fatherless home sustained by the efforts of two widows. Clémence painted water-colours of flowers and birds, which were sold as a means of income. Servières suggested that the caution and lack of ferocious originality that characterise the music of Saint-Saëns might derive from the civil-service mentality and subservience to commands, which were the necessary traits of the father. We might also speculate on the origins of Saint-Saëns's preoccupation with seeking out 'father figures' in music: chiefly Rameau, Bach and Beethoven, whose legacy was something of a patrimony and upon whom he admitted falling back in imagination for inspiration. He retained a childhood love of the Old Testament, the pages of which are full of father figures and tales of patriarchal power.

He was born into a troubled country. Charles X, last of the Bourbons, had been driven from the throne in 1830. Bigoted and reactionary – so devoted to hunting that he was nicknamed 'Robin des Bois' and the Minister for the Arts had been obliged to forbid Weber's *Der Freischütz* in its popularised version under that name – he had made a stately exit to the frontiers in a palatial coach with a colourful escort. A few men of action, in the confusion of the moment, succeeded in placing upon the throne a cousin, Louis Philippe, who took the title King of the French. An ideal ruler, in that he was intelligent, lived an exemplary life and provided France with several brave and gifted princes, he satisfied neither the royalists of the Right nor the republicans of the Left. There was little tradition of constitutional monarchy, no experience of cabinet solidarity and the King had an unlucky preference for elderly inarticulate soldiers as his Ministers.

Early cycles of the Industrial Revolution had produced unemployment and distress in the towns. In 1834 there were riots in Lyon and a general uprising was invoked in Paris, which ended in the 'Massacre of the rue Transonain': where twenty citizens, including women and children, were killed by government troops and national guards. From May 1835 until January 1836, during Clémence's pregnancy and the birth, a Grand Assize took place at the Luxembourg Palace – near to the rue de Jardinet – where soldiers with fixed bayonets held back the crowds while 121 of the 1500 insurgents arrested in Lyon and Paris stood trial and made inflammatory speeches to workers and students besieging the building. Saint-Saëns would later recall playing in the gardens of the Luxembourg as a child, but they were no place in which to wheel out an infant and the political situation, as much as the need for country air, may have hastened his departure for Corbeil.

In July 1835 the Fieschi assassination plot, one of many attempts on the life of the King, took place. Fieschi, a Corsican, with the complicity of Robespierrist fanatics, detonated an 'infernal machine', which consisted of a range of rifles firing simultaneously. The King's horse was wounded, the death toll was eighteen and the funeral of the victims produced counter-revolutionary demonstrations and severe Press Laws. The King was remarkably tolerant towards attacks upon his person, but Fieschi and his accomplices were executed four months after Saint-Saëns was born. Like many renegades, Fieschi had, in his time, been a police spy and informer, and it is interesting to consider that he and others might well have been recipients of the secret funds which Victor Saint-Saëns dispensed at the Ministry of the Interior. In June 1836 a republican fired at the King with a weapon disguised as a walking-stick and, in December, a further assassination attempt wrecked the royal coach and injured the heir to the throne, the Duke of Orleans. These facts are worth recalling, for the picture drawn in *Ecole Buissonnière* deals only with the calm of the ménage supervised by his 'two mothers', Clémence and Great-Aunt Charlotte. Also because the brief reference to his father as a 'sous-chef de bureau' omits the fact that the Ministry of the Interior under Louis Philippe had as many problems as modern governments in the Balkans.

There were, too, political events overseas that were to have a bearing upon the life of Saint-Saëns. In 1835 French troops suffered reverses at the hands of the tribesmen of Algeria, and began renewed efforts to conclude the campaign to subjugate the region. In 1837, after successes such as the capture of Constantine, the remains of the dead French hero, General Damrémont, were laid to rest to the sounds of the Berlioz *Requiem*. For the remainder of the century French colonists and capital transformed the Algerian shores into a French province, which became a favoured place for Saint-Saëns, where his health revived and inspiration flowed. In Egypt a usurper, Mehemet Ali, sought French assistance against the Sultan of Turkey and led Louis Philippe and his Minister, Adolphe Thiers, into rash entanglements, which they had to repudiate under stern pressure from Lord Palmerston of Britain. Yet, while Britain continued to strengthen its hold upon Egypt, the khedives enjoyed patronising French culture in preference to British. When Saint-Saëns was born

Mehemet Ali was in the process of presenting the famous obelisk of Luxor, which stands in the place de la Concorde. In the next century the composer was to have Egyptian palaces placed at his disposal, where he could write in circumstances of ease and luxury.

Despite political instabilities, Paris in the 1830s was rapidly becoming the cultural capital of the world. The revolution of 1830, although it disappointed many hopes, curtailed the influence of the aristocrats and opened up horizons to the young and ambitious. Louis Philippe was not a great patron of the arts. In the first days of the July Monarchy the choir of the Chapel Royal was suppressed, the subsidy to the Opéra questioned and the pension scheme for the Orchestra of the Conservatoire concerts ended. At the Opéra the Director, Dr Veron, economised by dismissing some of the orchestra players and the composer Fromental Halévy had to take to litigation to retain his post as joint chorus-master. Yet the arts benefited from new opportunities allowed to the middle classes. There were incentives to become prosperous as the franchise was governed by property qualifications. New groups emerged with tastes for opera and serious music, hitherto regarded as the perquisites of the nobility. In addition to the banking sector with all its ramifications, the nascent industries needed mathematicians, engineers and entrepreneurs, who formed part of a new educated public. Bourgeois taste began to dictate standards at the Opéra, where large-scale works, emotional in content and lavishly produced, caught the imagination. At the time of Saint-Saëns's birth Halévy's *La Juive*, a tragic plot interwoven into real historical events, had been the most recent triumph and Meyerbeer's *Les Huguenots* was in preparation. At the Opéra Comique artless pieces based upon slender romances and domestic misunderstandings entertained middle-class families in boxes, where bells could be pulled to summon refreshments. There were the beginnings of concert life where groups of talented amateurs performed, often reinforced by theatre musicians. The Société Philharmonique de Paris, founded in 1822, could bring together as many as eighty instrumentalists and forty singers. As the taste for German music and the efforts of Berlioz began to make greater demands on the players the necessity for wholly professional groups became more apparent. Chief of these was the Orchestra of the Société des Concerts at the Conservatoire, founded in 1828, which became the finest orchestra in Europe. Although its conductor, François-Antoine Habeneck, would occasionally pause to take snuff in the middle of a movement, leaving the players to go their own way, and two movements of a symphony might be played at the start of a miscellaneous concert and two at the end, it brought the symphonic music of Beethoven to Parisian audiences. On a smaller scale, to a devoted following, the Baillot String Quartet introduced the classical chamber works.

This music-making produced musical journalism. It was in 1835 that Berlioz began his work as critic for the *Journal des Débats*, to which he was recommended by the Duke of Orleans and for which he wrote for twenty-eight years. Within days of Saint-Saëns's birth the publisher Maurice Schlesinger took over the *Revue Musicale* of the learned musicologist Francois-Joseph Fétis and merged it into *La Revue et Gazette de Paris*. Many other music publishing houses had similar publications. Interest was invariably centred upon the virtuosi who flocked to Paris. In Autumn 1835 the pianist Sigismond Thalberg arrived in the capital and musical society was soon divided between the Lisztians and the Thalbergians, while journals fanned the flames of rivalry. Liszt returned to Paris in 1836 and gave what was probably the first performance there of Beethoven's *Hammerklavier* Sonata. These two giants were but the leading figures of a whole troop of aspiring celebrities. The 1830s saw the development and industrial manufacture of musical instruments, and piano-makers such as Sébastien Erard and Ignaz Joseph Pleyel held concerts, which were partly artistic but also commercial, to advertise their products. Extra pianos were often waiting in the wings on these occasions as strings snapped and keys crumbled under the assaults of those who copied the athletic manner of the two rival gladiators. Aristide Cavaillé-Coll was beginning his career as a great organ builder. In 1835 the organs of St Denis and Notre Dame de Lorette were under construction.

From the adulation that new heroes of the concert platform received, there naturally developed the feeling that artists had a role to play in the leadership of society, as guides towards the betterment of the people and seers spreading the gospel of art. It was during 1835 that Liszt produced his essay on 'The Condition of the Artist and his place in Society'. The duty of the artist to regenerate and uplift the world also found favour with sections of the Church and the Abbé Lamennais, who was known to Liszt, was one of several liberal Catholics who propounded this doctrine. Simultaneously with Liszt's essay came Alfred de Vigny's preface to his drama *Chatterton*, propounding the importance of the artist in society and the heed that should be paid to the strivings that shook the artist's soul. In old age Saint-Saëns was criticised for his readiness to write polemics on all manner of subjects not always musical, but for someone brought up in the shadows of Liszt, Hugo and George Sand the voice of art had a duty to make itself heard.

Clémence Saint-Saëns was aware of the route to success lying before a musical virtuoso. She had developed a fondness for the arts in the company of an uncle – 'who loved her very much, was passionately interested above all in music and had constructed for himself a "salon organ" which he played. While he combed her much admired black tresses he used to speak of art, music, painting, beauty in all forms' and she conceived the idea that, if she had sons, 'the first one would be a musician, the second a painter and the third a sculptor'. Michel Faure admits that he felt a certain chill when he read these words. For, although Camille drew a picture of childhood love of the keyboard and constant delight in his lessons, one cannot help feeling that ambition to rise in the world must have motivated the young widow and pushed her son into an arduous regime of training for which, fortunately, he had the most marvellous aptitude. Great-Aunt Charlotte, by contrast, who remembered the *ancien régime* and still adhered to its fashions in her dress, remarked that she would be happy if the child learnt to play sufficiently well to accompany dancing. She had not forgotten the servant role of the musician in the days before Beethoven.

It was she who first trained Camille at the keyboard. When he was two and a half the square Zimmerman piano was opened for his inspection and, instead of banging inaccurately up and down 'as the majority of children do at that age', he touched one note after another, lingering on them until the sounds died away. His great-aunt taught him the names of the notes and it was thought worthwhile to call in a tuner to examine the instrument, although in an adjoining room Camille was able to name the notes as they were struck. He later related how he triumphed over a Professor Zimmerman of the Conservatoire, who had doubted his sense of perfect pitch only to discover that he was being tested against an imperfect instrument. The story is doubtful, as different organisations and different parts of France had their own particular pitches and an agreed diapason was established only in the 1860s. Yet it reveals his precocity. A teaching primer, *Le Carpentier Method*, was mastered within a month. He 'cried like a lost soul' when the piano was closed and so it was left open and, from time to time, he would leave his toys, climb up on to the stool and express his thoughts in music. The two ladies were faced with a problem over which pieces he would consent to play. He found the writing for the left hand in popular children's pieces too dull and complained that 'the left hand did not sing'. The simpler works of Haydn and Mozart satisfied him at the age of five, but he refused to perform merely as an entertainer for gushing visitors and obliged only when he was satisfied that a discriminating, and possibly even critical, listener was expected. The audiences would appear to have been chosen with some regard to social advancement, for we are told that he was especially pleased at the helpful comments of the Vicomtesse de Ségur, an amateur violinist. His meticulous exactness came early. 'Which of these two ladies shall I accompany?' he asked with childish innocence, when one warbling duettist was out of step with the other.

He also began to write his own music. The date of the first composition is generally put at March 1839, when he was four and a half years old. Looking back seventy years later over these childish endeavours Saint-Saëns, while admitting that they were 'insignificant', found them free from faults in writing and marked by a harmonic correctness surprising from a child who had never studied the basic principles. One of the first to be written down (by his great-aunt) was a Galop, a popular form, dated 6 June 1841. Charlotte seems to have remembered at the last moment to squeeze in the time signature in the left hand (2:4) and in the chromatic rush back to the theme has mistakenly included a B sharp and a C natural. The key is G major, but there is a middle section correctly allotted to E minor with the rhythmic pattern neatly reversed. An Andante, dated 1 July 1841, seems, judging by the erasures, to have given the copyist more difficulty.

'*Variations* by Camille Saint-Saëns' is dated 25 August 1841, when he was still only five. The first Variation follows the pattern of harmony and restates the theme in weaving quavers, which is not remarkable, but the second turns it into a waltz in the major key and has a Coda that adds a flourish. A further taste of the later composer comes in a Violin Sonata on which is written '*Fini. Le* 8 Jan, 1842', where there is a slow movement in 9:8, which becomes quite elaborate and allows for short cadenza passages. This was no doubt the sonata performed by a young Belgian, Antoine Bessems, who had come to Paris to study under Pierre Baillot and was First Violinist at the Théâtre des Italiens. Seventy years later Saint-Saëns looked at the manuscript and did not find it good. Writing to his friend Charles Lecocq he said: 'There is a Sonata for Piano and Violin which is something frightful. I remember a man by the name of Bessems, a Belgian violinist, who played it with me! When I think of his frequent visits and of his kindnesses to me, I suppose that he had matrimonial intentions that my mother did not receive favourably. He was a very handsome man and my mother dreaded handsome men.' This piece is written out in a stronger hand and it may be that his mother had begun her long training in making transcriptions of his music. It was a labour she had to learn. When certain possessions of the composer were sold after his death, one observer was touched to note three whole concertos by Mozart copied by his mother for her son's use.

The first movement of the child's Sonata (which has no tempo indication) begins with a statement for the violin, which becomes material for a theme, and the Presto Finale is at least of a quality achieved by the contributors to albums for modest home performers. Another Andante (in G major), dated August 1841, has precise dynamic markings and introduces sudden scales and octave passages. We are told that sections such as this were too difficult for tiny fingers and had to be played for him by a family friend, Mme Raynard, sister of a singer, Giraldi. It was through her that Camille enjoyed a childhood friendship with the young and aristocratic Alexis de Castillon, which again suggests that his mother did not neglect useful associations. The same year also brought his first song, 'Le Soir', his 'First Romance' as the page proudly announces. It conveys the message – in A minor – that the dawn which is breaking proclaims in vain that the day is made for love. It is dedicated to Mlle Granger, the daughter of neighbours, whose father was an artist of distinction.

He had always been susceptible to natural sounds, which is no doubt why he treated as naïve the advice of Debussy fifty years later that musicians should harken to rustling leaves and waving trees; this he had done since infancy. As young as two, he had relished household noises such as creaking doors and striking clocks. His greatest pleasure was the 'symphony of the kettle', a large implement, placed every morning in front of the fire. He waited with curiosity for its first murmurs and the appearance of an oboe sound, which arose little by little until the water boiled. Much later, one of his valets, Paul Sabatie, raking over his recollections, said that he had heard Saint-Saëns recalling that he would rush to the kitchen exclaiming: 'Mama, there is an orchestra in the kettle. Come listen to it, Mama!' Of broader significance for his instinctive feeling for the eighteenth-century orchestral sound was his first experience of a concert. He had previously heard only the violin playing solo and he was ravished by the warmth of the strings in harmony. As soon as the brass burst in he uttered cries of dismay – 'Take them away; they are stopping me from hearing the music' – and had to be removed, wailing, from the premises.

At four and a half he accompanied the attentive Bessems in a Beethoven sonata in the salon of a Madame Violet. This was sufficiently notable to warrant a mention in the *Moniteur Universel*, where the first comparisons with Mozart were made.

> The oldest among us have not forgotten the excitement in Paris aroused by the precocious genius of the later immortal Amadeus Wolfgang Mozart [*sic*].
>
> The child of which we speak, Camille Saint-Sans [*sic*], aged four years, seven months, by his surprising musical instinct and by the rare aptitude that he shows at this tender age on the piano to seize whatever is impressive in melody, rhythm and harmony, makes one hope that, thanks to these exquisite gifts and with good nurture, the great masters will some day find in him a worthy executor. This plant, still so frail, must be carefully managed. It will grow of itself, if people who are concerned wish to coax it, while too much force-feeding and instant acclaim would be prejudicial.

It would be a strange child who was not delighted by these comparisons with Mozart and Saint-Saëns may have imagined some kind of mystical lineage. The counter-theme to the first subject of his First (unpublished) Symphony is the same as that which closed Mozart's symphonic writing, and the opening notes of his published Symphony in E flat are similar to those which accompany the rise of the curtain in *The Marriage of Figaro*.

Upon Clémence a stronger impression was made by the knowledge of Mozart's miserable end. She was swift to impress upon Camille the fickle nature of public opinion and was so thorough in this task that, when he gave his first recital at the Salle Pleyel, aged ten, he compared the tide of applause unkindly to a wave of muddy waters throwing up untouchable objects. While Clémence did not use the harsh methods employed by the fathers of César Franck and Claude Debussy (the first was trailed around the concert platforms as a slave to the father's ambitions and the latter was forced to practise eight hours each day[1]), she did not leave her desire to have a musician son to chance. In the 'Rule of Life', which Camille wrote out before his first Communion, we read the touching words: 'A day is such a short space and the time given over to Satan is irrecoverably lost.'

His powers of sight-reading were already uniquely impressive. At five and a half he read, without the slightest mistake, a score by André Grétry. At seven he began formal pianoforte lessons with Camille-Marie Stamaty, who had praise for the early tuition he had received from his '*Bonne Maman*', his correct posture and total reliance upon the fingers. Stamaty was the son of a Greek father and French mother, and had been the leading pupil of Frédéric Kalkbrenner, thus 'descended' from Muzio Clementi. Kalkbrenner had invented a '*guide-main*', a bar placed in front of the keyboard, which arrested all muscular action save that of the hand. It was excellent for developing evenness of tone and dexterity, very suited to the harpsichord and classical repertoire.

Although Saint-Saëns later considered Stamaty's training to be inadequate as preparation for the Romantic School or the exploration of the resources of the modern piano, his performing talents were totally moulded in the tradition exemplified in Stamaty's own treatise: *Rhythmic Training for the Fingers*. Chantavoine, who had as a young man heard Saint-Saëns play, described him as belonging 'to the school of clarity and correctness', where the arms intervene only as a last resort, when the resources of the fingers are used up. In the preface to the Studies by his pupil Isidore Philipp Saint-Saëns wrote, 'The pianist needs a hand that obeys him without resistance. Nothing but work will obtain this fortunate obedience.' He continued to exercise his fingers up to the last day of his life. According to the valet, Paul Sabatie:

My master had in Paris a magnificent Erard grand piano, but he

---

[1] Mme Bizet changed Georges's shirt while he practised the piano so that he would lose no time.

practised on an upright because his study was too small to contain the Erard. [He] practised daily without exception on an instrument even when travelling, sometimes during the night. For this he had a 'silent' piano of two octaves fitted with an adjustable screw to control the touch, light or heavy. Thanks to this he did not disturb his fellow passengers. At times, as I sat opposite him holding his silent piano on my knees, he did exercises to limber up his fingers and arms. He was frequently the object of chuckles, terminating in apologies and requests for his autograph, which he readily granted. He always rode second class. I must not forget to say that, in order to promote a greater manual suppleness and agility, he employed a small electric device of minimum voltage sending a very light current from shoulder to fingers. His sense of hearing was so acute that even at a distance from the music room he could say, 'The person playing in the next room is old (or young)' and that he or she touched a particular note with thumb, index or little finger etc. He knew the different strengths of each finger and was determined that no one should be able to detect this difference in his own playing.[1]

Writing of more modern methods of piano training, which stemmed from the demands of Chopin, Liszt and Rubinstein, Saint-Saëns deplored the invention of the 'perpetual legato so false and monotonous', the abuse of small nuances and the 'continual expressivo applied without discernment', but in his own piano concertos there are many passages where romantic ardour is called for. In 1844 *La Revue et Gazette Musicale* published an account of a matinée given by M. Saint-Saëns 'whose name is pronounced like that of a banknote representing half a thousand francs'. It was signed by Henri Blanchard, a foremost critic of the day and one who had been very severe upon the playing of the young César Franck.

He is an artist of eight years who commenced playing the piano at thirty months. *Historique*! He is evidently born to play the piano. Brought up on the works of Sebastian Bach, Handel, Mozart, he knows by heart the music of these illustrious masters of the art. In the Matinée Musicale which he gave last Wednesday under the

[1] The electrical device was stolen by a German soldier during the Occupation and the reference above comes from a letter from the ex-valet seeking some official compensation.

auspices of his teacher M. Stamaty, he began by loosening his fingers in playing the first part of the Second Concerto in A flat major by Field, a piece in elegant style and gracious character, then came the Sonata in C minor of Mozart for piano alone, then preludes and fugues of Bach and Handel, and finally a concerto of Mozart with orchestral accompaniment. If he lacks physical force to attack and make the bass strings resound, he compensates with a graceful tone, and as a musician who feels what he is playing. His slight alterations of tempo are always felicitous and come from a musical feeling which is inborn. His playing is neat and sufficiently firm and, if his trill is a little indistinct, he will perfect it by studying this aspect of piano playing which gives so much life to a performance. His little hands are well-placed on the keyboard; there is evenness in the sounds and expressions, which is not over mannered.)

Blanchard also attended a private concert at Mme Saint-Saëns's home in April 1846, and wrote that the 'company marvelled to hear this tiny but already great artist'. The boy played a work for four hands with his teacher, some fugues of Bach, a concerto by Hummel and the C minor (Third) Concerto of Beethoven. Blanchard noted with approval that there were no writhings at the keyboard, no tossing around of the hair, in fact, nothing of the *'enfant terrible'*. Both the programme and the manner of Saint-Saëns's performances would have appealed especially to Blanchard, who listed the faults of Romanticism and its 'fatal temptations: the scorning of fugue, a pronounced antipathy towards metrical regularity, a horror of the simple, an incessant need for tortuous melody, the use of luxuriant instrumentation and the need to give listeners a programme which explains the composer's thought'. Also in the same year, 1846, Camille shared a private concert with the seven-year-old Francis Planté, which was given in the salon of a Mme Pouquet. Planté, who himself became an eminent pianist, recalled the profuse embraces of the ladies present and a rewarding harvest of chocolate and cakes.

An 1846 public concert, given at the Salle Pleyel, passed into French musical legend. This time, instead of being accompanied by a double quartet, presumably all that could be squeezed into the family apartment, there was the Orchestre des Italiens, under its conductor Théophile Tilmant, to give support in the Beethoven Concerto No. 3, and a Mozart B flat concerto. In addition, Camille played an Air and Variations, a fugue by Handel, and a Bach prelude and fugue. Tilmant was a conductor admired by Berlioz and very much loved by his players. During certain difficulties in 1862 his musicians refused to let him retire. He lacked a theoretical education but had a strong musical sense and imparted a verve and sparkle to his performances. The occasion, however, was not one of high seriousness. This type of concert formed part of the social round and very often the interest was centred upon some new 'discovery' or musical sensation soon eclipsed by others.[1]

It is not often mentioned that his recital was interspersed with arias from popular operas such as *William Tell*, but all seem agreed that the concert was memorable. It had not received a great deal of publicity. The Salle Pleyel was the venue where Chopin had made his début with the least degree of publicity possible. The choice of pieces showed an unusual classical restraint: 'We thank the happy chance', said *L'Illustration*, 'that has provided for us one of the most lively musical delights of the winter, for which no announcement or advertisement had prepared us. We have just attended the début of a charming child of ten who in a concert given *chez* M. Pleyel has made known to us one of the most formidable talents of the day.' There was praise for his playing without scores before him and for the Cadenza, which he had composed for the Mozart concerto. 'Camille does not limit himself to performance . . . we are informed that he improvises and composes with wonderful skill and, in fact, in an intelligent cadenza, he succeeded in recalling the principal motifs of the piece wisely.' His playing had grown in strength and he was able to compete with the full orchestra, but he was praised, too, for his meticulous control in the gentler passages.

Saint-Saëns was fortunate in the time of his birth. The era of the solo recital had just arrived. Paris was not well endowed with concert

[1] Saint-Saëns was not alone among child prodigies. Another pupil of Stamaty, Louis Gottschalk, made his début in 1845 at sixteen, playing the Chopin E minor Concerto. Emile Paladilhe entered the Conservatoire at nine, won the Premier Prix for piano at thirteen and the Prix de Rome for composition at sixteen. Francis Planté made his debut aged nine at a concert in the Hôtel de Ville. As early as 1824 Charles-Valentin Alkan had won the premier prize for piano at the age of ten. Among the 1850 prize winners we find Planté aged eleven years three months and a violinist, Paul Julien, aged ten. In 1855 Victor Alphonse Duvernoy and Alexis Fissot, both under twelve, shared the Piano Prize.

halls. Liszt's father had had difficulty in finding a venue for his son and
this may be why Liszt, when older, chose to give one of his first solo
recitals at the Opéra. Normally, concerts were very haphazard affairs
and, in order to increase the audiences by bringing in families, several
artists were included. Heinrich Heine noted with some surprise a
concert in 1842 at which Liszt alone appeared on the platform, but
Liszt was also generous about appearing with other promising
performers and programmes were often lengthy. There was a fashion
for works played by instruments other than those for which they had
been composed. On one occasion an orchestrated version of the first
movement of the *Moonlight* Sonata was played, after which Liszt
performed the other two movements on the piano. It was only in 1839
that the recital, with all pieces transcribed or composed by Liszt, first
formed the basis of a solo performance. At all events Saint-Saëns
dominated this occasion and gave it the air of a solo recital. As an
encore he offered to play any one of Beethoven's sonatas. One
wonders whether even the young Mozart, given the difference in time
and place, could have mastered such works.

The widow of the Duke of Orleans, Louis Philippe's eldest son,
who had wished to preside over a great renaissance of the arts in
France, but tragically had been killed in a coach accident, asked to
hear the much praised child performer and a special recital was
arranged at the Tuileries. Stamaty, who had hastened back from a visit
to Rome, and his pupil were ushered through the State Rooms and
Camille, 'wearing a big white turn-down collar and a short coat', was
presented to the Duchess and her son, the infant Comte de Paris.
While Camille played Bach, Beethoven and Handel, the Comte, who
already possessed a small replica of the great organs designed by
Cavaillé-Coll, preferred to ride his rocking-horse. The Duchess gave
Saint-Saëns a gold watch as a reward for the 'young artist and future
teacher'. Saint-Saëns recalled that, as a result of the Salle Pleyel
concert, there was some discussion about his playing a Mozart
concerto at the prestigious Société des Concerts du Conservatoire and
there was even a rehearsal for the event. But the leading violinist,
François Seghers, later to be a great friend, was a spokesman for the
orchestra and expressed the view that the society had not been
founded to further the careers of precocious infants.

Some ill feeling arose between Mme Saint-Saëns and Stamaty. It is
difficult not to believe that the teacher had looked upon this

intelligent and promising child as something of an investment. The Saint-Saëns family was not rich; it is hard to envisage where the fees necessary to pay a distinguished Parisian teacher could have come from. Stamaty wished to grasp the opportunity and give more concerts, which would enhance his prestige. The mother did not wish to see her son pursuing the career of an infant prodigy and had legitimate fears for his health, for he was a pale and delicate child. Saint-Saëns later described a dispute over the merits of Chopin's music, which he felt as a gap in his education because of Stamaty's distaste for it. He seems to have been pressured into refusing to have Stamaty's name associated in some subsequent concerts. In the *Ecole Buissonnière* his somewhat grudging tribute is to say that Stamaty's greatest contribution was to bring him into contact with his first professor of composition – Pierre Maleden.

Maleden was a native of Limoges and still preserved his regional accent. Like Stamaty, he was unorthodox in his views and stood apart from other musicians. He had studied in Germany under Gottfried Weber (no relation of the composer), whose views on harmony he had elaborated and, in Saint-Saën's opinion, perfected. Weber's treatise placed less stress upon the mathematical correctness of harmonic writing and more upon the use of an 'inner ear' to divine what will or will not sound well. Over such matters Maleden and Saint-Saëns were not always in agreement, and lessons could be stormy. When Camille advanced ideas of his own, the tall lank-haired professor, otherwise described by his pupil as 'sweet and shy', would push his real and more vulnerable ears down to the table, asking him if he would change his mind. If the mind did not change, the teacher might admit the possibility of his own misjudgement. Maleden had a long-cherished wish to teach at the Conservatoire, but at the moment when Auber, the Director, was about to sign the necessary papers he had a rush of honesty and wrote to say that his methods of composition differed totally from those officially taught. Auber had second thoughts and Maleden remained an outsider. From both his teachers Saint-Saëns was given a training in dissent and was influenced towards an iconoclastic view of the received wisdom of the times, a characteristic which led him to be at first an advocate of the 'Music of the Future' and later to stand apart from the Franckists and Modernists, who advanced theories to which composing had to be subservient.

One teacher to whom he gave less attention in his recollections was his first tutor on the organ, Alexandre Pierre François Boëly. When departing for Italy in 1846, Stamaty advised Mme Saint-Saëns that her son should take private lessons while waiting to join the organ class at the Conservatoire. Boëly had been organist of St Germain l'Auxerrois since 1840. While supervising the rebuilding of the organ he had fitted a new 'German' pedal board with a greater compass and longer keys than those common in France at the time. Even so, the pedals seem to have been too short for the heels to be employed comfortably and, throughout his long career, Saint-Saëns played using only his toes, a remarkable skill which gave clarity and precise articulation. Organ manuals of the day contain exercises which show that toe-heel pedalling and substitution were practised, but Saint-Saëns, once again, seems to have begun with an unorthodox method. The new pedal board at St Germain had a compass sufficiently wide to enable Boëly to perform the works of Bach, to whose grandeur the pupil was introduced. According to Joseph d'Ortigues, friend of Berlioz, Boëly was one of the two or three Frenchmen 'capable of playing a fugue correctly', performing his own fugues 'with an ease of fingering, a purity of style and a severity of harmony worthy of Bach'. It was through Saint-Saëns that Berlioz himself, late in life, came to appreciate Bach. In the 1840s the Great Master was a figure little known in France, save to Boëly and the pianist, Alkan, who used a pedal piano at Erard's studio. The majority of French organs, not yet submitted to the ministrations of Cavaillé-Coll, were in poor condition, with unsteady wind pressures and unstandardised pedal boards. Camille had an opportunity to learn something of organ construction for, during the period of his lessons, the Clicquot organ was restored. The four manuals were reduced to three and a new and 'expressive' Récit (Swell) was added. Boëly himself inaugurated the new instrument in November 1850, but did not have long to enjoy its enhanced lustre. In 1851 he was dismissed during a drive for church economies, because his austere and serious tastes conflicted with those of the clergy and people. His pupil was later to endure similar reproaches and friendly relations with Boëly continued, for in the year that he died, 1858, the teacher dedicated a fantasie, Opus twenty-one, to the younger man and Saint-Saëns played for his funeral.

In view of all this expert tuition the story of Saint-Saëns's débâcle at the audition for the Conservatoire has the aura of a tale that grew with the years. Admittedly the instrument on which he had to perform was unworthy of its office, having been brought from the Tuileries and installed in two halves, one in the hall and the other in the adjoining ante-room. The great organ possessed only four stops and the pedals covered only one and a half octaves.

> I was put in front of the keyboard and was so overcome with awe at the extraordinary sound I produced . . . the whole class burst into laughter. I was thereupon admitted only as an auditor and allowed the humble position of listening to others. I was extremely assiduous and did not miss a single note or comment made by our teacher. At home I worked and pondered, and toiled hard at Bach's *Art of Fugue*. The other students were not as painstaking and one day, when there were few in the class and Benoist[1] had nothing more to do, he invited me to play. This time nobody wanted to laugh, I became a fully fledged student and carried off the second prize at the end of the year. I would have gained first prize had it not been for my youth and the inconvenience of making me leave a class where a longer period was necessary for me.

We might wonder why he chose to enter the organ rather than the piano class. Organ playing offered the better prospects of earning a living at one of the great Paris churches: an unexpected result of the 1830 revolution, in which churches and clergy had been attacked, had been a revival of fashionable religion. The Catholic Church was no longer so closely associated with the monarchy and several great preachers, such as Lamennais and Montalembert, envisaged an alliance of Church and people, which would be the foundation of a new social order. The rise of a middle class and its deference to respectability swelled parish congregations, and the ever present threats of republicanism and anarchy threw wavering souls into the arms of Rome. Without this religious revival France would not have been able to invest in so many new organs or furnish a living to such an exceptional group of great organists later in the century. It is interesting that Stamaty had shown particular interest in Camille's First Communion and wrote from Rome to Clémence to say that 'it

[1] François Benoist, Professor of Organ for fifty-three years. He educated more than one generation of French organists and pianists from Adolphe Adam, Félicien David and Louis James Alfred Lefébure-Wély to Léo Delibes, Georges Bizet and Raoul Pugno.

ought to occupy the dear child above all' for providence would then
make him a force in the restoration of Catholic art, which had fallen
into neglect.

Mme Saint-Saëns also wished to encourage her son's composing
abilities. When a friend learnt that young Camille was playing
Beethoven, then thought to be the acme of modernism, she enquired
reproachfully: 'What music will he play when he is twenty?'
Clémence, who, said her son, 'had a lofty and dramatic turn of speech',
replied, 'He will play his own!' The Conservatoire organ classes, with
their stress on improvisation and counterpoint, offered an admirable
training. The home was a religious one and the interest of influential
clergy in Camille's career was encouraged. The boy was fascinated by
the Old Testament stories and, with the aid of the exotic palm trees in
the Jardin des Plantes, conjured up images of the East. At the age of
eleven he had sketched out a tragedy, 'Moses at Mount Horeb', and a
little later he put to music a poem of Victor Hugo, 'Moses saved from
the Waters'. One idea in this youthful work, passages for four hands
on the piano in an orchestral score, was to resurface later in the Third
Symphony. Like Hugo he experienced the dramatic vigour of the
Bible and several of his most robust works, *Samson*, *The Deluge* and *La
Lyre et la Harpe*, were his own inspirations. In old age he returned to
what his admirer Emile Baumann called 'this terrible epic of the Book
of Exodus' when he composed *The Promised Land*.

Mme Saint-Saëns extended her quest for interesting and useful folk.
She had herself ability as a water-colourist and had taken lessons from
Pierre Joseph Redouté. Through neighbours, the Grangers (M.
Granger had at one time overtaken Jean Auguste Dominique Ingres in
the Painting Section of the Prix de Rome), Camille at five was
introduced to Ingres. The Saint-Saëns family would talk to him about
Mozart, Gluck and other pre-Revolution musicians.[1] Camille composed a short Adagio ('happily lost' he declared later) which he
dedicated to Ingres and he would play Mozart sonatas, which the
painter loved. In return, Ingres, whose talents on the violin Saint-
Saëns dismissed as a fictitious, if attractive, legend, bestowed on the
child a medallion showing the profile of Mozart and bearing the

[1] Berlioz in a letter to Liszt of 1839 speaks of Ingres's affection for music:
'I greatly admire the fanaticism of his great painter's musical passions and
you will heartily forgive him for loathing me when you remember that he
adores Gluck and Beethoven.'

words: 'To M. Saint-Saëns, charming interpreter of the divine artist'. An Adagio dedicated to Mlle Granger, dated 20 June 1842, has survived and is certainly Mozartian in its style.

The father of another young singer, whom Camille accompanied, presented him with the full orchestral score of *Don Giovanni* in two handsome red volumes with French and Italian texts. What a child of five made of the story, or whether his mother regarded the French text as wholesome, we do not know. The two volumes became sacred tomes to be studied. Hitherto he had known only a few conventional opera scores by Grétry and others. Now

every day with that miraculous ease of assimilation which is the dominant faculty of childhood, I immersed myself in *Don Giovanni* and almost unconsciously I imbibed its music, broke myself into score reading and became acquainted with the different voices and instruments. What joy I felt when, only a few years later, I was able to hear *Don Giovanni* sung at the Théâtre des Italiens by Grisi, Mario and Lablache. Yet, when you come to study the score closely how unremarkable are the means employed! Do all these marvels amount to nothing more than simple intervals of an octave, a few bars repetition in the bass of a very obvious rhythm, syncopations (which everyone uses), a little figure on the fourth string of the second violins and those scales, those terrifying scales, which are so restrained and do not go beyond an octave? It is true that these details seem of little or no account in themselves. Their value arises out of their placing, reciprocal harmony, contrasts and the overall balance. In these lie the style, the secret of genius. Unfortunately there is nothing more difficult to perform than this exquisite music in which every note, every silence has its value and where the slightest negligence, not only in the letter but in the spirit, will bring defeat. The big musical spectacles are more invulnerable: the Overtures to *Tannhäuser* and *William Tell* (you will see that I avoid prejudice) survive second-rate performances because, however many notes you mangle, there are always plenty left behind to ensure the triumph of the big battalions. The tree with a thousand leaves can weather the storm, but what becomes of a flower, a butterfly's wing, when they are rumpled?

In his use of solo woodwind, his sparing employment of the 'big battalions' and his refusal to thicken or extend scores for effect, Saint-Saëns continued to repeat the lessons he had learnt from the Mozart score.

A certain homeopathic Dr Hoffmann had married a female cousin of the Saint-Saëns family and built up a practice composed of admiring women, who had an opportunity at his home of meeting the handsome and romantic Charles Gounod, returned from his studies in Rome. Gounod's singing at soirées and his embracing smile helped to recruit patients for the good doctor. He was twenty-seven when he met Camille aged eleven. He, too, had been brought up by an adored mother and suffered from exposure as a child prodigy. Impressed by the boy's facility and given to making aphorisms, which were often cloudy but sounded profound, he murmured, 'You have not had a musical childhood.' He helped to increase the boy's already ardent interest in composition.

> May I be permitted to pay my tribute of thanks to the Master [wrote Saint-Saëns many years later] who, already in full possession of his talent, did not disdain to make me, the complete schoolboy that I was, the confidant of his most personal artistic thoughts and to shed his science over my ignorance. He held forth to me as an equal: it is thus that I became, if not his pupil, at least his disciple and that I finished by moulding myself under his shadow, or rather under his luminosity.

Without the influence of Gounod it is possible that Saint-Saëns, poring over Mozart scores, persuaded of the incomparability of Bach and also treated to eulogies of eighteenth-century French music at the Ingres home by the singer François Delsart, might have felt that the great age of music lay in the past. Delsart, uncle of Bizet and teacher of singing, was a great advocate of Lully, Rameau and their contemporaries. 'Delsart,' Saint-Saëns was to write later, 'the singer without a voice, the incomplete musician, the imperfect scholar', was guided by an intuition to explore the nation's artistic legacy. 'He left with all who knew him the memory of a visionary, an apostle. When you heard him talk with so much ardour of those works of the past that the world had forgotten, you began to think that such neglect must be undeserved and you wanted to know more about these relics of another age.' Another guest of the Ingres family was the composer

Henri Reber, who, at a time when all popular interest was centred upon opera, chose to write symphonies in the eighteenth-century manner (one of which the young Saint-Saëns arranged as a piano duet). To all this flood of antiquarianism Gounod brought optimism about the future, a degree of fame and a knowledge of contemporary Europe, for he had not only lived in Italy but had visited Austria and Germany, and been accepted by the Mendelssohn family as a friend. He was the first composer whom Saint-Saëns had met who embodied music as a living force. He took the role of an elder brother and, throughout his own somewhat wayward career, remained a friend and champion.

Of Camille's education in general subjects we know little. Some reviews of his concerts spoke of his being a polymath. He learnt Latin speedily from another Monsieur Benoist but found his Greek teacher uninspiring and, much to his regret, did not proceed with the subject. His curiosity was aroused by mathematics and sciences, especially astronomy. He would survey the skies through opera glasses that could be hired on the bridges of the Seine. The maths teacher, a Monsieur Raynard, a brother-in-law of the Giraldis, left the area after a family bereavement; the classics teacher appears to have fled from the effort of keeping ahead of a child who was determined to read Latin authors in the original. When science tuition was not to be had, he educated himself, planting seeds in window-boxes and observing germination, studying the accuracy of his mother's flower paintings, breeding caterpillars and investigating the life cycles of butterflies. Sometimes he travelled to Meudon and collected fossils and interesting stones with a geologist's hammer. One has the impression that he resembled those children in Victorian textbooks who respond with pertinent questions to commands such as 'Let us go for a walk, children, and observe the formation of the rocks'. He did not have very many contacts with children of his own age. Even his enthusiasms were calculated to elevate. A volume of Victor Hugo's poetry, expensively bound, excited him enormously. He devoured all the poet's work and a third of his songs were to be settings from it. He came slowly to an appreciation of Racine, in whose lines he found the same economy of means that he admired in Mozart. Such light relief as there was came from the novels of Dumas and Hugo, which sowed an interest in tales of brigands, gypsies and romance under Mediterranean skies, later to exfoliate in operas such as *Proserpine* and *L'Ancêtre*.

Thus, when he entered the Conservatoire at the age of twelve he was something of a phenomenon even for the remarkable times in which he lived, not just because of his pianistic skills, but because his mental processes had been absorbed by the continual contemplation of genius. Most composers have had to struggle on, stage by stage, towards greatness, but Saint-Saëns had breathed the air of the mountain tops since infancy. He had, from his teachers, acquired a strong independence of outlook and a suspicion of intellectual fashion, and though he recalled playing in the Luxembourg Gardens with at least two friends who remained close to him subsequently, Alexis de Castillon and René Thorel, he had been nurtured to achieve a kind of perfectionism which implied isolation. There *was* a gregarious side to his nature. He conducted a massive and witty correspondence, his tastes in the theatre and delight in the spectacular operas of Meyerbeer and the frivolities of Opéra Comique were those of the average bourgeois household of the time. He was a devoted and tireless participant in all the musical gatherings that he shared. Yet he remained always something of a slave to his own individual assumptions and the necessity of separating himself from the normal experiences of the great majority of beings, contented in his communings with his own intelligence or with selected heroes from the past. In old age he told a young admirer that he had never sought out advice in his youth and had never followed pieces of advice which he had been given.

2

The Conservatoire – Revolution and Repression

The Conservatoire National de Musique et de Déclamation had been founded in 1795 from the relics of a music school for the National Guard; its teaching duties were at the start combined with obligations to provide music for public ceremonies. It occupied a large space behind the rue Bergère and its façade had recently been reconstructed and embellished with four allegorical figures representing Opéra, Opéra Comique, Tragedy and Comedy. The instruction moved by stages from solfège and sight-reading, through singing and playing, to the theory of music and harmony. Pupils were admitted between the ages of eight and thirteen, so it is clear that Mme Saint-Saëns had kept Camille at home until the latest possible moment. Louis XIV had inaugurated prizes for study in Italy for painters, sculptors and architects, and Napoleon had extended this to musicians. The Prix de Rome was the Conservatoire's most prestigious award, although there were twice yearly examinations in most classes. For the pensionnaires who came from the provinces there were strict rules: no lights after 11 p.m., a 6.30 a.m. start in summer and 7.30 a.m. in winter, an allocation of two pairs of shoes per year and room inspections. The number of students had risen markedly during the reign of Louis Philippe, but conditions were, in many respects, archaic. In 1841, box 27 in the Concert Hall had collapsed and, at a prize-giving during one of the particularly cold winters of the time, the heating system had misfired so that the performers were barely visible through thick palls of smoke. We know, however, that Saint-Saëns had a great affection for the old buildings out of which came a great cacophony of sounds. He liked to compare much modern music to the babel of noise that greeted visitors to the entrance frontages.

His reminiscences of the teachers, like those of youth in all ages, centred upon personal foibles rather than tuition content. He considered Benoist, the Professor of Organ, an indifferent organist but an excellent teacher, and remembered his correcting ballet scores for the Opéra during lessons. He regarded his composition teacher Halévy as ineffectual, constantly distracted by visiting singers seeking auditions for parts in his operas. When he was a journalist on *L'Estafette* in the 1870s he recalled the excitement and parental frenzies of the competition days, which he compared to the 'steeple-chases of Chantilly', and defended the record of the Conservatoire against its critics. Yet we do not know a great deal about his time there and he makes no mention of the fact that he began his studies in the immediate aftermath of a stormy revolution.

The fall and flight of Louis Philippe in 1848 had been foreseen by no one. France was at peace and the government of François Guizot had a comfortable majority. There had been poor harvests in 1845 and 1846, and sufferings in the towns among the poor and unemployed, but the 'Bourgeois' Monarchy had seen the spread of industry and a rise in wealth reaching down into the community. As so often, it was a series of private scandals and a belief in widespread political corruption that led the restless nation to seek a change. The Duke of Choiseul-Praslin, who was charged with the murder of his wife, escaped the guillotine by swallowing arsenic. The Prince d'Eckmuhl stabbed his mistress, the Comte Mortier tried to kill his children and another peer forged the signature of the Secretary of the Jockey Club. The political sage Alexis de Tocqueville had denounced the moral state of the nation; and opposition parties, demanding an extension of the franchise, had opportunities to make capital out of such events.

Following a visit to Paris by Richard Cobden, founder of the British Anti-Corn-Law League, there was a desire to copy its methods of arousing public opinion and a series of political 'Banquets' ensued. These were not occasions for rich eating, but public meetings at which toasts were drunk after inflammatory speeches. The cancellation of the Banquets in Paris in February 1848 led to rioting and the erection of barricades in the streets. Young César Franck and his bride had to be lifted over one of these by the crowds before they could enter the church where they were to be married. The child Massenet, receiving from his mother his first and long-awaited piano lesson, had it rudely interrupted by gunfire from the streets below. The King, from whom resolution had been drained by the long struggle for survival, abdicated in favour of his grandson, the Comte de Paris, the same infant before whom Saint-Saëns had played the previous year. The Duchess of Orleans arrived at the Chamber with her son but, as the Chamber itself was besieged by a mob and no initiative was shown by Ministers, she was hustled from the premises, and the deputies and crowds alike responded to a call from the Deputy (and poet) Alphonse Lamartine, for a republic.

For some months the Provisional Government of Lamartine tried to calm the fears of the Right while doing something for the unemployed through a system of National Workshops. Such tasks as these provided were uninspired and consisted in planting 'Trees of Liberty' across Paris. They were organised by the socialist Louis Blanc, from the Luxembourg Palace very near to the rue de Jardinet. For a brief time there was an outburst of fraternity. On 2 April one such 'Tree of Liberty' was solemnly planted in the forecourt of the Opéra, renamed 'Theatre of the Nation'. The curé of St Roch arrived in procession with his clergy and held a cross aloft to bless the tree, for many clergy saw the new 'Second' Republic as another step towards the union of Church and people. The festivities continued with a free performance of Auber's *La Muette de Portici*, ever the musical accompaniment to revolutionary emotions, which was followed by a dramatised version of the forbidden 'Marseillaise'. A chorus from Halévy's *Charles VI*, 'Never in France shall England reign', was especially popular and sung frequently in the theatres. The sardonic English Ambassador, Lord Normanby, silenced complaints from English residents by observing, 'This is a distinction which assuredly none of us desire.' Some light reconstruction of the Conservatoire façade announced it as 'National' rather than 'Royal'.

A Constituent Assembly was elected, but by virtue of a strong reaction in the provinces it was predominantly royalist and frequently subjected to invasions by the mob, which in many districts still ruled the streets. The permanent Secretary of the Academy of Fine Arts, setting off for the Annual Session in his traditional court dress, was pursued and almost stripped as a representative of royal oppression. Projects for reform poured in upon the uncomfortable rulers of the new regime and the regeneration of music and the arts came under discussion. Before the elections it had been suggested that artists should be represented and Halévy had been prevailed upon to stand as a 'musicians' candidate. The future friend of Saint-Saëns, the Abbé Duguerry, graciously withdrew his own candidature to allow Halévy's name to go forward, though the composer did not win the seat. The attention of the Government was turned to the Conservatoire. Some critics appeared to think that it was a den of vice and wanted not only changes to the teaching staff, but isolated cells for study 'in order to achieve an establishment where a mother would be able to place her daughter without danger'. Under more liberal banners there were calls for an increase in state subsidies and support for the arts. 'Genius, immortal by its very essence, should not be muzzled.' The Government decided that the Grand Salle, hitherto the guarded sanctum of privileged subscribers, should be open to any musician who asked for it, though this does not seem to have been implemented. Alexandre Ledru-Rollin, Minister of the Interior, summoned Auber and the professors, and charged them to name a commission which would study proposed reforms. When the first report of the commission was given in July many suggestions were eminently sensible: the Conservatoire should play a greater role in the training of outside choral societies, which were popular means of elevating public taste; there should be classes in the history of music, lessons in Italian and an increase in the number of *pensionnaires*. Students of composition should be assisted to attend the subsidised theatres and be allocated a box. Finally, and the demand does not seem unreasonable, members of the jury on the great competition days were to be present from the start of the session.

Pamphlets on every subject circulated in the capital. One with the title 'Organisation of Work, A Plan for Musical Reform' was addressed to 'Citizen' Lamartine by a 'Citizen' Devillebichot. The author called for the Conservatoire to open its doors wider to the public and make musical tuition available through state subvention. It called for a 'National Society' of musicians. It placed great stress on the opportunities for young composers to hear their works performed. It wished to see all singers joining together once a week for choral work and all instrumentalists doing the same for symphonic work. Pupils should be admitted to Conservatoire rehearsals and concerts, and the works of student composers should be played at the request of professors. One assumes that the students themselves must have thought and argued about these proposals and surely the debates lingered on into the autumn of 1848 when the young Camille arrived. Thirty years later, when Citizen Devillebichot's pamphlet and many others had probably disintegrated on the bookstalls, Saint-Saëns founded just such a 'National Society' to assist young composers in hearing and appraising their works.

Anxious to imitate the tradition of the First Republic for mass festivals, Lamartine ('One of those poets whom Plato would have chased out of his Republic,' as the royalist Comte de Falloux remarked) celebrated a 'Triumph of Concorde' on the Champ de Mars. Students from the Conservatoire and Gymnase Miltitaire struggled to make themselves heard in patriotic song. Eight hundred composers entered a competition for national anthems. The titles of the entries show the mood of the times and some distinguished names appear in the lists. Artists had not been slow to embrace the republican regime: 'L'Harmonie des Peuples' by Ambroise Thomas, 'La Jeune République' by Pauline Viardot, 'L'Hymne au Fraternité' by Victor Massé and 'La Marche des Travailleurs' by Oscar Commentant may be noted.

The pious hopes expressed in all this hymnody were soon to be dashed in bloodshed, but in the final days before civil war state help for French composers was sought by a group of which Edouard Lalo was a member. A cousin of Lalo, Auguste Wacqez, outlined a detailed plan based on socialist doctrines. He began from the premise that artists were the victims of capitalist speculation, especially in the world of publishing, and wanted a national network of societies which would democratically elect a jury of eminent musicians to select works to be performed and published. He envisaged a Society of National Concerts and a journal, *Le Moniteur Musical*, to rehabilitate chamber and orchestral music. In a letter to a supporter of the scheme in Troyes, Lalo declared the wish of his friends to elevate French taste above the fashion for variations and pot-pourris on operatic airs, and suggested that such great names as Halévy, Félicien David and even Chopin would serve on this central jury and give young composers the chance to write more ambitiously. Swept away by the violent events in June 1848, these ideas resurfaced when Lalo was one of those who joined Saint-Saëns in the founding of the 'Société Nationale'.

While the new Republic was in theory friendly towards the arts, it was in practice facing insolvency. The theatres, after the first rush of revolutionary enthusiasm, were poorly attended. The revolution destroyed Adam's efforts to establish an 'Opéra National', forerunner of the Théâtre Lyrique. Many of the celebrities had left the troubled city for London. There was even discussion in the Assembly of a forced reduction in the budget for the Conservatoire. This roused great protestations, and Berlioz and Adam were among the signatories to a petition. Hugo spoke against the reduction in the Assembly and the credits were eventually voted. A major cause of government debt was the existence of the 'National Workshops', which drew masses of the unemployed from elsewhere into the capital. Unable to provide sufficient work to justify the daily payments, the Government could in the end offer only two uninviting alternatives: military service in Algeria or clearing swamps in the infested marshes of Sologne. As a consequence, in late June, there was a workers' rebellion in the poorest quarters of the city of so widespread and serious a nature that the Assembly gave General Cavaignac full powers to suppress it. There was desperate street fighting and a huge death toll.

For the Conservatoire the 'June Days' had one rather bizarre outcome. In the aftermath, the National Guard, drawn from more middle-class *arrondissements*, made itself the vigilant protector of public monuments and mounted night guards. This was the time of the competition for the Prix de Rome and the contestants, according to tradition, were to be sequestered in their rooms at the Institut to compose the Set Cantata. One moonlight night a nervous sentry rushed to his command post to say that gigantic shadows were moving on the cupola and roof of the Institut. It must be in the hands of the insurgents! When it was revealed that the Prix de Rome candidates, relaxing after long hours of work, had climbed up to fool about, there was relief in the National Guard, but fury among the Academicians. It was announced that no prize would be awarded, but fortunately the soothing words of Adolphe Adam, composer of *Giselle*, obtained a pardon for the culprits and the prize went to the nocturnal jester, Jules Laurent Duprato.

Other musicians were caught up in the events of the 'June Days'. Bizet witnessed recruits for the National Guard being drawn up outside the Conservatoire itself. The squad included François Delsart, who intended to defend the churches from left-wing insurgents. Despite toying with entry into the Church, Gounod very quickly learnt to shed his clerical habit when venturing into the streets.

Singers from the Opéra Comique joined the squad from the rue Bergère. Several were wounded or overcome by the heat and the Opéra Comique was unable to reopen for many days. By autumn, when Saint-Saëns entered the Conservatoire, the political situation had quietened, but so too had the many projects for reform and the spread of the arts. In 1913, writing on 'Religious Music', Saint-Saëns suddenly departed from his task and gave his general views on 'Reform'. 'My generation still remembers the 1848 revolution,' he wrote, 'carried out to deafening cries of "*Vive la Réforme*" advanced by the crowd which did not even know the meaning of the word. It was enough to ask any of the rabble at random to be convinced of this. Alas! very often the reform brought about, the "transfer of ownership" effected, men found themselves as before with their passions, their virtues and their faults; everyone just went back to bed. . . .' Did the boy really stop the rioters in the streets and ask them to explain their ideas of 'Reform'? It is possible that his redoubtable mother did so, as they passed the Luxembourg and the hungry crowds besieging it.

At the head of the Conservatoire was Auber, the esteemed composer of opera, less rigorous than his predecessor Cherubini, who had been heard to tell some candidates for admission they were too ugly ever to succeed upon the stage. History has not been kind to Auber's reputation, which is that of a light-hearted cobbler of stage works who despised the very art which brought him fame. As he moved constantly in high society, enjoyed riding in the Bois de Boulogne, attended race meetings and spent every evening at the theatre, the world wondered at which hour of the day he sat at his desk composing. He had invented a deterrent to unwanted callers by insisting on visits at 6 a.m. Even Wagner, in 1860, was obliged to conform to this schedule when he wished to discuss his music, as he had done with Rossini. Rossini had been unusually brusque but Auber, more courteous, had emerged from snatches of sleep from time to time to listen to his guest's theories. 'I like only women, horses, the boulevards and the Bois,' was his reply and Wagner, with high German seriousness, concluded, 'This man assuredly does not like music.' This was untrue; he would sometimes wake up opera singers at night with freshly written arias, but he had undoubtedly forgotten many of the thousands of pages he had written. One evening he went to the Opéra to hear *William Tell*, unaware that the programme had been changed. He settled back comfortably in his seat awaiting the beguiling tones of the violincellos. To his horror a brassy orchestral tutti struck his ears and, in rage at the unexpected, he tried to leave, becoming enmeshed in the feet of his neighbours and causing a commotion. Taking refuge in the corridor he realised that he had been put to flight by his own *Muette de Portici*.

For thirty years he guarded his role as Director jealously, not out of personal pride but so that he should not hand it on diminished. He procrastinated over the reforms proposed in 1848, as he did with the measures put forward by a later commission in the 1860s. Yet he introduced some changes which he judged useful and possible. On the vexed question of the moral tone of the Conservatoire he separated the singing classes into two groups, male and female. He enforced the strict timetables on the boarding scholars, convinced that the more hours of liberty they enjoyed the less work would be done. He encouraged the staging of prize-winning pieces with costumes and scenery, and placed his own talents at the service of the Conservatoire, writing music expressly for the examinations, pieces with rapidly changing keys for the solfège tests, passages of particular difficulty for instrumentalists and subjects for fugues.[1]

At the time he entered the Conservatoire Saint-Saëns was working on a symphony in B flat and a piano trio in G, both discontinued. Such ambitions were not entirely in accord with the curriculum, which aimed principally at vocal writing for the stage. The impression given by his memoirs is that of a rather solitary student; he refers to the hours that he spent reading voraciously in the library, though he does not tell us whether Berlioz, who drew a salary for duties there, was present. In 1917 when Fauré was Director, he was somewhat embarrassed to receive a *second* bust of Saint-Saëns. 'Since my new bust finds its place taken, could someone please put it in the library,' wrote the latter, 'where my education took place.' He describes how, in order to hear rehearsals for the orchestral concerts, which were forbidden to students, he would hide behind the rim of the boxes and crawl from one to another like some 'Phantom of the Opéra', evading the patrols of Lescot the janitor. He suggests that Lescot would sometimes delay his rounds to give young genius its opportunities.

The Société des Concerts du Conservatoire had first been mooted

[1] Saint-Saëns greatly admired the fact that Auber, as a young man, had written out seventy Haydn quartets to teach himself the art of composition.

on St Cecilia's Day in 1826, at a lunch given by the violinist Habeneck to fellow admirers of Beethoven. It slowly contributed to improved standards of orchestral playing. (The *Revue Musicale* in 1827 noted that half the Opéra orchestra was playing in the major key and half in the minor.) In French opinion the new orchestra was the finest in Europe. Beethoven figured prominently in the programmes. Soloists from the first desks, such as Auguste Franchomme the cellist, or Joseph Guillou the flautist, played pieces written by themselves such as florid variations on operatic melodies. As a mature composer Saint-Saëns was to be one of the first to write solos, deliberately providing such players with items of musical merit. If he were listening to Beethoven's Ninth in 1851 he would have heard an ophicleide imported because of the shortage of double-bass players. Jean Bonnerot suggests that the reports Saint-Saëns gave to his fellow students on the works that he heard earned him the reputation of being a dangerous modernist, but the programmes were conservative in the extreme, for even Schumann and Mendelssohn were scarcely acceptable.

There was talent among his contemporaries. In 1849 when he came second in the Organ Prize, the First Prize was won by Edouard Silas, a Dutchman, who later settled in London and became organist at the Catholic church of Kingston-on-Thames. In 1871, Opus 23, the Gavotte for Piano, was dedicated to Silas. At the same time the Prix de Solfège was shared between Bizet and Delibes. Henry Wieniawski took a piano prize and a Mlle Wertheimer (who was to appear later in Saint-Saëns's career) and Romain Bussine Junior came high in the lists of singers. Bussine, son of a star baritone at the Opéra Comique, was a particular friend. He helped to create the part of the High Priest in private performances of *Samson*, collaborated in the founding of the Société National in 1871, resigned in sympathy in 1886 and was buried in the Saint-Saëns family tomb at Montparnasse. The great song 'Le Pas d'Armes du Roi Jean' was dedicated to Bussine Senior. In 1851, when Saint-Saëns won the Organ Prize, Bussine the Younger came head of the Opéra Comique category and later he was Professor of Singing. In the same year Charles Lecocq, future composer of operetta, carried off an '*accessit*' for counterpoint and Bizet came second among the pianists. Auber permitted applause at the competitions, something that the martinet Cherubini had never allowed; he would bang furiously on his bell and threatened to clear the hall if audience reaction was evident. Other members of Benoist's organ class included Joseph Franck, younger brother of César, and Jules Cohen, the First Prize winner in 1852, who was also a great friend and later assisted Saint-Saëns in his organist duties. Jules Cohen's Cantata *Vive l'Empereur*, in homage to Napoleon III, was performed six times in 1861 alone.

As in all such institutions life was full of incident and articulate passions. The young Camille was particularly impressed by a contest for declamation between two young actresses, one of whom was more accomplished 'but the other in beauty and voice was so marvellous that she carried it off. There had been a demonstration, an uproar; today ... the prize would be divided.' Strange that he should have remembered this when he tells us little of the competitions in which he and his musical friends were engaged. The all-powerful Meyerbeer, to whose fame all young composers aspired, was a 'consultant' to the Conservatoire and sometimes visited the competitions. In 1849, a Mlle Constance Nantier sang an excerpt from his new work *Le Prophète*, and when his presence was noticed acclamations broke out and the whole assembly turned towards him with cheers and applause. One wonders whether Camille was part of this outburst of homage for he remained a champion of Meyerbeer to the end of his days.[1]

It was usual for government ministers to make speeches at the prize-givings. In 1849 when, as a Second Prize winner, he would have been present, the man from the Ministry expressed hopes for an increased subvention and the reopening of boarding facilities for girls. This would have been a more popular theme than that of the previous year: 'The Role of Music in Sparta'! Government was closely involved with matters at the rue Bergère. In 1850 a famous singer, Henriette Sontag, gained permission from the Ministry to have the hall of the Conservatoire and give six performances in Italian, semi-staged in costume. There was an outburst of fury and subscribers to the Société des Concerts claimed that the sanctuary of Beethoven and Haydn was about to be violated by selections from the Théâtre des Italiens; the Committee unavailingly signed a protest in the name of *all* the professors and pupils at the Academy condemning the flouting of tradition and invasion of rights of property.

[1] Reynaldo Hahn wrote, 'People of my father's generation would rather have doubted the solar system than the supremacy of *Le Prophète* over all other operas.

At this time Saint-Saëns was working on a second (unpublished) symphony. A long Introduction beginning with a unison D for the whole orchestra provides a theme, which is rhythmed into an accompaniment for the First Subject, but the work was abandoned after twenty pages, of which the chief portion is marked 'vivace'. A 'Serenata' (unpublished) appears to come from the same period but, as it also is in D and Saint-Saëns never followed a First with a Second Movement in the same key, it cannot be connected. In 1851 he was virtually unchallenged winner of the Organ Prize. From the same year, possibly earlier, he was admitted to the Composition Class of Halévy, the eminent operatic composer so often beset by aspiring singers anxious for auditions. In 1851 his latest work, *La Tempête*, was put on at the Théatre des Italiens, with the great singer Luigi Lablache as Caliban. In 1851–2 he would have been engaged in writing *Le Juif Errant*, based on a novel by Eugène Sue and in three months of rehearsals, which brought tribulations. 'If there were more activity at the Theatre, and I mean real activity, we would be making better progress', he wrote. 'Every instant there is some rehearsal, some scheduling requirement, which demands more work.' He was a kindly man, who at one time gave the impoverished Jacques Offenbach lessons free of charge and channelled commissions towards the needy Wagner. He was more efficient than he appeared to his students. He served as Secretary to the Academy of Fine Arts, headed the commission which established the definitions of note pitch, having collected information from musical institutions across Europe, and shared Saint-Saëns's interest in all manner of non-musical subjects. He is said to have been deliberately unpunctual, working on the maxim that 'to be punctual is to wait for other people'. Saint-Saëns recalled, 'Wholly wrapped up in his own work, he frequently neglected his class and came along only when he could spare the time. His students attended all the same and instructed each other – much less indulgently, I might add, than their master, whose greatest fault was over-kindness.' His class-mate Charles Lecocq was more caustic and spoke of their Alma Mater as the 'Renversatoire' where one learned the 'art of decomposition'. He and Saint-Saëns corresponded throughout their lives and, in 1892, Lecocq related a nightmare in which he believed they were both back in Halévy's class. 'Halevy was wiping his spectacles with a surly expression while Ferrière [some kind of surveillant?], crowned with his perpetual stove-pipe hat, summoned the pupils with the tones of a gendarme.' In the dream, Halévy, Thomas, Gounod and Auber were all in the pupils' desks and the teacher was Alfred Bruneau. Lecocq dreamt that Bruneau 'berated his pupils in no uncertain terms I can assure you'.

Halévy was not hidebound. He made efforts to import local colour into his scores. *La Fée aux Roses*, an opera set in India, offended the critics with its strange rhythms and unorthodox harmonics.[1] His greatest success, *La Juive*, made use of Jewish traditional themes, as in the chant of the Hebrews in Act One of *Samson and Delilah*. Yet Saint-Saëns acknowledged no great debt to him. Berlioz considered Halévy's orchestration too heavy, which could never be said of Saint-Saëns's, and the young Camille had already developed an interest in the mysterious East which owed nothing to his teachers. One of the first works which show an individual stamp was an attempt at *opéra comique* on a tale of Persia. Of this the Overture and an Aria (sung by one Saphi to a Leila) survive. The accompaniment to the Aria contains the characteristic touch of kettledrums employed *ppp* and a harp sweeps in on the line 'When on our harps of gold we sing her praises' as later it was to reinforce Samson's praises to the Lord. The unfinished Overture has a quiet classical opening which recalls Haydn's 'Austrian Hymn', but oriental touches are provided by the flute, oboe and pizzicato harp.

His studies in the library began to bear fruit in larger-scale compositions. A Symphony in A dates from around 1850 and may even have been completed before he joined Halévy's class. The symphony was not a form held in high honour at the Conservatoire whose principal concerns were training for the cantata, in preparation for the Prix de Rome, and, in the organ class, pedantic exercises in fugue and counterpoint. 'The symphony was considered as a school-exercise,' said the critic Tiersot in 1902. It was a test of talent but 'in the eyes of the judges, it had neither great importance nor elevated artistic significance'. Saint-Saëns's desire to follow the 'German' school is another example of his apartness. It also shows his preoccupation with form as a prime fascination in the art of composition. The cantata did not allow him to experiment with form; the symphony did and, in the shaping of the movements, he could

[1] He was, like Saint-Saëns, interested in new instruments and was one of the first to use valve horns in his scores. In the 1850 *La Dame de Pique* Berlioz thought the percussion was too prominent.

experiment with classical patterns. This first complete example of the genre is, as one would expect, very formal. In both the first movement and last, the exposition is repeated before the development; the Scherzo and Trio follow the accepted academic formula in full. By the time he had polished his first sketches he had added an Adagio Introduction, which finishes in Beethovian chords, followed by some calming woodwind passages before the Allegro begins. Beethoven sheds some influence in two other respects: in the stately Minuet which forms the slow movement the repetition of the opening statement is interpreted by a long passage in a more tempestuous vein in which the fourteen- to fifteen-year-old disturbs the tranquillity with rumblings and anguish. Later, in the Finale, he plays with the false anticipation of a peaceful ending, which turns unexpectedly into a rumbustious conclusion. A phrase from the Mozart *Jupiter* Symphony prominently underlies the first movement and is extended at the close of the development. The melody of the Minuet has a Handelian sound; the works of Handel were not well known in Paris, but Saint-Saëns had recently composed piano variations for four hands on the Chorus from *Judas Maccabeus*. The most original movement is the Finale, which, though it is in sonata form, has the impetus of a *perpetuum mobile*, demands the difficult feat of 'sempre staccato' in the rapid string passages, throws a new melody for oboe into the development and omits the second subject from the recapitulation to add to the sense of haste. When the first subject returns in the recapitulation the rhythm is accentuated by fortissimo chords from full orchestra. Then the time signature changes to the faster 2:4 and the strings play in unison while the woodwind stress an accelerando figure. He was already a master of the applause-raising climax. The Symphony was scored for a small orchestra and a separate version of the Scherzo with parts for single woodwind may have been designed for student performances. A symphony with chorus ('Les Cloches'), which also suggests Beethovian aspirations, was discarded.

In 1852, aged sixteen, he competed for the Prix de Rome. He was obliged to follow the traditional practice, which incarcerated the candidates equipped with only a piano for company, forbade the importation of letters or materials that might afford outside help and allowed only brief periods of assembling for meals. On this occasion the words to be set were entitled 'Le Retour de Virginie', but they failed to inspire. Saint-Saëns had suffered badly from illness of the lungs during the previous months. At times the pronouncements of the doctors had been gloomy. Augé de Lassus, a much later librettist and biographer, who must have discussed this episode of the Prix de Rome, speaks of him 'shorn of his strength and talent' and indicates that his mother's hopes placed too heavy a burden on his young shoulders. The Grand Prix went to Léonce Cohen, Saint-Saëns's senior by six years, another friend from the organ class, who had fared well in the competition the previous year. The Second Prize went to Ferdinand Poise, even more senior at twenty-six. The history of the Prix de Rome is famously littered with ironies. Cohen never produced any memorable work. Poise was prolific and his opera *Don Pedro* enjoyed some popularity in the 1850s. His other pieces suggest their nature by their titles: *Le Jardinier Galant*, *L'Amour Médecin*, etc. Saint-Saëns does not appear to have shown any rancour and, when he was a music critic in the 1870s, he found space to praise pieces by Poise. Augé de Lassus tells us that Auber thought the prize should have gone to Saint-Saëns, whose promise he esteemed more highly than the score in front of him.

Outside the Conservatoire his career as a pianist continued. In 1849 he played Beethoven variations at a charity concert organised on behalf of the poor of Paris by Meyerbeer's librettist, Eugène Scribe. Here he made the acquaintance of the singer Pauline Viardot, who in the same year enjoyed her greatest triumph as Fidès in *Le Prophète*. She toured the capitals of Europe in this role, but at her soirées in Paris she speedily made Saint-Saëns her favourite accompanist. During 1851 he played several times at concerts given by the new Société Ste Cécile, founded by the violinist Seghers (the same who had vetoed his performance of a concerto at the Société des Concerts in 1846). The Société Ste Cécile came into being in 1848 to introduce a more modern repertoire: Schumann, Mendelssohn and Berlioz, even early Wagner. It took its name from the hall in which the concerts were held and the programmes aroused a good deal of hostility, not only from the public but from the players themselves. It gave the first Paris performance of Schubert's *Great* C major; the Conservatoire had rehearsed but abandoned it during the 1840s. In January 1851, still only fifteen, Saint-Saëns played the Beethoven Triple Concerto and a month later Beethoven's Fantasia for Piano, Chorus and Orchestra, a work in which the piano writing finds many echoes in his own earlier pieces. Mendelssohn's lightness and clarity made an instant appeal to him, especially the *Scottish* Symphony. Schumann's power of feeling also exerted a strong influence, though he found the style dense, breathless and sometimes too heavy in its demands on players. Yet he adored the Quintet (his first major chamber work used the same forces) and the romantic Lieder. It was at this time that he began to write songs which have endured. 'Guitare' to words by Victor Hugo was composed in 1851, though unpublished until 1870, when he dedicated it to Augusta Holmès, who was but a child of four at the time it was written.

After its inauspicious start the acquaintance of Seghers and Saint-Saëns ripened and it was at the violinist-conductor's home that the youth first met Franz Liszt, who had entrusted the musical education of his two daughters to a pupil, now Mme Seghers. The friendship between Liszt and Saint-Saëns came later and was one of the most rewarding in nineteenth-century music. The Société Ste Cécile restored his spirits after the disappointment of failing with the Prix de Rome. In October 1852 he entered a competition for an 'Ode to Ste Cécile'. The Committee which judged the entries was a distinguished body and included Halévy, Adam, Reber and Gounod. His winning Cantata (out of twenty-two entries) was given a public performance on 26 December and two years later, in March 1854, it was repeated, a bonus which few of the Rome laureates enjoyed. Unfortunately, either for this or subsequent performances, the score and parts were scattered, for only copies for soprano solo, chorus and violins have survived. The actual orchestra employed was a large one; during the course of composition a cor anglais, three trombones, harp and harmonium were added. The lost work set a respectable seal on his growing reputation. He had, together with Bizet, been helping Gounod with piano arrangements of Incidental Music for a Five Act Tragedy, *Ulysse*, by the dramatist François Ponsard. He attended the opening night in June 1852 and described its failure: 'The play seemed boring and certain brutally realistic lines shocked the audience . . . they whispered and laughed . . . After the failure of *Sapho* and *Ulysse*, Gounod's future could have seemed dubious to the uninitiated but not to the élite which places artists where they rightly belong. He was marked with the sign of the chosen.'

3

The Parish Organist

The world into which Saint-Saëns stepped at the end of his studies was very different from that which existed when he first attended. During his first term the election of a President of the new Republic had taken place, but the victor was not Lamartine, who had favoured universal suffrage with his own triumph in mind, nor General Cavaignac, whose reputation was stained with the bloodshed of the 'June Days', but the almost unknown Louis Napoleon, nephew of Napoleon I, whose name captured the imagination of millions of provincial voters.

His sudden advent to power had not been anticipated by the political classes. Dominique Cavaillé-Coll, father of the organ-builder, visiting one of the Ministries on the morrow of the election, found it in total disarray. Louis Napoleon, a man of great ambitions, confused and contrary as they were, was the son of Bonaparte's brother Louis, and also grandson of the Empress Josephine, through his mother Hortense. One of the first signs of his ambitions was, at the end of 1848, to appropriate the boxes of the deceased Duke of Orleans at the Opéra and Opéra Comique. Within months, demonstrations in Paris had been dispersed and extremists forced into exile. The much heralded *Le Prophète* had been planned in 1848, but critics such as Blaze de Bury were not slow to point out the dangers of a major work portraying the religious risings of the sixteenth century: 'bands of Anabaptists preaching Communism to the distraught populations and coming to offer the sombre and prophetic tableaux of social revolution'. Both the President and the Chamber of Deputies were in their different ways conservative, but the Chamber, which was largely royalist in sympathies, was unable to agree upon a Bourbon or an Orleanist restoration. The tussle between President and Chamber was marked by suspicions and nervous attempts at pre-emptive strikes.

Berlioz remarked that to create works of art at such a time was like 'trying to play billiards on a storm-tossed ship'.

The President was surrounded by an unsavoury group including illegitimate scions of Napoleon I's grandees and on 2 December 1851 republican government was swept away in a *coup d'état*. On the previous evening the Opéra Comique quite inexplicably gave the première of a bizarre piece: *Le Château de Barbe-Bleue*, about a supposed niece of the English James II living near Madras and awaiting the restoration of the Stuarts. Restorations were the theme of the moment. The circle of Pauline Viardot was especially distressed by the *coup d'état* and gathered at her home to discuss the crisis. The house was searched and letters from foreign revolutionaries such as Manin (of Venice) and Kossuth (of Hungary) were taken away. A year later, while the august group of musicians sat in judgement on Saint-Saëns's 'Ode to Ste Cécile', the political Senate was asked to approve Louis Napoleon's elevation to the rank of Emperor. In the following month he married Eugénie de Montijo, whose deep brand of Spanish Catholicism gave a strong thrust to the power of the Church. 'It is the duty of the sovereign', said Napoleon III at Bayonne, 'to approach the altar in order to ask Heaven, through the intercession of its consecrated Ministers, to bless his efforts, to enlighten his conscience, to give him strength to do good and combat evil.' He supported church charities, restored buildings and allocated some of the millions he had confiscated from Louis Philippe's family to pensions for aged priests. At the outset of the new Imperial regime the Church, in turn, supported him as a champion of order. Early in his Presidency he had sent troops to Rome to crush the Roman Republic, restore Pope Pius IX and guard him with a French garrison. When he sought approval for his *coup d'état* by a plebiscite, the great preacher Montalembert urged support: '[His Coup] put to flight all the revolutionaries, all the Socialists, all the bandits of France and Europe. I recall such deeds as the liberty of religious instruction, the restoration of the Pope by French arms and the Church restored to the plenitude of its dignity with its Councils and Synods, the increase of its colleges and its charities.'

It is not surprising, therefore, that organ builders flourished and young composers such as Saint-Saëns found their first employments in a thriving, if often false, atmosphere of religiosity. In 1853 he was appointed organist of the Church of St Merri situated on the edge of

Les Halles. He had already some experience at the Church of St
Severin and it always gave him joy in old age to mount the steps of the
organs of his youth and renew acquaintance with their often antique
workings. At seventeen, he succeeded a seventy-eight-year-old at St
Merri, Vincent-Edmond Govin. He owed his appointment not only to
his prizes at the Conservatoire but to his mother's cultivation of a
friendship with the curé, Jean-Louis Gabriel. St Merri is a large
church and a census of 1863 noted a parish of 26,000 and 232
weddings a year. The fees from weddings and funerals added to the
modest salary. Among his nearest neighbours in the organ world was
Edouard Batiste, uncle of Delibes, in the huge St Eustache, who was
ranked as the second most popular organist in the capital (Lefébure-
Wély at the Madeleine indisputably held first place) and César Franck,
at the Church of St Jean-St François, who did not court popularity but
developed a severer meditative style, which matched Saint-Saëns's
seriousness.

Stories of the generally low standard of musical taste in the churches
abound. Montalembert himself had written in 1839 that the vogue for
playing tunes from the latest operas, waltzes and the like, was
'grotesque and irreligious'. Fétis wrote: 'Not one of them could master
the great compositions of Bach. All their attention is turned towards
special effects. . . . There have been no distinguished organists in
France since the seventeenth century . . . "Storms" have been standard
ever since.' On major Feast Days the overture to *William Tell* was
popular; hunting and even drinking songs would make their appearance as lively accompaniments to the services. The fact that few
organs had the capacity to meet the demands of major organ works
and the strongly ingrained tradition of improvisation lowered the
expectations of worshippers. The young Alexandre Guilmant from
Boulogne was recommended to Cavaillé-Coll as being so gifted that
he could read the works of Bach with hands and feet together!

Yet, by coincidence, 1852, when the Second Empire was born,
marked also a turning point in the history of French organ playing.
On the new Cavaillé-Coll instrument at St Vincent de Paul the
Belgian organist Jaak Nikolaas Lemmens gave an authentic perform-
ance of Bach's music marked by fine pedal technique. As a pupil of
Adolphe Hesse, pupil of Johann Forkel, who had studied with C. P. E.
Bach, Lemmens was in an apostolic succession. The audience,
including Gounod, Alkan, Thomas, Franck and Benoist, were struck

by the revelation and Benoist wrote to Cavaillé-Coll of the 'calm religious grandeur and serenity of style befitting the majesty of the Temple of God. In these times it is of great merit ... to remain faithful to the traditions of the Great Masters who, in the last century, have laid the foundations of the true art of the organ.' Cavaillé-Coll was more than ever determined to create a new school of French organ players and founded private and informal scholarships to send pupils to Lemmens at the Brussels Conservatoire: Guilmant, Widor and Clément Loret, teacher of Fauré, were among those he supported. At the same time he was using his technical skills to ensure a more steady wind pressure, to invent new methods of manual coupling hitherto impractical because of the heavy action required, to develop Swell enclosures, increasing dynamic expression, extending keyboards and pedals, creating a new range of orchestral sonorities and combinations of stops, which could be brought into play at a single moment.

St Merri was an abbreviation of Saint Médéric, who lived in the seventh century and was buried beneath the church. The seventeenth-century organ, restored by François-Henri Clicquot before the Revolution, had been badly damaged during the revolutionary wars, when vaporous saltpetre was manufactured inside the church building. The pedals had a range of only twenty-one notes, a compass which made the performance of Bach's music impossible, and two of its four manuals, the Récit and the Echo, were restricted. The machinery was in a poor state, which gave the organist, with limited duties, time to compose. Encouraged by Seghers, Saint-Saëns wrote another symphony. All works performed at the Société Ste Cécile had to be approved by the committee and Seghers knew that they were unlikely to recommend a major item by an eighteen-year-old already known to them. The Symphony in E flat was presented as having been sent by an unknown composer, probably German. Did not Liszt write to Berlioz when the latter was planning his first German tour: 'Germany is the country of symphonies; it is therefore yours!' The subterfuge does not appear to have aroused any suspicions and the programme carried three stars instead of the composer's name plus a note in small print: 'The manuscript of this symphony has been sent without the name of the composer to the committee, which after mature consideration has not hesitated to have it performed.' Saint-Saëns attended rehearsals with his mother and friends, and stationed himself near enough to Berlioz and Gounod to hear their comments and compliments. Georges Mathias, who had a piece in the same programme, recalled seeing the little group of Saint-Saëns's relations and friends, the young composer looking 'extremely serious'. When Gounod discovered the authorship of the work he recalled his early meetings with Saint-Saëns, then aged ten, and sent him a long-treasured letter laying upon him the solemn duty of becoming a great composer.

The E flat Symphony has been subjected to close analysis, but no one has made reference to the prominent military overtones. In the first movement there are fanfares and, even in the light and jaunty second movement, there is a strident call to arms. The Finale is introduced by a veritable 'marche militaire', which plunges into pure parade-ground music. This would be entirely in keeping with the mood of France in 1853. The name of Napoleon derived its magnetism from memories of military exploits and Napoleon III was obliged to show favours to the Army. It was Karl Marx who said that the *coup d'état* had been made easier by the lavish distribution of champagne and cigars to regimental officers. Once the Emperor was established a succession of commissioned cantatas greeted the birth of the Prince Imperial, the Crimean War, the fall of Sebastopol, battles in Italy and the despatch of troops to Mexico.

Although the Emperor was not at heart a warrior, military parades were conspicuous and Paris was a garrison town. Arthur Dandelot, impresario and biographer, remembered a young Prince Imperial, a babe in arms, being whisked through the streets surrounded by cohorts of cavalry. Although it might not be true to suggest that Saint-Saëns was proving in his symphony that he could write martial music with the best, it does display a truculence which was rarely an aspect of his music, but which reflects the mood of the early 1850s, when bugle calls were heard relentlessly across the land.

With astonishing assurance for this first attempt to storm the concert platform, Saint-Saëns does not hesitate to make some novel changes to the classical form, substituting a 4:4 'alla marcia' rhythm for the customary 3:4 Scherzo and placing it before the Adagio, reintroducing the introduction to the first movement with richer orchestrations at the focal points[1] and including fugal writing in the

---

[1] A recently discovered (and recorded) Quartet for Piano and Strings

Finale which omits a proper recapitulation. Apparently regardless of the shaky finances of the Société Ste Cécile he calls in the first movement for four timpani requiring two players and the Finale is scored for a very large orchestra, including piccolo, two flutes, two oboes, two B-flat clarinets, up to four bassoons, two horns in F, two chromatic horns in D flat, two valve trumpets in E flat, chromatic cornets and up to four harps. In order that the symphony should not escape notice he also added two saxhorns, from the family of instruments newly launched by Adolphe Sax and patented as recently as 1845.[1] In that year a contest had been arranged by the War Ministry to improve the quality of military bands and the saxhorns directed by the inventor had been officially recognised.

Their presence under Seghers's baton emphasised again the atmosphere of military flamboyance served by music. It is significant that Saint-Saëns seems to have begun his plans with the Finale. The brass is rarely preponderant, however, and the presence of harps provides much softer colouring most effectively in the ever-changing orchestration of the Adagio. The attitude to key structure is far from classical, the four movements following a scheme: E flat–G–E–E flat. To make the unusual – and unbroken – transition from the Adagio to the Finale, a long phrase mounts to A sharp, which becomes the B-flat dominant of the ensuing March. In the opening movement he modulates from E flat to C for the second subject, rather than to the classical dominant, B flat, possibly in order that the fanfares might have greater force.

It would have been impossible to exclude all influences upon such a young composer and there are reminiscences of Beethoven's repeated thumps in the first movement, of Mendelssohn in the second and Berlioz in the third. Yet it is clear that Saint-Saëns, later the archetypal conservative, was here allying himself with the moderns; perhaps with his aptitude for identifying with his performers he was following the policy of Seghers in furthering the cause of the Romantics.

The inner movements have generally been judged the most

(written between October 1851 and May 1853) uses the same device of prefacing sections of the sonata form with the identical introductory bars. But the idea is a clumsy one, especially in a smaller medium, and it was not repeated in maturer compositions.

[1] He was always interested in new instruments. A Psalm setting, 'Super Flumina', discovered after his death and posthumously performed at Versailles, adds a quartet of saxophones to strings and organ.

successful. The 'Marche-Scherzo', the kind of title he liked to invent, is a melodious foretaste of the composer's entertaining vein, a stroll through the Paris streets from the rue de Jardinet to St Merri by a young man whose mind is running on Mendelssohn's delicate scoring. The Adagio is astonishingly profound; a long, repeated song, the opening bars of which follow a contour reminiscent of the lament of Marguerite in the *Damnation of Faust*, but which moves on to the rising theme step by step so beloved of Saint-Saëns which reappears in the Romance, Opus 37, *La Jeunesse d'Hercule*, and the last Act of *Henry VIII*. The introduction to the Finale has such jauntiness of gait one wishes it did not disappear so swiftly. It leads to a solemn march, followed by several second subjects, which provide the material for the Fugue in the development and the boisterous Coda. His First (unpublished) Symphony apart, Saint-Saëns never quite solved the problem of a Finale, but the style, even if it falls into the bombastic, has a vigour which only Berlioz among French composers seemed capable of achieving.

The identity of the writer of this most innovative symphony did not long remain a secret. Blanchard, in the *Revue et Gazette*, said that it was by a pianist-composer pupil of Stamaty and that it had failed in a competition in Brussels to celebrate the birth of the Prince of Brabant. He described the Scherzo as 'a jewel of melody ... in the style of Haydn'. The Scherzo was the first extract to be played at the popular Pasdeloup Concerts (originally in 1863) and the whole symphony was performed by him in February 1872, but it fell into oblivion during the period when the composer was producing many major works.[1] In 1896, however, when there were Saint-Saëns celebrations afoot to mark fifty years of public appearances, the conductor Georges Marty approached the publishers for a copy of the score. Durand had bought the plates from the initial publisher, Richault, and informed the composer of this renewed interest with some trepidation, lest he would object.

My dear friend [wrote Durand], I forgot to tell you about the

---

[1] The symphony brought forth a somewhat typical burst of temper in 1919 when he heard a suggestion that he had put a 500-franc note into the score when submitting it to the committee. He wrote to the *Revue Musicale* that he had never at any time used such means to have his music performed and at seventeen he could not have 'afforded such liberality'.

surprise I was saving for you. It concerns the performance of your First Symphony at a Concert at the Opéra on Maundy Thursday and the Saturday before Easter. Marty came to ask me for it and I had no reason to refuse him a work which is in the catalogue ... He wanted an unpublished work but a performance of the Symphony would almost be a first hearing, since few people are able to remember having heard it at Seghers! Since then only fragments have been played – especially the Marche-Scherzo. This youthful work does not show its age; naturally the two movements which make the greatest impression are No. 2 for the public and the Adagio for the artists.... This exhumation is of the greatest interest.

In reply, Saint-Saëns expressed no disapproval but remarked, 'It will be necessary to place in the papers that I wrote this work at the age of seventeen, which excuses reminiscences of Mendelssohn, Schumann, Félicien David and also *Faust*, which was not composed until much later – but this, as you know is what one calls "pre-imitation".'

Meanwhile, at St Merri he was establishing his reputation as an organist. He studied the works of the Masters and some pieces by Liszt. The organ remained inadequate for either composers or performers of genius, as we learn from the modest proposals for improvement suggested in 1854, which refer to a proper covering of the keys with ivory for the white and ebony for the black, the revision of pitch to that of a normal orchestra and the replacement of the pedal board, 'which the organist uses only with difficulty!' Saint-Saëns must have registered some discontent as, several months later, the suggestions were shown to Cavaillé-Coll, who added the proposal that the four manuals should be reduced to three and that the pedal sounds should be deepened. He had in his workshop two organs awaiting delivery, one for a church in Ghent and the other for the cathedral at Carcassonne. He invited the Church Council to inspect them and secured a contract for the overhaul of the instrument. In a letter of June 1855, Saint-Saëns mentions that repairs would begin the following week. At some point in the year he visited Carcassonne and played, perhaps even inaugurated, the new installation. Work at St Merri consisted of modernising rather than constructing. In his invitation to the 'Solemn Reception' on 25 November 1857, when work was completed, the builder refers to the instrument 'which has just been restored and perfected'. The console was rebuilt but kept within the organ case, although it was his usual practice to detach and reverse it. The manuals were reduced to three but their compass extended to fifty-four notes and the pedal board was extended to twenty-seven. The pitch of the entire organ was raised a whole tone. The Diapason had been B flat rather than C and eleven combination pedals gave swifter changes to the player. Interestingly, he retained some of the antique stops at the insistence of Saint-Saëns, who felt that he needed them for the eighteenth-century pieces he so admired.

At the same time he became interested in the harmonium, another product of the inventive 1840s. Alexandre Debain had experimented with developing reed-tone colours operated from a keyboard and patented the name 'harmonium'. Rival firms produced a variety of similar inventions. Debain numbered his stops and these numbers, printed above music staves, instructed the players. The keyboard divided at middle E so that different registrations could be used for the left and right hands. In 1851, Debain also patented a 'Harmonicorde' which was a combination of harmonium and piano, in which a set of single wire strings were employed, giving the effect of a harp accompanying a wind instrument. In 1852 Saint-Saëns's Opus I appeared as Three Pieces for the Harmonium: 'Meditation, Barcarolle and Prayer'.[1] The Barcarolle was dedicated to Mlle Bertha de Tinan, who after her marriage as Mme Bertha Pochet de Tinan held a musical salon in Paris and at her summer residence near Le Havre. The first and third items were dedicated to M. and Mme Eugène Devivier. One assumes they had harmoniums. The Meditation is in rondo form, as no doubt many meditations are, but the hymn tune theme which reappears with tremulant does not have the customary rondo spirit. The Barcarolle is a single ABA melody with an accompaniment that becomes more complex. The inspiration for a Barcarolle probably came directly from Mendelssohn, whose 'Venetian Gondolier's Song' had been published ten years earlier. Saint-Saëns rather oddly seemed to associate the Barcarolle with the harmonium.[2] The surprising item is the Prayer, which is in the strange time of 11:4, one of the first examples of a bizarre metre in the

[1] Berlioz had published Three Pieces for Harmonium in 1845 but Saint-Saëns was one of the first of the great composers to write seriously for it.
[2] April 1897, unpublished Barcarolle for Violin, Cello, Organ and Piano. March 1898, Barcarolle Opus 108 for Violin, Cello, Harmonium and Piano.

nineteenth century. Opus 1 was published in 1858, intended for the new market as many bourgeois households were investing in these instruments whose tones exuded an air of piety. (The young Fauré began his interest in music improvising on a harmonium in an old chapel at Montgauzy near Foix, adjacent to his father's seminary.)

The Piano Quartet in E major remained unpublished.[1] Saint-Saëns must have been at work on it at the same time as his symphony and swimming against the tide, which bore composers towards the theatre. Quartets earlier in the century resembled conversation pieces in which one leader predominated, represented by the First Violin. Pierre Baillot (1771–1842) was the initiator of chamber-music concerts in France and he would play standing while the others were seated. The piano was slow to make its appearance, but its rapid spread into middle-class homes and the concerts given by the virtuosi (in 1837 Liszt played the Beethoven Trios in public and at about the same time Franck was the first pianist to perform the Schubert Trios) established it as a chamber-music instrument. In 1847 the violinist Delphin Alard gave concerts with the cellist Franchomme (from whom Saint-Saëns took some lessons in accompaniment) and the pianist Charles Hallé. These were interrupted by the revolution of 1848 and Hallé's departure for England. The genre appealed to the high-minded as being akin to intellectual conversation as opposed to mere entertainment, but chamber-music composers were not numerous. Georges Onslow, of English descent and private means, who succeeded to the Chair of Cherubini at the Institut, wrote almost seventy string quartets. Henri Reber, Professor of Harmony at the Conservatoire, enjoyed some success at the Opéra Comique, but wrote chamber pieces of which Saint-Saëns sometimes gave the first performances at the home of a M. and Mme Dien, professional musicians who taught by day and held weekly soirées in their apartment in the rue des Beaux-Arts.

Emile Baumann, who wrote a Study of Saint-Saëns's music and had conversations with him in the first years of this century, writes about contemporary composers and we can hear Saint-Saëns giving his views.

It is necessary to look again, *in spite of their defects*, at the Violin

---

[1] It has only recently been edited by Sabina Ratner in Editions Musicales du Marais in 1992.

Sonata and Quintet of Franck, so rich in ideas, so strongly constructed. The Trios of Lalo, _diffuse it is true_, are lively and high-spirited, recalling the countryside of the north with great nostalgia. There are Widor's elegant Trio and Quintet, the _learned_ Quartets of d'Indy, the _admirable_ Violin Sonata of Fauré, ardent as those of Schumann, with more suppleness in the rhythms and more subtle feelings.

As these words show, chamber music later became well established in France and Saint-Saëns was a leader in this field. The Quartet in E is simple but deft, with no problems of balance between the piano and strings. A Handelian opening, lengthy and cantabile, reappears at the end of the exposition and, in more romantic style, before the Coda. The piano dominates in the Andante, where it introduces a peaceful melody, so Brahmsian in character that one wonders why Saint-Saëns could never bring himself to appreciate his German contemporary. There is a middle section, a light Gavotte, which has the touch of elegance which Saint-Saëns brought to all his eighteenth-century pastiches. The Finale is headed 'Allegro con fuoco' and a dance-like figure flits through the pages which terminate in the usual Saint-Saëns invitation for applause.

A more accomplished work, and one for which the composer retained affection, was the Piano Quintet in A minor, written in 1854–5 and dedicated to Great-Aunt Masson. There were very few examples to guide him and the Schumann Quintet, which he came to admire after some hesitation, did not receive a public performance until 1865 with Charles Lamoureux and his colleagues. Beethoven's quintets were written for piano and woodwind, or for strings alone. Emile Baumann, whose partisan prose is always colourful, thought that the quintet contained in embryo many thoughts and feelings to which the composer later gave more opulent utterance. The march-like figure of the Allegro Maestoso, 'grave and with a holy sadness' provided by sighing strings, announces an inspiration 'drawn towards heroic and solemn forms'. Of the Andante he says: 'It is peace, the fullness of a pontifical fête beside a basilica.' This merges into the Scherzo, the first of Saint-Saëns's many essays into the 'fantastic' mood: 'rational and at the same time vertiginous', 'written with dry anger, frightening, lending to shadows the substance of real form'. These shadows disappear in flight and the quintet moves into the fugal opening of the Finale, which ends as 'victory remains with the forces of light'. (Baumann constantly emphasises the spiritual content of Saint-Saëns's music despite the composer's emphatic atheist views of later years.)

To modern ears there are clearer impressions. One is of the virtuosity of the piano part as befits the dedication. At times it is almost a concerto with cadenza and indeed Saint-Saëns performed it later with orchestral strings replacing the quartet.[1] It is also a demonstration of his move towards cyclical composition, for the chords of the opening reappear more than once and the Finale recalls themes from the first movement, with a great deal of superimposing of various ideas produced during the course of the work. Most significantly, the peaceful 3:8 hymn of the Andante only just survives curious interpellations, tremolo and pizzicato, which prefigure the linked Scherzo that follows. There are moments of sadness as in the viola solos of the Andante and an outburst for the strings in the Trio. Recapitulations are adorned with much ornamentation and, despite the stately theme of the Finale, the total effect is one of caution and a certain femininity, which dispels the assertive vigour of the opening pages.

When he had reached twenty, Saint-Saëns was no longer a precocious star and entered the period of harsher reviews from the critics. In the *Revue et Gazette* he lost the favour which had been shown to him by Blanchard, whose successor Adolphe Botte accused him of Schumannesque imitations, as well as a disregard for beauty and emotion. The quintet was harshly treated by Botte.

If the views of Pauline Viardot and her friends turned his mind to politics he had further cause for unease. Despite Napoleon III's promise that the Empire meant peace, he was soon trying to reshape the map of Europe as his uncle had done. The year 1854 was filled with preparations for the outbreak of the Crimean War with Russia. During the completion of the quintet, Frenchmen were dying of disease in the Danube delta and under the cannons of Sebastopol. Saint-Saëns had the opportunity to witness anxiety at close quarters as he was at this time preparing the vocal score of Berlioz's *Lélio* and Berlioz was fearful that his son Louis would perish in the diversionary

[1] It is interesting that the first published version in 1865, Opus 14, provided an additional part for the double bass.

campaign launched in the Baltic Sea. In 1855 Sebastopol fell and the event was celebrated in Paris with a revival of Ferdinand Hérold's popular *Le Pré aux Clercs*, and a Cantata entitled *Victoire* was put together by Adam in a matter of hours on a hastily written libretto.

It was also the year of France's first Universal Exhibition, following the example of Britain's Great Exhibition of 1851. Once again, many improvements in the quality of musical instruments were displayed.[1] Berlioz was one of the judges. In April the Berlioz *Te Deum* was performed at St Eustache with the composer conducting. Saint-Saëns, for whose intellectual accomplishments Berlioz had a high regard, was assisting with the vocal score of *The Damnation of Faust*. If, as is probable, Saint-Saëns was present in St Eustache, the occasion may have been confused with a performance of the Berlioz *Requiem* in 1852, of which he wrote, 'I had read the score and was dying to hear the effect. The Tuba Mirum surpassed my expectations. . . . It seemed as if each separate slim pillar in the church became an organ pipe and the whole edifice a vast organ. Yet even more I admired the poignant feeling of this marvellous work, the constant and incredible elevation of style, far more perceptible by ear than on reading, as is true of all the works of this composer.'

Queen Victoria visited Paris in August and at a gala performance of Auber's *Haydée* the chorus of the Opéra Comique was doubled by that of the newer Théâtre Lyrique. At the larger Exhibition concerts, Gounod conducted singers numbered in thousands. Napoleon III, who, as Berlioz remarked, 'execrates music like ten Turks', fingered his speech and rose nervously to make it before the Berlioz *Emperor* Cantata had run its course. His mildly despotic regime had indeed given France internal peace and hence prosperity, and this had assisted music in many respects. New theatres and halls were constructed, the Châtelet, Théâtre Lyrique and the first stages of the Palais Garnier Opéra. The Salle Herz, built in 1854 to hold an audience of 200 music lovers, added to the city's resources. The notion of technical progress, which had been apparent in the displays of musical instruments, spread to performances and the gap between professional and amateur players

[1] Two hundred and forty-three instrument makers were represented. Brass instruments were being developed with supplementary pistons. Cavaillé-Coll exhibited the Salon Organ, which became the property of Pauline Viardot and on which Saint-Saëns frequently performed. Not all ideas triumphed. One inventor had recently experimented with an octo-basse – a monster double-bass four metres high.

widened. At the Salles Pleyel and Erard, international artists such as Clara Schumann, Joseph Joachim and Rubinstein aimed at a more discerning clientele than the sensational wizards of earlier days. The grouping of industrial populations led to the establishing of many choral societies, which the Government regarded as welcome alternatives to political clubs. The audiences for orchestral concerts grew in numbers until new venues were needed, 'Orphéons' – male choruses – and wind bands recruited from the workers and petit bourgeois sprang up in the provinces with local rivalries sustained in competitions. In Paris itself, Gounod directed the Orphéon from 1852 to 1860 and dedicated a number of works to it.

Yet beneath the show of homage to art as represented in the gala performances and monster Exhibition cantatas (perhaps most of all in the Government's efforts to win prestige with the posthumous production of Meyerbeer's *L'Africaine* at the Opéra in 1865, with no expense spared) there was little official encouragement. The artists, who in the 1830s had believed in their mission to shape Society, could not sympathise with a regime, half-dictatorship, half-populist, and the tastes of the rulers were grandiose or frivolous. Romanticism was over and its leaders were either disillusioned like Berlioz, Théophile Gautier or Eugène Delacroix, or in exile like Hugo. Because of the prevalence of materialism, artists and writers became detached and movements such as the Parnassians elevating art for its own sake governed by its own rules grew, as did Positivism, seeking systems in everything as against the Romantic belief in inspiration and genius.

In 1855 Saint-Saëns's thoughts were also directed towards music flourishing in the provinces. He entered two large orchestral works in contests sponsored by the Société Ste Cécile, not of Paris but of Bordeaux. Bordeaux was a wealthy city with a larger middle-class population than most. In 1843 a Société Ste Cécile was founded as a private philanthropic body to assist musicians, amateur and professional. There was even a doctor appointed to see to the needs of members. Unlike the Leeds, Norwich and Birmingham Societies in Britain, which organised great festivals to support local hospitals, the Bordeaux group was more concerned with mutual aid. It developed an orchestra of its own, very probably comprising players from the Grand Theatre, and in 1853 sponsored an annual musical competition. In the first three years prizes were offered for a hymn, a Mass and a symphony. In the first two years the prizes were won by Antoine Elwart, a Prix de Rome winner and later Professor of Harmony at the Conservatoire. As Elwart was also a conductor at the Paris Ste Cécile, Saint-Saëns must have known of these competitions and Berlioz, who had conducted in Bordeaux, was aware of them. Later, in 1867, a member of the committee summarised the achievements and extolled the *variety* of the competitions as opposed to the 'Institut and its eternal Cantata'. In Paris the Société Ste Cécile had failed and been disbanded, many of its players being seduced away into joining the orchestra of Pasdeloup's Société des Jeunes Artistes. The competition in Bordeaux remained one of the few means of giving young composers an opportunity to write on a spacious scale. Works were submitted from Germany, Russia and Scandinavia. Entries had to be anonymous, bearing some kind of motto, and the winners, who could compete more than once, received a gold medal and 300 francs with, more important, a promise of public performance. Saint-Saëns may have entered several times; Bordeaux should be kept in mind when considering unpublished works. Certainly the Mass, Opus 4, written for St Merri, is dated 1856 and could well have been an entry for the 1855 contest. He was a winner in 1856 with his Symphony *Urbs Roma* (the motto he chose as a superscription), which he appears to have written swiftly in June and July. The prize was announced in January 1857 and the completed work was played in Paris in February under the direction of Saint-Saëns who took up the baton for the first time at the Société des Jeunes Artistes.

The motto 'Urbs Roma' is something of an enigma. Daniel Fallon suggests that Saint-Saëns might have intended a compliment to the capital of the South and its munificence. It is equally likely that he thought such a title might suggest a knowledge of Rome and imply the composer was a winner of the coveted Prize. Elaborate comparisons, for which there is little foundation, have been drawn between the music and the ruins of the Forum, or Rome as seen in the visions of Nicolas Poussin and Claude (Lorrain). Fear of (internal) barbarian attacks and slave rebellions were current in the 1850s, the working classes being regarded as 'barbarians at the gates'. But Rome had always fascinated the French. Berlioz was writing *The Trojans* at the time, an opera vibrant with the idea of the founding of Rome.[1] Even

---

[1] The scenario envisaged a vision of the Capitol with the word 'Roma' engraved at the back of the stage while Dido prophesied the Punic Wars.

in political life, Rome was a current topic as Napoleon III's troops guarding Pius IX were a source of pride to the French Catholics and anger to the opposition.

Great pains were taken over the Bordeaux performance. There exists a letter of June 1857 in which Saint-Saëns 'eagerly and gratefully' accepted the offer of conductor Louis Mézéray to hand over the baton to him and contrasts this with the attitude of the Parisian conductors. According to Bonnerot *this* was the first occasion on which Saint-Saëns conducted and it may well be that Pasdeloup in February had second thoughts and wielded the baton himself. Saint-Saëns accepted places in the principal loge for himself and his mother, and a wreath of oak leaves and laurel, a gift not always bestowed upon successful entrants. The *Urbs Roma* Symphony is another work revived and recorded in recent times, but it was not published in Saint-Saëns's lifetime. It is one of the first of his works for which two MSs exist. In general it was Saint-Saëns's mother who painstakingly wrote out the corrected versions of her son's work. It is not too hard to see why it was never published. Within three years he had written the so-called Second Symphony, in which he took great pride and which he endeavoured to have included in concerts on many occasions. His programme of work was increasing year by year and left little time to dust off old pieces and bring them to light. Most of all, the symphony would not have benefited from revision, for its faults lay not in the treatment, which is full of dexterity, but in the themes themselves, which lack distinction.

It is in F major and prefaced by a slow and solemn fanfare from the brass, punctuated by tutti chords from full orchestra; an impressive Prelude, emphasising the status of the competition, and hence flattering to the judges, is woven from the material. The fanfare returns, but not to mark divisions of the sonata form. Once again he reverses the order of the middle movements and puts the rapid one first. It is not called a Scherzo and is more in the nature of a boisterous country dance. A heavy rhythm is accompanied by pedal notes trilled out by other sections of the orchestra. This second movement is in the mediant rather than the dominant, in this case A minor with the Trio in A major. Saint-Saëns was only twenty, but shows his skills in utilising a large range of colours from the orchestral palette. If he decided against publication later, the reason was probably that he was dissatisfied with the overall shape of the work, which fails to reach a climax. The Finale shows his innovative talents, being cast in the form of theme and variations, but this very experiment precludes a convincing 'summing up' despite its felicitous moments. Whether or not he knew that Beethoven was familiar to the Bordeaux audiences, he seems to have been determined to provide a Beethovian slow movement: a Funeral March which, with its repetitions and a certain banality in the theme, becomes wearisome. It is one of the rare examples of Saint-Saëns going on too long, risking heaviness and boredom, though he remembered these pages and used them again in his film score for *The Assassination of the Duke of Guise*. It is entitled 'moderato assai serioso', but the serioso is unmitigated. A lyrical theme on the clarinet first in F and later in C major appears, but the 'Dead March' returns to extinguish hope. (Interestingly he had set 'La Porta dell'inferno' by Dante the previous year and the abandonment of hope seems to be the message of the movement.) Had it been written a year earlier it might have been taken as a comment on the Crimean War, but 1856 was a year of national rejoicing as the Tsar had sued for peace and, at the time of its composition, Paris was rejoicing at the christening of the Prince Imperial in Notre-Dame.

The Finale, by contrast, is all sweetness and light. The Variations gave further opportunity for Saint-Saëns to display his technical skills. The first variation is based on a rhythmic figure, the second is in 9:8 time and adds woodwind to strings and brass, as if it might be a 'Young Bordelais Guide to the Orchestra', the third is quietly lyrical and the fourth follows the classical pattern by moving 'l'istesso tempo' into the minor and featuring bold dotted rhythms. The fifth is in the unusual time of 5:4 and being only twelve bars in length could be thought of as merely the introduction to the final one. But Saint-Saëns sent careful instructions on conducting in 5:4 time. The last variation is attractive: the theme is syncopated and surrounded with delicate and rapid passages for the violins. A Coda is based on the theme itself and the symphony ends quietly with scale passages for the strings and solo woodwind, rounded off with a soft drum roll and muted chords.

His association with Bordeaux proved fruitful. He often returned to hear his works performed and in 1916 he was Guest of Honour at a Festival devoted to them. Three of the musicians who were to honour his work were born and educated in Bordeaux. Paul Taffanel, the great flautist, was responsible for establishing Saint-Saëns firmly in the repertoire of the Paris Société des Concerts of which he became conductor. Edouard Colonne conducted the first performances of the *Danse Macabre*, *Jeunesse d'Hercule*, the Fourth Piano Concerto and the première of *Samson and Delilah*. Colonne came from a poor Jewish family, lived by music copying and the violin, practising in a garret so cramped that it hindered his bow strokes, but became a noted champion of French music. Charles Lamoureux, though his programmes as conductor concentrated upon German music, reserved a place in them for the composer who was so highly esteemed in his home city when these men were young. In turn, Saint-Saëns paid homage to the achievements of 'a young Bordelais', Bernard Sarrette, as the true founder of the Paris Conservatoire, for which Cherubini had taken too great a share of the praise. 'There should be a statue of Sarrette in the middle of the courtyard. Justice would then be accorded,' he wrote in the *Voltaire* in July 1876.[1]

During these early years at St Merri he was also writing some of his most successful songs. He was fired with enthusiasm for the poetry of Hugo and Lamartine. His flowing Schumannesque setting of Hugo's 'Rêverie', a remarkably polished achievement for a boy of fifteen or sixteen, dates from 1851 and was followed a year later by Hugo's 'Le Pas d'Armes du Roi Jean', which so captures the zest and hollowness of medieval chivalry, courtly love, brutality about young death and religious sanctimony – all in a compressed space – that it is a miniature symphonic poem. Several songs were dedicated to Mlle Marie Reiset, the daughter of Frédéric Reiset, Curator at the Louvre, a collector of paintings both for himself and for the Orleanist Duke of Aumale. Bonnerot describes these songs, 'L'Attente' (Hugo), 'Le Lever de la Lune' (after Ossian), 'Plainte' and 'La Feuille de Peuplier' (A. Tastu), a duet 'Pastorale' (Destouches) and 'Le Sommeil des Fleurs' (de Penmarch), as 'spring-like homage' and they may indeed have been elements of a youthful courtship.[2] All the accompaniments, especially

---

[1] One of the first studies of his music was made by a young Bordelais, Gaston Sarreau, in 1904.

[2] Marie Reiset was later Vicomtesse de Grandval and a successful composer. She is usually described as 'a pupil of Flotow and Saint-Saëns', but she was five years older than Camille. No one acquired a greater cluster of dedications among his songs than Marie Reiset and their themes are romantic. There is no reason why a nineteen-year-old should not fall for a lady of twenty-five. The French film industry has long thrived upon just such a theme. Why or when she changed from being an object of 'spring-like homage' to professional pupil, for Saint-Saëns had very few of these, must be a matter for conjecture (or a film).

that of 'L'Attente', are designed to display the fascinating delicacy of
Saint-Saëns's piano playing. A duet for soprano and baritone, 'Viens'
(Hugo) could have been a piece in which Saint-Saëns hoped to join his
voice with hers, for he was always proud of his vocal chords, which
were greatly superior to those of most composers (or conductors.) He
loved song and thought the human voice the finest of all instruments.
Jacques Durand related a story in his memoirs (uncorroborated, alas)
that when Saint-Saëns was incognito in the Canary Isles he stepped in
to sing the part of Rigoletto when the local baritone was indisposed. A
further attraction of the Reiset household was that it was also
frequented by the Abbé Duguerry, priest of the Madeleine church,
whom Saint-Saëns met at dinner. 'If my organist leaves, I will take you
on,' said the Abbé. The more solemn song, 'La Cloche' (Hugo), was
dedicated to Pauline Viardot, though she does not seem to have been
quick to include his offerings in her public recitals.

The succession of these and other love-songs had some poignancy,
for his fragile health precluded his being a robust lover after the
fashion of Hugo, whose romantic moods inspired him. He was thin,
pale and short. Guarded by the two women, he lived for the most part
indoors, suspected of having inherited the malady which had carried
off his father. The Baron Haussmann's famous rebuilding of Paris
cannot have been immense fun for the residents. Acres of crumbling
old edifices were knocked down and replaced, so there must have been
massive quantities of dust and fumes clouding the air. Saint-Saëns's
whole body was sometimes shaken with coughing, fevers recurred and
he frequently had to take to his bed.

In 1857 he was taken to Italy by the Abbé Gabriel of St Merri to
whom he had dedicated a Mass the previous year. This is almost the
sole religious work that comes from the St Merri period. It was written
for four voices, great organ and choir organ, and a string orchestra
with flutes, cor anglais, trumpets, trombones and harp. The Abbé
Gabriel was a charismatic priest with powers of oratory and the saintly
appearance to match, a disciple of Lamennais and one who hailed the
revolution of 1848 as an opportunity for the Church to side with the
people. From the organ console Saint-Saëns, later the great anti-
clerical and rationalist, must have heard the Abbé's expositions of the
texts, for the work is infused with an appreciation of their implicit
drama. His Mass was greatly admired by Liszt, who divined a deep

devotional feeling in the work. Liszt returned his copy with suggestions for performance, but wanted it to be despatched back to him: 'I must possess this extraordinary work, which has its place between Bach and Beethoven.'

Even in much later days Saint-Saëns insisted that the task of music in the church was to aid worship rather than provide entertainment. Here the organ itself takes its part in the Mass, sometimes supplanting the voices in certain phrases and, in the Benedictus, carrying the entire message. It is the grand organ which leads the 'Kyrie', while the choir organ appears to express the worries and doubts of those pleading for mercy with its agitated phrases. In the final bars of the 'Agnus Dei' and the closing pages of the work both organs find a peaceful harmony in an interchanging dialogue, which they seem loath to end. Louis Vierne, organist of St Sulpice and Notre-Dame in the period before the First World War, called this section 'seraphic' and others have pointed out how much the echoing effects, as in the 'Hostias', prefigure Fauré. Vierne found particular virtues in every section: 'The "Gloria" is a marvel of composition and style, amazing when we know that the Master was only twenty-one.' As so often with Saint-Saëns, we find a history of music compressed into an entirely original work, not out of a desire to plagiarise ideas but rather as a recognition of the seamless nature of church worship over the ages. The Credo is based both in theme and style on the 'Messes Royale' of Henry Dumont, composer at the Chapel of Louis XIV. The 'O Salutaris Hostia' interpolated after the Benedictus, with its lovely counterpoint running against the plainchant of the sopranos in the Duguest setting of 'O Salutaris', brings us to the world of Bach's choral preludes. Haydn and Beethoven have made their presence felt in the 'Gloria' and we come to Saint-Saëns's own time in the inclusion of the operatic moments, which were customary in Paris churches, where the choirs and soloists often belonged to the operatic theatres. There are arias for the alto both in the 'Qui Tollis' section of the 'Gloria' and, to moving effect, in the 'Agnus Dei'. We may also sense the stage in the Grand March that opens the 'Sanctus', which is followed by the waltz-like figures for the accompaniment to 'Pleni Sunt Coeli', though the mood of the choir at this point is devout enough. Unity is provided by the frequent use of polyphony and fugue, of which Saint-Saëns had technical mastery. The final fugue of the 'Gloria', in which the voices soar beyond the church vaulting into clear blue air, is especially arresting.

The 'O Salutaris' section proved the most enduring. In 1904 the composer made an organ transcription, the only occasion when he arranged one of his own works for that instrument. It was dedicated to Gaston Choisnel, a cousin of his Durand publishers and a new partner in the firm. Saint-Saëns played his transcription for the first time at a benefit concert for the Association of Artists and Musicians at the Salle Pleyel in November 1904.

Other works from this period included the Six Bagatelles for Piano Opus 3 (1855), which have an interest as having been dedicated to Albert Libon, the high postal official who later left Saint-Saëns a substantial legacy. These were not given descriptive titles, but the composer later transcribed No. 6 for violin, which he called 'Meditation'. Another piece, which was not published for ten years but probably dates from his time at St Merri, was the 'Elévation ou Communion'. In its published version it first appeared in a 'Collection of Sacred Music for Women's Voices' edited by Louis-Désiré Besozzi, who had succeeded Saint-Saëns as teacher at the Ecole Niedermeyer. But although it probably came from a set of unpublished short pieces for organ or harmonium from the mid-1850s it seems to have exercised a fascination for the composer, who, in 1880, made two fresh editions for organ and harmonium, and later transcribed it for piano in 1886. By then it may have had nostalgic associations, for, when it was published in 1865, it was dedicated to a great friend, Alexis Chauvet, who had succeeded to Saint-Saëns's post at St Merri, after the five-year tenure of Benjamin Darnault. Chauvet was a brilliant organist, two years younger than Saint-Saëns and a Bohemian by nature, who affected long hair, wore his top hat at a casual angle and dressed in long trailing frock-coats. He was one of the many friends whom death removed, as he died of tuberculosis at an early age. His appointment to St Merri, after a competition, was believed to have been through the favouritism of Saint-Saëns, who admired his charm as much as his undoubted talents.

The development of instruments continued. At a concert in the Salle Herz in 1854 Saint-Saëns demonstrated the potentialities of the harmonicorde, and in 1855 an impressive array of musical notables, including Pauline Viardot and the cellist Charles-Joseph Lebouc, joined at a soirée, in which he played the Andante from Beethoven's Fifth on this strange hybrid. By 1856 several concerts had exhibited its qualities, and Queen Victoria and Prince Albert were said to have ordered not one but two. In 1857 Saint-Saëns made the acquaintance of the 'pedalier', an invention of a partner in the Pleyel Firm, Auguste Wolff. This was a piano with a pedal board on which two sets of strings resounded an octave apart, as on the 8ft and 16ft stops of the organ. At Wolff's private salon Saint-Saëns played the Bach D major Fugue and the *Revue et Gazette* commented that his feet showed the same agility as his fingers. It was also in this year that the renovated organ at St Merri was available for use. This not only enlarged his repertoire but inspired him to compose for the modern organ as we now know it. He wrote to one of his old colleagues from Benoist's class that he wished to play some Bach pieces, but would need a page-turner. He promised to take the friend to a dance as a reward: 'Madame Petit came by a while ago to say that she's having a dance next Thursday and that I can only take you on the condition that you come Sunday to turn the pages for me. But I am so good-hearted that I'll take you anyway.' The letter finished with the postscript: 'Alas!!! Today I am twenty-one and a half years old!!!!'

For the new instrument he wrote the Fantasia in E flat which remains a piece in the repertoire. The opening, with its syncopated effects of echoes from one manual to another, is clearly designed to display the new capabilities and the second section, with its flamboyant flourishes and operatic overtones combined with some complicated pedal work, is a show-piece for player and organ together. The MS referred to a dedication to Georges Schmitt, organist of St Sulpice, a better scholar than a performer in Cavaillé-Coll's opinion. Many years later old Saint-Saëns told the Scottish organist A. M. Henderson that, as he had composed the E flat Fantasy at St Merri, he would like his friend to hear it there. So one Sunday when the service was over the two men climbed to the tribune and Saint-Saëns played the fantasy 'with evident enjoyment'. Henderson thought that the opening section with its contrasts between manuals was 'especially effective on this old organ and in the concluding allegro, where some of the pedal passages are far from easy, he showed that his feet as well as his hands had lost none of their cunning'.

The fantasy was one of the pieces he played at the Inauguration of the organ on 3 December 1857, along with Mendelssohn's Sixth Sonata and the Bach D-major Fugue. At the start he indulged in a series of improvisations to demonstrate all the new stops and won praise from the critic Joseph d'Ortigues for giving these musical as well as technical interest. The final improvisation was a chorus of *voix humaines* over which the flute played an obligato, which brought to mind the cor-anglais solo from the *William Tell* Overture, a sure way to the heart of a Parisian audience. D'Ortigues praised also the triumphant use of the new pedal board in the difficult runs of the fantasy.

Another work which made its appearance in 1857 was the Tarantella for Flute and Clarinet. Pauline Viardot had introduced Saint-Saëns to Rossini's famous musical evenings in his apartment at the corner of the rue Chaussée d'Antin. These receptions were always thronged with flatterers but, when Rossini discerned that Saint-Saëns had genuine musical talent, he invited him to make a personal morning call. Along with two other young virtuosi, Planté and Diémer, he became soloist and accompanist at the musical evenings, and was admitted to the more serious discussions in the dining-room. The story of how the Tarantella was thought to be by Rossini, who then produced his young friend to hear the ecstatic comments, is well known. More important, the encounters with Rossini were the first that Saint-Saëns had made with legendary and successful genius. Of the two other great composers of his acquaintance, Berlioz was elderly and embittered and Gounod, to date, unsuccessful. It was important to have an image of the rewards that the career of composer could bring, to balance the disillusion and regrets which were such a feature of nineteenth-century musical life in Paris.

The Tarantella itself remains one of the composer's best-known pieces. The ease with which flutes and clarinet interweave their lines, the melodious central section and the customary invitation to applause in the rapidity of the final change of tempo continue to make it a vehicle for woodwind players to demonstrate their skills. It was performed in public for the first time at a Pleyel–Wolff concert by two of the most notable players of the day, Louis Dorus and René Leroy,[1] and was encored. The receptions of Pauline Viardot brought Saint-Saëns once again into friendship with Gounod, still struggling for success in the opera world. Despite Madame Viardot lending her talent and fame, his *Sapho* had been a relative failure.

---

[1] Berlioz found Leroy obtuse in learning how to interpret the famous clarinet solo which accompanies the entrance of Andromache in *The Trojans*. Furthermore, Leroy described the moving solo as 'pretty', adding to Berlioz's irritation.

As we have seen, Saint-Saëns had already worked in apprenticeship to Gounod on *Ulysses*.

Gounod played the piano competently but lacked virtuosity and had a certain amount of trouble in performing his own scores [wrote Saint-Saëns]. At his request I went nearly every day . . . and between us we played fragments of the emergent work from his newly written manuscript. Gounod was full of his subject and told me about his aims, ideas and desires. His great preoccupation was to discover beautiful colour in the palette of the orchestra and rather than take their ready-made systems from the classics he sought at first hand the shades necessary to his brush by the study of tones and combinations. 'The resources of sonority', he once said to me, 'are still largely unexplored.' He spoke truly. Since that time, what a magic flowering has grown from the modern orchestra. For the nymphs' chorus he wanted a special aquatic effect. This he achieved with a glass-plated harmonica and a triangle muted by muffling the stick with a skin.

The ever acquisitive brain of Saint-Saëns derived benefit from these sessions and, in addition to memorising Berlioz's *Treatise on Orchestration*, he acquired a fascination with effects such as the use of the xylophone in the *Danse Macabre* and the tiny cymbals in the 'Bacchanale'.

It was in the company of Gounod and Seghers that Saint-Saëns first heard the former's 'Ave Maria', which, as he said, 'brought Gounod popularity – at a price'. Gounod was at the piano and Seghers played the melody on the violin. In an adjacent room a small choir sang Latin words to provide the harmonic background.

These few bars [wrote Saint-Saëns] did more for his reputation than anything he had written up to that time. It became the fashion for ladies to swoon away during the second crescendo . . . Since then the choir has vanished to be replaced by a harmonium; violinists have distorted the ecstatic line by means of those tricks we know only too well, which change ecstasy into hysteria; then the instrumental line became vocal and resulted in an 'Ave Maria' more convulsionary even than before; and finally matters went from bad to worse ... the number of players was increased and an orchestra was added, not forgetting the big drum and cymbals.

It was in 1855 that Saint-Saëns had made his transcription of the *Lélio* of Berlioz, said to be one of the finest transcriptions of the orchestrally minded Berlioz in existence[1] (Saint-Saëns himself admired especially the piano transcription that Pauline Viardot, a fine pianist as well as a singer, made of the 'Royal Hunt and Storm', which had remained impervious to the efforts of others). After the E flat Symphony Berlioz had exclaimed: 'Apart from Saint-Saëns, a musician of nineteen years, and Gounod, who has just written a very fine Mass, I can see nothing but mayflies and mosquitoes hovering after the stinking morass we call Paris.' Though Berlioz was twice the age of Saint-Saëns they both had a disdain for the Italian music popular at the time. The older man could impress Saint-Saëns with his admiration for Gluck and, in return, Saint-Saëns was able to make Berlioz more aware of the greatness of Bach. 'I can still remember his delight and astonishment at hearing some Bach I played to him one day. He could scarcely credit that the great Johann Sebastian wrote such things, and told me that he had always thought of him as a sort of "super-swot", who manufactured learned fugues and was bereft of all charm or poetry.' The accounts Saint-Saëns gives of the tormented rehearsals through which Berlioz put his orchestras – 'I have seen him give twenty, thirty rehearsals to a single work, tearing his hair, smashing batons and music stands, without obtaining the desired results. The wretched players did what they could, but the task was beyond their powers' – are held suspect by Berlioz biographers, for Berlioz was undoubtedly the precursor of the modern conductor in control of performances. But that was the aspect of Berlioz that Saint-Saëns noted: 'He was unhappy as a result of his ingenuity at making himself suffer, in seeking and desiring the impossible in everything.' Neither Berlioz nor Gounod provided a great incitement for an ambitious young man to brave the critics and devote his life to composition. Rossini, by contrast, exhibited the rewards and eventually, when his long career was nearing its end, Saint-Saëns enjoyed

[1] It should be said that Berlioz, great as his admiration was of the young Saint-Saëns, thought Ritter's arrangement of *Romeo and Juliet* the finest piano version of his scores.

similar acclaim, this time on an international stage that was immeasurably broader than the Paris salons.

Four days after inaugurating the St Merri organ, and very probably to the chagrin of the church dignitaries who had borne the cost, Saint-Saëns was appointed as organist of the Madeleine, the official church of the Second Empire. Louis James Alfred Lefébure-Wély, the most popular organist in Paris, had resigned not in order to move to St Sulpice, as is sometimes stated (he did not take up the appointment there until 1863), but to compose a three-act *opéra comique*. Saint-Saëns's appointment had been arranged by the pastor at the Madeleine, the Abbé Gaspard Duguerry, who had met him at the Reiset home. The offer was not one which could be refused, for, as well as huge prestige, it brought the prospect of a much higher income. The 'irregular honorariums' to which the letter of appointment referred were the receipts of fees for weddings and private solemnities in this fashionable church. 'The committee asks that you be available for service to the parish 1 January 1858, inclusive. It will count on you for that day. It informs you, moreover, that the organ is at your disposal as of today and that you can use it, become familiar with it, and make all the necessary preparations.' The formal letter of appointment barely does justice to the career advancement thus accorded to a twenty-two-year-old, who was now recognised as one of the foremost instrumentalists of France.

4

The Paris Organist

The Madeleine, though one of the youngest churches in Paris, was the most illustrious. The foundations had been laid in 1764, but work was interrupted by the Revolution. The firm hand of Napoleon was needed to drive the enterprise forward and, in 1806, he ordered the construction of a Temple of Glory to the honour of the French Army. Previous plans were swept away and a design for a Greek temple surrounded by massive Corinthian columns was substituted. After Waterloo, the Catholic hierarchy resumed control and, in 1845, the completed building was consecrated.

It remains much as Saint-Saëns viewed it from the high tribune, opulent but sombre, lacking in flights of architectural fancy or the contrasts of colour and shade which give to French cathedrals a sense of mystery. It had the highest budget of any Parisian church and the organ, installed in 1846, was Cavaillé-Coll's second largest, with forty-eight stops and his first 'Voix Céleste'. The Vicar, Pierre-Henri Lamazou, who had once catechised the child Saint-Saëns, was personally interested in organ construction, wrote a history of the organ of St Sulpice and helped to plan the new organ at Notre-Dame. Less fortunately for Saint-Saëns, he had been a great admirer of Lefébure-Wély and his theatrical manner of playing.[1]

Lefébure-Wély combined the modern roles of star performer and publicity agent. He gave concerts with members of his family and would endorse any new instrument for domestic use. He wrote light pieces, markedly secular in mood, with titles such as 'Monastery Bells' and was famous for his 'storm' passages, during which he would have

---

[1] Saint-Saëns's famous remark (often paraphrased loosely) when he was reproached with eliminating light operetta items from his repertoire was, 'When I hear a page of Labiche [a writer of comedies] read as the sermon, I will play an appropriate voluntary.'

the lights dimmed. Rossini, with typical frivolity, professed great enjoyment of the Lefébure-Wély storms and would suffer many a Bach fugue, if a storm concluded the programme. Saint-Saëns considered him a much greater organist than his polkas and operatic selections indicated, and thought he had depths as an improviser exploring the organ's resources.

The *'titulaire'* was expected to play every Sunday of the year, save certain times in Advent and Lent. Each Sunday required three services: High Mass at 11 a.m., when the choir was present; 1 p.m., when the organ supported the greater part of the service; and 2.30, when the choir rejoined it in psalms and hymns. The afternoon services were concessions to society folk who found early rising a problem. The atmosphere was typical of the Imperial regime. The choir was dressed in scarlet and carefully choreographed to carry out movements in unison. Silence and reverence were supposedly enforced by uniformed ushers whose costumes reflected the Papal 'Swiss' Guards. The huge length of the Madeleine made it suitable for processions, especially on Feast Days and Festivals associated with Mary Magdalen, such as the Second Sunday after Easter. Crowds would wait outside the church to study the dresses of ladies in the congregation as they descended to their carriages.

As choirmaster colleague, the Maître de Chapelle, there was Louis Dietsch, who had, perhaps surprisingly for one who was also master of the chorus at the Opéra, been a prize winner on the double-bass at the Conservatoire. Members of the Opéra chorus and minor soloists would often take part in the Madeleine services. Dietsch has gone down in musical history as the man who wrote *The Flying Dutchman* on a libretto which Wagner claimed was a translation of his own and as the conductor who aroused Wagner's wrath and contributed to the 1861 disasters which overtook *Tannhäuser*. He was also a teacher of harmony and counterpoint at the Ecole Niedermeyer, where, within a few years, Saint-Saëns's sparkling teaching was to shine by contrast to his own.[1]

Saint-Saëns's own definition of the perfect organist was 'a virtuoso hardened to every difficulty and an ingenious improviser'. His fingers stayed close to the keys and his touch was rapid and immaculate. As arpeggios rippled up and down, sometimes in contrary motion, he

[1] When Dietsch's pupils were bored they would divert his attention to relating episodes from his quarrels with Wagner.

seemed able to reproduce his pianistic skills on this much heavier medium. The avoidance of heel work added to the lightness of the effect and excluded the long grinding sounds which characterised some contemporary playing. He was distinct from other great French organists such as Widor, Vierne and Dupré, who trained in the footsteps of the Belgian Lemmens and developed effects specifically designed for organ. His style, learned from Boëly, developed from what remained of the French eighteenth-century tradition. He would ask a friend to 'play me a Trio with a cornet in the soprano, a cromorne in the tenor and a grosse flute in the bass'. He avoided thick sonorities. As an accomplished orchestrator he enjoyed the power of the organ to reproduce orchestral effects. Just as he could compose in any circumstances and conjure up the Corsican countryside while sitting in a station waiting room, or depict the Mediterranean in the fogs of the Channel, no particular organ, not even that of the Madeleine, influenced his organ compositions. He differed, too, in avoiding excessive legato playing and too great a use of the Swell boxes to give expressive effects. It is recorded that the old organ blower of the Madeleine was heard to say: 'We have had the very best organists here: M. Dubois and M. Fauré – but only M. Saint-Saëns could make such beautiful effects with very little wind!'

It was as an improviser that he had unique powers. He believed that improvisation avoided monotony 'for all organists have very nearly the same repertoire'. Jean Huré, Gigout's successor at St Augustin, thought that all the eulogies lavished on his improvisations were insufficient.

His genius was of indescribable splendour. It was even more extraordinary than the description which Forkel gives of Bach's genius. ... Following a marvellously ordered plan he improvised counterpoint in two, three or four voices with such purity and logic in the progression of parts that the most erudite musician with the most experienced ear believed that he was hearing a carefully written down composition. So difficult were certain of his impromptus that it would have taken a year of assiduous work for our most skilled organists to play them.[1] ... For example, for the

---

[1] Auguste Durand said he had published many great works by Saint-Saëns, but the greatest of all were the ephemeral and fleeting unpublished improvisations at the Madeleine.

Sortie of High Mass, he would improvise a strict fugue in three real voices on the manuals. The incisive subject, the ingenious counter-subject, the inventive episodes, would continue in rapid movement until all of a sudden the last Motet sung by the choir was heard in the pedal and continued as the entrances came closer and closer together to the dazzling conclusion. This he called 'his little joke'.

Eugène Gigout would tell of Saint-Saëns improvising five- or six-voice fugues at breakneck speed and saying, 'If you don't hear, watch my fingers and feet! I have brought in the subject a number of times.' Jean Huré recalled an improvised 'Offertoire' in which the right hand moved in legato fifths and sixths, the left hand arpeggiated wide chords from one manual to another, while the pedal sang the melody in the tenor. 'And the rhythm did not falter for an instant.'

He lived in the great age of organ building and survived to hear his Third Symphony played on the 111-stop Austin organ at the San Francisco Exhibition. He is known to have played on over sixty instruments himself, but along with his suspicion of new ideas in composing went a certain conservatism with regard to practical advances in construction. He preferred combination pedals operated by the feet, which added or subtracted the reeds and mixtures, and disliked the unexpected results of novel combinations. 'In certain organs the combinations, far from being an accessory, seem to have been the builder's principal concern ... The organist seated before such a Chinese puzzle refuses to use them for fear of an inevitable gaffe.' He was not altogether happy with electrical action: 'One has the distinct impression of the intervention of an intermediary agent in the transmission of musical thought. You feel as though you are directing, instead of playing, because you don't feel the precise attack of the sound. Nevertheless, I have no reason to disqualify these types of action to which I have no trouble in adapting.' As he grew older he did become more cautious about the array of mechanical devices which confronted him. When he played in Karlsruhe in 1910 he made lengthy pauses while he altered the registrations, which certain of the couplers could have done in an instant.

As before, he was still living at home with the two widows. That at times he found the affection stifling we learn from a letter to Caroline de Serres written in 1910. Caroline had been suffering from depression and to strengthen her resolve he recounted depressions of his own. 'Do not tell me that there is no comparison between your sufferings and those I have endured. Those, no one has ever known; but when you know that my mother wished to read in front of me the letters that were addressed to me (I was twenty-four years old) you will be able to have some idea of the harassment I endured.' Friends spoke highly of Clémence Saint-Saëns. Cavaillé-Coll recalled to his children how for many years each Monday he had climbed the five storeys to the flat in the Faubourg St Honoré and later to the rue Monsieur le Prince for the famous musical evenings, 'unforgettable occasions illumined by the prestige of the Master and the shining spiritual face of his venerated mother'. Yet without siblings to share the weight of maternal ambitions, domestic life must have been warping and one cannot commend the habit of a mother accompanying her son to every concert and theatre as a matter of course.

He found pleasure in the lighter entertainments which Paris afforded, and the music of the café-concerts stimulated his imagination along with the works of Bach and Schumann, hence the luscious waltz in the Septet and the revelry of the Can-Can which ends the *Carnival of the Animals*. There is a lively tale recounted in Augé de Lassus's reverent biography. During one of his concert tours in France, Saint-Saëns found himself in a dreary Hôtel du Commerce which possessed a cheap piano. Someone, while waiting for the *patron* to serve, asked if anyone played. 'A little,' replied the unidentified visitor, who then rose and astonished the company by playing (and singing) a succession of café and music-hall songs. Work stopped in the kitchen and an audience gathered from adjacent bars. The general opinion was that the stranger must be a resident musician at the Alhambra or Alcazar, so vast was his knowledge of burlesque refrains and choruses. The performance, which had seemed inexhaustible, at last came to an end as the traveller mounted the stairs, candlestick in hand, to shouts for an encore the following evening. Next day the pianist had gone and there was a rush to the register to identify the hero of the previous night. 'Saint-Saëns' was deciphered as the occupant of room 46 and the residents learnt sadly that he had caught the express train in the early hours.

At Pauline Viardot's receptions he was not only welcome as accompanist on the serious Thursday evenings, but would share in the frivolities of the Sunday gatherings. Charades were popular and these included musical parodies at which Saint-Saëns was adept. In a mock version of Meyerbeer's *Robert le Diable* he acted the temptations offered to Robert – the vice of drunkenness was represented by the fashionable cup of cocoa – while Pauline Viardot herself accompanied the famous Dance of the Nuns performed by Romain Bussine and friends in white sheets wielding saucepans and wooden spoons on which the rhythms were beaten.[1] Saint-Saëns's skills in singing falsettos and cadenzas induced him to appear as a prima donna assoluta, costumed as Armide, singing 'Fuyez, plaisirs, Fuez!', or as Marguerite, his bearded face framed by a blue-and-white bonnet and flaxen plaits, singing the 'Jewel Song', which had brought particular fame to Mme Carvalho. With his acute sense of pitch he was able to parody the singer's tendency to sing sharp. In what can hardly have been a musical offering he donned pink tights and appeared as a corpse under the dissecting knife of Turgenev, whose unhappy love for Pauline had brought him to Paris. These nineteenth-century revels have long gone out of fashion and do not impress us as being very amusing. On the presumption that Mme Saint-Saëns did not attend we may see them as rather hysterical escapes from the atmosphere of severe expectations under the family roof. Paul Viardot, the violinist son of Pauline, wrote in the *Guide du Concert* forty years after these events that it was the free and unrestrained ambience in the Viardot home that Saint-Saëns relished. As his years at the Madeleine went by, the plots of charades and playlets became more elaborate and were often planned in the organ loft with Bussine, Fauré and others. Such frivolities continued into riper years. A Miss Goodwin, who claimed to be 'a great friend' of Saint-Saëns, told his English biographer Watson Lyle of an evening at the home of Léon Glaize the artist (who had just exhibited the composer's portrait at the 1899 Salon) where Raoul Pugno the pianist and Saint-Saëns improvised music for a comedy, 'La Blouse et l'Habit', graphically describing flood and fire as the plot required.

The old apartment in the rue de Jardinet was becoming cramped for his Monday musical evenings and, with his finances improved, he

---

[1] As well as being a great singer Pauline Viardot was an exceptional pianist. Saint-Saëns heard her play the Schumann Duet for Two Pianos with Clara Schumann and thought they were of equal virtuosity. In 1878 he told Durand that 'Mmes Montigny [Caroline] and Viardot play *Phaeton* very well together'.

moved, together with the protective women, to 168 rue du Faubourg St Honoré. The new apartment was on the fourth floor, much less enclosed by other buildings and faced a garden, long since built over, which separated it from the noise of the street. Most important, from the top floor he could view the heavens. He installed his own telescope, bought with the 500 francs he was paid by the publisher Girod for Six Duets for Piano and Harmonium. The duets, one of the first compositions to use the harmonium in harness with other instruments, had been requested by Alexandre Debain. They were dedicated to Lefébure-Wély. They comprised a Fantasia and Fugue, the subject of the Fugue being that of the Fantasia in diminution, a romantic Cavatina and a Chorale in which the piano, agitato, performs a study in rapid notes while the harmonium interjects several lines from the German Chorale version of the Gregorian 'Tonus peregrinus' in the harmonisation used by Bach in his Cantata No. 10. There was a link with the Psalm 'In exitu Israel' sung every Sunday at Vespers. There followed a Capriccio, a Scherzo prefiguring the Scherzo in the Second Piano Concerto (in the key of F sharp!) and a Finale.

The telescope was the result of a boyish enthusiasm rekindled by the purchase of Arago's *Astronome Populaire* in an old bookshop near the Odéon. Although Saint-Saëns always disclaimed any deep professional knowledge of astronomy and studied the stars for contemplative relaxation, this particular hobby remained a source of fascination and is always quoted as evidence of his wide-ranging interests. For a time he followed the progress of Donati's Comet and recorded his sightings; he liked to study the stars and thought that everyone would benefit from searching more deeply into the universe whither they had come, but, as he wrote, 'I have as much right to call myself an astronomer as the man who looks at pictures in the Louvre has to call himself a painter, or the man who hears Beethoven symphonies at a concert to call himself a musician.'

The move to the Madeleine demanded composition on a more persistent scale. The church required numerous pieces for its grand occasions, principally in the month of May, during which there were numerous services devoted to the worship of the Virgin. In May 1859 he wrote no fewer than eighteen canticles in French and Latin. Many pieces were written in haste, so that soloists and choir could rehearse, but some were later published, including a 'Veni Creator' for male voices, dedicated to Liszt. 'Who could believe with what éclat, with what uncanny prestige appeared the name of Liszt to young musicians in the early days of the Empire . . .' he wrote, 'a strange name, sharp and whistling as a sword blade which cuts the air, traversed by the slavonic "S", as by the groove of the lightning. The artist and the man seemed to belong to the world of legend.'

After many short religious works came the *Oratorio de Noël*, composed at the end of his first year and dedicated to the Vicomtesse de Grandval (Marie Reiset). The music, written in eleven days, was given to the choristers on 15 December, leaving them little time to rehearse for Christmas Day. The text was taken from the Latin words of the Christmas Office and the Midnight Mass. It was composed for five voices: soprano, mezzo, alto, tenor and bass, and scored for a small orchestra of strings and harp, combined with the great and choir organs. Berlioz's *Childhood of Christ* had been written only five years earlier, but the Saint-Saëns work, apart from a prominence given to the shepherds and a pastoral ambience,[1] is quite dissimilar, being very much a musical enhancement of the words of the Office, without interest in the human drama. As with the Mass, the music moves through the ages from the seventeenth century, with organs providing a rustic 'bagpipe' background. The words 'Fear not' (soprano) are interpreted in a very gentle 3:4 rhythm and the 'Gloria' has something of a march-like tread suggesting discipline in the ranks of the angels. The air for the tenor, 'Domine, ego credidi', reminds us of the links between the Madeleine and the Paris Opéra, as does the Trio 'Tecum principium', but in between there is a Bach-like duet for soprano and bass in the 'Benedictus' and the more vehement 'Quare Fremuerent (Why do the nations?)' where a phrase from the Eleventh Quartet of Beethoven comments upon the politics of war. Towards the close the pastoral image returns, the soloists take up phrases from the Prelude, brightened with Alleluias. The scene fades, giving the impression that the whole episode might have been a dream. There is a final chorus, short and full-bodied, in which the congregation may have joined. Vierne said quite firmly that Saint-Saëns did great things to rescue church music from the abyss of bad taste into which it had fallen, not

---

[1] Apparently the Madeleine clergy disapproved of the pastoral element, describing it as 'the sounds of a village fiddler'.

only through his aversion to popular music on the organ, but in his settings of Latin, of which many composers between 1830 and 1860 had been ignorant. The *Oratorio de Noël* guards the Latin text, giving greater richness than would have been possible in French. In the much praised Trio – 'Tecum principium in die virtutis in splendoribus Sanctorum' – Saint-Saëns's knowledge of Latin and appreciation of the classics enabled him to seize upon the key words and project them.

The first year at the Madeleine also saw the appearance of two concertos, one for violin; the other for piano. In the territory of the concerto Saint-Saëns was venturing where few French composers had gone before him. According to Dr Stegemann,[1] Saint-Saëns has never received the homage due to him as the establishing force in the French concerto. Lacking any tradition, the French before Saint-Saëns had accepted the Viennese model of three movements of classical design. But the swarming to Paris of the virtuosi had unfortunate consequences. Composers, who were often the performers themselves, were intent upon highlighting the solo part to which the orchestra provided an inconspicuous accompaniment. As a result there was little dialogue between soloist and orchestra, and little thematic development as the emphasis was on technical display. Opportunities for contrasting the timbre of the solo instrument with that of the various others was lost (one thinks of Saint-Saëns's frequent contrasts between the violin and the woodwind). Paganini kept his orchestrations as simple as possible for fear of theft, and since rehearsals were good moments for this, the scores were easy enough to read at sight. Parts would be collected immediately after the performance. The orchestral introductions were often just background music to the entrance of the soloists, who would bow to the audience, remove their gloves and prepare their opening bars with many flourishes. The 'virtuoso' concerto had produced some examples with musical worth and Henri Vieuxtemps and his pupils had introduced a certain lyricism into the concerto form which imported the 'singing' style of the operatic aria to provide moments of melody for the violin soloist.

Saint-Saëns had had some acquaintance with, and possibly advice from, the half-African violinist George Bridgetower (Beethoven's 'Il mulatto Brischdauer') and his First Violin Concerto, composed in

---

[1] Michael Stegemann, *Saint-Saëns and the Solo French Concerto from 1850–1920*, Scolar Press, 1991.

1858 but published as No.2 in 1879, was written in this energetic and muscular fashion. It is dedicated to Achille Dien, one of the musical hosts whose home he visited. It was played in Germany, but the first Parisian performance seems to have been given by M. José White, in the Salle Pleyel in 1862. It bears the hallmark of its predecessors in that the violin is rarely silent and is forced to such lengths of display that virtuosity sinks under its own weight. Yet there are original features: the slow drum roll and the steady re-entry of the orchestra as the cadenza draws to its conclusion, the familiar Saint-Saëns fugue in the Finale, which would rule out any notion that the work did not require orchestral rehearsal, and the long melody accompanied by the harp in the Andante, a contrast of timbre to which Saint-Saëns was often to return. There is no long introduction and the soloist enters at bar three, while the orchestra pounds C-major chords. In fact it is the orchestral tutti which comes second after the soloist's spectacular entrance. The first subject has both the opening flourish and a striking melodic phrase closely akin to it in shape. Saint-Saëns repeats this phrase at several moments in the movement, usually with very ornate embroidery, and it is superior to the more mundane sections in 6:8 rhythm. There is a further innovation in the linking of the second and third movements, though they are quite distinct, and both are captivating in their different ways. It is hard to see why the concerto (apart from its immense difficulty) has been so overlooked. The second movement with the harp accompaniment begins as a sad Celtic-sounding folk-song, but quickly becomes a romanza in which the violin makes Delilah-like advances. There is a fierce recitative, showing the operatic influences on the concerto at this time, a fanfare, a loud climax in which the orchestra gives out the theme while the violin weaves passionate arabesques above it, and a quiet close, all passion spent, until the third movement emerges. This is a gypsy dance, where once again the soloist leads and the orchestral tutti follows. The theme is well suited to a Rondo although the episodes are combinations of dance and exercise! In the fugato Coda and the concluding pages Saint-Saëns is, as usual, quite unashamed in demonstrating that dexterity has its place in music as much as in the brilliance of sport, athletics or the circus.

The First Piano Concerto was written in the same year. It is one of the marvels of his oeuvre that all five concertos for piano are quite different and the Fifth is as fresh and full of delights as the First. The

First has suffered unfairly by comparison with the Second. Even that constant admirer Emile Baumann describes it as 'youthful hyperbole; runs, arpeggios of exuberant proportions, an ambitious sortie into grandiose prolixity'. Yet there are some remarkably modern features about this work: a cautious venture into the cyclical form as both the 'horn calls' and the motto theme of the introduction return to blend with the closing bars. There is also the first appearance of a device, much later exploited to the full by Tchaikovsky and Rachmaninov, of taking the second, elegiac, subject of the Finale and turning it at the conclusion into a crashing rhapsody. The motto theme, which marks the various sections of the first movement (though with more subtlety that in the E-flat symphony) also shows that this concerto is a work of symphonic construction. Add to these features that, in both the outer movements, the piano is almost accompanist to the orchestra, or that they share themes (e.g. the piano completes rather than introduces the 'hunting horn' subject at the start, and the collaboration of piano and orchestra in the Finale with their alternating chords is essential to the whole concept), it is clear that, beneath the surface bravura, the concerto in France has taken on a new guise. In the Finale the piano solemnly intones the second subject, but is interrupted by comments from the woodwind; in the recapitulation a woodwind choir begins the same theme and is similarly cut short by the piano.

There is great originality in the slow movement, which begins with a slow lamentation over a bass figure which, together with a descending melancholy phrase, is four times interrupted by an insistent beating on the piano with odd bell-like chords like a repeated summons. The cascades of notes which follow these novel interpolations are without bar-lines and thus constitute a 'divided cadenza', in itself a new departure. They may be reminiscent of Liszt, but the whole movement has several passages which recall the Chopin of the nocturnes. As we know, Stamaty had withheld knowledge of Chopin from his pupil, but at this time he was close to the Vicomtesse de Grandval, who had had lessons from Chopin and, as an intelligent musician, could discuss his work. The close of the slow movement with strange trills at different points on the keyboard and muted chords at unexpected levels in the orchestra is quite unlike Saint-Saëns's 'romanza' style. In 1920 the composer wrote to his pianist pupil Isidore Philipp, in answer to an enquiry about the origins of this concerto, to say that it was inspired by the Forest of Fontainebleau. Its trees and rocks summoned up thoughts of Weber and the German forests, for the First Concerto is unmistakably Romantic despite its novelties.

In 1859 Saint-Saëns assisted Berlioz in the formidable task of editing the text of Gluck's *Orphée* for the Théâtre Lyrique under its impresario Léon Carvalho. Berlioz was able to dissuade Carvalho, who had a penchant for interfering with productions in every way, from including a pot-pourri of pieces from other Gluck operas. Saint-Saëns himself finished some of the essential rewriting, and the two men were close to each other. By date of birth Saint-Saëns was almost an exact contemporary of Berlioz's only and often estranged son. Interestingly, it was in 1859, also, that Berlioz visited Bordeaux at the invitation of the Société Ste Cécile to conduct a concert of his own works to great acclaim. The memories of his success there may have been a factor in persuading Saint-Saëns to write another symphony, which he did from July to September. This symphony, known as the Second, displays a greater confidence in dealing with the musical material than the First and the orchestration does not rely upon special effects: fewer kettledrums, no harp or trombones.[1] Baumann described it as having a 'scholastic severity' but once again Saint-Saëns experiments with the form. The opening in descending thirds is in an ambiguous key though by a change of rhythm it is turned into the subject of a vigorous fugue, a new departure in the exposition of a symphony. He reanimates the last phrase of the Adagio in the course of the Finale and also reintroduces the motif from the Scherzo, so he has chosen once again to extend the cyclical form. With changed rhythms the theme of the Adagio is reflected in the Scherzo. The academic nature of the first movement, added to the reputation he had gained at the Madeleine for eschewing waltzes and polkas, created the feeling that he was an academic musician who would never achieve popular success. This was to hinder him in his search for fame in the theatre, for, although he was in demand in the salons and backstage gatherings of singers as an accompanist, there was a reluctance to commission an opera from him. In the *Revue et Gazette Musicale* there was a reference to the first performance:

---

[1] Narcisse Girard, conductor at the Conservatoire, had rebuked Saint-Saëns for using trombones in a symphony. When Saint-Saëns pointed out that Beethoven had done so, Girard insisted that Beethoven had been similarly mistaken.

It is only just to thank M. Pasdeloup for being the only conductor who comes to the aid of composers, domestic and foreign, when they venture to take up the symphonic genre, their most difficult and important endeavours. At the last concert another new symphony of Saint-Saëns has been heard and through what other channel would it have been possible to reach the public? M. Saint-Saëns is one of our most celebrated young musicians. When the Société Ste Cécile existed he was already productive as a symphonist. He was very young at that time; today, when he has grown in age and talent, we find in him a little too much predilection for science with which he reaches the most lofty summits. He excels in combining groups of sounds and in confusing designs which, while not being completely impossible, are none the less strange and sometimes laboured. We counsel him to study the charm and melodic simplicity of which the father of the symphony, Haydn, will furnish him with delightful examples.

This would appear to refer clearly to the Second Symphony and yet there is mystery about the date of its première. Dandelot states that the first performance was given in 1862 at a concert in the Salle Pleyel monopolised by the composer who played part of a Hummel concerto, several transcriptions of his own, including the Kermesse and Waltz scene from *Faust* and a Caprice Brillant for Violin and Piano (with M. J. White).[1] In programme notes for an Ysaÿe concert, dedicated to Saint-Saëns in 1900, there are statements to the effect that the first appearances of the masterpiece were hesitant: 'The Symphony in A minor was performed for the first time in its entirety at the Châtelet concerts in 1880. The Andante [*sic*] and Scherzo had already been given in 1872 in one of the Conservatoire concerts.' Saint-Saëns in 1900 was in a position to give correct information, but it may be that the symphony was so coldly received that he had erased memories of its performance under the Empire.[2]

[1] The Caprice rarely appears in the list of his works, but apparently exists in the Sibley Music Library of Rochester University, USA.
[2] He did recall that when it was first rehearsed by Pasdeloup it encountered strong resistance from the orchestral players. It would not have been played well under Pasdeloup. The composer Paladilhe remarked, 'A composer must want to be hissed if he chooses to be played by Pasdeloup.' Jean Montargis, in *Camille Saint-Saëns, L'oeuvre, L'artiste*, 1919, recorded the first performance, in 1862 at the Salle Herz, by the Société des Jeunes Artistes under Pasdeloup.

As the Symphony was dedicated to Pasdeloup, it is odd if he did not perform it, although, as Dandelot remarks, conductors would be ill advised to perform every piece dedicated to them and Pasdeloup, who was no great musician, might not have appreciated a symphony which begins with a fugue. Saint-Saëns was always of the opinion that Pasdeloup did too little for young French composers. In the *Echo de Paris* in 1911 he wrote, 'He encouraged the efforts of the French School very little before 1870, contrary to the favourable opinion held on him on this subject. All I can find to quote on his behalf at the Society of Young Artists or the Concerts Populaires are two symphonies of Gounod, one of Gouvy, and the overture *Les Francs Juges* of Berlioz.' In a letter to Dandelot of 1907 Saint-Saëns was even more critical: 'Like so many others you have been deceived by Pasdeloup. Do you know that while everybody subscribed to a Festival in which I took part, alas, in the end with the aim of saving himself from poverty he had built a house at Fontainebleau. Be that as it may, I retain gratitude towards the courageous conductor who revealed to me and many others the masterpieces which his successors rendered with more profit and greater perfection.'

Jules Pasdeloup, a temperamental man with ginger-reddish hair, was the son of a violinist at the Opéra Comique who died young, leaving a widow and three children. Jules was the eldest and, having won a First Prize at the Conservatoire at fourteen, he undertook a wide variety of musical activity, sometimes playing the drums at popular concerts to support his family. During the revolution of 1848 he established himself with the Bonaparte family in a capacity unrelated to music and was put in charge of the paintings and furniture at the château of St Cloud. He also helped to organise musical soirées for Napoleon III and the Emperor's cousin, Princess Mathilde. Passionately keen on music and with a small gift of 500 francs from the Emperor, he organised the Société des Jeunes Artistes, which gave modest sums to pupils of the Conservatoire and provided them with the opportunity to play serious works, saving them from falling into the theatre orchestras or the bad habits which Auber deplored. He would travel to Germany each summer searching for scores of the Haydn symphonies and Beethoven figured prominently in his programmes. In his essay on 'Seghers and the Société Ste Cécile', Saint-Saëns accused him of using the Imperial favours to bribe the young players away. 'If Seghers had been more adaptable he might have secured resources but that was not his forte. Pasdeloup craftily took advantage of the situation. He had plenty of money and, as he knew what the financial situation was, he went to rehearsals and corrupted the artists. For the most part they were young people in needy circumstances and could not refuse his attractive propositions.[1] He killed Seghers's society and built on its ruins the Société des Jeunes Artistes, which later became the Concerts Populaires.' For eight years the concerts were held in the Salle Herz but as this venue would seat only about 300 people there were no profits and Pasdeloup decided to aim at a new concert-going public, paying lower prices in larger numbers. He owed certain ideas to Saint-Simon, the thinker and visionary earlier in the century, who wished to spread culture to the masses. He rented the Cirque Napoleon and on 23 October 1861 gave his first concert to an audience of 4000. Concerts were regularly given on Sundays amid the smell of horses and under a mixture of trapezes and circus apparatus. Saint-Saëns attributed Pasdeloup's reputation as a conductor to the fuzzy acoustics, which masked a host of faults, and to the fact that there were no rivals until Colonne arrived in the 1870s. Many new works were massacred, but at least the composers had a chance to hear them. 'How well Pasdeloup is led by his orchestra,' said Reyer. The Concerts were notorious for riots and demonstrations, especially for and against the 'New Music'.

At about the same time, in 1860, Saint-Saëns organised a concert of his own works at the Salle Erard. Adolphe Botte confirmed the opinion that the composer was dry and academic:

> Although young he has been composing for a long period but, after having quickly conquered the esteem of artists, he has scarcely made an inroad into public opinion. Everyone will tell you that they have read or heard somewhere that M. Saint-Saëns is a serious educated artist but no one will play his works. . . . We do not know, however, how we can praise this music without reservations. It is always interesting; if it captivates the intelligence, it is rarely beautiful or moving. The harmony, severely correct and often of

[1] Some as young as twelve or thirteen. The seventeen-year-old Charles Lamoureux was on the committee.

great strength, is hardly straightforward ... it seems to us that there is a recourse to all the coquetries of form when the thought is neither sufficiently large nor sufficiently free to go forward a little more easily and display itself more simply dressed. In the Quintet, in the Duets for Piano and Harmonium, in the Fantasy for Clarinet,[1] in the Tarantella, etc. there is talent enough ... even too much. If M. Saint-Saëns is able to join to the qualities which sparkle in his style that 'something' which remains the secret of thought, of passion, of nature, he will assuredly count as a much greater genius than 'a very meritorious composer'.

A few days later in the Salle Erard he gave a soirée which contained the Concerto in C for Violin, played by Achille Dien, the First Concerto for Piano and the Quintet in which the string players included Edouard Lalo and Jules Armingaud. As these two had been very active in 1848 in pressing for a National Society to further the interests of French composers, the old ideals were probably kept alive in discussion. That he had in mind the difficulties faced by composers of non-operatic music is illustrated by a letter he wrote to *La France Musicale* at this time: 'It is necessary for a composer of instrumental music to make a double sacrifice, the sacrifice of his popularity and the sacrifice of his fortune; it is not only that a composer does not become popular by writing quartets and symphonies, but it costs a great deal to mount these kinds of productions and have them heard. There is little encouragement.'

The Finale of the Second Symphony, the Tarantella, is at first hearing a somewhat frivolous close. It has often been compared to the Finale of Mendelssohn's *Italian* Symphony, but the manner is much closer to a Rossini overture, with all the trappings of tentative phrases, crescendos and noisy climaxes. Certainly Italy was in everyone's minds in 1859. In January of that year the Emperor had personally revised an article for the press, which stated that Italy should be liberated from Austrian domination and become a Federation under the Presidency of the Pope. Provoked by Piedmont, ally of France, the Austrians declared war and Napoleon III, with 200,000 troops, marched into the land which had witnessed his uncle's great triumphs. There were French victories at Magenta and Solferino, but so great was the

---

[1] This work is not recorded elsewhere; it might have been a religious solo in instrumental guise.

slaughter that the Emperor hastened to make peace. Henry Dunant, an observer of the carnage, was sufficiently horrified to establish the Red Cross. It is interesting that, according to Chantavoine, the sketches for *Samson and Delilah* go back as far as 1859 among Saint-Saëns's papers. The idea of independence for Italy rising against a foreign yoke may therefore have been one of the germs of the opera. At the beginning of June after the so-called 'victories', the theatres in Paris were brightly illuminated and many celebratory works such as Halévy's cantata *Italie* were performed.

It has often been said that Saint-Saëns avoided obligatory military service through the intervention of Princess Mathilde, at whose salon he accompanied recitals,[1] but it is doubtful whether his health at this time would ever have qualified him for service and later events were to prove that he was willing to join the colours. At the peace, France gained eventually the provinces of Savoy and Nice. A cantata, *L'Annexion*, celebrated these acquisitions.

There was a Victory Parade in the place Vendôme in August at which wounded veterans shouted '*Vive l'Empereur*', and captured Austrian cannon and standards rolled by. Meanwhile in the land of the tarantella, Garibaldi was waging his free-lance war on the Bourbons of Naples, and the remainder of Italy was convulsed by revolts and referenda. Bizet noted from the Villa Medici that the Italians were not over-enthusiastic in the cause of national unity: 'They know how to shout and form provisional governments but that is all.' The Pope continued to rely upon French troops to protect him in Rome and the threat to his temporal power caused alarm among French Catholics. Offenbach, whose jolly tunes from *Orpheus in the Underworld* had accompanied French soldiers marching to Magenta, produced in 1860 a topical piece, *Les Vivandières de la Grande Armée*. Italy must have been at the forefront of special prayers and Masses at the Madeleine with the clergy steering a difficult course between Emperor and Pope. At all events the South was surely prominent in Saint-Saëns's thoughts as he devised the Second Symphony. Beneath its effervescent surface the Tarantella Finale carries much craft. In form it combines the sonata framework with the traditional rondo. Its second subject is a

---

[1] Princess Mathilde's piano, certainly in her later years, badly needed tuning. It was covered with miscellaneous ornaments, which had to be removed before it could be opened. Bizet also played in her salon and probably he and Saint-Saëns were introduced there by Gounod.

cousin of the leading motif of the first movement. At one point a portion of the Scherzo is introduced and its pedal notes and arpeggios are also present. At other times the lower strings play references to it. The Adagio reappears as a chorale and the whole movement shows great inventiveness in its varieties of orchestration. Servières considered that it 'chases away the sentimental and plaintive ideas of the Adagio'[1]. It was twenty-seven years before Saint-Saëns wrote another symphony.

The year 1859 also saw the composition of the Second, so-called 'First', Violin Concerto. The swift plunge into yet another concerto for violin, while the first was still competing for attention, came about because of a meeting with the young virtuoso Pablo de Sarasate.

> Years have now passed [wrote Saint-Saëns in old age] since there once called on me Pablo de Sarasate, youthful and fresh-looking as the spring and already a celebrity, though a dawning moustache had only just begun to appear. He had been good enough to ask me, in the most casual way imaginable, to write a concerto for him. Greatly flattered and delighted at the request I gave him a promise and kept my word with the Concerto in A major to which – I do not know why – the German title of *Konzertstück* has been given. . . . Those who were in the habit of attending my Monday musical soirées have not forgotten the effect produced by my illustrious friend. This was so markedly the case that for several years afterwards no violinists could be prevailed upon to perform at my house, so terrified were they at the idea of inviting comparison. . . . By playing my compositions throughout the world on his magic instrument, Pablo de Sarasate had done me the greatest possible service and I am pleased to have the opportunity of paying him publicly the tribute of my admiration and gratitude, and of a friendship which follows him beyond the tomb.

In this century of genius, Sarasate, son of a Spanish military bandmaster, had given his first concert at the age of eight. Queen Isabella of Spain had provided assistance to send him to the Paris Conservatoire, where he won prizes in harmony and solfège, as well as

---

[1] It is interesting to note that in 1849 Berlioz had ideas for an A-minor symphony, but thought it would be ruinous economically and never set to work on it.

Premier Prix for Violin. He became one of the great platform performers of his day, travelling throughout Europe, invariably with a large French Brie for his own consumption, often losing his luggage or his tickets, but collecting an impressive array of works specially written for him by Max Bruch, Lalo and Alexander Mackenzie, as well as Saint-Saëns. He had a tone of silvery sweetness, especially in the high positions, but could be forceful and aggressive as the opening of the A-major Concerto shows.

Saint-Saëns was very often influenced by the personality of the players. This concerto has been as warmly praised as the C major has been ignored. The composer made one of his bold alterations to the rules by compressing his design into a single movement. Stegemann declares that he has not found any precedent for this 'individualistic interpretation of the concerto form'. The central slow section is very much akin to the Adagio of the Second Symphony, 'Theocritan' as Servières describes it, with muted strings, flute and cor anglais. The outer sections have much the same material in common, but when he returns to the opening section in part three he moves into the second subjects rather than the first, so the whole work is a kind of palindrome. The concerto is too short for an introduction or long Cadenza, but there is a brief cadenza-like section at the end of part one which ends with a long trill while the orchestra begins the slow movement. In the orchestration, much is made of the contrast between the higher registers of the solo violin and pizzicato accompaniments from the cellos and basses. Saint-Saëns was especially pleased at overhearing the comment at an early performance. 'The violin part is written as if the composer had been Joachim himself.'

Among lesser works written in 1859 was a *Bénediction Nuptiale* for organ, dedicated to Madame la Marquise de Mornay. Vierne, noting the muffled bells effect at the start, called the work 'that little masterpiece of written-out improvisation'. The long, sinuous melody moves – as so often in Saint-Saëns – step by step as if his fingers were just playing on the keyboard, and modulating at leisure. Two months after the composer's death this peaceful *Bénédiction* was played at the wedding of HRH Princess Mary to Viscount Lascelles.

The year 1860 saw many religious pieces. An 'Ave Maria' in A for 'two equal voices', following two others in the previous year, an 'Ave Verum', several canticles and motets. In addition he had the works of others sometimes thrust upon him. A report of the society wedding of the Prince de Polignac states: 'All the music for the Mass was composed by the Prince de Polignac, the youngest of four brothers of this illustrious family. The work was quite remarkable and testified to the composer's serious studies . . .'

There were further songs. 'Alla riva del Tebro' in the Italian style, 'Etoile du matin' (words by C. Distel) and 'Extase' (Victor Hugo). More remarkable was his setting of a poem from Hugo's *Les Châtiments*, that fierce attack on the Second Empire written in exile, 'Le Chant de ceux qui s'en vont sur la mer', in which the farewells of the sailor to the homeland are given a heavy and tumultuous accompaniment. It has been suggested that it was Saint-Saëns's interest in the drama *Spartacus* which lost him the favour of Princess Mathilde and the Bonapartes, but it is quite likely that a song such as this, dedicated to Pauline Viardot, in whose household there was a strong anti-Napoleonic feeling, could have been as damaging.

This was the year in which Wagner came to give three concerts at the Théâtre des Italiens and Saint-Saëns spent time studying the scores. He cherished hopes of impressing as a potential writer of opera and set to orchestral accompaniment a scene from Corneille's *Horace* as a dramatic duet. It was not until 1866 that he had an opportunity of hearing this work, which was given at a charity concert for the poor. He had also attempted to set the sleep-walking scene from *Macbeth* as a vehicle for Pauline Viardot, and considered *Kenilworth* as a possible operatic subject. A project for a ballet after the novel by Théophile Gautier, *Une Nuit de Cléopâtre*, had been rejected. Senators of the Second Empire, such as Prince Poniatowski, seemed to have their operas mounted; composers outside the charmed circle of the Tuileries had less success. Berlioz had presented a copy of *The Trojans* to Napoleon III, whom he described as 'having his twenty-five below zero look', and was told that the Emperor would read it, if he had the leisure.

Saint-Saëns at this time in any case had been forbidden by his doctor to fatigue his poor sight by too close a study of scores or by composition. It was a fortunate moment for French music when, forced to consider a temporary change in his musical activities, he accepted the post of Professor of Piano at the Ecole Niedermeyer. This school had been established in 1853 by Louis Niedermeyer, a prolific but only moderately successful composer, who had, however, enjoyed large profits from settings of Lamartine's 'Le Lac' and 'The

Lord's Prayer'. The events of 1848 had frightened Niedermeyer and he had fought against the workers under General Cavaignac during the 'June Days'. Although his Swiss origins were Protestant he regarded Catholicism as alone capable of barring the road to revolution and attempted to re-establish church music in its traditional forms. Romanticism and the neglect of schools of church music were alike blamed for the social evils of the time. His new foundation was favoured by the Archbishop of Paris and Napoleon III, desirous of having the Church as an ally, subvented it, awarded official prizes and ensured that Imperial functionaries in the provinces knew of it. It was thus that the young Gabriel Fauré, in the far-away South, was recommended by an official of the Corps Législatif.

The Niedermeyer plan was to train young organists and choirmasters who could then be employed by diocesan bishops. There was a certain rivalry with the Conservatoire, which, founded under the Republican Convention, was tainted with memories of revolution, but the new institution did not have the breadth of interests of the Conservatoire or any desire to furnish talent for the stage. The pupils were subjected to much church-going and lengthy sermons. Romantic composers such as Chopin or Schumann were considered unsuitable. There was a pedal-piano and an organ with twelve stops for pieces by Bach, Mendelssohn and Lemmens. Piano studies were restricted to Bach, Mozart and Beethoven. Alfred Bruneau, in a tribute to Fauré, greatest of all the alumni of the Ecole Niedermeyer, described the fifteen pianos in one room on which the pupils practised simultaneously. Three times a week there were singing classes under Dietsch, usually unaccompanied, but no secular singing, save on walks and outings. The interest in early church music was remarkable for its time and the harmony teaching, with its modal basis, was less pedantic than that at the Conservatoire. There was an element of the monitorial system in the tuition and older pupils taught the younger. Gigout was the teacher of Fauré in solfège and harmony, and later admitted to embarrassment when he recalled that he had corrected the counterpoint of 'our greatest composer'. Life was spartan but had inevitable undertones of boyish humour. Fauré and his friends would sometimes use coalbuckets, tongs and shovels in their joke scores. Gigout recalled an illicit visit to *Faust* when the pupils, who were not staying with their designated hosts as supposed, were forced to stay through the night in a café with scarcely a sou among them.

Niedermeyer died in March 1861 and the school became the property of his son Alfred, who, having little knowledge of music, appointed Dietsch as Director. Dietsch persuaded Saint-Saëns to take over the higher of the piano classes, 'a temporary arrangement' which lasted for four years. As a teacher, Saint-Saëns was a brilliant success. The episode is one of few in his life with no hint of controversy or rivalry. At twenty-six he was near enough in age to the pupils to arouse an air of camaraderie. Although in salons and society he lacked the physical attraction which ensured success, with schoolboys his wit and enthusiasm and warmth of nature were ideal qualities. So, too, was his advocacy of 'advanced' views regarded as subversive by the authorities. He turned the piano class into the most exciting seminars, playing and discussing Liszt, Schumann, Wagner and all others excluded from the official syllabus, and referring to his friendships with Berlioz, Wagner and Gounod. The youths were admitted to behold wondrous performances at the controls of the Madeleine organ, where they could see their teacher, elevated literally to great heights, outperforming anything of which they had experience. He had the additional teaching gift of being able to digress into all manner of subjects, bringing the lustre of a supposedly Bohemian world outside to his heavily disciplined pupils. Gigout recalled that the boys who were asked to dine at the Saint-Saëns apartment would be taken up to the roof and allowed to use the telescope while he shared his passion for astronomy. According to Fauré, although Saint-Saëns was not paid to teach composition, he encouraged the boys to write pieces of music and 'he read them with a curiosity and a care that only masterpieces would have merited. Then he distributed praise and blame, and accompanied them with examples and advice which impressed us, filled us with wonder and with courage.' He would also discuss with his class his own processes of composition. 'We drew from the same spring', said Fauré, 'the most fruitful teaching that it is possible to give.' Saint-Saëns would encourage frivolous compositions such as incidental music for charades and farces. There is even a suggestion that the *Carnival of the Animals* sprang originally from an idea mooted in this stern seminary. He conquered the hearts of all his pupils and in turn dedicated to six of them – Fauré, Gigout, Dietrich, Laussel, Lehman and Perilhou – transcriptions of J. S. Bach.

It was the handsome young Fauré who was his favourite and the friendship between the twenty-six-year-old teacher and the sixteen-year-old pupil was enduring and fruitful. Without the constant guidance and help of Saint-Saëns, Fauré would almost certainly have ended his days as a not very reliable provincial choirmaster. When Fauré eventually sat before the Director's desk at the Conservatoire, his first action was to write a letter of gratitude to Saint-Saëns. Fauré's two sons became substitutes for the children his teacher had lost and came to look upon the old man as a benign godfather. Other pupils such as Albert Perilhou and Gigout remained friends for life, though without the intense intertwining of personal and musical experiences. In 1914 when the name of Eugène Gigout came up in conversation with Jean Huré, Saint-Saëns suddenly said: 'Gigout? He was my little 106,' and explained: 'I promised him a fine reward if he would play Beethoven's *Hammerklavier* Sonata, Opus 106, by heart. He did it very well, hence I gave him the reward. I took him to *Faust*.'[1] For his Niedermeyer pupils he wrote playlets, *Le Château de Roch Cerdon* or *Les Cruartés du Sort*, his first attempts at written drama.

He was able to report on his meetings with the controversial Wagner. As he later pointed out, he had been the first in France to play the Grand March from *Tannhäuser* and he had composed paraphrases on *Lohengrin*. He had accompanied Pauline Viardot in a private performance of parts of *Tristan*. Both Liszt and von Bülow had made Wagner aware of his talents. He had accompanied Wagner at the Austrian embassy in renditions of sections of the *Rhinegold*, Wagner's voice 'a little too low to be tenor or soprano', and in 1861, when Wagner was in Paris for the performances of *Tannhäuser*, he invited Saint-Saëns to come to his apartment at 3 rue d'Aumale to play his scores with a finesse his own rough approximations could not rival. In *My Life*, Wagner wrote, 'I also got to know the astonishing dexterity and talent of this musician. To his extraordinary speed and his amazing facility in deciphering the most complicated orchestral scores, he added a memory no less admirable. He played *Tristan* without omitting any detail and with such precision that I could have sworn he had the scores in front of him.'

By the time this was written the hostility between France and Germany had caused a massive cooling of the mutual admiration and the reminiscence concluded with a chilly postscript. 'In the end I

---

[1] Gigout also submitted an attempt to orchestrate the sonata. Decades later Saint-Saëns remembered the schoolboy task and asked whether any copies remained.

learnt, it is true, that this amazing precocity in everything that makes up musical technique seemed to hamper in him the faculty of intense productivity. Whilst he made continual efforts to join the ranks of the composers I finished by losing him totally from sight.'

The historic failure of *Tannhäuser* at the Opéra in March 1861 was one of the principal reasons for Wagner's subsequent bitterness towards the French capital. The production had been advocated by Princess Pauline von Metternich, wife of the Austrian ambassador, who persuaded Count Walewski, illegitimate son of Napoleon I and recently appointed Minister of Fine Arts, to agree to a production, which his predecessor had not allowed. She was strongly supported by Baron Emile d'Erlanger, the banker and friend of the Empress, who to a great extent financed the rebuilding of Paris, but who was a good amateur violinist who played chamber music every evening after dinner.[1]

The reasons for hostility were mixed. There was dislike of Walewski's interfering policies at the Ministry and his blood relationship to the Emperor. The notorious grievance of the Jockey Club at the placing of the ballet in Act One before their time of arrival played some part. Exception was taken to the music, which, tame as it sounds to modern ears, provoked Prosper Mérimée to complain: 'I could write something similar tomorrow inspired by my cat walking up and down the keyboard. . . . Some say', he added, 'that Wagner has been sent to us to force us to admire Berlioz.' Auber called *Tannhäuser* 'Berlioz without melody'. Fétis, in the *Revue et Gazette*, had produced a damning condemnation of Wagner's self-advertised genius. At the première on 12 March the second act was disrupted by members of the Jockey Club. The majority of the audience had been either bored or amused before this incursion. Princess Metternich intermittently tried to lead bursts of applause, which never materialised. Five days later the opera was repeated. The Imperial couple arrived at the end of the second act and, some polite applause being taken as a tribute to the music, a reciprocal burst of hissing and abuse, with political as well as musical significance, followed. After the third of the four projected performances the work was withdrawn and Wagner left to nurse his grievances.

[1] His son Frédéric became a composer of operas under the name Frédéric Regnal.

At the same time there appeared a light little piece by Offenbach, *Monsieur Choufleuri*. The libretto was passed off as by the Duc de Morny, half-brother of the Emperor, though in fact it had been written mostly by his secretary, Ludovic Halévy. In the Birthday Honours Offenbach became a Chevalier of the Legion of Honour and the Goncourts wrote scathingly of 'Morny, Offenbach's patron, the amateur musician, the prototype man of the Empire, immersed and rotted in every sort of Parisian corruption'. There was growing disillusionment with the dependence upon Imperial whims and favours. Flaubert lamented: 'The moral sense is more and more on the decline. People wallow in mediocrity.' Baudelaire, also in 1862, said: 'You can't imagine to what extent the race of Parisians is degraded. Paris is no longer the charming place I used to know.' Gounod's *Reine de Saba*, a colossal failure in February 1862, seemed to embody the Empire's admiration for the grandiose. It lasted from 7.45 p.m. until twenty past midnight. Berlioz wrote sadly, 'There is nothing in the score. Nothing at all. How can I hold up what has neither bone nor sinew? Still I have got to find something to praise!' Berlioz had a great sense of the growing decadence around him, the 'pre-deluge' philosophy of those in power, which he translated into the 'Fall of Troy'.

Overseas, with more sinister consequences, Juarez, a revolutionary leader in Mexico, repudiated his government's debts, leading to a joint blockade of his country by Britain, Spain and France. Juarez offered to open talks, if the blockade were lifted. Spain and Britain agreed, but France refused and a French invasion of Mexico was begun.

Yet there were some faint signs of a greater future. A few days after the failure of *Tannhäuser* a Mass by César Franck was given its first performance – described ambiguously by Saint-Saëns as 'La Musique Cathédralesque'. At the Niedermeyer, Fauré presented his teacher with one of his compositions, a song 'Le Papillon et la Fleur' (on which Saint-Saëns drew one of his sketches depicting a lascivious butterfly gesturing to a flower). At the close of 1861, an Academy of Sacred Music was established as yet another effort to raise the standards of church music in Paris. Saint-Saëns gave his support, sat on the committee with his vicar, Abbé Lamazou, and was its official organist. During the following year its numbers rose to over 200, showing that a thirst for music more serious than the operettas of Offenbach existed.

On 29 April 1862 he took part with four others in the inauguration of the new Cavaillé-Coll organ at St Sulpice, the largest in France. Georges Schmitt played an Offertoire and Improvisations on a theme from *Judas Maccabeus*, Alexander Guilmant played a 'Méditation', César Franck a 'Fantasie in C' and August Bazille a 'Pastorale and Storm'. Saint-Saëns was entrusted with an Improvisation. It was received with modified rapture by the critic of the *Revue of Sacred Music, Ancient and Modern*, Louis Roger, who found it long-winded and over-complicated but concluded: 'He can sustain this criticism all the more since we don't need this instance to be convinced of his fine talent.' He may have been consoled on reading the same writer on Franck's contribution: 'that it had only one shortcoming; it did not end soon enough'.

In general he did not have an easy time with Parisian audiences. His fondness for the classical composers combined with advocacy for Berlioz, Wagner and Liszt ignored the middle ground of popular taste. The fact that he wrote chamber music, regarded as the preserve of the serious Germans, lessened his opportunities for operatic commissions. At this distance of time it is easy to forget that his fame rested on his prowess at the organ. When Princess Mathilde replied to an oblique request that she might use her influence with managements, the remark 'He plays the organ at the Madeleine and the piano at my house. Isn't that enough for him?' was not as facetious as is sometimes supposed. As today, it was the performer rather than the composer who commanded attention and enjoyed the prizes of success. Two weeks after St Sulpice, Saint-Saëns performed at yet more organs constructed by the ubiquitous Cavaillé-Coll: St Thomas d'Aquin and St Dizier, a town 200 kilometres east of Paris. Of this last recital the aptly named Canon Bourdon wrote a long account which gives a picture of his playing: he had given the obligatory 'storm' but also a Prelude of Bach and four improvisations. After the Blessing of the Organ he began a rhythmical motif, modulating effortlessly and slowly increasing the volume using all its new resources; he played with different groups of stops, giving the effects of a string ensemble, then a dialogue of woodwinds, and finally brilliant harmonies on the trompettes and bombardes. Again we can see that the organ to Saint-Saëns resembled an orchestra with its different sections and timbres, which he enjoyed contrasting.

Earlier, during the summer, Saint-Saëns was invited to pay a visit to the Fauré family at Tarbes. It was an extended and sociable tribe. There were excursions into the countryside and a musical recital at Bagnères. The lifelong correspondence of the two composers began. Fauré wrote of the impression that his brilliant teacher from Paris had made and how he himself had been the centre of attraction since. The boy's letters have an incipient flirtatiousness. The transcription of Bach dedicated to Fauré, one of the six rewarding prize winners, the overture to the Cantata No. 28, he describes as 'your little horror' because of its difficulty, but he intends to work on it when his headaches, 'which you don't feel strongly about I know', disappear. 'Do you know why I shall play it? Because of its key [D major], which is very fond of me and which I love very much myself.' Saint-Saëns's appreciation of Bach was still the exception. Paul Dukas found the cantatas boring as late as the 1890s. But in the reaction against the Romantics, interest in Bach was growing. Pauline Viardot subscribed to the Complete Edition, which began in 1850, and would sing arias of Bach and Handel at her private recitals with the Cavaillé-Coll chamber organ. As Bach was understood to be unemotional he appealed to the same inspiration as the Parnassian poets who put their faith in form, shape and restraint, with reason prevailing over excess. Bach, however, was staple fare at the Ecole Niedermeyer and it is no coincidence that Saint-Saëns's next piano concerto should have begun as if for fingers well trained in works for the clavichord.

Fauré sent imploring letters for the promise of a return visit, saying that he and his friends were preparing a little 'vaudeville' entertainment to which Saint-Saëns was invited and even telling him which train to catch, though he assumes 'death would be preferable to returning to this ghastly hole. Tarbes ... Adieu, my good friend and teacher; all my relations send you their best wishes ... as for me I cling for ever to your neck.'

Yet the visit was obviously an innocent one. The Fauré family might well have assumed that all Parisian tutors set off to visit pupils in the vacation and, being musicians, left items of laundry behind them (Gabriel promised to come back with the missing articles). Whatever the emotional undertones, Saint-Saëns never quite ceased to be the 'teacher' to Fauré. In his reply to these letters he plunges straight into encouragement to compose and speaks of another pupil at the Ecole, Julien Koszul: 'Koszul has charged me to say that your last "Romance" had a great success.' After saying that Koszul had sent 'a thousand *amitiés*', he sends to Fauré a similar number, adding 'it is 999 too many'. Fauré had some hopes of finding employment as an organist to the Senate, which possessed a small chapel. He quoted two Senators and an ex-Police Prefect who might be able to help him in his application in that age of patronage. All his relations had been urging him to be for Saint-Saëns 'the best pupil in the School and the best of friends outside it – they have no need to make these recommendations – in order to make you promise to return next year'.

The duties of teaching added to his daily obligations at the Madeleine and, combined with the doctor's warnings, seem to have restricted composing. From 1862 came only the song 'Soirée en Mer' (Hugo), a mazurka for piano and the Suite for Violincello, published in 1866 as Opus 16. It provides another example of Saint-Saëns, the pioneer of the cello repertoire in France, for this, as for many instruments, was very limited. It illustrates his double admiration for German music at this time; on the one hand Bach, whom he was determined to champion, and on the other Schumann, who was little known or admired in Paris. The Prelude is a more modern version of the Bach unaccompanied cello pieces. The piano lightly sketches the rhythm, but grows in the partnership and eventually introduces a phrase which becomes the germ of the fugue in the Finale. In fact, the cyclic tactic is once again used here and the 'Bach' movement reappears just before the close. The Serenade is a true serenade. The light piano figures suggest some sort of guitar while the cello sings phrases under an imagined balcony, which grow ever more amorous. The Scherzo, so called, is in reality more of a fast waltz, with the piano rushing up and down the keys, though both instruments in this very real duet share the melodies and counterpoints. We know that Saint-Saëns greatly admired Berlioz's orchestration of the Weber *Invitation to the Waltz* and there is more than one hint of that piece in this movement. The Romanza is a more complicated section than the usual treatment of this genre, with an impassioned middle section and emphasis on the lower, richer tones of the cello. The Finale is a bravura display with a bold initial theme, which later combines with the subject of a fugue in a battle royal until the cello retires into the safety of the eighteenth century. The Suite was played at a concert in 1866 where Berlioz, Liszt and Gounod were present and was published immediately.[1]

[1] When, many years later, Saint-Saëns orchestrated the Suite, he

The year 1863 was more productive. There was the '*Introduction and Rondo Capriccioso*', one of many mixed titles, written for Sarasate.[1] It follows the operatic pattern of recitative and aria and, familiar as the opening phrases are, they can still induce a *frisson* in the most jaded listener. In the Rondo there is also a contrast between the rhythmically firm opening phrases and the gentle guitar-like accompaniment to a seductive dance, the first of Saint-Saëns's many tributes to Sarasate's Spain.

Bordeaux chose as the subject of its competition in 1863 a 'Grand Concert Overture'. Saint-Saëns, inspired by the tragedy *Spartacus* by Alphonse Pagès, which he may have considered as the basis of an opera, wrote an overture, only recently discovered and recorded. In June, the jury awarded him first prize and, in November, he went south to hear it under the baton of Mézéray. It belongs markedly to the 'New Music'; Bordeaux must have been more adventurous than Paris. From the sonorous opening bars of the brass, Berlioz, Wagner and Liszt are all recalled,[2] though there is a lyrical central theme which could easily come from the mature Verdi and may have been conceived as a possible aria. Saint-Saëns, never a great friend of Italian opera, said once that he would have sacrificed all his works to have written *Rigoletto*. Carvalho had recently preferred Verdi's *Macbeth* to Saint-Saëns's projected vehicle for Pauline Viardot and made huge losses, but the Italian style was still the path to stage success. If there is a reason why Saint-Saëns never published this work it must be that it concludes with a conventional march (indicating the triumph of the Legions?), which has no thematic connection with the earlier dramatic moments and must have offended his ideas of form.

The MS of an unfinished Symphony in D exists at Dieppe, but it appears to have no connection with the Suite in D, Opus 49, which was not published until 1877. Servières said that the Suite was originally destined for the harmonium, though how the furiously rapid Finale could have been executed on a harmonium must remain a mystery. The Sarabande was the first movement to be composed and

diminished its youthful ardour. As the glittering piano passages in the Scherzo were not susceptible to orchestration, a Gavotte was substituted. The noble Finale, with its cyclical return to the eighteenth-century Prelude, was replaced by a concert Tarantella.

[1] Stamaty had in fact written a piece called *Rondo Caprice*.
[2] Gigout remembered hearing the astonishingly modern sequence which opens the overture, played to him as a Niedermeyer pupil.

would have proved more adaptable to a drawing-room instrument. The sequence – Prelude, Sarabande, Gavotte, Romance, Finale – suggests that the composer had been studying the age of Rameau. There is no evidence of a desire to impress, either with novelty or academic skill. It was orchestrated for the Litolff concerts at the Opéra in 1869, but the score is even less lavish than the Second Symphony and, apart from two trumpets cleverly employed in the Finale, there is no brass. There is an unusual uniformity of key and the movements follow the dance forms rather than any symphonic structure, save in the Finale, for even the Romance could be regarded as a slow and tristful Minuet. The Prelude is decidedly rustic, with piping wind and droning basses. The melancholic Sarabande is lightly scored and the Gavotte, with its twittering woodwind and decisive strings, has a plaintive episode which returns to the eighteenth-century world of aristocrats dressed as peasants. The miracle is the Finale, constructed virtually out of nothing except a few repeated notes, some nuances and cadenzas, and brilliant orchestration. A light, hammering motif runs from one set of players to another, as if a conductor had been forced to prolong the last bars of a Mozart overture while stage-hands hammered frantically behind the curtain. It has a vivacity totally French, which is its sole link with the preceding sections from an earlier age.

It has often been remarked that it is strange so brilliant a pianist wrote so little for solo piano.[1] Ten years separate the Mazurka of 1862 from his Gavotte in C minor. Among composer-pianists such abstinence is unique. The piano plays a major part in his chamber works, but he preferred the contrast of timbres between different instruments in his writing. Even the piano pieces he wrote for performance or for income were very often transcriptions of the works of others. It is possible that he found in the young Fauré a more pronounced 'poet of the piano' and devoted his energies to moulding the talents of his disciple. More prosaically it may be that, practising the piano each day, his thoughts wandered to the Opéra and concert hall. The Trio in F, Opus 16, was also begun in 1863, following

---

[1] Yet the guidance he received from Berlioz in their joint work on preparing the operas of Gluck produced the nearest thing to a piano sonata which he ever wrote: the *Caprice on the 'Airs de Ballet' from Alceste*. A noble first section is followed by an impression of tender eighteenth-century gallantry in 3:8 time, which moves into the minor nostalgically. The Finale is lively and exuberant. The slight title conceals a large-scale composition.

another visit to the Fauré family in Tarbes and a vacation in the
Pyrenees and Auvergne. It was dedicated to the cellist Alfred
Lamarche; the composer often performed it at his festivals and many
famous trios have included it in their programmes. It springs from a
happy period when he had the affectionate admiration of Fauré to
provide emotion and could escape the noises of the city as the area
around the Madeleine was rebuilt. Very little French music at this
time was genuinely inspired by the countryside and in this, as in so
much else, Saint-Saëns was a pioneer. The writing for piano in the
Trio is crisp and sparkling, and there are elements of humour as in the
Allegro Vivace when the listener is perplexed as to whether the tempo
is 2:4 or 3:4. Bonnerot describes how Saint-Saëns would play these
tantalising bars with nonchalant impassivity. The Andante has a
sorrowful theme played coldly by the piano in octaves, but a more
lyrical treatment is given to it by violin and cello. Its distinctive iambic
rhythm returns at intervals to check the emotion. The Scherzo, in
which the 'Trio' is heard twice, is a teasing interplay of single notes
thrown between pianist and pizzicato strings, and finishes with the
piano descending in semitones when we expect whole tones. In the
Finale, a final touch of humour, the piano appears to be leading off
into the well-worn path of a Saint-Saëns fugue. This proves to be
misleading and it is simply allowed a skittish coda of its own before the
final bars.

This was the year of the Congress of Paris, an outward sign of French
eminence, but it was also the time when the fabric of the Empire
began to crumble. The ruling clique, being to a large degree family
members, showed the readiness of families to divide. Walewski
supported the Poles in their rising for independence; Morny, with a
Russian wife, disagreed. The Empress supported the presence of
French troops protecting the Pope in Rome and, as Walewski stood
by her in her arguments, Morny expressed sympathy for the Italian
nationalists. But both Eugénie and Morny agreed over the importance
of French intervention in Mexico, the Empress because her Spanish
blood gave her an interest in remnants of the old Spanish Empire,
Morny because valuable profits could be made out of the venture. The
dreamy Emperor resurrected one of his uncle's less realistic schemes
for extending French power up the basin of the Mississippi. As a
starting point he offered the throne of Mexico to the Archduke

Maximilian, brother of the Emperor of Austria, whom he had entertained at the Congress. He hoped that this would re-establish good relations with Austria and also Belgium, as Maximilian's wife, Carlotta, was a Belgian princess. Auber wrote a national anthem for Mexico and was made a Grand Officer of Maximilian's Order. Prince Poniatowski set his new opera *L'Aventurier* in Mexico but, by the time that it reached the Opéra in 1865, Maximilian was fighting for survival.

Walewski, on retiring as Minister of Fine Arts, had given to the Théâtre Lyrique a subvention of 100,000 francs on condition that a three-act opera by a young winner of the Prix de Rome should be given. Saint-Saëns's friend Bizet had been the first to benefit and had been offered a libretto, *The Pearl Fishers*. Production was scheduled for September 1863. Although Saint-Saëns was a companion and admirer of Bizet this close association with the circumstances of the Walewski award made him realise that time was slipping by. It was his strong wish to reach the operatic stage, which motivated him in his strange attempt to sit once more for the Prix de Rome the following year.

Bizet, too, suffered from the general dislike of contemporary music. In 1863 Pasdeloup, in experimental mood, gave the Scherzo that survived from Bizet's plan for an 'Italian' symphony. Saint-Saëns was present at the performance and says that it was 'badly played and badly listened to, falling upon general inattention and indifference'. The rest of the programme was unimpeachably classical: Beethoven's *Egmont* and Mozart's Symphony No. 39. But the mere inclusion of Bizet resulted in Pasdeloup being deluged with correspondence from angry subscribers threatening to withdraw support. A week later, Bizet himself conducted the Scherzo at the Société Nationale des Beaux-Arts, a short-lived institution, not to be confused with the later Société Nationale, but a body with the similar aim of helping young composers. Saint-Saëns was also included in this programme and 'parts of a symphony' were given. The *Revue et Gazette* was very critical, especially of his conducting: 'A man may be very talented, write correctly, knowledgeably, in a very close, conscientious style and lack the tact, the experience and the special art necessary to a good orchestra conductor. M. Saint-Saëns proved this point very well that afternoon when he conducted two excerpts from one of his symphonies. The execution could hardly have been more hesitant, duller or more uneven.' The *Revue et Gazette*, though critical of Bizet's conducting, praised the music for a 'wholly French clarity and grace' and contrasted it favourably with the distorted and far-fetched style of Saint-Saëns. Saint-Saëns was still regarded as being too academic: Adolphe Botte wrote of his 'Fear of being common, love of colour and detail . . . the composer hurls his themes into waves of imitations and canons where they disappear immediately, pressed and stifled under a form which lacks tunefulness, under too tight a harmony, under a network of dissonances, cadences dodged, which makes the tonality lost to sight and disconcerts the ear. This monotony of surprises and affectations is not much better than the other sort of monotony.' The more savage P. Scudo, a failed musician who had taken up criticism, wrote violent attacks upon 'modern' music in the *Revue des Deux Mondes* and said of Saint-Saëns that he lived in a solemn, rather pedantic world – 'He has not convinced us that he is destined by God to compose great music.' Twenty years later Saint-Saëns recalled the concert of 1863, thinking no doubt of himself as much as Bizet. 'Failure then for us young Frenchmen was synonymous with death! Even success did not ensure a second hearing at these concerts.' He concluded that it was the mere fact of modernity which roused the hostility of the public: 'The public naturally enough finds difficulty in approaching a brusque genius like Berlioz who dwelt on inaccessible heights. But Bizet, the embodiment of youth, of gaiety and good nature . . . he sought above all things passion and life, whereas I ran after the chimera of purity of style and perfection of form.'

Although *The Pearl Fishers* had a cool reception in the press and some of the harmonic effects surprised, the première was not a disaster. Benoît Jouvin in *Le Figaro* found the opera 'an orgy of noise', but Berlioz devoted his final article in the *Journal des Débats* to it, praised certain sections and declared ironically that Bizet had returned from Rome 'without having forgotten music'. It was in November of the same year that Carvalho produced the emasculated version of Berlioz's own *The Trojans*, all that the great man ever heard of the work. Louis Gallet, later librettist for Saint-Saëns, recalled the jeers and animal cries which greeted an entr'acte and the crowds in the gallery singing the 'Soldiers' Chorus' from *Faust* by way of protest. The controversy over *The Trojans* – Bizet's support for it almost involved him in a duel – must also have persuaded Saint-Saëns more fervently towards the theatre, via the Prix de Rome. He was always combative and felt that, having gained access to the stage, he could strike one more blow against operatic conventions and with Bizet as comrade-in-arms do something for the improvement of taste.

His last attempt at the Prix de Rome at the comparatively advanced age of twenty-eight in the following year was humiliating. Although he could not yet be regarded as an important composer, he was known to and admired by many of the greatest musicians of the day, he was organist of the richest church in the capital and he had on record his previous successes in competitions. At the start of June the traditional incarceration at the Institut began. There were five finalists: Saint-Saëns, Adolphe Dannhauser, Charles Lefebvre, Titus Constantin and Victor Sieg, the last two being pupils of Ambroise Thomas. The words to be set were *Ivanhoe* by a Victor Roussy and, bad as they were, they had been selected from 127 entries. Exceptionally, the expenses of feeding the candidates were undertaken by the Institut, which implies that conditions were superior to earlier years. For twenty-five days composition proceeded and the first results were heard on 15 July. The Cantata of Saint-Saëns was played first in the Hall of the Conservatoire before a jury which had Auber as President and contained Prince Poniatowski,[1] Antoine Elwart, François Bazin, Duprato, and Ernest Boulanger, future father of Lili and Nadia. Bonnerot does not mention Berlioz although it is certain that Berlioz reproached himself for not having supported Saint-Saëns's candidacy more strongly. Mme Galli-Marié, the future Carmen, was one of the singers chosen to do justice to the works. After long deliberations in which a member of the Government, Camille Doucet, intervened, Victor Sieg was pronounced the winner of the Premier Grand Prix. In fact, two winners could have been elected, for in the previous year there had been no clear result, but, as if to underline Saint-Saëns's defeat, the minutes added that no one over the age of twenty-five had been considered worthy of the prize. Bonnerot, having examined the scores of the contestants, was in no doubt that Saint-Saëns's Cantata was superior to Sieg's. Chantavoine, writing much later, reported that Saint-Saëns had declared that there was a clique opposed to him from the start. Reyer remarked afterwards that Sieg must have owed his victory to his Christian name.

---

[1] Tuscan diplomat who had risen to favour with Napoleon III and may have represented an official view. He had composed successful operas in Italy and once starred as the leading tenor in his own *Giovanni de Procido*. The family remains important.

Sieg was greatly moved by his success, heard his *Ivanhoe* at the Opéra in November and then slipped into obscurity. For some years he was organist of Notre Dame de Clignancourt and an Inspector of Singing in Paris schools. When he died in 1890 Saint-Saëns had again to taste the bitter fruit of humiliation, as the obituaries referred to Sieg having defeated him in 1864. There might well have been political pressure. Saint-Saëns was a member of the Viardot circle, which included republicans and even revolutionaries from abroad. Louis Viardot had a great hatred of the Empire, and he and Pauline had recently moved to Baden. Saint-Saëns had set a poem from Hugo's *Les Châtiments* and written an overture on the slave revolts against Imperial Rome. He seems often to have taken part in mildly subversive artistic gatherings. For example, Gounod had written music for a play by Ernest Legouvé, *Les Deux Reines de France*, which dealt *en passant* with Pope Innocent III placing France under an Interdict. Because of political links with the Vatican the play was banned, but private performances were given in salons such as that of the Orleanist Bertins. Legouvé read extracts from the play; Gounod, the Vicomtesse de Grandval and singers from the Opéra sang the musical extracts, and Saint-Saëns and Bizet accompanied. The only other excuse for the jury is that they could have been seeking signs of genius in the midst of tentative effort and error, and considered that Saint-Saëns had reached his summit of proficiency. This would explain Berlioz's famous comment: 'He knows everything but lacks inexperience.'

It is ironic that many years later a Minister of Fine Arts had the idea that Saint-Saëns might be persuaded to be the Director of the Villa Medici and preside over the Prix de Rome winners. For a brief moment Saint-Saëns was attracted by the idea, but declined. He was always at pains to counter any suggestions that Auber felt animosity towards him. In a letter dated May 1899 from Las Palmas he wrote to George Mathias, pianist, that this was the opposite of the truth. 'Then, as later, he always showed me very great interest and sympathy – several times I have had to take up my pen to refute these falsehoods and I am happy to see you give the truth about him as in all else.' In fact, on the morrow of the contest Auber, realising that Saint-Saëns had entered in order to gain the promise of a stage production,[1] sent

---

[1] Significantly Paladilhe, a friend of Bizet, had been told in 1863 by Camille Doucet, Director-General of State Theatres, that composers who had *not* won the Prix de Rome could *not* be played at the subventioned theatres.

his secretary to Carvalho to ask for a libretto on which Saint-Saëns could begin work. The gesture was generous, but was to involve the composer in frustrations over many years.

Carvalho, real name Cavaille, had been born in Mauritius and was said to be of mixed race. He continued to send his French wine to Mauritius and back in the belief that a sea voyage improved it. He had sung minor roles at the Opéra Comique, but his talents were those of the impresario. He directed the Théâtre Lyrique, the third Parisian opera house, which had arisen from the ashes of an earlier venture, established by Adam before the 1848 revolution. From 1851 under its Director, Edmonde Seveste, it met Victor Hugo's call for a greater working-class interest in the theatre by charging moderate prices and having a larger repertoire made up of translations, works which had passed out of copyright and pieces by new composers. Between 1851 and 1870, out of 176 productions thirty-seven were new creations including works by Bizet, Gounod and Berlioz. Threatened by the rebuilding of Paris, it moved in the early 1860s from the boulevard du Temple to the place du Châtelet. Here, under Carvalho, it abandoned its more popular image for it incurred greater costs. Carvalho pursued a policy of attracting great singers such as Pauline Viardot and Christine Nilsson, had a great interest in expensive staging and an insatiable desire to 'improve' works in production. He is even said to have commissioned a new libretto for *Così Fan Tutte* based upon *Love's Labour's Lost*.

When he received Auber's request, which was almost equivalent to a command, he had by some fell mischance a libretto, *Le Timbre d'Argent*, a fantastic opera in five acts, by the noted collaborators Jules Barbier and Michel Carré, which was to be a scourge and source of fruitless labour to Saint-Saëns down to his seventh decade.[1] It had originally been given to Xavier Boisselot, but indolence and impatience had stifled any flow of music, and Carvalho was only too pleased to pass it on. Saint-Saëns was the fourth musician before whom it was placed but, accepting the challenge, he discussed changes with the librettists and retired to the charming village of Louveciennes, west of Paris, to begin composition.

[1] Barbier and Carré were, it is fair to say, at the pinnacle of their profession. They had collaborated with Meyerbeer in the *Pardon de Ploêmel*, a mainstay at the Opéra Comique's receipts, and with Gounod on the hugely successful *Faust*.

The year 1864 was not rich in other works, but he was active as a performer and, at the Salle Pleyel, gave a series of concerts which included all the piano concertos of Mozart and many Mozart trios and duets. The comment from the mordant Scudo on this achievement was: 'One is only able to encourage a pianist who has given proof of so solid a talent.' Yet, as with Bach, Saint-Saëns was once again the pioneer, for, in comparison with Beethoven, Mozart was less highly esteemed at the time. He was remembered as the child prodigy, but it was not until the production of *Don Giovanni* at the Opéra in 1876 that his genius as a composer was accorded proper acclaim. More remarkably, we have here Saint-Saëns, at the same time as writing *Spartacus*, imbued with the spirit of the 'New Music', calling attention to the spirit of the purest classicism. It is this dichotomy of taste that has always made him so difficult a composer to place in the scheme of things. As a pianist, though no one could deny the science of his playing and the dexterity of his fingerwork, his brusque gestures in crossing the platform, his impenetrable sang-froid through all pieces, grave and gay, and his emotionless acceptance of applause all added to the impression that he was a dry academic and this label was applied to his compositions.

His failure in the Prix de Rome helped in part to turn him back to the concert hall and triggered the commencement of his international career as a piano virtuoso. It is idle to speculate on his destiny as a composer had he been successful. Probably he would not have exchanged his lucrative post at the Madeleine for student life in the Villa Medici. We might have had an Italianate *Samson and Delilah*, produced at speed instead of being hammered out over the years without prospects of performance. It is more likely that a conventional libretto would have been provided for him based on a tale by Sir Walter Scott. His sources of inspiration remained classical and north European rather than Italian.

5

An Artist's Life

In 1865 the Paris première of the Schumann Piano Concerto was given with Saint-Saëns as soloist. He performed in Lyons and, in April, he participated in a Grand Concert at Dijon, which was intended to promote a monument to Rameau, whose greatness Saint-Saëns was also coming to recognise. A series of appearances with Sarasate was announced with the intention of bringing 'serious' music to the Parisians, but, after two different programmes had been publicised for the second concert, *Le Ménestrel* informed its readers that the artists had been unable to agree upon the works they would perform. In November Saint-Saëns travelled to Leipzig, and played his First Piano Concerto and a Bach transcription at the Gewandhaus. These engagements made it difficult for him to continue as a regular teacher at the Ecole Niedermeyer, where the death of Louis Dietsch had resulted in a change of regime, though he was elevated to membership of the jury at the annual prize-giving and his ex-pupils continued to stand in for him at the Madeleine.

He appears to have atoned for his absences from the tribune by a renewal of religious composition: another 'Ave Maria' (in A major for soprano, tenor and organ), an 'Inviolata' motet, sufficiently dramatic to be dedicated to Pauline Viardot, and the resurrected *Elévation ou Communion* for organ or harmonium, dedicated to Alexis Chauvet. The form is ABA, though in the final section Saint-Saëns combines two halves of former melodies into a third. There is a cadenza at the close which shows that the composer still often thought in terms of the piano at the organ keyboard. It was through his influence that Widor received a first engagement. In September 1865 he deputised at the International Exhibition at Oporto in a specially built replica of the Crystal Palace. Because of Britain's links with Portugal a British organ had been installed and Widor gained the experience of playing for both religious and popular concerts.

Saint-Saëns's major new work was the setting of Psalm 18, 'The Heavens Declare the Glory of God', for solo voices and chorus. There are orchestral parts although the main burden of accompaniment is carried by the organ. It was one of the most extended pieces he had so far written and displays new strengths. It is based upon the Bach cantatas; the Introductory Chorus becomes the Final Chorus, a feature added later. As the Madeleine must have been rich in baritones at the time there is the unusual feature of a quartet for four baritones where, by skilful use of imitations, he is able to distinguish four voices of similar range. There are, as ever, leaps forward to the nineteenth century and melodies characteristically French: in the chorus 'Exulta-vit ut gigas', voices in unison, doubled by trumpets and trombones over kettledrum rolls, describe the leaps of a giant ... The mezzo-solo, 'Domine adjutor meus', is a dialogue between the singer and violincello, to the exclusion of other instruments, emphasising the theme of humility. When the cantata was repeated at the Société Nationale several years later the soprano soloist was the Baronne de Caters, who afterwards introduced Saint-Saëns to Queen Victoria. The great Psalm appealed to Saint-Saëns because of its worship of order and the power of a kind of sun god in the universe – the same instinct which found expression in his many essays into the world of Hercules. The power of the sun is exalted in the roaring of kettledrums, the rushing of strings and an explosion of brass. To a serious student of astronomy there must have been power in the lines 'Day unto day uttereth speech and night unto night shareth knowledge', which are expressed musically. The final chorus is introduced by a kind of carillon of violins with contrapuntal lines (as later in the Third Symphony) emphasising a link between the harmonious spheres and the ordered music.

His social life continued to be active. In addition to his own Monday Evenings we catch a description of him by Hughes Imbert at Chabrier's musical soirées in the rue Mosnier: 'There was Saint-Saëns, with his Parisian sense of fun and prodigious musical memory. Massenet looking like a repentant Mary Magdalen ... Manet, leader of the Impressionists, and many others I have forgotten. Saint-Saëns sang and acted the part of Marguerite in Gounod's *Faust* with passionate ardour ... Among the instruments there was a remarkable organ, capable of the most bizarre imitations: the boom of the cannon, drums etc.' The artist Gustave Doré was a keen violinist and invited the company of musicians. One evening Saint-Saëns played piano versions of *Les Préludes* and parts of the *Dante* Symphony with Liszt himself as an onlooker. Such was the triumph of this performance that Berlioz dragged himself from his sick-bed to hear a repetition.

The songs of this period are bound up with his wish to embark on setting the libretto of *Le Timbre d'Argent*. 'L'Enlèvement' (Hugo) was dedicated to Carvalho's wife, the celebrated soprano Mme Miolan-Carvalho; 'Clair de Lune' to Mme Marie Barbier, wife of the librettist. The words of 'Clair de Lune' were by Catulle Mendès and show that Saint-Saëns was moving into new artistic circles. Mendès was born in 1841, grandson of Jewish bankers in Bordeaux. Passionately keen on Latin, the grandfather had not only translated the Book of Job into Latin verse but had imposed Roman names on his immediate descendants. Before he had reached the age of twenty, Catulle had set off for Paris aspiring to be a poet. Outstandingly handsome, with a mass of gold-blond hair, he was ambitious to occupy the literary throne that had belonged to Victor Hugo and to rival the achievements of all history's great heroes in some kind of glorious synthesis. He became the leading figure in a journal, *Parnasse Contemporain*, which assembled a diverse band of free spirits. They extolled an elevated view of poetry and wished to take over from the first generation of Romantics, affirmed the beauty and necessity of form, and desired to rid the language of sentimental insipidities. Their interests included the new civilisations revealed by exploration. It need hardly be said that the respect for form, precision of language and a fascination with Orientalism found an echo in the soul of Saint-Saëns.[1]

Mendès's chief idol was Wagner. Before he had even heard a note of the music he had devoured the poems of *The Flying Dutchman* and *Lohengrin*. In 1861 he founded the *Revue Fantaisiste*, in which he defended *Tannhäuser* and came to the notice of Wagner himself, who declared him a 'just and generous critic'. The musical passions of Catulle had led him to court the daughter of another keen (though unmusical) Wagnerian: Théophile Gautier. Judith Gautier

---

[1] The effect of the Parnassians on Saint-Saëns can be overstated. He did not subscribe to the withdrawal of artists from Society and continued to draw upon Hugo, Alexandre Dumas and others for his ideas.

dreamed of joining a sacred band that would defend Wagner against all creation. She and Catulle conducted a clandestine courtship through the services of the Gautiers' Chinese servant and measured the days of separation by reference to Pasdeloup's concerts. They were finally married in April 1866, but within a short space of time Catulle, who had Don Juan among his list of heroes, had become the lover of a remarkable female musician, Augusta Holmès, and fathered her four children. Once Augusta and Catulle were united in one of the famous and surprisingly stable unions of the time there was little space for other male admirers of Augusta. Epistles and poems she received from Saint-Saëns were bound to be unfruitful.

Augusta was the daughter of an Irish ex-officer, a man of literary interests, who lived at Versailles. She displayed precocious musical talents, studied harmony with Henri Lambert, the Versailles organist, and orchestration with Hyacinthe Klose, a pioneer of the modern clarinet. She sang with interpretative skill, emphasised by her extraordinary beauty, and was welcomed into the salon of Guillot de Sainbris, a wealthy patron of the arts, who supported the choral society of Versailles. Here she found herself in the company of talented young men including the poets Henri Cazalis (writer of the original *Danse Macabre*), Armand Renaud, and the painters Henri Regnault and Georges Clairin. Among the musicians were Gounod, Thomas and the still young Saint-Saëns. In later years Augusta was wont to recall the praise bestowed upon her by the elderly Rossini and by Wagner; she spoke less of the praises of Saint-Saëns, perhaps because she wanted to be associated only with the greatest masters of her time. But there was plenty of praise from Saint-Saëns at this juncture as from all who came under her spell.

The château of Versailles provided a suitable background for romantic evenings; there were parks and forests, fountains and lakes, and ghosts of the past surrounding evenings of poetry and music. André Theuriet, a novelist, described these occasions, which Saint-Saëns shared: 'After taking coffee and smoking in the garden one went indoors and, without being asked, Augusta seated herself at the piano. For more than two hours she bewitched us with her strange contralto voice, sometimes muffled and almost husky, sometimes extraordinarily vibrant . . .' After the music there were walks in the woods. 'The night is mild, the moonlight casts its spell across the clumps of trees, the chestnuts in bloom exhale a powerful scent. From time to time a voice sings out or artistic talk rises up through the branches.' When Saint-Saëns came to live at Louveciennes he was close to Versailles and became a visitor to the salons of de Sainbris and Major Holmès. He and Augusta both frequented the concerts given by Pasdeloup. Saint-Saëns inundated her with letters, poems and proposals of marriage:

> 'L'Irlande t'a donnée à nous. Ta gloire est telle
> Qu'un double rayon brillé à ton front; Astarte,
> . . .
> Sapho qui t'égalait n'avait pas ta beauté
>
> . . .
> Tu chantes, comme vibre une forêt superbe,
> Qu'agite la fureur des grandes vents déchaînés

His proposals were not accepted, but an affectionate friendship remained and Saint-Saëns corresponded with Augusta up to her death. The Astarte poem was found among her papers, written out with greater neatness than Saint-Saëns usually achieved in correspondence. She, too, had high ambitions as a composer. She wrote on a lavish scale; her *Ode Triomphale*, celebrating the hundredth anniversary of the Great Revolution, was performed in 1889 by 1200 musicians in the Palace of Industry. Her 'Hymn to Peace' in 1890 was given at Florence in commemoration of the death of Dante's Beatrice (1290) and Augusta was fêted as a genius who could match the demands of these massive occasions. She may at this time have regarded Saint-Saëns as a composer of church and chamber music whose aspirations did not match her own.[1] Added to this, she responded to the physical attractions of a man like Catulle Mendès whose glamour drew attention, even in her retinue of handsome young men.[2] What the musical results of a successful proposal on the part of Saint-Saëns might have been we can only conjecture. Hollywood was robbed of a screen epic that might have been built on the rivalry of their talents.

A major event at the Madeleine in 1865 was the State Funeral of the Duc de Morny. Although involved in a number of shady transactions

---

[1] And yet it was at this time that he wrote to an unknown female correspondent about his ambitions 'to become the greatest French composer, if that is possible'.
[2] The milieu was re-created in Act One of *Proserpine*.

(many of his papers were systematically burnt as he lay dying), he had been one of the more sagacious politicians of the time. Lord Cowley, the British ambassador, wrote: 'Morny is a great loss to the Emperor and the latter is much cut-up. In critical moments Morny had great calmness and firmness, and even his enemies admit that his judgement . . . when not warped by his own interests, was sound.' If he had lived it is possible that France would not have plunged into the disastrous war of 1870. Too close an association with the ruling clique was more than ever proving a disadvantage in the arts. When the architect Eugène-Emanuel Viollet-le-Duc was installed as Professor at the Ecole des Beaux-Arts as the Imperial choice, Count Nieuwerkerke, lover of Princess Mathilde, was driven from the platform in a hail of eggs and rotten fruit. A play by the Goncourts, *Henrietta Maréchale*, was hissed at the Théâtre Français, as the authors were known to be friends of the Princess.

Yet it was in 1866 that Saint-Saëns dedicated his 'Serenade' to the Princess, a piece for piano, organ, violin and viola or cello. Many arrangements were made of this including two by the composer himself, one for orchestra and another to words by L. Mangeot. The song is a poem of water which dreams in the moonlight of fleeting time and love. Moonlight was a popular theme, as was the supposed grace and calm of the eighteenth century. Between 1855 and 1865 Saint-Saëns wrote three songs which invoke the moonlight: 'Le Lever de la Lune' (Ossian), 'Le Soir descend sur la Colline' (Legouvé) and 'Clair de Lune' (Mendès). Verlaine was developing the theme of moonlight in his *Fêtes Galantes* published in 1869. The Serenade had a great success when played at a reception given by the Prince of Hohenzollern with Auber in the audience and the composer at the organ. It was repeated soon afterwards at a musical evening given by the cellist Lebouc, and at a public concert conducted by Jean-Baptiste Weckerlin, a musical scholar and archivist.

On the political stage the Emperor had talks with the Prussian Chancellor, Bismarck, who described him as 'half dreamer, half crook'. The ending of the Civil War in America boded ill for the Mexican venture; the United States government could now turn its attention to the unwelcome presence of French troops south of its borders and unemployed soldiers were seeking outlets for adventure. An agreement was reached with Victor Emmanuel of Italy whereby France promised to withdraw the garrison protecting the Pope. As French

Catholics were certain that Italian promises to respect the residue of the Papal States would not be honoured, the pulpits of the Madeleine and other churches resounded with denunciations of the agreement. The performance of Saint-Saëns's 'Psalm 18' at Midnight Mass on Christmas Eve 1865 painted an image of a divinely guided universe, a mixture of the biblical and classical sense of order and authority, which was very different from the political world before which it was given.

In the New Year, Fauré left the Ecole Niedermeyer with his Maître de Chapelle diploma and took up his first post as organist at St Sauveur in Rennes. Saint-Saëns, always the tutor as well as admirer, reproved him for being dilatory in thanking the Niedermeyer Director, who had recommended him: 'You have committed a serious offence, which you must rectify as soon as you can.'

In the summer of 1866 a group from the Versailles circle went down to Brittany for a vacation: Saint-Saëns, Henri Regnault, Georges Clairin, Emmanuel Jadin (who was about to set off for the Villa Medici) and another musician, Ulysse Butin. The friends spent the days painting and writing, made a pilgrimage to the 'Pardon' of St Anne de Palud with Fauré in the party and visited the Gulf of Morbihan, where Saint-Saëns sketched the *Trois Rhapsodies sur des Cantiques Bretons*, dedicated to Fauré and written for organ. One morning as he was embarking on a boat, 'a thin rustic sound' came to him and he discovered the captain playing an oboe. During the crossing the sailor played the tunes of his Breton region and these melodies, primitive and sometimes rough at the edges, were an attraction after the sophistication of Paris. Robust passages in the second Rhapsodie, based upon what could be a drinking song, remind us that religious festivals have been associated with merry-making down the ages. The term 'Rhapsodie' was suffiently novel; Saint-Saïns used it as a more colourful term for 'improvisation', in the knowledge that Liszt had made similar ventures into the folk-music of his homeland.

The first is ternary, the opening section being a 'missionary' cantique, repeated in the pedals with harmonies supplied on the keys. The central section consists of chords in the distant key of F sharp major, which recall the religious element; the first gentle theme returns against far-away sounds on the other manuals and dies away. There is throughout the work a contrast between sad feminine piety and a male roughness characteristic of the region. The second

Cantique contains an elaborate fugal section designed to give the organist an opportunity to offer his skills, and a quiet devotional movement, based on a Breton carol, 'Paraissez monarque aimable', repeated, extended and given a more metropolitan flavour. Section A returns with loud pedals at the close. The third Rhapsodie is even more unusual in form, double ternary, the repetitions being in shortened versions. Section A is a folk-song melody which serves as the basis for some improvisation. B has little relation save for rising notes within the same compass and, like the works of Schumann, it deceives over the placing of the bar-lines. C is another robust section which reiterates the basic theme up to a climax at increased speed and volume, and here there is a deliberate imitation of the Breton 'bagpipe', which had a share in celebrations as marked as the pious organist of the second Cantique. The third Cantique ends quietly and, strangely for Saint-Saëns, in a key different from that in which it began.

He had recently been playing the new organ at Rouen (where Aimabale Dupré, grandfather of Marcel Dupré, was organist). This was one of the first occasions when he was not inaugurating a Cavaillé-Coll instrument, for it had been installed by the rival firm of Merklin-Schutz. The reviewer in the Rouen paper found Saint-Saëns tedious compared with Auguste Bazille and his famous 'storms', but it is possible that Saint-Saëns was thinking of an organ of this simpler variety when writing the Rhapsodies. He was thinking, too, of Fauré. . . . We may guess that these pieces were an effort on his part to increase his protégé's popularity with the Breton congregation, for Fauré found Rennes boring and was on bad terms with his superiors.

During 1866 Saint-Saëns was also assisting Berlioz with the production of Gluck's *Armide* at the Théâtre Lyrique. Berlioz wrote to his friend Ferrand: 'Mme Charton-Demur, who plays the trying part of Armide, comes each day to rehearse with M. Saint-Saëns, a great pianist and a great musician, who knows his Gluck almost as well as I do . . . This morning in the "Hatred" scene Saint-Saëns and I shook hands. We were speechless. Never did any man discover such accents. And to think there are people who blaspheme this masterpiece.' Unfortunately the theatre felt obliged to cancel *Amide* while rehearsals were in progress. Berlioz at this time was seriously ill but, for three days in July, he joined Saint-Saëns, the organist Edouard Batiste and d'Ortigues on a jury for a competition in Louvain where, in the short time available, they were given sixty Masses to arrange in order of merit!

While these excursions to Brittany and elsewhere were taking place the map of Europe was changing. In the Austro-Prussian War, Prussia had driven its rivals from the German Confederation. Bismarck made peace swiftly, suspecting that Napoleon III might seek compensation for his neutrality. Austria grumbled at the lack of French support and Napoleon III's efforts to find alliances in the south German states proved fruitless. Events appeared to be passing out of control. Even Offenbach's *La Belle Hélène*, despite its overt frivolity, carried undertones of drift as the lovers set in train the catastrophic sequel to their passion. When the Imperial couple attended the Odéon, ribald shouts punctuated the performance and in their hurried exit a fleet of sewage carts nearby was hailed with cries of '*Vive l'Empereur*'. While Napoleon III was engrossed in writing (with academic help) a Life of Julius Caesar, French troops in Mexico were in retreat and Maximilian's wife Carlotta was touring the courts of Europe pleading for aid and displaying symptoms of approaching madness. Bad harvests, floods and a further outbreak of cholera added to the miseries of the poor. A façade of splendour, however, was maintained by the 1867 Universal Exhibition, which was intended to stamp the image of Paris as capital of Europe. The city swarmed with foreign royalty who had come to see the new boulevards and the unveiled majesty of the rising Opéra. As well as placing an accent upon achievements in industry and trade, the Exhibition established Paris as a centre of pleasure and indulgence. Offenbach's *La Vie Parisienne* made the point explicitly and his *Grand Duchess of Gérolstein*, though its heroine was nearer in personality to the meddling Eugénie than to the unpolitical Queen of Prussia, appeared to pour scorn upon lesser countries, subservient to military cliques. Yet the *Grand Duchess*, reinforced by Offenbach's subsequent *Les Brigands*, revealed secret unease at the existence of lands beyond the Rhine where regiments were drilling to martial refrains.

The 1855 Exhibition had done nothing for composers, but in 1867 a competition was announced for a hymn and a cantata. More than a quarter of a century later, when Saint-Saëns was a revered figure and President of the elaborate musical events at the Exhibition of 1900, the composer Alfred Bruneau recalled that 'the hymn inspired no one but the cantata threw the limelight upon a young man, then often dismissed, who was waiting only for the moment to hurl himself towards that glory into which he entered victoriously long ago. I have named our illustrious President'. An Imperial Commission was set up to choose the cantata, first a text submitted by nineteen-year-old Romain Cornut, still a pupil at the Lycée Bonaparte, and then the music. Saint-Saëns was tired and nervous, but was encouraged to enter by recent favourable comments upon his 'First' Violin Concerto, Opus 20 and the Tarantella performed in public. He finished the Cantata, *Les Noces de Prométhée*, only a few hours before the time limit expired. It was a document of thirty-two staves of a kind little used at the time and from this novelty arose the legend that, fearing the hostility of the Commission, he had the anonymous entry posted from England. Bizet reported 103 entries, Berlioz 104. Ernest L'Epine, Secretary to the Commission, revealed later that, of these, four were ridiculous, forty-nine passable, thirty-five good, eleven very good, three excellent and one perfect. Bizet, who had his work copied by a pupil, Edmond Galabert, so the writing would not be recognised, was among the last fifteen; Ernest Guiraud, Massenet and Weckerlin were the three 'excellent'.

The President of the Commission, Rossini, had attended rarely, Auber slept through many of the meetings, Ambroise Thomas voted for Massenet, Berlioz was a voice in favour of the Saint-Saëns entry. Paladilhe claimed that the thirty-two-stave paper came from Germany (it was in fact English), which made the jury think that the contribution might be from Wagner: 'They were disagreeably surprised when they opened the envelope and found the name of Saint-Saëns.' The winning cantata was headed with a quotation boldly selected from Victor Hugo, scourge of the Second Empire: '*La musique est dans tout, un hymne sort du monde.*' When published, it was dedicated to Saint-Saëns's old harmony teacher Pierre Maleden.

Berlioz was elated at his friend's success. On the day of the judgement he wrote, 'I have had the pleasure of seeing crowned unanimously the Cantata of my young friend, Camille Saint-Saëns, one of the great musicians of our age . . . How happy he will be. I ran to his house to tell him. He had gone out with his mother. He is a stunning pianist; at last behold something sensible happening in our musical world.' Bizet sent his congratulations, uncharacteristically concealing the fact that he had been a rival; Saint-Saëns, always anxious to help French composers, generously wrote to Massenet offering to use his influence with Liszt on the latter's behalf. 'There are such good and lovely things in your score that I've just written to Weimar asking for it to be played there.' Alas, the two musicians were foredoomed ever to misunderstand each other. Saint-Saëns maintained that his gesture had not been warmly welcomed. When, years later, Massenet wrote of his offer, 'Only great men can make such gestures', Saint-Saëns regarded the compliment as just another example of the other's notorious insincerity.

Saint-Saëns was not responsible for the poem, but it provided an interesting variant on the usual treatment of Prometheus, as hero in the struggle against the tyranny of the gods. Prometheus, in this version, weds Humanity, Justice attends the nuptials, Fraternity chooses its home on Earth. The accent is on the granting of favours and social unity from above, a reference to the well-meaning authority of the Emperor. Prometheus, prototype of inventors, has been delivered from the vultures of Tyranny and Superstition. Some dolorous music colours the discussion of the need for social unity and the customary Saint-Saëns harps hail Fraternity when she descends from Olympus (Olympus being always an analogy for the Court of Napoleon III). With its triumphal marches and marriage hymn, the cantata is very much a work of its time suggesting life under the rule of a benevolent Jupiter.

The performance of the work proved more difficult than the competition. It was scheduled for 1 July at the distribution of prizes awarded to inventors and manufacturers in the Palace of Industry. There were hesitations about giving it such a cavernous venue where the recitatives (and the finesse of the orchestration) would be lost. Saint-Saëns was not *persona grata* and officials of the Empire desired something more bombastic. Rossini himself came up with 'A Hymn to the Emperor and his Valiant Peoples' for large chorus and orchestra with military sound effects, from brass bands to gunfire. In the heady atmosphere of celebration Saint-Saëns was forgotten. Yet many members of the public wished to hear the cantata that had carried off the prize in the face of such talented adversaries. One journalist, Hippolyte Prévost, complained on the composer's behalf in *La France*. An assistant secretary of the Commission replied that the estimated time required of twenty-five minutes made it too long a work for an award-giving ceremony and repeated the concern that its delicate nuances would be lost in a large auditorium. Saint-Saëns paid a visit to Commissar-General Le Play and reminded him that there had been a promise to 'put at the disposition of the prize-winner all the necessary resources for a good performance'. Le Play confessed that all the money allocated had been spent. Other music concerts had also to be abandoned. Saint-Saëns gave an account of the interview in *Le Figaro* and, fearing a press campaign, Le Play made a token grant of 2500 francs to the composer.

The incident went some way towards softening public attitudes towards Saint-Saëns. The press supported the view that he 'had the right to more consideration as a man, as a prize-winner and as an artist long esteemed'. In fact he added to the 2500 francs a larger sum from his own resources and prepared a performance of *Les Noces de Prométhée* at the Cirque de l'Impératrice, a far from ideal setting as it was encumbered with circus paraphernalia. It was only under the Republic that the State made amends and rewarded the composer financially and artistically with a gala performance to open the Salle de Trocadéro at the Exhibition of 1878.

During the displays of arts and inventions in 1867, Saint-Saëns found himself in odd partnership with Wagner in advertising 'salon organs' as promoted by a company from Vermont, USA. He signed a bland testimonial praising the Estey Company organs: 'charmed by their tonal quality, which so closely resembles that of the pipe-organ', which the makers put side by side with the words of Wagner: 'The Estey organ is both wonderful and noble.' Such advertising was fashionable. Even Bismarck was once quoted in the English *Times* in connection with a particular cough mixture. Saint-Saëns also recommended the cabinet organs of Mason and Hawkins 'for the rendering of all sacred music and an indispensable auxiliary of the pianoforte in the drawing-room'. Almost all the leading Paris organists – Widor, Guilmant and Lefébure-Wély included – demonstrated the remarkable volume achieved by some of these instruments, designed ostensibly for domestic use.

As if the troubles caused by the Imperial bureaucracy over *Prometheus* were not enough, Saint-Saëns was pushed into further dilemmas by the interest finally shown by Carvalho in *Le Timbre d'Argent*. This was to rankle with him throughout the remainder of his long life. It was in 1864 that he had been given the libretto. When he went to Louveciennes to work on the score he seems to have been regarded as an oddity, for he must have taken with him a salon organ. The villagers, in the days before radio and recordings, had never heard some of the sounds which were emitted from his house, and imagined that weird and demonic spirits were being summoned to their quiet locality.

Two years elapsed before he was able to persuade Carvalho to listen to the music, but eventually he was asked to dine and was flanked at the piano by the impresario and Mme Miolan-Carvalho, suspecting that their gracious manner betokened a refusal. Gradually their musical taste overcame their reluctance and Carvalho declared that the opera was a masterpiece, which must go into rehearsal immediately. There was, however, an obstacle, for the principal female role was that of a dancer and the soprano had a smaller share of the music. Scorn has been poured on this libretto, but the idea of giving opportunities for a combination of opera and ballet was not in itself absurd. Momentarily the problem was solved by Barbier, who provided the words for the aria 'Le Bonheur est chose legère'. Old scripts in cupboards and in the memory were ransacked to find ways of adding to Mme Carvalho's share of the action, but never to her satisfaction.[1] One beneficiary of all this dealing was Fauré, for in 1868 Saint-Saëns arranged for him to be accompanist to Mme Carvalho on her tour of Brittany, where she consented to sing his 'Papillon et la Fleur'.

Saint-Saëns, who later wrote his own libretto for *Hélène*, might well have produced something more credible than *Le Timbre d'Argent*, but the work was an interesting comment upon the Second Empire. Conrad is an artist who longs for riches and for the dancer Fiametta. In a parallel with *Faust* a devilish figure, Dr Spiridion, presents him with a magic seal; at each blow a desire is fulfilled but a near friend dies. There is a parallel with the huge fortunes often mysteriously made by the financial manipulators of the time, and the sufferings of those who endured deprivation and danger in the toiling classes, as well as a reflection of the nostalgia for the preservation of rural simplicity in a society facing rapid growth in wealth-creating factories, banks and industries. The heroine, Helen, waits for Conrad in a simple but happy cottage hoping to win him back from city life, riches

[1] She is reported to have once pursued Gounod along a station platform, as his train moved out, demanding fresh additions to her roles.

and actresses. As in certain other Saint-Saëns operas, *Proserpine* and *Ascanio*, Helen and her sister Rosa show the goodness of charity to the poor, displaying their concern for a group of beggars. Eventually Conrad, believing he has caused the death of his closest friend, finding his monies looted and realising that his great palaces are insubstantial, smashes the 'Timbre' and finds that he has been having a feverish nightmare. The compression of the story into a dream has been condemned as dramatically weak, but the dream of riches was an obsession of the Empire.

Much is derivative. While Conrad lies ill at the start, enticing carnival choruses off-stage alternate with the pieties of Helen and Rosa, calling to mind the off-stage choruses which punctuate the opening scene of *Faust*. The visions of Fiametta as Circe and her nymphs suggest that perhaps the Venusberg had a touring company. Some of the ballet is in the older style of Adam and one has to assume that nineteenth-century ballerinas could think only in eight-bar phrases. Spiridion's 'Chanson Napolitaine', 'De Naples à Florence. Et de Parme à Verone', has strayed from the Parisian café-concerts and most curiously presages Cole Porter's 'We started in Venice' (*Kiss Me Kate*). The battle of Helen and Spiridion for Conrad's soul is a direct imitation of the final scene in *Faust*, yet it has considerable vigour. The overture begins with a swirl of sound which subsides into a slow waltz of great charm. The chorus, 'Carnaval, Carnaval', has a realistic violence and Spiridion's 'Drinking Song', with its low trills and hoarse irony, has a roughness which Saint-Saëns eliminated from later works. The chromatic writing that accompanies the scenic effects was unashamedly 'New Music' at the time.

Carvalho, a spiritual ancestor of modern producers, liked to make 'creative' additions to everything he undertook. The setting was moved to Vienna and the period to the eighteenth century – hence, probably, the Gavotte, which later became a piano solo. As the piece represented a dream, he thought of introducing animals. When he heard that Thomas's *Hamlet* had an underwater scene he was desirous that Mme Carvalho also should submerge herself to hunt for the fatal 'Timbre'. Despite his experience, he seemed unaware of the huge amounts of time and paper that changes impose upon a composer. He was also, like Conrad, in the throes of financial problems. In 1868 the Italian opera was instructed to release the Théâtre Ventadour for French opera three evenings a week and it was rented to Carvalho under the title of 'Théâtre de la Renaissance'. In March it was announced that *Le Timbre* would be performed and that a Mlle Brach, a dancer from the Opéra, had been engaged to play Fiametta–Circe *and* that there would be an underwater ballet. In May Carvalho was declared bankrupt and 200 creditors entered the fray, many of whom took part payment in scenery and costumes. When Pasdeloup became Director he had to suffer many arguments about the value of these things.

Pasdeloup was favourable to Wagner, who much preferred him to Carvalho. As a result of this rivalry Pasdeloup devoted much of the 1868–9 season to *Rienzi* at huge expense, while Carvalho endeavoured, without success, to retain his rights to *Lohengrin*. *Rienzi*, with its chorus of 120 and 200 extras, received full reviews, but no great outburst of praise. Gustave Bertrand wrote in *Le Ménestrel*: 'M. Wagner confirmed in a letter that M. Pasdeloup had only taken direction of the Théâtre Lyrique to perform his six operas. We hope that M. Pasdeloup will repudiate this bragging. If the Théâtre Lyrique is subventioned it is primarily to assist the French School, and M. Pasdeloup must never forget that. One Wagner opera will suffice for our enlightenment.' When the 1869–70 season was announced it contained a revival of *Rienzi*, various other works including Michael Balfe's *The Bohemian Girl* and, interestingly in view of Saint-Saëns's later fascination with the subject, plans for *Noah and the Deluge*, an unfinished work by the deceased Halévy which Bizet, his son-in-law, had been invited to complete – but no *Timbre d'Argent*. It is easy to see that Saint-Saëns, watching huge sums being expended upon *Rienzi*, would find the fascination of Wagner fading.

Fortunately, a greater project had its inception at about this time. An elderly music lover, knowing Saint-Saëns's affection for the old forms of music, attempted to interest him in writing an oratorio. There had been little composed in France in the tradition of Handel's biblical masterpieces, so widely applauded in Britain. (It was Messager who said that Handel would have loved Act One of *Samson and Delilah*.) Saint-Saëns had recently made what he called 'a charming acquaintance'. Fernand Lemaire, a Creole who came from Martinique, had married a cousin of a cousin of Saint-Saëns and, on the basis of this slender relationship, had had two poems set to music by the Master: 'Souvenances', strangely dated 1858 in the Thematic Catalogue, and 'Tristesse' dated 1868. The composer, as we know, had been deeply steeped in the Old Testament as a child and he approached Lemaire with the suggestion that he might turn the story of Samson into the text of an oratorio. It is significant that in 1866, when Saint-Saëns might have been meditating on his previous entry to the Prix de Rome, the subject set was 'Dalilah', the original title of the opera. He probably also knew Voltaire's libretto conceived for Rameau. In this work Delilah lusts after Samson and regrets her feebleness, while Samson, having betrayed his God of Combats, begins the final act with a lament for his faithlessness.

Although, as the opera grew, Pauline Viardot became recognised as the inspiration for the central role of Delilah there is also a touch of Mme Saint-Saëns's dominating presence, and her insistence on searching out the secrets of Samson are as powerful as we may imagine the composer's mother's demands to read his correspondence. Delilah's seducing is something rare in nineteenth-century opera, where heroines were usually pursued and vulnerable. In the music of her three great arias there are masculine as well as feminine emotions; they show no lineage from the much adorned heroine arias of Gounod and other predecessors. Indeed, in a different context, they would be quite suitable for male voices. Nevertheless, Delilah is portrayed as a beautiful and seductive woman and Augusta Holmès also must have contributed to the conception of the part, which she sang in its formative days. Georges Clairin, the painter, wrote of an evening in the studio which he shared with Henri Regnault at which Saint-Saëns was present, when Augusta sang Gluck's *Orpheus* in the moonlit room: 'That evening we were all in love with Augusta Holmès. When her father took her away, for it was necessary to return to Versailles, we remained dazed ... We did not have the strength to light a lamp ... Our sole desire was to hear the music again.' It should be noted that there is no explicit condemnation of Samson's sexual weakness in the Book of Judges. The theme of the strong hero undone by sexuality is one which Saint-Saëns introduces into the story, just as he dwelt upon the same idea in his treatment of the legends of Hercules.

Lemaire having declared himself in favour of an opera rather than an oratorio, Saint-Saëns began to work on the second act central to the meaning of the piece.[1] Parts of this, of which only the vocal lines

[1] The second act is the least 'Oriental' of the three. Much of it was written before his travels in exotic places had begun.

were written, were performed at one of his Monday soirées. He played the accompaniment from memory. Rubinstein and other musicians were present, but there was no great approval and the idea was put aside. Operas were expected to stay with classical or Romantic themes and there was some distaste at the idea of bringing Jehovah, a powerful force in the action, before the footlights.[1]

There were political overtones, not only abroad where nationalists in Italy, Poland and Liszt's Hungary still hungered for liberation from alien yokes, but at home also. In the aftermath of the 1848 revolution the populace still posed a threat. They either had to be bound in subjection or they would overturn the whole of society in another revolution. This opera is ambivalent. The Hebrews enjoy an early victory with the death of Abimelech and a successful revolt, as the people had done in 1848. Then the tide of triumph flows in favour of the Philistines, priest-led and hierarchical like the France of Napoleon III and Eugénie. Samson toiling at the mill mirrors the defeated aspirations of the downtrodden workers. Yet when the leader of the oppressed finally triumphs, the victory is so swift as to be almost illusory and we are not given any hymns of Hebrew joy or shown any scenes of benevolent Hebrew rule.

The myth of Samson was quoted often in the nineteenth century. After the failure of the 1848 revolution the historian Edgar Quinet wrote of the people as a 'blinded giant', who 'in the darkness would overturn the columns on which society rested and bury itself in the debris'. Léon Gambetta, the left-wing radical lawyer, spoke of 'overturning the foundations of the throne and the columns of the praetorium'. Furthermore, the search for a charismatic leader is endemic in France. It led to the rise of both Napoleons, to the waves of support which carried forward Gambetta, Jules Ferry and General Boulanger in the Third Republic, and exists still in the presidential system. It was never more clearly expressed than in the emergence of Samson *from the people* in Act One of *Samson* and the surge of orchestral force that carries forward the shout of 'Israel, Break your Chains'.

When Saint-Saëns had proceeded further – and it seems clear that it was he who decided the dramatic reduction of the biblical farrago and the balance of the three acts – another performance of Act Two was

[1] It has always been said that biblical subjects were excluded from the Opéra. But in 1846 it had mounted a work called *Le Roi David*.

given privately with Augusta as Delilah, Regnault, a fine tenor, as Samson and Romain Bussine as the High Priest. There were more encouraging murmurs on this occasion but no more enthusiasm. Lemaire, although his verse contained some of the most famous lines in opera, including '*Mon coeur s'ouvre à ta voix*', and wrote a masterpiece of compression, remains a mysterious figure. Saint-Saëns never returned to ask him for another libretto, but preferred to work with established writers. He remains as unknown as Drake's opponent in the famous match of bowls interrupted by the Spanish Armada.

Inspiration was flowing fully after the Exhibition success. The popular Second Piano Concerto appeared in 1868. He had come to know Anton Rubinstein, the Russian pianist with tumultuous energy, who 'could fill the Eden Theatre with resounding and graduated vibrations as if the piano were an orchestra'. Rubinstein's *Ocean* Symphony was one of the works which Saint-Saëns had amazingly transcribed on to the piano at sight. He conducted the orchestra at some of the concerts in which Rubinstein was solo pianist and left a graphic description of his attempts to decipher the MS scores while the huge Russian bear crashed and beat upon the keyboard, sometimes obliterating the orchestral sounds altogether. Rubinstein conceived the idea of conducting a concerto with the roles reversed. The Salle Pleyel had a free date three weeks ahead. In seventeen days Saint-Saëns had put together the G-minor Concerto, although he had been carrying some of the ideas in his head for months.[1] He played it in May 1868 but, much absorbed by composition, he had not mastered all of its difficulties and was dissatisfied with the première. He had also given himself an exhausting programme which included his First Concerto, a Bagatelle, probably one of the six of 1855, a Scherzo by Widor and a Mazurka by Adam Laussel, an old Niedermeyer pupil. Albert l'Hôte in *La France Musicale*, while admitting that he was baffled by the form of the first movement, which seemed like a brilliant improvisation, was full of praise for the Scherzo: 'with its zest, its activity, its rapid tempo ... this Scherzo is an exceptional piece where everything, piano and orchestra alike, is shaped by a master's hand'. Although named 'Scherzo', which indeed it is in spirit, this

[1] In view of this fruitful collaboration it is odd that in 1886 when Rubinstein gave his last great retrospective concerts in Paris, Saint-Saëns should have been forgotten. The Russian composer César Cui, a visitor to the West, wrote, 'I regret not having seen in these programmes any mention of Bramhs [*sic*], Saint-Saëns, Fauré and Franck.'

section is actually in sonata rather than scherzo form. Emile Baumann – who thought that the Second Concerto marked a great leap forward in the career of Saint-Saëns as the masterful composer – summed up admirably the average reaction to the first movement, which throws established form to the winds: 'The pianist arrives without knowing what he is going to play. He puts down a low G, which fixes the tonality of the movement and from his pedal, sustained as in an organ prelude, unfolds the magnificent exordium.' Saint-Saëns, in a letter of 1920 to his pupil the pianist Isidore Philipp, confessed, 'The Second [Concerto] must have been written for piano *à pedalier*. With your penetrating intelligence you will rediscover traces of this original conception.' In fact, as the fairly recent Suite in D and the Cello Suite had both begun with a prelude in the style of Bach, the famous opening should not necessarily have surprised. On this occasion, however, the music burgeons into a full romantic cadenza. 'One would believe', said Baumann, 'that the movement was going to follow an austere inflexible line, but, in developing, the music catches fire ... and an immense virtuoso passage similar to the curve of a rainbow gushes forth.' Within this passage is the germ of the principal theme, which Saint-Saëns took from a 'Tantum Ergo' that the young Fauré brought to him for inspection. There is a note of nostalgia both in the theme and in the Chopinesque slow section of this movement, which is not surprising, if Fauré were present in his thoughts. A letter of 1867 to Tarbes had concluded, 'Meanwhile a thousand kisses! But kisses on paper are not the same thing at all.' This is the high point of affection in the whole Saint-Saëns–Fauré correspondence. The adored pupil was growing up into a debonair male with other social interests. He had received scoldings from the Rennes clergy for smoking in the porch during sermons and arriving for an early service in evening dress fresh from a ball.

The 'Beethoven' chords which break in on the first cadenza illustrate that the content is directing the form. In reply to a journal which asked his opinion on criticisms of the work, Saint-Saëns said, 'The solo of a concerto is a role which ought to be conceived and rendered as a dramatic personage.' In a remarkable way he had evolved a concerto which neither reduced the orchestra to a few guitar-like strummings beneath the showy playing of the soloist nor magnified the solo part to overwhelming proportions in the tradition of Liszt and Rubinstein. The concerto was shown to Liszt by Henri

Regnault, who was in Rome, having succeeded in the (Art) Prix de Rome with a vibrant picture of Augusta Holmès as Thetis in an otherwise classical composition. His friend Jadin wrote:

> Regnault conducted me to Liszt's dwelling, a little palazzo ... He rang; a lackey came to tell us that his master was not in. Then Regnault scribbled on his card the object of his visit. We set off but he said to me, 'We won't rush things. He *is* here I am sure. He will come running after us.' Scarcely had we descended the staircase than we heard 'Pstt. Pstt'. It was Liszt who signalled us to climb it again. 'Could you hold on for a moment? I have to dispose of two Monsignors who are here.' It was wonderful to hear him sight-read this concerto as Regnault turned the pages.

In July 1869, Liszt received the published copy and wrote: 'The form of it is new and very successful. The significance of the three sections expands and you keep exactly the right balance between the impression of the pianist without sacrificing the ideas of the composer – an essential rule in this type of composition.' The third movement has been described for the purposes of a *bon mot* as 'from Bach to Offenbach', but that is wholly misleading. The Finale is a rough and raw piece inspired by Rubinstein's treatment of the keyboard. It has some affinity with Chopin's 'Tarantella' and the strident trills of the second subject have some similarity to Brahms's outbursts in the D minor Concerto published in 1861. Baumann compares it with 'the flight of a fantastic Mazeppa' and divines something frightening in its perpetual motion, but in all the concertos it is the weakest Finale and it is to be regretted that the Third Concerto has always been overshadowed by its predecessor. The Second became a great favourite in London concerts to the extent that Shaw was constrained to write in 1893 of a performance by one Slivinski: 'Saint-Saëns's Concerto in G minor, of which we have had more than enough lately. He made an attempt to treat it seriously with the result that it became very dull, whereas in the hands of the composer it is at least gay. The only really good bit in it is borrowed from the Prelude to Bach's Fugue in A minor, a favourite of Saint-Saëns as I guess from having heard him play it.'

Saint-Saëns was not allowed respite after this busy period. In June

1868 Versailles decided to celebrate the centenary of the birth of General Hoche, a hero of the First Republic. Emile Deschamps, an elderly admirer of Augusta, had composed the poem for a cantata and Saint-Saëns was commissioned to write the music, which was sung at the foot of the Hoche statue by combined choral societies from Paris and Versailles. The chorus had to have their parts to rehearse and the composer or his mother did not have time to write out a second version of the MS. The original was lost and Saint-Saëns apparently did not think sufficiently highly of the Cantata to make any serious attempts to retrieve it.

His supreme gifts as an organist were in demand. He was one of the seven chosen by Cavaillé-Coll to inaugurate the newly built organ of Notre-Dame in March 1868. The group included Guilmant, Widor, Chauvet, Auguste Durand, then organist of St Vincent de Paul, and Clément Loret. The builder had given five years of study and preparation to the Notre-Dame organ. Its eighty-six stops, though fewer than those at St Sulpice, were designed to fill the huge spaces with rich sound. So great was the crowd seeking admittance that there was pandemonium, quietened in one second by a mighty chord embracing thirty-two stops and mixtures. In the awestruck silence commanded by the chord, Darboy, Archbishop of Paris, made his entry. Widor, in a brilliant improvisation, showed off all the stops of the organ. Saint-Saëns played his march from *Prometheus*. A week later he gave a recital on the same organ, playing once again the march and his version of Liszt's *St Francis of Paola Walking on the Waves*. He even bowed to popular taste by providing a 'storm'. 'We don't like storms much,' said one journal. 'Even less in church, but we had to admit that the effect under the old Cathedral's vault was frighteningly real . . . As for the almost insurmountable difficulties present in the performance of this work by Liszt we would say, as everyone knows, for M. Saint-Saëns it is no more difficult on the organ than on the piano.' In August he inaugurated a smaller instrument in the Church of St Pierre in Dreux. Three days later, on 15 August, the major day in the Napoleonic calendar, he was awarded the Legion of Honour. His friend and patron, the Abbé Duguerry, had the pleasure of announcing the honour to him.

The Second Piano Concerto was repeated at a Pasdeloup Concert Populaire in December and a week later Saint-Saëns had the unusual honour of being a living composer included in the concerts of the

Conservatoire, which he accounted one of his most nervous moments ever. He was already undertaking some concert tours in Germany, though he did not wish to venture too far afield for his great-aunt, now eighty-seven, was in failing health.

Hector Berlioz died in 1869, removing one more sage of the great period of Romanticism and leaving a gap in the ranks of serious French composers. He had been sick for several months. A few days before his death Saint-Saëns had hurried through the streets to the rue de Calais to visit his old friend. The day was cold and when Berlioz, burning with fever, turned to grip the hand of the visitor, a contact which Saint-Saëns had wished to spare him, he uttered a groan and turned away. Yet the intimation of mortality and the reminder of Berlioz's faith in his talent spurred him on to fresh labours with *Samson and Delilah*. The handshake was a portent of death, but an invisible baton passed from one to the other. Saint-Saëns's major years of composition were about to begin.[1] He was not, however, included as a bearer of the Canopy at the funeral in the Trinity Church and the group consisted of Auber, Gounod, Reyer and Thomas.

The vagaries of operatic management played their part in turning him to other fields. Emile Perrin, Director of the Opéra, described by the playwright Victorien Sardou as 'the most volatile, capricious and changeable of men', was engrossed with a competition for setting a prize-winning libretto, *La Coupe du Roi de Thule*. He had invited Bizet to enter with a vague promise of success but, although Bizet had on the jury a good friend in the shape of Saint-Saëns, the competition was won by an amateur, Diaz de la Pena, a pupil of Victor Massé, with Massenet second. When the opera was produced in 1873 it was a failure. Bizet had been toying with an opera on the subject of Vercingatorix and the battles of the Gauls against Rome. He did not share his Emperor's fascination with Caesar: 'the insurmountable obstacle is Caesar. These wretched Emperors are generally not too musical.' This was certainly true of Napoleon III. Even when turning the barrel organ at Compiègne for quadrilles his sense of rhythm was so poor that he failed in this simple task.

His health was waning. Perpetually in pain because of a stone in the bladder, he could neither walk nor sleep with ease. Although some liberal reforms had been introduced, the opposition grew, especially in

[1] It is interesting to note, when thinking of Saint-Saëns's later travels, that Berlioz had expressed a longing to visit the Pacific Islands.

the large cities. Election campaigns were marked by demonstrations and vandalism and, in May, the opposition parties polled more than two and a half million votes. The Chief Minister was Emile Ollivier, son-in-law of Liszt, whose wife Blandine had died in childbed in 1857. Ollivier had become another admirer of Augusta Holmès and had sent some of her songs to Liszt, who, ever the flatterer, declared them the equal of Schubert's finest. He thought that in the song 'Sirène' she had pictured herself and would have persuaded Ulysses to succumb. Ollivier furnished letters of introduction when Augusta set off as one of the pilgrims to Munich, to hear the *Rhinegold* première, and to the Wagner home, Tribschen, near Lucerne in the summer of 1869.

Saint-Saëns journeyed in the same direction, but the party was not as compact as has sometimes been assumed. Augusta travelled with her father. Another group, consisting of Catulle Mendès, his wife Judith (Gautier) and the poet Villiers de l'Isle Adam, were going to pay homage. Villiers was bitten by one of the Wagner dogs, made wild accusations of infection from rabies and bored the Wagners with readings of his poetry. Judith Mendès was alarmed to hear of the approach of Augusta in Munich where she speedily made the acquaintance of Liszt, attended rehearsals of *Rhinegold* with him and even danced with him in his rooms under the watchful eye of Major Holmès. Hans Richter, recently appointed chief conductor at the Munich Opera and in charge of the production, although he did not like French music, fell wildly in love with Augusta and was in a state of emotional turmoil throughout the uneasy weeks of preparation. Cosima, who had been warned by Judith Mendès of Augusta's effect upon men, told Judith to let the Holmès party know that Wagner had 'departed for Cochin China or heaven knows where', but while in Munich, Wagner and Augusta met and had long conversations.

On 27 August the dress rehearsal took place. Saint-Saëns and the various French contingents were present, but separate. Musically the production was magnificent, but the décor and staging were disastrous. As the curtain fell, Richter turned to the 500 invited guests and said that he would not conduct this particular production. Catulle and Judith had sent a telegram to Tribschen, which described the stage machinery as 'absurd . . . and impossible'. Wagner, to the fury of King Ludwig II, forbade the performance. Ludwig, desperate to hear the work and filled with rage, sounded out Saint-Saëns to see if he would step into Richter's place. Saint-Saëns also braved the royal anger;

circumspect about association with the expected failure he declined the honour. With stage machinists brought in from other cities, a substitute Wotan procured and another Kapellmeister on the rostrum, the première of *Rhinegold* did take place on 22 September. The King was satisfied although the public, unaccustomed to opera without intervals, became restless and even surreptitiously hostile towards the end. The Mendès party had not attended in obedience to the Master's instructions, but when they returned to Tribschen they saw Augusta received by Wagner not only as an admirer, but also as a musician worthy of notice. She sang part of Erda's music from *The Ring* and some of her own songs and, later in life, gave thoroughly confusing accounts of the soirée to various reporters. It was even rumoured in the Parisian press that Augusta and Wagner would be announcing their engagement and formal denials had to be issued. In all these matters, save the offer of the conductor's baton, Saint-Saëns played no part, although Augusta's raptures over Wagner's greatness cannot have been welcome.

His visit to Lucerne, however, had a happier outcome in the Third Piano Concerto. He often wrote his works in pairs and this followed fast upon the Second. The opening was suggested by the noise of a river breaking the silence of the mountains and is one of the passages in which he admitted to a burst of impressionism. The whole work has an 'alpine' grandeur so the journey to Munich had its compensations. The key of E flat was that chosen by Beethoven for his most ambitious concerto and by Liszt for his first. The pattern is this time more formal, but Saint-Saëns the innovator is always present: at the start the piano, with its chords and arpeggios, acts as accompanist to solo announcements of the first subject in a rhythm similar to Schubert's *Great* C-major opening, but isolated, angular and rather strange. There is at the close of the movement, for the first time in a French concerto, a veritable conflict of great intensity between soloist and orchestra. The piano part is ferociously tough in these outer sections, but the development is divided very markedly into distinct parts, with two long piano solos: a long passage in which the themes are treated as in a nocturne, a crashing cadenza, then dramatic and rhythmic pages for orchestra with rich sequences. The orchestral writing, too, is muscular and emphatic, and Saint-Saëns's use of swirling arpeggios and scales is put to dramatic rather than decorative use.

The Andante, by contrast, is one of the most beautiful things he ever wrote. The indecisive harmonies at the outset, which we may agree with Baumann 'raise a curtain on chimerical horizons', and mysterious sounds from the piano lead into a hymn played by the strings, which, in turn, concludes with a beautiful melodic phrase that returns twice more, once with the voice of the oboe and later with piano and an inspired string obligato. In addition there is a solemn theme which employs the bass notes of the piano and later the lower strings. On its second appearance it is interrupted by signals of the Finale, for Saint-Saëns makes no break between the two final movements. Berlioz would have been enraptured by this section, its wistful melancholy and innovative harmonies. The principal theme of the third movement has a surging upward thrust, which spans almost the entire keyboard. A brief recollection of *Spartacus* leads into a more rhapsodic second subject, but inseparable from Saint-Saëns is the use of alchemy on traditional forms. In this Finale the first section is repeated and there is then continuous development until the final hectic bars.

The Concerto was given a rough reception on its first appearance at a Gewandhaus concert in Leipzig, the centre of classical tradition, hostile to the musical adventures of Liszt, Wagner and Berlioz. Saint-Saëns was regarded as their foremost champion. The chromatic chords at the start of the Andante, which seem mild today, led to shouts of protest and eventually to fights in the corridor of the hallowed building. The press was cold: 'Occasionally eloquent beginnings do not deliver what they promise and, despite heavy orchestral effects, which leave a distinct futuristic aftertaste, the work remains trite,' said the *Allgemeine Musik Zeitung*. In Paris, Bannelier in the *Revue et Gazette* saw in the first and second movements nothing but 'a regrettable aberration; it is comparable to everything incoherent and tormented in Liszt's late manner'. It was performed at the Salle Pleyel in March 1870 with Louis Diémer playing the orchestral part on a second piano and Elie-Myriam Delaborde, the dedicatee, played it at the Conservatoire. It was not until 1879 that the Third Concerto won any sizeable applause at a Delaborde concert and it then remained unknown for almost thirty years.

For a brief time Widor became Saint-Saëns's assistant at the

Madeleine but on 31 December 1869 Lefébure-Wély died and, on the recommendation of Gounod and Cavaillé-Coll, Widor moved on to St Sulpice. There was some opposition to the appointment because of his youth and the fact that he had not come through the Conservatoire. Both he and Saint-Saëns, together with Franck, Auguste Durand and Chauvet, played at the inauguration of the new organ at La Trinité. A further change in the organ world came about around this time with the news that Fauré had been dismissed from his post at Rennes having been, in his own words, 'an incorrigible religious defaulter. . . . When [the vicar's] hostility came out into the open it was again Saint-Saëns who rescued me and found me something in Paris.' This was an appointment to a church at Clignancourt, but once more Fauré seems to have been guilty of absenteeism, missing a service to hear *Les Huguenots*, and he did not hold the post for long. The Fauré parents were grateful for Saint-Saëns's continued protection of their son and the mother delighted in sending gifts of rural produce to the rue St Honoré. A gift of pâté evoked a high-flown poem by Saint-Saëns, which compared the butter coating to the golden robes of the Emperor of China. He hopes that Gabriel will be present when the golden robes are set aside, otherwise the pâté would be like a butterfly released from its cocoon on a rainy day, 'And my cheeks shrunken with sorrow would droop towards my breast. Like a forgotten peony in a waterless vase.' It is hard not to divine some romantic feeling in such phrases.

Fauré was a regular guest at the Monday Evening soirées, where he met Rubinstein[1] and was present at the performance of the Third Piano Concerto which Saint-Saëns gave at the Salle Pleyel with Louis Diémer. The performance 'sans orchestra' cannot have given much of an impression of the value of the work. Adolphe Jullien, however, wrote in *Le Ménestrel*: 'This is a very noteworthy work with an extremely innovative opening, charming and at the same time bizarre in its clashes and stark contrasts. The passionate admirer of the great German masters is recognisable in every bar of this glowing music, in the tremolos of the strings, the dark and mysterious melodies, and the gleaming flash of the brass.' In an article by Fauré, written in 1906 for

---

[1] Both the Second and Third Piano Concertos have elements which portray Rubinstein's manner of playing. The dedicatee of the Third Concerto, Delaborde, had many similar characteristics. He was a fencer and an oarsman. He kept parrots and cockatoos – briefly heard in the Finale.

the sixtieth anniversary of Saint-Saëns's first recital, he reminded pianists that there were other concertos beyond the second and the fourth; 'among them the Concerto in E flat merits especially to emerge from the shadows where it has been left to doze!' Saint-Saëns was very touched and referred to the article: 'Thank you for the "Concerto in E flat" for which you have a decidedly soft spot and that flatters me infinitely.'

Fauré's entry upon the Parisian musical scene via the Saint-Saëns soirées was of great importance to his future career. Outside this circle music was still much dominated by the stars and intrigues of the stage. Gounod's *Faust*, in a revised version for the Opéra, reached that pinnacle on 3 March 1869.[1] Saint-Saëns recounted that, in the ballet, the procession of 'Beauties of the Ancient World' carried vases of aromatic incense so powerful that sections of the orchestra were overcome. Meyerbeer had died in 1864, but his posthumous opera *L'Africaine*, cobbled together by a team of executors on whom Saint-Saëns expended considerable sarcasm, was intended by the Imperial Government to be a major event of the century, and much government interference and money went into the production, the orchestra being increased to over a hundred players. By comparison, chamber music, in which Fauré's talents lay, drew little attention and occupied far fewer public concerts. The public for it was, however, in slow process of creation. The bourgeoisie, unable to afford the splendid boxes at the Opéra and too serious to find anything to uplift the soul at the Opéra Comique, were beginning to find in home music-making something that raised them above the dull commercial routines in which they were engaged. In the French chamber repertoire there was still a void. Haydn, Mozart and early Beethoven had been the staple fare. From 1860 onwards, and with Saint-Saëns once again in the vanguard, French composers had begun to turn towards these smaller genres. The Armingaud Quartet, in which Lalo played the viola, had been founded as early as 1855, and in 1860 Lamoureux, with the support of Colonne, both subsequently outstandingly successful conductors, established his own chamber group. Immediately prior to the war of 1870 the pianist Léon Delahaye and friends founded a Société Schumann with the consent of Clara, the

---

[1] Gounod was in the throes of a spiritual phase at the time and offered to Saint-Saëns the opportunity to write the music for the requisite ballet.

composer's widow. The works of other musicians were included in its concerts: the Brahms Quintet (Opus 34) and even a quintet (Opus 1) by Saint-Saëns's young friend Alexis de Castillon. Interrupted by the siege of Paris and the Commune, the Society was refounded as the Chamber Music Society in 1872.

Among Saint-Saëns's smaller compositions of 1869 was another return to the world of Boucher and Fragonard in the song 'Marquise, vous souvenez-vous?' to an old-world minuet. It is not hard to write a pastiche of an eighteenth-century dance, but in this song, as in the later 'Sarabande and Rigaudon', Saint-Saëns achieves a level of elegance that has the inner grace of the originals. The three-part accompaniment suggests a small group of court musicians and the strict rhythm melts only at the close, when the Marquise forgets her curtsy. To this evocation of the *ancien régime*, a sharp contrast is provided by the march *Orient et Occident* for Military Band. This march, contrasting the musical styles of East and West, was written for the celebration of Fine Arts Applied to Industry. It has an interest solely as his first foray into oriental sound. He had not at this stage travelled in the East, where later he was to collect and study North African music, and write down characteristic rhythms and melodies on the spot. Later, he had friends who sent him material they had heard in Algerian cafés and bazaars. The march of 1869 was merely a signpost towards new pastures. Henri Regnault had spent much time at the 1867 Exhibition studying the Persian, Turkish and Egyptian sections and, had he survived the 1870–71 war, it is highly likely that he and Saint-Saëns would have travelled to these regions together. He had already journeyed through Spain with Clairin, who later designed the costumes for *Carmen*.

A more significant step towards orientalism and a presage of the later French preoccupation with the song-cycle came with *Les Mélodies Persanes* based upon poetry by Armand Renaud, which, prefiguring Impressionism, suggested the merest outlines of a story by a series of moods and reflections. A lover carries off a girl, she dies, he rushes off in despair to conquer the world, sword in hand, but ends by joining the whirling dervishes and destruction in opium-induced delirium. 'La Brise', describing the movements of a harem dancer, was dedicated to Pauline Viardot, still an image, vocally at least, for Delilah. Echoes of the habanera rhythm are in the mood of the later violin *Havanaise*. 'La Solitaire' was dedicated to Augusta Holmès and tells of the yearning of the girl to be swept off by a cavalier. Regnault, of whose voice Saint-Saëns thought highly – 'a tenor voice as enchanting, as irresistibly seductive as his penetrating gaze!' – was the first interpreter of the masculine songs in the set, including the very anti-monarchical–imperial 'Sabre en Main', which threatens to lift the mark of the yoke from the brow of humanity. The Eastern descriptions in the verse have not proceeded further than Delacroix, with references to jewels, ivories, eunuchs, nights of stars, etc, and musically the score is no more Eastern than Bizet's *Pearl Fishers*, but in the world weariness and the dizzy ecstasies (of great pianistic difficulty) there is an ominous impression of a new generation desiring the destruction of the old.

The start of the year 1870, which Queen Victoria in her *Journal* described as 'bloody, sad, eventful', found Saint-Saëns in Weimar, where he played an arrangement of Liszt's Hungarian music for two pianos with the Master. Later, in June, he accompanied Liszt on a second piano at the Beethoven centenary celebrations.[1] He may have been confident in his partnership with Liszt, but he expressed to his mother a certain dread over comparisons with the pianist Theodor Ratzenberger. The result was a diatribe which casts a harsher light upon her supervision of his career:

Dear Friend,

I found your letter upon my return from Mass. You make me ill with your fears. I used to think you a man; you are merely a coward. I treat you with contempt . . . I believed I had brought up a man. I have raised up only a girl of degenerative stock. . . . Play as you ought to play – an artist of great talent. Either you will play well, or I will renounce you as my child. . . . The Good Lord never abandons the man who has an upright and true heart. . . . You must show the genius of Beethoven to those who have never understood it.

After this exhortation he was in need of Liszt's encouragement! It was at this second meeting that he ventured to mention his *Samson and Delilah*. Liszt was Director of the Weimar Theatre, one of the posts which he held in the Grand Duchy, and the repertoire was known for

[1] He wrote an improvisation on themes from Liszt's *Beethoven* Cantata composed for this occasion.

breadth and bravery. His greatness extended far beyond his own creative aspirations. He questioned Saint-Saëns about the opera and then, without having seen a page of the music, promised that it would be mounted at Weimar when completed.

On his return to Paris Saint-Saëns was fired by this but once more the baleful influence of *Le Timbre d'Argent* deflected him. Emile Perrin at the Opéra asked if the work could be put on there. The honour was great, but so was the toil. No spoken dialogue was admitted, so the speech had to be turned into recitative or set to music. The Opéra also demanded a larger scale and Saint-Saëns had to re-orchestrate whole scenes. The roles were allotted to Mme Carvalho as Helen and the famous baritone Jean-Baptiste Faure, as Spiridion. Unfortunately, Perrin had under contract the notable contralto Mlle Wertheimer, whom he wished to use, and he insisted that the tenor role should be rewritten as a travesti part. The authors, Barbier and Carré, considered this impossible and much argument ensued, which the librettists won, but at the cost of alienating Perrin. Saint-Saëns felt in his heart that Perrin had lost interest. At this moment Perrin's nephew Camille Du Locle took control of the Opéra Comique and, hearing that his uncle wished to be rid of the *Timbre*, asked for it for his own theatre. The sung recitatives had now to be scrapped and the music reset to suit the traditions of the smaller house. Saint-Saëns received support from Bizet in his struggles. Bizet made the piano reduction of the *Timbre* and resigned from the *Revue Nationale* when the editor suppressed an article in favour of his friend. 'It is charming. True *opéra comique* tinged with Verdi,' wrote Bizet. 'What imagination! What inspired melodies! Of Wagner, of Berlioz, nothing at all ... Two or three of the pieces are a little vulgar in idea but they are very appropriate and are saved by the immense talent of the musician.' To the composer himself Bizet wrote, 'I am exhausted by the third act. It has exquisite tenderness and purity. The end of Helen's lovely song is indescribably glowing. It is excellent! The other big scene is superb too.'

As much of the music was in existence and Saint-Saëns wrote with great rapidity, an opera might have emerged intact from all these changes. At this moment the two librettists – 'united until then like Orestes and Pylades', lamented Saint-Saëns – decided to have a quarrel and would not communicate, a serious matter for *opéra comique*, where spoken dialogue had to be fitted to the acting capacities of singers. Saint-Saëns was forced to travel from one to the other bearing their heated exchanges. Du Locle thought he had found a ravishing dancer to play the central role, but she proved to be only a mime artist. Just as a proper ballerina, Luisa Trevisan, was engaged, the tenor refused to proceed with his part. Tenors were not easily replaced and, as Du Locle began his search, Mlle Trevisan was on her way from Milan with a contract and had to be employed.

Du Locle rushed hastily to Louis Gallet, a hospital official who could turn out verse, prose, speeches or scenarios for any occasion, and asked him for the plot of an opera-ballet. *Le Kobbold* was devised, a piece which could employ the ballerina until the end of the season. Day by day, the librettists sent instalments of the plot to Ernest Guiraut, who produced some appropriate music. *Le Kobbold* was notable in ballet history only for the fact that the tenor, Leroy, revealed unsuspected talents as a dancer, able to lift and reverse Mlle Trevisan. The première of *Le Kobbold* took place on 26 July 1870, while *Le Timbre d'Argent* was theoretically under rehearsal. That same evening, out in the streets, excited crowds were shouting 'To Berlin', for the war long anticipated and feared between France and Prussia had erupted. *Le Kobbold* was set in Alsace. On the false rumour of a French victory, Adolphe de Leuven, co-Director with Du Locle, inserted into the tenor aria the line 'To cross the Rhine is only a step', which had to be deleted when the news of crushing Prussian victories began to circulate.

6

Devastation, Seed Corn and Harvest

The Second Empire was dogged by scandal and discontent to the end. Earlier in 1870 Pierre Bonaparte, cousin of the Emperor, shot a journalist who had come to deliver a challenge to a duel. Crowds marched down the Champs Elysées demanding retribution and the murder trial was held in Tours to avoid disorder in the capital. Bonaparte was acquitted to great indignation, if no surprise, and Léon Gambetta, leading politician of the Left, scorned the regime in a Marseillaise editorial. 'For eighteen years France has been in the hands of these cutthroats ... Frenchmen, can it be that you do not think you have had enough of them?'

A diplomatic crisis began in Spain and grew to involve both France and Prussia. It was the French insistence upon making a drama out of a crisis which precipitated events. Napoleon III was persuaded into a Declaration of War, one which, in his heart, he knew he could not win. The French Army was unequal to the demands of campaigns, but there was immediate enthusiasm for an assault across the Rhine. The 'Marseillaise' had been forbidden under the Empire. At a performance of Auber's *Muette de Portici* the audience cheered the duet 'Amour sacré de la patrie' and demanded the 'Marseillaise' at the final curtain. The soprano, Marie Sasse, dressed in white with a tricolour sash, responded. After the first verse the audience rose and bellowed it with her. The scene was repeated nightly until the opera closed a few weeks later. She sang it also from her carriage as it passed through the streets. At the Opéra Comique, Célestine Galli-Marié and her colleagues performed the same ritual. Béranger's 'Forward Gauls and Franks', set to music by Delibes, was sung by the great baritone Léon Melchissédec (after which he read out army bulletins in the fashion of the First Empire). For 'Le Rhin Allemand' by Félicien David the chorus was dressed in the uniforms of various French regiments. 'In your militia regiment you will soon be engaged in driving out this pack of northern savages,' wrote Fauré's brother to Gabriel.

Meanwhile the military machine staggered to defeat. The Emperor, his cheeks rouged to hide his sickness, sought death by riding along the lines at the battle of Sedan, and then, braver than Napoleon I, who had a habit of abandoning defeated troops, drove through groups of sullen compatriots to hand his sword to the victors. When, on 3 September, news of the Prussian victory reached Paris, mobs invaded the Assembly and a Republic was proclaimed. Citizen guards at the Tuileries were thought to be unreliable and the Empress, who had imagined herself leading cavalry in defence of her son's rights, fled to the protection of her American dentist, who smuggled her across to Britain. On 5 September, *William Tell* at the Opéra was cancelled. On the 10th all theatres were closed by the order of the Prefect of Police and by the 15th Paris was virtually surrounded by the enemy.

The Republic did not consider itself bound by the Emperor's surrender and the war of the armies was transformed into the Siege of Paris. The siege did not ultimately alter the outcome, but it changed perceptions of the war and became an epic of French history, in which Germany appeared as the aggressor and France as the victim. With thousands of others, musicians took up arms. Henri Duparc was quick to enlist in the Mobile Guard; d'Indy and Arthur Coquard, a lawyer by profession but pupil of harmony with César Franck, joined him. Both Franck's sons volunteered and Franck himself (who managed to finish two sections of his *Béatitudes* during the bombardments) was given the difficult task of assisting with food and fuel supplies. Fauré joined a Militia regiment and took part in the skirmishes aimed at relieving the defences. Guiraud faced the enemy at a forward post. Massenet was an infantryman. Bizet, who had disapproved of the war – 'Our poor philosophy, our dreams of universal peace, world fraternity and human fellowship! Instead of that we have tears, blood, piles of corpses, crimes without number or end' – joined the National Guard, though as a Prix de Rome winner he could have been exempt. 'Tomorrow morning at seven I start my military drill,' he wrote. 'Our guns weigh fourteen pounds – heavy for a musician. These weapons kick back, spit, do everything possible to be more disagreeable to those who fire them than to the enemy.' Widor served in the artillery. The roof of St

Sulpice was damaged by Prussian fire and services were held in the crypt. Pasdeloup fought bravely in the National Guard, even contriving to give some concerts during the months of siege. He began by banning German music but, significantly, the absence of alternatives forced him to relent. The aged pianist Antoine Marmontel served in the same regiment as his son. Ambroise Thomas, aged sixty, volunteered for active service. Saint-Saëns himself became a soldier in the Fourth Battalion of the National Guard, and found himself on the ramparts and experiencing gunfire at a forward post, Arcueil-Cachan. Some have found the idea of Saint-Saëns in uniform a quaint image but, writing to a friend in a moment of depression in 1914, when his manservant Gabriel was seriously ill, he added, 'Alas! I have no longer the unquenchable energy of forty years ago, an exertion which won the admiration of my friends in the National Guard. I feel ashamed to have so little courage at the moment,' which suggests that he played his part. His mother suffered great anguish when she believed he was in danger. He wrote her a poem which sympathised with her trembling at the window listening to the far-off sounds of gunfire. Augusta Holmès served in hastily arranged fleets of ambulances. The foyer of the Théâtre Lyrique, like many others, was turned into a casualty station where female artists tended the wounded.

Employees of the Opéra were dismissed and had no visible means of support. Concerts were arranged on their behalf. In November Saint-Saëns wrote a cantata, *Chants de Guerre*, for soloists, chorus and orchestra, but Perrin refused it. The material was used by the composer for his *Marche Héroïque*, which in its first form was played on two pianos at a charity concert in the Grand Hotel by Saint-Saëns and Albert Lavignac, both in their uniforms. In November *Le Soir* reported that, after a performance of Cherubini's *Requiem*, M. Saint-Saëns, organist of the Madeleine, 'as his concluding voluntary played the "Triumphal March" of Beethoven. May this fine composition be the prelude to the impending success of our armies!' Forty years later he was to show a different attitude to German music in wartime. He gave a concert in aid of the Red Cross, which had its offices at the Palais-Royal, and, in December, played to a contingent of wounded Breton soldiers when his reminiscences of Breton carols brought tears of gratitude from the men.

The privations of the populace during the siege became historic. Animals from the zoo joined domestic pets on the café menus. Auber's beloved horses were commandeered for service or slaughter. As winter deepened, trees on the boulevards were cut down for fuel. Cavaillé-Coll, coming out of his workshop where wooden beams intended for 32ft organ pipes had been used to reinforce the building against bombardment, found one of his oldest workers trying to wrest a frozen stump from the ground for fuel. The siege prevented him from gaining the commission for the new Albert Hall organ and Saint-Saëns likewise failed to receive invitations to perform in London concerts.

Alexis Chauvet died from tuberculosis aggravated by the privations. A heavier blow came in January with the death in action of Henri Regnault. On the 18th there had been a musical evening at the home of Augusta. Against the noise of gunfire Regnault sang Augusta's patriotic 'Vengeance' and 'Au Cimetière' from the *Mélodies Persanes*.

> Seated on this white tomb
> Let us open our hearts
>
> . . . Roses today, and cypresses tomorrow!

It was strangely prophetic. Regnault sang it to the group in their military tunics, in a haunting fashion that was long remembered. On leaving Augusta's rooms he returned home to find an order to rejoin his battalion. The Provisional Government had long decided that further resistance was doomed, but the National Guard wished to persevere. General Trochu remarked in private: 'The only means of converting the Guard to the idea of capitulation is to have 25,000 men killed!' The attack at Buzenval, made with out-of-date maps, was a gesture to demonstrate the hopelessness of the cause. Saint-Saëns called on Regnault as he was leaving for the front. He remembered the artist making quick alterations to a canvas, then snatching up his rifle and departing. Regnault fought through the day but, as night fell, he was killed by a stray bullet during the final sortie. Augusta wrote that 'the last bullet of Buzenval has struck the sole painter of genius that France possessed'. Georges Clairin, at the burial, lamented that they were celebrating 'the death of all their hopes and their youth'. Saint-Saëns is said to have locked himself away for three days refusing food and comfort. He played the organ for the funeral and reminded his hearers of their loss with the sad strains of 'Au Cimetière'.

The war and siege had a profound effect upon French music. The frivolities of the Empire were in disfavour. There was insufficient money or stability for lavish stage works. Offenbach had not shared the perils, but had taken his family to Spain; his librettist Henri Meilhac ruminated that frivolous satire had weakened France. Ludovic Halévy disagreed, saying: 'I think we all paid too much respect. I saw the Empire at first hand during my intimacy with the Duc de Morny ... France never had a worse government; never a weaker one with pretensions to strength.' Germany could no longer be admired as the source of all that was profound. Italy had done less than nothing to aid France in her time of tribulation. There was a feeling that French music had for too long been subservient to foreign lands. On the eve of the capitulation Saint-Saëns, Bussine and other musicians met to found the Société Nationale to establish French music as a powerful force. Since the death of Berlioz, Saint-Saëns, still young, was the only composer of serious works who could wear his mantle, confident in his powers, and the most learned in masterpieces of the past. No one knew better the difficulties which faced the musicians. 'Not so very long ago,' he wrote later, 'a French composer who was daring enough to venture on the terrain of instrumental music had no other means of having his works performed than to give a concert himself and invite his friends and the critics. As far as the general public were concerned it was hopeless to think about them. The name of a composer who was French and still alive had only to appear on a poster to frighten everybody away.'

The initial thought of concentrating upon chamber music on grounds of expense seems to have come from Romain Bussine, first President, with Saint-Saëns his Vice-President. The Secretary, Alexis de Castillon, came from an aristocratic military family, but Saint-Saëns had interested him in music when both were children. On inheriting a title and income he had indulged his passion for music and taken lessons from Franck in composition. By the end of February Fauré had been brought into the group and others who showed an interest were Duparc, Lalo, Massenet, Guiraud, the flautist Taffanel, Charles Lenepveu (winner of the Prix de Rome in 1865, who had taken private lessons also from Chauvet), Théodore Dubois and Franck himself. Louis Bourgault-Ducoudray, a member of the first Committee, later became Professor of Musical History at the Conservatoire. He shared Saint-Saëns's interest in different civilisations and wrote a *Rhapsodie*

Cambodgienne performed in 1889. No mention is made of Bizet, but he had already made it clear that his interest was in the theatre. The Society adopted the motto 'Ars Gallica'.[1] Its constitution declared:

> The aim ... is to aid the production and popularisation of all serious musical works, whether published or unpublished, of French composers and bring to light, so far as is in its power, all musical endeavour, whatever form it may take, on condition that there is evidence of high artistic aspiration on the part of the author ... It is in brotherly love, with complete forgetfulness of self and with the firm intention of aiding one another, as much as they can, that members of the Society will co-operate, each in his own sphere of activity, in the study and performance of works they shall be called upon to select and interpret.

The reference to 'interpretation' shows Saint-Saëns's primacy in this venture, for he was the only member who could be said to have a public for his concert appearances. In humble roles, as accompanist and duettist, he was indefatigable in the first days of the Society. It was the intention to meet on Mondays, to examine works submitted, to watch over Pasdeloup's programmes and to seek out ways of promoting concerts. The earliest gatherings took place, sometimes in the rooms of Bussine, sometimes in a rented room at 4 rue Chabanais. When Saint-Saëns's Monday Evenings resumed, the committee moved to Sundays and proceedings ended with part-singing of vocal arrangements by Bussine, an entertaining thought.

Before the grand design could be put into action Paris was again engulfed by catastrophe. Citizens from the poorer faubourgs had many grievances against the new Government, now based at Versailles and headed by Adolphe Thiers, a veteran politician of many regimes. After the city's heroic resistance it resented a shaming peace treaty. The provinces of Alsace and Lorraine had been given to the new German Empire. That Empire had been proclaimed in the Hall of Versailles, where Louis XIV had once dictated to Europe, and Paris had been forced to accept a German victory parade down the Champs Elysées to the strains of Schubert's *Marche Militaire*. The Versailles Assembly,

---

[1] The name of the conductor Jules Garcin and an Emile Bernard occur in different lists.

elected by all France, contained a majority of royalists and there was everywhere talk of a restoration. Paris industries had been ruined; there were innumerable debts and non-payments. When Thiers attempted to disarm the city and tried to seize the guns on Montmartre, crowds, led by disaffected National Guards, ambushed the soldiers and murdered two generals. Their corpses, by an ironic twist of fate, were thrown into a house that had once belonged to Scribe, author of so many violent historical libretti. A Commune of Paris (the title recalled the powerful Commune of The Terror) was established at the Hôtel de Ville on 18 March, with a membership strong in left-wing rabble-rousers.

Saint-Saëns, though in the National Guard, did not wish to serve in its insurgent battalions and his mother did not believe he should be fighting fellow countrymen. He was living in one of the wealthier districts, was identified with the clergy of the Madeleine (the Commune was fiercely anti-clerical) and the air was thick with threats and rumours. His mother and great-aunt urged him to escape. Gathering small sums of money he rushed to the Gare du Nord, where, without having time to purchase a ticket, he threw himself on to one of the last trains to leave for the Channel before all city exits were blocked. Fauré also managed to escape with a forged passport, went on to the exiled Ecole Niedermeyer at Lausanne and spent the summer teaching. The young André Messager was one of his pupils.

In London an International Exhibition was opening. Saint-Saëns had not received the offers made to participate. His store of francs melted away and he was obliged to borrow. With some help from George Grove, he earned ten guineas by entertaining workmen at Crystal Palace by testing the organ, and shared his tiny emolument with another poor and hungry exile, Romain Cornut, the poet of *Les Noces de Prométhée*. There was a French colony in London. Gounod, who had at the start of the war written a patriotic piece, *To the Frontier*, and then straightway headed in the other direction, was awaiting performance of his Cantata *Gallia* in the Albert Hall. This was rapturously received and Saint-Saëns, always an admirer, wrote to his mother: 'France is avenged!' He earned a little money with some songs to English words: 'Voice by the Cedar Tree' (Tennyson) and 'My Land' (T. Davis). The latter, 'She is a rich and rare land', was in a style later adopted by Edward German for songs like 'Glorious Devon' and showed how rapidly Saint-Saëns could absorb local colour.

Another song, 'Là-bas dans un ciel de turquoise', to words of his own, was later used in *La Princesse Jaune*.

Back in Paris the Commune took over many churches as political clubs. On 6 May at St Sulpice a service in honour of the Virgin was interrupted by National Guards. In the days following, groups of Communards roared out the 'Marseillaise' and the 'Song of the Girondins', while the faithful sang the Magnificat. Eventually it was agreed that the building would be shared between Christians in the mornings and the 'Club de Victoire' in the evenings. Auber died on 12 May, watched over in turn by Thomas and Weckerlin. They did not desire a civic funeral under the Commune, so his body was concealed in the vaults of La Trinité and respectfully interred after it had fallen. Salvador Daniel, a left-wing music critic, was appointed to replace Auber, but was captured and shot as the Government fought to recover the capital.

At the end of May Thiers carried out the strategy he had urged upon Louis Philippe in 1848. He withdrew government troops to the perimeter of the city and began a systematic subjugation. Columns of soldiers recruited in the provinces assaulted the capital. The doomed Communards could do little but set fire to their shrinking domain and the royalist deputies looked on in horror from the terraces of St Germain as the flames rose and the great cupola of the Tuileries, packed with explosives, burst into fragments. Widor scribbled that all around him was burning and he expected to be roasted alive. The captured Opéra became for some hours a prison and death chamber while rustic soldiers jokingly tried on the costumes. The Théâtre Lyrique, ever unlucky, was set alight by missiles, the flames fanned by a south-east wind. The auditorium and stage were destroyed. The Director, Louis Martinet, who had been a picture dealer, lost valuable paintings with which he had furnished his office, but fortunately the archives and music scores were rescued. As the Ministry of Finance burned, the air was filled with acrid fumes of files and papers. Armand Renaud, poet of the *Mélodies Persanes*, kept many of his writings in his government office and lost them all. Debussy's father was a Communard and he and the son of a Mme Mauté, Debussy's piano teacher, were both taken prisoner and met in the cells at Satory.

In reprisal the Communards seized members of the higher clergy including Darboy, the Archbishop of Paris, and Saint-Saëns's friend Duguerry. The latter had denounced the murder of the two generals from the pulpit of the Madeleine and attacked the insurrection, refusing to flee as advised by his parishioners. On Palm Sunday he had fiercely criticised vandalism at the church of St Geneviève. He was arrested in Holy Week and imprisoned in the Conciergerie. On 23 May the Abbé Lamazou, who had courageously held services at the Madeleine subsequently, joined him in prison and on Ascension Day the Madeleine was closed. On 25 May, three days before Thiers triumphed, Darboy and Duguerry were shot by a firing squad. The Abbé Lamazou, who survived, announced the fate of their pastor to the remnant of his flock. Within a few days Saint-Saëns had returned home in time for Duguerry's funeral.

Bizet, viewing suburbs such as Neuilly and Meudon, said that the fifteen days of repression had caused more destruction than the siege of five months. Cavaillé-Coll, returning from a commission at Sheffield, found much damage done to his creations. Over fifty shells had fallen on St Augustin; one had exploded above the great organ of St Etienne du Mont. At St Médard the recently repaired mechanism had been smashed by rifle butts and St Sulpice had been showered with glass from the explosion of a powder magazine at the Luxembourg. At La Trinité, cannons had been placed behind the wind chambers of the great organ, attracting fire from Montmartre.

In peaceful England, however, Saint-Saëns had been able to arrange some future engagements. The new Willis organ at the Albert Hall awaited its inauguration. Six eminent Europeans were called upon to demonstrate it, including Bruckner from Vienna and Saint-Saëns from Paris. Mindful of Gounod's popularity in England, Saint-Saëns contributed the Church Scene from *Faust*, powered by the steam engine, which ensured an inexhaustible supply of air and delighted him especially.

The Société Nationale gave its first concert in November. The programme began with a 'Trio de Salon' of Franck, whose rise to prominence owed everything to the support of his new group of colleagues. Saint-Saëns's *Rouet d'Omphale*, his major composition during this distressing year, was heard in December. The works submitted were played in piano version and then voted on in secret. Even accepted composers seem to have been happy to submit to this procedure. It was agreed that the expensive orchestral concerts should be limited to two or three per season, but, in the rush of anti-German feeling, there was unexpected public enthusiasm and the membership swelled. The older journals looked on the venture with some condescension and *Le Ménestrel* called it a 'mutual admiration society', but it thrived. Early works by Fauré, Duparc, Chabrier and eventually Debussy owed their first hearings to the advocacy of Saint-Saëns. In December, the *Marche Héroïque* was played at the Concerts Populaires. Deeper than its title suggests, it paved the way towards the symphonic poems. The essence of the march is the theme of renewal and revenge, a restoration of vigour after the threnody to the dead. The men must rise from defeat and march on. It fixes, as in a photograph, the faces in the dull marches and monotonous routines of war. A second motif establishes a more virile resolution of revenge, while in the solemn central section a trombone solo has the accent of a funerary oration.

By contrast, the light and unusual orchestration of the *Rouet d'Omphale* betrays no suggestion of the recent tragedies. The first of his four symphonic poems, yet one more original conception brought to France by Saint-Saëns, it marks the opening of his most productive years. His meetings with Liszt had provided the idea but, where Liszt was discursive and rambling, he brought the virtues of brevity and significance to bear upon the music, in which a basic theme is preferred to a narrative. The work is dedicated to Augusta Holmès, but it is not purely a description of a heroic man enslaved by female charms, a risk that no doubt Mme Saint-Saëns had impressed upon Camille many times. It was based on the legend that Hera, jealous of the mother of Hercules, Alcmena, condemned him to fits of insanity. In one of these he had killed the brother of Iole whom he loved and was ordered as penance to go into slavery. He was sold to Omphale, Queen of Lydia, and set to women's work while his mistress put on his lion's skin and wielded his club. The dedication may allude to Augusta's admiration for Liszt, or to her aspirations to compose like men. The poem of Hugo, which furnished the idea, described the phantoms of the defeated monsters that roam in the cellars of the palace and we hear them groaning in the middle section. They represent dark forces at the base of society, which events such as the Commune bring to the surface. At that time Saint-Saëns, though not an admirer of Napoleon III, saw the monsters of anarchism and socialism released from captivity by the fall of the Empire.

It could be thought that, in the classical ABA pattern, Saint-Saëns is contrasting the light woodwind badinage of Omphale, such as he witnessed in the circle of Augusta Holmès, with the deeper and complex emotions that affected himself. The darker central theme is musically a version of the lighter one. The opening of the poem has an indecisive tonality as with the Second Symphony. He braved the opinion of many critics that descriptive music debased the art. Charles Bannelier, in the *Revue et Gazette*, objected to the whole idea of the symphonic poem: 'If this piece contains the skill of a master in the art of writing we do not admit the genre ... What a pity that the composer gave it a title which relates to a programme ... and that he wished to translate the untranslatable.'

It had been intended that Augusta would be his first partner in the two-piano performance. At the last moment she withdrew and de Castillon took her place. Although the spinning wheel was a medieval invention unknown in the world of legend, Saint-Saëns had recently seen a fine ebony wheel in the house of a friend and, soon afterwards, been shown a seductive picture of 'Venus' in the studio of a painter, Pierre Cabanel. The two images fused in his mind, the wheel suggesting the gossamer texture and the picture the taunting phrases of the enchantress. The evolution of the Hercules theme into light, mocking, staccato comments was a device to be used again for the part of Delilah.

The accent upon chamber music encouraged by the Société Nationale led to a closer contact with solo instrumentalists and a growth of pieces written for instruments which did not always have a large repertoire. Some were short, such as the Berceuse for Cello (Opus 38), which came from 1871. The purpose was to create something that would entertain an audience while giving a player the opportunity to display some virtuosity. A major work for the cello, the Sonata No. 1 (Opus 32) was written in 1872. Nine years had passed since his last important chamber work, the Trio, but instead of its light and extrovert style this sonata showed a fondness for low registers, doubling in octaves and a complex wrestling between cello and piano. Anger at the French humiliations has been suggested as a source of its energy and roughness. Also, it followed the death of Great-Aunt Charlotte whose vivacity and charm had alleviated life at home. He was now thrown back more than ever on his mother's company; she presided at his Monday Evenings and accompanied him to concerts everywhere.[1]

[1] Durand tells us that the sonata was first played at a Monday Evening

The sonata opens with a canonic dialogue. The tone is both turbulent and masterful. Two years before, Saint-Saëns had seen German fervour at the Beethoven centenary celebrations and, deducing that Beethoven's music might have contributed to the virility of German patriotism, estimated that a similarly masculine style might do the same for France. The key of C minor recalls Beethoven (Fauré also began a cello sonata in this key).[1] The Andante finds the cello singing and the piano playing staccato, although the roles are soon reversed and the piano lingers on a hymn-like tune, which paints a more amicable mood. An appassionato passage breaks out in the middle of the movement, although the chorale-hymn returns and the ending is a deftly syncopated duet. The piano dominates the Finale and, at the start, the cello contributes only the occasional comment. Much of the cello part is in the lower register. Saint-Saëns, looking down from the Tribune on the empty stall of the Abbé Duguerry, was often roused to anger. Baumann described the tussles of piano and cello in the lower registers as two masses of shade wrestling body to body 'as Jacob and the Angel'. According to Chantavoine the opening of the Andante is based upon a theme from Act One of *L'Africaine*. Bonnerot says it was the outcome of an improvisation at the organ of St Augustin, where Saint-Saëns had played for the funeral of Abbé Duguerry. The words of the excerpt, 'Afflicted by impiety and rebellion', would have been very appropriate. When the Andante was arranged for organ solo for Durand it showed the qualities of an organ work.

Camille Du Locle had resumed control of the Opéra Comique. He was small, dynamic, thought himself a poet and contributed to the libretti of *Don Carlos* and *Aida*. Composers arriving to play their scores

soirée. Everyone applauded, but Mme Saint-Saëns told her son that the Finale was execrable. Camille tore it up furiously and confined himself to his room for eight days, emerging only for meals. He then produced a Finale which his mother heard with satisfaction. There are certainly some grumpy passages in the movement.
[1] Fauré, completing his own Cello Sonata in 1917, wrote to his wife, 'Among modern French or foreign sonatas for cello there is only one of importance; that by Saint-Saëns. It is a masterpiece that is heard too rarely and that is because cellists pretend that their part is less brilliant than that of the piano! As if, in a combined work, the total effect does not result from the combination of different instruments.'

found the ivory of middle C disconcertingly missing from the piano. The tastes of his elderly colleague de Leuven (son of the Count Ribbing who had been involved in the real events behind Verdi's *Ballo in Maschera*) reflected an earlier age. Officials at the theatre would listen grimly to rehearsals of modern pieces, then stalk off with a condemnatory tread. After the recent turmoil, the *Timbre d'Argent* could not be considered for immediate production. They offered to put on a one-act opera if Saint-Saëns could supply such an item. Evenings of two or three such pieces were popular and enabled a director to keep composers simultaneously contented.

Du Locle introduced Saint-Saëns to the librettist Louis Gallet. He was Bursar of the Beaujon Hospital and a close neighbour of Saint-Saëns, an accommodating colleague with a necessary degree of tact. (An ignorant Minister of Fine Arts once told him that operas were usually written by the composer handing over the completed score and the librettist fitting in the words. 'It used to happen, but no longer,' murmured Gallet in a gentle defence of his role.) He and Saint-Saëns became close friends, and often exchanged views on current events in notes, drawings and verses. In the autumn of 1871 they decided to satisfy the recent passion for 'Japonaiserie' with a Far-Eastern fantasy. There had been an exhibition of Art Nippon in 1867. As modern warfare had recently brought Western 'progress' into disrepute, Japan seemed a symbol of timeless innocence and gaiety. Saint-Saëns, who was among the first Europeans to embrace 'Green' notions about the effects of industrialisation, wrote later in his *Rimes Familières* of the land of 'paper partitions', 'a little rice', 'work without haste, laughing all the while' and the 'poetising' of life in contrast to the machines that 'yell and whistle', the 'skies obscured with black smoke' and the dull colours and odd shapes of Western costumes. Du Locle was less impressed by the East and a compromise was reached by setting the slight tale half in Japan and half in Holland. It was written during the 1871-2 winter. For an off-stage chorus Saint-Saëns collected some genuine Japanese phrases: 'Good morning', 'It is nice weather', etc. (more salubrious than those Gilbert inserted in *The Mikado*), possibly in Antwerp or Holland, where he frequently gave concerts. Fauré, an admirer of *La Princesse Jaune*, made an arrangement of the exuberant overture for eight hands on two pianos and thought it merited revival. Pentatonic themes, perky and suggesting space, were included in the story of a young Dutchman, Kornelis, who, under the influence of drugs, falls in love with a Japanese figurine, fails to distinguish between the reality and the image of his real sweetheart Lena and awakens to discover that he has in fact confounded the two.

It was still usual to pay the leaders of claques in the theatre . . . De Leuven suggested fifty francs for the first performance and fifty for the twentieth. The second payment proved unnecessary. *La Princesse Jaune* joined Bizet's *Djamileh* and Paladilhe's *Le Passant* at the Opéra Comique in June 1872; *Le Passant* came off after three performances, *Djamileh* after eleven and *La Princesse Jaune* after fifteen. Du Locle had enjoyed designing the oriental costumes for both the latter works but the critics remarked that the music for one would have done as well for the other and *La Princesse* shared some of the criticism which Bizet's deliberate exoticism invoked. Saint-Saëns had already addressed to Bizet a sonnet, written on vellum sealed with red wax and signed with an elaborate double-S intertwined, in consolation for what Bizet regarded as poor notices. In it he contrasted the musical finesse of *Djamileh* with the bourgeois in their boxes, munching bonbons with the indifference of grazing cattle. *La Princesse Jaune*, despite the opulence of its love music and its piquant touches of colour, was received with the same incomprehension. The orchestration was described as 'detailed . . . with a great wealth of effects but no melody'. Jouvin, a notoriously harsh critic, said it was impossible to know in which key or time the overture was written.

Saint-Saëns was still regarded by some as a 'prophet of Wagner'. It was left to Reyer to point out that an apostle of Wagner would hardly have chosen the Opéra Comique to launch his crusade. He called *La Princesse* 'fine, elegant and colourful – full of pretty details, ingenious combinations of sounds and imitative effects which have not been rivalled'. (These included muffled temple gongs and a muted triangle adding to the impression of unreality, an off-stage chorus and sounds of little bells while Kornelis sings of the mirage of far-off cities.) Kornelis's declarations of love were stronger than the light serenades to which the Opéra Comique audience was accustomed and they disturbed it.

Fortunately, his place at the Madeleine meant that he did not have to worry financially about defeats on the stage. From the early 1870s onwards there was a steady improvement in the quality of organ playing. While Saint-Saëns remained the supreme master, many made

journeys to hear César Franck at St Clothilde. A younger generation
was in evidence. Gigout had been a piano pupil of Saint-Saëns at the
Niedermeyer, but his organ teacher had been Clément Loret. He
became organist at St Augustin, one of the churches which grew as
devout Catholics sought to atone for the recent disasters. Widor had
succeeded Lefébure-Wély at St Sulpice; Guilmant stepped into
Chauvet's place at La Trinité. An elevated view of the organist's role
was further strengthened when Franck was appointed as Professor of
Organ at the Conservatoire following the retirement of the sempiter-
nal Benoist. There is no reason to doubt Saint-Saëns's statement that
the post had been offered to himself and that he had recommended
Franck. Franck's biographers, however, tend to attribute the appointment to the advice of Théodore Dubois, Maître de Chapelle at the
Madeleine, who had influence with Ambroise Thomas, Director of the
Conservatoire. According to the children of Cavaillé-Coll, their father
was also consulted. Although Franck never succeeded in gaining one
of the Professorships of Composition, his classes embracing improvisation spread over into composition and he attracted pupils happy to
submit works for approval. Of the actual Professors of Composition,
Massé wrote light opera and was constantly ill, Reber and Bazin were
uninspiring. Vincent d'Indy carried off the Proxime Accessit prize in
his second year of studying under Franck and there was jealousy
among Franck's colleagues.

Saint-Saëns concentrated his attentions upon Fauré, encouraged his
composing and introduced him further into the Viardot circle. In 1871
he wrote the Duet 'El Desdichado' for two sopranos as a deliberate
amalgam of difficulties for two of Pauline's daughters, Claudie and
Marianne, through which they sailed with triumph. The Spanish text
had been adapted by Barbier and the fluctuations between major and
minor suggest that since the 'Guitare' of 1851 Saint-Saëns had made
the acquaintance of flamenco. The Viardot family had Spanish origins
and were also instrumental in creating a vogue for the habanera.

Another young musician to whom he tried to give practical help was
Alexis de Castillon. After the death of his great-aunt on 18 January
1872, Saint-Saëns did not appear in public again until March,
although he may have attended a Conservatoire concert in February,
when the Andante and Scherzo of his Second Symphony were
performed. It was Saint-Saëns who asked Pasdeloup to include the D-
major Piano Concerto of de Castillon in his concerts and Pasdeloup

who asked in turn that he should be the soloist, for his attraction as a virtuoso was uncontested. The programme took place on 10 March. Pasdeloup had played barely two bars when tumult broke out. He wished to call a halt, but Saint-Saëns motioned for him to continue. As the piece proceeded the noise rose, with Saint-Saëns in his piercing voice informing the mob that he would finish the concerto. In the orchestral passages he swept the audience with an irate glare, but the end was reached. 'Camille was superb,' said de Castillon justly, but the concerto was not heard again until 1899.

Fresh ground was broken with the First Cello Concerto of 1872. At first sight it appears to be a repetition of the experiment with form that had been ventured with the Violin Concerto in A. It is a single movement with the Andante in the centre and an apparent return to the first section creating a balance. Yet it showed the emergence of Saint-Saëns's characteristics in a different fashion. The initial section with its descending triplet figure, an artefact rather than a melodious outburst, is followed by a meditative second subject; but in its subsequent incarnation the triplets are succeeded by a more lyrical second subject, which owes something to the little minuet on muted strings which leads off the Andante. The Andante itself, with its cello solo, displays again Saint-Saëns's feeling for the derivation of the waltz from this older form. The third and final part not only contains much of the cadenza material, but one of the first of Saint-Saëns's brilliant drawn-out cantilenas on the known theme.

It is hardly necessary to say that the balance between soloist and orchestra in this difficult genre is maintained with consummate ease, solo woodwind being frequently used in contrast to the rich tones of the cello and the tutti being very strictly confined to Haydnesque flourishes. The concerto was dedicated to August Tolbecque and was first given on 19 January 1873. This was at the Conservatoire, in itself an accolade.[1] It was well received and the *Revue et Gazette Musicale* declared that the composer, if he continued in this vein, would recover much of the prestige he had lost with 'his all too obvious divergence from classicism and the tendencies in a number of recent works'. It was a favourite of Casals who played it at his London début in 1905.

[1] Tolbecque was over eighty. Soloists were sometimes allowed to suggest an item to be played. The conductor Edouard Deldevez took pleasure in pointing out to Saint-Saëns that otherwise he would not have been in the programme.

Rachmaninov expressed his admiration for 'its delicacy and beauty' to Saint-Saëns's English biographer Watson Lyle and may well have derived some inspiration from its extended and romantic final pages. It broadened the cello repertoire in France and its progress from minor to major in mood reflected a purer air of national optimism.

In 1872 Saint-Saëns began his career as a critic. A review, *La Renaissance*, had been founded and one of its directors was an amateur poet, Jean Alcard. Saint-Saëns set to music his 'Vogue, vogue la galère' as part of a vocal fantasie which survives only in the song. The association resulted in his writing some reviews under the name 'Phemius' over a period of fourteen months from October 1872 to December 1873. In them he defended the young French school, Bizet, Delibes, Guiraud and Dubois, and extolled the symphonic poems of Liszt. When the closed season for theatres and concerts arrived he penned a series on 'Harmony and Melody', which later survived as a title for collected articles.

In this year Debussy entered the Conservatoire. His admittance to the piano class had caused something of a sensation for there had been thirty-eight applicants and only eight male contenders had been chosen. Debussy had just turned ten years of age and was placed in the class of Antoine Marmontel, who perceived unusual talent: 'A true artistic temperament; much can be expected of him.' He also studied with Lavignac (Saint-Saëns's old partner in the wartime performance of the *Marche Héroïque*), who introduced his pupils to Wagner. So intent was the class upon argument over Wagner that on one occasion they found they had been locked in for the night and had to negotiate the decrepit premises in the darkness to find an exit. There was music from Massenet to attract the notice of 'Phemius'. In the oratorio *Marie Magdaleine* the title role was sung by Pauline Viardot and what d'Indy described as Massenet's 'eroticism, discreet and quasi-religious' was given its première on Good Friday 1873, the day following the failure of Franck's *Redemption*. The success of *Marie Magdaleine* was a turning point in Massenet's career. Saint-Saëns praised it highly as 'the most audacious experiment' since Berlioz's *L'Enfance du Christ*, but pointed out the debt to Gounod. Reyer thought it contained some unsurpassed moments of delicacy and purity, but the reaction of d'Indy, devout Catholic and ardent admirer of the Christian humility of his teacher Franck, was sharper. When he expressed admiration for the choral writing and heard Massenet declare that he did not like sloppy religious sentiment but gave the public what it wanted, d'Indy was shocked and henceforth regarded Massenet as frivolous.

The Société Nationale was the most fruitful, but not the only association to be founded in these early years of the Republic. For a brief time Saint-Saëns was entrusted with the conductorship of a 'Société Philharmonique'. In 1872 the publisher Georges Hartmann, inspired by intentions similar to the Société Nationale, rented the Odéon Theatre, recruited an orchestra and gave the direction to the thirty-five-year-old Edouard Colonne, until then known only as a violinist and conductor of operetta.[1] In March 1873 the first 'National Concert' took place. At the request of Hartmann, Saint-Saëns played his G-minor Concerto and accompanied Pauline Viardot in an aria. He had recently completed six more Bach transcriptions, which were dedicated to the pianist Mme Szarvady. A year later the 'National Concerts' (the title is further evidence of the serious and patriotic mood of the moment) moved to the Châtelet. After some financial difficulties they were reorganised with a membership and called themselves the Concerts Colonne.

With Fauré, Saint-Saëns played two-piano versions of various works; Fauré's Symphony in F, his own *Three Breton Rhapsodies* and the next symphonic poem, *Phaeton*. This last was dedicated to the hostess Mme Berthe Pochet, née de Tinan. He never lost an opportunity of recommending Fauré to these influential friends. He frequently asked him to deputise at the Madeleine and hoped to make him his eventual successor. Fauré had the privilege of hearing several of his piano pieces first performed by the great virtuoso: the first barcarolle, and three impromptus. He was introduced to the wealthy and artistic patrons who were building summer retreats on the Normandy coast. Together with his pupil and friend André Messager and the ever-peripheral Romain Bussine, he stayed with one such family at Ste Adresse. Nearby were painters such as Roger Jourdain, half-brother of Marguerite Baugnies. She had once considered marrying Saint-Saëns, but her parents had opposed the match, saying that large question

---

[1] Budding composers were obliged to applaud heartily at the Colonne concerts if they wished to be chosen, as Mme Colonne's eagle eye swept the audience. Colonne was autocratic after the manner of Pasdeloup. He silenced an audience demanding an encore of a 'Dies Irae' by shouting, 'No encores on the Day of Judgement!'

marks hung over his health. It was in these circles that Fauré first met the American sewing-machine heiress Winaretta Singer, later the Princesse de Polignac. Musical evenings were held in villas whose magic casements opened out upon the foam. Saint-Saëns could be satisfied that Fauré would have no difficulty in charming his hostesses.

Another young friend was less fortunate, for early in 1873 de Castillon died. During the war he had taken part in the battle to recapture Orleans. Forced to camp and sleep in the snows, the young soldier had suffered the ruin of his health. Hearing that it had worsened, Saint-Saëns rushed to his home, but came too late. 'He did not have the dolorous satisfaction of embracing living', wrote Gallet, 'him whom he had so often supported, encouraged and defended with all the force of his double talent as composer and virtuoso.' The Church of St Pierre de Chaillot was insufficient to hold the crowd of mourners who attended the funeral, including Saint-Saëns, Bizet, Franck, Lalo, Massenet and many others. De Castillon had sprung from an unmusical family, which had to elicit from Hartmann the names and addresses of the mourners to whom they should write as *'nous ne connaissons pas le gens de musique'*.[1] 'If he had lived he would have been a modern Beethoven,' wrote Hartmann to Gallet. He had been a student of the late Beethoven quartets, wrote many chamber works in his final years and helped to direct Saint-Saëns's thoughts back towards the need for more French chamber music. In his *Cours de Composition Musicale* d'Indy wrote: 'At a time when all his contemporaries were composing virtually nothing but operas, Castillon's temperament was one of the few clearly inclined to symphonic composition. He contributed so far as was possible to the development of the Société Nationale, which was really the nursery of the French symphony at the end of the nineteenth century.'

On 21 February 1873 the chapel organ at Versailles, dating from 1736, built by Clicquot and restored by Cavaillé-Coll, was inaugurated. Saint-Saëns played a Bach prelude and fugue, and Widor one of his organ symphonies. A few weeks later Saint-Saëns's Psalm 18 was performed on the Thursday of Holy Week by Colonne, together with Franck's *Redemption*, the latter suffering from lack of rehearsal time and poor copying of the orchestral parts, which d'Indy and friends

---

[1] Then he really must have had some talent,' said a relative, looking round at the rows of notable musicians. De Castillon had regarded Saint-Saëns as the greatest of them all.

tried to correct with much burning of the midnight oil and glasses of brandy. Furthermore, Franck had composed sections in keys difficult for brass.

Opinion in Paris at the time was not, however, concentrated upon comparisons between the professional Saint-Saëns and the emergent Franck. Capital and country were divided over the likelihood of the restoration of the Bourbon Comte de Chambord as Henry V. Thiers, after establishing the Republic as the form of government which 'divides us least', resigned in May and was succeeded as President by Marshal Macmahon, who had sympathies with the Right. The question had simmered ever since the Commune; the Minuet section of Saint-Saëns's First Cello Concerto showed that the *ancien régime* was not forgotten. An unforeseen obstacle arose in Chambord's refusal to accept the Tricolore as a national emblem and his insistence on the white flag of the Bourbons. Royalists rushed to his Court-in-exile at Frohsdorf and all manner of compromises were sought, including one fanciful suggestion that the national flag might be white on one side and tricoloured on the other. His supporters, representing provincial France, were powerful and had begun building the Sacré Coeur basilica to expiate national guilt for the godless Republics of recent memory. Yet the question of the flag, apparently trivial ('All that over a napkin,' Pius IX is said to have expostulated), was indicative of Bourbon intransigence. Chambord, truth to tell, preferred the romantic life of an exile, surrounded by courtesies, to the stressful tasks of government. Ardent Royalism did not fade away immediately, however. In 1874 the Government refused to allow St Henri's Day to be celebrated, although it had been made a semi-political rallying point for three years. Unexpectedly, fervent homage was then suddenly transferred to St Bonaventura who shared the same day in the calendar!

Phaeton was Saint-Saëns's principal exercise in the year 1873 and the finest of his symphonic poems. The myth of the young god driving the aerial horses of his father, Apollo, failing to control them, scorching the earth and finally succumbing to the thunderbolt of Jove, was clearly unsuitable for the operatic stage. Lully had used the story from Ovid's *Metamorphoses* as the basis of an opera, but did not attempt to depict the ride and introduced a heroine, Theone, who falls in love with Phaeton.[1] In the original story Apollo warns the youth of the

---

[1] Saint-Saëns possessed a copy of Lully's *Phaeton* (1683).

danger and this may well be the explanation of the sombre passage, which has greatly puzzled commentators and to which Saint-Saëns did not refer in his synopsis, placed as contrast to the sounds of the restless horses near the opening. It returns at a point in the Ovidian story where Phaeton's sisters, weeping by his riverside tomb, are transformed into poplar trees.

Saint-Saëns is not concerned to relate a story, but to draw an epic painting, and so brilliantly does he convey the images of a headstrong youth and the neighing and panting of the horses that one cannot understand why he should have opposed the representational efforts of the Debussyists in his later years. The *chords* which gallop even suggest the image of horses (plural) in harness. The theme of pride, which dominates *Phaeton*, must have been well to the fore during the year; the stubbornness of Chambord, the Sacré Coeur, both in different ways express the folly of hubris. Memories of the 1870 rush to war were every day revived in the laments that came from the severed provinces of Alsace and Lorraine. Musical form, however, is not sacrificed to meaning. Servières thought that the 'combination of themes, their amalgamation, division and extension, has an intensity of colouring that the composer never surpassed'. The scorching of the earth and its peoples are searingly portrayed by flaming roars from the brass. Any composer could orchestrate a well-aimed thunderbolt, but few could compress the growing disorder in the heavens by using fugal entries and thematic alterations with cool academic control. The chord of E flat (*ffff*) which denotes the intervention of Jove is the same as that which portrays the order of the universe at the outset. When peace has descended the cellos recall the moments of ecstasy and a flute gives a sad reminder of the first flush of success, a device which Strauss was later to use in *Don Juan*. It annoyed the composer when conductors took this lament too slowly. 'I have specified twice as slow; the measure ought not to appear changed.' Formal unity interested him more than pictorial effects.

Saint-Saëns's mother faithfully transcribed the corrected score. It requires a large orchestra with piccolo (ad lib), contrabassoon, full brass with tuba, two harps and four timpani with three players for chords on the drums, an idea that had been employed by Berlioz. Saint-Saëns himself wrote, 'Reicha, Berlioz's first teacher, had the original idea of playing tap drums in chords of three or four beats. In order to try out this effect he composed a choral piece, *L'Harmonie des*

Spheres, which was published in connection with his *Traité d'Harmonie*.' D'Indy, learning orchestration the hard way, was temporarily a timpanist in Colonne's orchestra at the time and may have contributed personally to these effects. As in *Omphale*, the rhythmic figure which unites the poem rises and falls in an arc. To depict the galloping of horses, composers had often used pounding triplets. Saint-Saëns follows the example of Berlioz in the *Ride to the Abyss* and uses a regular beat. The pounding of the hoofs is adroitly combined with the whinnying of outraged beasts. *Phaeton* was performed twice by Colonne at the Châtelet in December 1873. Its reception on the 7th was cool, but it fared better on the 12th. The critics were decisive in their condemnation of pictorial music and attacked the genre of symphonic poem as such. Most agreed that programme music was unworthy of a serious musician, who should touch the heart rather than feed the imagination.

Lighter music was again becoming fashionable. Lecocq, Saint-Saëns's friend from student days, enjoyed great success with the operetta *La Fille de Madame Angot*, set in the Directory period. Napoleonic themes were unacceptable and the Directory, that relaxed time between the Revolution and Empire, was now invested with nostalgia for a public satiated with political skirmishes. One line in the libretto, 'It was not worth the trouble to change governments', caused rival groups to demonstrate. Composers with their sights on the Opéra suffered a setback when the building was destroyed by fire. The new Opéra, planned under Napoleon III, was rising but still incomplete and productions were forced to move to the Salle Ventadour. Grand opera was no longer the sole preoccupation of composers, but Saint-Saëns, despite his diverse output, guarded his stage ambitions. He had suffered a long period of bad health and spent the end of 1873 at Pointe St Eugène near Algiers. He found a garden, a bubbling fountain and the tranquillity to resume composition of the third act of *Samson*.

As *Phaeton* had shown, he had arrived at a new peak of inspiration and, despite his overt disparagement of 'melody', he was able to develop his great melodic gifts while crafting a score that combined the Wagnerian ideas of thematic unity and continuous flow with traditional elements in grand opera. A note appeared in certain journals saying that he had just finished his 'oratorio' *Dalila* which would be given shortly at the Châtelet, but in fact the work was far from complete. It was in Algeria that the composer, penetrated by biblical images and classical myths, felt himself in a more exotic world and the intense colours, the perfect lines of the horizons and the novelty of the sounds began to permeate his music with ever greater frequency. Greatly improved in health, he began 1874 with further concerts. On 4 March, Alfred and Marie Jaell gave a performance of *Phaeton* arranged for two pianos at the Salle Erard and, on the 28th, played an unpublished work, dedicated to them, the Variations for Two Pianos on a Theme of Beethoven. It was the sole novelty from his pen at this time, but has remained one of his best-known pieces, both because of the ingeniousness of the idea and because two-piano works have always enjoyed a vogue in France.[1] By a strange coincidence Brahms, in the same year, was writing for two pianos his own extended treatment of a theme by a Great Master. Variation seven and eight of Saint-Saëns have a Brahmsian feel, despite the lack of mutual admiration between the two men.

But there are many 'echoes' in the Variations which treat the theme (from the Trio of the Minuet of Beethoven's Sonata Opus 31, No. 3, a series of wide leaps consolidated by narrower shifts of harmony beneath) as a guided tour of the post-Beethoven pantheon. Mendelssohn or Schumann treat the theme in the first Variation, certainly Schumann in the second, Liszt in the fourth and there is a reminder of Mendelssohn in the sixth. There is a variation 'alla marcia funèbre'. At the close, a fugue leads to a final Presto, with a barrage of repeated notes already used in Variation four (and later in *Africa*). Jacques Durand recalled an occasion when Saint-Saëns and Caroline de Serres (then Mme Montigny-Remaury) played the Variations at the Salle Erard. In the Finale Saint-Saëns allowed himself to be carried away. Mme Montigny pursued with all the strength she could muster and the result was an unrestrained steeplechase. It was discovered at the end that Saint-Saëns had won by a bar.

In July, he took part in the adjudication of the Prix de Rome which

---

[1] The idea of Variations on a Theme of Beethoven appears unusual but, of course, the content was not so very different from the Liszt 'paraphrases' which subjected a single melody to a sequence of elaborate treatments. Alfred Jaell had, like Saint-Saëns, given his first concert in 1846 as a child prodigy, though two years older at thirteen. The *Revue et Gazette* described his artistry as having 'miraculous qualities'. Marie Jaell had studied composition with Saint-Saëns (and Franck) and assisted Liszt with his correspondence at Weimar.

he had contested ten years before. Despite unfavourable reviews he was creating a reputation as composer as well as virtuoso. The interest in *Dalila* persisted and on 20 August Pauline Viardot, by way of a handsome surprise, arranged a private performance of Act Two. The setting was a small temporary stage in the park of a neighbour at Croissy, but care was taken with the scenery and costumes. Seeing the sumptuous draperies in which Pauline appeared at the start, Saint-Saëns at the keyboard could not refrain from the cry '*Que c'est beau!*' 'Her voice was then already impaired, especially in the middle register,' he wrote, 'but its upper and lower notes were wonderfully preserved and her performance of genius made me forget her age, which was unsuitable for Delilah, and the defects of her voice and everything else.' Her two colleagues were also stars of the stage: Nicot, who sang Samson, and Auguez the High Priest. The reception was the most friendly to date but Olivier Halanzier, Director of the Opéra, refused to commit himself to a production.[1] The biblical subject involved risks at a time when religious passions were running high. The plot, though it seems fine material to us, is wholly foreordained, and audiences, lacking our modern means of listening to the same works many times, enjoyed the twists and turns of a narrative with mistaken identities and the reappearance of lost relatives, etc.

Stage-managers, one imagines, could not have looked forward to the nightly destruction of the Temple of Dagon, burying the cast under the heavy and realistic scenery of those days. When Saint-Saëns approached the Minister responsible for Theatres to urge acceptance of *Samson*, he received a detailed criticism in which the Minister asserted that it was an oratorio by nature, unplayable on the stage. M. de Beauplan added that the entrance of Delilah in Act One was 'unprepared'.[2] But there was one outcome of the Croissy *Samson*: Edward Lassen, a Danish-born musician, who knew Liszt at Weimar and became Kapellmeister there, heard it, or was made aware of fragments in rehearsal. He was thus able to give substance to Liszt's general favour towards it.

---

[1] Olivier Halanzier had risen through provincial theatres. Son of an actress, he had managed his mother's company at Strasbourg at the age of fifteen. He had once played the flute, it was said, but had abandoned it.

[2] Wagner would have included a long narration (by an Old Israelite) giving the origins of the Philistine conflict and hinting at a mysterious priestess in the vicinity.

The summer saw Saint-Saëns, in company with Fauré and other friends, at the villa of Mme de Tinan. Fauré had by this time handed over his duties as assistant to Widor at St Sulpice to Messager and was undertaking more extensive work at the Madeleine. Saint-Saëns wrote for him a typically humorous account of his obligations at the services, prefaced by a drawing of a large-nosed figure at the manuals and concluded by the drawing of a matchstick man scuttling down the steps, interspersed with asides such as 'When the children in the Choir begin to fidget, the organ stops' or 'After the Benediction, exit. The organist goes to lunch at Richard Lucas' (a nearby restaurant). Messager at St Sulpice fared no better with the clergy than Fauré had done and later remarked that he had been to sufficient Masses to save him for the rest of his life.

At Mme de Tinan's there was much piano music and the hostess noted how closely Fauré modelled himself on his teacher. She told Saint-Saëns that Fauré had his clarity, simplicity and gentleness. 'He places his small hands on the keyboard just as you do, and give him your fire, in another ten years he will be a Saint-Saëns. But you have to goad him all the time.' In view of the present esteem of Fauré and the neglect of Saint-Saëns the comment seems ironic and, in fact, Fauré was soon to emerge with a pianistic style that derived more from the organ lessons of his youth from Clément Loret: legato playing and sliding fingers changing on the same note, moving thereby from key to key. Fauré was also ambidextrous and centred important passages in the middle of the keyboard shared between hands. He was still to his master the most promising force in French music. In November he was promoted to Secretary of the Société Nationale and was thus in the midst of the finest musicians of the day.

The summer, spent in the world of the salons, coincided with the composition of Saint-Saëns's Romance Opus 36 for Horn or Cello. Once again he was breaking new ground, for earlier in the century there were many instruments for which few pieces existed, yet every concert demanded solo items in the long programmes. Players had often to adapt operatic melodies themselves. Saint-Saëns began to supply this want and dedicated the Romance of 1874 to Henri Garigue, a leading horn player. It has parallels with an aria, with a more restless central section followed by a 'da capo' repeat. In this instance the long melody can be subdivided into quite distinct phrases with contrasting shapes, one of the features of Saint-Saëns's elusive style. A Romance in C for Violin followed, composed for Turhan – a friend of his youth and now leader of the Opéra orchestra – quite the equal of that in D flat for Flute or Violin (1871), which contains another characteristic in the step-by-step ascent of the melody.

In addition to spending some time at Le Havre, Saint-Saëns also made a visit to England. In 1873 he had the experience of trying out the largest organ which Cavaillé-Coll had built to date. It was in his workshop awaiting shipment to Sheffield. Widor, Guilmant and Saint-Saëns all gave separate or joint recitals, as did the British organist W. T. Best, a civil engineer turned musician, who gave the first concert when it reached its destination. In 1874, though he hoped that one of his own concertos might be selected, Saint-Saëns played the Beethoven Fourth Concerto – 'which I love passionately' – at the London Philharmonic Society and gave a recital at St James's Hall.

He was working on a third symphonic poem, the *Danse Macabre*, for part of the year. This exchanged classical legend for bizarre medievalism recreated in a contemporary poem by Henry Cazalis, a doctor (and early advocate of socialised medicine), who counted as one of the Parnassian poets. He was a friend of Augusta Holmès and Henri Regnault, whose biography he produced in 1872. Saint-Saëns set two of his poems, 'Dans ton coeur'[1] and 'Danse Macabre', which had appeared under the title 'Egalité, Fraternité'. The title was ironic and referred to death as the great leveller, twisting the revolutionary slogan; the poem described how the rich and great danced with beggars and outcasts in the graveyard. Cazalis described the sound of death's violin with the words *'Zig et zig et zag'*, included a lascivious coupling of a countess and cart-driver in the frenzies and added the dispelling sounds of the cock-crow at daybreak. Saint-Saëns must have approached the subject with amusement rather than awe. He first set the poem using the tritone, raw open fifths and a theme kept within the narrow confines of a minor third. It was published as a song by Enoch and then sold to Durand for one hundred francs while the composer, much under Liszt's spell at the time and conscious of Liszt's excursions into 'Mephistopholic' sounds, reserved the right to turn it into an orchestral composition. Before the poem, a piano

---

[1] Cazalis seems to have awakened strong murmurings of the mind in Saint-Saëns. In 'Dans ton coeur' this very orthodox composer put the voice part in flats, the rest in sharps, sharing notes in enharmonic relationships and with more modern chromaticism.

transcription and a version for small orchestra had been made in which a solo violin plays the tritone and fifths. In 1874 Saint-Saëns returned to the song, amplified the stage directions in the text with twelve notes ingeniously given to the harp to signify midnight, the xylophone to indicate clinking bones and the inclusion of the 'Dies Irae'. The xylophone had not been used before in full orchestra and it had to be described in 'notes for performance'. The mistuning of the solo violin to suggest disharmony in the cosmos must have been in its day a stroke as unexpected as anything by the 'moderns' he came to hate. Debussy said of it sarcastically: 'He showed in this work promise of becoming a very great musician.' The predominant rhythm is that of a waltz, although the poem mentions only the more stately sarabande.

Comments on this work, by which Saint-Saëns is remembered, have been wide-ranging. Baumann treated it seriously, as if midnight waltzing of the dead were a real phenomenon: 'horns and violins absorb with trembling harmony the silence of a winter's night', 'the bestial laugh of the terrible fifths', 'the final disbelief in salvation', etc. Servières omitted the poem from his analysis and Dandelot, more prudishly, omitted just the verse about the countess and the cart-driver. The Commune had aroused the idea of a society dancing a macabre farandole in which class and social gradation were lost. The cannon of Versailles resembled the 'patriotic' crowing of the cockerel. Chantavoine praised it musically and noticed that its brief points of narrative influenced the even more popular *Sorcerer's Apprentice*.[1] Undoubtedly the musical appeal of the poem for Saint-Saëns was very strong. He was able to interweave plainchant, as in his improvisations, in a secular and ironic context. The fugal treatment of the waltz theme (in its contours at least not altogether unlike Delilah's '*Ah! Réponds à ma tendresse*') could suggest the dislocation of the phantoms scattering and reforming. On personal grounds the 'amours' of patrician and pleb may have stirred his imagination; the waltz is undoubtedly lascivious. We are entering the age of Maupassant and Zola. Perhaps the Abbé Liszt spoke most truly when he wrote, 'The *Danse Macabre* takes hold of you so powerfully that you long to be there!'

Colonne played it at the Châtelet on 24 January 1875 and it was coldly received. The deployment of xylophone and castanets caused

[1] The driving rhythms, so prominent in unifying Saint-Saëns's symphonic poems, are also a marked feature of the *Sorcerer's Apprentice*, where it is by no means an obvious device to choose.

The forceful Madame Clémence Saint-Saëns, mère.

Camille Saint-Saëns, as a child.

Saint-Saëns, aged twenty (*left*), with friend.

Saint-Saëns in 1876.

Cartoon showing Saint-Saëns in
the uniform of the National Guard, 1870.

André, the son
who was tragically
killed in 1878.

1883: *Henry VIII.*
(*Above*) Act II: scene in Richmond Park.
(*Below*) Act III: scene for the trial of Catherine of Aragon.

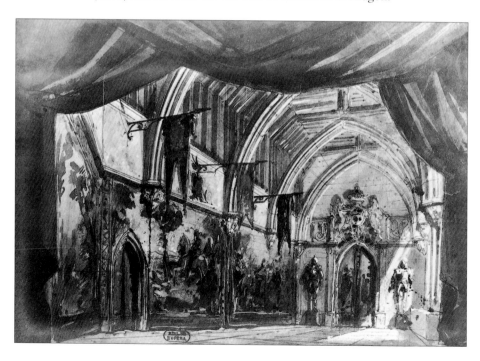

1887: *Proserpine*.
Artist's impression, including the famous convent scene (at base).

1888: *Ascanio*.
Act II: in Benvenuto Cellini's workshop.

This set - for Massenet's *Le Roi de Lahore* - had to be re-used
for Saint-Saëns's *Samson et Dalila*, Act I.

Artist's impression: Madame Deschamps–Jehin sings Dalila.

1893: *Phryné*.
Phryné's boudoir in Act II.

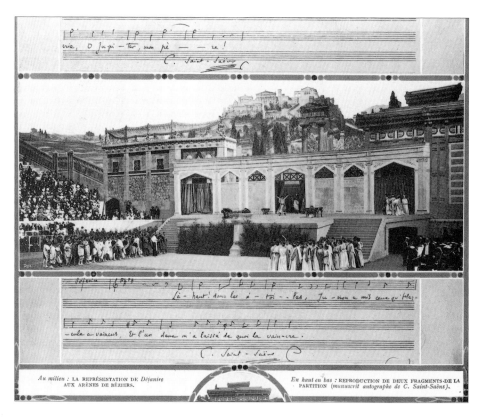

Au milieu : LA REPRÉSENTATION DE *Déjanire*
AUX ARÈNES DE BÉZIERS.

En haut en bas : REPRODUCTION DE DEUX FRAGMENTS DE LA
PARTITION (*manuscrit autographe de C. Saint-Saëns*).

The open-air production of
Déjanire at Béziers in 1898, with
musical quotations, autographed.

Castelbon des Beauxhostes (*right*),
the patron of the Béziers Festival,
photographed with his secretary.

astonishment. Adolphe Jullien called it 'a baroque composition, where there is everything except a musical idea, good or bad; one can only classify it under two categories: aberration or mystification'. On 7 February it received an encore, but some months later when it was given by Pasdeloup at his concerts, always inclined to great rowdiness, there was a demonstration against it with whistlers drowning the applause and rival groups threatening one another. It went into many versions. The composer arranged it for violin and piano, compensating for the missing xylophone by stipulating passages 'col legno' (i.e. with the wood of the bow). He used the pizzicato of the violin for the harp and preserved the timpani rhythms in the piano. He also made a two-piano version which the Jaells played at the Salle Erard and Saint-Saëns and Caroline de Serres at the Salle Pleyel.

It is at this time that we have an insight into Saint-Saëns's essential generosity. Caroline had asked him to join her for concerts in Lyon to assist the impresario M. Aimé Gros. Saint-Saëns replied that Gros had recruited many notable artists and had 'the wind in his sails'. He was himself going to Rennes to help another friend who had no great names in his programmes. However, he added typically, 'If you wish to give me very great pleasure, you will invite Fauré . . . in this way the public of Lyons will know my Variations and Fauré would have a chance to push himself forward.'

Feeling, perhaps, that he had gone too far in the direction of the programme music and conscious of his place at the head of the campaign to recognise chamber music, Saint-Saëns gave part of the year 1875 to his Piano Quartet Opus 41. He had complained that the Committee of the Société Nationale did not receive sufficient trios and quartets.[1] The quartet is interesting in several ways. Once again, with regard to form he emphasised the cyclical pattern. In the Finale the chorale theme of the Andante Maestoso returns, as do the first and third themes from the opening. It is also, for this normally silver-tongued composer, an angry work despite its peaceful opening.[2] In the Andante he uses the same device as in the Cello Sonata of a

---

[1] Even so, the critic Bannelier, not always indulgent, had spoken in 1874 in praise of the Société Nationale and 'an artistic future, which would have seemed an impossible dream a few years ago'.
[2] Sarasate was the violinist in the first performance, which would have enhanced the beautiful violin phrases in the First Movement.

chorale juxtaposed against a rhythmic patter shared between piano and strings. But the counter-theme, in this instance in an abrupt rhythm, is beaten out with disruptive force. Whether this represents his private feelings at the Tribune while hearing the religious plainchants arising from below or whether it infers something deeper as he moved closer to his impulsive and disastrous marriage it is hard to tell. The Scherzo is another *Danse Macabre* with a curious hiccuping motif and an agitated race between the instruments. The Trio is little more than a series of brushstrokes and, ignoring all the rules, the return of the Scherzo contains a series of recitatives and cadenzas for the participants.[1] Saint-Saëns, rightly, never ignored the element of excitement that virtuosity provides in concert performances. Finally, in the last of the three themes that introduce the work we have a foretaste of that elusive and wistful wandering style of melody which became so prominent a feature of his later works.

Early in 1875 Saint-Saëns organised a concert of his works at the Salle Pleyel. He played his E-flat Concerto, with the orchestra directed by Lamoureux, and in the Quartet he was joined by Sarasate, Turhan and the cellist Léon Jacquard. Servières thought the abundance of scholastic formulae had denied success to the quartet. Baumann speaks of a 'counterpoint exercise dramatised' and 'complicated mechanisms similar to the cogs of a clockmaker'. Although there are echoes of Schumann in the Finale, the mood of defiance was characteristic of a new buoyancy in France, responding to Bismarck's menacing gestures.

French Army reforms had made Germany nervous to the extent that export of horses across the Rhine had been embargoed. The French Foreign Minister had succeeded in persuading a number of countries that Germany was a dangerous power and the visit of the Tsar to Berlin was believed to be a brake upon Bismarck's wish to humble France yet again. Thiers had always dreamt of a Franco-Russian alliance, although the very thought of friendship between Tsarist Russia and Republican France had at first appeared preposterous. Now others began to entertain the idea, and links between the two countries were more frequent and open. French critics, Bourg-

[1] Although he was, in print, the great defender of classical forms, one cannot help thinking that Saint-Saëns was one of the first to break them down and introduce these abrupt pointillist effects, which have become so marked a feature of twentieth-century music.

ault-Ducoudray especially, found much to commend in Russian music and Saint-Saëns, during a visit to Moscow, obtained a copy of *Boris Godunov*. He did not esteem this rough-cast epic highly himself, but he lent the score to Jules de Brayer – a founder and contributor to the new *Revue Wagnerienne* who was said to have travelled to Bayreuth from Paris on foot – and ultimately it reached the hands of Debussy, who revelled in its unconventionality.

Another cause of French pride in 1875 was the Grand Opening of the splendrous Opéra in the Palais Garnier. Begun thirteen years earlier, it was an eighth wonder of the world. The King and Queen of Spain and the King of Hanover attended, along with 2000 guests; the Lord Mayor of London's coach left its native shores to bear him to the event in full regalia and even the stage-hands wore evening dress and top hats. The sculptures and paintings had occupied recent Prix de Rome winners without respite. The course of opera, however, never runs smooth. The female chorus threatened to strike over Sunday rehearsals; Christine Nilsson disliked the tenor and refused to rehearse before an audience. So her scenes from *Hamlet* and *Faust* were cut and replaced by episodes from *Les Huguenots*. Saint-Saëns regretted that there was insufficient room for the six harps required for the last act, but it seemed to re-establish Paris as the centre of the musical world.

The year became rich in composition, for he was working on his Fourth Piano Concerto and the oratorio *Le Déluge*. He also shared deeply with Bizet the complications that attended the mounting of *Carmen* at the Opéra Comique and its withering reception. The orchestra, accustomed to the easy scores of Adam and Auber, resented the complexity of Bizet's music and declared sections unplayable. The chorus, used to static formations watching the conductor, disliked their acting parts as cigarette girls flirting with soldiers. Bizet had wanted them to come on-stage casually with some semblance of street conditions. Du Locle declared this to be wholly against tradition. He and de Leuven were worried by the immorality of the story, for boxes at the theatre were used by bourgeois families in courtship rituals of the most proper sort. When a Government Minister applied for a box on the opening night Du Locle invited him to the dress rehearsal so that he could see whether it was suitable family entertainment. Saint-Saëns darkly, though probably mistakenly, suspected Du Locle of sabotaging the production in order to clear the way for more Verdi and recalled that 'in his sour and derisive voice' Du Locle would refer to Bizet's 'Cochin-China music' and declare that no one would understand it. The Government was in the customary crisis and there were fears that *Carmen*, depicting Spain as a land of brigands, would upset new diplomatic ties between Paris and Madrid.

The première was on 3 March. Saint-Saëns could not be present until a week later, but wrote: 'At last I have seen *Carmen*. I found it marvellous and I am telling you the truth.' 'Those three lines,' replied Bizet, 'signed by a Master, by a man like you, console me immeasurably for the insults of the Comettants and the Lauzières.[1] You have made me proud and happy and I embrace you with all my heart.' At the première the audience had grown colder act by act. Gounod, in his box, though he insincerely flattered Bizet to his face, was heard to claim loudly that melodies of his own had been stolen. 'Take the Spanish airs and mine out of the score and there remains nothing ... but the sauce that flavours the fish.' Galli-Marié as Carmen was a realistic actress and served Bizet well, but the tenor, Paul Lhérie, was undramatic and uncertain in pitch. In later performances d'Indy, who had won a ticket for the première donated by Bizet to Franck's organ class, had to sit behind the scenery at a harmonium to keep Don José in the correct key. At one moment when the seductress was singing pianissimo the bass-drum player mis-counted and hit two thumping blows, which petrified the house. The chorus were rebellious and the women who had to dance, fight and smoke complained of injury and illness. Early in May Bizet met the critic Comettant at the Conservatoire and there was a furious quarrel. Friends found him in an unsettled mood. He complained of deafness in his left ear and his voice was shaky. After an unwise indulgence in river-swimming – a favourite pastime – he fell ill, failed to struggle against his malady and died on 3 June.

Two fellow composers, Giraud and Reyer, both made mention of the strange premonition that had come to Galli-Marié in the card-scene, singing of death, that same evening. Gallet had been working on *Geneviève de Paris* and, meeting Mme Saint-Saëns, asked whether

---

[1] Achille de Lauzières was critic of *La Patrie* and the author of several unpublished operas; he was especially scathing on *Carmen*'s low moral tone. Oscar Comettant was a rival in the 'oriental' field, having written a piece called *Une nuit à Smyrne*.

Bizet had received the latest sections of the poem. Saint-Saëns's mother, in a voice that struck Gallet immediately as odd, kept on repeating that Bizet was ill and begged him not to visit. As she left, Gallet learnt by a signal from his wife that she had brought the news of Bizet's death. Saint-Saëns himself heard it on the staircase at the Madeleine as he was going to take the Evening Office. After a long silence he mounted the steps and went mechanically through the service.[1] He and Bizet had been comrades, almost Dumas's 'musketeers' or *Pearl Fishers* duettists, in their battles with the opera houses. Many years later he contrasted this camaraderie with the professional rivalry that beset his relations with Massenet. Once when he visited Le Vesinet to see Bizet in his country retreat, being unable to remember the number of the house he walked up and down the road singing the aria 'Je crois entendre encore' from *The Pearl Fishers* until he attracted Georges's attention.

He had himself recently experienced the spears of the critics after a concert performance of Act One of *Samson*. There was a smattering of applause from his friends but the audience was unmoved. Henri Cohen of the *Chronique Musicale* wrote, 'Never was there a more complete absence of melody to justify appreciation. Add to this lack of motifs, risky harmonies and orchestration which nowhere raises itself above the most ordinary level.' It was clear that *Samson* would not be the show-piece of the new Palais Garnier.

Fortunately, the constant repetition that he was an 'academic' musician brought a new career as the scholarly editor of eighteenth-century music. It was in 1875 that he was summoned by a Mme Fanny Pelletan to assist her in the huge undertaking of a chronological and annotated edition of Gluck. The *Iphigénies* had been published and *Alceste* was in proof when her first collaborator died in February. Saint-Saëns had early caught the enthusiasm for Gluck from Berlioz. He accepted the task and took over the project when Mme Pelletan died a year later. It occupied him, amid all his other labours, for almost thirty years. He had assistants, but his unfeigned passion for scholarship was given full scope. His future biographer Arthur Dandelot, finding himself as a very young man working on the life of Gounod in the

---

[1] Pierre Lalo recalled that he had just returned from school and was sitting at table when Saint-Saëns burst in, distraught and gasping: 'Bizet is dead.'

Opéra library, recalled that he 'had illustrious neighbours such as Camille Saint-Saëns collating with love the scores of Gluck and Rameau for the model editions of the House of Durand. On a certain day when the Master had just recopied a rough version . . . destroying the original work. . . . I let him leave and then later with care gathered together the torn pieces from the waste-paper basket. Returning home I re-collated them on a white sheet, reconstituting the precious MS completely. It became one of the favourite items in my cherished collection of autographs.' The scraps he collected were Saint-Saëns's notes on the range of eighteenth century flutes!

Before the performance of *Samson* Saint-Saëns had played his G minor Concerto, together with transcriptions of Bach, in Brussels. The success of his appearance had persuaded him to embark on his Fourth Concerto and this he played at the inauguration of Colonne's 'Artistic Association' concerts in October 'To the memory of Georges Bizet'.

The new concerto demonstrated yet another experiment with classical form. Instead of three movements there are two, each subdivided into two sections, so that we have the form of a four-movement symphony in two halves. There are themes common to both, which come in metamorphosised patterns. Daniel Fallon found in an MS a version of the slow movement with an almost illegible date, May 1854, twenty years earlier. He interpreted this as a sketch of a slow introduction to a symphony and, if so, Saint-Saëns would have had a four-movement work in mind when he resuscitated it. The composer branches out into new paths from the start. There is no orchestral introduction as in the Concerto No. 1, no solo piano introductions as in Concertos Nos 2 and 3. Instead, piano and orchestra alternate in phrases, a theme and variations of Protestant sobriety. The same theme in part two is transformed into a galloping Scherzo and is joined to one of Saint-Saëns's outbursts, rare enough, of joyous vulgarity. The last 'folk-song' theme of the Finale, simple but strangely memorable, comes first mysteriously veiled as a chorale. Baumann speaks of Saint-Saëns's 'Biblical and Christian' phase, and asserts that, without even knowing its date, we would place it in the same period as *Samson* and *Le Déluge*. He compares its ordered arrangement of contemplation, turmoil and revelation with Wagner's *Parsifal*, composed in the same year. He discovers Saint-Saëns's equivalent to Beethoven's 'Ode to Joy', with 'the shivering of sacred trumpets' and a 'vivacity unlimited, an idealisation of the City of the Elect'.

A rationalist interpretation could equally be found by hearing the concerto as an expression of the ideas of Ernest Renan and those who desired a regeneration of France based upon a sturdy agrarian society (hence the 'folk-song' in the Finale) and emancipation from romantic and religious notions. Such ideas were strong in the salon of the singer Marie Trélat, which the composer frequented. The concerto moves from static introspection to vigorous popular celebration.

More recently Dr Stegemann has described it as the high point of Saint-Saëns's career in the concerto forms and observes that it signifies a 'perfect union of Classic intellect with the structural freedom of Romanticism'. It is certainly remarkable for the strict control that governs its progress from quietism to celebration, and the piano part from simplicity to vertiginous soarings, which suffuse the last great outbursts of brass.

Bannelier, who had admired the recent quartet, objected to the mixing of styles and described it as 'an orchestral fantasy with solo piano rather than a concerto'. Cohen detected 'aberrations of modern style that M. Saint-Saëns adores, and of which he is one of the high priests'.

The energy and exuberance of the final pages coincided with marriage to Marie-Laure-Emilie Truffot. Until the Saint-Saëns archives are fully explored, and even perhaps after, we are unlikely to know the whole truth of his sexual inclinations. When Jean Bonnerot wrote the first edition of his biography in 1913 the composer was alive, but he made no mention of the marriage and prefaced the volume with a statement, unusual for its day, that it was not 'a psychological study'. Little more was inserted when the second edition was completed in 1922. Saint-Saëns forbade publication of his correspondence without Bonnerot's permission and his secretary lived on until the 1950s. There has thus never been a fully documented life and all is left to conjecture. The assertion that 'the homosexuality of Saint-Saëns was notorious' has crept into some learned volumes.

Accounts of the courtship, when he was almost forty, generally describe his nineteen-year-old fiancée as the 'sister of a pupil', Jean Truffot, to whom he had dedicated his *Caprice on the 'Airs de Ballet' from Alceste*. The date given tentatively by Octave Séré for the writing of this is 1867, at which time Marie would have been only twelve (unless the dedication came later). It is an important piano work, almost the nearest approach to a piano sonata he wrote. Yet at no point is a Jean Truffot mentioned in musical circles and we know from Pauline Viardot that Saint-Saëns was highly selective in his choice of pupils. We do not find Truffot being pushed forward at the Société Nationale, or La Trompette, or any other body. When the marriage ended we hear no more of him at all, either in defence of wife or husband.

In the otherwise very conventional *Life* by Arthur Dandelot, having said that the marriage fell apart after terrible tragedies, and reflected upon the hasty marriages into which many artists enter, he adds the mysterious paragraph: 'Saint-Saëns, in his forties, was bathing at the "School of Natation" Deligny with a friend, when the latter, having known that the musician wished to marry, put forward the claims of his own sister. Some time later, after the acquaintance was made, marriage was agreed and accomplished in the following month.' The Deligny Baths by the Seine, in later times certainly, had a reputation as a homosexual gathering place.[1] Either Saint-Saëns had a strange confidence in the judgement of the young man, who was presumably much nearer nineteen than forty, or (since similar situations are not unknown) he may have forced upon himself a confusion of brother and sister, imagining a similarity of relationship, just as Kornelis confuses the figurine and the real girl in *La Princesse Jaune*.

We know that he was fond of certain women and do not have to go through motions of inventing supposed romances as a smokescreen. He had proposed to Augusta Holmès, he had discussed marriage with Marguerite Baugnies, daughter of a rich and important family. It has been said that her family did not favour a pianist with no private fortune, but this hardly fits with her subsequent weddings to a painter and a sculptor. Saint-Saëns, at the Madeleine, was far from being a penniless Bohemian. It is also said they had worries over his health, which may be a euphemistic way of referring to his homosexuality. Augé de Lassus, who liked to emphasise Saint-Saëns's vitality and humour, tells us that he conceived a passion for the soprano Christine Nilsson, but that when he heard her say that Mozart was 'boring' he

---

[1] Even in his 1935 revision of this story after correspondence with Marie Saint-Saëns, Dandelot still referred to 'frolicking swims'.

speedily disengaged himself. In 1878, after his marriage, we find him writing to Durand about a singer, Mlle Bellocca, heard in Strasbourg, who is 'adorable, ravishing', whom he hopes Pasdeloup will engage. She later sang an aria of Delilah in London. His admiration may have been purely musical but the enchantment sounds genuine enough.

When he went, as a very elderly gentleman, to the San Francisco Exhibition in 1915 John Philip Sousa, the famous bandmaster, recalled that: 'Saint-Saëns and I became the best of friends. We used to wander about the grounds together and he seemed always to have an eye for lovely womankind. Slim beauty seemed to make little impression on him and when one with territorial expansion hove into sight he would nudge me, calling my attention to "yonder beaming beauty!" '. Since no one dissembled his feelings less than Saint-Saëns, one has to assume that his eye for the pretty girls was honestly focused.

There were other women, such as Caroline de Serres, with whom he kept up lifelong friendships. Yet none of these bear the seal of sexual interest. We have stray comments which refer to homosexual relationships: his attending soirées at the home of Count Fersen, a notorious homosexual, where so-called 'ballet roses' involving youths in tableaux were presented; the biography of Augusta Holmès by Gerard Geffen (1987), which says of her rejected suitor that, after leaving his wife, he 'led a long existence as a traveller in the company of a faithful domestic who was perhaps more than that . . .'; a comment by the actor Pierre Bertin in his autobiography that 'Saint-Saëns liked the young men very much'; and his friendship with the accomplished salon musician Reynaldo Hahn, whose homosexuality was undisputed.[1] Many allusions were made during the bitter press skirmishes of World War One, when he sought to have German music banned, and his opponents made reference to his visits to North Africa and his sexual preferences. The correspondence published by Pierre Aguétant, a young poet, which dates from the time when Saint-Saëns was eighty, makes it clear that the old man liked to have young male company, but tells us no more than that. James Harding's biography came out in the 1960s, when the subject was still difficult to broach, but he has made it clear that some of his informants declared Saint-Saëns to be homosexual. More recently Michel Faure makes reference to handsome Arab servants, a familiarity with his manservant Gabriel and a

[1] It was Hahn who said that Saint-Saëns went to North Africa and the Canaries to 'hide a vice to which he never made the least allusion'.

comment by the critic Louis Laloy about a young friend 'who accompanies Saint-Saëns as a shadow'.

The environment in which Saint-Saëns grew up, consisting of the 'two mothers' and containing a real mother of strong personality and religious views, would have been sufficient to deter any early heterosexual adventures. As time went by, Mme Saint-Saëns's opposition to any potential wife in particular, combined with a desire for grandchildren in general, must have engendered frustration. A young English girl, Amina Goodwin, who had won a scholarship to the Conservatoire related in all innocence that Saint-Saëns had invited her to his home and 'would not let me leave until he had introduced me to his dear old mother'. It is more likely that the mother wished to cast a stern eye over any female visitor on the premises. Among the *petite bourgeoisie*, sexuality had often to be repressed by a puritanism which concentrated total activity upon intellectual pursuits to climb the social scale. It is surely significant that the myths of Samson and Hercules, so prominent in his work, deal with the disasters that overtake the heroes when sensuality dominates ambition.

The Romantic composers, who affected his adolescence, were never averse to translating their private emotions into music. Among those he most admired – Schumann, Berlioz and Liszt – biographical confession was an industry. While he retained a classical reserve and put form before feelings, he showed in the works where he had a choice of subject a strong attraction towards themes with homosexual connotations. *Omphale* describes a man of great power, dressed as a female and brought low by desire. The *Danse Macabre* is voluptuous rather than sinister and the embraces of couples far apart in social class is a phenomenon more prevalent in homosexual than heterosexual circles. *The Youth of Hercules* sets out the conflict between pleasure and duty. Duty had to triumph in the nineteenth century, but the portrayal of pleasure veers very definitely to the exotic. While both Massenet and Puccini drew large profits from their operatic portraits of desirable women, two of Saint-Saëns's plots depend upon the attractions of a handsome male: in *Proserpine* the courtesan commits murder for the love of Sabatino and in *Ascanio* the Duchesse d'Etampes is prepared to do the same through a greedy passion for Cellini's young apprentice. In both cases the young men have conventional love affairs against which these unconventional emotions must rage and beat.

Conversely, those who believe that Saint-Saëns had a private life of unruffled normality could argue that when he first visited the Canary Isles incognito and was followed everywhere by suspicious police spies there was no evidence of anything irregular. His visits to Algeria and Egypt were undertaken for genuine reasons of health. Nowhere do we have any indications of an obsessive need for homosexual encounters such as exist in the papers of Tchaikovsky. His grief at the death of his mother suggests domination, but the same may be said of many contemporaries on whom no shadow rests. The dedicated mother was the mainspring of many artistic careers in this time of social mobility.

His marriage took place in February at Le Cateau, a small industrial town in the north of France. This indicates that the mother was not closely involved in the plans and some sort of desire to escape. Yet he brought his bride to live in the family apartment. There was no time for a honeymoon, for there were concerts and his duties at the Madeleine to be fulfilled, and at the close of the year he undertook a concert tour of Russia. In 1935 Dandelot retold the story and placed the encounter at the Deligny Baths at a date when the girl was only eight years old. It was, he said, twelve years later when the request for marriage was addressed (in sufficiently humorous terms) to Marie's father and consent was given, despite the age difference. Dandelot admitted that he had been incorrect in saying that Marie had no musical interests. Saint-Saëns had confidence in her opinions and dedicated the score of *Le Déluge* to her. The rupture did not come immediately after the death of the elder son, but there was a separation which it took three years to complete. Marie, by this time a widow, endorsed his version, though in fact *Le Déluge* remains, as published, one of the few works which have no dedicatee.

The year had been eventful. It also saw the establishing of a contact with the publishing firm of Durand, which acquired sole rights to new compositions and began the process of buying the copyrights of previous publications. The contract stipulated that he was to offer all his works to Durand, who would pay 500 francs per quarter. On 1 April 1880 he was to receive five per cent commission, but was guaranteed 2000 francs per annum for ten years. By 1889, 4000 francs are mentioned in a draft contract.

There were soon two sons to the marriage: André and Jean-François.

Saint-Saëns was writing in a fast and powerful fashion. The popular

'Allegro Appassionato' for cello and piano appeared amid other and larger works. When he returned from much applauded concerts in Moscow and St Petersburg he found in his accumulated mail a notice to say that *Le Timbre d'Argent* was being advertised at the new Théâtre Lyrique for October 1876, a surprise for which he had hardly dared hope. The hard campaigns of recent years appeared to be ending in possibilities of operatic success.

7

Saint-Saëns 'Agonistes'

At the time of *La Princesse Jaune* Saint-Saëns had asked Gallet to compose a poem for him from the sixth chapter of Genesis on the subject of the Flood. With customary speed Gallet brought him a 'Symphonic Drama in three parts'. Before and after a description of the deluge are passages paying homage to the wisdom and power of the Almighty. In part one the orchestra consists of strings and harp, giving a picture of the simplicity of the first days of Man. The Prelude is built upon a theme developed fugally and concludes with the famous violin solo representing hope and redemption. After a chorus which gives utterance to the Divine disgust – 'I will exterminate this race' – contralto and bass announce the Flood and the rescue of Noah through divine foreknowledge. In part two the orchestra is augmented drastically. Horns, trumpets and trombones, (five in all) saxhorns and tubas, gong and timpani depict the steadily rising waves, the lashing of rain and the cries of terror uttered by the engulfed people. Camille Bellaigue, who considered *Le Déluge* superior even to *Samson*, describes the picture: 'It is no longer an orchestra ... it is a waterspout, a cataract. The second part of *Le Déluge* is putting into music the symphonic transcription of Niagara.' Inured as was the audience to organ 'storms' in church, this music in the concert hall was as provocative as the *Rite of Spring*, to which an older Saint-Saëns reacted with such horror.

The classical orchestra returns to accompany the human sentiments of part three where the earth is gradually reborn. Complex harmonies paint the return of light, the birds cross the heavens and the chorus gives the pardon of a relenting God. 'I will no longer curse the Earth; Go Forth and Multiply.' A fugue is the aptest means of obeying this last injunction and the oratorio ends with the Prelude theme given out with full vigour.

The story of the Flood had appealed to the Romantics. Alfred de Vigny, godfather of Augusta Holmès, had treated it. Halévy had left an unfinished opera, *Noë*, which his son-in-law Bizet completed and which was staged in Karlsruhe in 1885. Saint-Saëns's approach is impersonal, framed at the opening and close in the classical fugue form. When he conducted the Prelude he would insist: 'No vibrato! No expression! God is all by himself in Heaven. He is bored!' But there are features imported from the symphonic poems. The curse theme of part one is transformed musically into the theme of forgiveness. The storm arises slowly after an ominous silence broken only by the crackle of woodwind. After part two has modulated through every key there is a final decrescendo and a *ppp* close as the Ark drifts towards a featureless horizon in darkness. The instructions to build the Ark are set in measured workman-like phrases. There is a fine phrase descriptive of Noah opening the window of the Ark. The moment in the Prelude when the full complement of violins move in to support the soloist is a passage of sheer beauty, which Saint-Saëns only once surpassed, in the Adagio of the Third Symphony.

Le Déluge was first given by Colonne on 5 March 1876. Saint-Saëns played Beethoven's 'Fantasia' for piano and chorus in the same programme. There was some opposition to the strident sounds of part two by Cohen of *L'Art Musical*, and *Le Ménestrel* judged it the work of 'a very great musician but a musician led astray'. Sections of the audience, however, responded to the hissing with shouts of applause and calls for an encore. Part two had to be restarted. Octave Mercier made an allusion to the fact that 1876 had been a very bad year for rain and described it as 'torrential'. Another critic compared it to Donizetti's *Il diluvio universale*, which he is unlikely to have heard, and regretted that Saint-Saëns had not matched its 'large and spacious melodies'. The oratorio was given in 1878 by Pasdeloup and in 1879 at a festival organised by the impresario Albert Vizentini, when the violin solo was played by Paul Viardot, son of the singer, but it was not until 1 February 1891 that it was given at the Conservatoire, where, according to Vierne, the relatively small hall could barely withstand the tumults. It thus took almost as long as its partner at birth, *Samson*, to be accepted as a masterpiece. Despite its kinship with the English choral tradition it has never established itself in the 'Land of Oratorio'. The composer found it hard to classify. '"Oratorio in three parts", "Poème Lyrique", "Cantata biblique"?' he asked Durand. '"Oratorio

Biblique" seems to me a kind of pleonasm!' The religious aspect is divorced from the Liturgy unlike the Mass or *Oratorio de Noël* and has an air of Protestantism: biblical, direct between God and the individual; which reminds us that in the salons there were admirers of reformed religions such as Renan, Georges Sand and Taine, unbelievers but ready to accept responsible Christians separated from the more intense Catholic Ultramontanes.

Following his winter tour of Russia, Saint-Saëns set off again in March, passing through Lyon, where for Aimé Gros, conductor and friend, he performed his Third Piano Concerto. He continued to Vienna for further concerts, one devoted entirely to his compositions. On 1 May he wrote to Durand, The '*Danse Macabre* has electrified the public. The violinists will no longer tune their chanterelles (E strings) in anything but E flat.' He returned in April to take part once more in judging the Prix de Rome and, in the Chapel of Versailles, his Motet *Tecum Principium* was given for the benefit of the victims of a genuine flood in the Pas de Calais. On 4 July he came to London. He gave a concert at the Musical Union, founded by John Ellis, who had been a pupil of Thomas Attwood, pupil of Mozart. At the Union the players sat in the middle, which was an excellent means of hearing chamber music. It also pioneered the use of programme notes, which were distributed to subscribers on the previous day. Hermann Klein, later his librettist, went to hear 'the famous organist of the Madeleine'. The only original work was the set of *Beethoven* Variations. The performance he thought brilliant, but not as perfect as the one that was given with Caroline de Serres a few months later. Klein mentioned this discrepancy. 'There was a good reason for the difference,' said Saint-Saëns chivalrously. 'With one lady there had been no opportunity to rehearse; with the other I had already played the duet at a dozen concerts in France.' On 6 July he joined his old Conservatoire friend Edward Marlois in the two-piano *Marche Héroïque*.

In May 1876, Léonce Detroyat, a former director of *La Liberté*, whose wife had known the composer in childhood, founded a new periodical, *Le Bon Sens*, and gave Victorien Joncières the task of music critic. Joncières did not please the public and, in June, Saint-Saëns was appointed in his place. *Le Journal de Musique* hailed this second venture into journalism – 'There are few writers in the field of music who know the first thing about it; we are happy to have one more among those who know whereof they speak' – and detected signs of apprenticeship to Berlioz in the art. He seized the opportunity to diminish the attractions of Italian opera. Reviewing *La Favorita* of Donizetti, he welcomed the opportunity to hear the beautiful voice of Mlle Rosina Bloch, 'condemned' to the role of Leonora, but observed that she interpreted it with a boredom which was 'both profound and excusable'. In the same article (26.6.76) he referred to the symphony, 'born on the other side of the Rhine' and 'shown forth in all its glory at the concerts of the Conservatoire, whose hall became the Sinai of a new religion'. The time had arrived when France should no longer 'push into the limelight . . . the masterpiece of the foreigner' . . . 'She must force herself to produce them and impose them on the world – to create a new art responding to the new aspirations of the public and the incontrovertible progress of French music.' This new wave he compared with the literary movement of the 1830s and he declared it an irresistible force.

Le Bon Sens merged with another journal, *L'Estafette*, with Detroyat as Director, and it was under this title that most of his articles appeared. He was witty and provocative. He reviewed a revival of *Der Freischütz* and parodied a scene in which some new composer took the work along to the Director of the Paris Opéra. 'How the devil can you hope that a French audience could understand this tale of the dark huntsman, the casting of magic bullets, all this bric-à-brac from across the Rhine? . . . All these badly dressed peasants will not make a colourful spectacle. We have to have fine materials, weavings of silk and velvet. We must have fine processions, ballets, opportunities for the electric lighting.' As for the Wolf's Glen, 'I have thunder produced by sheet metal, wind machines, lightning and real water. I don't need your music for all that.'

He could dispense criticism as wounding as any he received. A tenor was given low marks for his ponderous delivery which, 'despite the desperate beatings of the excellent conductor, M. Deldevez, went at a pace slow enough to irritate the nerves of even the calmest and sweetest of musicians'. He reflected upon a recent choir festival at Dieppe. He enjoyed the brass bands, fanfares and singing in the streets, and opposed the attitudes of the elderly who condemn the young to nights of silence in public places, while they play cards. 'Youth has need of pleasure, movement, turbulence even; condemned to silence it atrophies, physically and morally. . . . These festivals are excellent things, often involving hard work, an enriching of heart and spirit, and they make vibrate chords in the soul which would otherwise be silent. If all this disturbs M. Prudhomme and his wife – if songs ring out at 2 a.m., that is no great evil.' He is, of course, critical of the quality of the music provided for these 'Orphéons' and believed it a duty to write for them. His own competition pieces contained challenging entries, unisons and counterpoint. His *Soldiers of Gideon* of this time, words by Gallet and an offshoot of his Old Testament readings, even had some political significance for the efforts of the Republicans against the right-wing President Macmahon. Saint-Saëns was closely identified with the Republic, which gradually loaded him with honours, and he sees the troops of Gideon as marchers towards the Promised Land, much as its supporters were endeavouring to establish the Republic firmly. 'Let us march. The hour is nigh. Our sudden attack will for ever break our chains!'

Ambroise Thomas had been expected at Dieppe, but his failure to attend a performance of *Mignon* had given some offence. 'People who have never directed a Conservatoire', said Saint-Saëns, 'do not understand that the composer of *Hamlet* may sometimes be forced to remain in Paris to preside over examinations and competitions where his presence is indispensable.' He was equally generous about Massenet and the news of a new commission from the Opéra: 'Day is dawning at the Académie Nationale de Musique.' He hears Galli-Marié in *Mignon* and considers the decline in ornamentation in singing: 'It was the fashion in the heyday of the Italians to express even the most tragic sentiments in trills, arpeggios and scales; it is the fashion at present to cry the abomination of desolation at the tiniest vocal ornament. These exaggerations have no *raison d'être* . . . all forms are good when they are employed suitably. Art is mocked by absolute rules and empirical systems.' Finally he recounts that he was somewhat nervously cajoled into judging an Art Exhibition but he 'reflected that over a long period, painters and sculptors were not uncomfortable about judging musicians and sentencing them to deportation in the least musical city in the world' – so his scruples vanished.

He attended another festival in honour of Rameau at Dijon in August and took part in recitals with the flautist Taffanel. This visit was a prelude to an important assignment at Bayreuth, where Wagner was presenting *The Ring*. He was able to send *L'Estafette* seven comprehensive articles between 19 and 25 August. They were later

edited for the volume *Harmonie et Mélodie* and show the admiration he
had for Wagner the musician, even though he had been outraged –
and remained so into his last years – by Wagner's crude literary attack
on the French, 'A Capitulation', in which Wagner had gloated over
French humiliations in 1870–1. Many were surprised that Saint-Saëns
was not an uncritical supporter since he had so often been branded
with 'music of the future'. His survey of *The Ring* remains a classic
appraisal, although he could not resist touches of humour at its
absurdities.

He begins by accepting that Wagner is rarely written about with
objectivity and that he detests France, though that does not affect the
merits of his music. French writers 'who have covered him with gross
insults for fifteen years find him ungrateful and perhaps they are right,
for nothing has done more for his fame than these incessant attacks'.
He points out that the poem of *The Ring* had been completed in 1863
and had no relevance to recent warfare. The study of Wagner's music
had long been one of his chief delights and the pleasure of the
Bayreuth productions had left an impression which no discussion of
theories could efface. But there is music other than Wagner's. The
idolaters, such as Mendés, Judith Gautier and their circle, make
themselves ridiculous by refusing to accept any genius save the one
they revere.

> Neither Handel, Mozart nor Mendelssohn has written a bearable
> note. The French School, The Italian School, have never existed.
> At the hearing of all music other than Wagner, the visage of the
> Wagnerian expresses profound disdain, but it does not matter
> which product of the Master, be it the ballet from *Rienzi*, it plunges
> into a state of exultation difficult to describe. . . . They would
> immolate themselves with joy on the altar of their idol, if the
> fantasy of demanding human sacrifice had occurred to him.

He recounts how a female admirer, a 'writer of great talent and
imagination' swooned at the 'extraordinary and incredible' chord she
had heard in the score of *Siegfried* and which she forced the weary
Master to repeat on the piano though he assured her it was a simple
chord of E minor that she could easily play for herself. Such worship
had its counterpart in the fury of the anti-Wagnerian, who turned

purple and forced Saint-Saëns to break off after a few bars of the major chords that begin the entry of the gods into Valhalla.

He applauds Wagner for realising his dream of a purpose-built theatre in a choice location. The idea, he thought, arose more naturally in Bavaria, where theatrical presentations out of the ordinary were a tradition. He cites Oberammergau, where a specially constructed theatre presents its offering from 8 a.m. to 5 p.m. and 'the interminable piece which could be intolerable in a closed hall is followed without undue fatigue'. Given the dedication of the cast, the commitment of the audience and the backcloth of Bavarian scenery, he finds nothing unusual in the four nights *The Ring* takes to unfold.

Wagner achieves his effects and avoids monotony by doubling the number of instruments and adding the battery of brass against which the singers could hardly contend if the 'symphony' were not contained in its submerged pit. When the sunlight strikes the gold beneath the Rhine amid 'cascades of sound' it seemed to Saint-Saëns that the combination of scenic effect and music 'defied description'. He admired all the stage effects, though he thought Valhalla, home of the gods, 'funereal' and reminiscent of 'the cemetery of Père Lachaise'. He 'found it hard not to smile' at Alberich's transformation into a snake and, rightly, judged him an imbecile for turning himself into a toad capable of being crushed underfoot. Describing the subtle as well as the thunderous ways in which Wagner used the orchestra as 'a rich carpet on which the personages of the drama walk', he defends him against critics who regard him as noisy. Many 'light' operas made much more noise, 'where the big drums and cymbals are beaten without pause, where trombones and cornets seethe with fury, and where singers, in spite of desperate cries, can only make themselves heard intermittently . . .' It is certain that the flimsiest operetta makes more noise than *Rhinegold*. In the first act of *The Valkyrie* the strings are used with tenderness and the scene is full of peaceful reticence. Yet these pages have been penned by someone described as 'the man of noise, the horse-breaker of ferocious instruments'. He relishes passages when the characters are silent but the orchestra speaks for them. Yet he could appreciate the orchestra in full flood. Of the 'Ride of the Valkyries' he writes, 'Who has not heard it does not know what power music can reach.'

The praise which he bestows on the *Ring* cycle makes it strange that he should both have disappointed Wagner's devotees in Paris and

stored up unpopularity in Germany itself. The parting of Wotan and
Brünnhilde, he declares, 'has an Aeschylean grandeur', *The Valkyrie*
ends on a tableau which 'is a feast for eyes and ears', *Siegfried* could not
have been written without the abandoning of all the old operatic
clichés. One has to hear the first act of *Siegfried* to understand how a
composer can infuse such interest into long conversations between
two characters. He was aware that a break occurred in the composition
while the composer created *Tristan* and *The Mastersingers* and, from
the third act of *Siegfried*, he begins to be bewildered by the strangeness
of the harmony, the 'fatiguing' complications of the score and the less
restrained use of the immense orchestral resources. He found much to
admire in the awakening of Brünnhilde, but thought the final duet too
static and too confused in its use of several themes, so that the ear did
not know which one to follow.

After the reservations over *Siegfried* he found *The Twilight of the
Gods* magnificent. 'One is dominated by the situations of the drama,
swept along by the whirlwind of modulations, incoherent in appearance, which do not leave a moment of repose and make you lose a
sense of time by a kind of magnetic effect.' He cannot give any idea of
equivalent music, for it resembles no other. The final act has an
immensity that seems almost supernatural. His phrase 'like the chain
of the Alps viewed from the summit of Mont Blanc' was a noble
tribute.

After giving space to an account of the performers – the tenors were
inferior singers to those at the Paris Opéra but better actors – he
describes the staging. The absence of footlights means that there is
not much coming forward from the depths of the stage; the lack of a
box means that prompters have to lurk in the wings or behind pieces
of scenery. There is much steam used on-stage, billowing forth and
adding to scenic illusions. He found Wagner's comments, in a speech
where he said in substance, 'France has an art, Italy has an art; if you
support my efforts, Germany will have an art', less offensive than some
critics'. 'For a long time his admirers have known that his tactlessness
equals his talent.' Detaching himself from extremes he concluded:
'Wagnermania is an excusable absurdity; Wagnerphobia is a malady.'

He returned to Paris and used a review of Meyerbeer's *Le Prophète*
to defend '*musique savante*' as against 'melody and inspiration'. He
began by quoting an anonymous review of the opera on its first
appearance in 1849. No doubt it gave him pleasure to remind the

critics of how they had wrongly castigated a revered masterpiece: 'musical marquetry, a mosaic without colours, a garden without flowers . . . a practical course in musical theology without true faith, etc.' He recalled Pauline Viardot in the role of Fidès and her portrayal of 'burning maternal passion . . . this maternal love more fierce than the flames of Eros himself'. He pointed out that many great moments in music have nothing to do with 'melody' in its conventional sense.

He had a keen eye for the mistakes of producers. When the prophet, John of Leyden, called upon his followers to rally round him there was no one nearby on stage. He appeared to be addressing members of the orchestra, 'which lends itself to hilarity'. He wishes that the Opéra would follow the example of the Théâtre Français, where the great players often take small parts, if the occasion demands. One inexperienced singer in a Meyerbeer ensemble can ruin the whole effect.

He was equally combative in his article on 2 October, which expressed his hostility to the idolising of Bellini and Italian opera. By contrast, the fate of French composers was less enviable. 'There has been for some years a wall of ice between the public and musicians of the young school.' His views brought him into argument with other critics. A Jules Ruelle in *L'Art Musical* declared that Saint-Saëns was peevish and hinted that *Le Timbre d'Argent* might suffer the caustic comments that were being dispensed to other works. Later in October, Saint-Saëns mentioned that the overture to Adam's *Giralda* had been wildly applauded though it consisted of a mazurka theme repeated twelve times and such music could be heard more easily in cafés. He thought that it had a Spanish flavour 'only to the extent that Schumann in his "Spanish Lieder" had made an Andalusia of Leipzig'! Yet he could be generous and was delighted to see revived *Les Charmeurs* by Ferdinand Poise, his old rival in the Prix de Rome.[1] He paid a warm tribute to a recently deceased fellow organist, Edouard Batiste of St Eustache.

Verdi's *Force of Destiny* had just suffered a cold reception, but 'no matter how dead Italian operas appear to be, they are always capable of being resuscitated'. He would have much preferred to see Arrigo Boito's *Mefistofele*. There was praise for Pasdeloup following the loudly

---

[1] Also in a letter: 'Give my compliments to Poise on his success. He is an old comrade of mine, I will always be happy to see him succeed.' From Weimar, November 1877.

hissed 'Siegfried's Funeral March' with Berlioz's 'Royal Hunt and
Storm'. Drawing on long acquaintance with the great French
musicians he was able to recall that Berlioz had not allowed the 'Royal
Hunt' to be played in concert form, not even as an entr'acte, without
the appropriate staging.

The arguments with M. Ruelle intensified. He was attacked in *L'Art
Musical* for pronouncing a funeral oration on the Italian School and
described as having a wish to tear pieces apart like a cat putting out its
claws. *L'Estafette*, it was said, allowed him to indulge his terrible hates
too freely. Ironically, Ruelle accuses him of modernism in terms that
he would cheerfully have applied to Debussy thirty years later –
'tiresome harmonic discoveries', 'dissonances sought out with great
difficulty', 'chromaticism sufficient to induce sea-sickness', 'cadences
continually avoided'. Ruelle scorned the notion that these things
marked 'progress'.

> You, M. Saint-Saëns, are the revered pontiff of young French
> chromaticism. Not only do you soar in the Empyrean beside the
> God, Wagner, but you keep your feet on the ground by means of a
> journal where you are allowed to sing the praises of your friends and
> publishers. Ah well! The bourgeois will judge you one of these days.
> It will listen to the work so long awaited, *Le Timbre d'Argent* . . .
> Take care that the public still unconverted to your Wagner idolatry
> does not prove too hard to please.

Saint-Saëns replied a few days later, expressing surprise at the anger
unleashed upon 'his humble personality' and protested that he had
always fought for French music. He realised that all came down to a
quarrel over the admirers of 'melody' who found it only in Italian
works. From the point of view of posterity it was unfortunate that he
chose the same moment to point criticisms at Verdi's *Requiem*,
recently heard in the unlikely venue of the Opéra Comique and its
'atrocious modulations and inextricable fugues'.[1] He also made an
early use of the word 'impressionism', saying that critics had a duty to
assess all aspects of a work 'if they did not wish to see Music fall into
anarchy and impressionism'.

---

[1] When in Weimar at the end of 1877 he wrote to Durand, 'I have just
heard the Symphony of Brahms. It is a hotchpotch!'

In the *Timbre d'Argent* he had given a hostage to fortune and fellow critics, even before its appearance, were dipping their pens in vitriol. Octave Mirbeau said that he 'dared to hope that its reception by the public would be such that no impresario would again entertain hopes of putting on a composer so notoriously unpopular and so incontestably lacking in talent as M. Saint-Saëns, and that the latter would not have the audacity to present himself, score in hand, in the face of the hoots and whistles of the public'. Four days later, in the journal *L'Ordre*, Mirbeau gave a whole column to the destruction of Saint-Saëns, describing him as 'a grotesque dwarf, whose sole wish is to display his mediocrity in broad daylight.... All the insults this powerless, malevolent character has thrown on everything we respect will be thrown back in his face. So much the better; it will be his chastisement and our vengeance.'

Before this could be done Saint-Saëns, in curious circumstances, had resigned from *L'Estafette*. The occasion was the long-awaited première of the opera *Paul et Virginie* by Victor Massé at the Théâtre Lyrique. The incident was related by Durand in a note which found its way into the files of the Bibliothèque Nationale. Saint-Saëns had taken Durand with him and was chatting with Auguste Vaucorbeil, Director of the Opéra, in the foyer, when Detroyat boomed at him from the top of a staircase, 'I hope that you are going to slam this in no uncertain fashion. Instead of a box for six people on the first floor, these folk have given me one for four people on the second floor. The music of Massé has nothing to do with it. Agreed! But if you do not write an article on these lines I will have you replaced.' Saint-Saens, who was not enthusiastic about Massé's music, but wished to praise the piece in order to save the Théâtre Lyrique for his own *Timbre d'Argent*, sent in his resignation. Detroyat then had to write the review himself, which he did under the transparent pseudonym 'Léonce de Tortay'. As the dispute had been heard by others he could not make himself ridiculous by castigating *Paul et Virginie*, so he restricted himself to praising the libretto with vague compliments about the music 'which has been widely praised by experts'.

Before leaving 1876 it may be noted that a cloud appears to have passed over relations with the Viardot family. Pauline resigned membership of the Société Nationale in November. In September Fauré had written to Marianne Viardot, expressing a hope that the quarrel had been sorted out and Saint-Saëns should not feel

misgivings about the affection of Pauline towards him. Fauré's Violin
Sonata was given its première in January 1877. It had been dedicated
to Paul Viardot. Fauré wrote to his patrons, the Clercs, that it had had
a greater success than he could ever have hoped for and that he had
heard Saint-Saëns lament that 'he felt the sadness that mothers feel
when they see that their children are too mature to need them any
longer'. Saint-Saëns could not be accused of failing to place his
services at the disposal of colleagues. In January he gave the première
of Chabrier's Impromptu in C (dedicated to Mme Edouard Manet),
one of the first works to show Chabrier's rhythmic skills and
imagination. In April we find him returning to Fauré, praising the
Violin Sonata and its composer's 'profound musical technique', 'rich
abundance of melody' and 'unconscious naïveté, which is irresistible'.
He had introduced Fauré to Louis Gallet, since the Viardots thought
that he should attempt an opera. Some years later, when Fauré heard
that Messager had seen his *Requiem* in MS, he wrote to Marguerite
Baugnies, 'Tell Messager that showing him my new compositions
makes me tremble; that creature terrifies me more than Saint-Saëns
does.' Fauré had fallen heavily in love with Marianne Viardot. As a
pensionnaire far from home since childhood, he was constantly
searching for a female figure in which there were maternal elements, a
role which Marianne felt unable to sustain. The year was thus one of
emotional storms and it was to console a rejected Fauré that Saint-
Saëns took him to Weimar in December 1877 to meet Liszt and hear
Samson and Delilah.

The new year was an important one in Saint-Saëns's career. *Le
Timbre d'Argent* reached the stage of the Théâtre Lyrique in February.
The premiére of *Samson* in December coincided with the birth of a
second son, Jean-François, and the gift of a munificent legacy. The
fourth, and last, of his symphonic poems, *La Jeunesse d'Hercule*, was
played on 13 January by Colonne. It never achieved the popularity of
the earlier poems and lacks their unified structures. The subject is
closer to those favoured by Liszt, with philosophical implications. It is
the only one of the four to finish with a triumphant Finale but, with its
sections and sub-sections, it lacks the driving energy which impels its
companion pieces. He prefaced the score with an explanation: 'the
story recalls how Hercules at the beginning of his life had two routes
open to him: that of pleasure and that of virtue. Insensible to the
seductions of the nymphs and bacchantes, the hero enters upon the

path of struggles, at the end of which he glimpses the reward of immortality through the flames of the funeral pyre.[1] Liszt's *Tasso* had used the symphonic poem to portray a tussle between Virtue and Pleasure. Pleasure for Saint-Saëns was portrayed by the sinful sounds of a Bacchanale and this is a milder version of the more powerful and oriental one composed for *Samson*.

He was fond of *La Jeunesse*, which he included in programmes when demand for the *Danse Macabre* waned. Dedicated to Duprato, it was not received with enthusiasm. The critics thought that states of mind were not suitable subjects for musical treatment. Among his biographers, Servières thought 'the virtue of Hercules does not run into grave dangers'. Jean Montargis pointed out that the initial Andante Sostenuto hovers between two tonalities, indicative of the indecision of the hero. Watson Lyle made the interesting comment that the 9:8 rhythm of Pleasure was 'fancifully suggestive of beckoning hands'. Baumann considered that the use of kettledrums at the start signalled a thirst for action and that the tranquillity of the Hercules theme as first announced was that of the strong, silent hero; its vigorous suffix, which has some affinity with the Second Symphony, showing him flexing his muscles. He thought that the first appearance of the Bacchanale had a note of triumph, showing him young and successful even in pleasure, admired the 'fanfares which introduce the grand version of the Hercules theme at the close' and the 'dolorous roaring of the trombones', which depict the dissolution of the hero's earthly remains while his essence is wafted above.

Although *La Jeunesse* is not as compact and incisive as the other poems, it is splendid to listen to and full of effects drawn from the large orchestra required, cornets added to trumpets, a 'petit bugle' in B flat, three trombones and tuba, tambourine, triangle and bass drum added to the percussion. Its failure, or its own message of submission to the eternal laws, appears to have caused Saint-Saëns to draw a line under this phase of his composing career and no more symphonic poems followed.

Late in February the Théâtre Lyrique put on *Le Timbre*. The première had been fixed for 15 January, but had to be postponed as the orchestra needed extra rehearsals. The Minister of Fine Arts had promised a subvention to Director Vizentini, but there had been many

[1] The 'choice' is related by Socrates in Xenophon's *Memorabilia*.

delays and it was not certain that the money would ever be paid. Gounod attended the first night, following the work from a score, and heard a neighbour say to his lady, 'There is a person who likes everyone to know he can read music.' He subsequently wrote to Saint-Saëns, 'I sing "Demandez à l'oiseau" and encore myself.' The critical reception was diverse. Its Wagnerian moments, the combination of all the 'seduction' themes in the final struggle for Conrad's soul, the transformation of the theme of fortune into that of death, and the symphonic episodes required for the appearances of the dancer–*villainaisse* angered the anti-Wagnerians. The Wagnerians complained of desertion from their ranks and saw in *Le Timbre* an eclectic opera in the nineteenth-century tradition. After eighteen performances (a better showing than the four prophesied by Saint-Saëns's enemies), it disappeared from the hoardings. According to Bonnerot (and hence one assumes Saint-Saëns's memory) Vizentini realised too late what a success he could have enjoyed if he had had the confidence to give the opera more support, for the union of opera and ballet would have had a spectacular appeal. Vizentini became, in time, an admirer and said that if ever he were Director of the Opéra Comique he would revive *Le Timbre*. It was given at Brussels in 1879 and at Monte Carlo in 1907. Just prior to the First World War the grand opera score was rediscovered and performed, but by then tastes had altered and it seemed dated. Although it has been consigned to oblivion, it was created during the same years as the undisputedly great *Samson* and its themes, deriding the mad search for riches and the return to a 'Green' past, are contemporary. A splendidly mounted revival must remain a mirage, but a mirage delectable to contemplate.[1]

January had brought another attempt to establish the Third Piano Concerto. It was given at the Conservatoire by its dedicatee, Elie-Myriam Delaborde. It received a cold review in *Le Ménestrel*, which foretold the death of the concerto and the inferiority of the genre to even the 'lowliest symphony.... M. Saint-Saëns did not hit upon ideas that could rescue him from his musical audacities. The Société des Concerts made a mistake in accepting it and would do better to remain classical and leave these experiments to Pasdeloup or Colonne.'

[1] Servières recalled seeing *Le Timbre d'Argent* and reflected that Bizet, who made the piano version, probably gathered some inspiration for a bolder form of *opéra comique*, more dramatic than the insipid examples of his time.

In April, Saint-Saëns was in Lyons after giving successful concerts in Geneva. He wrote to Durand, telling him where to collect and send on the special iron castanets required for a concert performance of *Dalila*. The Director of the Grand Théâtre of Lyons, Aimé Gros, commissioned a new project. Gros began his career as a violinist, attended the Conservatoire in the 1850s and astonishingly once obtained First Prize in the class which contained Sarasate and White. All three were friends and were christened 'the Three Chanterelles'. After the war, Gros had come to Lyons and worked hard to establish symphonic concerts, appealing to old friends, now celebrities, to come and play. Appointed as Director he immediately offered to put on an opera by Saint-Saëns, mentioning that his corps de ballet was so numerous and well-trained that a Grand Divertissement would raise no qualms.

The composer was at this time anxious to produce a series of stage works on the history of France. This may have been inspired by the historical legends that Victor Hugo had produced, or because 1877 witnessed yet another political crisis, which threatened the collapse of the Republic. In May, President Macmahon sent Prime Minister Jules Simon a letter stressing disagreement over the Press Laws and the activities of Municipal Councils. (This last question may seem pedestrian to us, but was close to the subject of this next opera.) Simon resigned and his successor, the Duc de Broglie, represented a long association with the Monarchist–Orléanist Right. The Left was meanwhile growing stronger under the leadership of Gambetta. On the extreme Left, journalists like Henri Rochefort sent manifestos from exile, in efforts to inflame the populace. 'Move from words to deeds; from the ballot-box to the barricades.' Macmahon and the Senate voted for the dissolution of the Chamber of Deputies. The elections which followed were a battle in which the Government won extra seats, but still faced a strong anti-monarchical Republican majority. Attempts were made to unseat various left-wing deputies, but many were subsequently returned. Paris was in turbulent mood and street demagogues were much in evidence. We can understand, therefore, that the story of Etienne Marcel, fourteenth-century Provost of Paris and leader of a municipal revolt, had great topicality. Since 1872 the reconstruction of the Hôtel de Ville, burnt down under the Commune, had focused attention on civic history. Etienne Marcel, hitherto a figure known mainly to scholars, became a hero of the struggles of the bourgeois corporations against the powers of the Valois kings. Gallet and Saint-Saëns selected the episode as the first in the series of historical dramas. Gallet had no difficulty in constructing a plot out of Froissart and the history books. He added a conventional love story matching Beatrix, daughter of Etienne, with Robert de Loris, squire to the Dauphin.

Saint-Saëns's incessant travelling, often ascribed to the separation from his wife or the death of his mother, was evident long before either of these tragedies. Prior to the long awaited production of *Samson* at Weimar he undertook a tour which carried him to Leipzig, Warsaw, Dresden, Berlin, Schwerin and Breslau. The chorus and orchestra parts of *Etienne Marcel* were written out during his travels. At Leipzig he played his Fourth Concerto, together with Bach transcriptions and the demanding Liszt arrangement of the *Danse Macabre*. He reported to Durand that sixty-five pupils of the Conservatoire there had signed an Address thanking him for the pleasure he had given. At Warsaw his concert was attended by the Governor of Poland and an organ recital attracted a large audience. He hoped to include Warsaw in future tours. Rehearsals for *Samson* were now in full spate and he refused other engagements: 'I no longer move from Weimar and therefore can't go to Stuttgart for the moment. I am playing at Leipzig only because of its extreme proximity. Dalila before everything!'

Liszt had first proposed the singer Marianne Brandt as Delilah and recommended her to the Grand Duke as 'the German Viardot'. 'She is described as ugly,' he wrote to the Princess Sayn-Wittgenstein. 'I find her very beautiful in the theatre.' The role went in the end to a relatively new singer, Mlle von Müller. The fact that she had sung the roles of Senta and Pamina suggests a soprano, but she had a very expressive middle register. In a letter long afterwards to M. Henri Collet, author of a monograph on *Samson*, Saint-Saëns described the tenor, baritone and orchestra as excellent and the '*chanteuse*' as adequate – he was still thinking of Mme Viardot in the part. He was less pleased with the chorus and later told Reynaldo Hahn that he was horrified at the volume and persistence with which they sang out of tune. The first performance had to be postponed to 2 December ('*Horresco referens*,' wrote Saint-Saëns to Durand, for this was the date of Louis Napoleon's *coup d'état*). It was attended by the Grand Duke, his family and the Court. Saint-Saëns had brought Fauré, his friend Romain Bussine, Durand, Armand Gouzien, Director of the *Journal de Musique* and Charles Tardieu, a critic from Belgium. These were the only Frenchmen present and the opera owed its appearance in the list of great stage works entirely to its German admirers. Lassen conducted badly at the start, having begun to celebrate too soon. One grievous error restored sobriety and the performance went forward in triumph. There were vociferous curtain calls after the second act and the composer was dragged from his box to acknowledge the cheers. After the third act there were renewed calls, crowns were offered to him by the orchestra and 'The Ladies of Weimar'. The Grand Duke congratulated him at length. A private supper at the hotel where the French party were staying rounded off the evening and Saint-Saëns proposed the toast 'To the Master that one cannot forget at Weimar, the dear Abbé Liszt'.

The Paris press gave the event little attention. The *Gazette Musicale* republished the report which Tardieu had sent to the *Independant Belge* in which he defended Saint-Saëns from accusations of having slavishly imitated Wagner. The same idea was expressed by von Bülow, who wrote after subsequent Hamburg performances, 'Saint-Saëns is the only contemporary musician who has not let himself be led astray by Wagnerian doctrine, but who has drawn from it salutary teaching.' It seemed that the road to the Paris Opéra lay open; yet for fifteen years the piece had to wander from city to city before it reached this destination.

It was Liszt's promise that the score would be played, whatever it might be, that saved *Samson* from all the cuts and changes that afflicted other operas. It evolved as a unified work of art, the central act embodying the essential theme, and the first and third framing it in a political and religious context. Whether the work is oratorio or opera is irrelevant. Handel tended to treat oratorio dramatically and opera discursively, using a musical language common to both. Mendelssohn's *Elijah* has been staged on occasion and many oratorios have contained passages that can be visualised in terms of costumes and scenery. It was Saint-Saëns's imagination which saw in the Old Testament the kernel of a narrative as powerful as those provided by the classical writers. In a letter to Mme Charles Tardieu of 1882, Liszt accepted that *Samson* had humanised oratorio with undoubted success. 'Amorous scenes introduced to the theatre in biblical subjects offend me, save in the *Dalila* of our admirable and gallant friend Saint-Saëns, who has made a superb love duet perfectly suited for Delilah and Samson to entangle amorously, while in the *Marie Magdaleine* and *Hérodiade* of Massenet the thing is just theatrical convention.' Saint-Saëns presents the love duet as something elemental, an expression of a feeling which comes from beyond the boundaries of the plot. He was 'Wagnerian' in the sense that he allowed the primary emotions as much force as the 'New Music' could express. It is these external factors which give the opera much of its impact. Even in the most rapturous love duets of Puccini we do not feel that the fate of nations is involved, or a glowering Almighty is judging events. Yet Saint-Saëns involves the gods without Wagnerian monologues and with a much more economic use of musical effects. 'The anguish of Samson, the pleas of Delilah, the effusions and avowals of the two lovers up to their supreme struggle beneath the growlings of the tempest,' wrote Paul Dukas. 'Each of the phases of this scene of love and treason is rendered with an incomparable musical power.'

There is homage paid to the Greek ideal of dramatic unity. The Old Testament story is an extraordinary mishmash of adventures, riddles and deceptions. In the opera we can believe that little time elapses between Samson leading the Hebrew uprising and his downfall at the hands of the temptress. Where a passage of time has to be indicated, as Samson groans in servitude, heavy chords depict the slow revolving of the treadmill. The simple design does, however, support a vegetation dense with elements: the majesty of sacred texts, the conflict between priest-ridden warrior overlords and the toiling agrarian classes whose solidarity is shown in the more traditional forms of plainchant and fugue, a mingling of sexuality deliberately associated with orientalism.

The Prelude is linked immediately to Israelite lamentations. The violas suggest an unseen procession of mourners. The voices express themselves in groans and sobs, while the orchestra carries the continuous flow. When the orchestra reminds the Hebrews of their plight they break into a measured fugue and here also the form matches the emotion. The fugue, with its regular repetitions, emphasises recurring griefs, while in its muscularity and construction it hints at energies that lie dormant. The first great burst of melody comes when Samson (who symbolically emerges from the chorus rather than making a grand entrance) preaches the invincibility of

Jehovah. Sweeping harps accompany his lyric outburst; Saint-Saëns enjoyed using harps whenever possible, but here they remind us of the Psalms and the Harp of David. The arrival of the Philistine, Abimelech, to quell the riot caused the composer one of his rare mental blockages. He had to work at the scene grimly. He was staying with friends at the time and one day, very absorbed at the breakfast table, he confessed he was having great trouble 'getting into the skin of Abimelech'. This seems to have been taken literally by the children of the house and every morning he was expected to appear in Abimelech's skin. In the end he decided upon exaggerated stiffness as in a frieze of Assyrian soldiers. The horns and the rare ophicleides in unison with the voice give a picture of a rigid sacerdotal despotism, unfeeling and wooden. The little dance-like replies and light cymbal taps suggest off-stage mocking retainers and a corrupt regime. The raging of the High Priest when Abimelech is slain contains no great thematic materials, for the Philistines must not be shown to have unconquerable strength. Strength is to be found in the hymn by which the old men of Israel welcome the dawn, which symbolises liberation. Saint-Saëns's interest in the Orient serves to create a feeling of timeless, monotonous chanting, exclusively male, but also humble and resigned.

This in turn melts into the entry of the Philistine priestesses. The female chorus was a quintessential feature of the late nineteenth century. Here it is dramatically in place; the weaving designs of strings and flute paint the garlands and draperies that float about the girls. The 'New Music' of the School of Liszt and Wagner here serves the cause of Dagon rather than Jehovah, and the trio of Delilah, Samson and the Old Hebrew introduces a new type of chromatic melody in which conflicting voices are divided, as against the unity which characterised the Hebrew chanting. The Dance of the Priestesses is no mere foretaste of the Bacchanale. Lightly scored, it has a pointed archness akin to the music of Omphale and emphasises that the seduction of Samson is as yet at a tentative stage – shimmering veils, poses and glances. In similarly pictorial fashion Delilah's first long aria, slow and carefully moulded, has about it a feeling of incantation, a temple procedure where the female icon moves slowly through ritual observances.

In the second act, although outwardly the scale of the action is reduced, the dimensions of the drama are greatly increased. First the echoes of the distant storm indicate an Old Testament God watching from afar; the solo of Delilah summoning Love to her aid suggests that she, too, has allies watching from deep subconscious regions. We learn that she is motivated by hate rather than love and her solo has no feeling of femininity. The scene between the High Priest and Delilah is rescued from convention by a restlessness which belittles the protagonists, compared with the mighty duet that is to follow. When the High Priest, in recitative, recalls the recent victories of Samson, syncopated strings portray the palpitations of his anger, the double-basses expose the roughness of his thoughts. Delilah is brought to the summit of her will to avenge her people, by bass clarinets and contra-bassoons, which depict lurking evil. Yet, although recognition must be given to the role of the orchestra as commentator upon the action, as in Wagner, theatre music is to Saint-Saëns above all vocal music. Throughout this act the drama unfolds in the vocal lines, which become ever more expressive and impassioned until in the final moments of the lovers' tussle the orchestra is unleashed to maximum effect because of its long submission. When Samson enters, his hesitancy is made apparent; Divine wrath rumbles in the timpani though the storm is still far off. The early stages of the duet may seem simply an alternation of religious motifs (him) and seductive motifs (her). What is cunning, however, is that Samson's motifs cover a narrower range than his triumphant verses in Act One, while Delilah invents new motifs such as 'a god more powerful than yours' on which the clarinet lingers and ultimately the irresistible 'Softly awakes'. The contest is thus between responses that lack conviction and those freshly minted by a vivid imagination. At the end the return of the Abimelech theme, cold and metallic, announces the victory of the priest-led warrior caste.

In the third act a brief episode in the action has to be transformed into a third of the opera. There was little in operatic tradition, or in Wagner, to suggest the scene of Samson at the mill, expressing his remorse and enduring the jibes of the Israelites his weakness has betrayed. There is a symphonic balance with Act One, which also began with the Hebrews crushed but passing on resilience down the generations through the textures of fugue. As Act One moves from Jewish woe to pagan decadence, so too does Act Three. The Bacchanale is always a good target for critical sallies. The latest – 'operatic orgies always tend to be funny rather than salacious and when performed to the decorous music of this Bacchanale, producer and choreographer are on to a loser' (*Sunday Telegraph*, 4.2.96) – is easy to make, if one thinks of unrestrained savagery as the only means of depicting sensuality. Saint-Saëns's music, though it is certainly no *Rite of Spring*, derives from an age when lavish décor, jewellery and fabrics enfolded the courtesans and oriental motifs adorned the palaces of sex. Orgiastic violence played no part.

The third act was extensively rewritten and revised in Algiers. We are reminded that the Bible story is set in the Middle East, lands of tents, harems and tribalism. The oboe theme 'malconico' which introduces, and the blatant Arab theme which dominates, the Bacchanale come directly from Arab streets and markets. They reflect the ambiguity which marked the Western view of the East in Saint-Saëns's lifetime. The reality was that the West, with its arms and weapons, was ruthlessly subjugating vast regions of the East. By contrast, the art of Delacroix, Regnault and others portrayed the East as decadent and cruel. Saint-Saëns had great sympathy for many aspects of the Orient. If he had wished to paint a musical fresco of Philistine revels he would not have portrayed them as devoid of glamour or romance. As Delilah and the High Priest pour libations on the altar, another rigid musical form, the canon, is employed and it is apposite, for the interweaving of the two voices sustains a picture of incantations. From this point all is compressed. The images follow one another rapidly as they might be seen by a reporter at the scene of a disaster. The moving cry of Samson for one final inspiration from the Lord, the reprise of the first-act phrase 'Israel break your chains!', the sinister impression of an Angel of Death passing over the celebrations and the descending scales of the trombones as the Temple cracks, appear without any obvious abruptness within the progressive crescendo of festive music. No final chorus appears at the end to moralise. The choral works of César Franck consist almost entirely of moralising; Saint-Saëns sees the story as an episode in a struggle; and we are left with the feeling that the pendulum might well swing back and the Israelites pay heavily for this outrage. Saint-Saëns was already moving far from the pieties of his childhood to his pessimistic view of the human condition, in which it is far from certain that Good will have the ultimate victory.

The year of two operatic productions was also one in which he relinquished his duties at the Madeleine. For some time he had had to rely on deputies when he undertook concert tours, but he had to appear for the great occasions. When Liszt pressed him to come earlier to Weimar he replied that he did not have the leisure, 'losing time to a thousand useless annoyances' and wishing the 'organ, the Conservatoire and the Institut with the devil'. Since the death of Duguerry he had lacked a friend among the clergy. The curés who succeeded took little interest in the fame of their organist. They deplored the controversy that so often surrounded performances of his music and reproached him with the austerity of his taste. He was exasperated when they thought, during a performance of Liszt's *St Francis Preaching to the Birds*, that he was tuning the organ in public.

In the second week in April he used his commitments elsewhere to tender his resignation. He was succeeded by Théodore Dubois, Maître de Chapelle, but he was able to ensure that Fauré was given the latter's post. He also moved his growing family to the rue Monsieur le Prince on the Left Bank. The lease in the rue Faubourg St Honoré had expired. A friend, Albert Libon, Director of the Posts in Paris, to whom he had dedicated *Le Timbre d'Argent*, had a nephew who resided in the rue Monsieur le Prince and had often expressed the view that Saint-Saëns should live close to this nephew so that he could visit them together. When the nephew, Armand Rousseau, found that a flat on the fourth floor of his house was available, Saint-Saëns rented it straightway. Libon, however, did not survive to make many visits. He fell seriously ill and when Saint-Saëns tried to visit him he was told that Libon was not at home. Libon had, in fact, named the composer as a very considerable beneficiary in his will and did not want his friend to be accused of attending his deathbed with expectations. Returning from a concert in London,[1] Saint-Saëns learnt of Libon's death and a bequest of 100,000 francs for a Requiem to be performed a year later. A codicil had been added which absolved Saint-Saens from this obligation – 'I have given way to a feeling of vanity that I cannot explain, but I leave him 100,000 fr. in order to enable him to leave the organ of the Madeleine in order to devote himself to music for the theatre, his long-felt desire.' Despite this absolution, the Requiem was written and performed. The bequest came after he

[1] His Trio and Quartet had been well received. Contrasting this work with the failure of Massé's *Paul et Virginie* he commented to Durand, 'It shows the English public is not so stupid.'

resigned from the Madeleine, but it left him free from financial worries.

While working on *Etienne Marcel* Saint-Saëns also produced a Romance in D for Cello and Piano. It was dedicated to Aldolphe Fischer, who had recently played the Lalo D minor Concerto for Cello under Pasdeloup. He also produced his first Six Studies for Piano. These represented a challenge in a field where he had great mastery. Chopin had made of the Study a means of extracting poetry from technical exercises. The form demanded conquests of new peaks of performance combined with a flowing sense of melody. Liszt in his *Transcendental Studies* had combined virtuosity with poetic evocations of times and places, thus fusing the prowess of the performer with the interpretative gifts of the poet. In his piano works Saint-Saëns makes few attempts to delve into the 'soul' of the instrument. His affinity with the eighteenth-century harpsichordists is underlined by the fact that two of the Studies are Preludes and Fugues: the F minor Fugue dedicated to Anton Rubinstein shows him linking music and performer. It demands muscular strength and the theme returns in octaves. Two Studies have an explicit technical purpose: the 'Daily Exercise' and Study 'For the independence of the fingers'. The sixth, in the form of a waltz, was dedicated to Marie Jaell. The violinist Eugène Ysaÿe transcribed it into an equally difficult piece for the violin in 1901.

The International Exhibition of 1878 was intended to be a symbol of the resurrection of Paris. Macmahon, who had survived the political tumults of the previous year, remained as a dignified totem to host State occasions but there was no gathering of monarchs as in 1867. The Shah of Persia was the only royal visitor. The frieze above the stage in the new concert hall at the Trocadéro, which showed France summoning all the nations of the earth, was therefore over-optimistic, but tourists came in droves to see the completed Opéra. The Festival of the People was moved from 14 July to 30 June as demonstrations were feared, but was marked by a revival of the ostensibly forbidden 'Marseillaise' by the band of the Republican Guard. The Republic atoned for the sins of the Empire by ordering a performance of *Les Noces de Prométhée* to inaugurate the Salle des Fêtes built upon the Trocadéro site, opposite the Champ de Mars.

Cavaillé-Coll's initial bid to install the organ had at first been rejected and by the time the committee had changed its mind there was too little time to build a new instrument large enough to fill the great arena with sound. With ingenuity, the builder added a fourth manual to an existing organ in his workshops. With great 32ft towers on either side it dominated the hall, though it was not ready for the opening ceremonies since, because of acoustical problems, it was heard twice. Guilmant was the first to give a recital on 7 August and twice-weekly performances followed. They were of great importance for French organ music, for it was heard outside the churches for the first time. Admission was free and large crowds attended. The future President Carnot came to every recital. Franck played the première of his 'Trois Pièces'. Saint-Saëns gave a prodigious recital on 29 September, which included his own Breton Rhapsodies and the prelude from *Le Déluge*, Bach's B-flat Prelude and Fugue, and two pieces of Liszt: *St Francis Preaching to the Birds* and the first performance outside Germany of his 'Grande Fantasie and Fugue on the Chorale from *Le Prophète*.'[1] In the extract from *Le Déluge* the composer achieved such sweetly coloured tones and received such an ovation that an encore had to be given before the programme could proceed.

The Festival showed some recognition of the labours of the Société Nationale, for concerts of French music were proposed. The Ministry of Beaux-Arts organised a competition for a symphony. An elderly composer, long forgotten though like Saint-Saëns he had been a child pianist, Louis Lacombe, took down from his shelves a symphony entitled *Sapho* and submitted it. Several jurors had never heard of him. '*Et quoi!*' cried Saint-Saëns. 'You do not know Lacombe? I shall acquaint you with him.' Then, with his prodigious facility, he took the large orchestral score, rapidly transformed it into a piano version, occasionally singing the melodies, and gave such a superb rendering that *Sapho* was chosen as the winning entry. He did not use the Exhibition to further his own compositions but, when a Handel Festival was suggested, he drew attention to Berlioz, Gounod and

[1] Saint-Saëns himself described this as 'the most extraordinary organ piece in existence. . . . It lasts forty minutes and the interest does not lag for a moment. Just as Mozart in his Fantasie and Sonata in C mi[nor] foresaw the modern piano, so Liszt, writing this Fantasia more than a quarter of a century ago, seems to have foreseen today's instrument of a thousand resources.' The aged Liszt did try the Trocadéro organ himself, with the assistance of Widor.

Massenet as choral composers and pressed especially for Halévy's *Prometheus* ('unjustly neglected') and Dubois's *Paradise Lost* ('a colossal work').

Of all the great musicians whom Liszt unselfishly assisted, Saint-Saëns was the sole one who tried to repay the debt. Not only was he almost the only French pianist to play original works by Liszt but, early in 1878, he arranged a concert at his own expense in the Salle Ventadour to present some of Liszt's orchestral compositions. The programme included the *Dante* Symphony, *Festklänge*, seventh of the symphonic poems, and excerpts from *Christus*. It was not the success for which he hoped. He complained that his modest posters had been pushed out of sight to the top of the billboards. One newspaper, under an absurd misapprehension, announced that Liszt himself, 'under the direction of M. Saint-Saens', would give a concert of his works. The orchestra, brought together for the occasion, did not like the music; the critics were still influenced by the opinion that a virtuoso could not be a great composer. Bannelier, a critic virtually ignored by both Bonnerot and Dandelot in their biographies, declared that Liszt had 'completely rejected classical and even romantic ideals' and criticised the 'indeterminate poetic element which . . . replaces specific beauties such as formal writing and developmental interest, which are essential in a classic work'. In the same year Bannelier was to describe d'Indy's first symphonic poem as 'a bastard genre'.

There were concerts in Antwerp (where he conducted *La Jeunesse d'Hercule*), Strasbourg and Basle. Saint-Saëns reported to Durand that his C minor Concerto had been given a great ovation and had been described as combining the force of Liszt with the suavity of Chopin. The local paper had hailed him as head of the French School as both pianist and composer. Generous in assisting colleagues, he had included a Scherzo by Dubois in his recital, but he had not been able to procure any promises with regard to *Dalila* from the Strasbourg Opéra. After an organ recital at Basel he retired to Berne to write, in a short space of time, the *Requiem* requested by Libon. It is hard to believe that the work could have been despatched by someone whose mind was in such a ferment with projects. A letter, which begins with his problems over the rhythm of the 'Ora Duplex', goes on to discuss his correspondence with Liszt, the Théâtre Lyrique and the Ministry, his dismay that the Théâtre Lyrique was to open with an opera by Flotow, his progress with *Etienne Marcel* ('the first two acts are orchestrated, the third three-quarter sketched, the fourth is short' – he could let a director have the vocal parts and finish the orchestration in time for the final rehearsals) and plans for a concert performance of *Dalila* in Brussels, where he jokingly suggests a Mlle Ritter *en travesti* as Samson, who is proving difficult to cast.

Samson was given in oratorio form at Brussels on 5 May in the presence of the King and Queen of the Belgians. On the 22nd came the first performance of the *Requiem* at St Sulpice, with Widor at the organ and Saint-Saëns conducting. There was little time to rehearse the soloists who play such an important and closely integrated part; the performance took place in the morning with little advance publicity, but was agreed to be a dignified treatment of the text. The scale of the *Requiem* had to be relatively intimate – to commemorate a Postal Official with the apocalyptic thunders of a Berlioz or Verdi would have been injudicious – but the drama of the *Requiem* is realised.

It opens with a combination of stabbing brass chords, which alternate with cries of woe from the violins. In contrast to the extended treatment of the 'Kyrie' in his youthful Mass, it is here given to the chorus, which bursts in with the words while the quartet seek 'Requiem aeternam'. The opening of the 'Dies Irae' portrays the nervous apprehensions of the people rather than the wrath of the Deity. In the calls of the brass, which come between the loud chords of the great organ, there is a sense of spatially arranged orchestration after the manner of Berlioz. The various pleas for mercy are treated dramatically, even operatically, with the tenor and chorus exchanging phrases over accompaniments which suggest the theatre. In the 'Ora Supplex', where the supplicant's heart is 'crushed almost to ashes', the woodwind nearly whine in unusual descending chromatic figurations, until once again the chorus bursts in upon the quartet with the cry 'Lacrymosa dies illa'. The whole section concludes with a long and rich 'Amen'. The 'Hostias' set from the 'Offertorio' refers to a sacrifice of praise and prayer and Saint-Saëns treats it as a hymn or chorale sparsely accompanied. The words of the 'Sanctus' are heard against luminous strings and the 'Hosannas' are separate exclamations against an excited string background. Woodwind arpeggios introduce and decorate a gentle 'Benedictus', which is the quiet blessing inferred by the text. The initial cries of grief return before the 'Agnus Dei', which is a slow, extended melody of deep melancholy against which first the quartet and then the chorus declaim the words. The orchestral sound is slowly dissolved, there is a return of the setting of 'Requiem aeternam' and with a stress on the word 'Rest' the soul of the departed is quietly cast upon eternity.

Despite his private scepticism, Saint-Saëns believed that music written for the Church should aim to inspire contemplation and, though the words are interpreted, there is no attempt to compose a drama for the concert hall. Despite the occasional operatic mood which affects his religious works, he makes no concessions to entertainment in music written essentially for worship.[1] It was a sign of his mental versatility that, even as he was completing the almost overdue *Requiem*, he was engaged upon a comic piece he was committed to compose for the 'Garde Volnay', an artistic group which met in Paris. A libretto had been written by a member, based upon an imagined episode between the Beaumarchais characters Dr Bartolo and Rosina. Nine musicians collaborated to produce sections of the score, including Guiraud, Joncières, Duvernoy and some obscurer still. It fell to Saint-Saëns to compose the Finale of this *opéra bouffe*, *Nina Zombi*. The composite score was performed, no doubt with great hilarity, on 11 May, five days before the *Requiem*.

This *Requiem*, like Mozart's, was destined to mark greater woes than were ever intended; the respectful acclaim at St Sulpice and the revelry of *Nina Zombi* gave way to tragedy. The lives of great artists have always had what seems to be more than a fair share of human afflictions. Those which fell upon Saint-Saëns were of a nature that scarcely bear contemplation. On 28 May, the elder of his two sons, André, was playing in the fourth-floor apartment. His mother was preparing to go out and his grandmother was elsewhere in the flat. The maid, who had been doing laundry, opened a window to let in some air; the child, hearing shouts below, climbed on to the sill, fell and was killed on the stones of the pavement below. Saint-Saëns, returning from rehearsals for the *Noces de Prométhée*, could only nurse a broken corpse. Worse was to follow. His wife, desolated by the tragedy and the inquests, public and private, which followed, went to her mother in Reims to recover. She took the baby, Jean-François, with her but, only six weeks after André's death, the younger child

[1] In 1892 he expressed his pleasure that the Société des Concerts was going to perform his *Requiem* in preference to Brahms's. It would be 'better for the public' as 'Brahms is a soporific of the first grade'.

succumbed to pneumonia. It, too, was a sufficiently painful death. Lalo, writing some weeks later, reported to a friend: 'Saint-Saëns had the misfortune to lose his second child – of convulsions following from an inflammation of the chest.'

Given the high infant-mortality rates of the time and the youth of the mother, a different pair might have begun to build a new family, but Saint-Saëns's fragile marriage was broken. Despite his many absences abroad he appears to have concentrated great devotion and hope upon his children. Henri Ferrare, a relative of Caroline de Serres, although a child at the time, was able to recall the impact of the death of André upon the musical circles of the day. He spoke of a note arriving in the early morning, his mother going pale upon reading it and workmen hastily raising the barriers across his window. When Saint-Saëns came to the house a few weeks later Henri was not called to the salon, as the sight of children was too agonising for the composer. Servières speaks of a grief which persisted far into old age, so that if anyone mentioned a child, ill or dying, the old man's eyes would fill with tears. Beneath the philosophic mask there was a poignant sense of isolation which surfaces in the Adagio of the Organ Symphony and several of his latest works. It was particularly ironic that 1878 should have been the year in which he was writing to Victor Hugo seeking permission to set two poems, 'Chanson de grandpère' and 'Chanson d'ancêtre', the first an artless round suggestive of children dancing and the second exhorting the young to a joyous and virile patriotism ('The blood of a people flows through the heart of a single man').

The performances at the Exhibition kept his mind occupied and a successful visit to London came in the summer. 'I have done marvellously with the G mi[nor] Concerto,' he wrote to Durand. 'I have read the word "triumph" in the papers, which are not always kind as you know.' With Wieniawski he played chamber pieces and with Carl Rosa he had discussions that he hoped might lead to the production of *Le Timbre* or *Etienne Marcel* at Covent Garden. In August he had moved on to Geneva and wrote to say that he needed rest as he was suffering from heart strain and faintings, 'natural enough after all I have suffered'.

The Minuet and Valse Opus 56, written at this time, is a curious work, not only because it represents an essay into solo piano writing, but because it portrays the disintegration of a stately court minuet into a languorous waltz, which increases in tempo to prestissimo before returning to the initial measures. It thus carries implications similar to Ravel's *La Valse* a generation later, when the waltz itself had come to represent stability and confidence in the old order of things. Like Opus 59, *König Harald Harfager*, two years later, it leaves an impression that it might have been intended as the kernel of a symphonic poem.

To the miseries of his devastated home there was added the first professional set-back of the kind which made him suffer. His early brushes with the critics he had endured in the knowledge of his own superior grasp of music and musicology. His tribulations with theatre managers were the lot of every composer and he had faith in eventual victory. '*Dalila* is and will remain my masterpiece,' he told Durand while writing the *Requiem*. But it now seemed that he could be dethroned as the major figure among French composers, as it was the time when Massenet's career began to overshadow his own.

Le Roi de Lahore had been put on sumptuously at the Palais Garnier the previous year. The huge sum of 200,000 francs had been spent on the costumes alone. The President had attended, together with the Emperor of Brazil. Gounod, with his unstoppable *bonhomie*, had embraced Massenet with the words '*Dans mes bras, mon fils! Embrasse Papa!*' Massenet had been appointed as Professor of Composition at the Conservatoire through the influence of Ambroise Thomas. Later in the year the death of Bazin left a vacancy in the Fine Arts section of the Institut and both Massenet and Saint-Saëns were candidates for election. Saint-Saëns had tactfully refused to compete with Ernest Reyer two years before, but in 1878 there was a great deal of canvassing among members of every faculty and Massenet had an inexhaustible supply of charm, which he lavished widely. After the first ballot both men were left in the race, together with Ernest Boulanger. The votes of the music section had placed Saint-Saëns narrowly in the lead with thirteen votes against Massenet's twelve and Boulanger's six. Public excitement and involvement in such matters were normal. Gounod, Massé, Reyer and Reber were in combative mood on behalf of Saint-Saëns, but in the second round Massenet achieved the required minimum of eighteen votes and became the youngest member of the Académie. Saint-Saëns had not added to his original thirteen. Massenet's apology to his rival, which lamented that the

Institut had been guilty of a grave error of judgement, received a gruff and whole-hearted endorsement.

To Durand, Saint-Saëns wrote: 'Behold us beaten!' He went on to say unconvincingly that he detested all official institutions, *conservatoires* and academies with their time-wasting committees and boredom which 'don't make up for the little satisfactions of vanity which one draws from them'. On the Wednesday following the election both composers were at Lalo's. Lalo pressed Saint-Saëns not to display his rancour but to chat with Massenet as usual. With a lisp 'more harsh than ever' Saint-Saëns replied that he had said all he had to say to Massenet. He suspected that the rivalry came from Massenet, despite the latter's silky manner. At a festival concert given towards the end of the year the conducting was shared between the two men and Gounod. On the night of the performance Massenet arranged, unbeknown to the others, for extra brass to be added to the orchestra. Saint-Saëns, who was an uncertain conductor, fumed at the problems of balance with which he had to contend; Gounod accepted the situation and embraced everyone in sight; Massenet, who had judged exactly what he needed, produced a blaze of sound to ensure that the items from his *Roi de Lahore* were the triumphs of the evening. Lalo wrote of these Vizentini concerts at the Hippodrome that 'Massenet is the victor of these concerts where 15,000 people squeeze in. I am not selling any wares there – where Saint-Saëns and even Gounod have been driven from the field by Massenet – the ladies' blue-eyed boy.'

Massenet did not, however, have his rival's versatility. To thank all those who had taken part in the Trocadéro recitals Cavaillé-Coll, in November, gave a banquet in the hall of his factory. Before his employees and workmen Saint-Saëns, Widor, Guilmant and Gigout all played on one of the workshop organs and spoke a few words in honour of the designer. *Le Ménestrel* described the occasion. 'It is futile to speak of M. Saint-Saëns's playing. It is simply prodigious. As for his registration, it is a reflection of the orchestral palate of the composer of the symphonic poems. M. Cavaillé-Coll . . . stated with satisfaction that, after numerous hearings of the organ, it was still possible to draw new effects from his superb instrument.' The critic referred to the long list of musicians who had made their way to the Madeleine to hear the famous Saint-Saëns improvisations and was disappointed that the Exhibition audiences had not had the opportunities to hear them.

*

When 1879 dawned, preparations were well advanced for the première of *Etienne Marcel* at Lyons. Opera-house problems had not been lacking. A Mme Mézéray, who was to sing Beatrice, furious at not being applauded on her entry in Act Two of *The Huguenots*, had undermined Act Three, withdrawn from the company altogether and then apparently returned to the fold. Saint-Saëns helped out at the piano with rehearsals for Guiraud's *Piccolino* and was pleased at its success. For the city of Lyons *Etienne Marcel* was a major event. Notables from the Rhône Valley filled the boxes. This was an audience which had been known to hoot down the third act of *Faust*, but the reception of *Etienne* was rapturous. A feature of the work was the prominence given to an active chorus which, far from being static, shared with the hero the thrill of revolt, followed by disillusion, anger and treachery. The dances assigned to the people in the square of Notre-Dame aroused such applause that the orchestra was drowned, and the dancers could not hear a note and became confused in their movements. In the evening a party was held and Saint-Saëns had the pleasure of hearing himself hailed as the leader of a growing and brilliant French School. One critic declared that the unity of the ensembles and the strong alliance between plot and score made one imagine that it had been composed in a single day.

Etienne is the Provost of Paris who leads a revolt of the citizens against the Dauphin, who rules while his father, King John, is captive in England. The third act, in which the civic officials process before Notre-Dame in great pomp, allowed Saint-Saëns to write a march and some lively choral and ballet music. Faction grows within the city, however; Etienne is persuaded to open the gates to King Charles the Bad of Navarre (one of the few aptly named French kings), another claimant to the throne. Jean Maillard, a more extreme rebel, refuses to hand over the keys and, although the Dauphin is prepared to issue a pardon to the Provost, the latter refuses it and is murdered by Maillard. In a final scene the Dauphin is welcomed back to Paris and Etienne's daughter, Beatrice, is reunited with her lover.

This happy ending to an essentially tragic story remained a weakness as audiences grew accustomed to the anguished denouements of Verdi and others. The story combined two themes from recent history: the revolt of the Paris Commune and the anticipated entry of Chambord as King Henry V. The libretto made it clear that rebels fall out among themselves, but lacked a decisive political message, royalist or republican. The descending fifths, which play a prominent part, indicate that political revolt spirals downwards and there are indications that the crowd has a warmer heart than the rich merchant class, but heroes and villains are found in both camps. Use is made of the leitmotif, which was beginning to have some popularity in bourgeois circles; listeners could understand something so simple and feel educated. 'Motifs' appealed also to the Wagnerians, but they found too many traces of Meyerbeer. The ballet music survived for a time in the concert hall and, if the anachronism of a waltz in medieval Paris was criticised, Saint-Saëns was able to reply that in *Polyeucte* Gounod had provided both a waltz and a mazurka for the early Christians. Sadly, for an opera that depicted Parisians, *Etienne* never reached the Opéra.

The Grand Théâtre of Lyon received a subvention of 20,000 francs from the Ministry of Fine Arts, the residue of funds from the deceased Théâtre Lyrique, for the Government looked temporarily with favour on the decentralisation of the arts. Unfortunately for French musicians, this largess was spent on a production of *Aida* and no further lustre was shed upon national composers. Abroad, Saint-Saëns's reputation continued to grow. The King and Queen of the Belgians attended a performance of *Le Timbre* at Brussels in February. In the same month he visited Dresden, Hanover, Leipzig, Königsberg and Pressburg, reaching Vienna by March. At the same time he was composing sections of a cantata, *La Lyre et la Harpe*, for the Birmingham Festival. He had also to deal with performances of his works elsewhere. We find him asking Durand in his ironic style to send a copy of *Jeunesse d'Hercule* arranged for two pianos to Diémer, 'who is going to perform this incomparable masterpiece with me on Saturday at the Société Nationale'. At Hanover he was soloist in his Fourth Concerto and conducted the *Danse Macabre*. He told Durand that von Bülow had his picture in a coloured frame, side by side with that of the Wagners, and he was proud to note that the great conductor, who never bothered with ballet, was pleased to conduct Delibes's *Coppélia*. At Leipzig he played the Beethoven G major Concerto but the concert included his Second Symphony, which he was delighted to hear well performed by the Gewandhaus orchestra. At Stettin the programme included selections from *Etienne Marcel*. From Königsberg the only news was that 'the town lacks interest and the women I have met are not pretty'. In Vienna he played the

Beethoven C-minor Concerto, gave an organ recital to a packed audience (though he found the instrument 'ridiculously complicated and wheezy which killed *St Francis Preaching to the Birds'*), and gave a very successful concert version of *Dalila*. He hoped the Vienna Opera might stage it during the following season. Birmingham had demanded the chorus parts of the Cantata earlier than expected and these were despatched to Durand during his travels. Visits to Mainz, St Gallen, Stuttgart and Brunswick followed. In April he was for a short time back in Paris, but then set off for Liège to supervise a performance of *Le Déluge*. By the beginning of May he was in Milan, from where he wrote in frivolous Italian to 'Conte Augusto di Durando [at his] Palazzo di Parigi, Piazza della Maddaleno' about a concert which included pieces by 'Ambrogio Thomaso'. He gave piano recitals and conducted two of his symphonic poems, the Bacchanale from *Samson* and his Second Symphony. He was ceremonially received at the Milan Conservatoire and gave a piano recital by way of thanks. The publisher Ricordi pressed a libretto, 'Il Macedone', on him, but it was not judged stageworthy and nothing came of the project. One wonders whether, with Ricordi's powerful backing, Saint-Saëns as an opera composer might have enjoyed some of the success which came to Puccini. At Turin the *Danse Macabre* was encored.

He moved on to London, staying with Mme Dieudonné in Ryder Street, St James's. The Symphony in A minor was repeated, together with the Fourth Concerto. He was recalled to Paris for a special charity concert in aid of flood victims from the Hungarian district of Szegedin, organised by the pianist, Mme Wilhelmina Szavardy, whose husband came from the region. The occasion was a further opportunity to show his gratitude to Liszt who had been engaged upon similar charitable work. Saint-Saëns conducted his *Danse Macabre* and a piece called *Rêverie Orientale*, which was later included in the *Algerian* Suite. He returned to London and played his Second Piano Concerto on 2 July. He took advantage of the organ in St James's Hall to perform Bach's Prelude and Fugue in A, even though this instrument was known among professional organists of the day as 'The Beast'. Shaw, otherwise an inveterate spoiler of Saint-Saëns's reputation, often recalled his admiration of this fine performance.

He was now able to concentrate upon the cantata that had been commissioned by the Birmingham Festival committee. This festival, dating from 1768, was founded to raise funds for local hospitals. It gave opportunities to large numbers of people to gather and sing joyously the choral music of Handel and had a proud tradition of commissioning major works, including Mendelssohn's *Elijah*, but this was the first time it had approached a French composer. Even Gounod had to wait until 1882 for his *Redemption* to be heard in the Town Hall. Saint-Saëns had at first entertained the idea of setting a Breton legend and rumour had it that a 'young poet' was providing a libretto. Instead, Saint-Saëns turned to Hugo and found inspiration in the *Odes et Ballades*, Book Four, where Christianity and paganism are sympathetically contrasted. This represented some detachment from the mood of the 1870s when the Church had enjoyed a vitality expressed in the foundation of numerous monasteries, convents, hospitals and schools. In terms of music the pinnacle of devotion was reached in February 1879, with the first performance of Franck's *Les Béatitudes*, on which he had been working for ten years.

La Lyre et la Harpe was given its first performance on the third day, 28 August. The tenor soloist had been withdrawn to preserve his voice for Rossini's *Moïse*, but the quartet was sufficiently distinguished. Saint-Saëns particularly admired Mme Helen Lemmens-Sherrington for her beautiful voice and musicianship. He observed to Durand that the harpists 'scratched' with enormous enthusiasm, though not with perfect co-ordination. He found two old friends in the orchestra: the first violin, Prosper Sainton (later the teacher of the young Edward German at the Academy), and the leading cellist, Lasserre, who had both been his partners in chamber works. The forces employed were large: a chorus of 340 (which included forty-five male altos) with an orchestra of 186. Saint-Saëns admired the singing and wrote of 'accuracy, precision in time and rhythm, finesse in the lights and shades, charm in the sonority ... this wonderful chorus combines everything'. Refuting the accusation that the English were unmusical, he added, 'If people like this are not musicians, they do exactly what they would do if they were the best musicians in the world.' He attributed the taste for oratorio to England's religious tradition, neither Catholic nor Lutheran. 'England is a biblical country and the Old Testament enjoys almost as high a place in its religion as it does with the Jews. Hence the great success of works like *Israel in Egypt*, *Elijah* and *Solomon*, all of them subjects which would never appeal on the Continent as strongly.'

La Lyre et la Harpe attains a standard infinitely higher than many of the composer's commissioned works. Hugo's words did not make any crude comparison between paganism and Christianity, and the ambiguity appealed to the composer. The poem set out the dignity of the pagan world, as well as its delight in pleasure, and pointed to the equally worldly and human appeal of the Christian message with its obsession with images of mother, outcast and a marriage of souls such as existed between Jehovah and his chosen people. It remarked upon the poetry on which both pagan and Christian adoration depended. The music must have seemed curious to the Birmingham audience, for the musical differences between pagan temptations and Christian virtues are not profound. Saint-Saëns identified church music with plainsong and the improvisation on themes relevant to the Mass. He was less acquainted with English cathedral music and its tradition of sweet restfulness. As a result, the opening chorus, 'Dors! O fils d'Apollon', has a distinctly Anglican sound similar to hushed Introits heard in English chancels. So, too, has the fugue, 'Olympus is born of Parnassus; the poets have made the Gods'. In the opening of part two, Hugo contrasts the eagle and the dove as symbols of pagan and Christian belief. In Saint-Saëns's treatment, it is the dove which has the seductive aria, which many English listeners would have found operatic and hence pagan.

Saint-Saëns himself had commented on the similarities between the music of Gounod, in which religion was allied to sensuality, and the Renaissance paintings of Raphael, in which holiness was linked with physical beauty. 'Raphael and Ingres were among those who retained the cult of beautiful forms and pagan nudities, and would have found it hard to depict moral beauty allied to physical ugliness.' Only in the baritone solo 'Jouis! C'est au fleuve des ombres', a waltz (which has echoes of Wagner's 'Dance of the Apprentices'), is there the merest suggestion of licence. Aware that British concert halls had organs installed, he was able to write for organ and orchestra in a way which furnished experience for the later Organ Symphony. The contrast between the organ at sacred moments and the light but brilliant orchestration of paganism furnish the listener with the chief means of distinguishing the modes of faith. As he expressed surprise at the excellence of the Birmingham chorus, he may not have had great expectations and the writing is not over-intricate, but there are fugal passages and some strong mass sounds accompanied by brass fanfares at the climactic moments. *The Times* referred to 'Wagnerian' aspects of the score and it is true that, while the voices express Hugo's thought, the orchestra carries the main stream of the music especially in the sections devoted to the lyre. The sparkling background to the choral hymn to the gods of Olympus are scintillating pages.

There were growing tensions between Saint-Saëns and Marie. Some months before, writing from the Truffot home in Reims, he had requested Durand to lower the charges on items of choral music required by the local Choral Society but in August 1879 he refers to the impending arrival of his *diablesse* from Reims and mental strain. He had certainly not been close at hand to console the grieving mother, though he seems to have spent time in the autumn of 1879 in Paris. He returned to England to give two concerts in Manchester and, in an article in *Voltaire*, raised the subject of the secular use of the organ. Manchester had a magnificent Cavaillé-Coll organ in the City Hall. Could not the Hôtel de Ville in Paris contemplate something similar? English critics had said he played the organ in too 'orchestral' a manner, but the range and variety of the French organ was just coming to England. Saint-Saëns compared the change to that which confronted the harpsichordists when they faced the new pianoforte. The best style was that which made fullest use of the sonorities available.

In October he reviewed *Aida*, which he found more comprehensible than *Trovatore*, though he could not understand why the daughter of the Pharaoh should enter into romantic rivalry with a slave-girl she could dispose of with a flick of her fingers.

The success of *La Lyre et la Harpe* persuaded Pasdeloup to ask for it as the inaugural piece for his Concerts Populaires in January 1880. Mme Lemmens-Sherrington came expressly to sing the soprano part and the performance was so well received that it had to be repeated two weeks later. On 1 February the Symphony in A minor was given by Colonne. The success it had enjoyed abroad persuaded Saint-Saëns to revive it in Paris after eighteen years of neglect. He was still a controversial figure, however, and after the brief Adagio a few cries of 'encore' from his partisans unleashed shouts of protest from his enemies. The fracas was about to become ugly and had to be silenced by a hasty plunge into the Scherzo. At the Cirque d'Hiver, the Second (in fact the First) Violin Concerto was also revived with Marsick as the soloist. *Le Ménestrel*, while having reservations about the 'originality' of the theme of the Finale, praised the opportunities afforded for both lyrical playing and virtuosity. The success was sufficient to turn him again to writing for the violin and during the year he composed not only the Third Concerto but also a *Morceau de Concert*, which absorbed at least one theme superfluous to the well-endowed concerto, but too good to waste.

On 17 January, at the Société Nationale, Saint-Saëns played the piano part in Franck's Piano Quintet, which was dedicated to him. He was seen to be in an increasingly bad humour and marched from the platform leaving the inscribed score on the instrument. He endeavoured to discourage a second hearing and the Bonnerot biography makes no mention of the first performance or the dedication of this work. It may be that he had relied too heavily upon his brilliant powers of sight-reading and found them sorely tested. The explanation, which appeals to those who prefer hidden dramas, is that the Quintet relates a story of passionate and reciprocated love between Franck and Augusta Holmès; that Saint-Saëns's temper was tried by noticing the expressions in the score, unusual for Franck, 'tenero, ma con passione', 'con molto sentimento', and by the surging nature of the music itself. Even some of Franck's admirers found the Quintet disturbing. Augusta had become his pupil in 1875. Although Franck was subsequently painted as an elderly saint, he was at this time only fifty. Augusta liked to attract the worship of lofty souls. She had enjoyed the attentions of Liszt and Wagner; she had tried to make an impression on Victor Hugo. At the moment she came into Franck's life his creative powers were awakening after long years of drudgery spent with a severe wife, who was forever listening at the door to condemn his compositions as 'uncommercial'.

The Franck family regarded Augusta Holmès as something of a vampire, but her own inspiration at this time also showed new sources of strength and originality, and she submitted a large-scale work, *Les Argonauts*, for the Ville de Paris Competition. Saint-Saëns reviewed it, giving much space to discussing the symbolism of rejecting love in order to gain the supreme object, be it the Golden Fleece, the Rhinegold or the Grail. He made much of the desire of women composers to conceal their sex by outdoing males in the force and ferocity of their orchestration. He nevertheless voted for the work, along with Franck, Massenet and most of the great musicians, when it came before the judging committee. The first prize was awarded to *La Tempête* by Duvernoy with an *ex aequo* award made to Guiraud, but Augusta was pleased by the support of Saint-Saëns and other musicians, and consoled herself with the thought that against her had been simply 'the Prefect of the Seine, Ambroise Thomas and the municipal councillors'. At the première of the quintet it would be far-fetched to assume that Saint-Saëns felt personal jealousy over any words or deeds of Augusta, but the situation may have aggravated emotions of bereavement and marital disharmony. It is more likely that he disliked the thick and heavy Germanic nature of the music and sensed that Franck was having a stronger impact on the younger generation of composers than himself. It did not help that d'Indy, in his review of the quintet, criticised French writing for the piano in previous years: 'the "avalanche" of fantasies and plethora of concertos, which contained much music of poor quality'.

In February he was again off on his travels, with a series of concerts in Amsterdam, The Hague, Rotterdam and Utrecht. Momentarily he included Berlin, where his concert was attended by the German Empress and her visiting brother, the Duke of Edinburgh. Back in Paris, he had discussions with the Directors of Covent Garden, with a view to the production there of *Etienne Marcel*. He played two of his recently composed Piano Studies at the Société in March and subsequently, at the Salle Erard, gave a recital which included his 'Minuet et Valse'. Portions of *La Lyre et la Harpe* were admitted to the programmes of the Conservatoire, and Mme Watts, who had come to Paris to sing the contralto part, appeared at the end of March in a concert performance of the final Scene from *Samson* at the Châtelet, with the composer conducting. In April he performed Liszt's great B minor Sonata in the Salle Pleyel. This again marked him out as an advocate of the 'New Music' and mystified the conservative Bannelier, who wrote, 'New things require new names. Why keep the classic designation for a work whose liberty of form is driven to excess? . . . No doubt there is an underlying programme; we were not given it, but we are not too sorry.'

Saint-Saëns himself may have meditated a fifth symphonic poem; his Opus 59 (*König Harald Harfager*), a piece for piano duet based upon a ballad by Heine describing the fate of a mortal dragged down to the ocean depths by his love for a mermaid. By contrast, the Third Violin Concerto reverted to a clearly structured three-movement form. There were individualistic touches: the orchestral prelude was omitted and a harsh theme from the solo violin introduces the first movement, while the Finale is preceded by a recitative with a Spanish flavour. Dedicated to Sarasate, who gave the first performance at one of the Monday soirées, the solo part is prominent throughout. In the Barcarolle, which is the second movement, the violin dominates many delicate exchanges with solo woodwinds. At the close, it ascends into ethereal regions and disappears into wispy harmonics. The orchestra, which is continuously and subtly strengthened through the first movement, shares in the long Finale, in which there is a great richness of melodic material.[1] It was no doubt the very profusion of themes that caused him to write, almost simultaneously, the *Morceau de Concert* for Violin, which had in its central section a typical theme, divided in its elements but beautifully fashioned in its ultimate form.

Late in April we find him thanking Durand for trying for greater tolerance on the part of Mme Saint-Saëns towards her husband's long and frequent absences, 'making my wife understand that if there are advantages in being the wife of a composer there are an equal number of inconveniences'. He was in London for long periods from May to July. Between his visits he also made a journey to Baden-Baden, to a meeting of the Association of German Musicians, which was a further opportunity to meet Liszt. He played his Fourth Concerto, conducted *Phaeton* and gave an organ recital which included a Breton Rhapsodie and, as yet another advertisement for a fellow countryman, a sonata by Guilmant. Back in London, he played his First Concerto, the *Beethoven* Variations with Mme Montigny and with her, Agnes Zimmerman and Joseph Wieniawski, brother of the more famous Henri, his *Marche Héroïque* for eight hands. At the Steinway Hall he gave a programme which included works by Fauré, the first occasion on which he had been played in England. He took part in a gala concert organised by Sir Julius Benedict, but had a bad fall over some trapdoor mechanism. 'Anyone else would have been killed,' he wrote to Durand. 'I have not left my bed for two days.' Fortunately his fingers had been undamaged and he was able to play at the remaining concerts even if his bows, always stiff and almost indiscernible, were now impossible.

[1] Sarasate, asked if he would ever play the Violin Concerto of Brahms, had said he would never stand alone on the platform, violin in hand, while the oboe played the single melody to be found in the whole work.

'The few hairs which remain to you are going to stand on end on your venerable head,' he told Durand. He had been invited to Windsor to be received by Queen Victoria and was met at Windsor station by the Baronne de Caters, daughter of the famous singer Luigi Lablache and now singing teacher to the Princess Beatrice, as her father had been to the Queen. The Baronne had recently sent to Paris for a collection of Saint-Saëns songs published earlier by Richault. These had arrived worn and with many loose sheets. The Princess had expressed no surprise and had said – as he told Durand – that she was accustomed to music arriving from France in this state. In a later essay he described his first meeting with the Queen.

> I had been somewhat intimidated by the stories told of the coldness Her Majesty affected at this sort of audience. Imagine my surprise when she arrived, stretched out both hands to take mine and talked to me with great cordiality. Her Majesty wished to hear me play the organ (there is an excellent one in the Chapel at Windsor) and then the piano. Finally I had the honour of accompanying Princess Beatrice in an aria from *Etienne Marcel*, which she sang with great purity of style and diction. It was the first time Her Royal Highness had sung in front of her august mother and she was dying of fright.

The Queen was so impressed that she summoned to Windsor Mme Albani, wife of the Director of Covent Garden, and asked for *Etienne Marcel* to be included in the repertoire, a wish that was never granted. While in London he regained access to the library of Buckingham Palace, studied the MSS of Handel oratorios (even he was disconcerted to discover the speed at which Handel composed) and discovered the theme which he was to use for his next opera, *Henry VIII*.

There had been a change in the Directorship of the Paris Opéra. Vaucorbeil, the new incumbent, had some musical knowledge. Son of a French actor, he had studied at the Conservatoire under Cherubini, had been briefly Professor of the Vocal Ensemble there and had written a certain amount of music himself. Reyer observed that a little knowledge was a dangerous thing. The unmusical Halanzier had accepted Gounod's *Tribute of Zamora* as brought to him; Vaucorbeil had made him rewrite whole sections and indicated how improvements could be made. Reyer added that he left the Director's office after a reading of his own *Sigurd* feeling as if he had faced a criminal court. Vaucorbeil, however, was not hostile to Saint-Saëns and was keen to commission a work. He offered the opportunity to write a ballet, but Saint-Saëns insisted that an opera must come first. The Director was a great friend of Detroyat, Saint-Saëns's former employer at *L'Estafette*, who had long dreamed of writing a libretto for the Opéra. He had in his files one called 'The Schism in England', based upon a play by Pedro Calderón. It was a dark drama, enlivened by a court jester who might have been a distant cousin of Rigoletto. The libretto had been offered to Gounod and Joncières, but no progress had been made. Gounod made one of his gnomic pronouncements by saying that 'Even Saint-Saëns had the right to enjoy a failure at the Opéra' (to which Vaucorbeil ruefully replied that Gounod's *Tribute of Zamora* had been quite enough to be going on with). Detroyat and Saint-Saëns were brought together and asked to collaborate.

Saint-Saëns, still meditating a series dealing with great moments in the history of France, had been, like Bizet before him, contemplating an opera about Vercingetorix and the Gauls. During the summer of 1880, however, a fresh war of religion began in France and the intertwined themes of a foreign Pope and the right of divorce gave the reign of Henry VIII great topicality. In March 1880 the Jesuit Order was banned. In July, *The Times* in England reported disturbances as the Archbishop of Paris sought to break the seal on the Jesuit Chapel in the rue de Sèvres and remove the Host to St Sulpice. Jules Ferry, a leading Minister and anti-clerical, pressed for the restriction of Church influence in education, the laicisation of teaching personnel and the re-establishing of divorce; measures which aroused the wrath of the Right. A playwright, Armand Silvestre, was asked to rewrite the Detroyat libretto and we hear of him reading extracts from the text to high-ranking politicians. Saint-Saëns, as the composition proceeded, found himself with collaborators imposed upon him, intense analysis given to the various scenes and innumerable difficulties. Later he wrote of his experiences as 'a Calvary which he would not mount again even to have a piece performed at the Opéra'.

For the time being, however, he was more immediately concerned with the Algerian Suite, summoning up memories of the Mediterranean while watching the waves of the English Channel, giving tentative thought to his next opera, *Proserpine*, which appeared to

interest Covent Garden, and planning a tour of Spain. He requested
that a copy of the *Beethoven* Variations be sent to Madrid in order that
it can be given 'to the victim who is charged to play it with me'. He
also noted (to Durand) that Ferry, being unable to find a Foreign
Minister, should take the post himself and help to find *Etienne Marcel* a
destination in the capitals of Europe.

At Madrid, in October, the *Danse Macabre* was encored. Saint-Saëns
performed his Fourth Concerto, which he describes as having a
'stunning' effect. Paul Viardot played a concerto by Benjamin Godard
and the Prelude to *Le Déluge*, which was also encored. At Saragossa
Saint-Saëns made an arrangement of the Spanish *La Jota* for violin and
piano, which he intended later to orchestrate. He added humorously
to Durand that, if he could have the rights to *La Jota* in Spain, 'I will
give you the rights in England in exchange'. From Jerez he reported
indescribable enthusiasm, ravishing *Andalusiennes* and a young amateur
of music with a fine cellar who promised a gift of his best sherries if
Saint-Saëns would dedicate a piece to him. A series of concerts in
Lisbon followed. One was attended by the Court and a barcarolle, *Une
Nuit à Lisbonne*, was subsequently dedicated to King Don Luiz.

He returned to Paris late in November. The composer Henri Reber, a
member of the Institut, had died on the 24th. Without waiting for his
Chair to be declared vacant, the Parisian press put forward the names
of Saint-Saëns, Delibes, Franck, Lalo and others as claimants. In
earlier days Saint-Saëns had played chamber music with Reber and
only eighteen months before had made him the dedicatee of *La Lyre et
la Harpe*. On 21 January 1881, the Music Section of the Institut classed
the candidates: (1).Saint-Saens; (2) Delibes and Guiraud; (3) Joncières;
(4) Duprato. There were thirty-three voters in the election and a total
of seventeen votes was required for the winner. In the first ballot
Saint-Saëns tied with Delibes with fourteen each, but in the second he
received twenty-two votes against Delibes's nine and Duprato's two.
(Delibes, strange as it may seem, was regarded in some quarters as a
dangerous Wagnerian.)

On the evening of his election, Saint-Saëns hurried straight to the
chamber-music society, La Trompette, where he was a revered
member. This society had its origins in the early 1860s in a group of
young students at the Imperial Military Academy. During breaks from
study they would gather in corners to play instruments. The guiding

spirit was a young Breton from Quimper, Emile Lemoine, who became a notable mathematician, and who built up a cell of music lovers in this predominantly scientific institution. The gibe '*Allons. Les voilà encore à la trompette*' had been hurled at the amateur musicians by fellow students hurrying off to lighter amusements. When the group left the Academy they continued to meet, often in artists' studios where, surrounded by half-finished paintings and statues, they would concentrate on a very classical diet of quartets by Beethoven and Mozart. Lemoine was autocratic. He would keep out late-comers, reprove chatterers and announce further performances of works that had not been appreciated. He discouraged the bringing of children who occupied valuable seats and threatened to discontinue concerts if the practice continued. One atelier they hired was near the new railway terminal at Sceaux and Lemoine thought that the whistles of the trains were expressions of disapproval at Beethoven's quartets, which resulted in a severe lecture. In the early days women were excluded as having a regrettable fondness for Offenbach.

The society came to rest eventually in the Salle de l'Horticulture, amid test-tubes and botanical drawings. The name of Saint-Saëns first appeared on the programmes in January 1875 and Lemoine speedily enlisted his support to raise the quality of performances. Young composers had opportunities to hear their works performed and great players such as Saint-Saëns, Diémer, Jaell and Delaborde would often act as accompanists for songs and string pieces by others. It was Saint-Saëns who insisted upon proper rehearsals and an end to the practice whereby enthusiasts would rush in with sheets of music and give inaccurate renderings of their recent fancies.

Lemoine had long been anxious for an original work from him. Saint-Saëns had refused, saying on one occasion to the persistent requests, that he would 'write a concerto for twenty-five guitars; to put it on you will have to depopulate Castile and Andalusia'. Eventually he succumbed and in January 1880 produced a piece for trumpet, piano and strings. The presence of a double-bass caused some overcrowding on the platform. The trumpet dominates the subservient strings, a hint of Lemoine in charge of his 'salon' (though we are told he wept for joy at the opening bars), but on the strength of its excellence he was able to ask for voluntary additions to the subscriptions. By December 1880 Saint-Saëns had added for the same combination the Minuet (again linked to a waltz), Gavotte, Funeral March and Finale. M. Teste, a well-known trumpet player, took part in the famous Septet at its première on 28 December. The evening was notable for another departure from tradition, for the assembled company, led by Mme Henrietta Fuchs, sang the Bacchantes chorus from Gounod's *Philémon et Baucis* and a movement from Rossini's *Stabat Mater*.

Saint-Saëns had promised that his first engagement as an Academician would be at La Trompette. During a programme of the classics to which had been added an extract from Massenet's *La Vierge* and a piece by the Russian, César Cui, Lemoine mounted the platform. The audience, many of whom expected the customary reproofs for chattering or for using the chairs 'as cloakroom extensions', perceived he was in solemn mood. He asked to be given a minute for his eloquence instead of the usual fifteen seconds, linked himself with the applause and emotion that had greeted the arrival of Saint-Saëns and brought out a rosewood baton, mounted with silver on which had been engraved the emblems of the trumpet and the palm leaves of the Academy. Quoting the words addressed in the legendary vision of the Emperor Constantine he presented it saying, '*In hoc signo vicisti*, behold the instrument of your victories.' There was thunderous applause and the two men, 'the great musician and the great listener', embraced.

It was a circle in which Saint-Saëns was both friend and colleague. A few weeks later he participated in the Bach Four-Piano Concerto with Diémer, Pugno and Charles-Wilfrid Bériot, a rare constellation of pianistic talent. After his ventures into North Africa and Iberia, the Septet represented a return to the typically French notion of the suite. The problem of containing a trumpet in a small chamber group seemed at first bizarre, but was overcome with deceptive ease. Lemoine, though an opponent of Napoleon III (he had played music to political prisoners under the Second Empire), had taken part in the Franco-Prussian War and various military trumpet calls mark the Prelude. The Minuet and Gavotte are both sparkling pieces and prove Saint-Saëns to be one of the few French composers who could infuse gaiety into serious forms.

Baumann, who must have been in a revanchist mood when writing of the Septet, thought that the Funeral March was that of a hero and the lively trumpet part resembled the 'call that on the morning of victory on our field of battle the trumpet will be able to sound'. The likelihood of warfare against the German Empire was never far from the mind during these years. Saint-Saëns had chosen the key of E flat for the Septet, the same as Beethoven's. It is a piece which has to be seen as well as heard, for despite the contrasts of the three timbres – piano, trumpet and strings – there is great dexterity in the ways in which themes pass from one player to another. The trumpet gleams, the piano and strings shimmer, and the composer seems as happy in the *ad hoc* collection of instruments as Bach in his *Brandenburg* Concertos. The piano writing in the Finale, as in all his chamber works, requires virtuoso technique and exalts the instrument to a principal role.

In the same month, the *Suite Algérienne* was played at the Société Nationale by Saint-Saëns and Fauré in the latter's transcription for piano duet. Algiers was to become a second home to Saint-Saëns. It was not unusual for composers to employ regional touches in their works. In the same year Chabrier produced his *Pièces Pittoresques* for a Société Nationale concert and it included a 'Mauresque' section. British composers might write Imperial marches, but they did not consider incorporating the actual sounds of Indian music. Saint-Saëns was a pioneer in blending genuine themes from Islam with Western-ised patterns and orchestration. The *Suite Algérienne* was written in 1880. The Prelude, in C major and 9:8 rhythm, describes the emotions of the traveller as he is wave-born towards the white buildings of Algiers. The persistent chords and the muffled drumming of the timpani paint increasing anticipation as the boat rolls to and fro. The noises of the town become more complex and at the close the shrill sounds of bugles announce the French military presence. The 'Rhapsodie Mauresque', which follows, sets some Arab themes. The string sections are divided, the rhythms alternate between 2:4 and 3:4, and there are suggestions of an indolent guitarist strumming a thin instrument, whose meagre strains are swallowed by the clamour of street dancing. The 'Reverie du Soir' brings East and West together as the Conservatoire musician contemplates the disappearing colours of twilight, the earth relieved from the rigours of the midday sun. The tambourine beats an obscure rhythm and the flutes intone a form of chant, which introduces a viola solo that seems to place the movement at some definite moment of inventiveness. The final movement is a French military march, Algerian only by its high-spirited style, characteristic of the African troops whose swords seem to whirl and flash as the cavalry prance by. It exudes confidence and reminds us that plans were afoot at this time to expand the French Empire in North Africa. French troops crossed the Tunisian frontier, initially to deal with troublesome tribesmen, but ultimately to establish French influence further along the coast. The Archbishop of Algiers, Cardinal Lavigerie, set up a mission in Tunis, began the building of a cathedral on the old citadel of Carthage and made it a headquarters for a new Order. Although such actions caused offence to the Italians, numerically strong in Tunis, the 'annexation' was a notice to the French people that the defeat of 1870 would not prevent the spread of empire.

A biographer of César Franck has said of the *Suite Algérienne* that at best it deserved a place in a 'programme of popular seaside music', which is to overlook the fact that of all the French composers, Berlioz excepted, Saint-Saëns is the only one able to write with a masculine robustness which attracts the non-musical listener. We do not denigrate this ability in an Elgar or a Walton and their popular marches are not used as arguments against their genius. There are no French composers whose span extends over so wide an arc of musical taste as Saint-Saëns's.

8

The Traveller with Lined Paper

By the spring of 1881 relations between the composer and his wife had become increasingly strained. During a March tour of Switzerland he wrote to Durand that he had not replied to any of her letters. In July 1881 the couple went for a brief holiday at the health spa La Bourboule. One morning, in a fit of bad temper, under the pretext of visiting the home of Auguste Durand, Saint-Saëns disappeared without giving any warning. Panic-stricken, his wife caused searches to be made throughout the countryside. She was able to return to Paris with the help of Henri Duparc, a guest at the same hotel, but a letter from her husband and the attitude of her mother-in-law convinced her that she must resign herself to a total break. Three days before his disappearance Saint-Saëns had written to Durand, 'Life is made up of sadnesses, but I will never become accustomed to them. Something about divorce would be crushing for the composer of *Samson*.' A divorce was never arranged. Marie returned to her family and eventually lived out a long life of comparative solitude through the two World Wars and the Occupation. She died in January 1950, aged ninety-five, taking to the grave the secrets of the extraordinary relationship. In 1935 she told Dandelot that the separation had caused great surprise to friends, as Saint-Saëns had often been told that, when people saw the couple together, they felt an urge to marry. The mysterious brother appears to have made no attempts at reconciliation. Ten years later Saint-Saëns, in a letter, compared her condition with that of a retired organ-blower from the Madeleine: 'They are both alike; unemployed and miserable.' He was fortunate in her lifelong silence and in the admiration she expressed for his music, but the episode is a strange one, complicated further by the fact that Saint-Saëns's music from this period, unlike Tchaikovsky's in similar circumstances, bears few traces of stress or depression.

He did, however, pour some feeling into *Henry VIII*. Queen Catherine of Aragon, childless and abandoned, is his most sympathetic female operatic character. King Henry, monster as he is, does not transfer his affections to Anne de Boleyn [*sic*] without some mental turmoil. The yearning phrase which embodies Henry's lustful desires, as powerful as anything in *Samson*, is a master-stroke both by its shape and its lack of satisfactory completion. It speaks of a desire for freedom from a marriage that has lost its attractions and the call of an alternative longing.

One of the compositions from these months of domestic discord was the *Hymn to Victor Hugo*, the poet who was now a national icon. The *Hymn* had been destined for the inauguration of a statue, but subscriptions had come in slowly and the chagrined Hugo cancelled the event. The music was performed at a concert in the Trocadéro in May. Despite his enthusiasm for Hugo's poetry, Saint-Saëns knew that, like a number of French poets, he had no ear for music. Some time previously a practical joke had been played on him. He was persuaded that a commonplace music-hall tune was by Beethoven and would be a sublime setting for some of his lines. Vanity convinced him that the combination of two such geniuses as himself and Beethoven would be incomparable, and he took pleasure in having this hybrid offering played at supper parties. Saint-Saëns worked the banal theme into the *Hymn* with some intricate counterpoint, a touch of wit in an otherwise solemn tribute. Hugo, who rarely made public appearances, attended the concert and was loudly cheered. As a result, Saint-Saëns became a frequent guest of the venerable poet and dined with him in select supper parties where the host sat 'Jove-like – an ageless and immortal human being whom Time would never touch' at the head of the table. Among the writers present were Paul Meurice and Auguste Vacquerie, and it was out of these literary suppers that the melodramatic opera *Proserpine* evolved later. The critic Julian Tiersot thought the *Hymn* a remarkably fine work and regretted that, after cheers for the poet, it had been coldly received. This may have been because of a quotation from the 'Marseillaise' on trumpets, which would have startled an official audience. Tiersot thought it worthy to be in the repertoire as firmly as the Organ Symphony and its Andante theme as excellent as that of Beethoven's Ninth. 'Never has one seen a work, generous and superb, received so frostily' (*Revue Musicale*, October 1935).

Reading through the Durand *Thematic Catalogue*, one is constantly reminded of how much paper Saint-Saëns covered in his eventful life; of the *Hymn to Victor Hugo* he wrote not only the full score but the two-handed piano version and a two-piano four-handed version. These were in addition to a four-handed single piano version by Guiraud and an organ arrangement by Guilmant. The same is true of many other large-scale works.

The year 1882 began with a further tour of Germany and Central Europe: Breslau, Leipzig, Prague, Frankfurt, Mannheim, Karlsruhe, Bremen and Berlin. In Berlin he directed the *Suite Algérienne* and thereby possibly reminded the Germans that they were being slow in the race to seize Africa. In Prague he conducted *La Lyre et la Harpe* and found opportunities to coach the tenor Hermann Winkelmann as Samson, in preparation for Hamburg. Although there were rounds of applause and encores (he was especially pleased that *Jeunesse d'Hercule* had been a great success at Karlsruhe) he detected a certain coldness in his reception and attributed this to German preoccupations with the Wagnerians v. Brahmsians, both parties being 'unable to understand a simple natural melody'. At Mulhouse the Concordia Society organised a great festival in his honour and brought together the Choral Society of Strasbourg and the Orchestra of Basle to give *La Lyre et la Harpe*. There were concerts of his songs (he appeared as pianist and organist), official welcomes and speeches. His visit coincided with Hugo's eighty-first birthday and a congratulatory telegram was sent by the civic dignitaries. The seized provinces were never averse to celebrating their traditional links with Paris and Saint-Saëns was keen to lend his name to efforts at maintaining French culture.

In March he was in Lille conducting *Le Déluge* and in Hamburg for the first three performances of *Samson*. It had proved difficult to produce and rehearsals had dragged on for six months, but despite the criticisms (which he confided to Durand) Saint-Saëns begged his publisher to report that it had been a great success. He was pleased at von Bülow's intention to attend – 'Hamburg has one box in which to wedge people coming from the four cardinal points.' He thought the Delilah, Mme Lucher, 'adorable' and Winkelmann 'marvellous'. Von Bülow hailed the opera as 'the most significant musical theatre work of the last twenty years'.

Another stern epistle winged its way from his mother to Hamburg, to urge on his confidence in *Samson*: 'I hope you are like me. True talent follows its own path, without paying attention to what others say . . . work with the gifts the Good Lord has given you . . . One fine day you will feel strong like a man . . . but leisure plays no part in the process . . . You have come into the world to make music. Then do so!'

In July the Association of German Musicians met in Zurich. He revealed his prodigious powers as an organist with a performance of Liszt's Fantasia on the Chorale from *Le Prophète*, with Liszt himself in the audience. A few weeks earlier Liszt had written, 'Very honoured friend. I still remain enraptured by your "Preaching of St Francis to the Birds". You use the organ as an orchestra in an incredible style . . . the most skilful organists throughout all the world can only hold you in reverence.' Fauré had been taken to Zurich. He wrote to Marie Clerc: 'I saw Liszt – an emotional occasion! Saint-Saëns claims that I went green when he presented me to the Master and words cannot describe the welcome Liszt extended to me.' Fauré presented his Ballade, apologising for the fact that it might seem too long, to which Liszt replied that a composer must abide by his instincts. Liszt began to play but, probably out of kindness, complained 'he had run out of fingers' to cope with its complexities and asked Fauré to continue. A signed photograph and a profession of goodwill followed. It was through Saint-Saëns that Fauré came to know the poetic treatment of the piano in Liszt's works and it was he who, at the end of 1882, gave the first performances of Fauré's First Impromptu and First Barcarolle at the Société Nationale, and encouraged him in the writing of the Valses-Caprices.

In the same year he also lent his support to Lalo. There had been a 'Monbinne Prize' instituted in 1876 to be awarded every two years to the composer of an *opéra comique* by the Académie des Beaux-Arts. The Music Section, led by Saint-Saëns, Reyer and Massenet, expressed the view that, as no *opéra comique* justified the prize in 1882, it should be given to Lalo for his ballet *Namouna*. This was a work which had caused the composer grief at a time of illness, as he was given only four months to write the score for the Paris Opéra. 'Even Saint-Saëns – he who writes the fastest among us – said to me after my illness that he would never have accepted such a galley-slave task.' There had been opposition from Thomas, Barbier and Heugel, composer, librettist and publisher of *Françoise de Rimini*, which they wished to have performed, and the Ministry of Fine Arts had to be invoked to defend Lalo's score. This outraged Thomas – 'the Mikado of the Conservatoire' as Lalo called him – and the two men faced each other as they made amendments to their respective works in the copyists department. The angry Thomas feigned ignorance of Lalo's presence. 'He detests my music, as he has a right, as I have to detest his "Under-Usher's Music".' The upshot of all this was that the full Academy rejected the opinions of Saint-Saëns and his friends, much to their fury, and a half-prize only was awarded to Poise. In relating this story to Adolphe Jullien, critic of *Le Français*, Lalo added an amusing reminder of Sarasate's proverbial forgetfulness. 'When you have news of Sarasate tell me if he has not forgotten his violin in one station, his hat in another, his cardigan in the next and his shirts in a hotel in Toledo.' Saint-Saëns's Third Violin Concerto, although dedicated to Sarasate, had not pleased the great violinist, who thought it did not satisfy the public. It was only when Ysaÿe played it with enormous success that Sarasate's interest revived and he included it in his programmes. At a Colonne concert, where Ysaÿe was recalled many times by the audience, he did not wish to efface Saint-Saëns from the success and modestly asked the first violin of the orchestra to make way for him at the desk so he could lead the next item, the *Jeunesse d'Hercule*. His magnificent tone inspired the strings, and Colonne and the orchestra gave a memorable performance.

As the composition of *Henry VIII* took up a great part of the year the output of other pieces was slender. There were two choruses, *Calme des Nuits*, whose entries on long sustained notes made it a testing piece for amateur choirs, and *Les Fleurs et les Arbres*. Encouraged by his recent election to the Academy, Saint-Saëns wrote the poems for both. In May the first reading of *Henry VIII* took place in Vaucorbeil's office; the roles were allocated and the staging ordered. In August it was announced that the opera would form part of the winter season, but the months that followed were filled with arguments and rewritings. To complete the orchestration Saint-Saëns rented a villa in Le Tréport, close to the summer retreat of the Durands. Guiraud was a guest of theirs and there were young friends with whom Saint-Saëns enjoyed visits to café-concerts around the harbour. In the town was a junk shop kept by a local character known as 'Mother Jacob', whose fondness for drink made it hard to complete a purchase. Saint-Saëns's young secretary Albert Guinon wrote a poetic lament on the 'Bazaar of Mother Jacob', which so appealed to Saint-Saëns's sense of humour that he set it to music and conducted a choir of young people to serenade her premises. The composer would also entertain the Durands with his party pieces and his baritone voice. He knew the words of a popular song 'Joseph est en voyage', about a wife whose husband is travelling, put on a grandmother's hat and cloak and sang it in stentorian tones, the other guests joining in the chorus. The weather was hot, the windows were open and groups of evening bathers assembled with curiosity. A young sculptor, Jules Franceschi, advanced to the door, called for silence and announced that the singer was the great Maestro Camille Saint-Saëns, who was rendering one of the most significant pages from his new opera, a statement received with proper reverence by the crowd.

In October the Maître de Ballet produced a scenario portraying the loyalty of Henry's subjects. Saint-Saëns found a collection of Scottish and Irish airs belonging to Mme Detroyat and used some as a basis for the ballet score, although it was an anomaly to include Scotland in Henry's dominions. The first stage rehearsal took place on 2 December. All the ensembles were written, although parts of the fourth act were still unfinished. Years later, Baumann questioned him on his methods of composition and what took place at the moment of inspiration. Saint-Saëns replied that he was quite ignorant of the process: 'The ideas come as they wish and it is sufficient that one chases after them.' He added, 'While I was working on *Henry VIII*, having arrived at the fourth act and the aria of Catherine of Aragon, I was finding nothing. I left the Romance – I thought no more about it. Eight days later, crossing by the avenue de l'Opéra, suddenly I heard my motif. I ran home to write it down and *only then* I perceived it was in 5:4 time!'[1] In the original score, when the duet between the repudiated Katherine and the fearful Anne Boleyn is interrupted by the angry arrival of the King, the impetus of the scene was lost. Mme Gabrielle Krauss (Katherine) suggested that she should be the first to be aware of the King's presence. This inspired Saint-Saëns to press forward with the great quartet about which he had been doubtful. He had already told the singers he 'did not wish to rewrite the quartet from *Rigoletto*', but he achieved a greater ensemble of the highest musical complexity and dramatic unity where the shifting key-changes (based on a gross inflation of Henry's original phrase 'Who may

---

[1] As finally conceived 5:4 is juxtaposed with 3:4.

command, where he loves') mirror the unanswered questions that rack the four protagonists,[1] an operatic ending unlike any other.

Jean Montargis, in his biography, repeats the criticism that, because of the many amendments made to the score during composition the work was thematically confused and it is a commonplace of criticism of Saint-Saëns that he lacked a theatrical sense. (Even Tchaikovsky, who admired him, wrote to Mme von Meck of his 'conviction that Saint-Saëns will never write a great dramatic work'). Reservations are unjustified: *Henry VIII* is superbly dramatic and Saint-Saëns was very proud of it. In 1909 he wrote to Durand from Aix-les-Bains after a rehearsal: 'The work stands out brilliantly. Why it is not in the repertory everywhere is what I refuse to understand.' In 1920, anticipating a revival, he wrote to the Opéra: 'I believe that your baritones will not be sorry to appear in such a rewarding part. There are not many things in opera like the Grand Duo in the second act, not to mention the Finale in the first act, the aria of Katherine or that of Henry which is famous among singers.' At the same time he was aware of the difficulties. In 1906 he informed Rudolf Ganz about the roles of Henry and Katherine: 'It is always difficult to find singers capable of performing them. If, as you say, the baritone, Aubert, was admirable, he is all the more laudable as the part is terribly difficult. One does not often find voices like that of Lassalle or natures like that of poor Krauss who was so marvellous.'

Henry's music has a caressing hypocrisy. The plot hinges upon the King's passion for Anne Boleyn and his desire to put away Queen Katherine. As his will is thwarted by the Papal Legate he casts aside the Catholic religion and proclaims himself Head of the Church in England. There are anomalous references to the recent Decree of Papal Infallibility and the inhibiting effect of Papal authority on national sovereignty. Tudor historians could complain that the libretto ignores the crucial factor that Katherine could not produce a male heir, so vital to the peace of the realm, but there is a powerful contrast between Katherine, self-sacrificing and loving, and Anne Boleyn, determined not to become a discarded mistress like her sister, but fearful that the terrible monarch will take revenge for any unfaithfulness. The device of the letter, which reveals the previous love of Anne for the Spanish Ambassador Gomez when both were at the French

---

[1] Katherine, Anne, Henry and Don Gomez, Anne's lover.

Court, is part of age-old libretto machinery, but its treatment is given a rare dignity. In the final scene Katherine withdraws the letter from her prayer-book, refuses to hand it to the King, who tries to goad her into jealousy by insincere expressions of passion towards Anne, and dies, hurling it into the fire. Anne and Gomez tremble at the dreaded prospect of revelation and Anne has premonitions of the scaffold, which returns the plot to historical reality. The drama was combined with all the pageantry the Opéra commanded. Act Three begins with the imposing March of the Synod, redolent of heavy copes and mitres, and concludes with a chorale, which combines the grandeur of a nation breaking from Rome with a flavour of Protestantism. The background of 'The People' is present both in the sturdy regional sections of the ballet and in the development of the chorale, contrasting with the soft choruses and amorous music of the Court. There is unity to the first act, built around the off-stage execution of Henry's former friend Buckingham. Katherine's failure to win a reprieve reveals her waning influence with her husband. Henry's cruelty to those whom he has once loved becomes apparent and the fate of Anne Boleyn is foreshadowed as the funeral cortège, sounding 'De Profundis', passes under the palace windows as the King is declaring his unequivocal love for her.

Research was done on old manuscripts and drawings to re-create the Tudor Court. When the opera was in rehearsal at Covent Garden in 1898, Queen Victoria asked the composer about the origin of the old melodies used in the score. He recounted his story of finding a theme in sixteenth-century harpsichord arrangements in the Buckingham Palace library 'buried under a tangle of arabesques, the theme of so lovely a character that it is the framework of the opera'. A letter from one of the royal princes later reported that the Queen had talked with interest about this discovery in her collection.

The dress rehearsal, to which critics had been invited, left the audience cold and unconvinced, but the reception of the première was cordial. Saint-Saëns's first work at the Paris Opéra had attracted everyone of social and artistic distinction. The composer sent a letter to the conductor, Ernst Altès, 'How the slack and indecisive playing of the rehearsal turned into the admirable rendering of the first night and the marvellous playing of the second – how the pupa has become a startling butterfly – I am not aware. What I do know is that the Orchestra of the Opéra has proved once again that it is the best in the world. The Société des Concerts will not take offence at these praises. The Society and the Opéra represent the God of Music in two persons.' Altès had had to conduct from the MS score, so many had been the cuts and rewritings during rehearsal. One scene had gone, in which the Legate pondered on the fatal pride of kings. There was sufficient evidence already in the libretto to show Republicans that a royal sceptre could become a threat to liberty.

The reviews were long, detailed and complimentary. Edmond Hippeau's critique eventually ran to a volume of eighty pages. The *Revue des Deux Mondes*, which had hitherto taken scant notice of Saint-Saëns, printed a notice of thirteen pages. Some critics detected Wagnerian elements and indeed there are many leitmotifs, each character having more than one, throughout the opera. Adolphe Jullien, however, a leading Wagnerian, decided that Wagner would find nothing of himself there and the inconsistencies of style recalled the diversities of Italian opera. Louis de Fourcaud, in *Le Gaulois*, ignoring the achievement represented by a fusion of lyric drama and conventional opera, protested that the mixture of forms 'engendered monotony', but the general impression was that France had produced a great opera. The warmest tribute came from Gounod, who wrote in the *Nouvelle Revue* of April 1883: 'Saint-Saëns is one of the most astonishing musical organisations which I know. He grasps his craft as well as anyone; he knows the Great Masters by heart; he plays and amuses himself with the orchestra as he does with the piano – that is to say completely. He is gifted with descriptive powers quite rare; he has a prodigious facility for assimilation; he will write at will a work *à la* Rossini, *à la* Verdi, *à la* Schumann, *à la* Wagner. He knows them all from head to toe, which is perhaps the surest means of imitating nothing.' In a eulogy almost modelled on orations over the departed, Gounod recalled meeting the child Saint-Saëns, his 'intelligent and generous mother', the long-delayed theatrical success and the security of his reputation.

As a political statement *Henry VIII* triumphed. Divorce became legal in July 1884, the same month as that in which Saint-Saëns was made an Officer of the Legion of Honour. Laicisation proceeded in education and other areas of social life. Where Calderón in the original play had described the accession of Katherine's daughter Mary to the throne and her marriage to the Very Catholic Majesty Philip II of Spain, Saint-Saëns's librettists left Henry very much in charge of his own destiny and his young nation state. Yet *Henry VIII* was not the hardy perennial which Gounod and others anticipated. Difficulties arose with the third performance. The question of understudies had been overlooked. First Jean Lassalle and then Mme Krauss fell ill. The third hearing had to be postponed until 14 March. Throughout April the première danseuse, Mlle Sobra, had a sprained foot and was missing from the ballet, a serious matter at the Opéra. While thirty-one performances brought high receipts in 1883, there were subsequently only a few widely spaced representations. Built upon the traditional ingredients of solos, duets and ensembles, it did not have the great solo arias of *Samson* and its peaks depended heavily upon rich orchestration, of which piano reductions gave no adequate impression.

French Wagnerians who hoped to see a leading champion of the 'New Music' take the Opéra by storm were disappointed that so much of Meyerbeer remained. As Hippeau showed in his study, the leitmotifs in *Henry VIII* are used in a manner very different from Wagner's, whose motifs are plastic and changeable, altering according to the needs of the drama and the inner thoughts of the characters so that they take on a life of their own similar to the dramatis personae. In *Henry VIII* the themes are more like those of a formal symphony, which contrast with one another and are balanced in a musical way. Moreover, there are whole pages in which the leitmotifs are left aside, such as the melodic chorus of courtiers disporting themselves in Richmond Park in Act Two and the antique dance based upon 'The Carmen's Whistle' of William Byrd with which Anne seeks to beguile the suspicious King in Act Four.[1] Wagner's motifs, although treated with cunning, announce themselves with such prominence and force that the dimmest intelligence must eventually respond to them. Those of Saint-Saëns are interwoven with the music in a way that makes them a commentary upon the action rather than a symphonic substitute for a stage play. Saint-Saëns wanted to have his scenes engraved each as a continuous whole. It was only because the publishers thought that amateurs would consider this 'Wagnerian' that – until *Ascanio* – they were printed in the traditional format of recitatives, arias and ensembles. He did not wish the motifs to

---

[1] Apparently Rubinstein had included 'The Carmen's Whistle' in a series of programmes on the 'History of the Piano Repertoire' in 1880.

dominate the process of composition or halt the music's flow. Writing of his later opera, *Proserpine*, he declared that the listener should allow himself to be carried along by the current of the music 'as the boatman lets himself float on the current of the water, without worrying about the chemical components of the waters which carry him'.

In Wagner the voices have to assert themselves against heavy and often contrary forces, but he saw the function of opera as the dressing of voices in fine raiment. In the two arias of Catherine, the first pleading her cause before the Synod and the second lamenting her long exile from Spain, he shows a tenderness for the vocalist which precludes the use of distracting orchestral motifs.

As soon as *Henry VIII* reached the stage Saint-Saëns set off for a long rest in Algiers. His doctor was disturbed at the condition of his lungs and urged immediate departure, even though this precluded answering his critics and caused inevitable rumours of 'flight'. He was exhausted after the wrangles, political and managerial.[1] His stay at Pointe St Eugène proved to be too short and having returned to Paris he was forced to travel again to recuperate in Béarn while the young Messager deputised for him (and met his future bride) at a series of concerts in Le Havre. It was characteristic that he used the success of *Henry VIII* to benefit younger colleagues and suggested to Vaucorbeil that Messager, whose career had been slow to prosper, might be asked to write a ballet. There was no immediate result, but Saint-Saëns persevered and in 1885 was able to tell Messager that Vaucorbeil was waiting to see him in his apartment in the rue Miromesnil; the resulting score was *The Two Pigeons*.

Recovering in the Pyrenees, Saint-Saëns had his old pupil Perilhou for company. 'Perilhou says it is a "laughter-cure"; indeed I need it,' he told Durand. A later letter indicated that he felt much restored. 'In the shack which pompously calls itself "Casino" – I have danced a quadrille!'

There was, not surprisingly, a reduction in his rate of composition, but 1884 saw new piano works, which included the *Rhapsodie*

---

[1] He later recounted his troubles to Albert Carré, Director of the Opéra Comique. He had to 'make an uproar from Hell' to have clarinets on stage for Act One as brass only was normally allowed. For the last act he thought Vaucorbeil had deliberately reduced the set to exclude the on-stage instrumentalists.

d'Auvergne, an Andantino and the *Piano Album*. The *Rhapsodie* was his first work for piano and orchestra that was not in concerto form and, since it used airs from the Auvergne region, owed something to Liszt's *Hungarian* Rhapsodies. There is the Lisztian pattern of a melancholy song, in this case based upon a melody heard sung by women doing their washing at a stream. It is interspersed with trills in thirds and gives way to an insistent bass rhythm and a 'gypsy' dance, which comes to a climax in strong chords. There is a further dashing dance embellished with runs down the keyboard, a reappearance of the introductory song and the most scintillating of all his spectacular final displays. The work was written in three versions: piano solo, piano and orchestra, and duet for four hands. It was a piece he chose to perform in an embryonic recording process pioneered by a piano manufacturer, Edwin Welte, in the early years of this century.

The *Piano Album* was made up of Prelude, Carillon, Toccata, Valse, Chanson Napolitaine and Finale. The collection comprised various genres of 'studies', souvenirs of travel and salon pieces. The future enemy of impressionism incorporated the effects of muffled bells at the close of the Carillon and strumming strings in the Chanson Napolitaine. The Prelude is a development of the Mendelssohn 'Song without Words', though with moments of passion and virtuoso passages. The Finale is written in a grand eighteenth-century style and comes to a spectacular close. The Carillon has the unusual feature of a 7:4 metre.[1]

The Chanson Napolitaine is very different from the traditional sprightly tarantellas and paints the heavy toil of fishermen with hints of an Arabic connection in its languid close. In the winter of 1883–4 Saint-Saëns had journeyed in Italy and North Africa, for he was too unwell to make many public appearances. He found little to raise his spirits in the architecture at Pisa and Siena – 'a passion for the ugly torments men' was his comment. He lamented his illness to Durand, saying he had 'great projects' in mind and he endeavoured to interest some of the Italian opera houses in *Henry VIII*. At Pompeii he seems to have ascribed the death of the city to the Christians and forgotten the eruption of Vesuvius. A deep-seated fear of the overthrow of a settled order by revolutionaries (Christians in the Roman empire and

[1] The *Album* was dedicated to Anna Hoskier. M. Hoskier was Danish consul in Paris, a wealthy music lover. One of his daughters married the pro-Saint-Saëns critic Camille Bellaigue.

Communards in contemporary France) was mingled in his thoughts with an increasing impatience with the Church. 'The burnings at the stake of the sixteenth century were the equivalent of the ferocious beasts of the amphitheatre,' he wrote.

Like many of those who have risen to a position in Society by their own efforts, he had a horror of its collapse under pressures from visionaries. Soon after his return he composed his part-song 'The Titans', in which there are exhortations to make war upon Olympus, an allegory of the battles which the bourgeois Republicans still felt to be necessary against the ingrained religious reactionary outlook. Yet, incongruous mixture that he was, he chose this period in which to write two more settings of 'O Salutaris' (in E major for baritone and organ, and E flat for soloist and organ) and a religious motet, 'Deus Abraham', dedicated to Renée Richard, who had sung the role of Anne Boleyn.

On the return journey he paused in the South of France, where the *Danse Macabre* and the ballet from *Henry VIII* were played at the inauguration of the Nice Casino, and in April he went south again to Toulouse to supervise rehearsals for *Henry VIII* and conduct a Saint-Saëns Festival, which included extracts from the *Oratorio de Noël*, the Romance in F for Horn and Orchestra and two of the symphonic poems: *Omphale* and *Phaeton*. From his next stop, Barcelona, he told Durand that Detroyat was proposing a new work for the Antwerp Exhibition in the following year. The Director had given Detroyat a choice of Gounod or Saint-Saëns and he had chosen the latter. Alas, he was too busy and too unwell to contemplate another operatic score. He was surprised that *Henry VIII* had not been put forward as an alternative. He was in Paris in May to sit on the jury of the Prix de Rome, which was won by a favourite pupil in Guiraud's class, Claude Debussy. Guiraud and his pupil had long nocturnal cigarette-smoking sessions in a café, where they would play billiards until closing time, then walk to and fro between their lodgings. Guiraud had spoken enthusiastically of Debussy to Durand and took great pains with the preparation of his pupil's *L'Enfant Prodigue*. At the preliminary hearing before the Music Section, where there was great argument, Debussy received the votes of Guiraud and Saint-Saëns only, but after a fine performance before the whole Academy and long discussions, during which Debussy waited anxiously, he was declared the winner. The musicians (save for Saint-Saëns) had maintained their objections, but the victory was won by the votes of the painters who admired the imaginative touches in the score. Durand sent a note with an offer of publication and next morning found Debussy on the steps of his office with an equally excited Guiraud beside him.

Saint-Saëns proceeded to Weimar to join Liszt at a Congress of Musicians, returned to Paris to attend the funeral of Victor Massé, where he held one of the cords of the pall, and went on to Dieppe. He wrote to Caroline de Serres to say that he was still far from well, that he hoped to hear from her in London and that he had just visited a sad and lonely Pauline Viardot. 'She was very sad; her pupils are gone, she is alone in the world and feels cruelly the void left by her husband and Turgenev.' He told Durand that he was 'setting off for Old England' to hear *Tristan* at Covent Garden, and drew a cartoon of Britannia and a ship crossing the Channel.

In September he published a letter in which he took issue with those Wagnerians who claimed that Berlioz had had a great admiration for his German colleague: 'May I be permitted, apropos of *Tristan* to recall some personal memories . . . Berlioz detested this score. He had other personal hates, notably that which he nourished for Meyerbeer's *Le Prophète*. As I had candid conversations with him, it never bothered me to argue with him and express to him the admiration which the general conception and a large part of the work of the great Richard inspired in me.' Saint-Saëns added that he had very occasionally been in agreement with Berlioz and referred to an 'atrocious' passage in the second act of *Tristan*, which he had tried hard to understand and appreciate. While his letter contained much that was complimentary to Wagner, criticism of anything was a blasphemy in the eyes of the Wagnerians. The opinion that Saint-Saëns, once an admirer, had become a critic of his former idol spread in this distorted form.

His reputation was not enhanced by a mismanaged production of *Etienne Marcel* in Paris at the Château d'Eau. A project for a new Théâtre Lyrique had been announced many times without result, but the possibility of civic funds persuaded the tenor M. Garnier to launch a company called Opéra Populaire, with which he hoped to mount *Etienne* and further his own singing career. Unfortunately the production ran into immediate difficulties. Chorus salaries were unpaid; the chorus called off a strike on the day of the première only out of respect for the composer. Garnier had instituted some sort of booking system, which was intended to make large profits, but ended by turning away the public. The baritone Auguez was well cast as the heroic Etienne, for he had been wounded and decorated in the 1870 war, but Garnier was a corpulent Robert de Loris who had trouble rising to his feet at the end of the love duet with Beatrice. Another singer from Marseilles was described as delivering her lines 'with an accent straight off the Canebière'. Subscriptions had to be returned and the theatre closed. The failure was more bitter for 1884 saw one of Massenet's greatest triumphs with *Manon* at the Opéra Comique.

In October Saint-Saëns gave a lecture to the Five Academies on 'The Past, Present and Future of Music'. In theory, he was prepared for any new experiments which might change the orthodox notions of Western music. He believed that the system of tones and semitones was only an approximation and the human ear, as it developed, might well become dissatisfied with a limited range of sounds. If a new art based upon more subtle gradations were eventually to be substituted the scores of his own day would come to be regarded like works in Latin or Greek, where masterpieces are recognised though the language is no longer in daily use. He expressed the view that the exclusive use of major and minor keys was ending, and ancient and oriental modes were being introduced, which would inject new life into melody. He foresaw the rapid extension of rhythmic patterns to include exciting new possibilities. He had always believed that there was more to music than its ability to express emotions and that musical architecture and form could give equal pleasure. 'When nothing but emotion is sought,' he said, 'art vanishes.' In practice he was to prove less welcoming to the collapse of key structures and violent experiments with new sounds and rhythms, which came earlier than his survey predicted, but the lecture reinforces the impression that deliberate craftsmanship rather than inspiration moved him more deeply. He also stands out from many notables of his own day in *not* regarding his own age as the pinnacle of Man's evolution.

In November he was in Geneva, where a new Salle Victoria was being opened with the patronage of the British consulate. He conducted *Le Déluge*, in which Marsick played the famous violin solo. A successful tour of Switzerland with Marsick followed and, in gratitude for the collaboration, the composer later wrote and dedicated to him his First Sonata for Violin. As the Chair of Victor Massé was now vacant in the Institut, Reyer, supported by Saint-Saëns, wished to put forward the name of Lalo for election. Delibes was eventually successful, but Lalo wrote to Saint-Saëns to express his gratitude for 'the courage necessary to throw my name into the midst of a gathering whose hostility, more or less disguised, I know'.

In the years immediately following this period of illness, Saint-Saëns's outlook oscillated between ambition and amusement. This is the period of the Violin Sonata and Organ Symphony, both with their long extended double movements and, at the same time, the *Wedding-cake Waltz*, *Carnival of the Animals* and *Gabriella di Vergy*. This last was written for La Trompette, a satire on Italian opera, '*un drama lirico*', a 'youthful work by a former organist'. There was already a Donizetti (and a Michel Carafa) opera of this title, but the audience enjoyed the purely satirical offering. Pauline Viardot was at the piano and there is even mention of a M. Franck on the harp. There was little scenery on the platform of the Salle d'Horticulture but, as the presenters announced, the Italians had never bothered much about scenery anyhow. The text, in basic Italian, consisted of exclamations such as '*fatal presaggio*', '*funeste pressentimento*', '*forza del destino*', '*facciamo brindisi*', etc. At the close the heroine, having been served the heart of her lover by the enraged husband, seizes a dagger and poses the question of suicide with much hovering over 'yes' and 'no'. Finally she stabs herself and expires. Augé de Lassus believed that Donizetti and Verdi would have appreciated the light touch with which they were mocked. Pierre Lalo, reviewing *La Favorita*, once said he preferred Saint-Saëns as a writer of Donizetti operas. Saint-Saëns was not at the first performance, but he came on future occasions as the parody proved popular.

Disputes over German opera were more serious. In 1885 *La Revue Wagnerienne* was founded, which aimed at exploring Wagner's philosophies and artistic theories rather than his music and gathered contributors such as Mendès, Huysmans, Verlaine, Mallarmé and other names from literature and art. By a coincidence, the publishers Calman-Lévy brought out in the same year a selection from the articles which Saint-Saëns had written in *L'Estafette* and *Voltaire*. In the preface, the admiration for Wagner was somewhat attenuated and there was a reiteration of his dislike of fanatical Wagnerism. In this he shared the view of many Frenchmen. Augé de Lassus said of Wagner's long acts that to expect the French to sit through two hours of music without prattling was to ask for the superhuman. When the Marsick Quartet in 1884 played the *Siegfried Idyll* one listener, bred in the land where music evolved from the dance, was heard to remark loudly, '*Ce n'est pas très dansant.*' But as Wagner gained increasing favour in Germany his compatriots began to regard Saint-Saëns as one of his principal French detractors.

The Violin Sonata indicated that Saint-Saëns's period of furious energy was beginning to fade. A meditative quality intervenes and infers that there are moments that can be dedicated to pause and recollection, though it has an athletic ending. The cyclic pattern is once again employed; the second subject, if such it is, of the first movement returns in the *perpetuum mobile* of the finale, is combined with the rapid theme of the latter and finally hammered out in octaves on the piano before the whirling close. Although the clear division of the two movements is in the classical pattern of four – Allegro Agitato, Adagio, Allegretto and Allegro Molto – there is very little adherence to classical forms. Despite the gulf which was to open between the ideas of Saint-Saëns and those of Debussy, it is noteworthy that in this work Saint-Saëns appears to consider it quite appropriate to 'play' with themes and adjust them, rather than develop them in the traditional fashion. The first 'movement' has no clear development section and the Allegretto only the merest suggestion of scherzo and trio, interrupted by a very solemn passage on the piano that makes the transition to the next 'movement'. The wayward melody at the opening, swaying between 9:8 and 6:8 in rhythm, has always been a strong candidate for the model of the Vinteuil Sonata in Proust, though it is hard to see why it should have exercised such great fascination. Saint-Saëns wrote many more inspiring melodies than this.[1] The first has always been the more favoured of his two Violin Sonatas by players, and Servières considered it an unsurpassed example of the composer's craft. The Finale, with its virtuoso runs alternating with a theme of passionate stridency, gives the work a climax admirable for the platform.

In the same year Saint-Saëns presented to Caroline de Serres the wedding gift of a Waltz for Piano and Strings, unique and delightful, although the title of the *Wedding-cake Waltz* gave the opportunity to some to identify him with lightweight trifles. In the previous year

---

[1] Proust wrote to a Jacques de Lacretelle that the phrase came from the Sonata of Saint-Saëns, 'a musician I am not fond of'. Many years later, he heard Enesco play the Franck Sonata at the time Vinteuil was introduced into the novel. To please Hahn in 1895 Proust wrote two articles on Saint-Saëns in *Le Gaulois*.

Caroline had asked Franck for a concertante piece and Franck had written *Les Djinns*, in which the orchestra represented forces of evil and the piano forces of light. If Saint-Saëns felt any jealousy over Franck's intrusion it did not show in this romantic *Valse-Caprice*, whose principal melody is familiar to thousands barely aware of Saint-Saëns's existence.

As well as ensuring that the Prix Rossini went to two young composers, Lucien Lambert and Georges Mathias, Saint-Saëns had to extend support to Fauré, who was greatly distressed at the death of his father. Fauré had married early in 1883 and his elder son, Emmanuel, had been born in that December. He had anxieties over household finances, the health of his wife and his teaching and travelling. 'He must have been very distressed at losing the best of fathers,' wrote Saint-Saëns to Marie Fauré. 'This is the first real sorrow to strike him in his life ... Fortunately in you he has the greatest consolation.' In Antwerp, Fauré sorely needed Saint-Saëns's forceful aid to sort out confusion at the Festival. 'Such ineptitude, and so casual an attitude all round that I am half surprised anything in fact takes place at all ... There isn't a rehearsal room in the entire city. There is a German faction, tenacious and crafty, which wants to make the French Festival collapse.' As the Concert Hall had been usurped by a floral exhibition it seemed as though Fauré's symphony might have to be performed in an open-air bandstand to a strolling audience, but Saint-Saëns was able to ensure better treatment for the symphony and his own Fourth Piano Concerto.

He remembered another Niedermeyer pupil in dedicating his Polonaise for Two Pianos to Julien Koszul who eventually became Director of a Conservatoire at Roubaix (where he taught Roussel). Sympathy for the fate of partitioned Poland was common to all Saint-Saëns's generation. In addition he maintained his nostalgia for the memory of Chopin, whose acqaintanceship had been barred to him. He had a great detestation of George Sand, for what he thought was her 'harmful' effect on the composer. His own Polonaise has the same sad note of a call to battle of which the doomed outcome is never in doubt, but a move into the major at the close may betoken a future resurrection of the country. A notable performance of this duet was given at Vevey in 1913 by the composer and Paderewski. There was huge enthusiasm and Saint-Saëns wrote to Durand to say that the hall would not hold all those wishing to attend.

Towards the end of the year a much larger work began to seize his imagination. On 4 July the London Philharmonic Society considered 'an invitation to compose a new orchestral work for next season to be sent to Gounod; if he refused, to Delibes, Massenet or Saint-Saëns'. On 1 August it was resolved 'that Saint-Saëns be invited to play a concerto at one of the concerts, either his own or not, as he prefers'. Francesco Berger, the Secretary, offered five dates from March to June 1886. Saint-Saëns, who was answering appeals from Fauré to help him rehearse the Saint-Saëns *Requiem*, chose 19 May and suggested two possible programmes: his Fourth Concerto and *Rhapsodie d'Auvergne*, or Beethoven's Fourth and his own Septet. He agreed to play a number of solo items, asked for a fee of fifty pounds: and closed significantly by saying he would be pleased if the Society would include a symphony of his in one of its programmes. Berger replied that the Philharmonic was an artistic rather than a profit-making body and suggested a sum of thirty pounds. The smaller fee was agreed. Berger asked if he would be able to compose a new symphonic work for the following season, to which Saint-Saëns replied that 'without making a formal commitment I will make every effort to respond to your wish and write a new symphony for the sake of your Society'.

In November he embarked on another concert tour with the violinist Raphael Diaz Albertini, to whom two years later he dedicated the *Havanaise*. They played at various towns in northern France and Brittany. By December he had crossed to England, where he attended a performance of Gounod's *Mors et Vita*. A concert which included the Fourth Concerto and the Septet earned him some respectful comments from Shaw, who received the Septet 'thankfully' since so little chamber music had included the trumpet since the days of Bach and Handel. It was in London that the first thoughts on a symphony came to him.

At the start of the new year, 1886, he began a tour of Germany, where the atmosphere was much less emollient. There had been a production of *Lohengrin* proposed by Carvalho, which caused a section of the French press to stir up trouble. Lalo wrote to von Bülow in December about 'a stupid struggle' impending and said that he would fight for the Tetralogy or *The Mastersingers*, but felt less inclined to do so for Wagner's earlier works. In the end a nervous Carvalho cancelled his plans.

Saint-Saëns's Berlin audience, believing some national foe was in their midst, greeted him with catcalls. Police ejected the protesters and the concert continued. On the following day a more private recital was peaceful, but the press suggested he had fled from the concert hall. He was depicted in cartoons as leaving a platform under a hail of vegetables. At Cassel the welcome was even colder. His agent received a letter from the theatre intendant, which condemned the French musician's 'incomprehensible' lack of tact with regard to German art and declared his presence to be incompatible with official policy. The *Musikalisches Gazette* of Leipzig urged that all theatre directors in Germany should follow suit; the intendants of Dresden and Bremen swiftly fell into line behind their brother at Cassel. Saint-Saëns does not appear to have learnt the lesson of the 'Ems Telegram'[1] as he wrote to Emperor William I asking for a denial of certain remarks made about his antipathy to Wagner.

Some voices were raised in his defence. Eduard Hanslick deplored the attacks and support came from Angelo Neumann, Director at Prague, to whom Saint-Saëns protested that he had been among the first to plead for *Lohengrin*. Having been virtually banned from Germany he played in Prague and Vienna, where he was much fêted, for there were many in the Austro-Hungarian Empire suspicious of Germany's dictatorial attitudes. Caroline de Serres, whose second husband was a director of the Austrian railways, gave a great reception in his honour and played a two-piano version of the ballet from *Etienne Marcel* with him. On his return to Paris Saint-Saëns poured out his thanks: 'You are quite adorable, quite exquisite, quite yourself. There is not an equal in the world. There are no terms to thank you and I will not even try.'[2]

Meanwhile, he had snatched a moment of repose in a quiet Austrian village and there, so strange are the mysteries which govern inspiration, he emerged from his *via dolorosa* of cancelled engagements with the score of *Carnival of the Animals*. He was simultaneously working on his Third Symphony and confessed to Durand that he found relief in this lighter task. He wished to offer the pieces to

---

[1] The telegram message from William, edited by Bismarck, which precipitated the war of 1870.
[2] His humour reasserted itself rapidly. 'Don't distress yourself,' he told Durand. 'My music will be in future for Germany like that of Wagner for France – the taste of forbidden fruit.'

Lebouc, a cellist who gave chamber concerts and was about to retire. They were written for two pianos, two violins, viola, cello, bass, flute, clarinet, harmonium, xylophone and celeste. He had had ideas for these humorous musical sketches ever since the Ecole Niedermeyer. French music since the days of Clément Jannequin's *Réveil des oiseaux* contained examples of bird and animal imitations. Etienne Méhul, in *La Chasse de jeune Henri*, had tried to convey the barking of dogs, and in the early 1850s a certain M. Saint-Léon had written a piece, *Une Matinée à la campagne*, for the Théâtre Lyrique in which his violin interpreted all manner of farmyard noises. In the 1880s Chabrier had also tried his hand at some humorous pieces.

The fourteen short movements which comprise *Carnival* are remarkably varied. In the 'March of the Lion', Saint-Saëns specified 'style persan' as leonine roars shared the Dorian mode with parts of the *Mélodies Persanes*; the 'Poules et Coqs' followed the examples of Rameau and other bird noise experts, 'Hemiones' employed rapid piano runs to suggest the wild gallops of this somewhat untraceable species, the 'Tortoises', represented by the Galop from Offenbach's *Orpheus in the Underworld* played adagio, continue on their obstinate way oblivious to all harmonic obstacles and, in the manner of the fable, reach their goal. The 'Elephant' is pure parody with the double-bass lumpenly murdering Berlioz's 'Dance of the Sylphs', with allusions to Mendelssohn and Meyerbeer's *Les Patineurs* thrown in. The 'Aquarium' is a highly impressionist piece with its mixture of celeste, piano and violin sounds, which even Debussy might have thought adventurous. The 'large-eared' asses make braying sounds[1] but poetry returns with the 'Cuckoo', where string passages suggest limitless forests from whose depths the solitary cuckoo sounds. Flutes, as custom dictates, people the aviary and then, surprisingly, come the 'Pianists' practising Czerny-like exercises and reminding the listeners that, for a composer, piano players in a neighbouring apartment are troublesome beasts. The fossils are both real and metaphorical: skeletons from the *Danse Macabre* jostle with musical relics, which include a Rossini aria and songs such as 'J'ai du bon tabac'. Another

---

[1] The 'personages with long ears' seems to have been a current phrase. Lao writes of 'The possessors of long ears who admire *La Juive* and *Hamlet*, but regard the word "Symphony" disdainfully ... the ideal of these folk does not go beyond cantilenas and cavatinas.' The conjunction of uncritical opera lovers and asses would not be unwelcome to Saint-Saëns.

change of mood introduces 'The Swan', where the lines of the melody suggest the graceful contours of the swan's neck, which, despite its many versions, is best heard as the cello solo, while the two pianos magically suggest the ripples and water-drops of river foliage through which the majestic creature glides. The Finale harks back to the mood of the Second Empire, a 'carnival' in its way, and various figures from the bestiary join in a 'can-can' romp. The suite displayed his interest in new instruments, for it was in 1886 that the celeste was first displayed by Alphonse Mustel.

Feeling that the Cat had been unfairly omitted, Bourgault-Ducoudray began composing a sequel and searched out low-class lodgings to study the mating calls of street cats. They failed to oblige him and, being a stickler for exactness, he left the work unfinished. At the first performance of *Carnival* the pianos were played by Saint-Saëns and Diémer, and among the other players were some of the finest instrumentalists of the time such as Taffanel and Turhan. Lebouc, the cellist, was elderly and his laboured breathing was a cause for comment, but on this occasion there was an emotional display of homage and the image of the swan-song seemed movingly appropriate.[1] Some days later 'La Trompette' had the privilege of hearing the suite at its mid-Lenten celebrations. Two hundred people had to stand – so great was the gathering. Liszt was in Paris for his *Legend of St Elisabeth*. Saint-Saëns and Pauline Viardot were guests in his box at the Trocadéro and he asked if he might hear the much discussed *Carnival*. A special performance was arranged for him in the strictest privacy, for the composer foresaw, with good reason, how speedily his reputation might be lessened when identified with a musical prank.

In May Saint-Saëns was again in London for the first hearing of the Third Symphony at a concert attended by the Prince and Princess of Wales. He played the Beethoven Fourth Concerto and then mounted the rostrum to conduct his new symphony, the first that he had written for twenty-seven years. The form had recently returned to favour in France with the Lalo Symphony of 1885 and Fauré's a year earlier. D'Indy was simultaneously working on his *Symphonie Cévenole* and the Franck Symphony was finished before the Organ Symphony

---

[1] In 1938 Leopold Godowsky, the great American pianist, crippled by a stroke, asked some friends to play his transcriptions of 'The Swan'. 'This wondrous melody from the pen of his erstwhile master and protector was the last music the doomed man heard on earth.' It was almost the last Saint-Saëns heard.

was played in Paris. Saint-Saëns made his first sketches in B minor and the opening bars have an affinity with the Schubert *Unfinished*, but this plan would have involved a Finale in B major with its many difficulties and the work moved into C.[1] He provided an analysis explaining the two-movement structure 'to avoid the endless resumptions and repetitions, which more and more tend to disappear from instrumental music under the influence of increasingly developed musical culture'. This analysis, incidentally, is written almost entirely in terms of the 'feelings' he later dismissed as superfluous in music: the first theme 'sombre and agitated', the second 'with a feeling of great tranquillity', 'vague feelings of agitation', 'fantastic' elements in the Scherzo etc. The suggestion of the 'Dies Irae' in the first movement and the fact that the dedicatee, Liszt, died at about the time of its appearance gave rise to the belief that it was a funeral tribute, but Liszt was alive when it was written and wrote a month after its début, 'Very dear friend. Pleased by the kindness of which you have given me such proof. I am wholeheartedly grateful to you. The success of your Symphony in London gives me great pleasure and it will continue "crescendo" in Paris and elsewhere. For the purposes of the dedication I ask that you use only my name ... which I must now append to these few lines because of my poor eyesight. With devoted and cordial affection, Franz Liszt.' The 'Dies Irae' could have been in Saint-Saëns's mind with reference to himself rather than another, for he had been severely ill in 1883–4 and had written to Liszt saying he had nearly succumbed to his sickness.

The St James's Hall organ had recently been replaced and he did not know the new instrument. He did, however, intend that the score should be followed exactly; the pedal should not be used until the third bar of the Adagio and the 32 ft depths should not be sounded until the Adagio theme is played by the full orchestra. *The Times* appeared to be more struck by the use of the piano in place of the harp than the addition of the organ, although it expressed admiration for the restrained use the composer made of the large forces assembled: 'M. Saint-Saëns is a master of his craft and, what is more, he makes that mastery subservient to the expression of a poetic idea.'

[1] An 'unfinished' symphony did not, of course, have to encounter this problem! The initial phrase came to him on a rainy day in a London street. A surprising moment of illumination, as two weeks of rain stopped all work on *Ascanio* at a later date in Paris.

Among its many remarkable gestures of patronage, the Philharmonic Society had commissioned Cherubini's Symphony in D as far back as 1815. Saint-Saëns's symphony, with its imposing proportions, its fugal intricacies and its robust manner, manifests a proud declaration of the Conservatoire traditions. Yet the struggle between classical and Romantic was no less strong in him than in Brahms and from Berlioz he had inherited the imaginative faculty that refused to repress personal feelings: hence the restlessness of the first movement, the rich sadness of the Adagio, the chaotic syncopations and 'unclassical' key changes – F, E, E flat, G – of the Trio and the huge batteries of brass and organ at the close ('like Napoleon hurling in the Imperial Guard at Waterloo,' as Augé de Lassus described it). The final pages, it is true, do not achieve a grandeur sufficient to match the earlier mood of turbulence and tragedy, exciting though they can sound.

Saint-Saëns did not have the powers of the titans of the symphonic form. He lived under a Republic that never knew total self-confidence. D'Indy, who was identifying a 'School' of César Franck with increasing enthusiasm, wrote of the Organ Symphony that it seemed 'like a challenge to the traditional laws of tonal structure' and thought it gave 'a final impression of doubt and sadness', where the Franck symphony represented 'a continual ascent towards pure gladness and life-giving light'.[1] D'Indy also disparaged the attempt to combine the sounds of organ and orchestra, and quoted Berlioz, 'the genius of the chemistry of timbre', on the misguidedness of combining them: 'The orchestra is Emperor; the organ is Pope. It is better not to renew the Investiture Contest in Music.'

Paris ignored the new symphony for some time but Garcin, conductor of the orchestra of the Conservatoire, put it on the programme for January 1887. So great was its success that it was repeated three times during the season, an event without precedent. The concerts were still suspicious of living composers and it was only from the time of Garcin, and his successors, Taffanel and Georges Marty, that new works were promoted with enthusiasm. The London programme was translated into French, the first time that programme notes were introduced into French concert halls, and at the end of the

---

[1] In the programme notes he supplied, Saint-Saëns made reference to the 'defeat of disturbing and diabolical elements'. This may have been a gift to the English public, which liked to feel a moral message behind music.

première Gounod introduced Saint-Saëns to a friend in a voice which was intended to be heard by all: 'Behold the French Beethoven!'[1] Lecocq wrote, 'the trumpets of glory are resounding to the echoes with your name. The entire critical world inclines before your magnificent work. Even the terrible Pougin [Arthur Pougin of *Le Ménestrel* and other journals] himself begins to believe that you may have some talent.' Fauré attended with the score, 'something which ensured I did not miss a single note', and wrote: 'This Symphony will live much longer than us two, even when putting our ages together!' Fauré asked if Saint-Saëns could come to the Société Nationale to hear his new Quartet. Saint-Saëns replied sadly that he no longer attended the Société: 'I certainly thought about your Quartet and, had I not been tied to some unavoidable work, I should have asked to hear the rehearsal.'

His absence from the Société symbolised a blow which had fallen even before the Organ Symphony reached Paris. For ten years Henri Duparc and d'Indy had been Joint Secretaries. D'Indy had been efficient in his military fashion, but he and Duparc were anxious to lift the ban on foreign music. They argued that the standard of national art would be raised if there were opportunities to compare French works with those from abroad. These proposals were met with darkened brows on the part of Saint-Saëns, especially when plans were put forward to include excerpts from Wagner. 'The day that Wagner is played in Paris, what will become of us?' he asked. He had some justification, for Wagner's music was available in orchestral concerts and could not be described as 'interesting' new work from other countries. Italian operas swamped the French stage and the Société he had founded and served for sixteen years had proved its worth in giving a generation of French musicians an unparalleled starting point. Vallas, biographer of d'Indy, suggests that Saint-Saëns might have worried about royalties as he did not have the independence of the aristocratic d'Indy, but Wagner inhabited only the operatic stage whereas, through Durand, the works of Saint-Saëns in many genres and countless arrangements for voice, piano, violin and duets were on the market. Ironically, French music had become strong enough in the years since 1871 to withstand competition from abroad and Saint-

---

[1] Godowsky observed that Saint-Saëns had a photograph of Liszt inscribed 'Au Beethoven français'.

Saëns was wrong in adopting a Maginot Line mentality. The widening of the Société's programmes proved a strong attraction to Russian and Spanish composers to come to Paris, and other countries developed similar musical forums.

In November 1886, d'Indy was successful in passing a resolution that allowed into the Société's concerts 'works still unknown in France, as well as important selections from the masterpieces of Bach, Rameau, Gluck, etc. restored to their original editions'. This last phrase suggests a gesture towards Saint-Saëns, but Vallas is clear that the resolution was designed to deliver the Société to the Franckists. Saint-Saëns and Romain Bussine, the original begetters, resigned. Only fifty-one, Saint-Saëns appeared to younger musicians as belonging to the past. Although Franck, who succeeded as President, was older, the same attitude did not prevail towards him, for his composing career had just begun and masterpieces were coming in swift succession. In a letter to Hugues Imbert of August 1887 Franck made reference to Saint-Saëns, 'for whom I have passionate, wholesale friendship and deep gratitude'. It was his disciples who made of the relationship such a tale of rivalry. Saint-Saëns had, on his side, a peppery wit, which he could not resist, and had pleasure in pointing out that in Franck's Prelude, Chorale and Fugue the Chorale is not a chorale and the Fugue is not a fugue. (At least he could not deny that the Prelude was a prelude, as someone remarked!)

At the start of 1887 Le Déluge was also given at the Conservatoire. It was an appropriate overture to a year which was thick with political scandals. In 1886 the British ambassador had remarked that the Republic had lasted sixteen years, 'about the time it takes to make the French tired of a form of Government'. General Boulanger, Minister for War, had enjoyed publicity as the result of some Army reforms and became the hero of fervent nationalists. The young Jacques Durand was doing his military service at the time and long remembered the frenzied cheering which greeted the General at the 14 July celebrations. In April there was an incident on the Franco-German border when a M. Schnaebele, a French official, was arrested, supposedly on French territory, by German agents. Saint-Saëns indirectly became a victim of the 'Schnaebele' incident. It was not the moment at which to launch Lohengrin in Paris and its first performance at the Eden Theatre was almost as notable a fiasco as the Tannhäuser of 1861.

Lamoureux's production took place amid a storm of abuse in the press. The audience (including General Boulanger, as it happened) had to take shelter inside the theatre while a hail of missiles and refuse rained upon the walls and windows from angry crowds. Lamoureux had hoped to include *Samson and Delilah* as part of his season, but was persuaded to abandon the whole project before public order collapsed.

The necessity of a strong leader such as Boulanger seemed greater than ever, but a change of government removed him from the Ministry of War and before 14 July 1887 parades took place he was posted off to the Auvergne. At the Gare de Lyon his supporters lay down on the railway tracks to prevent his train from leaving.

A minor social scandal unexpectedly led to accusations that the Government of President Jules Grévy had been involved in selling honours and decorations. The source of corruption was traced to the Presidential Palace and Grévy's son-in-law, Daniel Wilson, who, as it happened, was brother of a Madame Pelouze who had employed the young Debussy as a private musician and helped to found the *Revue Wagnerienne*. The revelations threw Paris into uproar. Ex-Communards proposed marches on the Hôtel de Ville and there were rumours of gymnastic clubs which would suddenly turn into revolutionary cadres. After months of unrest Grévy resigned. Jules Ferry was the strongest man in politics, but the Left disliked him for his part in suppressing the Commune, the patriots for turning French military force into colonisation rather than revenge, the Catholics for his education policies. The choice of President fell upon Sadi Carnot, a descendant of the hero of 1793, chosen, as Clemenceau put it, 'for his perfect insignificance'. Carnot did, however, have the distinction of being an early member of La Trompette.

Anarchism raised its head once more. The apartment of Madeleine Lemaire, a friend of Saint-Saëns, salon hostess and painter, was burgled and set on fire. The perpetrator, Clément Duval, killed the policeman who tried to arrest him and proclaimed at his trial 'the right of those who have nothing, to take from those who have'. When d'Indy was rehearsing one of his orchestral works he found a note pinned to the rostrum, saying, 'Death to the aristocrats. Next time we will finish you off, you and your kind.' It was not surprising that Wagner should have appealed to some whose minds swam in a miasma of gods and heroes. Emile Dujardin, who was a member of Guiraud's composition class and a convinced Wagnerian, another founder of the

Revue Wagnerienne, was, though a gentle character, a member of an anarchist circle called 'The Batignolles Panthers'. Saint-Saëns admired the talents of another anarchist student, Victor Fumet, and tried to rescind the cancellation of his scholarship at the Conservatoire.

Even Saint-Saëns plunged into melodrama with his next opera, *Proserpine*, and reality proved more cruel than melodrama when the scenery and costumes were destroyed in a conflagration at the Opéra Comique which cost over seventy lives. As recently as 12 May 1887 there had been a question in the Chamber referring to the dangers of fire at the theatre, which had been rebuilt after an 1838 conflagration without allowances for the increase in personnel. By 1887 there were 450 artists and backstage people, all necessary for the lavish choral and scenic requirements of grander operas. Employees in the dressing-rooms and workshops were linked only by two wooden bridges to exits. On each side of the seven-storey building were vertiginous stairs of up to 170 steps, less than a metre wide in places. It was on 25 May, during Thomas's *Mignon*, that sparks falling on some torn gauze scenery spread out of the control of the cast, which tried at first to stamp them out. The first spectators to leave had time to descend and collect their cloaks. A second wave rushed for the exits when flames appeared and the sudden opening of the doors caused a rush of inward air, which carried the fire upwards. The chief gas controller, fearful of an explosion, turned off the supply and lights were extinguished, so that audience, orchestra and singers struggled blindly through smoke-filled labyrinths lit only by the fires on stage. Those behind the scenes were trapped. The costumiers fled to the roof, courageously slid down as far as the entablature and were eventually rescued, but four ballerinas perished in the corridors. A leading singer escaped after clinging to a window-sill for almost an hour. A team of *pompiers* had been on duty, but they wasted precious minutes trying to communic-ate. Hoses were unrolled without water; robinets spouted water without the hoses being unfurled. As in all theatres where the repertory changed frequently, the scenery was close-packed and dry with age.

The events had been terrible enough, but press accounts maximised them further; Carvalho, whose career had brought him to the Opéra Comique, was condemned to three months in prison and André, a fireman who had been negligently watching *Mignon*, received a sentence of one month. Productions moved for a time to the Châtelet but *Proserpine*, although the score was rescued by the conductor Jules Danbé, could not easily be restaged and became one of Saint-Saëns's least known operas. The composer felt it had been strangled at birth and long carried its failure in his heart. He placed it along with *Samson* and *Henry VIII* as one of his favourite stage works.

Proserpine was born at one of Hugo's dinner parties, though Saint-Saëns had suggested the idea as far back as 1880 when Carl Rosa had talked of a commission in London. The story came from a book of youthful verse by Auguste Vacquerie, an associate of Hugo in exile, and centred upon the story of a courtesan in Renaissance Florence. Vacquerie agreed that Gallet should construct a libretto from his poem and together the composer and librettist sketched out the work the following day. Gallet completed his script and, drawing on the merest reference in the text, invented the Convent Scene in Act Two as a contrast to the general violence and perversity of the story. He was a talented artist who sometimes helped out puzzled designers. The Convent Scene was staged on the basis of his water-colours. Saint-Saëns went to Florence in the summer of 1886 to absorb something of the atmosphere of luxury and treachery in the old Medici palaces. During August and September he sketched *Proserpine* at Chaville on the outskirts of Paris and the first night was fixed for March 1887. On the evening of the prèmiere, the Opéra presented a revival of *Aida*, but most of the critics chose to come to the Opéra Comique. The second act, which shows the heroine, Angiola, in the Convent while her friends chatter, the poor come to seek alms and religious services sound in the distance, was rightly acclaimed as a wonderful, coherent and symphonic episode. At a revival in 1899 the entire act was encored.

The story of Proserpine, a courtesan whose lovers come from high and low society, 'the count in his palace of marble and the fisherman on the lake', recalls the promiscuous noblewoman of the *Danse Macabre* and, by implication, the collapse of social barriers in the underworld. Her admirers discuss her in a sparkling 'vivacissimo' at the outset. True affection can bring only torture and misery. She believes that she has a genuine love for the handsome Sabatino, one of her past lovers, but he is directed towards the virginal Angiola by her brother Renzo. We may see a parallel between Angiola waiting for her betrothed in the convent and Saint-Saëns's Marie, brought to the notary at Le Cateau to marry a virtually unknown husband at a brother's command. The clear divide between respectability and the lawless lower classes carried a contemporary social message. Proserpine finds an ally in the villain, Squarocca, whom she enlists in a plot to kidnap Angiola. It is better for Sabatino that he finds a bride from his own class and better for those in the middle class – if, like Saint-Saëns they have risen upwards, or, like his great-aunt, known a sharp fall – to avoid sympathy with sansculottes lest all regress into a plebeian morass.

In the 1887 version, the jealous Proserpine stabs Angiola and is, in turn, fatally stabbed by Sabatino. Later the plot was revised and Proserpine stabs herself, having failed to despatch her rival. Saint-Saëns, who did not normally make alterations to completed works, made other later emendations to *Proserpine*, introducing a gypsy tarantella in the third act and suppressing an unusual symphonic prelude before the fourth, which was intended to portray the pursuit of Sabatino by the lustful Proserpine so that he will not become subject to a higher and purer love.[1] In Act Three she invokes the classical goddess Proserpine, who reigns at intervals in the underworld. Like Delilah, she is thereby seen as submitting to occult forces which give her strength. Servières criticised the composer for choosing a slight horror story as the vehicle for a major opera and summarised the plot as 'Love me pretty boy or I will slay your fiancée'.

Saint-Saëns tried on occasion to give the work a greater depth of meaning. Referring to an ironic declaration of love which Renzo obliges Sabatino to make to Proserpine he wrote, 'Two young men play with the heart of a woman and this woman dies as a result. Angiola is the Day; Proserpine is the Night.' The opera has brilliant passages, notably in the sparkling accompaniment to Proserpine's admirers in Act One, and the style marked a move from Meyerbeer, Halévy and the large ensemble writing of the earlier works.

The scene in which Proserpine leaps from concealment to interrupt the romantic exchanges of the young lovers reminds us that the story originated in the circle of Victor Hugo, with its thunderous romances and unlikely coincidences fashionable earlier in the century. On an insufficiently grand scale for the Opéra, it did not entirely suit the Opéra Comique, where the audience looked for a happy ending and was to be troubled by a final scene which had echoes of *Carmen*. Soon

---

[1] The device used by Puccini to link episodes in *Manon Lescaut* (1893).

afterwards the composer wrote of a synthesis of declamation and symphony, 'which I seek and which one day others will find. Both heart and head impel me to pursue this aim and to this I must adhere.' He clearly felt that the Wagnerian model in which music is ultimately subordinated to text was not the final answer.

Within a few weeks of the opera reaching the stage Saint-Saëns set off on a major tour to St Petersburg in the company of three distinguished wood-wind players, Taffanel, Gillet and Turhan. He had been engaged to conduct seven Red Cross concerts in the Manège, normally used for riding-school manoeuvres by the Imperial Guards. He had before him the orchestra of the St Petersburg Opera and, because he was able to correct a mistake by counting the bars in Russian, he won its joyful co-operation. Contacts with Russia continued to increase at this time. Fauré had met Tchaikovsky in 1886 and had given him an inscribed copy of his Second Quartet. César Cui spent time in Paris and commented upon French music in the *Revue et Gazette* and *Le Ménestrel*.

Saint-Saëns's first gala concert was attended by grand dukes and duchesses but, when the Opera reopened, several principal artists disappeared and the Russian winter took effect. In the vast Manège the temperature was freezing; even a Russian public could not brave the conditions. Nevertheless there was great interest in the soloists, as wind players in solo items were unfamiliar. An oboe concerto by Mme de Grandval was put into the programmes and Saint-Saëns had brought a suite of his own, based upon Russian and Danish songs. This was intended as a tribute to the Tsarina, Marie Feodorovna of Denmark, sister of Alexandra, Princess of Wales. The first performance in Paris was given by Taffanel at his newly formed Society of Wind Instruments. Having completed the Third Symphony and *Proserpine* in the previous twelve months, Saint-Saëns could be excused for devoting his energies to smaller and less exacting works. In addition to the Caprice for wind instruments there was a piano work, *Souvenir d'Italie*, and a *Feuillet d'Album* for four hands on the pianoforte. Italy seems curiously Arabic in Saint-Saëns's memory; the cymbal and castanet effects are demanded of the piano in a vigorous but harmonically sterile 2:4 section.

The *Feuillet d'Album* was arranged by Taffanel for flute, oboe, two clarinets, two horns and two bassoons. Taffanel, son of a theatre musician in Bordeaux, entered the Paris Conservatoire in 1868, gaining the premier prix for flute in 1860 and subsequently prizes for harmony and fugue. He became principal conductor of the Conservatoire concerts, a tribute to his musicality, for the post was normally given to violinists. It is possible he first met Saint-Saëns when the latter had his *Urbs Roma* Symphony performed at Bordeaux in 1857 and Taffanel was one of the city's promising young musicians. They would doubtless have met later in Paris, for Taffanel's teacher, Dorus, was one of the players of the Tarantella at Rossini's soirée. Taffanel attended Saint-Saëns's Monday Evenings and his name appears as Assistant Treasurer in the early days of the Société Nationale. He was a profound admirer of Saint-Saëns whose Romance for Flute and Orchestra Opus 37 he played in Germany and England, as well as on the Russian tour.

Saint-Saëns became godfather to his third child in 1882. He was hesitant about approaching a man who so recently had lost two sons and parted from his wife, and first he got in touch with the composer's mother. Some time later he wrote again, urging her to forget the idea if she had not already mentioned it and on the following day received a letter: 'My dear Friend, I had vowed that I would not be a godfather ever again. I have two reasons for this. The first you can guess and the second is my antipathy to religious ceremonies. Nevertheless, it seems to me that we could get round this by having some friend or other to represent me at the ceremony. On that condition I shall accept and with great pleasure ...' He was a diligent godparent and made frequent enquiries about little Marie-Camille.

The year 1887 also saw the *Morceau de Concert* for Horn Opus 94. This was a more ambitious work than the previous Romance for Horn and was dedicated to Henri Chaussier, leading horn player at the Conservatoire concerts, who had recently taken part in the success of the Organ Symphony. The opening theme, which is followed by variations, has an eighteenth-century ring. Saint-Saëns had a great interest in the Court of Louis XIV. The combination of the pomposity of the horn and a stilted dance rhythm brings to mind the Grand Monarch leading off, as was his wont, in court ballets. There follows a section which explores the more mysterious qualities of the 'horn calls' and a conclusion, which introduces more elaborate variations and opportunities for display.

A part-song, 'Les Guerriers', from 1887–8, aimed at the provincial choral societies, mirrors the patriotic anger of the time. The words expressed a heedless chauvinism, as the call is made to inscribe the name of France on the faces of the warriors who have chosen to die for their country. A *pas redoublé* for piano duet, a *marche militaire*, appeared also in a version for military band. Popular marches kept a martial note alive in both drawing-rooms and local parades. The result of the 'Schnaebele' incident had been to submerge all local and private quarrels in a mood of national assertiveness.

A more original work was the setting of Hugo's 'La Fiancée du timbalier'. Written for voice and orchestra, it contains an ominous march motif as the hired warriors go off to war, with a softening on the mention of the girl's fiancé among them, and ominous chords as a warning of the gypsy is recalled; rich orchestral colours describe the robes of the barons, darker colours as the depleted troops return, and contrasts between excitement and despair as the drummer is missing from the cortège.

In London he gave his first four concertos and Wilhelm Ganz, the conductor, found him as fresh at the conclusion of this marathon 'as if he had done nothing at all'. His mother, who had always encouraged him in his foreign tours, now began to regret his prolonged absences. Her sight was weakening and she was prone to depressions. 'I begin to find your travels a little lengthy . . . when you are not present my brain suffers a little . . . I have so little time to live . . . my years seem to pass more quickly than those of others . . . I have a need to see you.' He wrote to her almost daily.

It was at this time that Saint-Saëns was visited by a young pianist, Leopold Godowsky, of Polish extraction, almost self-taught: Godowsky had toured Canada with Ovide Musin to whom Saint-Saëns had dedicated the *Morceau de Concert* for Violin. He came to Europe to study with Liszt but, on arrival, saw the news of Liszt's death in the newspaper headlines and immediately made for Paris and the man whom he considered the second-greatest pianist and musician of the time. He found Saint-Saëns quick to listen and praise him, but slow to give instruction and advice. 'When I played for him, even his own compositions, he would invariably say *"Mais, c'est charmant"* or *"Admirable"* to *"Epatant, mon cher"* or something of the same sort and, even though spoken from the heart, this hardly amounts to constructive criticism.' The relationship was a curious one and Godowsky was given the impression that he was replacing the dead sons. 'He wished to adopt me, but with the proviso that I should take his name, but this I refused to do and it made him very angry.' Saint-Saëns enrolled both of them in a gymnasium. They would spend whole Sundays together, Godowsky playing what he had prepared and Saint-Saëns supping copious draughts of hot chocolate. In the evenings Saint-Saëns would play his own works and transcriptions. He arranged for Godowsky to play his compositions at La Trompette and introduced him to Tchaikovsky as a surprise. There were moments when Godowsky suspected that more interest was shown in him as a surrogate son than as a pianist, but in fact Saint-Saëns was deeply impressed by their similarities of technique: the dextrous finger work, the care over phrasing and the sparing use of the pedal. Through Saint-Saëns the young Godowsky gained an insight into French thought and valuable introductions to the great musicians and the patrons of the time. The relationship lasted until 1890 when he resumed his career in the United States.

This did not diminish interest in the progress of Fauré. Addressing the now more domesticated Fauré as 'My fat cat?' he refers to someone whom he has just met who wishes to buy all Fauré's music and thinks it puts Chopin's output in the shade. He concludes by saying that he is slaving away himself at Fauré's piano works 'and at present getting nowhere. The more I look at them the more I love them. Especially the Nocturne in B ma[jor] which I find absolutely entrancing. I shall ask you for a lesson some time.' At the same time Fauré, asked for some personal details for a publication, *L'Independance Musicale*, mentioned his interest in certain contemporaries and concluded, 'As for older composers, apart from Saint-Saëns for whom I have my passionate, wholesale friendship and deep gratitude, I cannot bring myself to take much interest in all these people like Massenet and Salvayre – the only exception being Reyer and certain lighter pieces by Delibes, which have grace and charm.'

The *Havanaise*, a virtuoso violin piece with orchestra, although it breathes the warm air of the Spanish Indies and is intended to depict the seductive movements of a dark Spanish girl, had been begun two years earlier in a cold hotel in Brest during the tour with Diaz Albertini who had Cuban origins. Saint-Saëns had managed to make a small fire in his room and the crackling of the wood gave him a melodic idea to which he added decorative phrases suggesting caresses. The habanera rhythm brings in the violin in the introductory section and soft drumbeats give reminders of it from time to time, especially during a quiet and reflective close. A rapid section leads to two more romantic themes, but there is in this instance no sharing with the orchestra and the violin not only dominates melodically but interposes phrases which suggest flirtatious glances, with chromatic runs and trills, and scales in thirds.

Concerns over health began to reappear towards the end of 1887 and he wished to avoid the Parisian winter. He set off for Algiers, taking with him the poem of another Gallet opera, *Ascanio*, based upon a play, *Benvenuto Cellini*, by Paul Meurice. Meurice had been a member of the team of assistants employed by Dumas in the writing of the original novel, *Ascanio*, which he had been allowed to dramatise. Saint-Saëns knew Meurice, for his neighbour from the days of the rue du Jardinet, Mlle Granger, had been his first wife. The story gave the opportunity to put into theatrical form the meeting between François I and the Emperor Charles V at Fontainebleau in what was a glorious moment in French history. The new Directors of the Opéra, M. Ritt and Pierre Gailhard, were in need of new works for the proposed 1889 Exhibition and granted a contract. The title *Ascanio* was selected in preference to *Benvenuto Cellini* to avoid confusion with the opera of Berlioz.

Cellini has been summoned to France by the connoisseur King François I. His favourite pupil, Ascanio, is a source of attraction to the Duchesse d'Etampes, an important figure at Court, but Ascanio is in love with the sweeter and younger Colombe d'Estonville. Benvenuto himself feels an affection for Colombe and this arouses jealousy in his former mistress, an Italian model, Scozzone. To save Colombe from the vengeance of the duchess, Benvenuto arranges for her to be conveyed secretly to a convent in a reliquary that has been commissioned. The duchess seals the reliquary in the belief that Colombe will slowly suffocate inside but, when she comes to open it, she discovers the corpse of Scozzone who has suffered remorse at her part in the plot and substituted herself. All this is interwoven with the theme of the creation of works of art, for, at the moment when the duchess touches the cold dead hand of Scozzone, a chorus announces that Cellini has cast a new masterpiece, his statue of Jupiter. The image of the artist struggling to create perfect forms outshines the malevolence and fluctuation of events. The two monarchs, François and Charles, both seek the services of the great artist and are willing to treat him with humility. Government and workshop come together. The music of the opening pages describes the bustle of a busy and happy bourgeois enterprise – and the patronage of the great and wealthy, symbolised in the celebrations at Fontainebleau, reflects the kind of support essential to composers such as Fauré, who was receiving help and encouragement from the Princesse de Polignac, the Countess Greffulhe and other great hostesses.

Saint-Saëns had completed the first act by 14 December. He returned to Algiers and installed himself in a quiet villa on the outskirts of the city where he could compose without distraction. In the evenings he would wander into the Arab districts and listen to the music in cafés. He wrote to his mother of the Festival of Mahomet being celebrated with metal castanets and 'symphonies which have all the charm of active metal factories'. Despite the need to rest and combat anaemia it was a happy time for him and soon the second act of *Ascanio* was finished. Gallet and Saint-Saëns corresponded at a distance. By September 1888 the score was complete, save for the ballet.

Almost at once difficulties arose. It had been decided that *Ascanio* would open during the Paris Exhibition of 1889. The role of Benvenuto had been written with Lassalle in mind. The great Jean de Reszke had sought the role of Ascanio but, on discovering that it was secondary, had retreated. A soprano expressed a wish to sing the dramatic role of Scozzone although it had been written for a contralto. Singers discussed the allocation of roles among themselves, there were delays in ordering the décor and the press was filled with false conjectures on progress, for the two Directors contradicted one another; an agreement secured from one was likely to be undermined by the other.

Saint-Saëns composed little in 1888 apart from *Ascanio*, but there was vigorous activity by others. Lalo's opera *Le Roi d'Ys*, rampantly Wagnerian in orchestration, had its première. Franck added further to the piano repertoire with *Prelude, Aria and Finale* and was working on a tone-poem, *Psyche*. This musical description of the seduction of Psyche by Eros was interpreted by d'Indy and other admirers as a Christian allegory of Divine Love. Mme Franck, who saw the shadow of Augusta Holmès athwart the score, carefully mislaid her ticket for the prèmiere at the Société Nationale, now a Franckist stronghold. Franck also used the theme of a song by Augusta Holmès in a collection of harmonium pieces he was putting together and dedicated to her the second of his Three Chorales for Organ. Augusta had her own musical triumph with a Grand Oratorio, *Pro Patria*, given at the Conservatoire in June. Marguerite Baugnies organised a tombola in her salon to raise funds to send Fauré and Messager to Bayreuth. A happy result of the excursion was the *Quadrille on Themes from Bayreuth*, which they put together on their return. Debussy, too, made his first journey to the shrine to hear *The Mastersingers* and *Parsifal*.

Across the political stage there grew the spectre of a military-style dictatorship under the increasingly popular General Boulanger. Dismissed from the Army but elected as a Deputy in several constituencies, financed by the wealthy Duchesse d'Ezes, he was supported by sections of the press. In June he produced a list of reforms, which in essence criticised the Republic and invoked a reply from Prime Minister Floquet, who pointed to the absence of military victories in the General's career. 'At your age, General Boulanger, Napoleon was dead!' There were fears of a *coup d'état*. The military governor of Paris, expecting a kidnap, had doubly strong locks fixed to his doors. Flaubert's old friend Maxime du Camp thought democracy was doomed. 'Like Peru, Haiti and Mexico, France slides towards intermittent Ceasarism.' Boulanger's demands for a dissolution of the Chamber led to a duel with the Prime Minister. Floquet was an elderly lawyer, but he had the better of the contest and for two days Boulanger was at death's door. All this must have made the plot of *Proserpine* seem tame enough.

Old Mme Saint-Saëns died on 18 December at the age of seventy-nine. Having ventured out into the cold weather she caught a chill, which turned to pneumonia. Camille wrote immediately to Fauré, whose mother had died almost exactly a year before. 'I too lost my mother this morning at nine o'clock. Not much point in saying more is there. . . .' He had been at her bedside and received her final kiss. At the funeral he maintained a cold composure, but observers noted his pallor and suppressed anguish. The moment when she was laid to rest in the family tomb at Montparnasse, beside the bodies of his two children, was one of the utmost poignancy. The loss of the principal force behind his arduous existence marked the close of a childhood that had lasted long into middle age. She had guarded the composer and tried to mould him in the image of genius which the long shadow of Napoleon laid across the nineteenth century. Lecocq remembered her saying, 'To do great things a great character is the sole necessity.' The effect of her death was to exacerbate the restless and nomadic existence which already monopolised much of her son's life-style. For a brief while he transferred his affections to the mother-in-law of the young Jacques Durand, Mme Louise Marcotte. He liked to stay at her property on the edge of the Forest of Fontainebleau, enjoyed the company of her dogs, composed his Suite for Piano Opus 90 there and dedicated it to her.

For the moment, however, he was anxious to escape from the home of sad memories and disputes at the Opéra. He left Gallet to supervise the preparation of *Ascanio* and departed on New Year's Eve. He spent some weeks in the Bay of Tamaris, suffering from insomnia and even talking of suicide. He had already embarked for Algiers, where he rested until May. He was unable to work and spent his time walking, reading old copies of the *Revue des Deux Mondes* and corresponding with Gallet. The latter had many difficulties to report. By the end of February 1889 the décor had not even been ordered. To celebrate the centenary, the Opéra proposed to revive Gounod's *Romeo and Juliet*, saving the costs of a new production. Then attention was switched to Thomas's *The Tempest*, which was produced in June. Saint-Saëns was back in Paris in May, but without the will or strength to combat the mysterious opposition to *Ascanio*. In September he spent two weeks at St Germain-en-Laye to console Diaz Albertini, who had also lost his mother, and wrote, at the request of Auguste Vacquerie, now editor of *Le Rappel*, articles on the musical instruments displayed at the Exhibition. The appearance of the Far-Eastern musicians, which so famously stirred Debussy, did not have the same delirious effect upon Saint-Saëns. 'Nothing could be more strange to behold than the enormous success of the Annamite theatre of the 1889 Exhibition,' he wrote. 'One heard only the cries of animals having their throats cut, wailings resembling so closely those of cats that one asked oneself with misgivings, after having heard them, whether cats do indeed have a language of communication; as for the instrumental part, take a badly greased pulley, your kitchen implements, a dog with food poisoning and do some carpet beating on the lot; you will have something very close to the effect.'

He also wrote a review of Augusta Holmès's *Ode Triomphale*, a massive pageant-cantata, which required assistant conductors placed upon plinths under orders from an autocratic Colonne to control the participants. Saint-Saëns was kinder to the *Ode* than he had been to the *Argonauts*. He recalled the happy evenings in Versailles long ago: 'What a shining memory they have left me, those riots of youth, art, music and poetry.' He praised the skill with which she had written for such large forces and subdued 'the orchestral sea whose waters, sometimes swirled up, sometimes calmed, under the trident of M. Colonne, filled the great Palais with its waves'. Having temporarily lost the faculty of composing he turned to poetry and tried to confide his feelings in verse. Gallet wooed him into accepting a libretto on the Merovingian queens of Gaul, Brunehilde and Frédégonde, but he could summon no musical inspiration and handed it on to Guiraud. He no longer felt any attachment to the apartment in the rue Monsieur le Prince. He had his furniture, pictures, *objets d'art*, manuscripts, medals and the letters he had received from musicians throughout Europe sent to Dieppe and made a gift of them to the town, to be housed in a museum. In October he gave his lawyer general powers of attorney and set off again for Spain, hoping 'to return with the swallows'.

9

Collapse and Recovery

His journey began in Andalusia, plagued again by insomnia, fears of madness and what he called 'a night feeling in his mind'. He was experiencing trouble with his eyes and made his way with some difficulty through the narrow streets and over cobbled pavements. He wrote to Gallet that 'he could not submit his poor vision to ruled paper'. He visited the Alhambra. 'Regnault could never tire of it and I understand.' He was preoccupied with his poetry. 'I have become a true fount of Hippocrene. I write verse from morning to evening and even at night. There are too many poems to send you.' In the gardens of the Alcazar he picked an orange illicitly and was obliged to tip the guard generously. He paused at Cadiz to write the sole musical work which dates from these travels, the strange Scherzo for Two Pianos, which he dedicated to Philippe Bellenot, choirmaster at St Sulpice, and his wife. It was played soon afterwards by Diémer and his pupil Edouard Risler, at the Châtelet. Saint-Saëns had drawn on the title page a strange bird clinging to the letter S and the use of the whole-tone scale, the tritone prominent in the themes and the total lack of sympathy between the themes made it appear as if the composer were casting aside his old classical vocabulary. To the purists there were passages that appeared to be echoes of the current anarchism. He himself wrote, 'I am at the mercy of the unexpected; I had no intention whatsoever of writing a scherzo. . . . There are some oddities. . . . Sight-reading it must be fairly painful; it is a piece one should not play until it has been mastered.' There is something odd in this conventional composer, in a moment of deep depression, writing involuntarily a piece that prefigures music of the next generation and in which the two instruments pass by one another without merging closely.

Augé de Lassus referred to a performance of the Scherzo by Saint-

Saëns and Diémer as a magnificent entertainment with 'an inexhaustible abundance of criss-crossing ideas'. In 1908 the composer was programmed to play it in Manchester with a Mme Chailly. The lady's son recalled that, quite naturally, she had assumed the celebrated Maestro would play the first piano and she rehearsed the second. Saint-Saëns returned from Egypt via Monte Carlo and arrived two days before the concert. He seated himself at his piano at rehearsal and said, 'Naturally, you will play first piano.' 'But, Master, I have worked at the second.' 'Not at all. Not at all. I am going to play the second and you will play the first'. Somehow she struggled through the reading and spent the next forty-eight hours working remorselessly at the principal part. On the day of the concert Saint-Saëns took the stage with white gloves, offered her his hand and led her with great ceremony to the place of honour. The family appears to have remained on friendly terms during the years following.

His letters from Cadiz mention a little Italian actress, Dora Lambertini, who was immensely talented but full of charm, a contrast to her sister who was of 'incredible beauty' but of no intelligence. He met a Portugese vice-consul at a local brasserie, but did not reveal his identity, gave his name as Charles Sannois and made excuses for not having a visiting card.

It was under this name that he arrived in the Canary Isles at the end of December 1889. Still in bad health, disgusted with life, taxed with overwork and pressures of all kinds, he wished to cut all cables and find the means of rebuilding himself. In a letter from the Hôtel de France, at Cadiz, he would not even give Gallet his destination. 'When you receive this letter I shall be travelling between sky and water, sailing towards a destination you will know later'. He had sent the Directors of the Opéra his instructions for *Ascanio*, rejecting any further changes and requesting that Guiraud should supervise rehearsals. *Lohengrin* had been played at Weimar without Wagner, *Aida* at Cairo without Verdi; *Ascanio* could be mounted without Saint-Saëns. Three days before he embarked at Cadiz he read in a café that Henri Verdhurt, manager of a new Théâtre Lyrique at Rouen, had expressed a hope that it would open with *Samson*, but even this news did not tempt him to return. When he landed at Las Palmas he asked for his trunk to be taken to the Four Nations Hotel, reputedly the best in town. While the servants dealt with his luggage he amused himself by examining the exotic flowers in the foyer, then signed himself 'Charles

Sannois, Merchant'. For some days he remained in the simply furnished room 15.

His habits puzzled the patron, since, oddly for a merchant, he appeared to write and receive no mail. His sole occupation was to take solitary walks, pausing at odd moments to scribble some words in a notebook. He dined alone, principally on fish and fruits, and answered questions in vague and monosyllabic replies. He was punctual and paid promptly, but other guests began to ask questions. 'Was he an invalid seeking the sun? A political refugee expelled from his country? A disappointed lover keeping his distance?' Sometimes, when he was out, the staff would be asked to search his room for evidence. All that could be deduced was that he liked music, for three times a week there were concerts on the promenade by municipal bands to which he would listen raptly. Suspicions that he was a spy grew when he purchased a sketching pad and was seen making drawings of the coastline.

Although he double-locked his door when indoors, the chink in the keyhole enabled the curious to see him jotting down hundreds of little signs on lined paper. This was clearly some sort of code and it was decided to inform the police. A functionary was appointed to follow him secretly and report. Saint-Saëns soon became aware of the plodding figure who dogged his footsteps. He ordered a carriage, packed his bags, paid his bill and moved to another hotel on the opposite side of town.

He resumed his solitary existence. One evening outside the local theatre he met the conductor bewailing the sudden absence of the timpanist. He offered his services, but the man was doubtful of the capacities of a volunteer and declined. A touring opera company arrived and Saint-Saëns placed himself in the second row of the stalls. When the overture began it was noticed that he was becoming agitated, beating time with one hand, shaking his head and muttering under his breath. His neighbours started to complain, but worse was to follow when the first act began and the tenor broke into an aria. Snorts and noises of dissent came from his place. The conductor turned round and asked him either to be quiet or leave, while attendants rushed to calm the fractious section of the audience. M. Sannois shrugged his shoulders and departed. The incident became a talking point of island life.

This was as nothing to the furore in Paris over the question of the vanished composer of a work being expensively prepared at the Opéra. Rumours flew to and fro. He had gone mad from overwork and was confined in an asylum, he was in prison, he had been left a fortune and an island by a relative in America and was living like the Count of Monte Cristo. Reporters followed in the steps of Gallet and Durand, sniffing for clues. Musical problems continued, for the Opéra had no contralto capable of singing Scozzone. The provinces were scoured, but no suitable or disengaged contralto could be found. Guiraud helped to transpose the part with some trepidation, for the composer had left orders that nothing should be touched and his temperament was well known. Scozzone's aria, 'Fiorentinella', could be altered into the mezzo range without difficulty and somehow the ensembles were doctored to meet the crisis. The première was a great success and redoubled the efforts of the press to locate the composer. Lalo reported that he had 'heard fearful things' about the opera before the first night, but that he had been astonished at the refined orchestration and the interesting timbres explored by this composer of symphonies and concertos.

By now it was April in the Canaries and, as the rains had come, it was impossible for Saint-Saëns to take his long walks. He began to explore the town with a guidebook and was naturally attracted to the cathedral. One day, as he was crossing the adjacent *Place*, he passed some little girls playing but, when he had gone a few paces further, he heard a cry and turned to find one of them wailing in misery. She had fallen, bruised herself and was covered with mud. Saint-Saëns and a passing stranger lifted her up, dried her tears and gave her a sweet. The girls ran off to resume their game, but the stranger recognised the prominent features he had just seen in a magazine sent from Paris extolling the triumph of *Ascanio*. He murmured that it was a great honour to have so famous a Frenchman in Las Palmas and, when Saint-Saëns dissembled, produced from his pocket the picture of 'M. Saint-Saëns de l'Institut'. By evening the town knew of his presence. The identity of the suspected spy or the disgraced English aristocrat (no supposition was too wild to be entertained) was revealed and all the musicians of Las Palmas beat a path to his door to ask for auditions and concerts. He wrote to Gallet: 'For three days I have led an insupportable existence. I no longer have a moment to myself; I am scratching these lines to you while engaged in conversation; if what I write does not make sense do not be surprised. I have to write a

Romance for Baritone (with orchestra) and a comic duet for the Little Lambertini whom I have rediscovered here. I had to employ violent means to escape from the cheering of the local populace! As compensation I have been shown the treasures of the cathedral among which is a marvellous jewel-setting by Benvenuto himself, which is authentic.'

His friends in Paris were correct if they feared that the news of changes to *Ascanio* would provoke an explosion. The plot was complicated even by the standards of opera and Saint-Saëns had tested his virtuosity to the limit in weaving a coherent musical structure out of its diverse elements. His first words were

> The news of *Ascanio* does not please me! No contralto and a major scene cut. This habit of desecrating a piece because one scene does not make the whole impression that is expected never makes total sense. The dress rehearsal of [Massenet's] *Esclarmonde* was very doubtful, but nothing was changed and the première was a triumph. I could have wished that we had shown the same boldness. What dramatic reason can there now be for the Duchesse to wish for the death of Colombe? It has been turned into the Theatre of the Absurd, which I detest.

His anger vented, he included a note of thanks to Guiraud, for he believed that the musical aspect would have been rendered faithfully. Guiraud was 'a sure and devoted friend and impeccable musician who has watched over my notes that were in danger'.

He told Gallet that he intended to publish some poems; this would provide more fodder for the critics who loved to batter away at him and were reluctantly coming round to the view that he knew something about music. His *Rimes Familières* were published in 1890 and a 'Prelude' announced that he had become a 'prisoner of the lyre, Apollo had made himself my gaoler'. The poems are in no way autobiographical, but there are references to the rivalries and recriminations from which creative artists must suffer. 'Lines to a M. Jacques D—' (Durand surely) warns him that, if he enters the lists on behalf of art, he must expect lying eyes, hypocrisy and the 'masks of friendship hiding jealousy'. A second poem to Augusta Holmès speaks of the envy that success will bring: 'The strong are feared'. He writes of Venus as an ideal dream of love, 'pure as water of the lakes and deeps', which he has not found. In 'Adam and Eve' he describes the horrors of life outside Eden, but surmises that they have discovered love, which compensates for all the deprivations. These are the kind of thoughts which came inevitably in the months of depression following his mother's death, though whether the misery came through sadness – for she seems to have been greatly loved by all his friends – or through regrets over the wasted years of emotional bondage is uncertain. The image of the destroying female epitomised in Delilah, Proserpine, the Duchesse d'Etampes and later in *L'Ancêtres* comes in a verse play, *Botriocephale*. In this joyless playlet a faun laments his ugliness while a Fury disguises herself as a nymph, flirts with him and persuades him with flattery to dance. At the moment of a kiss, to which he is enticed, she turns frighteningly into her form as a Fury and returns to Pluto.

His book of verses was hardly likely to challenge the great poets, but there are some striking images, as when on 'Death' he observed that Man had been wont to believe that under the cold stone there opened up a 'gulf of light', or when in 'L'Arbre' he pictured the roots struggling in the darkness in order that the upper branches should wave in splendour – a metaphor for the social system of his day. 'Le Pays Merveilleux', which is a recollection of his holiday in the Pyrenees, dedicated to Albert Perilhou, is almost a programme note for Strauss's *Alpine* Symphony. Among various poetic tributes to Pauline Viardot, Fauré, Gounod and others were meditations upon the fratricidal destruction likely to descend upon Europe and hopes that regeneration would come from the wisdom of the East.

As he caught up with the news that he had missed in his absence he was angry to discover that some Spanish newspapers had questioned his loyalty to the Republic. He declared wrathfully that even the Duke of Aumale (the most distinguished of Louis Philippe's sons) would vouch for his impeccable Republicanism. While he had been on his travels General Boulanger had been totally discredited. In January 1889 he had triumphed in Paris elections. His supporters expected that he would march on the Elysée Palace and overthrow the Republic. The *coup d'état* never came, for the General hesitated to grasp power illegally, was distracted by a love affair and, after days of indecision, fled across the frontier.

At almost the same moment the Eiffel Tower was opened as a focus for the Exhibition. As the lifts were not working officials at the opening had to mount the 1792 steps to the summit (the number was a reminder of the heroic days of the First Republic in 1792) and plant the Tricolore.

Saint-Saëns had also missed the first performance in France of *Samson* on 3 March 1890 at the Théâtre des Arts at Rouen. The enterprising Director, Verdhurt, had summoned an advisory council which included Fauré. The young Paul Dukas, a great admirer of Saint-Saëns, was doing his military service near Rouen and undertook to coach the tenor, Lafarge, in his off-duty hours. Durand had begged Fauré to assist at the rehearsals, for the composer's friends still had no idea of his whereabouts.

Verdhurt found a young singer, Mlle Bossy, and engaged her as Delilah. The costumes did not arrive in time for the dress rehearsal and those who were admitted saw the strange sight of the Old Testament epic unfolding in modern dress. Special trains had to be arranged from Paris to transport the notables who wished to attend and there were stories of hotel rooms being commandeered by brute force after noisy disputes. Georges Clairin, the composer's old painter friend, was in Rouen stirring up enthusiasm. At the première the excitement mounted from act to act and was at fever pitch when the final scene was reached. The collapse of the Temple of Dagon had been a victory for the stage machinists and Verdhurt was so thrilled with the effect that he was reluctant to lower the curtain. Fauré, conducting, had to repeat part of Act Two while the audience contemplated prostrate Philistines under the ruins.

Durand *Fils* and friends had much to tell Saint-Saëns when he reached Paris and they rushed to the Hôtel Terminus to impart news of *Samson* and *Ascanio*. Somewhere *en route*, however, he had come across a newspaper report of *Samson* and the repetition of Act Two. He was not pleased, fearing something clumsy. His head was in the wash-basin covered with soap, but this did not prevent him from being voluble on the subject. When he learnt that Fauré had supervised the music and ensured a wonderful presentation he became all smiles and the tirade was stilled. Verdhurt brought *Samson* to the Eden Theatre, Paris, a large edifice, originally a circus, but used for ballet spectacles. It enjoyed further success, although the crushing of Samson's foes under the Temple brought screams of terror from the hired extras, who were not conversant with the plot. The scholar and critic Camille Bellaigue advised the Government to withhold its subsidy from the

Opéra and hand over wads of bank-notes to Verdhurt as a token of its esteem. Arthur Coquard, a follower of Franck, brought to César news of the first night and the warm reception. Franck was dying. 'I can see him still,' said Coquard, 'turning his worn and suffering face towards me and saying eagerly and almost joyfully in that deep and vibrant tone, so familiar to all his friends, "Very fine! Very fine!"' At last the Directors of the Opéra were forced to reconsider their opposition to the work.

Ascanio was less fortunate. There was criticism that it was neither old-fashioned opera nor lyric drama. Gounod wrote a note of appreciation in *La France*, in which he praised the careful underlining of the drama in the accompaniment and deprecated judging it by the piano score 'because of the number of musical intentions that find their justification, their sanction, only on the stage and the constant richness of the orchestration spread over the entire work'. Lassalle, who had elsewhere sung Hans Sachs, made a great impression as Cellini, a similar conception, in which the older man sensitively suppresses an affection for the heroine in favour of a younger suitor. The ballet devised by Gallet showed the fêtes offered by François I to Charles V. Various Olympian deities descend and preach a doctrine of love and reconciliation. This too had some contemporary relevance as sections of French Society sought to use events such as the Exhibition to conceal social inequalities under a lavish display of entertainment. Shaw, having gone to Paris to hear *Ascanio*, wrote, 'I am strongly of the opinion that the Channel Tunnel should be proceeded with at once' (a view shared by Fauré) and did not reckon his trip worthwhile as he persisted in finding Saint-Saëns derivative and Paris 'a pedant-ridden failure in everything it pretends to lead'. His only good words were for Lassalle, who 'can hardly believe in the part of Benvenuto Cellini but believes immensely in Lassalle and so manages to make things go with conviction'. Somehow, in 1890, Saint-Saëns had found the time to make two piano transcriptions: one from the scene where Ascanio and Colombe show charity to a beggar, the other from the ballet, which he inscribed to Paderewski. The Polish pianist played the Fourth Concerto at a festival dedicated to Saint-Saëns by Colonne at the Trocadéro, in which a sensational sonority was achieved in the Finale.

César Franck died in November. Several sources state clearly that Saint-Saëns was a pallbearer at the funeral along with Delibes, the

organist Henri Dallier and a relative, Dr Ferréol, but Franck's
biographers seem sceptical. 'Good manners were never Saint-Saëns's
strong point,' says L. Davies and 'Saint-Saëns decided to issue his
grudging respects before departing for Egypt'. D'Indy deplored the
absence of Ambroise Thomas and talked of 'excuses' from the
Conservatoire, but it was a time of appalling weather and Thomas was
not robust. Jacques Durand, when he met the sturdy-looking Verdi,
could hardly believe that he was the same age as the frail-seeming
Thomas. There was a great gathering of musical talent none the less.
Chabrier, in whose career Franck had taken a strong interest, gave a
moving oration on 'the unrivalled teacher whose wonderful instruction has produced a whole generation of musicians marked by energy,
faith and serious intention' and 'whose counsel was always sound and
whose words were always kind'.

One of the first acts of Franck's disciples was to remove the name of
Augusta Holmès from the dedications of his last organ pieces and
substitute another. D'Indy succeeded as President of the Société
Nationale and its policy continued to be dominated by Franckists,
there and elsewhere. Widor was now Professor of the Organ at the
Conservatoire. The Franckists appeared to be determined to prevent
Widor's pupils from receiving the First Prize, and the shy and docile
Vierne was unsuccessful on at least three occasions, before noisy
demonstrations against the jury by students and calculated exhibitions
of rage by Widor procured him the coveted place.

In July 1890, the Musée Saint-Saëns was opened at Dieppe. A cousin,
Léon Letellier, librarian, had acted as recipient of the MSS and
papers, which together with the furniture and valuables formed the
nucleus of the collection. The composer regularly sent fresh acquisitions, as well as bundles of his correspondence. By the time of his
death it held more than 15,000 letters addressed to him, a vast archive
for the study of nineteenth-century musicians. In 1923 the museum
was transferred to a fifteenth-century castle overlooking the Channel,
but during the war the collection was dispersed and difficulties were
experienced in reassembling it.[1]

*

[1] It is only in more recent years that Professor Yves Gérard has begun the
work of cataloguing and making sections available to (mainly American)
research students. The present Director, M. Pierre Ickowicz, is pressing
forward with this work.

Saint-Saëns's travelling plans for the winter of 1890–1 were the most extensive to date as he was taking an interest in the East, more practical than Debussy's, and making for Ceylon. He travelled second class on the packet boat *Messagéries* and once again signed himself 'Charles Sannois'. He carried with him the libretto of a lyric drama, *Eviradnus* by Alphonse Pagès, but it brought no spark of inspiration. The Commandant believed him to be a Dutch Jew trading in diamonds. He took pleasure in discussing astronomy and botany with a M. Jacquet on his way to Saigon as Director of Botanical Gardens established in these new 'Vietnamese' colonies. He also met a young doctor, Felix Regnault, *en route* for Calcutta, who later became one of his correspondents. He had his first view of Egypt, the Sphinx and the Pyramids when the boat stopped at Alexandria, and he paid a visit to Cairo. No one suspected his identity and when, one evening, a passenger sat down at the piano and played a fragment from *Etienne Marcel* he kept silence with some difficulty. On the final evening, however, he thought it polite to reveal himself to his two close friends and agreed to play for them. A lady passenger realised that this was no ordinary pianist and remembered his face from photographs. Fortunately there were only a few hours left in which he had to endure celebrity status and he disembarked in good spirits, his cough and winter fever dispelled. He stayed in Ceylon for almost three months, scanned the night sky to see the stars of the southern hemisphere, showed an interest in the wildlife and made friends with a baby panther.

He carried out some of the alterations suggested by Vacquerie to the score of *Proserpine* but, much rested, he began to rediscover musical inspiration and on his way back he revisited Cairo, where the composition of *Africa*, a Fantasy for Piano and Orchestra, which he had been carrying in his head, signalled the return of buoyant skills. The Fantasy evokes many images of the Arab countries, using a compressed form that was becoming increasingly characteristic. *Africa* is an exciting work in rhapsodic form. It falls into two sections, although the introduction is an Allegro in which the piano plays a subordinate part. Its principal task begins with a Cadenza, then the mood flits between the reedy dance-like themes such as might be drawn from Arab instruments and a languorous Andantino, culminating in a 'Tunisian' theme suggesting a whirling finale by Arab dancers. There are passages of repeated chords, requiring the great dexterity of wrist which Saint-Saëns possessed, reminiscent of a passage from the *Beethoven* Variations and the third of his Studies, rising 'as a swarm of drunken wasps', as Baumann described them. Two features of *Africa* strike the listener: in the first place it is as 'impressionist' a piece as *Iberia* or similar works by which later composers sought to create moods and, in the second, it shares with Chabrier a muscular vigour for which one searches in vain in much French music of the time.

The first performance was given by Mme Roger Miclos, to whom it was dedicated.[1] Shaw, who heard the pianist in London, described her 'cold, hard, swift style on one of those wonderful steel dulcimers made by Pleyel'. *Africa* shows that Saint-Saëns's exuberance had returned and may also be seen as a gesture of disregard towards contemporaries. Not only is it a reminder of his virtuosity, for even among his own works it provides an exceptionally sparkling role for the soloist, but it revels in his love of travel. Other composers might add the label 'Espagnol', but he had been further afield than anyone and imbibed the music of places that to contemporaries were merely dots on the map. Also, in its multiplicity of themes and the steady increase in tension reflecting the movements of Arab dancers, this Fantasy makes a bold statement for joyous revelling in sounds as against the sombre and dark-grained works on which Franck's disciples were so often engaged.

The Piano Suite of 1890 was a return to the eighteenth century, comprising a Prelude and Fugue, Minuet, Gavotte and (an innovation for Saint-Saëns) a Gigue. The celebrations of the Great Revolution (the Exhibition of 1889 and great street processions planned for 1892) had the natural effect of turning people's minds to the *ancien régime*. The more aesthetic aristocrats were not slow to encourage a nostalgia for *fêtes-champêtres* and courtly routines. Musicians obediently produced pavanes, nocturnes and barcarolles to feed the image. But Saint-Saëns had always been fascinated by eighteenth-century Court life (he confessed great affection for Mme de Pompadour) and had been an early pioneer in the revival of the eighteenth-century Suite. In this instance the first piece pays homage to Bach, though the left hand emphasises powerfully the harmonies which Bach might have left implicit, the Minuet once again refers to the derivation of the waltz, while the playful Gavotte is turned almost into a polka.

[1] The composer gave her a gift of some Arab jewellery.

He rewrote some music which Lully had provided for the Molière play *Le Sicilien*, giving strength to the orchestration but remaining faithful to the 1667 score. This was part of a larger interest in seventeenth-century stage music, which emphasised that the *ancien régime* had encouraged culture. It was important to the Countess Greffulhe and others like her to make the point that they too patronised the arts, in order to ward off attacks by radical Republicans on inherited wealth. Saint-Saëns unearthed music for *Le Malade Imaginaire* by Marc-Antoine Charpentier, performed in November 1892, and in the following year Fauré wrote incidental music for *Le Bourgeois Gentilhomme*.

While journeying homewards he spent time in the museum at Naples studying the stringing of lyres and *cithares* in antique drawings, and pondered a thesis on the subject. A liver complaint took him back to Algiers and Tunis for a long period of convalescence. There was at this time a demand for new concert pieces by the great conductors of the day and, now an eminent composer, Saint-Saëns had to maintain a balance, sometimes reworking old material in new forms. For Colonne he had rewritten the *Mélodies Persanes* as a cantata, *La Nuit Persane*, and for Lamoureux he created a *Rhapsodie Bretonne* out of the first and third of his earlier organ pieces. *La Nuit Persane* was the larger work; Saint-Saëns copied the plan of Berlioz who had welded his *Scenes from Faust* into the *Damnation*, with declaimed recitative. To the five original songs he added further verses from Armand Renaud, 'La Fuite' for tenor and chorus, and 'Les Cygnes' for tenor and contralto. The picture of the Persian Orient was still one of languour, whisperings and a constant twilight, punctuated by bursts of unrestrained vigour as in 'Sabre en Main' and the final 'Songe d'Opium', in which the strings were able to depict the increasing delirium with added realism while the dirge was this time shared between tenor and bass. In 'La Fuite' reverie and action combine, the chorus sings of nightingales and roses contrasting with the nervous gallop of the rider. In the *Rhapsodie Bretonne* the transfer to orchestral sounds as opposed to imitations on the organ gave a lighter and more dancing tone to the pieces. At the close a dance motif returns in the cellos and dies away as the pilgrim procession disappears in the distance. A 'Chant Saphique' for cello was dedicated to Delsart, a teacher at the Conservatoire with a great interest in the bass viol and other seventeenth-century instruments.

There had been another change of regime at the Opéra. Ritt and Gailhard had departed, their places taken by Auguste Bertrand, an ex-Director of the Variétés, and Campo-Sasso, a former Director at Marseilles, where, like several provincial managers, he had put on *Samson*. There was talk of producing Reyer's *Salammbô* but there was still no news of *Samson*. Saint-Saëns, at the Pointe Pescade near Algiers, considered a final severance with Paris, imagining *all* promises to be hypocritical. Before the change of Directors could take place Ritt and Gailhard hastened to produce *Lohengrin* in their final months. Lamoureux was given full control of the choice of artists and designers. The blessing of Cosima Wagner was obtained. (Reyer suggested that to please her further a Bayreuth-type orchestra pit might be excavated from the Opéra foundations and trumpets announce the themes down the avenue de l'Opéra before each act.) Jean-Antoine Constans, a firm Minister who had stood out against General Boulanger, promised total tranquillity on the streets. *Lohengrin* passed off without anti-German demonstrations, although one elderly gentleman shouted for the 'Marseillaise' to be played after the Prelude and had to be asked to leave. To forget his quarrels with the Opéra Saint-Saëns wrote a prose comedy, *La Crampe des Ecrivains*, based upon an anecdote he had picked up on his travels. In March 1892 it was put on at the Municipal Theatre in Algiers and was some years later played at Béziers. He rejected Gallet's attempts to interest him in another grand opera but finally, with Bertrand as Director and Colonne as conductor, *Samson* reached its destination at the Opéra in November 1892. It could not be said that no expense was spared, for the first act used recycled scenery from *Le Roi de Lahore* and for the second the painters covered some stock sets that were found in the store-rooms. There was little difficulty in finding a Prison Scene for Act Three 'at the Mill', but new designs were required for the final Temple scene. The machine effects were only partly successful, for the pillars were badly joined and wobbled before Samson had an opportunity to test his new-found strength. At the moment of supposed catastrophe the dome descended majestically, but not with a speed to threaten life and limb.

Musically, however, the results under Colonne were entirely worthy. Mme Deschamps-Jehin, a singer with a very expressive and dramatic voice, creatrice of Herodias and Margaret in *Le Roi d'Ys*, who had sung Delilah at Monte Carlo earlier in the year, repeated her performance, although Saint-Saëns was wont to express a fondness for Rosina Bloch who had taken the role at the Eden Theatre and died young. He came to Paris to supervise the rehearsals, down to the minutest details. He had tiny cymbals made specially for the dancers to play in the Bacchanale. At one rehearsal, feeling that his wishes were being ignored, he rushed across the ramp set up over the orchestra pit brandishing his umbrella, which he then used as a partner to illustrate the movements required. The electricians were given marked scores to cue in the Storm in Act Two, but they were unable to count the bars and a cousin of the Durands, Gaston Choisnel, a better musician though not a trained electrician, was put in charge. At the dress rehearsal the lightning flashes were so blinding that members of the audience needed to close their eyes; the effects had to be modified so that the action could be followed.

During these rehearsals the composer heard that Mount Etna was erupting and rushed to spend a week contemplating the spectacle. Otherwise work was so intensive that the première was postponed from 18 to 25 November, to give the artists some rest. President Carnot and (significantly) the Grand Duke Vladimir attended. The reception was triumphant, since the opera was already acknowledged as a masterpiece and the reviews mattered little. *Le Journal* published a large illustrated supplement. *Le Figaro* took the opportunity to launch an attack on Massenet, to the indignation of Lecocq, who wrote to Saint-Saëns: 'One knows very well that Massenet is a sensualist and he takes care to make his declarations of love to the public in his music.' Saint-Saëns, in replying, recognised in Massenet 'the indefinable and special charm of which only he has the secret', though he added that Massenet was capable of malice in everything that concerned his musical reputation. Lecocq concluded, 'One feels for him the infinite indulgence that one accords to a pretty woman.' Camille Bellaigue wrote a great eulogy, which elicited from the composer a warm letter of thanks. 'Chance, which sometimes has a mind of its own, put your marvellous article before my eyes yesterday. To compare my music to the verse of Racine and Delilah to Athalie touches me to the heart . . .' After referring to Bellaigue's well-trained pen and their friendship he concluded, 'Yes, classic I am, nourished on Mozart and Haydn since my earliest childhood. I would like to find it impossible for me not to speak in a clear and well-balanced language.' In a rare mood of magnanimity he added, 'I do not blame those who do otherwise, as

Victor Hugo apropos of certain poetic innovations. I find certain developments good for others!' *Samson* reached its hundredth performance at the Opéra in 1898 and by 1906 had been played 227 times. *The Musical Times* in England remarked that it was popular with the management because its comparative brevity enabled it to be a 'curtain-raiser' for the three-act ballets, a merit it shared with *Rigoletto* and *Der Freischütz*!

In the following month his Second Trio for Piano, Violin and Cello was given at the Salle Erard. It had been begun at the Pointe Pescade, Algeria, in March and finished at Geneva in June. Into the fourth and fifth movements he wove fragments from an unfinished string quartet and he offered the dedication to an aristocratic pupil, the Vicomtesse de Guitant. He had planned it while writing *Ascanio*, but it was set aside like many other projects. The first movement has the imagery of waters lapping at the Pointe on an evening of idyllic peace and is pervaded with a calm that contrasts with the more frenzied portrait of Arab life in *Africa*. The second, in 5:4 time, begins with hints of Schumann's humorous play with the bar-lines, goes from B major to the minor and passes through complicated modulations. There is a rich Andante based upon downward scales for the cello. The fourth movement is in 3:8, a kind of waltz; the Finale has a vigorous theme from the unfinished quartet, expressed in unison. There are many rhythmic transformations of the ideas and great technical difficulties. It is a much larger work than its predecessor of thirty years earlier.

The Trio pianist, Isidore Philipp, was one of Saint-Saëns's most outstanding pupils. He later recounted his first meeting with the Master. Of Hungarian origin, he had studied with Stephen Heller, who gave him a letter of introduction. Nervously, the fourteen-year-old pressed the bell of 14 rue Monsieur le Prince and, to his surprise, the door was opened by Saint-Saëns himself, who read the letter, made some flattering remarks about Heller and heard his visitor play a Beethoven sonata. 'Good, but you are terribly shy; it is necessary to correct that,' said Saint-Saëns. 'I also have been shy and it has greatly harmed me. . . . Come tomorrow at nine o'clock. We shall get down to work.' The lesson which ensued next day was a nightmare. Cries of rapture were succeeded by shouts of rage and torrential wrath. At one moment old Mme Saint-Saëns put her head round the door. Philipp thought she must have imagined he was being strangled. 'But, Camille, you are throwing this poor boy into a panic,' she said. 'No,

Maman, he is too shy. Stupidly shy. I want to cure him . . . and he will stay to lunch.' From such an unusual beginning came a long friendship and Philipp later spoke of wonderful lessons, which displayed Saint-Saëns's prodigious memory and original views.

He had occasion to witness something of his master's private generosity. One day a lesson was interrupted by an old orchestral horn player who asked for a short interview. Saint-Saëns said he could speak before the pupil and it transpired that the man was in straitened circumstances. 'Mama!' cried out Saint-Saëns. 'How much money have we here?' 'Two thousand francs,' replied the mother. 'Then bring me half,' he shouted and, handing over the money, he murmured, 'Not a word of thanks, I beg you.' When Philipp was himself a famous pianist, Saint-Saëns came to hear him at the Société des Concerto. Philipp had written the cadenza for the Mozart Concerto. 'Your cadenza is bad,' was the judgement, but next day he received a package in which there were two cadenzas composed by Saint-Saëns overnight.

Always full of surprises, Saint-Saëns now plunged into operetta. The young author Augé de Lassus had written and discarded a verse comedy about Phryné, an Athenian courtesan, who was said to have been a model for the sculptor Praxiteles. He then thought it might serve as the libretto for a light opera and approached Saint-Saëns, whom he knew to be greatly entranced by the ideal of Ancient Athens. It was at the time of the composer's breakdown and nothing came of his plan. The two next met by accident at St Germain; Saint-Saëns talked of Gluck but made no mention of 'Phryné'. Once again they ran into one another near the Pont des Arts when the poem was far from the author's mind. '*Et Phryné*?' asked Saint-Saëns. 'She is waiting for you,' replied Augé de Lassus. 'Well bring her tomorrow morning,' said Saint-Saëns.

Phryné is another work which portrays the *femme fatale* who puts the moral order at risk. But the mood of the 1890s was more relaxed than the days of *Samson* or *Proserpine* and French writers had been expressing admiration for the sexual freedoms enjoyed by the classical Greeks. The name Phryné was a challenge, as she and her wild friends were reputed to have been responsible for the desecration of statues of the god Hermes. Her lover, Nicias, is indeed a type of Alcibiades, and the original verse-comedy appeared to mock the famous Mutilation of the Hermae before the doomed Sicilian expedition. Saint-Saëns, proficient in Greek history, knew that the Athenians, far from laughing at the incident, regarded it as a dread augury. The plot was amended to revolve around the statue of a civic official, Dicéphile, a pompous upholder of morality, who complains that the statues of Praxiteles and others display too much nudity. There were many very well-clad statues to local dignitaries going up in French provincial cities and Saint-Saëns parodied the sound of municipal anthems. Although Dicéphile is outraged when his statue is mocked, Phryné succeeds by her allurements in melting his austere views and tricks him into a ludicrous declaration of passion. For a touch of her hand Dicéphile promises to lay at her feet Laws and Justice, and all the panoply of the moral order. The theme is very different from that of the *Jeunesse d'Hercule* two decades earlier, when virtuous action was decisively preferred to sensual pleasure and Saint-Saëns is clearly on the side of the courtesan and Nicias. He appears to have been aiming for an audience which had a hankering for Aristophanes and Offenbach. He wished to show his own versatility and to reassert tradition. Paris, in the concert halls at least, had recently had a strong diet of late Wagner.[1] There were moves, too, being made by the Franckists towards the foundation of the Schola Cantorum, as a severe rival to the Conservatoire, which would elevate the standards and impact of religious music. The death of his mother had also removed an impediment to this celebration of licence and misrule.

Much of *Phryné* was written in Algiers. Saint-Saëns asked for the description of the heroine returning from a sea bathe and being mistaken for Venus arising from the foam, to be given to Phryné herself rather than another character ('the incident of the sea bathe, fifty centimes, peignoir included,' he wrote to de Lassus remembering his days on the Normandy coast, adding 'this work entertains me beyond anything you can imagine'). A further letter suggested that Venus should be mentioned by name; 'the Queen of Paphos and Cnide' would not mean very much to 'the ignorant audience more conversant with Panama than Mythology'. (The 'Panama Scandal', in which Deputies had been discovered taking bribes from the Canal

---

[1] The solemnity of the Wagnerians was well illustrated in 1893 when, at the Opéra, before the scenery of the bridal chamber from *Lohengrin*, Catulle Mendès, at a table, read out the poems of *Rhinegold* and *The Valkyrie* with commentaries, while Debussy and Pugno played sections of the score on two pianos.

Company, had recently been a huge gift to the press.) He certainly seems to have enjoyed the heterosexual images with which *Phryné* was loaded: 'I see Phryné before my eyes all the time . . . and this evocation is wholly agreeable. But what woman would ever be able to realise such an ideal!' Later, when he has been sent some extra verses, he writes of 'clothing the nudity' of the words with 'amorous sharps and flats'.

Detroyat had recently opened the Théâtre de la Renaissance as a venue for operetta. He began with Messager's *Madame Chrysanthème*, but financial failure loomed and Messager was distressed. Saint-Saëns had originally promised *Phryné* to Detroyat, whose venture failed. Carvalho, back at the Opéra Comique, was anxious to have the première and telegraphed urgently to Algiers. To help Messager recover his confidence the composer gave the first act to him to orchestrate. On 11 March 1893 he wrote that he had finished the second act on the 5th but

I am not sending it to you, because I am orchestrating it myself while you finish orchestrating the first. You know that we are being put on immediately, there is therefore no time to lose. I will leave to you only the Finale, which is composed of reprises from the first act with light modifications. What a pity your ravishing *Chrysanthème* has been sacrificed. Perhaps *Phryné* will have the power to bring it to the Opéra Comique. The press has been unanimous in its praise and it is possible that, in time, you may not have to regret this venture. The theatre is a funny place . . . You will grow in stature I have never doubted. . . . Don't call me Master any more [he added]. You are another. And I see you thriving more and more with pleasure and a certain pride, for I imagine, perhaps wrongly, to have worked at your education as Gounod formerly worked at mine.

Somehow he had to find time to practise the piano in the midst of all this light-hearted composition. The object was a forthcoming Chicago Exhibition and he added, 'Who knows, if Christopher Columbus had been shipwrecked I would not be forced to practise scales and octaves.' It would seem that the part Messager played, because of the pressure of time, was not generally known although Saint-Saëns was quick to publicise it later in *Musica*. 'Messager rendered me the more than unpayable debt of putting his elegant pen at my disposal and to write the orchestration of the first act.' Carvalho had succeeded in procuring the beautiful star of Massenet's operas, Sybil Sanderson, for the part of Phryné. Saint-Saëns was at first reluctant to hand over the role intended for Mlle Simonet, the original Angiola of *Proserpine*, but he could not have hoped for a more celebrated artiste to launch his *opéra bouffe*. Lucien Fugère, who played Dicéphile with huge aplomb, was a veteran who had sung parts such as Papageno and Leporello in performances innumerable. Those who had regarded Saint-Saëns as an academic, 'algebraic' composer had the ground cut from under their feet by the light touch displayed. The municipal bands were parodied, the Archonte was epitomised in Sullivan-like references to Handel and grand opera, and a bassoon chortles in the background of his homilies. (Saint-Saëns regularly visited the Savoy Operas during his visits to London.) The arietta of Phryné's servant, Lampito,[1] describing her boudoir, has sugary harmonies that point a finger at Massenet and in the seduction scene the discrepancies in rhythm between Phryné and her elderly admirer paint a breathless agitation. By contrast, the narrative of Phryné, describing how the fishermen took her for Aphrodite, depicts the movements of the waves along with a hymn to perfect beauty, which proved to be one of the composer's most remarkable pages. Saint-Saëns missed the rehearsals under Carvalho, who worked himself into such a lather in the dances that he required frequent changes of clothing. The première was a great success and the operetta was played over fifty times in the first year. Gounod, who was dying at St Cloud, heard of the applause and almost the last letter he wrote complimented Saint-Saëns on his 'pagan victory': 'Thank you for your delicious *Phryné*. I shall hear it through my eyes, those second ears of the musician. . . . I embrace you in love, "Imo Corde".'

---

[1] Lampito had been assigned a difficult part in the Ensemble. Saint-Saëns thought he should be given an aria, as a good singer would be needed – an indication of his acquaintance with the practicalities of the theatre.

A National Musician

Other manifestations of success coincided with *Phryné*. The Cambridge Musical Society wished to celebrate its fiftieth anniversary by granting honorary degrees to great European musicians. Verdi and Brahms headed the list, but Brahms was averse to sea travel, even in its briefest forms, and Verdi, engaged in the production of *Falstaff*, was too old to make the long journey without risk. Gounod was the French composer best known in Britain through *Faust* and his pious oratorios. Musicians, however, were sceptical of his worth; Hallé declared he would refuse to rise from the dead if the Last Judgement were accompanied by the strains of his music. Gounod, alas, risked arrest if he set foot in this country because of a debt incurred as the result of a court case. After him, Saint-Saëns was highest in English estimation. He had visited London to conduct and play his own works almost every year since 1871. Invitations were sent to Saint-Saëns, to Max Bruch (since Germany would need to have a representative balancing France), to Boito, a worthy substitute for Verdi, since he had supplied libretti for his compatriot and had enlisted under Garibaldi in the Risorgimento, to Edvard Grieg, who enjoyed great popularity, and to the lesser known Tchaikovsky, an alternative to the revered but wayward Rubinstein.

Saint-Saëns was the first to reply. He accepted the honour with 'heartfelt gratitude', but was planning to appear at the Chicago Exhibition in June, where he hoped to introduce Americans to some of Fauré's works as well as his own. Fauré had suggested several piano pieces and concluded his reply: 'All my affectionate good wishes and I hope you experience as little fatigue as possible, many dollars and, above all, good health.' The Chicago visit did not materialise; Saint-Saëns hinted that he had cancelled his trip in favour of Cambridge.

It was expected that the five composers would participate in a great concert. Boito, fastidious about allowing his music to be heard in public, while he polished it endlessly in private, had published little except the opera *Mefistofele*. Charles Villiers Stanford, Professor of Music and in charge of the celebrations, could do little other than put the Prologue (for soloist, chorus and orchestra) into the programme where it bulked large. Bruch had opted for the Banquet Scene from *Odysseus* and when Saint-Saëns suggested his 'Psalm 18' Stanford regretted he could not include one more large choral work in this copious bill of fare. The fact that Boito had composed no suitable orchestral work did not endear him to Saint-Saëns. 'You will see that it is unfortunate for me that M. Boito has written, as you tell me, nothing other than *Mefistofele* and that I should be therefore forbidden to give a large-scale vocal work and be forced to let him produce the biggest and most impressive musical effect. It would be possible . . . to remove the Septet, which is very long, from the Psalm; one could even cut it short at the end of the chorus in A flat; one would then have something sufficiently abridged to allow M. Boito to spread himself to his heart's content. . . .' He suggested *La Jeunesse d'Hercule* or his Fourth Concerto. 'I beg you not to see in this the slightest trace of ill temper towards anybody, particularly M. Boito, for whom I have had the deepest regard for many years.'

Saint-Saëns wrote this from Algiers and, when Stanford replied that he feared the Fourth Concerto would be too long and hoped for an original work, Saint-Saëns put forward *Africa*.

It is certainly less substantial than a concerto; however, at the Lamoureux concerts where the audience is difficult (and even rather stuffy) it scored such a triumph that it had to be given a second time; at Liège and Baden it succeeded to the same degree and I enclose a review of this latter performance which was sent to me recently. . . . All I ask in return for my abnegation is that the orchestral accompaniment should be rehearsed with as much care as if the work were a symphony, because it is of great importance and not just a mere accompaniment. There are in particular some extremely delicate oboe solos.

He left it to Stanford's 'erudition' to decipher the extract from a Mannheim newspaper and dig out phrases such as 'unmistakably a work of genius'. Stanford had toyed with the idea of the Tchaikovsky

Piano Concerto No. I (not as well known as it is today), but the Russian candidate was a less efficient correspondent and was finally asked for an orchestral piece, which turned out to be *Francesca da Rimini*. Grieg was to be represented by the *Peer Gynt* Suite (which was not a favourite of Saint-Saëns. '*Peer Gynt* which is dinned into our ears too much,' he once complained).

Hearing that so many famous musicians were to visit England, Francesco Berger, Secretary of the Philharmonic Society, tried to secure their services for London. Saint-Saëns, who had almost thirty years of concerts ahead of him, at first declared his performing days to be over.

> I no longer wish to perform in public but this exceptional event, the Chicago Exhibition, having persuaded me to shed my reserve I see no reason for refusing to appear one last time on the programme of the Philharmonic Society. I shall therefore play, as is your wish, my Concerto in G mi[nor], unless you would prefer something new in which case I would propose my Fantasy, *Africa*, which has had a huge success at the Châtelet Sunday Concerts and at the Cirque des Champs Elysées [the Colonne and Lamoureux concerts respectively]. I leave the choice to you. For the orchestral work I shall conduct the symphonic poem in A, *La Jeunesse d'Hercule*.

Berger put him and Tchaikovsky in a programme for 1 June. When Saint-Saëns heard that a Tchaikovsky symphony would be included he asked if he could play two piano works.

> This way it will not look as if we are competing against each other – something that is always unpleasant – for we will then be as far as possible on different ground from one another. I therefore suggest to you as my second piece my Fantasy *Africa*. However it is also in G minor, or at least it begins in that key before passing into many others and finishing in G major. It is an extended piece in which the orchestra is important. If you see any problem in the similarity of keys you can replace the Second Concerto with the Fourth in C minor; as far as I am concerned I don't see any problem, assuming that presumably Tchaikovsky's symphony will come in between the two pieces; unless that too is in G minor!

He added a footnote expressing his pleasure at the reception of his celebration of the French North African Empire. 'This Fantasy *Africa*, which I am offering you, has had an absolutely remarkable success in Paris.'

When all was settled he was seized with an impulse to conduct the Philharmonic Orchestra once more. Even the hostile Shaw thought he compared very favourably with English conductors. In February, Saint-Saëns wrote, 'Since the last time I had the honour of writing to you I have reflected, and the idea of *not* conducting your fine orchestra – of forgoing such a rare pleasure – is really too distressing to me. May I once again offer a change of plan? Don't you find me really rather an idiot? I'd like, after having played my Concerto in G minor, to conduct *Le Rouet d'Omphale*. If the programme arrangements demand that *Le Rouet d'Omphale* should precede the Concerto I don't mind either way.'

Berger, though he must have wondered whether matters would ever be finalised, certainly did not consider Saint-Saëns an idiot. In his *Reminiscences* he declared, 'With the solitary exception of Mendelssohn, modern times have produced no musician of such varied eminence as Dr Camille Saint-Saëns. . . . He has done everything that a musician can do and done it successfully.' The Frenchman came higher in his estimation than Grieg, who had refused to appear for twenty-five pounds, demanding fifty, and whom he found patronising. On the evening of the concert itself Tchaikovsky, who spoke no English (when rehearsing Symphony No. 4, wanting more brio in the Finale he could only shout, 'Vodka, more Vodka!'), almost failed to gain an entrance to St James's Hall. The seats had all been sold; the staff could do no more than repeat this fact to a foreign gentleman who stood on the steps repeating the one word 'Tchaikovsky', which they took to mean a wish to hear the composer's work.

The concert was a great success although Tchaikovsky had been worried lest Saint-Saëns should take up too much rehearsal time, as he had a reputation for being fussy. The audience, 'by five times recalling Saint-Saëns after a brilliant performance of the Concerto, expressed in a manner unmistakable the cordiality of their feeling towards a musician of whom not France alone but all musical countries are proud'. The *Illustrated London News* declared: 'M. Saint-Saëns was greeted as a friend of many years' standing and, after he had played his Concerto with splendid vigour and aplomb, he was treated to one of the loudest and longest ovations that has been witnessed lately in a concert room.' The hall had been packed. Even Sarasate had gained admittance only to a standing place. Shaw, who dismissed the Tchaikovsky Symphony as 'Scythian Savagery', thought the *Rouet d'Omphale* 'trivial enough to satisfy even the weariest of unhappy persons who go to the Philharmonic for the sake of culture under compulsion of fashion or their parents'. As for the applause, he remarked that Saint-Saëns 'was recalled again and again after playing his C minor Concerto in the hope that he would throw in a solo. This, however, he evidently did not understand; and the audience had at last to give over the attempt.'

A dinner was given to honour the two composers. They had known each another since Saint-Saëns's visit to Moscow in 1875. Modest, brother of Tchaikovsky, recorded that

> this short, lively man with his Jewish type of features attracted Tchaikovsky and fascinated him not only by his wit and original ideas, but also by his masterly knowledge of his art. [He] used to say that Saint-Saëns knew how to combine the grace and charm of the French School with the depth and earnestness of the great German masters. . . . One day the friends discovered that they had a great many likes and dislikes in common, not merely in the world of music. In their youth both had been admirers of the ballet and had often tried to imitate the art. This suggested the idea of doing a dance together and they brought out a little ballet, *Pygmalion and Galatea*, on the stage of the Conservatoire. Saint-Saëns aged forty played the part of Galatea most conscientiously while Tchaikovsky aged thirty-five appeared as Pygmalion. Nikolay Rubinstein provided the accompaniment. Unfortunately, apart from the three performers no spectators witnessed this singular entertainment.

When Adolf Brodsky visited Paris in 1881, he and Saint-Saëns tried to interest the Parisian conductors in Tchaikowsky's as yet little-known Violin Concerto. Tchaikovsky had a special admiration for *Phaeton* and *Danse Macabre*, and said of the G-minor Concerto that it was 'exceptionally beautiful, fresh, elegant, and rich in fascinating detail'. In 1888 Tchaikovsky visited La Trompette and Lemoine was keen to stress that the Society had been the first to welcome him in France.

For the great Cambridge concert Saint-Saëns listed the nine themes used in *Africa*. The programme, although arrived at circuitously, gave him foremost place, even though Boito and Bruch took up more time, for *Africa* has a most spectacular solo part. 'It has none of the darkness of Africa about it,' wrote the *Daily Graphic*. 'On the contrary, it is of the gayest, most brilliant and exhilarating character. M. Saint-Saëns took charge of the piano part and played it with a verve and unfaltering dexterity which fairly brought down the house.' He himself found much to admire in his friend's *Francesca da Rimini*: 'the gentlest and kindest of men has unleashed a terrifying hurricane with as little pity for his interpreters and listeners as Satan for the damned. But such are his talent and colossal technique that one takes pleasure in this damnation and torture.'

At the dinner in King's College Saint-Saëns's placement showed that he was pre-eminent among the guests (Grieg had been prevented by illness from attending in person). He sat between the Provost, Augustus Austen-Leigh, President of the Cambridge Musical Society, and Lord Leighton, a major figure in the artistic establishment. In his letter of acceptance Saint-Saëns had confessed to the Provost '*Vous savez que je ne parle pas anglais, sauf avec les cabmen et les waiters* [sic]', but Lord Leighton moved with ease from French to Italian with Boito on his other side. In any case Saint-Saëns was always more proficient in English than he cared to make out.

In his speech, Stanford light-heartedly expressed a fear that 'with so many representatives of the Great Powers, he should drop a word which might endanger the peace of Europe'. He observed that the musicians had already trespassed freely on foreign territory: Bruch into Greece, Boito into Germany, Tchaikovsky into Italy, 'while Saint-Saëns, boldly plunging into the wilds of Africa, had hit upon some smiling oasis amid its Saharas'. Which composer should have the privilege of replying? Stanford had fixed upon age as the criterion and told a little story of how an impresario, obliged to arrange a gala ballet in which four star ballerinas appeared all claiming to be the youngest, had stuck grimly to this yardstick for the order of precedence. Saint-Saëns wittily thanked him for comparing four weather-beaten composers to '*quatre jolies femmes*!' He did not have the voice for public speaking, but later wrote that his fellow Doctors had been well satisfied with the speech on their behalf. At a lower table, far removed from the concourse of talent grouped around the Provost, was the young undergraduate Ralph Vaughan Williams.

The conferring of degrees began with a procession around the Senate House Green. The Doctors of Music wore robes of cream, gold, red and black, and wide black berets of Tudor design trimmed with gold cord. There were other recipients of honours from the wider world, including Lord Roberts of Kandahar VC, most popular of generals, Lord Chancellor Herschell and the Maharajah of Bhaonagar, who had given generously to charities in his princedom. Saint-Saëns was greatly impressed by the head-dress of the Maharajah, who had been excused from wearing the traditional cap and sported a turban studded with precious jewels. Four native servants in scarlet and gold were stationed at the Senate House to bow on his approach. Saint-Saëns was paired with Bruch in the procession and, in a temperature of about eighty degrees, found the atmosphere torrid. May Week celebrants were crowded into the galleries. There were loud cheers for Lord Roberts and when the undergraduates burst into a sincere but unmusical rendering of 'For He's a Jolly Good Fellow' the *Pall Mall Gazette* noted that it caused 'M. Saint-Saëns to twist his fingers'. When Saint-Saëns came forward there were cheery calls for a song rather than a speech. Dr Sandys, Public Orator, stuck to his brief and hailed Carolum Camillum Saint-Saëns in the customary Latin.

The *Daily Graphic* reported that all four musicians were applauded but 'particularly M. Saint-Saëns and most of all M. Boito who looked strikingly handsome in his gorgeous gown'. Boito, something of a dandy, was very proud of his robes and put them on to entertain friends when he returned to Milan. Tchaikovsky found the student ribaldry a dreadful ordeal.

The guests made their way to Christ's College. At luncheon the musicians were on secondary tables but Saint-Saëns was again in the company of Austen-Leigh and the University Registrar, J. W. Clark, an unmusical enthusiast of drama, who had the strange wish to go to Bayreuth purely for the sake of Wagner's libretti. Saint-Saëns was faced with a conversation on the philosophical import of *The Ring*. After a tea party arranged by some '*femmes charmantes*', Saint-Saëns set off for Trinity, where he had persuaded Stanford and Alan Gray to allow him an organ recital. The Trinity organ had been renovated in 1889 and was one of the finest in Cambridge. Because of the tea party or the '*femmes charmantes*' he was half an hour late and during the waiting period Alan Gray, the regular organist, had played Bach to the large audience. The new Doctor now rushed up the organ steps and launched into a brilliant extemporisation, followed by another in the form of a fully developed fugue. He went on to play his Fantaisie in B flat and a Bach prelude in the same key. The *Cambridge Review* described his performance as 'nothing short of marvellous'.

A renewed interest in the organ was an aspect of his return to better health and spirits in the 1890s. He had left the Madeleine disenchanted with the ecclesiastical use of the organ and the attitudes of the clergy. Now he sometimes returned to the once familiar church of St Severin, where his old pupil Perilhou was organist. The original fourteenth-century instrument had had several rebuildings, most recently in 1890, but the renovator, John Abbey, had left some of the old stops from the days of Saint-Saëns. His delight in this fact and his affection for Perilhou brought him to St Severin for eleven o'clock Mass every Sunday when he was in Paris and he fascinated his hearers with magnificent improvisations. He usually arrived near the end of High Mass and seated himself at the end of the Tribune until the Service was completed. He had a scarlet silk scarf, which he took from his overcoat and wound around his head against draughts. Fauré, still choirmaster at the Madeleine, would come to join the party and before departing for lunch the three would take turns in improvising. On one occasion an uninvited visitor who had climbed the organ steps stood transfixed in the doorway at his first sight of an organist manipulating keyboards, pedals and stops. The man's astonishment appealed to Perilhou's sense of humour and he indicated to Fauré that the latter should slide into place and continue without an apparent break. Fauré did the same to Saint-Saëns and the intruder left, bewildered by his discovery that organ playing was normally done in relays.

In 1892 Perilhou introduced the young, almost blind, Louis Vierne, who had come as assistant on the recommendation of Widor. Vierne later said of Saint-Saëns:

Sometimes a difficult personality, he nevertheless was always kind and tolerant to me. . . . He enjoyed having me improvise the Sortie at the end of Mass and laughed until he cried at my dreadful harmonic mistakes. 'Very good! You don't expect it but it is very musical, youthful and earnest, and the counterpoint does not get lost. You will go far, young man, when you are a little older and through experience have lost some useless things. In the meantime sow your wild oats; I see nothing wrong with that. What is important will show itself.

Two years later, as he was handing out Diplomas at the Conservatoire, he greeted Vierne as First Prize winner with the words: 'Great organist! Excellent musician!' Vierne went on to be organist of St Sulpice and Notre Dame.

In September Saint-Saëns was again in London to direct rehearsals of *Samson*, which was to be given in oratorio form for a new impresario, Mr Farley Sinkins. He was granted an orchestra of 100 and chorus of 300. The chorus did not respond well and there was a week of difficulty at the end of which Saint-Saëns went back to Paris, as did the tenor Lafarge. The Delilah was despatched to persuade Lafarge to return, but failed in her mission; she then would not sing with the replacement tenor 'out of respect for the work', though Saint-Saëns suspected that her voice was tired. The whole incident gave great amusement to Shaw, who spoke of 'the composer and tenor representing the French nation', who 'have done their best to save us by bolting at the last moment. . . . The story of their flight,' he went on, 'and of Mr Sinkin's diplomatic masterstroke of sending the soprano to win them back, and of the fugitives rising to the height of the occasion by capturing the soprano, has already been told though not explained . . .' Substitutes were found. '*Samson* with the part of Samson read at sight is perhaps better than *Samson* with the part of Samson left out,' said Shaw, but the episode did not serve to advance the cause of the opera, still under censorship as a biblical subject, in Britain.[1]

Gounod died in October. Mme Gounod realised that Dubois at the Madeleine would have to participate in the Funeral Service, but wished Saint-Saëns to play and requested that he used a theme from the third part of *Redemption* for his improvisation.[2] He had been

---

[1] In December 1896 *Samson and Delilah* was given more successfully at the Queen's Hall under Randegger, after which it became popular as a concert-hall work.

[2] Fauré, at the choir organ, was having problems with discipline during rehearsal and referred to the 'cruel choirboys'.

preparing a score for Sophocles's *Antigone* in a new version by Vacquerie and Meurice at the Comédie-Française. The classics were enjoying a return to favour, for Romanticism was associated with revolution, and there had been an extension of classical teaching in the 1880s. In the Antique Theatre at Orange, for example, the tradition of presenting light operas had given way in 1888 to a notable production of *Oedipus Rex*. There were many, both in Paris and in the provinces where the local legitimists and gentry took the lead, who thought that classical training would afford a bulwark against decadence, disorder and other sad effects of Romanticism. In place of Mendelssohn's Romantic music, which had been used in the Odéon production of 1844, the producers turned to Saint-Saëns, who tried instead to reproduce the sounds of ancient Greece itself. In his preface to the score he said he had wished to make 'a line drawing, heightened with tinted plates whose charm comes from extreme simplicity'. The orchestra consisted of four flutes, two oboes, two clarinets, harp and strings. The choruses were inspired by ideas of Greek modes and unison singing. *Antigone* is, of course, a drama which elevates opposition to the State to a duty, but the general feeling was that the classics denoted a certain stability and permanence. In addition to *Antigone*, which ran for almost fifty performances in the first year, Saint-Saëns some months later produced his *Hymn to Pallas Athene*, the protectress-goddess of the State, for the Festival of Orange. Whereas the Republicans had had to battle against the Right to establish their principles, they were now faced with threats from the socialist Left. Strikes were more frequent, socialist deputies and international socialist organisations were new phenomena and anarchists, often confused with socialists in the bourgeois imagination, were increasing their attacks. In 1893 a bomb exploded close to the Madeleine and damaged the offices of Durand and Co. One result was a decline in anti-clericalism in journals and even moderate subventions to institutions such as d'Indy's Schola Cantorum. Pope Leo XIII, sharing the belief that militant socialism was the greater threat, urged French Catholics to rally more loyally to the Republic, even at the expense of deserting royalist principles.[1]

Saint-Saëns did not attend the première of *Antigone* but, tired with

[1] A unison song, 'Vive Paris, Vive la France', words by Alfred Tranchant, music by Saint-Saëns, was also a contribution in restoring the social fabric, at a less exalted level than Greek drama.

the year's exertions and affected by melancholy at the death of Gounod, set off at the end of October. He stopped at Toulouse to supervise rehearsals of *Proserpine* and moved on to Valencia and Cadiz. 'There by force of solitude and quinine, with a noticeable amount of sun, I have waited for the return of my strength,' he wrote to Gallet. He greatly relished singing and dancing in the Spanish form of folk-song cabaret, Zarzuela. 'This Zarzuela is my joy . . . embellished with seguidillas, tangos, malaguenas and all that follows. An inexhaustible melodic abundance, the very devil animates these little works . . . I am going to lie low at Ismaila in deep solitude and try to do our big scene, which makes me a little frightened . . .'

This last remark referred to the score of *Frédégonde*, an opera left unfinished by Guiraud, which he had undertaken to complete. Even this work paid some sort of tribute to the Christian religion as a civilising force in barbaric Gaul. Gallet had devised the scenario for Saint-Saëns, but it had been handed on to Guiraud, who was fired by the story and composed as he received the libretto in portions. He was working on it at Wimereux near Boulogne in May 1892, when he died suddenly.

Guiraud is best known for his connections with other musicians since he orchestrated *The Tales of Hoffmann*, wrote the grand opera recitatives for *Carmen* and was the teacher of Debussy and Dukas. Perhaps his greatest contribution to French music was rescuing Bizet from a fight with a gondolier in Venice, since if Bizet had ended up in a canal there might have been no *Carmen* or *Pearl Fishers*. Saint-Saëns once described how Massenet was ruthless in refusing to see visitors until the day's composing was achieved and contrasted this with Guiraud's openness with those who usurped his time and curtailed his achievements.[1] He was fond of Guiraud and on the news of his death wrote to Gallet from Marseilles: 'This first letter written on the soil of France will not be joyful. At the moment of leaving Algiers I learnt from the *Petit Journal* of the unexpected end of our friend, Guiraud, and you can imagine what impression this news had produced on me. I

---

[1] Guiraud's absent-mindedness was also familiar to his friends. He kept the subscriptions for a statue to Marmontel, the pianist professor, in an old trunk and forgot about them. Many had expired before the committee made enquiries. He had once been a theatre drummer and his expert flourishes brought a halt to Méhul's *Burlesque* Overture, which a group of great musicians were playing in *Toy Symphony* fashion.

am astonished that [indecipherable] had not telegraphed it to me. He
did not wish to upset me but he was wrong. I know how to endure the
cruelties of life. I have experience of them.' He hinted that he might
finish the opera. 'Behold, Frédégonde and Brunehilde fall back into
your arms. We shall talk about it. Perhaps my courage will return. I
dare not say anything positive yet.' He tried to write an article on
Guiraud, but doubt and depression set in. He scribbled a letter on
Marseilles Station the following day: 'It is not my fault if devotion,
modesty, self-denial, conscience, respect for the masters do not roam
the streets ... I think it preferable to keep silent at least for the
moment. I will certainly find one day the occasion to sing the praises
of his clear memory as is befitting.' He did, in fact, do much more. He
wrote to Gallet from Toulouse that, feeling himself in debt to his
supportive friend, he would finish 'Brunehilde', as the work was then
known. 'I only ask not to be hurried to work quickly as in former
times; the idea of spending long months seated immobile before a
writing desk frightens me. We shall between us try to arrange with the
Opéra the best way of leaving me the time to carry through this task
without too much fatigue.'

There have been examples of pupils finishing the compositions of
the Great Masters, but rarely has an eminent composer given time to
the completion of a half-finished work by an inferior contemporary.
Progress was slow by Saint-Saëns's standards. At the start of 1894 he
had decided to return to the Canary Isles.

> I have found in a not particularly smart hotel a ravishing lodging; a
> salon giving on to the Promenade, two large rooms with the
> pleasure of a terrace. I have a good little fellow from the district to
> look after me and have bought some furniture with which I have
> decked out my prison quite well [he told Gallet]. This is truly the
> place in which to pass the winter. Today, the 8th January, I have
> noted 21 degrees centigrade; the locals complain of the temperature
> and say there has not been so rigorous a winter for a long time ...
> During this ever so rigorous weather I have slept with the window
> open! [He enjoyed sketching.] Yesterday I made a first serious
> promenade accompanied by my 'slave' who carried an album of
> great size. Armed with a menacing pencil I have clambered up a
> road deprived of all shade, as is the case everywhere here, and I had
> the pleasure of sweating profusely. When I arrived at the top of the

road I found the viewpoint . . . but too late. I will return there in a carriage and then the great works of art will begin. Joking apart, I find that a bad sketch, poor as it may be, still has a flavour that a photograph will never have. . . . I like to be here much more, ignorant of all that is going on, warming myself in the African sun and doodling over drawings and water-colours . . . Would that I could sent you the magnificent palm trees – a species special to the region – whose immense fan shapes resembling long green plumes sway in front of my window. I see with alarm that it is the 10th January, that a third of the month has flown away . . . One ought to be able to prolong the happy times and curtail the others, which is exactly the opposite of what takes place.

He always reported on standards of female beauty during his travels: 'The girls have retained a pretty custom of walking with a mantilla of white muslin, which envelops the face and drops down below the waist, which gives them a virginal and Biblical air, which makes me think all the time of the introduction to *Marie Magdaleine*.' Gallet must have enquired about the progress of *Frédégonde*, for he subsequently wrote,

Do not torment yourself on the subject of 'Brunehilde' . . . at the end of March I will definitely leave Las Palmas . . . for the last week of April I am going to live at St Germain and then we shall put ourselves seriously to work. Calm yourself then on my account. You recommend the sky of Paris to me, but it is my enemy and I am afraid of hackney cabs and spiders – I am not nervous about anything else other than the water, which I drink only when I am assured of its purity. In this fashion I avoid all irritation of the bowels . . .

He intended to go on to Oran, but there was some difficulty in procuring a berth. 'The Isles are charming but one does not always leave as easily as one would wish.' In April the weather was colder and he was affected by influenza. As he could not go out for walks he read and practised the piano. He still did not feel able to tackle a project as large as *Frédégonde* and in the meanwhile he turned to philosophic discourse. *Problèmes et Mystères* discussed the future of society and was published in the following July. The book begins with thoughts on the metronome and the unequal use composers made of it. Schumann must have had a defective metronome since his indications do not always make sense.[1] Having praised the beauties of inanimate Nature he described the slow spread of thought involved in the long evolution of Man. The tiniest of organisms will show traces of thought – moving towards the light, for example. No one disputes the presence of intelligence in animals. The idea of the Soul, however, is an invention, as our thought is the product of natural elements and agents, as a few drops of alcohol will demonstrate.

He gave a brief history of nineteenth-century religion from the resumption of Church power at the Restoration, and the opposition of religion to science. He referred to the attempts of both Renan and the Positivists to establish a kind of religion without mystical faiths, but granted that the mystical element was a source of art. There were no higher summits in Berlioz than his *Te Deum*, *Requiem* or *Enfance du Christ*, though no one was less of a believer. Societies have been built on theocratic principles but, therefore, when religion crumbles society may crumble with it. Atheism had come into the world, but hitherto it had been badly presented and confused with freedom from moral constraints. Seekers after God have pointed to the limitations of science but each day science pushes further forward into the darkness. To preserve a steeple from lightning or a town from the plague, a lightning conductor is better than a cross and sanitary precautions better than processions. Chinese civilisation has survived because of its emphasis on the family. Christianity, on the other hand, if we take its injunctions seriously, denies the family, work and saving, the basis of all social order. Taking no heed for the morrow and food or drink naturally led the Saviour into eating with outcasts, for all idlers must eat where they can. An emphasis on communistic sharing and chastity

---

[1] Saint-Saëns was not wholly blameless in this respect. Max d'Olonne had rehearsed 'Le Cimetière' from *La Nuit Persane* and he and the tenor were to perform before the Master. On the eve of Saint-Saëns's arrival, he discovered to his horror that the metronome marking was much more rapid than seemed appropriate. As soon as Saint-Saëns descended from the train d'Olonne sang him a snatch of the song at what seemed a ridiculously perky speed and asked if it was correct. 'Precisely,' said Saint-Saëns. 'I wrote it down, metronome in hand.' As the pair panted their way through 'The Cemetery' at rehearsal, Saint-Saëns stopped d'Olonne. 'Why rush your tenor? Let him sing at this ease!' Normal speed was resumed and the composer listened happily.

must each alike lead to the breakdown of society, for the first will lead to inordinate consumption and the second to the elimination of the race.

Forced to contemplate what would motivate a society that no longer had the weapons of heavenly rewards and punishments held over it, he returns to the fleeting metronome, now a metaphor for the ever-ephemeral present. We must look to the past and the future, which alone exist. It should be the duty of children to look after the aged, to conserve masterpieces and the intellectual inheritance. Parents must have solicitude for their young, for education, health and the environment such children will experience. In a moving passage the childless wanderer speaks of the duty of parents to explain the insects and weeds which children so often produce for inspection and are told irritably to throw away. How much more valuable it would be to use the opportunity to introduce some science than retail bizarre legends of the plagues of Egypt and chariots of fire. *Problèmes et Mystères* was typical of the period in which curé and schoolmaster were locked in combat in every parish. Yet a musician depends upon popular approval; this philosophical essay was evidence of the author's indifference to it.

Music was not totally neglected during his stay in the Canaries. The *Caprice Arabe* for two pianos was written in 1894. In January he told Durand that he had come across some Arab documents acquired earlier, which he thought that he had lost, and found sufficient thematic material to make 'a little *Africa* for two pianos'. When the work was nearing completion he described it as having a quality which distinguished it from his other efforts to explore oriental sounds. Although the title suggests the salon there was a real intention to explore Arab rhythms, especially conflicting rhythms, which the four hands enabled him to do. The sound of the Arab derboukas was suggested. It is true that he wove Arab themes into Western shapes, but that was in keeping with French policy, which always sought to turn colonial territories into outposts of metropolitan France. Even so the *Caprice Arabe* has some unfamiliar harmonies and whiffs of Eastern spices. There is no great chasm between its sultry opening pages and Debussy's *L'Après-Midi*, which appeared in the same year.

He also composed his *Thème Varié* for Piano, containing many difficulties and booby traps, as a test piece for the Conservatoire Piano Prize. In 1894 the prize was won by Ricardo Vines. Alfred Cortot did not fare well in this competition, which might in part explain his unsympathetic attitude towards the composer's piano music.

The time that he spent in Paris in 1894 was one of the shortest periods of residence. The capital continued to be disturbed by anarchists. In February Auguste Vaillant, who had thrown a bomb into the Chamber, wounding several politicians, was executed. Soon afterwards, Emile Henry, son of a Communard, threw a bomb into a café near the Gare St Lazare, which was not patronised by the rich but by their supposed 'lackeys'. Henry was executed in May and a further series of attacks in the smarter hotels and restaurants followed. In June a twenty-one-year-old Italian, Caserio, shouting, '*Vive la Révolution! Vive l'Anarchie!*', stabbed President Carnot with a six-inch knife. Carnot had refused to pardon the revolutionaries and his assassination resulted in severe laws, removing trial by jury from many political cases and restricting the reporting of them.

Saint-Saëns's fame as an organist lingered on, for he was invited to play at Carnot's State Funeral in Notre-Dame. The organ there was being overhauled and Saint-Saëns asked Widor to send two pupils to assist in pulling out the stops. One was Vierne, who thus had his first experience of the Notre Dame console. Saint-Saëns now published his Three Preludes and Fugues (Opus 99), dedicated to Widor, Guilmant and Gigout respectively. The first two names were closely connected with the Conservatoire and the recent *Thème Varié* had been inscribed to Ambroise Thomas. The dedications were no doubt part of a campaign to install Fauré in some Conservatoire post. Fauré and Saint-Saëns continued to submit their compositions to each another. In October 1894, Fauré mentioned a new Waltz, Nocturne and Barcarolle 'that I will play to you very badly on Wednesday morning if you wish'.

The Preludes and Fugues for Organ were major works which, together with a further three published as Opus 109, mark Saint-Saëns as one of the greatest composers for the organ, though curiously the association does not readily come to mind. All three pay homage to Bach with preludes that allow the resources and contrasts of tone to be displayed and fugues that build up to strong climaxes, especially in the 'Gigout' Fugue. Vierne thought that these three works, along with their 1898 companions, should be in the repertoire of all organists worthy of the name as much for their superb style as for their virtuoso

demands. The No. 1 Prelude begins devoutly with a rippling figure
that passes from keyboard to keyboard with chords interposed and a
slow crescendo, which leads to its repetition in stronger colours. It has
been compared with an aqueduct where running water resonates over
the columns of strong indestructible arches. The Fugue subject is
conventional, capable of harmonisation in its interstices, and at the
same time of contrapuntal treatment, variation and extensions. There
is also a link between the subjects of Prelude and Fugue.

No. 2 is less conventional. The Prelude is a fluttering, gossamer
thing with delicate rhythmic surprises where a romantic barcarolle
melody sings out below and is eventually shared between the pedals
and high registers of the keyboard. The Fugue has a quirky theme,
such as might be set as an amusing exercise, which begins with a little
triplet twirl. By the end it has attained the dignity worthy of the great
instrument for which it was destined. Prelude No. 3 follows the
pattern of the Widor Toccata in having a bold pedal theme sounded
under a cascade of repeated figures on the keyboards. In this instance
the theme is longer and more elaborate. The Fugue in 3:4 time calls
all the resources of a grand organ into play with sequential passages, a
prominent counter-theme near the close, rapid flourishes and a
majestic chordal close, a blaze of sound introduced by a forceful
introduction on the pedals.

At the end of the year Saint-Saëns set off for Saigon, his longest
voyage to date. He took 'Brunehilde' with him and composed down
the Red Sea and over the Indian Ocean. The last page of the score
bore the inscription 'Saigon. 1895. Avril'.[1] It was ten years since
French advances in Cochin-China had almost come to grief. A
garrison at Tuyen Quan had been besieged; there had been defeats
and disasters. Ferry, the Minister responsible for a colonial policy, had
been attacked by both Left and Right, accused by Clemenceau of high
treason and besieged in his Ministry by crowds threatening to throw
him into the Seine. He had hastily concluded a Treaty with Imperial
China, which gave the French rights over the lands of the Emperor of

---

[1] 'I shall finish the last scene in the midst of monkeys and coconuts. . . . I
attacked our last act in the open sea . . . a marvellous blue unknown in the
North. It appears I shall arrive . . . for a great Chinese Festival which lasts
several days!' Yet 'Brunehilde'–*Frédégonde* deals with Merovingian Gaul in the
Dark Ages. Saint-Saëns's mental agility was astonishing.

Assam. A long process began whereby French officials came out to rule the area in the interests of trade and good government. They included acquaintances of Saint-Saëns. Indeed, when he was in Saigon he saw the arrival of Armand Rousseau, his old neighbour from the rue Monsieur le Prince, as Governor. M. Jacquet, newly appointed Governor of a penal settlement at Poulo Condor, a group of eleven islands off the Mekong Delta, invited him to spend a season in this remote spot. He took great delight in the vegetation, especially exotic trees, hitherto only seen painted on screens, and he made journeys to the islands to study huge lizards, which croaked their names, and birds with plumage of all colours. 'I was made to live in the tropics; I have missed my vocation,' he observed. One of the favourite subjects of conversations was the fauna and flora he had seen in his travels. Once in Indo-China he just drew back from stroking an emerald-coloured serpent, discovering later that a single bite would have been instantly fatal. There was already a French opera house in Saigon where the airs of Gounod and Thomas could spread civilisation in the Far East.

He arrived back in France in May and handed over the task of orchestrating Acts One to Three to Paul Dukas, a pupil of Guiraud, for whom he had a high esteem. Rehearsals began in September. In addition to completing the two final acts he had introduced a ballet into Act Three. Guiraud had set the lyrical parts of the score with delicacy. Saint-Saëns added a robustness, most markedly in the ballet based upon French provincial airs, and a large ensemble, 'The Anathema of the Bishops', which Baumann considered as great as any choral scene in French opera. As the title 'Brunehilde' had obvious associations with Wagner and the completed work would disappoint the keener Wagnerians, the rival Queen Frédégonde rose to stardom in the new title. The première took place on 18 December. Saint-Saëns had remained in Paris for the winter beyond the call of duty. The reception was enthusiastic, but it remained in the repertory for only eight performances, a very bitter blow to him, more on account of the slight to Guiraud than because of his own labours. For a time he vowed he would not write anything further for the stage. Augusta Holmès had suffered a similar set-back in June when her *Montagne Noire* had been put on at the Opéra. Remarkable as it had been for a woman to succeed in forcing an entrance where so many aspirant males had failed, Augusta's work was heavily criticised by Bellaigue and others. Through the singer Mme Heglon (Frédégonde), Augusta learnt that her old admirer had spoken warmly of her work. 'How much pleasure I had to learn through your fine interpreter, Mme Heglon, that you approve of and like my *Montagne Noire* for which I have been tied to the stake and crippled with arrows and clods, as for the *Ode Triomphale*. Your vote, impeccable Master, effaces all outrage and injustice. I am going to send you the score. I would have liked to see you but I have just been ill with a terrible liver complaint ... confined alone, taking only some milk.'

Another epic voyage, this time into scholarship, beckoned. Alberic Magnard, a musician whose father directed *Le Figaro*, used its columns to call for a complete edition of the works of Rameau. The Durands, especially Jacques, who was emerging from a Wagnerian phase ('Guiraud and Saint-Saëns had cured me of my shrill Wagnerism'), favoured the project and decided that it would require a leader of undisputed prestige in both musical and academic fields. Saint-Saëns, who had read the Magnard letter, accepted this role.[1] The Durands chose as collaborators Charles Malherbe, an archivist with a wide knowledge of music collections and an expert on the eighteenth century, and Léon Roques, their chief proof reader, pupil of Ambroise Thomas, and friend of Massenet and Diémer at the Conservatoire. Many others participated: Jean-Baptiste Weckerlin, Librarian of the Conservatoire, Delisle at the Bibliothèque Nationale, and d'Indy who had conducted many performances of Rameau. Debussy, Dukas, Guilmant and Reynaldo Hahn, all at some stage lent their expertise. The tasks involved textual comparisons and discoveries of unpublished pieces. There were interpolations and ornaments to clear away, adaptations made for modern instruments and transposition of parts. Saint-Saëns insisted upon supervising much of the detail himself and each year would devote some weeks to the preparation of the monumental series, which occupied its researchers year after year. It was a matter of national pride to prove that France had possessed a genius worthy to rank with Sebastian Bach.

In January 1896 Saint-Saëns set off for Egypt, via Milan where the première of *Henry VIII* took place with Mme Félia Litvinne as Anne Boleyn and where he was able to congratulate Toscanini on achieving the correct tempi in the *Danse Macabre*. He enjoyed periods of repose

[1] Lecocq had kindled his enthusiasm for Rameau when they were students and his friend had arranged a vocal score of 'Castor and Pollux' as a labour of love.

in both Cairo and Luxor. Magnard had spoken enthusiastically about Egypt and persuaded the young Durand to travel there where he, too, heard the song of the Nile Boatmen, which Saint-Saëns used in the Fifth Piano Concerto. Fired by his enthusiasm, the composer and his painter friend Clairin made the expedition to Luxor. Clairin wrote a description of Saint-Saëns making a purée of the local onions, stirring 'his horrible soup' with one hand and writing music with the other. 'He is furious because he was not able to go to market yesterday. He is always delightful with gaiety, youth and simplicity.' A *Valse Mignonne* was completed for the Princess Bedia-Oman, daughter of the Khedive, and a duet for tenor and baritone, 'Venus', for which he wrote his own lyric, was dedicated to two of the singers in *Frédégonde*, Albert d'Alvarez and Maurice Renaud. He voyaged up the Nile to Aswan and Philae, and wrote his Second Sonata for Violin and Piano. He then retired temporarily into seclusion to write the new piano concerto, putting into it many of the impressions he had gathered on his travels in both the Middle and Far East. Renewed pleasure in instrumental music consoled him for the frustrations of the theatre.

He returned to Paris to participate in the celebrations for the fiftieth anniversary of his first recital at the Salle Pleyel in 1846. It was planned by his friends in the same venue and given in aid of the Association of Artist Musicians. The programme contained memories of the child prodigy, including the Mozart B-flat Concerto. There were new works: the Violin Sonata played by Sarasate and the Fifth Piano Concerto to which others gave the name *The Egyptian*. Taffanel played a Romance for Flute and Orchestra; there was a fragment from *Phryné* and, as a reminder of how often the careers of the two men had been intertwined, a paraphrase on Massenet's 'Death of Thaïs'. During the interval the composer came forward to read a poem of his own, which described the impressions of the pale and delicate '*garçonnet*' who had wrestled with Mozart and Beethoven fifty years before. There was a tribute to the 'incomparable woman' his mother, somewhat veiled as, in determining that her son would be a musician, she had not comprehended how that path led to grief as well as fame. Her pleasure in old age had been for someone very different from the real Saint-Saëns. He harked back to his teachers, Stamaty – one of whose sons was there – and Maleden, and the conductor of the 1846 concert, Tilmant, and made particular mention of his childish distaste for rapturous applause which 'rose like a tide of flotsam' around the platform. Fame is a hollow thing, for art is like the sea, one day, as on this anniversary, resembling the joy of a blue sky and calm waters; tomorrow will come the storms and buffeting. He was now too old; before, he had been too young for the part he had to play, but he hoped his audience would encourage him and help to blow a few of the dying cinders into life.

There was irony in the burst of acclamation from the press, for only a few months had passed since the failure of his noble rescue of *Frédégonde*. *Le Temps* described this anniversary as 'a procession of uninterrupted ovations'. The new concerto 'proved his extraordinary vitality . . . a work of fantasy ornamented and coloured like one of the prettiest buildings of the Alhambra . . . the acclamations which greeted it do not salute only a great past, but the proof of splendid artistic renewal'. Many of the hardest critics were obliged to pay some homage. Louis de Fourcaud in *Le Gaulois*, although he thought some of the works lacked a personal stamp and were marked by '*bizarreries*', conceded that Saint-Saëns was the musician who brought the greatest honour to his country and his art. 'The Parisians have learnt to esteem him slowly when already in foreign countries his name has resounded among the most famous. Acclaimed in Germany, Russia, England, even in Italy, in Paris he still fights battles on his own and others' behalf!' Nowhere in Europe could one find 'a more complete musician'.

In *La Liberté* Joncières, an art student turned musician, a convinced Wagnerian who had left the Conservatoire after disagreements with his tutors over Wagner's 1860 concerts in Paris, devoted columns to the anniversary, describing it as 'a very rare spectacle . . . A French composer has been acclaimed and received the unquestioning witness of sincere admiration in which is mixed a sort of "national pride", a sentiment which for far too long seemed completely extinguished among us at least in musical matters.' He reminded his readers that no critics had been invited to the concert and no free tickets distributed to friends. 'Not a single listener had obtained a complimentary ticket for this artistic jubilee, and each had to pay twenty francs for the right to applaud the illustrious Master. And it has been necessary to exclude the world at large, for the Salle Pleyel would have been too small to contain all the devotees of the great virtuoso composer, and the takings could have been 10,000 francs.' In *L'Eclair*, Samuel Rousseau praised again the time-honoured French genius for 'clarity, logic and form; even when he appears to give way to the most bewildering fantasies, building up a thousand witty and exquisite episodes, he co-ordinates logically the most unexpected elements and in impeccable form he gives the impression of excellent and absolute completeness. No one better than he will be able to apply to himself the famous line: "Living he has entered into immortality".' Hugues Imbert, who in 1888 had written harshly about Saint-Saëns in his *Profils de musiciens*, numbering him among those 'intelligent and independent minds . . . only half engaged in the movement of change . . . [whose] reputations will perhaps not go beyond the century in which they lived', reserved a definitive judgement. *Le Temps* had observed that the triumphal soirée at which Liszt made his farewells to the public in Vienna in 1873 did not have more splendour than this occasion. Unlike Liszt, however, Saint-Saëns did not enjoy being lionised. After this historic concert he made his way back to his furnished rooms and dined alone with his much loved dog Delilah.

The Fifth Concerto entered rapidly into the repertoire. In November the Conservatoire season opened with a performance by Diémer, the dedicatee, with Taffanel conducting. In December Diémer played it again at the Colonne concerts. The sudden realisation that the composer had been working among them for fifty years seemed to surprise the musical world and some of the critics veered into hyperbole. Edward Mangeot in *Le Monde Musical* said of the Concerto, 'Never have we heard a work more colourful or gripping; it is from Rubens, from Raphael, from Michelangelo, for one finds in it fantasy, grace and power, and the listener admires at the same time the incomparable structure, chief quality of the greatest musician of our time and this prodigious imagination which gives us new and singularly captivating impressions.' Saint-Saëns described it as 'a kind of voyage in the East, which goes even as far in the F-sharp section as the Far East. The passage in G is a Nubian love-song that I heard sung by the boatmen on the Nile when I was going downstream in a "dahabieh".' Once more he was being innovative, for this is the first French *concerto* to incorporate 'exoticisms', previously confined to suites and shorter pieces. The orchestration of his piano concertos had been steadily expanded: the Second had added trumpets and timpani to the woodwind and strings of the First; he added three trombones (which play a large part in the contests with the piano) in the Third. While retaining these forces for the Fourth he now put in a piccolo and two additional horns. He never exhibited his talents as an orchestrater flamboyantly. He was fond of using percussion quietly. The muffled timpani introducing the Scherzo of the Second Concerto are familiar; in the Fifth, the gong makes a similarly surreptitious entrance while the piano is hammering out an oriental motif and the strings are buzzing away in a high-pitched 'jungle' drone.

The mood of this concerto mirrors the happiness that Saint-Saëns found increasingly in the East. Allowing for Baumann's over-fanciful imagination, there is something convincing in his image of the fresh opening bars, *in medias res*, so unlike their counterparts in all previous concertos. 'It is the morning, he opens his window, he is free, he has left behind the servitudes and troubles of existence. The air is spotless, a light illuminates his table, touches the pages of an MS begun – immediately he *sees* the initial phrase in F major, which dances and smiles, a group of the Muses with delicate interlacing of hands – light tints of its melody develop without being able to leave perfect chords.' Perhaps more strangely, as Dr Stegemann has pointed out, these chords, lilting and fresh, are really a broken chorale.

There were innovations, too, in the form of the first two movements, for the second is very much a 'fantasy' and the first, though it has a feeling of being in sonata form, has a pattern of its own. In the more regular Finale the impressions of a journey homewards are marshalled in more regular fashion, although, by what is a freak coincidence, the first subject has a marked resemblance to the piano style of Scott Joplin.[1] The second subject falls into two sections using almost the same patterns, but where the first is lively and dancing the second is tender and rhapsodic. This extension of a second subject into a romantic postlude was later employed spaciously by Rachmaninov. All in all, the notion of foreign travel is emphasised by the unusual scoring which Saint-Saëns normally based upon strings with woodwind solos and additions. Here there are unusual combinations of woodwinds and new timbres such as horns with piano. The Nubian love-song relaxes into the homely key of G major. It is the left hand which draws the melody while the right executes harp-like figures which, as in 'The Swan', represent ripples on the waters. There is a section of almost forty bars in which muted violins play a repeated

---

[1] Saint-Saëns had told Isidore Philipp that the Finale expresses 'the joy of a sea crossing, a joy that not everyone shares'.

C sharp, while the left hand of the pianist dances and the right makes castanet sounds pianissimo, evoking an image of finger cymbals, although Saint-Saëns is said to have told Diémer in rehearsal that this passage portrayed the croaking of frogs at twilight. Tremolo bars for the strings at the close are reminders of one of the features of Egyptian singing.

The Finale bristles with so many difficulties it was for many years a test piece at the Conservatoire and formed the basis of a huge 'Study' by the composer, dedicated to the pianist Pugno. Towards the close there is a gigantic series of chromatically interlocking octaves from bottom to top of the keyboard. In a letter Saint-Saëns said, 'It is virtuosity itself I mean to defend. It is the source of the picturesque in music, it gives to the artist wings to help him escape from the prosaic and commonplace. The conquered difficulty is in itself a source of beauty.'

The restrained new Violin Sonata was an unexpected companion piece. Writing to Chantavoine, Saint-Saëns said that he preferred it to the First, but Chantavoine thought this a difficult opinion to explain. One can agree with Saint-Saëns, however, for the Second Sonata breathes an air of total contentment. Instead of a programme and impressionistic effects we have a first movement in an approximately classical form even if the recapitulation is barely differentiated from the development. There is a Salon Waltz–Scherzo with a mildly academic Trio and reminiscences of a minuet. The slow movement is a romanticised choral prelude in which the violin carries a sustained melody accompanied by broken chords, pages of great beauty interrupted only by a playful moment of dialogue between the two instruments. Even the Finale is light and based upon one of Saint-Saëns's compound themes made of more than one configuration.

In June it was played at a celebratory soirée arranged by Gigout, whose pupils performed a selection of the Master's organ works including the Fantasy written in 1895, Opus 101, dedicated to the Queen of Romania, who was known in Parisian artistic circles as a writer under the name of Carmen Sylva.[1] The Fantasy is an extemporisation from a four-note figure, which is at first accompanied by rippling notes on different manuals, then harmonised in chords, is adapted to become an episode in a fugal middle section and reappears

---

[1] The Queen of Serbia, not to be outdone, asked Saint-Saëns to write an opera on a libretto of hers. He thought it 'amateurish' and declined.

in the Allegro, which seeks a full-blooded display of the organ's resources before closing in quiet flute arpeggios. Reminiscences of César Franck come in the passages which link an Andante to the Allegro. Rejoicing in his revived love of the organ, Saint-Saëns made a tour of Switzerland, its churches and cathedrals, in late September. His companion on the programmes was a singer, Mlle Baldo, who included Franck's 'Panis Angelicus', Saint-Saëns's own 'Deus Abraham' and Gounod's 'Jesus of Nazareth' as contemplative additions between the Preludes and Fugues, his Fantasie and a *Rhapsodie Bretonne.*

Although the anniversary recital of 1896 was acclaimed, among the public the event on which much greater attention was focused was the visit of Tsar Nicholas II, who landed at Cherbourg and made a loudly cheered entry into Paris. Isolated in Europe, France had at last found an ally in the unlikely guise of autocratic Russia. 'At last we are not alone!' was the cry. The French colonies were given prominence in the processions and Algerian chieftains in white cloaks with flashing scimitars escorted the Tsar to the Arc de Triomphe. 'How much better to be a wine merchant at the moment,' wrote Fauré to his wife Marie.

He was much preoccupied at the time with manoeuvres at the Conservatoire. Ambroise Thomas had died from the excitement brought on by a performance of an excerpt from his *Françoise de Rimini* at an Opéra gala. Saint-Saëns took a keen interest in the sequel. Massenet, Professor of Composition since 1878, was an obvious Director but would accept the post only on condition of being elected for life. When this was refused, he resigned his Professorship. Théodore Dubois became Director and resigned his composition class and his post as organist at the Madeleine, where Fauré succeeded him. Thomas had disliked Fauré, who had recently been defeated in the election for the Institut by Lenepveu, and Fauré was worried that the official musical world was against him. He wrote privately to Dubois asking if his fears were justified, and protesting that he would retire from competition and 'continue to perpetrate my work, which is probably detestable and inferior'. Saint-Saëns advised him to apply, not for one of the two vacant composition classes (Massenet's and Dubois's) but for Widor's organ class, letting Widor take Massenet's composition pupils. 'It [the organ class] hurt neither Widor nor Franck.' He no doubt felt that Fauré needed to consolidate his fame and security as an organist, and he knew Fauré was uncertain of his worth as a teacher of composition. In the end Widor, whom the younger man found self-satisfied and fickle in his promises, took Dubois's pupils and Fauré was given Massenet's.

As for the Institut, Fauré wrote, 'My only hope would be to succeed you in forty years [by which time Saint-Saëns would have been 101] but I swear to you that I like you very much more than the Institut.' The composer George Enesco found Fauré a much better teacher than he imagined himself to be. He was the opposite of the expansive Massenet, brief on technical details and proverbially unpunctual, but he had an aura and was inspiring. One of his first pupils was Maurice Ravel. Saint-Saëns was pleased that the art of composition was taken out of Massenet's hands.

After a rush of composition Saint-Saëns seems to have thought he would retire and, remembering the success of *Phryné*, on a light note. There was a rich vein to explore in the geographical and social variety of the French provinces. He became interested in a ballet scenario submitted by J. L. Croze, a godson of Gallet, who had recently written verses for him, which was set in Provence. Mindful that Dubois had recently produced a 'Farandole' he suggested a move to the Nivernais region and a story from Boccaccio, which told how two lovers had substituted a little white donkey in the girl's room to deceive an old Marquis into believing her safely immured. The ballet was intended for the Folies-Marigny where Croze was employed, but the theatre went bankrupt. The Directors of the Monnaie in Brussels were approached, but were nervous of the donkey, so the story was rewritten. It was, in effect, a version of Hérold's *La Fille Mal Gardée*, in one act and three scenes and the title, *Javotte*, was chosen by Durand. The similarity of the two ballets has eclipsed the scintillating score of *Javotte*. Saint-Saëns admired Delibes and wrote the music in similar style, but combined a boulevardier zest with inescapable academic touches. There are Rossinian echoes in the opening, slow waltzes, romantic solos for oboe, violin and viola, and a march for the local *pompiers* with cornets and saxhorns which matches anything in French light music. The bassoon sings inflected phrases, which almost speak the words as the parents mime a search for their missing daughter. There is a Finale in 5:4 time for full orchestra and a series of rustic rhythms which weave popular exuberance into the more aristocratic dance patterns.

He began the score at Aix-les-Bains and finished it at St Germain. The Monnaie abandoned its rights, but these were speedily taken up by Vizentini who was now Director at Lyon. Vizentini had also agreed to revive *Proserpine* and the role of Angiola was sung by a Mlle Duperret, whom Saint-Saëns had heard in Saigon two years before. He supervised the rehearsals from mid-November and conducted the two first performances. *Javotte* was well received and was seen as part of a renewed interest in the provinces, where residual support for the political Right was there to be nurtured. Several journals asked Saint-Saëns if his latest score was a postscript to his career in more serious composition. His replies referred to his opera scores, which were collecting dust in management offices awaiting presentation. He did not see the necessity of hoarding useless scores in chests of drawers. Once again, fire had struck the Saint-Saëns repertoire, for a blaze in the rue Richer in 1894 had destroyed many of the décors stored there by the Opéra. The State intervened to assist with the costs of replacement, but *Henry VIII* and *Ascanio* were left off the list for rehabilitation and only *Samson* was still to be found on the *affiches*. Even after a year of considerable triumphs the composer left Paris with bitterness against the Opéra and its Directors.

The solitude of the Canaries revived his spirits.

I have found once more the sweetness of the air, the little red, yellow and blue houses, the pretty girls in bright skirts, their heads and shoulders enveloped in the white mantillas of wool ... There is always a superabundance of dogs and, worried that there might not be quite enough, someone has put a whole bronze collection of them in a town square, where they sit enthroned in various postures. It is original, very original ... In return someone has destroyed the captivating fountains where water, which came down from on high, was collected by women with long rods armed with a sort of funnel. I weep for them silently, content that 'progress' has made no other ravages.

While in the Canaries he wrote a long study of Gounod for the *Revue de Paris* and showed his erudition in a correspondence with the critic Bellaigue who had just reviewed the *Egyptian* Concerto. Saint-Saëns described the review as a 'feast'. 'It exceeds the bounds of thanks. You have put me in this position before, but this time it is worse still and I feel myself blushing. Please, I am only human and to hear such things before the whole world ...' Bellaigue had written on 'Exoticism in Music' and Saint-Saëns referred to Beethoven's Dervish Chorus in the *Ruins of Athens*. He had seen 'these mystic spinning tops' in Cairo. 'Have you not noticed the similarity of the triplets played by the flutes which accompany them ... For me it is impossible that Beethoven simply by intuitive genius had divined that. He must have had at his disposal an authentic document.' He moved on to discuss Handel and the scores he had studied in Buckingham Palace library. He believed that Handel owed his superiority not so much to his musicianship as to his descriptive powers. 'The masterly capacity to write choruses, of dealing with fugues, others had as well as he. What he brought was colour, the modern element ... Look from this point of view at *Alexander's Feast*, *Israel in Egypt* and above all *L'Allegro and Pensieroso* [*sic*] and try to forget all that has been done since. You will find at each stage a search for the picturesque, imitative effect. It is real and very intense for the milieu in which it was produced – where it seems to have been previously unknown.' He had some months earlier been in correspondence with a M. Litta on a study of expression marks in the works of Bach and the harpsichordists. He put forward the suggestion that a study of Bach's word-setting in the cantatas sometimes provided clues to the moods and colouring of the Preludes in the *Well-Tempered Clavier*, although he himself preferred impassive performances to the 'combat areas' of 'high emotions', which certain artists cultivated.

He was not, in fact, allowed to enjoy any kind of retirement from the theatre. In the southern town of Béziers an old arena, built originally for bullfights, was being restored. Money had run out, but work was sufficiently advanced to give a wealthy amateur musician, M. Castelbon de Beauxhostes, vice-consul of Spain, the idea of imitating Orange and presenting spectacular productions. Castelbon had already patronised local culture, seeing, like many of his ilk, a sound alternative to trade unions in municipal bands and choral societies. He had, by this time, founded a band, La Lyre Bitteroise, which he conducted, and was contemplating a festival with a famous name at its centre.[1] On his return to France Saint-Saëns had given a series of

---

[1] A Saint-Saëns Festival in emulation of Bayreuth had once been discussed at a private dinner with Eduard Lassen and Nikolay Rubinstein. Saint-Saëns, disappointed at the failure of *Etienne Marcel* in Paris, had seemed thoughtful

Dieppe welcomes Saint-Saëns. Cartoon at the time of the opening of the
Saint-Saëns Museum, featuring operatic characters carrying suitcases.

Saint-Saëns (*far right*) crossing the Channel. Snapped by a fellow passenger.

1903: Saint-Saëns in Béziers, with a group of young friends.

1906: Saint-Saëns at Monte-Carlo for *L'Ancêtre*, with Geraldine Farrar and M. Renaud.

Saint-Saëns at
the rostrum.

Cartoon: Saint-Saëns
seeking inspiration in
the Orient.

(*Facing page*)
Statue of Saint-Saëns
by Laurent Marqueste,
1907. Presented to
Dieppe but destroyed
in the Second World War.

Piano duettists:
Saint-Saëns (*right*)
with Paderewski.

Saint-Saëns playing a
'Danse Macabre' for Germany.
A German eagle is captive
under his keyboard.

au Parthénon

Saint-Saëns at the Parthenon in 1920. An ambition at last realised.

The family tomb. Montparnasse, Paris.

organ recitals in the Midi and he was asked to test the acoustics at Béziers. The scientific aspect interested him, for he had already carried out experiments at Orange. Gallet was at the time working on a tragedy, *Déjanire*, derived from the *Trachiniennes* of Sophocles and *L'Hercule sur l'Oeta* of Seneca. Hercules, whose sensual weakness fascinated Saint-Saëns, was a popular image as part of a French 'classical' response to Germanic toughness. In 1894 France had played a leading part in the revival of the Olympic Games. Gymnasiums spread and Alpinism became popular. Saint-Saëns planned with Gallet to present the work, not as an opera, but as an antique tragedy in the Greek tradition with sung choruses and symphonic interludes. The principal parts would be declaimed, but music would accompany the entrances and exits. While Gallet worked on *Déjanire* at foggy Wimereux, the composer made an extensive tour which embraced Stockholm and Copenhagen. On the eve of his departure from Denmark he was invited by Queen Louise and her daughters to the royal palace where he played for them his *Valse Mignonne* and *Rêverie Arabe*. The Queen reminded him of his great-aunt Charlotte.

In October he was at the Brussels Exhibition, where he conducted his Third Symphony and played the organ in *La Lyre et la Harpe*. He visited the French section and demonstrated the effects of the harmoniums and celestes. With the young Edouard Risler he played his Gavotte on a special double piano invented by Gustave Lyon, to whom in the following year he dedicated his transcription of the Duos for Piano and Harmonium Opus 8, rewritten for two pianos. In the autumn the Salle Saint-Saëns was opened at the museum in Dieppe, followed by a banquet, a festival and the renaming of a *place* in his honour. He became a considerable patron of clubs in Dieppe and subscribed towards a racing skiff for the Club Nautique. He was awarded a medal by a local Shooting Club, which he must have supported for patriotic rather than sporting reasons. Many musical festivals were held to celebrate his anniversaries. The museum declined into Social Security offices when the contents were removed to the château.

All this was preliminary to a visit to Madrid in November where his success was phenomenal. He supervised rehearsals of *Samson* and at a

and did not dismiss the idea, which was mooted for somewhere in the Auvergne.

major concert he appeared as composer, conductor and pianist. Each item in the programme was encored: the Prelude from *Le Déluge*, the Tarantella, the *Rouet d'Omphale* and the Second Symphony. Finally the *Danse Macabre* had to be thrown in as well. On the next day he gave a recital which included his First Trio and harpsichord pieces by Rameau. He had a further encounter with royalty. Queen Christina was a redoubtable lady. As Regent she had swept aside all objections that, heavily pregnant with the heir to the throne, she should abstain from visiting the victims of a hurricane and, with the same independence, had refused to listen to cautions that the number thirteen in her son's title would be unlucky. She wished to hear Saint-Saëns on the organ and a Cavaillé-Coll instrument was located in the church of San Francisco. Some great ladies of the palace expressed their disapproval of a church visit for anything other than divine service, whereupon the Queen came to the recital no longer incognito but with the infant King, the Court and fanfares sounded along her route.

I had written a religious march for the event and the Queen kindly accepted it [wrote Saint-Saëns]. I was a little flustered when she asked me to play the too familiar melody from *Samson and Delilah* which begins '*Mon coeur s'ouvre à ta voix*'. I had to improvise a transcription suited to the organ – something I had not dreamt of doing. During the performance the Queen leant her elbow on the organ, her chin resting on one hand and her eyes upturned. She seemed rapt in ecstasy which, as may be imagined, was not displeasing to the composer.

On the following day, after three hours of rehearsals, he made his début as a Spanish speaker, at the Ateneo Society, apologising for his lack of fluency and giving his address half in Spanish and half in French. It was here he repeated the offer he had first made as a child of ten to play any Beethoven sonata. The A flat (probably opus 26) was selected by the committee and he prefaced it with a sixteenth-century Spanish piece he had just found in a collection and transcribed.

These long absences from Paris are no doubt the reason why we have so little written by him on the Dreyfus Case, which was now bursting upon France. Captain Alfred Dreyfus had been arrested in 1894 on the

charge of passing information to the Germans and his trial took place
in the wake of a press campaign on the dangers of foreign spies, waged
especially in *Le Petit Parisien*. For over two years the Dreyfus family
had been protesting his innocence and the case gradually attracted
attention. It was in January 1898 that Emile Zola published his famous
letter in *L'Aurore*, alleging that the conviction had been false. Zola's
trial lasted into July, keeping opinion in ferment and rioters on the
streets. The artistic world was divided like all others. Debussy
criticised the opera *Messidor*, by Alfred Bruneau, based on a text of
Zola, who was of Italian origin, as 'non-French'. Edgar Degas fired his
favourite model because she was Protestant, and all Protestants and
minority groups were believed to be Dreyfusards. Proust attended
Zola's trial and persuaded Anatole France, who had been a Boulangist
in his time, to sign a petition supporting Colonel Picquart, who had
asserted Dreyfus's innocence. Meanwhile the Army yearned for
another Boulanger who would crush the Republic and silence the Left.
When railway strikes broke out and the stations were occupied by
troops the Dreyfusards spread fears of a military *coup d'état*. Dreyfus
and his family were Jewish and in contrast to the heroic mood of
Samson the Jews were now seen not as champions of liberty, but as
foreign infiltrators subverting French national life. The once accepted
life-style of Catulle Mendès came under attack as decadent. Augusta
Holmès, incensed that after his divorce from Judith Gautier in 1896
Catulle had remarried someone else, was passionately anti-Dreyfusard.
Saint-Saëns received a letter from her which ran: 'Do you know that
Clairin has become a fierce Dreyfusard? One cannot speak to him any
more. When one reflects that to our hero, Henri Regnault, he was like
a brother, the whole thing appears unbelievable.' Often regarded as
over-combative by nature, Saint-Saëns appears in his reply to be
moderate: 'Yes, my dear friend, I knew about this and I feel as sorry
about it as you. But please show some indulgence to an old friend from
long ago. Clairin saw Dreyfus and has the impression that he was not
guilty . . .' With his Jewish features Saint-Saëns did not escape some of
the charges that now fell upon the Israelite fraternity, but he was a
much decorated and strong supporter of the Republic and was not
disposed to throw in his lot with the radicals and protesters.

He had been abroad during the first weeks of the furore. Grieg,
however, formerly popular in Paris, was openly a Dreyfusard and for
some time concert promoters dared not advertise his works for fear of

demonstrations. By coincidence, Jacques Durand, while in the Army, had sat next to Dreyfus at a Mess dinner. He had been in the habit of giving piano recitals to entertain fellow officers and Dreyfus had come to one of these as a guest. Durand also knew Picquart, who was musical, and had had conversations with him about Wagner and Bayreuth.

While Paris became heated over this great drama of modern history, Gallet and Saint-Saëns were turning back the clock to ancient drama. The French School at Athens had brought to light some fragments which appeared to illustrate the staging of Greek plays. Reinach, an archaeologist, had discovered and deciphered a *Hymn to Apollo* in 1893 and asked Fauré to harmonise the result. While it was tempting to return to authentic staging, however, it was impossible to emulate the Ancients completely. The amount of sound required to fill the huge arena, the nature of the public hoping for entertainment, and the need to use local and unskilled musicians persuaded the authors to provide a work with wider attractions. In some ways the Festival at Béziers came close to that union of art and people which Hugo von Hofmannsthal envisaged for Salzburg. Local wind bands from towns and villages were assembled to produce the necessary volume; the chorus was made up of workers from the vineyards and mills. There was a vast orchestra with over a hundred strings and a phalanx of harps placed high on the perimeter, at Saint-Saëns's request, so their sound should not be muffled.

The writing of *Déjanire* took place in a busy year. At Las Palmas Saint-Saëns had written three further Preludes and Fugues for Organ, and the *Caprice Héroïque* for two pianos. His compositions were featured frequently in the Paris concerts and he himself played the Fifth Concerto under Lamoureux in February. In April 'Sunrise on the Nile', a poem with musical accompaniment, words and music by Saint-Saëns, was declaimed at a new series of Colonne concerts and, in July, *Henry VIII* was put on at Covent Garden. The London audience was provided with an analysis of the motifs and a translation of the eulogy which Gounod had written in 1883. The performance took place on 14 July 1898 and representatives of the French Government attend-ed.[1] The opera was given without the ballet demanded by the Paris

---

[1] The year was one of huge tension between England and France because of disputed claims to Fashoda, in the Sudan. It is remarkable that a French opera about English History reached the stage at all.

Opéra which, as *The Times* observed, had 'taxed the imagination somewhat severely by presenting a troop of Highlanders dancing in Richmond Park'. Fauré, who had been in London in June, wrote, 'Isn't it today that *Henry VIII* receives its première? How I would have loved to stay for that.' He had just received the Preludes and Fugues for Organ, 'which I shall never be able to play properly and to my great joy I saw my name at the top of one of them ... My regrets at not having written the organ piece you *commanded* are all the deeper as a result.' The visit to London included Philharmonic concerts (the Scherzo of the Second Symphony pleased the audience so much it had to be repeated), matinées *chez* the Duke and Duchess of Connaught and a second meeting with Queen Victoria at Windsor. Saint-Saëns then went on to Brussels, where he appeared with the violinist Ysaÿe, whose talents persuaded him to consider a string quartet, a form of which he had hitherto been nervous.

A new generation of players was emerging. The young violinist Jacques Thibaud had enjoyed a sensational success in the Prelude to *Le Déluge* in March;[1] for a first performance of the *Caprice Héroïque* Diémer was joined by Alfred Cortot. In order to finish *Déjanire*, whose mass forces presented another new challenge, the composer settled in Lyon. He had again visited Béziers *en route* to study the ground plan and measure the distances.

At the start of August he came south to supervise rehearsals while the actors studied their roles in Paris. He was surprised at the high standard of the chorus, for many had not even been able to read music at the start of the enterprise. He gave hours to rehearsals under the hot Languedoc sun. The first performances of the spectacle took place on the 28th and 29th. The visual impact alone was immense. The scenery – naturalistic and gigantic, set up where it caught the sun most fully and the furthest portions depicting high mountains – stood out against the clear blue skies. Saint-Saëns was amused that several spectators were surprised to find that they had failed to notice a mountain range in the area during previous visits. At the centre was the life-sized entrance to an ancient city and, as the early evening sun began to set, the stage picture was bathed in golden light. Real cascades of water fell from the rocks and no expense was spared in

---

[1] In the following year Thibaud also revealed the potentialities of the *Havanaise*, until then neglected.

suggesting the opulence of the Persian Empire. Among the great moments of the production were the arrival of the jealous wife of Hercules, Déjanire, in her horse-drawn chariot and the tortures inflicted by the Shirt of Nessus, which caused the hero to hurl himself into the pyre, lit to celebrate his union with Déjanire's rival. Ten thousand spectators attended from the whole of France. Saint-Saëns conducted the bands and the orchestra with its eighteen harps and twenty-five trumpets. Before the era of Pop concerts no musician had ever received such crowd acclaim. The multitude surged down the aisles crying, '*Vive Gallet! Vive Saint-Saëns! Vive Castelbon!*' Gallet wept. It seemed as if culture had been freed from the aristocratic trappings of gilded expensive theatres and brought, as in ancient Greek cities, to the populace. The Minister of War had authorised the participation of Army musicians, for the festival was an opportunity to halt the growing divide between the military and the citizenry. Other Government Ministers travelled long distances to subsequent festivals, for these were seen as a means of encouraging civic patriotism at a time when the Dreyfus Case was driving Left and Right to separate extremes.

Avenues were named after Gallet and Saint-Saëns. Parts of *La Lyre et la Harpe* were given, along with a new song appropriate to the region: 'Les Vendanges'. The large-scale production, together with the success of *Henry VIII* in London and the fact that his name was featuring on the Conservatoire concert programmes almost as often as Beethoven, combined to push Saint-Saëns nearer to the position of a national hero. Members of the Paris press attended *Déjanire*. The correspondent of *Le Figaro* was especially dithyrambic: 'It is a colossal work. More than that, it is a veritable triumph. The admirable grandiose work of Gallet and Saint-Saëns encompasses a double problem: artistic decentralisation and an attempt to rejuvenate the theatre. Both have been solved brilliantly.' Saint-Saëns was described as 'the great master of the French School' and the journal looked forward to cities all over France recruiting peasants into choral societies and mounting their versions of Greek civic drama. When *Déjanire* in modified form was given at the Odéon in Paris in November, the President of the Republic, Félix Faure, attended and invited Saint-Saëns into his box, the signal for a great ovation. The occasion was, however, clouded by tragedy, for, while the Odéon was preparing the new production, Gallet died. He and Saint-Saëns had collaborated for twenty-six years with an almost daily exchange of scripts, scores, scribbled verses and parodies embellished with drawings. Saint-Saëns paid a tribute to the writer in the *Revue d'Art Ancien et Moderne*.

The Three Preludes and Fugues for Organ (Opus 109) had been published. The first in D was dedicated to Fauré. Although the key is the same as the Bach transcription of Niedermeyer days and had a significance for the two men, the Prelude and Fugue have a thick and Germanic texture which is hard to associate with Fauré's lucid Gallic style. The Prelude has a distinctive tread in the first section and becomes more polyphonic in the second. The Fugue takes two subjects, one from each half of the Prelude. Both subjects are combined as the Fugue proceeds and the ending after many complications comes in long sustained chords. There is an element of grief and mourning present, which does not match the lively and humorous correspondence that went to and fro between them. The Second and Third are dedicated to Perilhou of St Severin, and Henri Dallier, organist of St Eustache and successor to Fauré at the Madeleine in 1905. The two works may be said to contrast the intimacy of St Severin and the imposing spaciousness of St Eustache. The 'Perilhou' Prelude is peaceful and cheerful, adapted to the lighter stops. The Fugue theme is given out with the counter-subject and, with its little upward run, is recognisable in its numerous appearances and disguises. The 'Dallier' Prelude is large-scale and flamboyant, a typically French toccata with brass and reeds in lusty voice over loud pedal motifs based upon a downward scale. The Fugue theme is very modern and its chromatic intervals give little indication of key, which remains amorphous throughout. These intervals recur, sometimes faster, sometimes slower, on both manuals and pedals accompanied by running figures, which lead to pages of such complexity that one imagines eight or nine hands and feet are busily at work. There are some final flourishes and arpeggios, and loud pedalling introduces a massive chordal close. The work has a Lisztian grandeur, which Saint-Saëns emphasised in his own recitals now that he had returned to the instrument.

In March he produced a Barcarolle for violin, cello, piano and harmonium. It was premièred at La Trompette with the composer this time at the harmonium and Diémer at the piano. At a subsequent performance in Barcelona, which Saint-Saëns could not attend though

it was given in his honour, the young Pablo Casals played the cello
part. A *Valse Nonchalante* for piano belongs to this period, as do
transcriptions of pieces for the lute discovered in Spain. Many
performances of his works new and old took place at La Trompette
and Lemoine must have sought his assistance in receiving some State
recognition. Saint-Saëns wrote very warmly of the contribution which
this musical club had made to French cultural life.

> You have been able to create a special milieu where the greatest
> artists, the most nobly titled, the old fogeys like myself (Oh! No!)
> love to come forward, where the everyday rivalries and pretensions
> are banished and where geniuses who are enemies elsewhere meet
> one another fraternally.... At the price of what fatigues, what
> difficulties, what self-sacrifice this outcome has been achieved I
> alone, perhaps, after you can know; and if it depended upon me
> alone you would be very rapidly decorated with the recompense
> which is so markedly owing to you.

When Lemoine did eventually receive a State decoration it was for
services to mathematics rather than music.

More controversial was the letter he wrote reacting to a request that
he should join the committee proposing a monument to Franck. It was
alleged that he had commented 'that the influence of César Franck
had been disastrous to French art'. From Béziers he felt obliged to
write to the Director of *Le Monde Musical* to give his version of the
snub.[1] 'Dear Monsieur, The information which you report is correct
or only very slightly wrong. I had written "his influence on the French
School has not been happy" and I have nothing to add to this except
that a statue to Rameau, Méhul or Hérold would seem much more
appropriate than that which has been suggested.' The admirers of
Franck have regarded such comments as outrageous, but Saint-Saëns's
views showed concern for the future of music. In a letter of 1898 to
the *Revue de l'Art* on 'Contemporary Movements in Music' he had
deplored the constant search for novelty and the rapid discarding of
established models, which had taken long ages to perfect. 'The West
gladly mocks oriental immobility. The East might well mock the

---

[1] The exertions of Béziers had some alarming effects on his health. Once,
while accompanying the violinist Johannes Wolff in the arena, the keyboard
suddenly turned blood-red. He had to play with his eyes closed.

instability of the West; the impossibility of retaining for any length of time a form, a style, its mania for seeking novelty at any price, without aim and without reasons.' Mozart, for example, left an ideal form for opera: arias, duets and ensembles based upon the situations. Now fashion demands that whole acts should be 'cast in bronze in a single span'. He deplored the existence of any 'School' in which everyone tried to write like everyone else. Wagner's genius had become a blunt instrument in the hands of imitators: 'The world is full of young composers who struggle hard to lift up this club of Hercules.' He had always been aware that there was a danger in fashionable trends and had usually been opposed to them. There were now among Franckists and would soon be among Debussyists those who would take a precious and élitist view of the artist's vocation and ignore the achievements of all those on whose discoveries they built. He took a more historical view and one day confided to Charles Malherbe: 'When I start to read again the fugues of Bach, the symphonies of Beethoven, the oratorios of Mendelssohn, so, as in times past Anteus rediscovered his strength by touching the earth, I also have regained confidence by contact with these giants. I would study afresh, make comparisons and, feeling that the truth was in the furrow they had ploughed, would once again urge myself forward.'

At the end of 1898 he went back again to the Canaries to draw and write verses in the sun. One of his pleasures upon returning was to show his friends the sketches he had made of various scenic spots. Reasons of economy, too, led to these frequent visits. When he was very old he told Pierre Aguétant, his young admirer, that he always returned from the Canaries not only with memories of delectable places but wads of banknotes, which otherwise would have melted away in Paris. The *Caprice Héroïque*, another invented title, almost an oxymoron, was written at Las Palmas for two Russian lady pianists. The composer referred to some unexpected accidentals which would call for a trained eye, but the piece ends with a joyous 'Galop', aiming at a public surely much broader than the salons.

His next long voyage took him westwards across the Atlantic to Buenos Aires. A friend had invited him to give some chamber concerts in which he was joined by local string players. He spent June and July in Argentina, and thus was far distant from all the political upheavals which afflicted his country. In February President Faure died in the arms of his mistress. He was succeeded by President Emile Loubet, who was believed to have been implicated in the Panama Scandal. At the Auteuil Races on 4 June Loubet had his top hat beaten in by a boisterous aristocrat, who had promised a lady-friend that he would thrash the 'odious Dreyfusard'. The day before, a High Court of Appeal had quashed the decision against Dreyfus and ordered a retrial. This took place at Rennes as it was feared a hearing in Paris would be too explosive. There was, nevertheless, rioting in the capital which left over a hundred people wounded and twice as many in gaol. The astonishing verdict at Rennes that Dreyfus was guilty 'but with extenuating circumstances' pleased neither party. If guilty there could be no extenuating circumstances. A Presidential pardon did little to assuage the wrath of the Dreyfusards, and angered others who thought that the fight for one man's innocence was discrediting the Army and postponing for ever the reconquest of Alsace and Lorraine.

Back in the peace of Las Palmas, Saint-Saëns chose 1899 to face the challenges and difficulties of a string quartet. Fauré knew of his worries in attempting this form. 'Saint-Saëns had a fear of it and only risked himself there towards the end of his life.' He had several times sketched out quartets, but drew back in favour of other projects.[1]

When the violinist Ysaÿe was beginning his career Saint-Saëns had been encouraging and revealed some of the ideas behind the B minor Concerto. In his turn, Ysaÿe became an incomparable interpreter of Saint-Saëns. Half-way through the composition it was decided that this new work should be dedicated to him. Aware that he was thought to write too rapidly and that he was accused of improvising his works, Saint-Saëns spent almost a month on the first movement, polishing the interplay of at least three themes. The Quartet was finished in April and mailed off to Durand with a Coda following. Ysaÿe was greatly touched by the dedication and finished his letter of gratitude by hoping that Saint-Saëns, like Beethoven, would crown his career by writing in this genre. 'All musicians have been astonished and have regretted not having a string quartet from you to interpret . . . Today

---

[1] A young musician, Fernand Le Borne, brought him a string quartet which had received a measure of praise from certain teachers. Saint-Saëns hurled the pages on the floor, saying it was crazy to attempt the most difficult form of music at the outset of one's career. He went out, slamming several doors, leaving his mother to console the tearful student who was retrieving scattered sheets.

without knowing this Quartet I am convinced that the enthusiastic welcome which is reserved for it will induce you to compose a series. This would be a worthy crown to your works and will complete one of the most beautiful musical monuments of the century.'[1]

Even some of his greatest admirers, such as Baumann, have failed to detect a warmth of emotion behind the inventiveness of this work. Servières thought the form needed 'an effusion of the heart which emanates rarely from a sexagenarian, even if he remains as alert as Saint-Saëns'. D'Indy, in his *Course of Composition*, singled out the Quartet for analysis and endeavoured to show how it derived from a single figure and cyclic forms in order to be able to say how much more clearly Franck had achieved similar designs. In fact, the pattern of the opening movement is characteristically Saint-Saëns, with sections returning, but not necessarily in sequence, and a reminder of the quiet opening before a hectic and demanding conclusion. The Scherzo, in 2:4, is based upon a very simple pattern, repeated with many elaborations – almost a passacaglia. The Trio, which is in part repeated, contains a fugue and some rumbustious peasant-like measures suggesting a dance. The Scherzo comes to a quiet ending and the repeated theme fades out pizzicato. The Adagio begins in the mood of the *Déluge* Prelude, but the first violin does not have the advantage of contrasting orchestral timbres and much indecisive pensiveness and cross-rhythms give an impression of undue length, rare in Saint-Saëns, despite the charm of some innocent diatonic episodes. The Finale, in the nervous style of Schumann's repeated rhythms, has sudden capricious changes of mood. If the Quartet fails to impose itself, it is perhaps because it gives the impression of attempting too much. There are numerous changes to pizzicato, to unison and to vibrato as if to broaden the limited palette available. In order to achieve the balance of forces, despite the importance of the first violin, there are many repetitions, as one instrument picks up the theme from another, and this, together with the great variety of agitated undercurrents in the accompaniments, rarely allows the listener to relax and enjoy the music's flow.

The Quartet was first heard at a private performance for the benefit

[1] It was Shaw who said of Ysaÿe that 'his combination of Latin finesse of execution with a German solidity of tone, and occasionally with a German obtuseness of intonation, all stamp his share of original sin as distinctively Belgian'.

of Durand. In September Saint-Saëns wrote to Ysaÿe following a concert, 'My dear Friend, You were divine, marvellous – that's all one can say, but it is not all; the publisher would now like to hear the Quartet and you yourself have said you wanted to play it . . . So if you can do us this great honour we shall meet at 19 avenue rue de l'Alma (it is high up, but there is a lift) at four o'clock; you will work with your bows and then everybody will meet again for dinner at my house at seven o'clock. I am really ashamed at the inconvenience I am causing you with my vile music. Give my best wishes to Mme Ysaÿe.' The first public performance was given at the New Theatre under the auspices of Colonne in December.

The long hot summer, which had served up a climate suitable for rioting, did at least ensure the success of *Déjanire*, revived at Béziers. Castelbon had hoped for a new work, but Saint-Saëns, engaged upon a two-piano version of four pieces from the early Duets for Piano and Harmonium, refused; he put forward Fauré as the conductor for 1899 and a composer for the following year. One of the purposes of Saint-Saëns in undertaking the strenuous labours for Béziers had been to open up new ground for young composers away from the intrigues of Paris. After Fauré, others such as Max d'Olonne,[1] Déodat de Sévérac and Henri Rabaud benefited from commissions from Castelbon and the picture often painted of Saint-Saëns as an egoist determinedly hanging on to his laurels and giving no encouragement to the next generation must be dismissed.

Carvalho had died in 1897 and the Direction of the Opéra Comique had devolved on Albert Carré who was keen to give *Javotte* its first showing in Paris. After illnesses in the cast and a decision to dance the role of Jean *en travesti*, *Javotte* reached the stage in October. The critic of *Le Soleil* noticed many of the clever touches in the score.

It is solely a pretext for dancing and M. Saint-Saëns, who asks nothing more of it, gives himself to the task with a light heart, borrowing for his muse the most popular rhythms, inserting here and there some distorting features which sharpen the flavour.

[1] D'Olonne was first introduced to Saint-Saëns as a boy of ten, at a piano recital at Rennes. The hall was three-quarters empty, perhaps because of Saint-Saëns's reputation for austere performances. He pulled out a two-piano version of the *Algerian* Suite and asked d'Olonne to play it with him. Many years later he heard d'Olonne at a competition in Paris and remembered the initial meeting perfectly.

Witness the Bourée in D with the suppression of the leading note, and the Variation in the third scene where the tonality of E flat is ceaselessly menaced by a grumpy D flat, which glides wickedly into the melodic design. There are some beautiful motifs to applaud like that which personifies Javotte, the rapid steps with which the young girl soothes her solitude and the very musical scene of the contest of dance. The rest is written effortlessly with abundance and with simplicity, though with a verve which never fails.

In *Le Journal* Catulle Mendès saw *Javotte* as another of the composer's musical jests: 'I do not blame at all the great and learned musician of the symphonic poems, the inspired creator of *Samson and Delilah*, for having participated in such a light work. The great sculptors have shown the ability to create finely chiselled miniatures.... The real Saint-Saëns allowed glimpses of himself in certain phrases, warm and rich, and in the fine mischievousness of rhythms, and in tiny details of orchestration one sees the science of a superb artist.' Henry Gautier Villars praised him for not investing a village romance with the voluptuous resonances of *Samson*, but thought certain passages were too reminiscent of 'fragments of Clementi Sonatas cleverly orchestrated'.

A promise to revive *Proserpine* was also kept by the Opéra Comique after many years of excuses. Saint-Saëns wrote to Fauré, 'My Fat Cat, I have very much regretted missing the chance to hear your music, which I adore, but I have been rehearsing from one to six, doing the piano part myself. I was exhausted to begin with; today I shall have the orchestra, which will not be too hard.' At the same time he summoned Fauré for an 8 a.m. practice for the eight-hand version of the *Princesse Jaune* Overture and the *Marche Héroïque*, which he and Fauré, together with Diémer and Cortot, were to play at a concert in aid of a monument to Louis Gallet. On this occasion, Saint-Saëns played the *Beethoven* Variations with Princess Alexandre de Bibesco and, alone, his *Valse Nonchalante* and *Valse Mignonne*. He spent the last days of the century correcting the proofs of a new book, *Portraits et Souvenirs*, made up of collected articles containing memories of musicians, some anecdotes and comments that had appeared in various reviews. In the Preface he mocked the devotees of incomprehensible music who found perfection in sounds they could not understand. It marks the point at which he became established as a conservative spokesman.

Proserpine was played in its revised version and the second act was tumultuously applauded and encored. The critic Etienne Destrayes thought it Saint-Saëns's finest work after *Samson* and produced a pamphlet analysing the score minutely. It was seen as a compromise between traditional French opera, with its set pieces, and the Wagnerian method of casting whole acts in symphonic forms.

The *Second Book of Piano Studies* closed the century. No. 1, based upon major and minor thirds and redolent of the 'Forest Murmurs' in *Siegfried*, was dedicated to the Belgian Arthur de Greef. The second was a vertiginous series of chromatic passages inscribed to a M. Livon. In both, Saint-Saëns followed the example of Chopin and aimed at musical merit as well as exercise. The third was a Prelude and Fugue, less exacting and dedicated to Charles Malherbe, who was a scholar rather than a virtuoso. The fourth, surely sufficiently 'impressionist' to satisfy the Debussyists, was called *Les Cloches de Las Palmas* and was a study in sonorities and a combination of bell-like sounds, the carillon having an irregular beat. The fifth contained elements of the first and second combined. Ten years later Saint-Saëns, who had had trouble with his fingers, wrote triumphantly to Gaston Choisnel from Monaco that his strength and dexterity had returned. 'I play like Saint-Piano himself, my Study in chromatic thirds.' At the end of his life he reported that he could still play it, but only for his private satisfaction. It was dedicated to Edouard Risler, pupil of Diémer. The sixth and final Study was dedicated to Raoul Pugno, whose portly frame often shared a platform with Ysaÿe. It combined both the piano and orchestral parts of the Fifth Concerto Finale at an enhanced speed, something of a Mount Everest of the piano repertoire. The degree of sheer notation demanded in all these Studies was a sure indication that the energy of the Master was unflagging.

11

'I Would Like to be Idle but Have Not the Time'

The new century brought yet another Great Exhibition. Its theme, 'The Triumph of Science', was near Saint-Saëns's heart. He agreed to compose a cantata, a setting of a poem, 'Le Feu Céleste', by Armand Sylvestre, which extolled the blessings of electricity. He was also selected as President of a Commission which would oversee the programmes of French music to feature in official concerts. He was thus elevated over twenty-four of the most illustrious musicians in France, including Massenet, d'Indy, Reyer and Dubois, and was able to demonstrate progress made since the foundation of the Société Nationale. The cantata was dedicated to Taffanel and was a success at its first performance. He enjoyed using his gifts as an orchestrator to provide 'electrical effects'. A recitative, 'This flame to the vault of heaven flown', is accompanied by eight cellos, 'divisi', two harps, solo first violins and muted violas, giving a strange shimmering sound. The opening is a huge climb in fifths through the orchestral range, and arpeggios rush up and down the scales resembling flashes of lightning. Ravel could still recall the effects over a decade later. A theme of the poem was the avenging by science of the disasters incurred by heroes of mythology, among whom Saint-Saëns met old friends: Phaeton, 'burning with magnificent madness'; Prometheus, 'great thief of sublime fire'.

On sending the score to Taffanel he wrote a letter typical in its solicitude, insistence on details of performance and impish humour.

My dear friend,
    It seems you have allowed yourself the luxury of being ill and that does not surprise me; I have always thought that the combination of

the Societé, the Opéra and the *professorat* constituted too heavy a burden for your physical strength and that sooner or later you would have to reduce this commendable but overtaxing work-load. Be sensible. I needed the entire month of January to get my poor brain back into a state for composing music; the bustle of Paris had overwhelmed it. I got down to work on February 1st; I began by sketching a little piece, *La Nuit*, then I went on to the Cantata, which will be called I think 'Le Feu du Ciel'. I have abandoned the idea of giving you a choice; only the Cantata is suitable for the official concerts that you are conducting. It won't be very long because I have made up my mind to have all the first half declaimed with orchestral ritornellos. A soprano and choir take care of the rest. There is a part for organ, eight trumpets (but that's nothing like what I have done in this genre), there is a grand fugal chorus more in the style of Haendel than in that of François Bazin,[1] which is perhaps regrettable, but one does what one can; there is a big violin solo, a long virtuoso passage in demi-semiquavers for the first violins of the orchestra; there are to be pluckings of the harp and fierce beatings of the tam-tam, the largest and most terrible that can be found, which will not prevent the violas from indulging themselves at one point by donning mutes (wicked fellows) while eight cellos divided into four parts (or reunited in four parts if you prefer it) make a fuss at the bottom of the page.

Electric wires could be placed under the listeners' seats to give them a violent shock at each strike of the tam-tam; think about it! I'm afraid you are going to find this effect a little too advanced and '*fin de vingtième siècle*'. If you have another work of mine played – which I doubt – I suggest that it should be the *Hymn to Victor Hugo* written, like 'Le Feu du ciel', with the auditorium of the Trocadéro specifically in mind.

Taffenel replied in March, having seen the score.

'Le Feu du ciel' will kindle us so well that the audience will thrill without any of your mischievous devices. How can I fully explain to you the joy that I felt on learning that you had dedicated 'Le Feu du

---

[1] Professor of the Conservatoire and author of a course on harmony. César Franck's first pupils at the Conservatoire were amazed to learn that he had never read Bazin's *Treatise*.

Ciel' to me? So often I have envied those whose names you put next to yours – and this time you thought of me'.

The Commission wished to pay tribute to its President and has placed you at the head of the first official programme. That's as it should be ... But ... the date is fixed for the 1st May! Will you be among us? ... And are we to carry on if you are not there? ... Moreover, the verdict is unanimous for you to open these festivities ... What's to be done? ... Speak and thou shalt be obeyed.

The Exhibition, as well as celebrating science, was intended to symbolise peace and harmony. It was opened by President Loubet in April and Saint-Saëns returned to Paris in May for his cantata, now named *Le Feu Céleste*. There was also a special performance of a work by Rameau, *Quam dilecta tabernacula*, which he had reconstituted. He was promoted Grand Officer of the Legion of Honour, he played before the President at the Elysée Palace and was appointed by the German Emperor, William II,[1] to the place on the German Order of Merit vacant since the death of Verdi. The Exhibition had caused him to cancel a second visit to South America, a decision which no doubt pleased Augusta Holmès, who had written in February with maternal solicitude, 'I very much wish that you would not go again to Buenos Aires. It appears that it is full of all sorts of sicknesses, including the plague ... Inquire about it before setting off.'

In addition to composing, there were at least ten great concerts to plan, including sixty works to be selected, ranging from François Joseph Gossec, who helped to found the Conservatoire and brought the symphony to France, through Berlioz and Gounod, down to the large number of composers arising in the last quarter-century. After finishing a large work, he liked to settle to the composition of smaller pieces. At Las Palmas at the start of the year he had begun the setting of a poem, 'La Nuit', of which he finished the first draft in February 1900. It was a 'small cantata' for soprano, solo flute and female chorus, dedicated to Colonne. Saint-Saëns described it as 'quite pleasing' and suitable for 'concerts or social gatherings wherever there is a light – a very light – soprano, a female chorus and a flautist, none of which are

---

[1] William preferred *Pagliacci* to *The Ring*. After Saint-Saëns's death a Frankfurt newspaper commented: 'William II, badly advised as always, had the misfortune to give Saint-Saëns the Order of Merit, he who spat venom upon hearing a few bars of Wagner.'

hard to come by as you know'. In November it was conducted by
Colonne at a Saint-Saëns festival which included the Symphony in A
and the Third Violin Concerto played by Ysaÿe. *La Nuit* illustrated a
theme which had been prevalent since the Romantic age and had
inspired numerous nocturnes, barcarolles and serenades. The female
chorus becomes a humming chorus, until even its faint harmonies are
extinguished.

A more robust work was called for when, at the start of 1900, the
playwrights Victorien Sardou and Pierre-Barthélemy Gheusi compiled
a libretto which they hoped would provide a spectacle for the Antique
Theatre at Orange to rival that of Béziers. The story 'Les Barbares'
was based upon the history of Orange itself in the first century BC,
when Roman settlements in Gaul were invaded by hordes driven from
the Baltic coasts by the inrush of the seas. The tale of a German
menace coming upon peaceful Gallo-Romans had echoes of contemporary fears. Saint-Saëns was thought of as first choice to compose the
score, but he had seen the massive Roman theatre and foresaw
problems. 'One could do nothing in that immense theatre without
considerable modifications to the stage, which would be very
expensive and the acoustics become detestable as soon as the wind
blows.' The two librettists were persistent, promised him that the
theatre at Orange would be adapted to his every wish, that the Paris
Opera would put on the work later and that he could have any changes
he wished in the scenario. The collaboration did not at first run
smoothly. In *Le Guide Musical* of September 1935 Gheusi recounted
the storms. Saint-Saëns took the MS to Algiers, immediately reduced
the seven scenes of the first act to three and made alterations in the
text, which caused Sardou to exclaim: 'These are no longer the
barbarians; they are the *pompiers* of Nanterre.' 'Thunder of God,' he
wrote in March, 'he is wearisome, our Orpheus. It is not a
collaboration; it is a combat.' He almost refused to sign the text, but
when, at the end of the month of March, he heard Saint-Saëns play
the music of the first two acts he thought it magnificent and was won
over.

Despite the honours which were flowing in his own direction[1] the
event in 1900 which gave him the greatest pleasure was the success of

---

[1] Saint-Saëns was regarded as Dreyfusard; Sardou as anti-Dreyfus. The
even-handed government of Waldeck-Rousseau made both Grand Officers of
the Legion of Honour.

Fauré's *Prometheus* at Béziers. He wrote proudly to Durand that all his fears that Fauré might not match up to the 'breadth and nobility of character of the subject' had been put to rest. 'I know of no one else capable of achieving lines of such dimension or such simplicity within this severely contoured work, myself included.' Having failed to meet Fauré one morning in April, he finished his little note: '*Mon Dieu*, great musicians are difficult to meet.'

In June Fauré apologised for not being able to show Saint-Saëns the completed score. 'It has gone to the engraver, or the copyists, or to Montpellier, *chez* Eustace.' (Eustace was the Bandmaster of the Second Regiment Engineers who had helped Saint-Saëns with the military band scoring for *Déjanire* and was now assisting Fauré. Saint-Saëns had written a work which has no opus number, a 'Franco-Espagnol Hymn', which Eustace had also arranged.) Fauré was surprised to find himself a much greater celebrity than he had been as conductor of *Déjanire* the previous year. Some friends and helpers had been invited to meet him. 'The unfortunate people were rooted to the spot, they didn't dare speak. At a stroke I have become Saint-Saëns himself.' At rehearsals, although he was a southerner, he found the accents of the chorus obtrusive. 'The men's chorus is good at learning things by heart,' he wrote to Marie, 'but they have terrible accents and sing jerkily and harshly.' In another letter he referred to the military musicians. 'The poor old infantry, accustomed to playing polkas, marches or fantasias on *Robert le Diable*, is having a dreadful time with the exigencies of its task . . .'

Saint-Saëns lost no time in spreading news of the success of *Prometheus* and reported the prowess of his pupil at the Institut. The scale of the work was no less prodigious than *Déjanire*. There were 400 musicians from local and regimental bands, a hundred string players drafted from Paris and more contingents of eighteen harps and thirty trumpets. All in all, 800 performers took part before an audience of 15,000. The weather was less kind than it had been to *Déjanire*. A thunderstorm two days before the première did heavy damage to the set and lightning struck the exact spot from which Prometheus was to steal the fire. Fauré himself was twice drenched: once by the downpour and a second time when the tanks used to supply the artificial waterfalls overflowed. Saint-Saëns wrote to Lecocq that 'the two performances were listened to religiously right to the end and lengthily acclaimed. The orchestra is that which I thought up for

Déjanire – two wind sections separated by a strong group of stringed instruments and a phalanx of harps behind. There was in addition this year a third military band concealed in the middle of the rocks to accompany the gods, who sing too far behind to be accompanied by the other orchestras – that was an excellent effect. In brief, an admirable festival of art which owes nothing to the North and German influences.' His admiration for the score was surprising, for it contained many harshnesses and modernisms, representing humanity searching for fire. But he told his pupil: 'With your *Prometheus* you have beaten us all, myself included – and I experience no pain – on the contrary.'

In October, Fauré was in Brussels for a performance of his *Requiem* conducted by Ysaÿe. While there, he not only reported the première of 'a dreadful Italian work called *La Bohème*', but met Saint-Saëns and Durand, who were in the capital to hear the fiftieth performance of *Samson and Delilah* at the Monnaie. Saint-Saëns had not been well and had only a cup of tea instead of the expected dinner. He left the following morning for a meeting of the Institut, so Fauré had to report to his wife that the two musicians had spent little time together.

Saint-Saëns had revisited Orange on his way to Béziers, and he and the librettists spent much time during the autumn discussing staging and the placing of actors and chorus. He lived for a time at St Germain and worked on his sketches. Gailhard, once more a Director at the Opéra, was impatient to hear the completed acts, but also wanted to preserve some secrecy over the score. A special meeting was arranged at the Durand offices, a somewhat comic affair, with Gailhard, a fine bass-baritone in his time, sight-reading all the parts and Jacques Durand struggling to make a piano reduction in the absence of Saint-Saëns. When they came to the duet between Marcomir, the barbarian chief, and the virginal priestess Floria, Durand raced away so ardently on the piano that Gailhard was left breathless.

Fleeing the winter once again, Saint-Saëns travelled through Lyon and Marseilles to Algeria, where, at Bône, he settled to the completion of *Les Barbares*. He had thought that he might join the recently widowed Caroline de Serres in Corsica but, as he wrote, 'I have more confidence in Algeria. I am writing to you near an open window in the rays of a fine setting sun. I have said goodbye to the fires and the heavy winter clothes. . . . Do you know that the music of our friend Liszt begins at last to be treated with the justice we showed to it long ago. The *Faust* Symphony had a great success at the Concerts Lamoureux. It is a great joy for me and I am sure it will not leave you indifferent.' By March 1901 he had despatched two completed acts and was at work on the third, which included a ballet, when word came that the Ministry charged with repairing the arena at Orange had decided to postpone the work, which meant it would be impossible to stage an opera. The librettists urged Gailhard to put it on at the Paris Opéra, but this necessitated much rewriting, as it had been conceived for open-air performance with massed effects. The labours of revision taxed the composer and in May 1901 he was forced to rest. He had intended to write a second ballet, this time for Béziers. But, as he was unwell, he confided the task to the young winner of the Prix de Rome, Max d'Olonne, giving him advice on the resonances of the setting.

Les Barbares was also intended, when destined for Orange, to be a work of civic reconciliation. After the withdrawal of the barbarians a farandole was to be launched upon the stage, which would gradually spread to the terraces until cast and audience wound their way, dancing, into the streets. This would bring Dreyfusards and anti-Dreyfusards, Republicans and reactionaries together under the banner of art and consolidate the peoples of Gaul against northern Germanic threats. It would also demonstrate social solidarity against internal disturbers of the Republic. 'The Barbarians' was a term used by Maurice Barrès and other right-wing authors for 'our communards, our socialists, our plebs', who must be forced to retreat.

As with the *Hymn to Pallas Athene*, the ancient links between Provence and Greece are invoked. There is a hymn to the sun, which shone on a classical Greece as it does on a modern Provence. Saint-Saëns could well have identified the Wagnerians among the northern hordes. It was Reynaldo Hahn who said of *The Ring*: 'I love Apollo and the Muses too much to sympathise with the disagreements of those repulsive bearded figures.' The barbarians retreat before the light of the classical world.

The story centres upon the priestess Floria (*La Vestale* might have been a more apt title if Spontini had not already appropriated it). The pillage of Orange is averted because Floria gives herself to Marcomir, the Teutonic chief, as the price of the city's safety, but he is killed by Livia, widow of the Roman Consul slain defending the city. The opera was famously criticised by Debussy as being a vehicle unworthy of the composer's talents. The première, however, was one of the great events of the 1901 season and it shared with *Phryné* the distinction of being an opera by Saint-Saëns that was received as a success.[1] Taffanel conducted and received a letter of thanks from the composer addressed to the whole company.

Gauthier-Villars, in *Echo de Paris*, compared the marvellous cleverness of the orchestration with a finely filtered wine where no roughness or sediment remained. Catulle Mendès, in *Le Journal*, forgave the composer for deserting the forward shock troops of the Wagnerians at an earlier date. 'Saint-Saëns is one of the highest glories of modern music.' He admired the constant change and experiment, which was a feature of the Master's output. 'They reveal a perpetual need for renewal, diversity, change, to become something which will be better; the aesthetics of Saint-Saëns are only attempts to achieve the impossible in surpassing himself.' The opera had an overture, unusual in his operas, which was intended to give a picture of the menace of barbarian pillage. Before commencing composition he had been to see Gluck's *Iphigénie en Tauride*, and the work has the broad and statuesque character of Gluck, as distinct from the miniatured interpretations of the text, which marked the Renaissance story of *Ascanio*.

Once again a large work was accompanied by a smaller one and 1901 saw the appearance of *Lola*, a brief *opéra comique* with words by Stephan Bordèse. It was a story of low life in the verismo tradition that was becoming popular and which Massenet followed in *La Navarraise*. Lola is a young gypsy who is tyrannised by her master. One day she flees from him and encounters a patron of higher social class, Don Benites. Like Carmen, she bewitches the Don with her singing and dancing, but stabs him with a stiletto when he tries to force himself upon her. The music included a habanera–tango rhythm, which indicates a link with Carmen. Charles Koechlin[2] was recommended by Fauré to help with the orchestration of this mini-opera, which had been promised to the Colonne concerts. It was subsequently seen in a

[1] Live oxen were brought on stage in an ensemble and gave the management many problems of housing and feeding during performances.

[2] Durand accepted Koechlin's Suite for Piano as part of the transaction. In 1946, in a broadcast, Koechlin repeated a remark of Saint-Saëns: 'Do you want to be a composer? It is a martyr's profession!'

stage version at the Théâtre de la Renaissance in May 1901, but Saint-Saëns does not appear to have pressed for its publication. If *Lola* has a moral, it would appear to be that the respectable classes should beware of alliances with the lower orders, as the latter lead a life of unrestricted selfishness and happily destroy those who seek to better their lot.

In March 1901 there were celebrations of Saint-Saëns in London in which Ysaÿe participated with the Third Violin Concerto and the *Rondo Capriccioso*. Ysaÿe wrote to his wife:

> I shall always remember this concert as one of the supreme moments of my career. Saint-Saëns was wildly applauded and, after the concert, we had to come back six times holding hands. . . . Colonne who was present told me he had never heard me play so well. There was similar enthusiasm after the *Jeunesse d'Hercule*. In fact the whole thing was a triumphant success for the great-hearted French musician . . . and at the same time it was a great pleasure for me to feel that I had contributed to it. This morning at the station the aged master embraced me affectionately and when I realised the warmth of his feelings for me I felt immensely proud, far more proud than all the applause of the crowd, or the praise of silly journalists could ever make me.

Saint-Saëns was in equally good spirits when he visited Béziers in the summer for the revival of Fauré's *Prometheus*. Fauré found that the music was unfamiliar after a break of a year and the string players left something to be desired. The Government and Army again loaned military bands to win popular support, but with a certain amount of disdain for the composer. Fauré wrote to his wife that the second performance had been rather less successful than the first, 'because of the rather strong wind and the untimely arrival of the War Minister. Having entered the arena in the middle of an act he was the cause of a demonstration from the entire rabble and we were compelled to break off. He had to go for his train in the middle of the last act so he disturbed us again.' Saint-Saëns does not seem to have been unduly upset and told Fauré that 'the Minister had been bowled over and very impressed'. It was at this Festival that Saint-Saëns met a young composer, Roger Ducasse.

After a party including Castilbon and his family had visited the spa at Lamalou, Fauré wrote; 'Saint-Saëns was in incredibly good form.[1] He is completely under Ducasse's spell and finds him remarkable in every respect.' Fauré used the occasion to speak of his own gratitude to Saint-Saëns, assuring his teacher that his feelings were expressed infrequently because he was so convinced that the Master knew of them. This appears to have restored Saint-Saëns's confidence and caused some emotion. His warm feelings overflowed into extra large presents to the Fauré boys in the autumn. 'Never have I been present at such an explosion of joy,' wrote Fauré, and his wife added: 'You are like a parent to us and your name is constantly on our lips.'

Ducasse fared better than Paul Dukas, whose Piano Sonata was dedicated to Saint-Saëns. Dukas played it at the Durand offices with the editor turning the pages and it caused them such emotion that at the end they threw themselves together in an embrace. Legend has it that Saint-Saëns did not like the work and ignored it, but it seems that he did offer to transcribe it for two pianos, as he had done with the Chopin and Liszt sonatas. This task was never carried out, for pianistic ability was increasing and there was less demand for four-hand versions.

In the autumn of 1901 before leaving for Egypt, Saint-Saëns, as President of the Academy of Fine Arts, had to make the customary speech recalling the virtues of deceased academicians and sending young winners of the Prix de Rome on their way. He urged the musicians, painters and sculptors to study foreign arts without imitating their exterior forms, to study nature . . . the eternal source of beauty and not to strive to be 'modern, which is the surest way of ageing more rapidly'. He set off in late November for Cannes and spent two weeks on the Côte d'Azur. Then he sailed to Egypt, where a splendid property on the Island of Rodah in the Nile was placed at his disposal by Mohammed Aly Pasha, a brother of the Khedive. Decorated in the style of the Alhambra and surrounded by palms, fig trees and roses, it was an exotic location in which to write the semi-oriental music for *Parysatis*. The famous 'Air du Rossignol' was derived from some trills and roulades by a singer in a Greek café in Alexandria, where he went to take part in the festival for the centenary of Victor

[1] His moods were changeable. The songs of 1901, 'Elle' (Lecocq) and 'Désir d'Amour' (Perpina), are full of melancholy reflections on the failure of love and the loss of happiness.

Hugo. His *Hymn* to the poet was sung by an Italian opera company in the city.

The organisers at Béziers considered that it was time the presiding genius of the Festival should produce a new work for 1902. *Parysatis* was a drama in three acts with prologue, written by Jane Dieulafoy, an archaeologist and scholar who affected to wear men's clothes. It was set in ancient Persia; the scenery drew upon researches which the Dieulafoys had made in the ruins of Suza, and mosaics and reliefs brought from Persepolis to the Louvre. The story told of a contest for the throne between Artaxerxes and Cyrus at the Court of Queen Parysatis. There were choruses for women of the harem and the Magi. Twelve songs were included, of which the 'Air du Rossignol' became a favourite concert piece for sopranos. The prelude was composed in the dorian and hyperdorian modes. Dances were flavoured with oriental ingredients and there was a warlike march for Artaxerxes returning from the battlefield. Paul Viardot conducted the ensemble, which once more comprised 800 performers. A moment in the score said to have been unforgettable was the oboe lament for the death of the heroine Aspasia, played as sunset lit the arena with a softened glow. Fauré was present at the première and reported to his wife that Saint-Saëns had had a great ovation, that the evening skies had been perfect but some thought the music a shade meretricious. 'In addition to worries about the weather we learnt about eight that the principal singer had had a miscarriage during the night. Fortunately another young performer (who must have been delighted with the turn of events!) knew the part and could replace her ... In fact, everything ended in a great apotheosis. Saint-Saëns and Mme Dieulafoy in her little jacket and breeches kissed each other on the stage and general rejoicing ...' Béziers stretched its appreciation so far as to put on stage productions of Saint-Saëns's *Botriocephale* and the farce he had devised called *Writer's Cramp*.

In Britain, 1902 was the year of the Coronation of the Francophile Edward VII. Saint-Saëns had composed a march and diplomatic initiatives were launched to put it prominently into the Service. It was a period when France and Great Britain were drawing into a closer entente. Britain had been alarmed at finding itself without friends during the recent Boer War and at the rejoicing in Europe at her early defeats. At the French Foreign Office, the Minister, Théophile

Delcassé, worked constantly to find the allies whom France might need in the future. Sir Frederick Bridge, organist of Westminster Abbey, had been sent all manner of anthems and marches from would-be laureates, but the British ambassador in Paris, Sir Francis Bertie, put in a special word of commendation for Saint-Saëns. Bertie reported that the French ambassador in London had mentioned to the Foreign Secretary, Lord Lansdowne, that M. Saint-Saëns, who had had the honour of performing before the Queen on several occasions, had composed a march in honour of the King's Coronation and was anxious that it should be played during the ceremonies. When Lord Lansdowne and both ambassadors were involved we may deduce that there was political pressure to forward Anglo-French friendship. Sir Frederick accepted the proposal with alacrity. 'I at once replied that I should be honoured by being made the recipient of a work ... by the doyen of French musicians.' Saint-Saëns came over to rehearse his 'Coronation March', but could not be present at the actual event, which had to be postponed because of the King's operation for appendicitis. A curious myth persisted that the Cross of the Order of Victoria bestowed upon Saint-Saëns gave him the title of baronet and the right to be addressed as 'Sir'. One imagines this to be some jest of his own, which found its way into circulation. The 'March' itself was based upon the sixteenth-century air used in *Henry VIII*, the chorale of English provenance, preceded by a huge eighteen-bar fanfare and much embellished.

The year also saw the appearance of a Second Cello Concerto, thirty years after the First. Opus 119 was dedicated to Joseph Hollmann, who had a large, muscular style of playing, and the work is one of technical ferocity. Whereas in the First Concerto the soloist is joined in close proximity to the orchestra in the musical flow, the Second has many solo passages beyond the normal usage of the instrument and seeming at times like a study in double-stopping or bow technique. Two staves have to be employed to indicate the huge runs and leaps, and the cello at times provides both melody and harmony in the manner of Bach's unaccompanied suites. In places the cello virtually accompanies solo passages from woodwind and brass. In the second part – for Saint-Saëns reverted to his two divided movements as in the Fourth Piano Concerto – the Cadenza gives the impression of an operatic dialogue using both pizzicato and arco passages. Chantavoine thought he detected an element of satire in the piece, and an over-emphasis on the 'thrown-about hair, the stormy shoulders, furious brow and athletic double stopping of Hollmann'. This would form a counterpart to the *Carnival*, where the cello is romanticised and the pianist is mocked. Yet the concerto has a brisk liveliness, not least in the Haydnesque flourishes which open the first and fourth sections, both with intrusive triplet figures that give an air of a performance before a monarch or court. In the slow section (two) the cello descends to regions deep in the bass clef, normally unfamiliar when it is in romantic vein.

A celebration close to his heart took place in March when a monument to Liszt was inaugurated at Weimar. At the Annual Public Session of the Five Academies he read a learned paper on 'Lyres and Zithers' and methods of playing these instruments in classical times. During his travels he had visited museums and studied the handling of them on vases and murals. He was also meditating a four-act play, *Le Roi Apepi*, based upon a novel of the same name by a Victor Cherbuliez.[1] In addition, he was maintaining his interest in astronomy and lent a telescope to Marie Fauré, who shared this enthusiasm. His principal lens was undergoing repairs, but he sent a smaller one, for 'as Jupiter is at this moment easy to observe I think it would be rewarding for you not to wait. Anyhow one sees easily with the size 60 lens while with the 170 difficulties commence. It is necessary to make use of the Finder and to acquire the fingering technique.'

Debussy's *Pelléas* was put on at the Opéra Comique, conducted by Messager. Romain Rolland considered the dress rehearsal on 28 April one of the three or four major dates in the history of French lyric theatre. Saint-Saëns, meeting Jacques Durand, announced that he had stayed in Paris in the heat of summer only 'to speak ill of *Pelléas*'. This might have been braver than it sounds for there was a painter, Paul Robert, swarthy and sinister, who frequented Parisian cafés and would physically assault any detractors of Debussy. Nor was Saint-Saëns alone in his disapproval. A voice from the Gallery ordered Dubois to applaud, as he sat expressing disapprobation in his box.

June 1902 was the centenary of the birth of Niedermeyer and a festival of his works was arranged at the school, now settled in Boulogne-sur-Seine. Saint-Saëns did not take part, but he wrote a

[1] *Le Roi Apepi*, in which a novelist tries to ensnare a rich aristocrat, repeats the theme of feminine threats to a settled order of things as in *Samson*, *Proserpine* or *Lola*.

tribute in which he praised the part that Niedermeyer had played in settings of contemporary French poets creating a new art analogous to German Lieder. Had he had more faith in himself and not turned aside to study Church music he would have been a song writer worthy to be ranked with Gounod and Fauré.

Pelléas was not the only matter to disturb his calm. In the autumn of 1902 there was a brush with the Artists-Musicians of France, a Union of which Gustave Charpentier was President, which had supported a strike, the first ever, by orchestral musicians. Saint-Saëns was so outspoken in his denunciation of this action and his belief that it was a privilege to serve in the cause of art that the Musicians of Paris in General Assembly decided that, until further notice, they would not play any of his music. The issue had rumbled on for over a year. In 1901 he had been invited to join a Syndicate–Union of Musicians on the Committee, but had declared Unions to be the enemy of free will and individual liberty. When the strike was organised he pronounced it 'ridiculous'. In a letter to Charpentier he said, 'Art is a cult, not a form of merchandise,' and declared that musicians had turned themselves into workers. The embargo does not seem to have lasted long.

He had an instinctive dislike of the overturning of the past symbolised in *Pelléas*. He wrote a preface to a collection of pieces by his old teacher, Boëly, which came out at this time and described him as having 'that unique trait of drawing his inspiration from the past. He took great pains to write in the style of Scarlatti and Bach, the object of his greatest admiration ... an artist steeped in such a tradition need not depend upon the approval of his contemporaries; he only attracts attention later when the current issues no longer exist.'

While in London he had been asked by Sarah Bernhardt to compose an overture and incidental music for her production of *Andromaque*, in which she intended to play the rival part of Hermione. His Overture represents the torments of Hermione rather than the peace of Andromaque. Bold brass themes depict the male characters sometimes with great harshness. The music was well performed, but the production was controversial and Sarah's stage emotions, like Saint-Saëns's dramatic and agitated music, were beginning to seem old-fashioned. The Overture was published, together with the Prelude to Act Four, rich and full of melancholy.

Before *Andromaque* was put on in February 1903, an approach had been made by Raoul Gunsbourg, Director of the Theatre of Monte Carlo, who had already lured Massenet to participate in his winter festivals with the opera *Le Jongleur de Notre-Dame*. Gunsbourg wrote to Prince Albert of Monaco to inform him that 'M. Saint-Saëns, a colleague of Your Highness at the Institut and one of the greatest French composers, has just formally promised to reserve for Your Highness's theatre during the 1903–4 season his next opera, on which he is presently working and which he hopes to be able to submit to Your Highness next March. M. Saint-Saëns has delayed his journey until tomorrow evening so that he can present his respects to you and, if Your Highness decides to receive him, I shall have the honour of introducing him tomorrow about six in the evening.' The composer decided to write a piece that he had long meditated on the story of Helen of Troy. Since adolescence, Saint-Saëns had been moved by the tale of her elopement with Paris, a legend seminal to so much great literature. He had been deeply offended by the frivolous treatment given to it in Offenbach's *La Belle Hélène*. He thought about confiding his theme to a collaborator, but in the end decided to be his own librettist, and buried himself in classical literature to find inspiration to depict the emotional scene in which Helen flees into the night from her palace, is pursued by Paris, struggles despairingly with her feelings and finally joins him in his fateful voyage to Troy.

While he was at work in Egypt the Director of the Khedival Theatre in Cairo conceived the plan of a Saint-Saëns Concert on behalf of Breton sailors. For a time the composer had to forget his plans for *Hélène*, resume his piano practising and rehearse the other artists. The peace of the island palace was abruptly interrupted.

I dumped *Hélène* very regretfully and, when I wished to resume my task, found it impossible. I was completely disorientated. I had to leave my delightful stay in Cairo to go and seek out a solitary retreat at Hanaibin in the middle of the desert, bathed in light and silence, to find inspiration. Hanaibin is a fine place that I recommend to all lovers of solitude, a solitude alleviated anyhow by a very civilised group of people of both sexes employed by the Suez Canal, surrounded by their families, a little élite colony in which I even came across two talented poets. As these people are happily occupied, they provide company without disturbance. In twelve days I had written my poem. Then I set off for Port Said to return

to Paris, where the preparations for the revival of *Henry VIII*
awaited me.[1] When this revival was completed I wished to settle
down to write the music of *Hélène*. More setbacks, the rehearsals at
the Opéra had tired me. My brain was not functioning. I spent eight
days at Biarritz, another eight at Cannes in complete idleness . . .
Then I remembered the watering-place of Aix in Savoy, which
stands on a mountain covered in flowers surrounded by a
marvellous panorama to which one can climb without effort by
means of a funicular. I fled swiftly to Mont Revard, where I
sketched almost all the music of *Hélène* which I finished later in
Paris. One always ought to work like that in peace and silence safe
from all distractions and demands – and with the great spectacle of
nature under one's eyes surrounded by flowers and scents. Practised
under these circumstances work is more than a pleasure; it is an
exquisite delight.

Augusta Holmès had died in January while he was abroad, her beauty
long since faded and her life one of solitary misery. The funeral
service had been thinly attended, but Saint-Saëns on his return
arranged a more fitting ceremony at which he played a paraphrase on
her first song, 'The Song of the Camel-Driver', and had engraved on
her tomb lines of her own verse which began 'Glory is immortal; the
grave ephemeral'. The painter Clairin was especially touched by Saint-
Saëns's tributes to the former beauty. 'My rusty autumn leaves flutter
at the memory of those green days of spring.'

Fauré had recently become music critic of *Le Figaro*, which meant
many evenings occupied with concerts. In April he forgot to invite
Saint-Saëns to a performance of his (Fauré's) songs and chamber
works, and received an unusually sharp reprimand. 'It is a good thing
that your music is more comprehensible than your actions!' Fauré was
able to soothe his master with an article celebrating the 200th
performance of *Samson* at the Opéra. 'I count it one of the greatest
happinesses and one of the most emotional experiences of my life that
I was able to be present at the first performance of *Samson*. Paris owes

---

[1] One can appreciate the remark made to Marie Fauré in a letter written
on his return to France (February 1904). 'You say that all men are lazy. I
would be delighted to be so if I were able, but I never have the time.' His
insistence upon being on-stage for rehearsals wherever possible was in the
tradition of Meyerbeer himself.

this double atonement to the greatest of our living musicians.' Saint-Saëns could not but relapse into his jocular mood. 'Ungrateful wretch! The burden of gratitude ... is too heavy for my shoulders to bear. I am now in *your* debt.'

In August Saint-Saëns went again to Béziers, where there were performances of *Parysatis* and *Déjanire* in the Arena and *Le Roi Apepi* in the town theatre. In the autumn he paid a lengthy visit to Germany and attended the unveiling of a statue to Wagner in Berlin. He played and conducted in several German cities, and arrived in Geneva for a festival of his works. Prince Mohammed Ali Pasha was rewarded for his hospitality with the dedication of a *Valse Langoureuse*. The waltz can move easily from the languid and dreamy mood to the zest of a faster speed. The *Valse Langoureuse* has sudden changes of mood and a glittering middle section, and is akin to a postcard reminder of the delights of Paris as known to an Arab potentate.

At Monte Carlo two performances of *Samson* were given early in February in honour of Saint-Saëns, who had arrived to attend the rehearsals of *Hélène*. As *Hélène* was a one-act opera, it was coupled with Massenet's *La Navarraise*. Librettist as well as musician, Saint-Saëns faced the critics on two fronts. In old age in 1918, he wrote to a friend, 'You are too indulgent towards the verses of my libretto for *Hélène*. They are not *bad* but that is all; and your compliments give me great pleasure without inflating the opinion I have of my poetic work. They make a happy counterweight to the severities which welcomed the libretto on its appearance.'

Gunsbourg was adept at attracting the finest singers of the time and Helen was played by Nellie Melba, to whom Saint-Saëns had spoken of his project with such enthusiasm that she cancelled the second half of her American tour and learnt the role travelling in trains between engagements. Saint-Saëns was deeply impressed by her stage presence. 'She did not play. No. She *lived* the Helen I had dreamed of.' She, in turn, thought the composer 'one of the most amazingly youthful old men' she had ever met. 'He was still writing music of a vigour and freshness that he never surpassed. We used to trot about Monte Carlo together, he usually taciturn, but sometimes letting loose a volley of observations on music, opera and life in general.' When Saint-Saëns came to her residence to rehearse and the servants were absent he would play crashing chords on the piano to summon her. An enterprising business manager arrived from England to demonstrate to them the merits of a new invention called the 'gramophone' and Melba was sufficiently impressed to present a machine to Prince Albert and make some recordings.

The *Journal de Monaco* predicted that *Hélène* would be the success of the season and it was revived the following year with a fresh cast and in conjunction with Mascagni's *Amica*. Eventually, however, it joined the ranks of Saint-Saëns's many neglected stage works. It was played in London with Melba once again as Helen, but London audiences had a decided preference for old favourites and as a one-act opera it was difficult to fit into traditional programmes. Even Saint-Saëns's admirers were reserved in their opinions. Fauré thought it 'interesting because of the staging and the orchestral role'. Messager, who came to London especially to conduct it, though he described the later pages as 'among the most beautiful that the Master has written', felt the effects of the slow and retarded period of composition in the opening scenes. It is clear, however, that no piano reduction gives an adequate impression of the orchestration, for, as in Wagner, 'the statue is in the orchestra, the pedestal on the stage'. Messager declared, 'No one knows better than Saint-Saëns how to make the orchestra speak. One asks oneself whether one admires more the constant novelty of his sonorities or the simplicity of the means by which he expresses them. One can be certain of meeting in each one of his works some new effect. I will cite in *Hélène* the employment of the wind section in the distance, which accompanies the apparition of Pallas, as well as that of the contre-bass clarinet, whose sounds are simultaneously solid and sweet.'

For the London production a translation had been made by Hermann Klein. It was not totally successful, but Saint-Saëns gave Klein a beautiful old Greek coin, which was said to represent Helen herself. The opera proceeds by sections as in a cantata. Outside the Palace of Menelaus, voices are heard singing the praises of the King, his wife and the princely guest, Paris. The action moves to the sea-shore, where Helen arrives weeping to ask the gods to help her escape her feelings for Paris. She is about to drown herself, when a vision of Aphrodite surrounded by nymphs comes across the waters and gives her the fatal advice to listen to the voice of love and think of the glory her beauty will bring her. Dark clouds gather on the horizon and a clap of thunder announces the arrival of Pallas, who represents reason and comes as the messenger of Zeus, to warn her of the consequences of illicit passion and to paint an image of Troy in flames. Paris, in pursuit of Helen, declares himself ready to sacrifice his father and brothers sooner than give her up. Inspired by this declaration Helen, too, states that she will abandon her Greek homeland and her family. The darkness vanishes, the sky is radiantly blue and the lovers are glimpsed finally in a vessel bound for Troy.

Saint-Saëns himself was the first to see that the vision of Pallas bore a resemblance to the appearance of Brünnhilde to Siegmund in the second act of *The Valkyrie*, but he did not see how the drama could be played differently. The conflicting advice given by Aphrodite and Pallas can also be seen as a choice which affected music; whether it should surrender to impulse and sensation, forgetful of consequences, or abide by the precepts of reason as exemplified in the Age of Enlightenment, of Mozart and Haydn. In society, too, the choice had to be made between the bourgeois virtues of thrift, honesty and relative chastity, or the enjoyment of wealth and the cult of self-indulgence which might ultimately lead to the breakdown of social order. Once again there were voices summoning France to return to the agrarian basis of society and restrict the new industrialised cities, which sucked in large populations to be exploited and depraved. The theme of 'the family' is stressed, both in the praise for Menelaus and his household at the start and in the prophecies of the break-up of King Priam's family, which will result from the elopement.[1]

He returned from Monaco to Paris, where the Société des Concerts offered him a Grand Matinée in April. He played a D-minor concerto of Mozart, moved on to the organ to participate in his Third Symphony and completed the display of his talents by conducting *Le Déluge*. In May, in London for *Hélène*, he gave a recital with the violinist Johannes Wolff. Shaw had once referred to Wolff as 'playing difficult pieces as if they were easy and easy pieces (Raff's Cavatina and the like) as if they were immensely important and difficult'. It was to Wolff that Saint-Saëns dedicated his next important violin work, the *Caprice Andalou*, which utilised popular Andalusian themes picked up on his travels. It gives great scope to the soloist and the orchestra is kept subordinate, simply adding harmonies and providing a rhythmic

[1] It should not be overlooked also how inventive a serious one-act opera was. Those familiar to the Opéra Comique were almost always brief and frivolous. Saint-Saëns once again created a new form with no model before him. *Salome* appeared in 1905. *Electra* was not staged until 1909.

background to the violinist's flights of virtuosity. Saint-Saëns referred
to the '*chevaliers de l'archet*' who would enjoy the dashing 'moto
perpetuo' at the close. He wondered whether the Dutch-born Wolff
would have the hot Spanish blood required to give the work its true
character. He thought of it as an encore piece to come in the second
part of a concert where the first part had included a serious concerto,
and ruminated with satisfaction on the traps it contained for unwary
conductors.[1]

After the London concert he made a trip to Scotland and gave a
recital with Thibaud in Edinburgh. In June came *Hélène* at Covent
Garden, after which he embarked for a second visit to South America
and concerts in Buenos Aires, Montevideo and Rio de Janeiro. He was
particularly delighted at the warm reception given to a Fantasy by
Perilhou, which he had already played in London. In Uruguay he
wrote down the setting for a national hymn for use on public
occasions. In September he set off back to Paris. It is remarkable that
he could find the time to carry out tasks such as arranging his
Bénédiction Nuptiale for four hands (pianoforte) and a transcription of
his 'O Salutaris' from the Mass for Organ. He hired a room near his
apartment in the rue Roussell and would sometimes spend weeks
there, composing and transcribing, while everyone thought he was in
Egypt or the Canaries. He also gave a lecture to the Astronomical
Society on 'The Effects of Mirage', which drew on his experiences in
the Red Sea and the Isthmus of Suez.

In November he was in Milan for *Hélène* and writing to admonish
Fauré for his criticism of Berlioz.

> To do distinguished criticism it is necessary to know how to
> appreciate what one does not like. Handel found Gluck less of a
> musician than his cook. He saw only his inadequacies of writing; he
> saw neither his colour nor his dramatic power. It is not thus that a
> critic should judge. The defects of Berlioz hit the eyes; he redeems
> them by greatness of character, by his personality, by his astonish-
> ing creation of modern orchestration. It is necessary to say to you

---

[1] A Léon Moreau records a story of Saint-Saëns in Spain at one of the
café-concerts he so enjoyed. One singer attempted some French popular
songs. 'Absolutely dreadful!' snorted Saint-Saëns. 'Shut up. You know *nothing*
about *music*,' said the girl with the collecting plate. 'You are the first person
who has ever used that expression to me. You deserve this,' he said, putting a
large sum on her plate.

that we do not (in France) have such a great number of great composers. Leave to others the task of denigrating them. *Dixi*. Pardon my tyrannical attitudes, the bitter fruit of my incurable affection – and present to your family my most tender regards.

Fauré accepted the lecture with good grace and protested only that Berlioz had set a bad example to the moderns who believed that genius would always compensate for the absence of talents. 'I know that *Hélène* has obtained an enormous success at Milan and I am very happy for that.'

By December Saint-Saëns was in Cologne, where the *Timbre d'Argent* was in rehearsal. In a year of such travelling it is not surprising that he either did not attend or failed to show a sufficient immensity of grief at the inauguration of the monument to César Franck in October. D'Indy contrasted the poor attendance at Franck's funeral years before with the important figures who gathered before St Clothilde on this occasion. Henri Marcel, Minister of Fine Arts, spoke of Franck as an 'immortal genius' who justified the existence of humanity. D'Indy described the general enthusiasm but, clearly not having studied the section on 'Brotherly Love' in Franck's *Rédemption*, added 'with the exception of a member of the Institut whose implacable jealousy pursued Franck beyond the grave'.

This was a time of controversy and throughout the Colonne season there were battles over the validity of the concerto form. Wagnerians thought the future belonged solely to combinations of music, drama and spectacle. Socialists and syndicalists thought the exaltation of the soloist and the subordination of the orchestra a vile relic of the class system. In February, the soloist in Saint-Saëns's Second Piano Concerto was hissed and a few days later Paderewski received similar treatment in a Beethoven concerto. There were suggestions made that the concerto arose from the coming together of a group of instruments each one of which represented some facet of the soul or some character in a drama (as in Wagner). Mozart came under criticism for establishing the tradition of elevating one instrument as soloist and thus subordinating the others. In *Le Gaulois* Saint-Saëns defended virtuosity. 'Nothing is more relative and the lowest pupils at our conservatoires execute in performances what seemed inaccessible to our fathers.'

To those who opposed the concerto on the grounds that it

promoted individualism rather than social cohesion, or cheap thrills
rather than musical thought, he pointed out that, often in Mozart
concertos, the piano remains silent so that the listener can attend to
the orchestra expressing many and varied moods. He made the novel
point that one or two concertos would have met all Mozart's needs,
since he travelled from town to town and never had the same
audience. But Mozart had an irresistible need to produce. With
Beethoven the concerto reached its apogee, as did the quartet and
symphony. Schumann thought so highly of the form that he confided
to it 'his poem of love and the story of his union with Clara Wieck, the
celebrated companion of his life'.

12

A Corsican Vendetta and Scholarly Polemics

S aint-Saëns braved the onset of winter in Paris to supervise rehearsals at the Opéra Comique of *Hélène*, in which the principal role was taken by Mary Garden, the original Mélisande. The première took place on 18 January 1905, after which he left immediately for Algiers. He received a cordial letter from Prince Albert of Monaco requesting another opera for the 1906 season, when a special place would be reserved for him in the programme. He replied from Algiers that, although the theatre no longer attracted him and *Hélène* had been intended as his farewell, 'how could one resist a desire that your Serene Highness condescends to express with an insistence so flattering to me?' On 25 April the *Journal de Monaco* published letters from the Prince and Saint-Saëns announcing that a new opera by the composer, *L'Ancêtre*, would figure in the 1906 season. Saint-Saëns had hoped that these would be published earlier, for he had been asked to produce a new work for the Paris Opéra (and such an agreement generally involved Government Ministers) and he wished to provide as an excuse that he was already committed to Monte Carlo (which privately he much preferred). He probably did not want to write another full-scale opera as part of government policy. Gunsbourg, however, had delayed publication until the close of the 1904–5 season in case the announcement overshadowed the operas of Massenet and Pietro Mascagni, which remained to be heard.

The composition of *L'Ancêtre* was combined with prose writing and polemics. In a preface to the thirtieth volume of *The Annals of Theatre and Music* he suggested the abandoning of horseshoe-shaped halls and considered the merits of the hidden orchestra, an achievement of Wagner that he praised unreservedly. He then entered into the debate on Church music raised by the 'Motu Proprio' of Pope Pius X. The struggle between Church and State had continued, and the Dreyfus Case had not eased the situation. For several years bodies such as the Monks of Solesmes had researched into plainchant as a means of emphasising the historical traditions of the Catholic Church in France. In 1894 the Schola Cantorum, which in Reynaldo Hahn's words 'condemned all music which sought to please', was established to revive ancient music. In 1903 the papal 'Motu Proprio' prescribed the almost exclusive use of plainchant or sixteenth-century polyphony and stated that modern works would be disallowed, if they had any taints of the theatre or employed secular instrumentation. In the following year Pius set up a commission to prepare a Vatican edition of chant-books and there was some astonishment that Saint-Saëns, Widor and other learned French musicians were not included. In 1905, editions began to appear and Widor, certainly, thought the researches at Solesmes too uncritical. The setaceous Saint-Saëns was more sweeping, for much of his own religious music and that of Gounod was affected by an operatic style. While he sympathised with the exclusion of sentimental rubbish, he pointed out (in the columns of *Le Figaro*) that sanctity and profanity in music are very much in the minds of the listeners. The madrigals of Palestrina have a religious sound to modern ears and the secular and sacred arias of Handel are virtually interchangeable. He could not see the rationale behind abolishing cymbals and drums when the paintings of the Italian primitives showed angels having pleasure with such things. 'Did not trombones sound in the Temple of Solomon? . . . In paintings of Fra Angelico and other old masters do we not see angels in Heaven playing all the instruments then in use: viols, zithers, sackbuts, tambourines, oboes . . .?' Some years later, in his autobiographical *Ecole Buissonnière*, he recalled celebrations of the Mass he had heard in Andalusia, 'constructed on popular rhythms and accompanied by castanets and Basque tambourines; there the Church is not satisfied with laughing – it dances'.

One might feel that his attack on the Schola Cantorum, and the suggestion that choirmasters died in poverty and disgrace because they were unable or unwilling to comply with the 'Motu Proprio', was melodramatic. Yet Henri Malherbe said that he personally knew two old dismissed organists in distressed circumstances to whom Saint-Saëns sent regular pensions. On the 1st of each month a letter of encouragement and a payment of money (necessary for their survival) would arrive.

In February 1905 he published in *Le Figaro* the discourse intended for the oft-postponed unveiling of the statue of Gounod in the Parc Monceau. As one would expect, he praised Gounod for being a leader and an inspiration to French composers. He was almost bound to say that no statue could capture the smiles and the charm which exuded so freely from the Master. With his own originality he pointed out that Gounod was one of the few composers who added something to the literary characters he portrayed. 'Marguerite, Juliet, Mireille, daughters of Goethe, Shakespeare and Mistral ... the musician has had them reborn, belonging to him by right, creations less complete but nearer to us, more accessible to the masses, given by their music a universal appeal.'

On 5 February Hollmann performed the Second Cello Concerto at the Société des Concerts. It bewildered some critics accustomed to Saint-Saëns's more mellifluous manner. René Doire in the *Courrier Musical* declared: 'M. J. Hollmann played majestically and with a conviction that we admired but did not share the Second Violincello Concerto of Saint-Saëns, a work perilously acrobatic despite a sentimental Romance, which wishes to be suave but would have remained banal only if the cello of M. Hollmann had not sung it so exquisitely.... It is certain that this new Concerto is far from equalling the First ... it will not gain the same favour with instrumentalists and listeners.' None of the criticisms daunted the composer from joining this concerto with another cello sonata as he had done thirty years before. This Second Sonata in F, begun at Alexandria but written at Biskra, is much more conventional than its concerto partner, although full of intricacies and dashes of old-fashioned romanticism. There are four movements, of which the second is a Scherzo: theme and variations. This is unusual in that the theme is not a staid melody that can be turned into more elaborate versions, but is itself a bustling tarantella figure. The variations are ingenious: elaborate figures for the piano with whispered asides from the cello, an irate dialogue, transmutations both lyrical and fluttering, and leaping fugal treatment that has a suggestion of the *Carnival* characters. The final variation is a passage in the wild, 'will-o'-the-wisp' style that Saint-Saëns often used in a Scherzo movement with sinister trills from the cello and a final disappearance of both participants into the ether. In the Adagio the piano is subordinate. The composer observed to Durand that it would 'draw tears from those members of the audience that it did not put to sleep'. It is not, however, a straightforward 'Romance' and there are modal effects and echoes of the East, as if the cello were Cantor in a synagogue ceremony. The Finale is a toccata in which once again the cello has moments of simply underlining the harmony. One particular romantic phrase recurs in the general bustle, which concludes with crashing fortissimo and virtuoso effects. Throughout, there is a certain harking back to Schumann in devices such as the repeated rhythmic figures and capricious treatment of the bar-lines.

Such archaisms appear to be more deliberate if one reflects that 1905 was also the year of Strauss's *Salome*. A 1905 *Ode to Horace* for a mixed chorus underlined conservative ideals and reflected an admiration for the supposed immobility, permanence and peace of the classical world. A bomb thrown at the President and King of Spain as they left the Opéra injured over forty bystanders at this time.

The seventieth birthday was celebrated by messages of goodwill from musical bodies everywhere. There were Saint-Saëns festivals at The Hague and at Marseilles. At the latter, on 2 April, he conducted his Third Symphony, then gave an organ recital of works by Bach, Liszt and himself. In May he took part in a soirée at the Société des Concerts to raise funds for a Beethoven monument, giving a profound performance of the *Emperor* Concerto. In August he travelled to Burgos to see a total eclipse of the sun. Knowing the interest of the Fauré children in astronomy he wrote to say that they had been in his thoughts during 'the most marvellous spectacle that awaited me'. Much of the year was spent preparing *L'Ancêtre*. Augé de Lassus, his collaborator in *Phryné*, had offered a very different libretto, recounting a brutal Corsican vendetta. The plot had come to him in a dramatic fashion as one day he was walking down a deserted road near Ajaccio when, from the bushes, two shotguns appeared, pointing at him and following his path, before being withdrawn by unseen fingers. He realised that he was not the traveller expected and devised a scenario to explain the dangerous moment.

Saint-Saëns in turn went to Corsica, under his old assumed name of M. Sannois, to seek inspiration in the terrain and the moods of the peasants. Corsica was as little known in metropolitan France as any foreign land. The score is a further example of Saint-Saëns, never a folk-song collector, arousing interest in the regions of France through music. He went on to Lake Maggiore to begin composition, then to Thun in Switzerland. As changes had to be made to the denouement, Augé de Lassus came to Thun. At seventy, Saint-Saëns was wont to swim in the waters of the River Aar during the male bathing hours, then return to his hotel refreshed and play scenes from *L'Ancêtre* on the piano, which de Lassus described as having 'resonances like cracked saucepans'. The final pages of blood-stained action at the end of the opera were written at Pontarlier, in the waiting-room at a stop between two trains. The visit to Burgos then intervened and on the journey back to Dieppe the orchestration was completed.

It may have been on one of these journeys that another incident involving hotel pianos took place, for Augé de Lassus recounts it. Saint-Saëns, incognito, moved tentatively towards a keyboard abandoned by some small girls as if he would like to try it and sympathetic guests gave encouraging nods. He continued their catalogue of errors with horrific mistakes, jarring as only a trained musician could supply. The following evening he approached the piano again. This time guests fled into the streets prepared to brave the elements rather than endure a similar ordeal. Those who failed to reach the door were this time treated to renditions of Mozart and Beethoven by an interpreter of genius.

Before leaving 1905 it should be noted that this was the year of the 'Affaire Ravel'. Maurice Ravel had been the most gifted pupil to pass through Fauré's composition class but, despite his successes in the musical world, he had failed to win the Prix de Rome, his nearest achievement being third place in 1901. Saint-Saëns had shown an interest in his cantata *Myrrha* and wrote to Lecocq that 'the third prize winner whose name is Ravel appears to me to be destined for an important career'. In 1905 Ravel was rejected in the preliminary round and the list of finalists contained a superfluity of names from Lenepveu's class. The critic Pierre Lalo then took up the matter in *Le Temps* and, scenting a newsworthy incident, other journalists followed. Famous names entered the fray and Romain Rolland, although Ravel's music was not to his taste, protested that the whole concept of the Rome Academy was being compromised if recognised talent was so arbitrarily excluded. As a result of the uproar Dubois was obliged to resign as Director of the Conservatoire and Fauré, who had never been a student there, was chosen as his successor. In a most touching gesture his first action, seated at the Director's desk, was to write eloquently: 'My dear Camille, As it is you who brought me up and it is to you I owe what I am, it is only right and proper that the first words I shall have written at the Directorial table should be addressed to you.' Although Saint-Saëns resigned from the council in order that he should not appear to be a power behind the throne, he maintained a constant interest in Fauré's plans of reform and the inevitable combats with colleagues. There were also problems with the ancient buildings. 'The awful thing is that the Queen [Alexandra] wants to visit *our* Conservatoire and go to some of the classes!' Gabriel wrote to Marie in 1908. 'She is deaf but not blind and will no doubt be taken aback by our miserable conditions.'

The première of *L'Ancêtre* took place at Monte Carlo on 24 February 1906. The décor and costumes were designed by Visconti, Senior, and Saint-Saëns had his wish for Mme Félia Litvinne ('I have convinced myself that I will never be able to do the great final scene of Act One with a contralto. It is a great soprano that is necessary. I see only Mme Litvinne who has the superhuman stature necessary') fulfilled. The American soprano Geraldine Farrar played Margarita. The *Journal de Monaco* described the evening as 'brilliant'. Saint-Saëns was escorted into the Prince's box, from which he acknowledged the plaudits of the fashionable audience. The story describes the feud of two families: the Fabiani and the Neras. Tales of rustic passion were popular at the turn of the century, but Saint-Saëns made an effort to recreate the presence of nature and the violent contrasts which the countryside of Corsica presented. A hermit, Raphael, who tries to reconcile the families, lives by cultivating bees, which gave the composer opportunities to write colourful pages,[1] giving expression to an admiration for rural life. Fauré travelled to Monaco for the occasion. 'My music is too opportunist for you,' wrote Saint-Saëns. 'Nevertheless I hope that in my new work there are some features that will not displease you.'[2] At

---

[1] His interest in natural history extended to the tiniest insects. René Thorel said that a 'fly drowning in a glass of water' would find a saviour in Saint-Saëns. A passionate interest in bees was here translated into evocative sounds.

[2] It is a sign of his eminence that, by 1912, *L'Ancêtre* had travelled to Paris (Opéra Comique), Toulouse, Prague, Antwerp and Montreal.

the same time he acquired an MS copy of Chopin's Second Ballade, which he presented to the Director of the Conservatoire and on which he wrote an article for the *Monde Musicale* in 1920.

The sixtieth anniversary of Saint-Saëns's first concert in the Salle Pleyel also came in 1906. The occasion was celebrated by a Charity Concert of songs, two-piano works (performed by Francis Planté and Léon Delafosse) and the Master himself in Beethoven's *Emperor* and the *Rhapsodie d'Auvergne*. Fauré, in *Le Figaro*, praised the ever youthful abilities which Saint-Saëns displayed at the keyboard and reminded virtuosi that three other concertos existed besides the G minor and C minor 'and among these the Concerto in E flat deserves particularly to emerge from the shadows where it has been sleeping'. Saint-Saëns was greatly touched by this reference. The year was also the 300th anniversary of the birth of the dramatist Pierre Corneille. The words of a celebratory cantata were written by Sebastian-Charles Leconte, which evoked characters from *Le Cid*, *Cinna*, *Polyeucte* and *Horace*. Men of letters and musicians were assembled by an under-secretary of state to select the composer most worthy of setting the poem and the choice fell by acclamation on Saint-Saëns, who was able to frame part of his early setting of a scene from *Horace* with portrayals of characters from other plays. Vast aggregations of brass and unison tributes hailed the city of Paris 'where thought and art are worshipped'. *La Gloire de Corneille*, a very spacious and melodic work, dedicated to Fauré, was played at the Opéra in June.

Saint-Saëns had passed part of the spring in Italy, where he gave an organ recital at the Saint Cecilia Music Academy in Rome and an orchestral concert in Florence. In August he visited Salzburg for the festival in honour of the 150th anniversary of Mozart's birth, contributing an organ version of the latter's Grand Fugue and Fantasie in C major. At the end of the year, tired with concerts despite a period to recuperate in Spain and Portugal, he set sail for North America. While at sea he fell gravely ill and, on landing in New York, he was placed under the care of a doctor who had serious fears as to whether he could survive a tour and insisted upon a resident nurse. Saint-Saëns, anxious to avoid the ministrations of an Amazonian battle-axe, was delighted to find that the nurse was young, slender and entertaining. 'It appears that these charming nurses frequently marry their patients after the latter have recovered,' he mused. He was keeping in touch with the overthrown Dubois: 'I have to play my old G minor, *Africa* and other trifles.'

Despite his poor health he gave performances in New York, Washington, Philadelphia and Chicago, and surprised himself by his enjoyment of the New World. He had expected to find it a place of restless and excited crowds, 'something like an exasperated England'. He discovered that the invigorating effects of modernity compensated for the absence of historic buildings. Certain architects dream of making New York an artistic city; their dream will be realised. 'They are lavish with the finest marbles and costliest wood. At night, when the windows are illuminated to an incredible height and the electric lights are shining all around, the sight is wonderfully fantastic.' He was delighted by the squirrels who came up to beg for nuts in Central Park. The battalions of female admirers and patronesses of the arts did not compare unfavourably with the hostesses of Paris. 'I was afraid I might meet some bachelor women with short hair and harsh expressions, and was agreeably surprised to find it was not so.'

He had high praise for the orchestras 'often composed of French performers' and conductors. 'Mr Walter Damrosch is sympathetic to French composers. Nor is he alone in this ... in New York ... a successful performance of *La Croisade des Enfants* by Gabriel Pierné was given and in all the towns I visited I found in the repertoire the works of César Franck as well as my own.' He was thrilled by a performance of *Samson* in Philadelphia by an amateur chorus of 250 voices. 'I had to endeavour to recover my fingering of past days in order to play my Concerto in G minor, which everybody wished to hear interpreted by the composer. This did not please me by any means for nowadays young pianists play it better than I do; I prefer to play the Fifth, which is more symphonic and more fitted to my present powers. Well then, I played the G minor at Washington before President Roosevelt, who, after receiving me most affably, did me the rare and signal honour of coming to listen to my playing.' His patriotism was aroused by the many statues and memorabilia of Lafayette. 'The Americans have one quality which touched me greatly; they are not ungrateful; they have not forgotten the part played by France in their independence.' He enjoyed the *en suite* bathrooms, the private telephones and, as a connoisseur of railway travel, the efficient ticket system, which avoided a scramble for places. 'One consequence of this is that Americans move from place to place with astonishing ease; I was continually coming across people whom I had seen the previous week six hundred miles away.'

His ardour in defence of animals strikes us as extremely modern. His thoughts on American zoos led him far from his subject into an eloquent harangue against the imprisonment of wild species. 'Dens for lions and bears! In New York I saw foxes and wolves shut up in narrow cages where they could scarcely move. Yet carnivores include the finest animals in creation! Would it not be more interesting to see them gambol and sport about than eternally pace to and fro in prison houses? I appeal to civilised Man for whom it is disgraceful to act like a savage incapable of reflecting and understanding Nature.' He loved La Fontaine because the author of the *Fables* had credited animals with intelligence when 'in the seventeenth century under the influence of Descartes all intelligence was refused them'.[1]

One piece he had taken to New York with him was the *Fantasie pour Orgue-Aeolian*, written for a mechanical device, which used the punched rolls associated with pianolas to create works too complex for human hands and brains. Volume and speed of playing were to be controlled by pedals and levers following complicated multi-coloured instructions. The work had been begun in London, which he had visited to accompany Hollmann in the Second Cello Sonata, and some features of the sonata were repeated, including a brilliant start and a set of variations. Particular effects of the Aeolian organ were, however, incorporated, such as the echo, the harp and chimes, all of which lent colour and breadth of treatment to the 'chorale' sections and the accelerated close. The Aeolian Company advertised its links with him with American thoroughness, although few musicians had less need of a machine to release a performer from normal limitations.

He returned to France, still in very bad health, visited Paris, 'which seemed to me like some pretty bibelot, but how glad I was to see it again', then travelled on to Cairo to convalesce. He paid Prince Haida Pasha the compliment of setting a poem to music, 'L'Etoile', and responded to a request from the playwright Eugène Brieux to compose incidental music to *La Foi*, a drama set in ancient Egypt. Brieux was a serious dramatist admired by Shaw. (He was also the author of a play translated into English as *Damaged Goods*, dealing with the problems

---

[1] Hatred of cruelty to animals was another emotion he shared with Berlioz.

of venereal disease. During World War II it toured Great Britain with official backing.) *La Foi*, under the guise of dealing with the ancient mystery religions of Egypt, plunged into questions of science and religion, and priests imposing ideas of the supernatural upon the credulous. Such a subject would appeal to Saint-Saëns[1] and was highly topical. The year 1906 had seen the separation of Church and State in France, with passions aroused on both sides. In Franck's former church St Clothilde, for example, where Charles Tournemire was organist, there was fighting with right-wing activists who blockaded the building against government officials, who wished to make inventories of the church treasures.

From the lengthy score, which was of operatic dimensions, Saint-Saëns extracted the material to make *Three Symphonic Tableaux*. Together, these form a remarkable exception to his general taste. The work is post-Wagnerian in style, the orchestral tutti are immense, on a Straussian scale, and the mixture of scene-painting (the dark Nile, the temple trumpets, a certain oriental voluptuousness), combined with psychological struggling (heavy orchestration in the lower instruments, strings vibrato, meditative phrases in the woodwind), could be mistaken for Mahler. He had a great admiration for the music of *Parsifal* but one wonders at times whether Wagner is being classified with the purveyors of mischievous religiosity. At the same time he made use of his knowledge of Egyptian scales and chord sequences. 'Unfortunately,' as he said to Fauré, 'after *Salome* such things appear diatonic!'

The composition hung fire for some time, but was begun early in 1908. He took great pride in the fact that it was French archaeologists who had restored the monuments of Karnac. As a scientist he was interested in the means by which Egyptian painters had worked in comparative darkness within the tombs.

It was during these early years of the century that Emile Baumann recorded a typical interview and his impressions of the composer at work.

Despite constant worries over health, his appearance was robust; an

---

[1] He had already expressed similar feeling in his own words for the song 'Lever de soleil sur le Nil': 'Sphinxes in their heavy silence tell us that the gods are dead.'

interior force appeared to manifest itself through the solid build but tired shoulders of the continuous worker. The visage of the very eclectic musician bore no resemblance to any musician of times past or present. He did not have, like Reyer, the physique of an officer, nor the solemn pedantic face of a Franck, nor the artistic head of a Massenet. He showed an aversion to compliments and scarcely appeared to believe them. All his conversation was very direct, accompanied by quick gestures and sudden alternations between pleasure and anxiety. He has just returned from Egypt, and describing a site or a mirage he quickly seizes a pencil and sketches on whichever MS happens to be in front of him. Five minutes later Berlioz's *Childhood of Christ* is mentioned and he is at the keyboard, but he rarely returns to develop a striking idea or a new thought. He sings an operatic extract giving the illusion of the accompanying orchestra; despite his lisp he recalls the voice and mannerisms of a long dead actress.

He appeared to be impervious to his surroundings and showed no instinct for property or collection. Photographs of friends, a portrait of his mother, a recent score are the only objects of interest. When writing he will ask himself aloud questions about the instrumentation. 'Shall I give that to the horns or the violas?' His memory seems to be working powerfully as he writes. His nose has its despotic curve, the tight mouth shows a disdain for stupidity. A pince-nez, ever present, assisted his poor sight and concealed a slight squint, but the open nostrils give the impression of exuberant appetites which must necessarily have been repressed. Beneath the sharpness and the rapid flow of remarks one discerned the sadness that came from many conflicts and tragedies. 'One rediscovers the joy of living,' he had recently written to a bereaved friend, 'but the gaiety no longer penetrates the heart of things.'

Baumann felt that, despite the wide travelling which the composer undertook, he carried with him the restricting shackles of a constant need to compose. This was an inevitable part of the work ethic enjoined upon Camille since childhood.

His articles and reviews continued throughout 1907, a restless year in general. The blessings of *Le Feu Céleste* appeared more doubtful when an electrician's strike plunged Paris into darkness. In succeeding months there were strikes of building and postal workers. Mutinies broke out even in the wine-growing districts around Béziers. *Salome* was given at the Châtelet in May. Saint-Saëns, sensing a connection with anarchism, addressed a letter to *Le Temps* in which he praised the 'prodigious talent' of Richard Strauss and 'the artistry of Mme Destinn' but condemned much of the music. 'The completest liberty reigns: while one group of instruments covers one tonality, another has no scruples about battling with its neighbour, while the voices travel along elsewhere.' Lecocq agreed that, while certain passages were delicious, 'others surpass in horror the deepest circles of Dante's Hell'.

A German journal, *Die Standarte*, in an open letter to Saint-Saëns tried to prove that Wagner's 'A Capitulation' was not an insult to France, to which he replied: 'Sir, An old proverb states that insult is allowed to the vanquished, not to the victorious. In reissuing this Prose in his Complete Works, Richard Wagner has committed a blameworthy act.' On hearing that there was to be a translation of Wagner's theoretical works he wrote to *Le Ménestrel* on 'Light and Clarity'. 'Clarity is the health of style. Not long ago it was the hallmark of everything. Provided that one was clear and precise it was permitted to be dull, flat, or even vulgar and the most beautiful things were rejected, if it was necessary to make the least effort to understand them. Today it is the contrary; the absence of melodic ideas, incoherent and even discordant harmony, disorder in the structures, everything is allowed, everything admitted into music making it possible to be obscure and incomprehensible.' Having plunged into a general attack upon modern trends he returned to Wagner in his peroration. 'One thing disturbs me, the opinion that the author has of himself. "It is strange," Wagner said one day. "When I reread my former theoretical works it is impossible for me to understand them." After all, not to understand oneself, is that not the ultimate limit where progress in the incomprehensible ends up?!' Wagner's 'A Capitulation' was a grievance of which he could never rid himself. He was attending a festival at Pézenas in honour of Molière when 'suddenly ... the "Ride of the Valkyries" broke out'. When the Government Minister present remarked that he thought the music rather fine, there was a hail of Saint-Saëns's criticism. 'Deprived of the vocal aspect, mutilated in its development, the "Ride" is no longer beautiful. ... My protestation had no effect but to put me on bad terms with the Minister.' Saint-Saëns objected strongly to Wagner played by French military bands – 'He, the insulter of defeated France!'

The Honorary Doctorate he received from Oxford University in June 1907 was not in celebration of a primarily musical occasion as at Cambridge, but part of a generous distribution of honours by the Chancellor, Lord Curzon. The Prime Minister, Sir Henry Campbell-Bannerman, and a host of dignified figures including Rudyard Kipling, General Booth of the Salvation Army, Edmund Warre, Headmaster of Eton, and the sculptor Auguste Rodin were similarly honoured. The presence of Saint-Saëns and Rodin, and references to 'Dulcium Gallicum' in the Latin oration, point to further political cultivation of Anglo-French friendship.[1]

There was some confusion as the Honorands assembled and Prince Arthur of Connaught and the politicians received their degrees, while the others were kept outside in the courtyard. 'What is the name for this ceremony?' asked Saint-Saëns of Sir Hubert Parry. Not wishing to become involved in explaining the word 'Encaenia' in French, Parry simply replied, 'Momentary confusion!' Saint-Saëns consoled himself by playing with the handle of his umbrella, from which, despite his medieval robes, he would not be parted.

He had already, in January from Cairo, had a correspondence with Bellaigue on the subject of Wagner's theories.[2] 'How, my dear friend, with your judicious intelligence do you let yourself fall for the Wagner mirages? How do you not see all that is specious in "this chimerical phraseology"? I am unable to comprehend how a passionate phrase expresses the "evolution of a passion" rather than its lasting state. If that is to say that Wagner has very well expressed *desire* it is a lot of fuss about nothing.' He poured equal scorn on Wagner the Apostle to the People. 'Wagner writing for the masses. I must laugh! There Nietzsche is correct; the aspirations of the populace are small and easy to satisfy. Melodrama, farce and, in music, easy and vulgar tunes. That is what pleases them. The only work slightly popular of Wagner is

---

[1] When the invitations were issued an elderly don, possibly remembering the Cambridge 1894 ceremony, suggested sending one to Tchaikovsky. Dr (later Sir) Hugh Allen said it would have to be sent to heaven as Tchaikovsky had been dead for fourteen years. Glazunov was eventually asked.

[2] It is worth recording that in 1892 Wagner wrote to Felix Mottl, the Austrian conductor: 'So you adore Saint-Saëns. Between ourselves you are *not* mistaken.'

Tannhäuser because one finds there arias, ensembles and even some vulgarities.'[1]

He believed that works of art obeyed aesthetic rather than sociological laws. '*The Huguenots* and *La Juive* are apologetics for the Reformation and Hebrewism, and veritable indictments of Catholicism. No one thinks that, when hearing them, and no Catholic is shocked.' Warming to his theme he continued, 'Have you ever been tempted, coming out from hearing *Tristan*, to kill yourself, in order to love Mme Bellaigue more fully, and do you think she would have savoured this sort of love? I yield to her judgement. For me, when people wish to make works of art enter into other realms, they enter into the realms of madness. Richard Strauss is in process of showing us the road.' There was also an immensely long exchange of views with Bellaigue on the use of expression in the works of Palestrina – 'The "molto espressivo" which the Schola Cantorum scatters in its editions appears to me a monstrous error; it denatures the music by inflicting these whinings upon it.' The discussion led to a hardening of his views upon 'expression' in music. 'If the search for expression constituted progress in art, the Laocoön would be superior to the Hermes of Praxiteles, Guido superior to Raphael. It was thus that Stendhal understood Art.' Bellaigue, also Camille, replied as 'a modest and cognomial homonyme' that the music of Gounod and Saint-Saëns would not be worthy of existence if it were just form or formalism; 'if behind these melodies, harmonies, rhythms, the fugues themselves, sometimes, there was not spirit and heart'. He did prefer the Venus de Milo and the Hermes to the Laocoön 'but I do not grant that the form, the form of this young man or this young woman, expresses nothing. They express very lofty, very general and profound things; an ideal conception of life and the world, while the Laocoön (whose children anyhow are very ugly even as forms) represents only a state of physical suffering, violent, one evil moment which is a passing thing.' In Monte Carlo for rehearsals, Saint-Saëns continued the argument: 'I say that emotion in art is the germ of death; it is the same sort of thing as love in life. Have you understood?' Bellaigue then defied him to analyse any work of great music without having to use a vocabulary of feeling in the soul, and finished with a veritable reproof: 'Monsieur,

[1] An admirer of Wagner had recently written that to understand the character of Kundry in *Parsifal* it was necessary to read all the old patristic theologians. '*Diable! Voilà qui est laborieux,*' was Saint-Saëns's answer.

you do not deserve to be the great artist which you are. Is it necessary to explain to you, since you don't understand it at all, the emotion that your music causes, and which is there in the first note of the organ of the Adagio of the C mi[nor] Symphony[1] and the languor when the voice of Delilah melts during the triolets *"cachent ma tristesse"*, similar oboe notes in the scene at the mill and the poetry of a duet in *La Lyre* and the pagan outburst of that other verse?' . . . The two men were, however, reconciled by a mutual dislike of *Salome.* 'This horror has had thirty-eight performances in Berlin,' wrote Saint-Saëns. 'A pathetic comment on the times we live in. But, as I have said, the public no longer creates success; it has success imposed upon it.'

In October he broached the subject of vocal display in *Le Ménestrel*, addressing himself to the critic Julien Tiersot, who had found merit in the vocal fireworks which crown the aria of Electra in *Idomeneo.*

The ostracism of vocal display in our time [wrote Saint-Saëns] is to my mind an error as great as the abuse made of it in the time of Rossini. But I will go further than you and I would defend against Berlioz the vocal display in the great aria of Donna Anna. The staunch avenger foresees at this moment a better future. She opens her heart to hope, and the delicate arabesques which support the retardation of the strings are in no way in disaccord with the situation. It is necessary to add that Berlioz, so intransigent in the matter of vocal displays, did not deprive himself of the pleasure of writing them. They are there in *Benvenuto* and *Beatrice and Benedict.* It is true they are quite extraordinarily gauche and maladroit.

In February, Monte Carlo mounted Massenet's *Thérèse*, a short opera set in the time of the Revolution. Massenet and his party left the Palace almost immediately before Saint-Saëns moved in for a revival of *Le Timbre d'Argent*, first performed thirty years earlier. It is difficult to account for Gunsbourg's wish to revive *Le Timbre*, but there had been two productions of it in Germany in 1904–5, reminding the world of its existence. It was given three times, the cast included

---

[1] In 1899 Bellaigue wrote to Saint-Saëns to say that he had heard the Third Symphony again and 'it caused me one of the greatest musical emotions I have ever experienced'.

Maggie Teyte and there was the usual ceremonial dinner in the composer's honour.[1]

It is to be hoped that he enjoyed his dinner better than one given in his honour during a festival in northern France. Saint-Saëns informed the President that he could not dine out as he was on a strict diet. The President said he would be given whatever dishes he chose. Saint-Saëns said that the doctor allowed him only the glutinous and edible parts of pig's trotters. While the guests feasted around him he wrestled with the trotters, displaying a crescendo of indignation, and finally stormed out, deaf to all entreaties to remain.

From Monaco he continued to Bordighera to rest, and there he wrote his Fantasia for Violin and Harp; the zephyrs of the Italian Riviera and his recent thoughts on 'clarity' contributed to this delicate combination of instruments in a work dedicated to two sisters: Marianne and Clara Eissler. It falls into sections and in the first, which has a tentative and improvisory nature, the single line of the violin is contrasted with the arpeggios and broken chords of the harp. In the second the violin asserts itself in double-stopping, while the harp dwells on a more throbbing, oriental accompaniment. The violin elaborates a lyrical theme, which leads to cadenza-like passages with echoes of a concerto. The third section adds further contrasts of timbre. At one moment there is a skittish chase; at another the violin strikes low keynotes on which the harp elaborates. Section four presents the harp in bell-like tones, repeating patterns of notes while the violin resorts to outbursts, often of passionate intensity. The work ends with repetitions of the opening motifs and brief recollections of the first lyrical passage. By economy of means and delicate use of faintly exotic but acceptable harmonies, the work serves as a riposte to *Salome* and its orchestral tumult.

In April the Monte Carlo Opéra paid a visit to Berlin. This was an endeavour to improve relations after Germany's efforts to thwart French penetration in Morocco. The repertoire included *The Damnation of Faust*, *Carmen*, *Mefistofele* with Chaliapin, *Don Carlos* and Xavier Leroux's *Theodora*. On 12 April Prince Albert and his suite, Saint-Saëns, Massenet and Leroux (along with Grieg, who was in Berlin at the time), were invited to lunch by the Kaiser and entertained in his

---

[1] He wrote from the Palace to Renaud, organist at Versailles, 'As for the roulette. Don't worry! I never play there.'

private apartments. In the evening the composers dined with Prince Albert,[1] then went on to a performance of *Salome* by a German company. Finally, on the next day the Monte Carlo Opéra gave separate acts from *Samson*, *Hérodiade* and *The Barber of Seville*. Saint-Saëns and Massenet, the two old rivals, shared a box at this gala evening and acknowledged the applause of the audience from their places, before being received into the Imperial box. The artists taking their bows wore French and German colours intertwined in ribbons. Saint-Saëns had an advantage over Massenet on this occasion. As the various composers and producers were decorated with the Order of the Crown of Prussia he received an autographed photograph of the Kaiser since he already held the much superior German Order of Merit. While in Berlin he was able to enjoy some library researches and he wrote for *Le Ménestrel* a study of the Beethoven MSS at the Berlin Library. In June he conducted Beethoven's Ninth at the Opéra to help raise funds for a Beethoven monument. As a result of his researches he departed from the tradition in certain of the tempi, notably in the Scherzo and the *allegro energico* of the Finale.

He had entered into the company of those granted monuments to themselves while living. A statue of the composer, showing him seated with a score on his lap and hands modelled from life by the sculptor Laurent Marqueste, had been presented at the Salon of 1907. A female admirer, Mme Caruette, wished to give it to the town of Dieppe. There were some satirical comments by those who thought a statue to the living musician premature. The monument to Gounod had only recently been put up at St Cloud. In spite or, perhaps, because of the erection of one to Marshal Macmahon in his lifetime a law forbade the inauguration of statues to the living. But significantly, government intervention enabled the ceremony to take place in the foyer of the Dieppe Theatre. 'Since one only puts up statues to the dead, it follows that I am now counted among their number,' he remarked. 'You will excuse me therefore from making a speech.' The orchestra of the Société des Concerts du Conservatoire attended, the local Orphéon, the 'Children of Wilhelm', sang and Félia Litvinne was one of the soloists along with members of the Caruette family with musical

---

[1] Prince Albert, incidentally, had been a strong supporter of Dreyfus and invited him to the Palace at Monte Carlo on his release.

aspirations. The programme included excerpts from *Henry VIII*, the Allegro Appassionato and 'The Swan'. By a stroke of irony, the statue of the musician whose relationships with Germany were so volatile was melted down by the Germans during World War II for armaments. Also in 1908 he wrote a cantata for the Children of Wilhelm at Dieppe, to be sung before a monument raised to the dead of the 1870 war, *Aux Morts de la Patrie*.

After a period in Switzerland he informed Caroline de Serres about the programme of a concert in which he would share the baton with Colonne. 'I will be the one who conducts your pieces and thus you can rest at ease. You will see how I accompany you! ... If you come to discuss matters with them, the Septet and the Wedding Cake would be a kind gesture as, with you, one is sure of success; you have the authority to establish compositions.' He added that his great admirer, the violinist Johannes Wolff, was to be married. 'He is wedding a widow younger than himself and appears to be delighted. I am a witness of the marriage ... and after, I set off on holiday. The liver and kidneys are not in good shape and I have headaches. I am not able to work and try to give my brain a rest, travelling incognito, which should bring results as it has done in the past.' A singer had asked him for a companion piece to 'La Fiancée du Timbalier' but he could not find a suitably inspiring poem 'even in Hugo. ... Happily that has not made me pine away.' He did, however, set two poems by the Comtesse de Noailles, 'Soir Romantique' and 'Violons dans le Soir.' The latter, with its tale of sobbing and frenzied violins breaking the evening calm, has a part for solo violin, sometimes echoing the smooth vocal line and sometimes making shrill and striking comments. The piano part is subdued, the atmosphere has a hint of Spain and the 'expression' demanded is in contrast to his views so insistently addressed to Bellaigue.

The 1908 season at Monte Carlo included *Henry VIII*, which demanded some spectacle. It had a most unusual première in March in aid of the League of Hygiene, a body formed to protest against the tar dust raised on the road from Nice to Menton. Gunsbourg sent a telegram to the absent Prince Albert to say that the opera had been a great success and Saint-Saëns had been acclaimed. To celebrate his recent journey to America he composed a large-scale setting of Psalm 150, 'Praise Ye the Lord', words in English, for double-chorus, organ and orchestra. It was dedicated to a New York architect, Whitney

Warren, who was a Foreign Associate member of the French Institut. The inclusion of harps, drums, cymbals and all manner of percussion, which the psalmist describes as acceptable to the Lord, constitutes a direct challenge to the 'Motu Proprio' and the Schola Cantorum. In April 1909 he wrote jokingly to Fauré: 'I know you have a horror of the frivolities of *Phryné*, but I hope to mount again in your esteem when you get to know my Psalm that I hope to conduct this summer in England.' This expectation was not fulfilled and the psalm remained a work which he never heard performed. Fauré was working on the opera *Pénélope* and Saint-Saëns forbade him to waste time on letter writing. 'I absolutely forbid you to reply to me. When one is working all day, to write letters is a torture; that I know and wish to spare you.' The choice of *Pénélope* as a subject had its political resonances, for the return of Ulysses was a symbol for the resumption of normality after a period of disorder. The Government had been taking a strong line against strikes and demonstrations; states of emergency were declared and strikers dismissed.

For military band, Saint-Saëns wrote an occasional piece, *Sur les Bords du Nil*, and he continued to feature in the Colonne concerts. In November there was a large assembly at the Conservatoire for a Memorial Concert for conductor Georges Marty. Messager conducted the orchestra for the first time and Saint-Saëns played a C-minor concerto of Mozart. He gave the concert his full support, writing to many titled people and patrons, asking them to subscribe, as the concert was in aid of Marty's widow. The biographer Arthur Dandelot cited this concert as an example of the composer's outstanding generosity to fellow artists: 'Too much is said about his asperity and not enough about his fount of discreet benevolence.'[1] The asperity was under some subjugation at this period, though his criticism of a publication of Couperin's pieces for strings and harpsichord gives an insight into his massive learning. He told Fauré that it was particularly wrong to have errors in exercises and he considered Dukas, the editor, to have been insufficiently familiar with ornaments and grace-notes in

---

[1] Saint-Saën's personal kindnesses were evident at all stages of his adult life. One New Year's Eve Augé de Lassus found an old ragged musician blowing painfully on an ophicleide outside the composer's apartment in the rue Monsieur le Prince. Saint-Saëns listened, leaning out of the window with apparent pleasure. 'I have seen him much less patient with many less cruel cacophonies!'

old music. 'I was no better until I had studied the question in the Violin Method of Mozart (*père*) where the question is treated in depth'. There were three editions of Mozart *père* in the Conservatoire library but the oldest was the one that should be studied. 'This is not a matter of taste; it is a matter of erudition; it is a matter of knowing uniquely what the composer wished to write.'

He himself was turning to a completely new medium: the cinema. From recording simple processes such as a train arriving at a station, film techniques had moved on to devise imaginative re-creations of fairy-stories or science fantasies with special effects. Fairgrounds and arcades had film halls into which the public crowded. Many of Saint-Saëns's best-known pieces had already been pressed into service as background music. There were some who thought that the art should aim higher. A 'Film d'Art' company was founded, which prepared a production, *The Assassination of the Duke of Guise*, depicting an event of the sixteenth-century wars of religion. The script was by a member of the Academy and the players were drawn from the Comédie Française. The action was 'theatrical' and unsubtle; the story was condensed into a series of tableaux which showed King Henri III summoning the Duke of Guise to a council, handing out daggers to his bodyguards and inspecting the corpse of the victim. As an echo of the Dreyfus Case a letter is found on the Duke's body suggesting treasonable relations with foreign powers. After perfunctory religious rites the body is burned while the Duke's mistress collapses with grief. There were no lavish court scenes that required fanfares or spectacular dance sequences. The music accordingly concentrates upon the atmosphere of intrigue and suspicion, and Saint-Saëns, jotting down ideas while he watched the flickering screen, was able to rescue the slow movement of the *Urbs Roma* Symphony from oblivion. With limited resources at his disposal he was grateful too for his knowledge of the harmonium, which gave a useful adjunct to strings and piano.[1] He was the first international composer to write for this new form of film entertainment, but at the time musicians were more excited by the appearance of Diaghilev's Russian Ballet.

He spent many hours during his winter travels in supporting Fauré's candidature for the Institut. 'I have written forty letters and I will write some more still.' He advised Fauré to drum up support among his

---

[1] Durands speedily made a version for piano alone for the use of cinemas with even slenderer resources.

female admirers to counter those of Widor, his principal opponent. He believed the Countess Greffulhe, to whom Fauré had dedicated his Pavane far back in 1887 and for whose daughter he had written a wedding anthem in 1904, was a key figure. 'It is above all by women that one arrives at the Academy.' He left the Canaries and braved the Paris winter to be present at the election. 'Saturday the battle,' he wrote to Lecocq. 'It has been rough and, when I saw at the fifth ballot that Widor had gained two votes and Fauré had lost one of them, I believed the cause lost, everything spun around me and I had an attack . . . a congestion of the lungs which had not disappeared by Monday morning.'

Fauré himself was nervous of the outcome and, possibly fearing that Saint-Saëns's support would be counter-productive, was quite unable to concentrate on a rehearsal in Barcelona where he was appearing with Marguerite Long. He heard finally that he had defeated Widor by the narrow margin of eighteen to sixteen. Although Fauré was fifty-nine at this time, Saint-Saëns does not seem to have thought it wrong to write to him as one might to a boy, reminding him to send letters of thanks to Mme Greffulhe and other supporters. Fauré was having problems in his efforts to reform the Conservatoire and its disputatious professors at a time when music was changing at a pace hitherto unknown. In 1908 Nadia Boulanger scandalised the academics by submitting an instrumental fugue for the Prix de Rome instead of the usual vocal one. Demands for her disqualification were led by Saint-Saëns, not because he disapproved of female composers, but because he believed that all writers of music should be conversant with vocal writing. The Minister of Fine Arts decided in her favour and she gained Second Prize. In 1909 there was a breach in the Société Nationale initiated by Ravel with the support of many young colleagues.[1] A new body, the Société Musicale Indépendant, proposed to give space to young musicians, a reaction against the

---

[1] Ravel had a high regard for Saint-Saëns and often had the latter's scores before him on his desk. Reviewing a performance of a Liszt symphonic poem, he wrote, 'Within this form, often clumsy, always effusive, doesn't one distinguish the embryo of the ingenious, facile and limpid development of Saint-Saëns?'
On the songs of Fauré which disregarded form, he wrote, 'Fauré's songs do not bear the slightest imprint of the continual pursuit of architectural design found in the shortest works of Saint-Saëns, who truly created new techniques of development.'

preponderance of the Franckists. As early as 1899 Ravel's *Schéhérazade* had been accepted only after strenuous efforts by Fauré and, in 1907, his song-cycle *Histoires Naturelles* had been heavily criticised by the academics. D'Indy had rejected a symphonic poem by his own pupil Maurice Delage, claiming (erroneously) that it contained an unplayable low C for the horn. Fauré accepted the Presidency of the SMI, hoping to keep both the new and the old school in some sort of harness, but the gesture did not please his old friend. Emile Vuillermoz, another pupil of Fauré and a founder of the SMI, wrote that his master 'received from the composer of *Samson* a letter which shook the columns of the new temple and charged his former pupil to break immediately with "the little anarchists" who were jeopardising his reputation, casting him in a dangerous role'. Fauré, with some courage, wrote back to say that the 'anarchists' had talent and must have opportunities for hearing their works.

The quarrel was not lasting, though each reserved his position. For Saint-Saëns other polemics began in 1909, arising from the production of *Iphigénie en Aulide* at the Opéra-Comique. There had been erroneous interpretations of the composer's intentions. '"Andante" in the eighteenth century did not imply slowness,' he said in a letter to *Commoedia*. 'The marking "Andante Allegro" was not rare in Handel, where today "Allegro Giocoso" would be used.' It was for lack of knowing such things that the habit of taking the air 'Divinités du Styx' with solemn slowness had arisen. It should be played with passion as Berlioz, who had seen the works of Gluck when they were still in the repertoire, used to interpret it.' Treatment of recitatives, so important to Gluck, was marred by even greater errors. This he traced back to the singer Gilbert Duprez, who made every recitative portentous and lingered for ever on the notes. Recitatives should reflect all the many rhythms and speeds of ordinary speech. Since modern works have become so ponderous and boring – he added for good measure – it is unfortunate that ancient works should be made unnecessarily ponderous also.[1]

Messager had been able to revive *Javotte* at the Opéra and Saint-Saëns had a rare moment of pleasure in his dealings with that

---

[1] A year later he was pressing for *Orphée* to be done at the Opéra. He said the Pelletan Edition – in French – was the only good one, not just because he had worked on it. 'There is a magnificent German edition ... which is completely erroneous.'

institution, lavishing praise on the conductors, designers, the players and the 'ensemble of personnel of which, elsewhere, the least coryphées would be stars'. In April *La Foi* was finally put on at Monte Carlo. Charles Malherbe reviewed the score: 'Egypt and Antiquity. These are two words which speak always to the imagination of a composer such as Saint-Saëns, two colours that shine with a special brilliance on his orchestral palette.' The theatre critic of *Le Temps* noted the effectiveness of the 'archaism of the brass' at the Gates of the Temple and the 'suavity' of the Intermezzo in the third act where flute, cor-anglais, harp and tambourine mingle together. Malherbe also referred to the oriental scales which were combined into a 'harmonious design'. Saint-Saëns did indeed 'Westernise the music of remote regions', reflecting the policies of the Colonial Powers in every other field.[1]

In July, he was at Aix-les-Bains rehearsing *Henry VIII*. 'This morning a magnificent rehearsal . . . singers chorus and orchestra form a fine ensemble and the work stands out brilliantly.' He wrote to Bellaigue that he had relished a review of *Henry VIII* at the Opéra: 'to see appreciated the delicate touches I have bestowed on that noble figure, Katherine. Do you know that, if I have rendered to your satisfaction the miseries of the dying Katherine, it is that I was myself sufficiently moribund when I wrote the fourth act. I do not know how I was able to emerge from that bad stage in order to reach my present age. The adieux to life – I believed I was making them myself and that is why I have made them with such sincerity.'

He was now surprised at the adulation which Mussorgsky was receiving from Debussy and others. 'Is it [*Boris Godunov*] such a great masterpiece?' he asked Bellaigue. 'I have found to my astonishment some parts very feeble. It has the advantage of coming from afar off with the prestige of another race and another language. I find a different mastery in Glinka and in *Onegin* of Tchaikovsky that the critical world affects to despise.'

The *Revue de Paris*, in August, contained his long defence of historical subjects in opera against the fashion for legendary subjects then so popular. He traced the growth of mythological subjects in

[1] It was in 1909, after *La Foi* was completed, that he heard an Egyptian muezzin singing in remarkable half-tones – a sound between that of a bird and a man. Even Saint-Saëns was unable to write it down in any useful notation.

French opera in the eighteenth century and historical subjects in the nineteenth. He reaffirmed his admiration for the great operatic success that had so nearly coincided with his birth. 'Who would have said that one day it would be necessary to come to its defence, when *The Huguenots* shone in the repertoire of the Opéra like the sun in the firmament?' The critic Pougin, in writing on the opera, had let fall some criticisms. Saint-Saëns, in defending the aria of Marguerite (de Valois), became most eloquent: Meyerbeer, who had intended to write a grand aria, 'makes of this Queen, young and beautiful, surrounded by her women and her pages, a "Court of Love". From the first notes of the introduction, played by the cellos, repeated by the flutes, an atmosphere of feminine charm envelops us; and, when the delicious phrase "Oh! Beautiful land of Touraine" unfolds accompanied by harps, one is transported into a world of amorous elegance which one encounters nowhere else.' He had lived through epochs in singing, as in composing, and recalled the impression Mme Carvalho had made in the role which over the years had become too statuesque and regal.

He did not think that French legends had the same misty fascination as those of Scandinavia and wondered whether French composers would slavishly have followed Wagner if the latter had decided to write operas about historical persons such as Frederick Barbarossa. He defended his own choice of *Henry VIII*, admitting that legendary subjects gave great scope for miraculous devices, but could hardly raise the same emotions as real people. 'Who would endure the interminable discourses of sad Wotan without the marvellous music with which they are accompanied?' In the clear daylight of French rationalism he did not understand the emotions which lurk in the clouds of the subconscious, so strangely symbolised in Wagner's dramas and which, even as he wrote, were being explored by Freud and Jung. He also ignored the fact that in *Samson* he had used characters that were scarcely less legendary than Wagner's.

Of course, Old Testament characters were as real and historical to the church-going public, in Britain, as Queen Victoria and her Ministers. *Samson*, regarded by most as unquestionably historical, was finally given at Covent Garden. The *Illustrated London News* stated that 'It is rumoured that the prohibition was removed at the request of the Queen [Alexandra]'. Saint-Saëns, who came to London[1] to supervise

---

[1] While staying at the Grosvenor Hotel he found time to write a letter in

rehearsals, was loudly cheered at the close, but already *Samson* belonged to a passing age. The current issue of the *Musical Times* noted the growing popularity of Debussy, who had recently crossed the Channel to conduct his *Nocturnes*, and, by popular demand, had included *L'Après-Midi d'un Faune* in his programme. The Société des Concerts Français devoted an entire evening to Debussy.

In June his friend and publisher, Auguste Durand, died. This was a personal blow, but the son, Jacques, had known Saint-Saëns since childhood. Saint-Saëns 'inspired in me a certain fear when I was a child', he wrote. 'I discovered later that he had a heart of gold under his slightly gruff appearance.' Jacques was anxious to promote French music and organised concerts featuring a wide range of modern works at the Salle Gaveau.

In order to visit Germany, Saint-Saëns had, as he wrote to Caroline de Serres, to cross the huge stretch which separated the former frontier from the new one – 'it is impossible for me to love the German Empire'. This, despite a 'rapturous reception at Darmstadt'. He recommended Caroline to find a good quartet and attempt his youthful Quintet, 'but, Heavens, it is difficult!' Some piano compositions (MSS at Dieppe) were unpublished and he wrote some incidental music for *Poème Antique* by a relation of Caroline de Serres, which was given at a private matinée. He poured scorn upon the scheme of a M. Ecorcheville to invite composers to celebrate Haydn with pieces based upon the notes H–A–Y–D–N. (There was some whim floating around at the time for extending the letters used in the scale.) 'Never, very much never, have I seen the notes Y and N.' He asked Fauré to join him in his repudiation of the idea, to which several major composers acceded, 'a ridiculous enterprise which could make us the laughing stock of musical Germany'. His Three Extracts from *La Foi* were read through in October for Colonne. 'Mme Colonne offered me flowers, both embraced me, a touching scene with orchestral accompaniment.' Caroline de Serres had sent him a birthday gift. 'This plump chicken came to me exactly on the day. I have to give dinner to M. le Directeur du Conservatoire in person and his charming Secretary M. Bourgeat! And it is a marvellous chicken. As it comes from you it will be more marvellous still. The fingers are going to be licked right up to the

support of his friend René Thorel, who had initiated a campaign against pigeon shooting and the maiming of birds to assist the marksmen. 'Cruelty to animals is unworthy of a civilised society.'

shoulder ... At one o'clock I have a rehearsal with orchestra for *La Princesse Jaune*. Oh! I have no time to become bored. When will I get to Egypt to work in peace?' He finally succeeded in escaping there via Naples. From Cairo he made efforts to elicit a Légion d'honneur for Jules Loeb, now Professor of the Violincello at the Conservatoire and one of the creators of the Second Trio.[1]

At the end of 1909 La Trompette celebrated its fiftieth anniversary (1910). Casals and Suggia were both members of a cello quartet. The principal item in an outstanding programme nevertheless remained Saint-Saëns's Septet.

The year 1910 saw a resurgence of composition. For the opening of the Oceanographic Museum at Monte Carlo he wrote a Festival Overture. Once more, music was employed in the service of science. He was uncertain what to call the mixture of march, overture and symphonic poem. It certainly could not be *La Mer*, already associated with Debussy. 'In German, *Fest-Ouvertüre* would be good, *Ouverture de Fête* in French is senseless, *Ouverture Triomphale* would be too ambitious,' he told Durand.... '*Ouverture pour l'Inauguration du Musée Océanographique de Monaco* would be the correct title, but imagine putting that on a concert programme ... no one would be able to say *Ouverture Océanographique*.' He portrayed the beauty of the calm sea and the exploration of ocean depths, which brought marvels to light. There follows a picture of the sea in wrath and the subjection of nature by ever-resourceful mankind.

In memory of Mme Caruette of Dieppe he wrote a grand duet for violin and cello, with piano accompaniment. As later orchestrated, the work stands as one of the few contributions to the double concerto form. With its changes of mood and tempo it has the quality of an improvisation, an art which Saint-Saëns feared was under threat from German influences. 'This is the negation of eloquence. Consider what the senate, the pulpit and the courtroom would be like if nothing were heard but speeches learned by heart!' The title *La Muse et le Poète* was invented by Durand and Saint-Saëns objected to it. *The* (English) *Times*, which gave the piece a poor review, thought the idea had been inspired by de Musset's 'Nuit d'Octobre'. It would be just as likely that

---

[1] From Cairo he also joined in protests against the closure of the Salle des Concerts at the Conservatoire. 'Its disappearance would be criminal. As an acoustic it is too little for the great orchestral development of modern works – but it was a marvellous temple for chamber music.'

it depicted Mme Caruette and her blandishments, as the tetchy old composer alternately repulsed and accepted her plans for the statue.

The work was premièred in London in June by Ysaÿe and Hollmann. The occasion was the twenty-fifth anniversary of Saint-Saëns's own first concert in London and was devoted to his compositions. He played in his Piano Quartet, there were some songs and he was joined by Raoul Pugno for the two-piano Scherzo. The programme concluded with the Septet and covered his years of composing from *Le Timbre* to *La Muse*. During this London season he performed twelve of Mozart's piano concertos at the Bechstein Hall. *The Times* remarked that these were heard insufficiently and one discovered their remarkable individuality when they were given in sequence. In September he was at Aix-les-Bains for *Proserpine*. He told Caroline that his health was excellent and his legs recovered, but the work of rehearsing the opera, 'which I love so much and hear so rarely', was allowing too little time 'to look after my fingers in view of the Munich Festival, where I fear to shine "like an underpowered light bulb" '. He hoped that by mid-September he would have had time to train his fourth finger. In the spring of 1910 he arrived in Munich for the Festival of French Music. The organisers expressed their regret that they had not been able to find a choir sufficiently well-trained to perform the *Béatitudes* and *Rédemption* of Franck without adequate rehearsing. 'So much the better; things will be a little less boring,' was his rejoinder. He did, however, plead for at least the 'Pie Jesus' from the Fauré *Requiem* and shook the hand of Leo Sachs, the Secretary, most warmly when he heard that an overture by Dubois was in the third concert. A project to have three French symphonies in one programme (his own C minor, Franck's and d'Indy's) was abandoned. 'It would have been a sacrilege,' said Saint-Saëns. 'What would one say about a dinner which consisted of three roasts!'

Sachs commented upon the absence of piano sonatas from his pen and ventured to suggest that Beethoven was a difficult predecessor to follow. 'Too true,' said Saint-Saëns. 'That good man has killed off the sonata!'

In October *La Muse et le Poète* was given in Paris with the same soloists. Saint-Saëns wrote to Ysaÿe, 'You were marvellous, my great friend! You expressed the idea of my *Muse* as though you yourself were the author. And the "Rondo", which the whole world plays, you succeeded in playing better than all the world. What miracle made your tone more beautiful than it ever was before? That wonderful tone which had never been heard until then. I was not the only person who noticed it. It is a real happiness to have such interpreters. Your grateful and devoted Saint-Saëns.' He was equally generous to Messager, whose opera *Fortunio* was revived in November. He regretted that Messager, now a director of the Opéra, had spent so much time on administration. 'We would now have had a string of masterpieces – and there are so few. This clarity and wit, this charm, the distinction of the orchestration – what a difference from the fashionable hullabaloos! I would speak about it at length if I had the time to write long letters.'

It was natural that his visits to Egypt should re-awaken his strong interest in the Orient and some sort of wish to 'ride in triumph through Persepolis'. An idea that had remained dormant since 1898, to return to the myth of Hercules (a notion completely at variance with his recently expressed views on legend and history in opera) and transform *Déjanire* into a full lyric work, came to fruition. As Gallet had died, Saint-Saëns himself had to do much rewriting to turn the verse-drama into a libretto, but he included Gallet's name as co-librettist. His labours were stimulated by the offer of a production at Monte Carlo. Many pages were written by the Nile and after a visit to the tombs of the Kings and Aswan he returned to Cairo celebrating his journey down the river in verse:

> *Large et lourd, le beau Nil s'épand dans la clarté*
> *Sa puissance est égale à sa tranquillité*

The Seine must have heard his words and wished to emulate the Nile, for there were major floods in Paris, submerging the streets as far as the Gare St Lazare.

The première of *Déjanire* was given at Monte Carlo in March 1911 with Mme Litvinne in the principal role, but much of the critical commentary was reserved for its staging at the Paris Opéra in November. He spent part of April at Menton, from where he wrote to Caroline: 'My illness has one good aspect, that it does not give me pain and, as all the world believes I am travelling, I hear no news and enjoy a peace that I have not known for a long time.' His devoted servant Gabriel prepared tisanes and warmed milk for the invalid. 'He also brings me the papers, for I do not go out. I only go to take a seat by the edge of the sea. There is only one road to cross.' With his binoculars he watched vessels passing on the horizon. 'One would not say these are riotous pleasures. Very rarely I tinkle away at the piano in order not to lose the habit.'[1]

Guilmant had died in March. Widor had set his heart upon Vierne as successor as Professor of Organ, and Vierne, at Notre-Dame, was of sufficient stature. Fauré wanted Gigout, his old friend from the Ecole Niedermeyer. When he heard that Widor had been criticising him to mutual friends he enlisted the help of Saint-Saëns to persuade a reluctant Gigout to stand, as a gesture of retaliation.

Still convalescent in Paris, Saint-Saëns broke his own rule not to interfere in the affairs of the Conservatoire to press the claims of Gigout. 'He has the most admirable technique, but more than that he is a marvellous improvisor and, with him, one would be sure not to see it collapse, the fine art of improvisation, so French and in my opinion so necessary.' Fauré was able to tell him that Gigout had been nominated after 'quite a battle'. Saint-Saëns more than once told friends that, if they wished to hear the finest improvisations in Paris, they should visit St Augustin to hear Gigout. Some years later he told Gigout that he had been at St Clothilde and had heard a most marvellous 'Tantum Ergo'. When he discovered that it was by Gigout, his old pupil, he had, as he said, 'burst with jealousy'.

Colonne had died in March. *La Nuit*, the choral piece for female voices and soprano soloist dedicated to one of Saint-Saëns's most stalwart champions, was given at the Société des Concerts. He spent some of his time sorting out his papers, 'a mountain of old archives', and wrote to Lecocq that he had 'rediscovered the masterpieces of my youth, one of which was written at the *age of four*. These masterpieces are modest, as you might believe.'

His illness did not incline him towards religion. In his correspondence with Dr Felix Regnault the questioning of faith continued. He believed that so-called 'religious feeling' would disappear because 'it always takes the form of the love of God *made Man* or of the Holy Virgin. Everyone will know, inevitably, some day that there has never been God made Man nor a Virgin, Mother of God.' He believed that the improvisation of an Introit should establish a mood of devotion and his dismissal of religion was not done in a jeering spirit. In a letter

---

[1] He added, 'I would have preferred to enjoy Naples, drinking to the health of the volcano in the wine of Syracuse ... while nibbling fresh fruit.'

of June 1911 he admitted to Dr Regnault certain odd superstitions. 'An uncle of my great-aunt Masson had a servant who – in her sleep – indicated where one would find lost objects and perceived what people she knew were doing in their own surroundings. For me, for several years I have had the strange faculty of divining the arrival of visitors some moments before the doorbell indicated their presence and, over two years, no less strange, in playing dominoes to choose with a sure touch the domino I needed.' The ageing aesthete and dandy Robert de Montesquieu made efforts to win Saint-Saëns's friendship. There was some affinity in their addiction to young company and talent, for Montesquieu was the ardent patron of the pianist Léon Delafosse and the relationship served Proust as a model for that of Charlus and Morel. Yet Montesquieu's aim appears to have been to convert Saint-Saëns from rationalism. He called in a Father Mugnier, but the priest enjoyed his conversations with the composer too cheerfully to embark upon conversion.[1]

The year saw more prose writing. At its start he drew up for the *Courrier Musical* a conservative declaration against modern music under the title of 'Musical Anarchy', protesting against atonal systems and the abandoning of traditional rules of harmony. He produced a series of columns for the *Echo de Paris* on Sundays, which treated a range of topics in addition to music. He wrote of his many encounters with royalty, citing his meetings with Queens Victoria and Alexandra of Great Britain, Christina of Spain, Amelia of Portugal, Marguerite and Helen of Italy, and expressing particular affection for the Queen of the Belgians. He was drawn into a controversy by a group of French composers led by Xavier Leroux, who protested against the 'invasion' of French lyric theatres by Italian composers. In a letter to *Le Temps* Saint-Saëns observed that Puccini was the only Italian composer who posed any kind of threat,[2] whereas eight works of Wagner were in

[1] Many attempts were made to reconvert Saint-Saëns. In 1914 he wrote to an Abbé, 'The death of my sons did not destroy my faith, lost earlier. They might even have restored it, but that was impossible.' A young priest who hoped to begin a correspondence received the peremptory reply: 'I am not a virtual disbeliever. I am an *utter* disbeliever. . . .' In 1920 he told a correspondent: 'I hope I have rid myself of ideas of the future and eternity, and I await with the greatest calm the moment when I will rest for ever from my laborious life.'

[2] From Cairo in February 1910 he admitted having taken pleasure from *Tosca* and *Fedora* (Umberto Giordano) 'when they were new, before singers had added their traditions'.

the repertoire of the Opéra and *Salome* had just been added. A provincial Director was unable to promise him any productions as resources were being lavished upon *The Mastersingers* and *Hansel and Gretel*. His opposition to Wagner and the Wagnerians did not eclipse his admiration for the old Germany, however. For the *Courrier Musical* he wrote on Schumann's Variations and acknowledged that his own style owed a great deal to him. 'Never have I been able to forget the profound impression that the Lieder of Schumann first produced on me when I came to know them through the baritone [Julius] Stockhausen. It was, I believe, the cycle *Dichterliebe* and it was for me the revelation of a new world. Soon I was in possession of the piano works ... I was probably the first French pianist who gave them in Paris, in spite of the unconcealed opposition of the listeners.' After dealing with Schumann's habit of separating the rhythm from the bar-line structure he praised the composer's 'colour, life and penetrating charm, qualities that I have sought in vain, alas, in composers of instrumental music who have succeeded him'. This last comment was no doubt a judgement on Brahms, the musician on whom Saint-Saëns and G. B. Shaw were in agreement.

His essay on Chopin caused him to recall his lessons with Stamaty.

I never heard Chopin and I am inconsolable about this, for I could have heard him and it was my piano teacher ... who prevented it and threatened to dismiss me from his house if he learnt that I had heard the great artist. It was not at all that at ten years I was what one would call an infant prodigy; I was an artist and a very undocile pupil when the master's demands did not fit in with my own feelings – and that happened only too often, for Stamaty constantly demanded nuances, the 'molto espressivo' of which I have kept traces ... As a result – appalling scenes: I had no musical feeling ... Time was wasted in giving me lessons ... If it had been possible he would have discouraged me.

Then, fearing he had been rather harsh, he added, 'There were, however, good things, even excellent, in his teaching. ...' It is odd to think of Stamaty demanding nuances and at the same time forbidding the boy to listen to Chopin, though it reinforces the modern view that Chopin did not perform with the expressive abandon of many interpreters. Saint-Saëns had been initiated into Chopin's style by

Pauline Viardot and the Vicomtesse de Grandval. He referred to such features as 'the simplicity without affectation, the maintaining of the beat in the accompaniment of "rubato", the limited employment of the pedal ... the trill launched by the higher note'.[1] There are many nostalgic traces of Chopin in his own concerto slow movements and in the salon waltzes, and something enigmatic in his final summary that the '*odor di femina*' invaded everything written by his idol. In his own musical framework his Chopinesque moments are framed by the protective masculinity of Beethoven or Liszt.

He defended his role in setting French poetry to music. 'I have heard it said that Duparc and Fauré were the first in France to take as texts for Lieder the verses of the "great poets". Now these two gentlemen were my disciples and I have shown the way to them by taking as texts the poems of Victor Hugo, which passed at that time as intractable to musical setting. Before me, Gounod with Musset, Niedermeyer with Lamartine, had already traced the route.' He wrote with heat against a suggestion that he had said Haydn's pictorial sketches were light and faint. 'The Storm of *The Seasons*, the Hunt, the Vendanges. Little pictures! These are great canvases brushed with large strokes by a master-painter, overflowing with life and colour, and there is nothing greater than the last chapters of this marvellous poem. Every composer should study "The Seasons".'

His autumn programme gave little indication of recent ill health. *Proserpine* was revived at the Trianon-Lyrique Theatre and *Déjanire* had its Paris première at the Opéra. A letter to Caroline reported also on a visit to Heidelberg for a festival in honour of Liszt at which both he and Risler performed.

Ma chère Caro,

When will I be able to see you? I don't know. In rehearsals at the same time at the Trianon-Lyrique and the Opéra with a bundle of things all around. I have not been able to put my hands on a piano for two days although it is necessary for me to do two hours' work daily with the prospect of playing on Sunday week my Fifth Concerto at Lille ... Yesterday we put on the stage the first act of

---

[1] The Allegro Appassionato of 1884, piano solo, with orchestration added later, links the styles of Chopin and Fauré in a remarkable way, despite the passages of technical difficulty intended for a Conservatoire test-piece. The message for students was not purely one of finger-work.

Déjanire. Everyone is wildly enthusiastic and all went like clock-work, no friction, no bad tempers. . . . I am happy to see this work in its true setting. Today I am going to work on *Proserpine* at the Trianon. You will see tomorrow in the *Echo* the account of the Festival of Heidelberg,[1] of the astonishingly cordial welcome I found – Richard Strauss was assiduous in his attentions. Behold me back again in the Society founded by Liszt with the title 'Member of Honour' . . . It is a complete linking. . . . In spite of this crazy life I am getting along well at the moment. Let's hope that it lasts for I have not the time to be ill. It is different from having time and wasting it. There are, however, new remedies for migraine. You must try them. I embrace you.

While he was in Paris he lived in the rue de Courcelles. In June he wrote to Bellaigue to correct a recent comment. 'Permit me to say that it was not at five years but at eighteen years that I was accused by Gounod, so delightfully, of "lacking inexperience".[2] At five years, you must believe me, I had something still to learn . . .'

In July came the 'Agadir' incident when Germany despatched a gunboat to Morocco to place a curb on the ambitions of the French. Debussy and Fauré both refused to attend the French Festival in Munich. Saint-Saëns did attend and, in a gesture of friendship, joined with Richard Strauss in an informal concert where he played his *Valse Mignonne* and Strauss his waltzes from *Der Rosenkavalier*. As early as 1890 in his *Rimes Familières* Saint-Saëns had pondered the possibility of colonial rivalry leading to European conflict. Yet he was in certain ways an 'official' composer and was in a position to be obliged to give expression to patriotic moods, sometimes deliberately fostered to obscure class conflicts. *La Gloire* was a cantata produced in 1911 to words by Augé de Lassus in a musically confident style. It spoke of the laurels adorning the 'hecatombs' of the dead, a reference to the war of 1870, but an unhappy premonition of the one to come.[3]

[1] Saint-Saëns and Risler played pieces by Liszt at this festival. Risler's life had had parallels with his companion's. He lost a wife and daughter in swift succession. Like Saint-Saëns, he became a ceaseless traveller, but his playing lost its lustre.

[2] Still confused with Berlioz. See pages 42 and 122.

[3] *La Gloire* must have been a response to the spread of anti-militarism in working-class circles, a message preached by Jaurès at the Socialist Congress, Stuttgart, in 1907, an alarming prospect in view of worsening international relations.

His hymn *To Aviators* with words by his secretary Jean Bonnerot was, however, inspired purely by admiration for science.[1] Hymns to the miners and workers which followed were not so disinterested. Just as the barcarolles and pavanes of the late nineteenth century had been partly intended to lend glamour to an aristocratic and hence stratified society, thought was now given to casting an aura of nobility over 'labour' to divert attention from the gulf which lay between different class expectations. The *Hymn to the Miners*, dedicated to a choir in Roubaix ('Strike the hammer without pause against the black coal'), urges the miners to sing to the rhythm of their blows, to regard the pick-axe as a sceptre and to encourage the young to follow them into manual labour ('Let the son of a miner be a miner also'). When, as at Courrières in 1906, an explosion brings heavy casualties they must regard themselves as martyrs in man's struggle against nature. There was no one who knew unremitting toil more than Saint-Saëns, but clearly here he identifies himself with a bourgeois class, which wished to guard the gains it had made and had no desire to distribute them more widely.

Messager conducted the première of *Déjanire* at the Opéra on 22 November. The décor by several designers used ideas derived from the excavations at Mycenae. Saint-Saëns attended nervously, fearing some disaster – forbidden by his doctor to go outside, he had made the journey by underground passages. Fauré praised the opera in *Le Figaro* and the manner in which material from the old spectacle had been interwoven. 'The role of Iole in particular is drawn almost entirely from music of the scene which characterised her when the role was declaimed. The majority of the choruses, so firm and vigorous in design, have remained intact ... But Saint-Saëns has rebuilt with suppleness, art and a style so suitable the most recent pages with the former ones, that only the bold impression the latter made at Béziers thirteen years ago enables one to disentangle them from the variety of effects.' As for the theme from *La Jeunesse d'Hercule*: 'The recent years have not lessened the noble and vigorous character ... it has, on the contrary, come to its full and magnificent flowering in the present *Déjanire*. ...' Having praised the dignity of tone, aptness of expression and interest of orchestration, Fauré concluded, 'There is not a

---

[1] This chorus was commissioned as a test-piece for the highest category of choirs at an International Festival in Paris.

musician in France or elsewhere whose works are able to the same degree as his to be offered as shining examples.'

Adolphe Boschot was similarly enthusiastic about his colleague in the *Echo de Paris* and did not find the opera antiquated. 'Nothing of the modern soul is foreign to Saint-Saëns. Every curiosity, every desire for novelty or rarity, every form of intellectual activity (even archaeology and astronomy) have found in him a sympathetic welcome. These distractions . . . have never caused him to forget that he is above all a poet, a creator in the world of sound. But they have infused in him an admirable facility for renewal. This many-sided and abundant enthusiasm, comparable to that of Goethe, or a master of the sixteenth century, has conserved in him the fire of youth, ceaselessly rekindled.' To a generation confronted with *Electra* and the huge orchestras of the post-Wagnerians, Boschot praised the balance of forces that Saint-Saëns maintained. 'A drama in which one takes an interest in the characters and wishes to hear their words ought not to be drowned in the orchestral mass . . . If he confides to the voice the most important and necessary melodic designs, he takes care to give it orchestral support, the atmosphere of which states or suggests what the voice is unable to say.' The composer had, of course, been able to elaborate the choruses much more freely than those written for the amateurs of Béziers. In the final act he took a text from Greek literature for an 'Epithalamium' and wrote the music in a Greek mode. His own opinion was that *Déjanire* was a new work and the old was just an embryo.

By December he was back in Algeria and had moved from the heat of Blidah to the fresher climate at a thermal station, Hamman R'Ihra. 'Tomorrow the bath treatment begins,' he wrote to Emile Renaud. 'I hope it will soon allow me to take a walk in the woods.' A few days later he reported that he had walked four kilometres. During his time in Algiers *L'Ancêtre* was given at the Opéra there. He showed a strong interest in the work of a young composer, Henri Fevrier, whose *Monna Vanna* was being produced at the same time. He attended the rehearsals and the première, and exhorted Fevrier not to surrender to fashion.

Despite his lack of religious beliefs he continued to do battle with the 'Motu Proprio', almost as if he wished to fill the pews with worshippers. He repeated his opinion that, as there was no under-standing of how plainchant had been performed originally, all versions were arbitrary. If all motives redolent of the theatre were to be excluded, the 'beautiful prelude to the Church Scene in *Faust*' would go; if solo lines were to be excluded, so would the 'exquisite' 'Pie Jesus' from Fauré's *Requiem*. In support of musical instruments he cited the muffled drums and cymbals from Gounod's *St Cecilia* Mass and the gong used in a Mass by Liszt. A piano might be thought out of place in a church, but could be an excellent substitute for the harp.[1]

Massenet died in August. The rivalry of the two composers was well known and Saint-Saëns was too honest to deny it. 'Some have spoken of the friendship that united us. My friends were Bizet, Guiraud, Delibes – they were brothers in arms. Massenet was a rival.' In his article, however, he ascribed many virtues and refuted criticisms of Massenet's 'lack of depth', though there may have been a faint air of malice in devoting space to such a theme. 'The Greek artists whose work fills us with admiration were not "deep". Their marble goddesses were beautiful. Beauty alone was enough for them. . . . The rose with its fresh colours and scent is in its own way as precious as the haughty giant oak.' He turned aside to deal with modern music. 'Happiness is disapproved of in the music of our time. Haydn and Mozart are to be reproached with it. We modestly turn away our faces at that giant explosion of joy which ends the Ninth Symphony . . . Long live sadness! Long live boredom!' Then, with a thought for his own reputation, he praised the sheer quantity of Massenet's output, adding that the artist who produced little might be interesting, but could never be defined as great. He joined a committee which considered plans for a statue to the composer of *Manon*, but the coming war held up its consultations.

There was now a vacancy in the Institut. The musicians, among whom Saint-Saëns was the senior figure, refused to recognise the claims of Gustave Charpentier, but the painters and sculptors forced his election through acclamation. Charpentier was, like Saint-Saëns, from comparatively humble origins, but his early life-style had been proletarian and he had taken a lead in the unionisation and the strikes of musicians. 'It is the Revolution which has entered the Institut,'

[1] He remained certain, however, that music in church should atmospherically enhance reverence and thought the 'theatrical efforts' in Beethoven's Mass in D too secular for church performance. 'One is no longer in the church, one does not know where one is.'

exclaimed Saint-Saëns and he refused to attend for many months. It was a further instance of old-age prejudices obliterating earlier kindnesses, for Charpentier's student work *Impressions d'Italie* had been bought by a publisher for the large sum of 1500 francs because of the very enthusiastic report Saint-Saëns had given to the young man's Envoi from Rome.[1] When the score of *Louise* was published Saint-Saëns studied it carefully and wrote of it to the composer with genuine warmth. Charpentier's *Sous les Cimes* had contained a section dedicated to Saint-Saëns and some saw reproduced there the Master's cunning modulations (e.g. the D-minor to C-major episode in the 'Bacchanale').

After the Institut election there was an amusing incident when Charpentier was given the only free table in a restaurant in Nice, which forced him to have Saint-Saëns as a neighbour. The old man's companion was anxious to make conversation, but Saint-Saëns plunged deeply into 'his copious bouillabaisse' and kept a grim silence. *Louise*, as well as its sympathy with the Parisian poor, had a feminist theme and there was some strong though ill-informed indignation in 1912 when Lili Boulanger, younger sister of Nadia, was unsuccessful in the Prix de Rome. On this occasion the contestants were immured at Compiègne. The jury contained Saint-Saëns, Widor, Dubois and Paladilhe, but it was said to have been Saint-Saëns who insisted that the subject of the cantata be kept completely secret beforehand. The jury were very severe on contestants in the preliminary round and found only four, (less than the permitted number), worthy of going forward. Lili Boulanger was forced to retire through that same ill health which brought about her early death, but there was a feeling that the misogyny of the judges was responsible for her failure. Two women, however, inspired Saint-Saëns to composition in this otherwise silent year. Caroline de Serres lost the use of her right arm in an accident. Saint-Saëns ingeniously composed his Six Studies for the Left Hand and went so far in friendship as to do for her all the necessary fingering. This Opus 135 is one of his most delightful compositions and the Studies form a suite with a Bourrée, Gigue and Moto Perpetuo included. In all sections the absence of a right hand is concealed and the music employs the length of the keyboard with

[1] As distinct from the reactions of Ambroise Thomas, who, when Charpentier's Envoi, *Vie de Poète* was played, marched out of his box, slamming the door loudly.

dexterity. There was even a Fughetto; to write a fugue for a single hand might seem an impossibility, but Saint-Saëns's wizardry succeeds. In a letter to Caroline of November 1912 he expressed his concern that she had, in addition to her injury, caught a cold at a very bad performance of *Déjanire*. 'Two-thirds of the score too slow and it was glacial and deadly boring.' He was at Marseilles for a production of *Proserpine*. 'The artists are perfect, full of talent and good intentions. We work every day and I bang away on the piano some three hours, ending up with sore fingers of which I am ashamed. I hope very much that you are better and you have recommended "tormenting the ivory" as Berlioz used to say.'

He mentioned the Studies but had had little time to work on them. He was correcting proofs for the collection of his essays, which were soon to be published under the title *Ecole Buissonnière*. He also mentioned to Caroline his admiration for the royal family of Belgium. For Queen Elizabeth, a violinist, he had composed a Tryptique for Violin and Piano. One 'Congolaise' movement took him across the Sahara to the Belgian Empire in mid-Africa, which was certainly, musically speaking, uncharted territory. A movement in 5:4 time was a tribute to the Queen's professionalism. The Belgian King and Queen were his special royal favourites and their photographs had pride of place on his piano. He would extol their combination of culture and intelligence at length and when he had an invitation from them to play it was noted that he would practise more assiduously than ever several days before. It was from Brussels that there came a wish that *Le Timbre d'Argent* might be revived in its once short-lived grand operatic form as that version had reappeared among his papers. On 1 April 1913 he told Renaud that he was off to attend *Proserpine* in Brussels 'and that was not an April Fool'. He wrote to Caroline to say he was working on the fingerings of the Studies, 'which will assist you in practice. I have scarcely any time to touch *my* piano; just sufficient to prevent my fingers from becoming rusty.' He concluded on this occasion: 'I went yesterday to see *The Girl of the Golden West*. I left after the first act.'

Major composition resumed with an oratorio, *The Promised Land*, for the Three Choirs Festival, which, in 1913, was to be held in Gloucester. English words had been adapted from the Bible by Hermann Klein. It was the first French work commissioned by the Festival for 180 years. He had sketched it out in Cairo at the same time as he was completing the Six Studies, and he continued with it in

Paris, Algeria and Cairo once again. 'I am much too busy to become old. There is simply no end to my interminable career,' he told Henderson, a Scottish critic and his future biographer, who complimented him on his magnificent performance of the E-minor Prelude and Fugue from Opus 99 at the Salle Gaveau. In May 1913 he wrote to Caroline after a day of practice at the piano: 'My agility has come back completely but that *evenness* of which I was so proud is no longer as beautiful as in the past and I have to pay more attention to it,' adding, 'How lucky are those who never play well in public for, as the years go by, they only play less well and nobody notices.' He endeavoured to practise for two hours a day until the last day of his life. One feature of his piano music which gave him great pleasure was the revival by Marguerite Long of the Third Piano Concerto, which, she claimed, had not been heard for thirty years. She worked at it with Saint-Saëns accompanying her on a second piano. 'His problem was that he tended to play too fast! Rehearsing the Concerto with him was a wild chase.' She tried to follow him, then had to stop. 'Master, I cannot keep up with you.' He would candidly reply, 'Oh! I may have rushed a bit. No?!' He was grateful for her love of this neglected concerto and wrote: 'I could never thank you enough for devoting yourself to this extremely difficult work. You give me one of those extreme pleasures that are too infrequent in the life of an artist and console for many an unhappiness.'

During the early months of 1913 it was not his own *Promised Land* which preoccupied him so much as Fauré's opera *Pénélope*, which had its first performance in Monaco in March. Burdened with his Conservatoire duties, Fauré had taken five years to complete this major work and even at the end the production had to be hastily mounted. Saint-Saëns darkly suspected that *Pénélope* was a victim of Gunsbourg's vanity, as the latter had somehow written an opera, *Venise*, orchestrated by his long-suffering conductor Léon Jéhin which swallowed resources in the same season. *Pénélope* was dedicated to Saint-Saëns, but disappointed him. He was dismayed that Fauré discarded the tradition of arias and ensembles in favour of recitative and complete modernism in the musical language – the features of *Pelléas* rather than his own stage work. Lecocq received his complaints. 'Travelling through all the keys without stopping, one experiences an unspeakable fatigue. Just as Grétry would have given a "louis" to hear a "chanterelle" [an oratorio of Méhul had dispensed with violins], so would I give two just to be able to rest on the tonic! I greatly regret that Fauré did not write an opera twelve years ago when he composed *Prometheus*. There was a masterpiece.'

His immediate reactions to Fauré were more guarded. He blamed the acoustics of the hall for some noisy brass and failure to hear the words. He thought the version unclassical and disliked the cavortings of Penelope's suitors with the female servants. He spilled much ink on the minor matter of whether the librettist knew the difference between tightening and drawing a bow, which must have tested Fauré's patience after his long struggle to complete the work. He praised the music for the dances and admitted that no piano version gave an adequate impression of the score, but told Lecocq that he had to make 'superhuman efforts' to understand the conception and of his disquiet at students of the Conservatoire seeing the Director 'constantly breaking the rules he teaches them'. The point had already been made in his *Ecole Buissonnière*, published at the start of the year: 'For me, music is an art which has its laws, its grammar and syntax, things that do not receive attention where there is only a desire to create atmospheres and ambiances.' The phrase reminds us of how much of Saint-Saëns's music is in effect conversational both in its improvisations and its unwillingness to impose. To him, music, like talk, had to be in a language that all participants could understand. And although his ever curious mind leapt forward with interests in science and its achievements, his heart remained, not unnaturally for a seventy-seven-year-old, firmly in the past. Even in his polyphonic *Hymn to Work* the emphasis was on the scythe, the spade and the anvil, as though the conditions of the factory workers of 1912–13 resembled the 'joy from morn to eve' of merry peasants of the past.

In May he attended a festival at Vevey where Paderewski played his Fourth Concerto and they both joined in his Polonaise for Two Pianos. 'This combination . . . attracted such an extraordinarily large audience we didn't know where to put them.' At the same festival he played the organ part in his Third Symphony. In July, feminist harmonics again resounded in the Prix de Rome. The jury was much the same as in 1912, although Charpentier and one or two other new names were included. Saint-Saëns was the senior figure, however, and we may gauge an impression of how he was regarded from remarks of Emile Vuillermoz in *Musica*: 'The misogyny of the jury was known. The entry of an Eve into the earthly paradise of the Villa Medici was dreaded by certain patriarchs as the equal of total catastrophe.' Although Marcel Dupré was first in the preliminary round, Lili Boulanger gained five out of eight votes in the Music Section and an overwhelming vote from the full Academy where Saint-Saëns had a reduced role. The controversy does not seem to have prevented him from writing a *Valse Gaie*, which Servières considered the most interesting of all his salon waltzes for the variety of ideas and the elegance of the decorative passages.

A traveller without family, he made some efforts in his later years to establish links with a circle of relatives. In July he wrote to Renaud to say he was taking a week off to see a cousin, Valentine, at Béziers whom he had not met for two years.[1]

He was also working on an Overture in G 'to an Unfinished Comedy'. This was a piece begun when he was nineteen, which had presumably surfaced during his sorting of papers, and it was performed on 2 June at the Queen's Hall, London, prior to the Three Choirs Festival at Gloucester. There was some mystery about the announce-ment of a seventy-fifth anniversary, but it was explained that this celebrated the mastery of his first Piano Manual at two and a half![2] As the political skies darkened it seems that no opportunity was lost to emphasise the mutual regard between the English and the French. Queen Alexandra was patron of the Saint-Saëns Festival and Sir Alexander Mackenzie, a prominent figure in English musical life, spoke of 'the delightful qualities of his music, a combination of grace, wit and learning ... his popularity is nowhere stronger than in England'. Saint-Saëns's own part in the concert was amazing for his age: the Scherzo from the Second Concerto and the Finale from the Fifth, together with *Africa* and a Mozart concerto. Beecham con-ducted the C-minor Symphony, ringing applause greeted the com-poser at every appearance and he was presented with a tribute signed by every leading British musician (in which, somehow, Winston Churchill was included!). 'With progress for your watchword and with unique versatility, you led the advance of French music in every

[1] Mme Valentine Nussy-Verdié was the granddaughter of a Mme Lesuerre, sister of Mme Clémence Saint-Saëns, hence unconnected with the several Dieppe relatives.

[2] The overture was given in Paris at the Colonne concerts in October where it received a thrashing from Octave Séré, who thought it 'empty and dry. ... May it please the gods that M. Saint-Saëns, or those who rummage about in his fading papers, are not reserving similar surprises for us.'

branch,' declared Sir Alexander, 'and you are justly acknowledged today to be its most gifted and exalted representative.'[1]

He attended Covent Garden to see Kirkby Lunn once again as
Delilah and, when he came on stage after the second act to
acknowledge tumultuous applause, he was given a huge emblem of
laurel leaves bound in red, white and blue ribbons, the colours of both
nations.

At the Gloucester Festival on the third morning, traditionally
reserved for new works, three were heard: *The Promised Land*, Parry's
Te Deum, and Stanford's *Ye Holy Angels Bright*.[2] As *The Times* pointed
out, all three composers were well past middle age and the current
dearth of younger people called for action. Saint-Saëns gave a concert
on the evening before. 'Everyone in Gloucester rightly felt that he was
doing very great honour to the Festival by undertaking all the fatigue
which the production of a new work entails,' said *The Times*. 'More
than that he gave the keenest delight by his exquisite playing of
Mozart at the Concert . . . so that personal admiration for him both as
a man and an artist has been raised to a very high pitch.'

The text of Saint-Saëns's piece related the sufferings of the
Israelites who had come out of Egypt, the miracle of the water
springing from the rock, the admonitions to Moses and Aaron, and the
death of Moses within sight of the Promised Land, 'buried in a valley
in the land of Moab; but no man knoweth his sepulchre unto this day'.
Saint-Saëns, as we know, had been fascinated by Old Testament
figures since childhood and was a great admirer of the British tradition
of oratorio. He had some hopes that he might hear *The Promised Land*
at the Albert Hall, sung by choruses of the massive size which he had
heard in Gounod's *Mors et Vita*. The death of Massenet may have
brought to mind his version of *La Terre Promise*, which, though
written at the height of his fame, had sunk into oblivion. The war
prevented Saint-Saëns's oratorio from gaining a place in the repertoire
of choral societies.

Despite the colourful scoring, as in the rush of water from the rock,

[1] Although he affected not to understand English, one of his jokes was to
sign letters in French 'Your Obedient Servant'. On this visit he entertained
his English friends with imitations of the imposing Cosima Wagner receiving
at Bayreuth, and showed a talent for giving impressions of musical
instruments when discussing leitmotifs from *The Ring*.
[2] The genial Parry warned Saint-Saëns that he should not expect ecstatic
applause in an English cathedral setting.

the melodic strengths and the skills in choral writing with great double choruses etc., the work could not by its very theme provide the spiritual uplift which was so strong a characteristic of the British choral tradition. God, like the God of *Le Déluge* and like the composer himself, trembles on the edge of moods of impetuous rage. The special sin of Moses was to smite the rock rather than speak to it as the Lord had commanded. The disparity between so venial an offence and exclusion from the Promised Land which punishes the great leader diminishes spiritual elevation. *The Times* found fault with the double chorus 'The man Moses was very meek', pointing out that Moses was anything but meek. When the work was given by the Royal Choral Society in London in November the paper returned to the subject, dwelling upon discrepancies in the Old Testament and the poverty of real incident in the libretto, and adding: 'The importations from other books, Job and the Psalms, contribute what is certainly not drama. In one passage where the librettist departs from the actual text he writes what is certainly not grammar. The title is a curious misnomer, for the Promised Land is not granted but denied as far as the story of the oratorio is concerned.'

By autumn, Saint-Saëns was in Berlin for the hundredth performance of *Samson*. At home he had been given the Grand Cross of the Legion of Honour[1] and from Berlin he wrote to Arthur Dandelot concerning plans for an intended Final and Farewell Concert in Paris. It was to be given in the Salle Gaveau in support of a military charity with which his old childhood friend, René Thorel, was associated.

> Here are the main outlines of my programme. I will play on the piano my Quintet and a concerto of Mozart; on the organ one of my Breton Rhapsodies at the start to give late-comers a chance to arrive and the Grande Fantasie of Liszt on the Chorale of *The Prophet*. That lasts forty minutes and it will be the second half of the programme. M. Diaz Albertini will play my *Havanaise*, Mlle Anckier pieces for the lute from the sixteenth century, which I have arranged for the harp. These two will play together my Duet for Violin and Harp. It will be necessary to price the places at 20 fr, 10 fr and 5 fr.

Although he hardly ever courted press publicity he asked Dandelot to

[1] According to Hahn, this could only be done after Massenet's death.

announce the concert 'in aid of the patriotic work of the Maison du Soldat. Fifteen affiches with my name in very large letters. Later you will announce what I will play.' There was some trouble over the soloists. 'How can I give you a definite programme when I do not know if I have a violinist?' The choice fell eventually upon Jules Boucherit, who had once come *ex aequo* in competition with Thibaud and was the teacher of Ginette Neveu. He played the *Rondo Capriccioso* with Saint-Saëns at the piano. Another change was the substitution of the *Marche Religieuse* to accommodate the late-comers. A newspaper report that he would be playing the Liszt *Ad nos* for organ *and orchestra* produced another letter to the impresario: 'Where in the devil did you discover that the Liszt Fantaisie was with orchestra? ... I hope you will correct this mistake.' The Quintet was to be accompanied by the whole String Section, conducted by Pierre Monteux.

The concert was under-advertised but the hall was full and there were crowds in the corridors and on the staircases. The composer made his usual curt entry and marched to the organ to begin. After Liszt's colossal organ piece had ended three hours of multi-faceted labour, he still found the energy to give a second concert at a supper party for organisers and friends. Guests shouted out little-known works by Chopin and Liszt, testing his memory to its limits, but always with a response. With his streak of music-hall humour he imitated Mozart's trick of playing central notes with his nose while his hands moved at the extremities of the keyboard. The impromptu recital lasted until the early morning, after which he left again for the South. Francis Planté had been unable to attend the concert because of ill health. His letter to Dandelot shows the awe and regard in which Saint-Saëns was held by fellow musicians. 'What happy news you give me. Our great Saint-Saëns having the extremely noble idea of dedicating his concert and huge virtuosity on the piano to the creation, so patriotic and French, of the "Cercle National" for the Paris Soldier. ... To applaud alternately ... our illustrious French Master ... as pianist and organist is a rare and marvellous stroke of good fortune for our Parisian public. It is at the same time an unforgettable festival of art ... All Paris will be there.'

Caroline de Serres died early in 1914. 'You must know that your mother was one of the great affections of my life. During the little time which remains to me in this life I will not cease to regret her, to think of her and revive in my memory so many wonderful discussions and manifestations of a talent she preserved in all its brilliance to the day she took to her bed never to leave it.' The production of *Le Timbre d'Argent* in Brussels revived his spirits, for he had always had a fondness for this troublesome work. He was helped by Pierre Barbier, son of the original librettist, who rewrote much of the prose dialogue in verse for musical setting. The production was delayed owing to difficulties in mounting *Parsifal*, but it proved successful. The health of his devoted manservant Gabriel was causing concern. 'I will have with me here a boy who has looked after me in Algeria and Egypt,' he told Renaud. 'He came to Brussels and has been able to attend the revival of *Le Timbre*, which sounds well in its new form.' In late February and early March there were two unusual concerts at The Hague and Amsterdam in which the first halves were given to Saint-Saëns and the second to Debussy. He still had hopes that the Paris Opéra would re-stage *Henry VIII* and made a gift of the score to its library. The three volumes were written in his neatest hand and comprised 1130 pages, the last dated December 1882.

In March he attended the première of Messager's opera *Béatrice* at Monte Carlo, the only famous musician present. He returned there for the twenty-fifth anniversary of Prince Albert's coronation and conducted the second act of *Samson* as part of the festivities. He told Renaud that he had kept himself going on the journey from Dijon with a huge slab of gingerbread. He was obliged to sit through a pageant of historical costumes given in honour of the Prince and wait upon news of a possible performance of *Les Barbares*. Gabriel was now extremely ill and an operation was required. 'It is I who am frightfully depressed by all these exertions and have not had the courage to come and see you,' he told Renaud, who was staying at Nice. 'Please excuse me. I will . . . come and see you tomorrow.'

Les Barbares had been given at Dijon and there had been a grand concert at which a sonnet had been declaimed in his honour. He was 'inspired from Heaven' – a Samson who had not overthrown the pillars of harmony but made a temple to French art . . . 'the shade of the great Rameau takes the emblem from his crown and puts it on your immortal brow'. (A few weeks later Saint-Saëns himself burst into verse to celebrate Widor's appointment as Secretary of the Academy of Fine Arts, calling on Minerva the warrior to protect him.) The Festival inspired further studies of Rameau. At the home of the

Princesse de Polignac he gave a Rameau recital and conducted the Overture to *Zais*. He resumed work in the library of the Conservatoire and the Bibliothèque Nationale, revising *Zoroastre* for Maison Durand, and left his intensive work only to supervise rehearsals for *La Princesse Jaune* at the Opéra Comique.

As the debate on religious music had rekindled old interests he wrote some short anthems: an 'Ave Maria', a 'Tu es Petrus' and a little hymn to St Camille de Lelis for a monastic community. When the MS of this last was lost in a fire in a matter of weeks, he wrote out a second version, which, in turn, was destroyed by the German invasion. In the midst of study and composing he found the time to travel via Bordeaux to Lisbon for the production of *Proserpine* and during the five days of the voyage began setting verses which the poet Georges Ducquois had selected from his collection *La Cendre Rouge*. He wrote to Fauré: 'As I will write no more operas will you allow me to reply to your flattering dedication of *Pénélope* by offering you a collection of ten pieces for singer and piano ... It would give me great pleasure to see your glorious name on my collection. I dare not call it a collection of songs for it is something different, which I don't know how to define. They are for several tastes but not for all tastes.' They were pieces with simple titles such as 'Silence', 'Jour de Pluie', 'Amoroso' etc. and did not aim at any of the deep penetration of feeling or the invention of effects which characterised contemporary song-cycles.

Like many busy people, he stretched his energies even further by constantly repeating lists of his activities on paper. To Renaud he wrote in June:

I would have come to see you yesterday, but had to have the benefit of Sunday peace in order to work on the article for *Echo de Paris* – knowing that in days to come I will be in turmoil and work will be impossible. I am going to have to occupy myself with rehearsals for *La Princesse Jaune*, who at last is going to come before the footlights. You will be pleased to hear that *Phryné* at the Gaieté [performed in aid of a musicians' orphanage] has had an extraordinary success, so that the Director has decided to put on *Proserpine* in October, which prevents me from going to Vienna as I had promised.'

He had recently played with Diémer a Waltz for Two Pianos by Renaud and he reported that it had been much admired. 'Gabriel has good and bad moments. He is not too unwell at present, but faces his operation.' It was at this time that Chantavoine, future biographer, paid him an afternoon visit. Saint-Saëns had been invited to dine that evening with the President and was already in evening dress. He was engaged in practising Czerny's simplest exercises just in case he should be asked to play some short piece after the repast. By contrast one evening, feeling depressed by Gabriel's illness, he went to dine at a night-club called the Magic City where he found the almost nude female dancers heavy and uninspiring 'and they had the sulks!'

He returned to the Institut and was, as ever, a powerful voice in the competitions for the Prix de Rome. Henri Busser, organist at St Cloud, had recently given an excellent recital of some of his works and he made the rash Herodian promise: 'My dear Busser, Ask me what you would like and I will give it you.' Busser immediately pressed him to break his boycott of the Institut and support Marcel Dupré. Dupré himself gave a slightly different account. Saint-Saëns was not present when voting began and Dupré and Marc Delmas tied on the first ballot. Widor begged Saint-Saëns to leave his studies of Rameau and come to break the tie. He then told Dupré to call on the great composer 'to thank him for your prize. He wants to know you better.'

Having prepared and memorised an impressive greeting, I arrived at the Master's, very nervous, knowing that the great musician was not always agreeable [recalled Dupré]. He opened the door. 'What do you want?' 'Master, I have come to thank you for your kindness...' The fine greeting was allowed no time. 'Kindness nothing. I voted for you because you deserved it. I read about you in this morning's paper. Is it true you were a child prodigy?' I remained still. 'But why not admit it? So was I!' From that moment he was charming and interesting.... He kept me a long time talking about Dieppe, Rouen, the great organ of St Ouen, Cavaillé-Coll, for whom he had a deep admiration, then about technique and orchestration. I left in ecstasy.

We have a good description of Saint-Saëns at the moment when Europe was on the brink of war from Hermann Klein, who had been hoping to publish a collection of the composer's letters. Meetings in Paris having proved impossible, Klein agreed to break a journey to

Switzerland at Namur. 'I am going to Namur in July to play at a musical festival which the King and Queen of the Belgians are to attend,' came the composer's message. 'Be there at the Hôtel de la Citadelle on Wednesday, 29 July, and you will find me.' In fact he arrived a day later and, as the taxi climbed up to the Citadel of Namur, they spoke of the possibility of war. Klein said he did not believe it would happen. '*Moi non plus*,' said Saint-Saëns. 'I saw the King at Brussels this morning and he assured me he would be at Namur with the Queen during the week. I hope there is a good piano at the hotel or I shall have to find one in the town.'

'Later, after tea we went for a walk on the heights overlooking the Meuse. He gave vent to some not flattering remarks about Germany and her detested ruler. He was interested to hear that at Dinant that morning I had found people fearing the worst and, a bad sign, the 'Agent de Change' had refused to change a five-pound Bank of England note. 'What!' he exclaimed. 'Do they possibly imagine that the Germans will have the effrontery, the incredible wickedness, to invade Belgian territory? It would bring down all Europe on them. It would mean a World War – they cannot be so mad! You are off to Switzerland to enjoy your holiday. I am off to Aix-les-Bains to enjoy mine. Don't let us worry over this scare.

At dinner, while they were discussing the absence of advances in orchestration since Wagner, the proprietor of the hotel came to tell Klein that a message had just come from Brussels; the Belgian Army was being mobilised, the festival was cancelled, the King and Queen would not be leaving the capital. Klein was asked to tell Saint-Saëns as the proprietor was too upset, believing his hotel was doomed to destruction (as indeed turned out to be the case). The old man took the news better than expected. Shaking his fist he uttered one word: '*Canaille*'. He declared his intention of going on to Aix but, at the mercy of swift events, was soon back in Paris. 'The whole cortège of griefs and ruins that war brings is going to come about,' he wrote to Lecocq. 'One asks oneself whether it would not have been better to die young than to see so many evils and horrors.'

13

War Service at the Keyboard

Before the war had run many weeks he had made his own translation of the British national anthem, 'Sauve le Roi', and provided a piano accompaniment. It was widely circulated in French homes and ran through several editions. He abandoned his half-hearted decision to give up public recitals. He spent September at Houlgate near his friend Dr Regnault, who was in charge of a hospital and offered to care for Gabriel. He gave concerts for the wounded and on behalf of war charities. War, at first, did not diminish his fine tastes in food. He told Renaud that he was off to dine with friends who had just been given a 'fabulous' turkey and would teach his hosts the proper method of eating pineapple. 'The cutting into thin slices which is inflicted on us makes a wasted opportunity of a delicious fruit and was invented when pineapples cost 20f in order to supply the smallest possible amount.' He added that he had begun a 'great symphonic poem' for the San Francisco Exhibition. 'Who would have said that at my age I would be doing such things?'

The war had begun with the enthusiastic participation of the press and journals were replete with tales of German atrocities. In *Echo de Paris* he began a series of anti-German articles which his admirers found hard to justify. Messager lamented to Fauré: 'Poor Camille is becoming ridiculous with his need to engage in polemics and make foolish remarks.'[1]

Something has to be said in defence of these statements later published under the title: *Germanophilia*. On a personal level he was consumed with worry over the health of Gabriel and reported

---

[1] When his young protégé Max d'Olonne tried to reprove the Master, he received the disarming reply: 'One suffers by being as the Trojan Cassandra who sees clearly and is not able to open the eyes of others. . . . I hope you will continue to regard me as one of your best friends.'

deteriorations to Renaud with frequency. His affection for innocent Belgium derived not only from his personal devotion to its musical Queen, but the frequent gestures Brussels had made on behalf of works such as the *Timbre d'Argent*. He belonged to the age of Hugo and George Sand, when the 'Artist in Society' was believed to have a mission to pronounce on political and social matters, adding qualities of imagination to the popular debates. Furthermore, he put himself at some risk by an anti-German crusade. Widor, in a Paris restaurant frequented by members of the General Staff, overheard that Paris would not hold out for three days and would probably be plundered and burnt.

Read without the presupposition that it is a diatribe, *Germanophilia* is a lively piece of musical criticism in which there are reservations as well as percipience. It is studded with theatrical reminiscence and a wide range of witty observation. When condemning the sheer mass of writing devoted to Wagner he adds that he has just had yet one more 'enormous analysis' of *The Ring*.[1] He tells the public that its admiration for Goethe rests upon the transformation of the unexciting Gretchen into the Marguerite of the French *Faust*, whereas the 'masterpiece' of Goethe has sections 'impenetrable even to the Germans themselves' and 'ends mysteriously in the drying out of marsh-lands'. He recalls that, although some French conductors never failed to include Wagner in their programmes, the choice was a very limited one. 'It was always the Overture to *Tannhäuser*, the Prelude to *Tristan*, the 'Ride of the Valkyries'. He asserted that deep in the score of *The Ring* were embedded bars for instruments that Wagner had only imagined, though allowing that others might be substituted. When a statue to Bossuet had been planned and *Le Déluge* was to be given at the Trocadéro to raise funds, the concert was constantly postponed because of the time taken in rehearsing Wagner. When *Samson and Delilah* reached the Opéra the costs of *The Valkyrie* were so exorbitant that old statues of Indian Gods had had to be rescued from Massenet's *Roi de Lahore* and used in the scenery. He could not be accused of self-promotion in criticising Wagner, for he had always defended French composers who could be regarded as rivals.

He never attacked Wagner's musical creativity, but his analysis of the logical absurdities in *Parsifal* show him as brilliant in journalism as

[1] He observed on his travels that 'wherever there are Germans, even at the ends of the earth, there are committees raising funds for Bayreuth'.

in all else. Remarking on the 'audacious' talents of Richard Strauss and his descent into the purely massive compositions, he observes that works like *Ein Heldenleben* and the *Sinfonia Domestica* would never have been performed had they been signed with a French name. In the Recognition Scene of *Electra* three different keys are employed. 'One can derive the same sensation at the Fair at Neuilly with several orchestras playing within earshot.'

His opponents replied, often in colourful fashion. He was obliged to deny that he had cavorted in the dress of an Egyptian dancing girl, although his youthful appearances as a bearded Marguerite must have given rise to such stories. His basic premises that there is a link between a people and its music (as in Naples, Andalusia and the Arab world), that indigenous French genius had perpetually been thwarted by the idolisation of foreign examples and Wagnerism had become an industry fuelled by those who took refuge in misty sensationalism ('Schumann never thought of invading the rest of the world') contained some truth. Brahms, he thought, had been fortunate in his initial, B, which linked him luckily to Bach and Beethoven, but despite being a supreme exponent of 'indigestible Germanism' he was at least serious.[1] Now even Viennese operetta was conquering Paris, a genre in which the French had always been paramount.

In a simultaneous correspondence with Bellaigue he was at the same time exonerating his idol Beethoven from certain excesses of behaviour, while reminding his friend that he had celebrated the defeat of the French at Vittoria with a most mediocre composition, but added that the liberating soul of Beethoven was very different from the spirit which was to be found in the cult of German music as a national force. Saint-Saëns had clearly ignored Lecocq's observation (August 1885) that 'when musicians do not write on *ruled* paper what they set down remains insignificant'. But *Germanophilia* is not as crude a work as is often suggested. One can now see the First World War as Europe following, almost eerily, the rush towards self-immolation which climaxes so many Wagner operas. Saint-Saëns was at least consistent in returning German decorations to their homeland.

The editing work he did for Durand at this time – the sonatas of Mozart, the concertos of Beethoven, the rhapsodies of Liszt and

---

[1] Did Saint-Saëns know of and resent Brahms's *Triumphlied*, which set lurid texts from the Book of Revelation to celebrate the Fall of Paris in 1871, a work at least as triumphalist as Wagner's 'A Capitulation'?

various eighteenth-century violin works by French composers – show no anti-German bias. His setting of a poem, 'Vive la France', was sold on behalf of soldiers' charities. He gave generously to artists impoverished by the war and refused to leave Paris for the first time for many winters, although it was within earshot of German bombardments and the weather was unusually cold. 'I am going out today sporting my furs,' he told Renaud.

He had been working on a huge cantata, *Hail California*, which he had been invited to conduct at the San Francisco Exhibition. It was the climax of his many official pieces and was written for organ, orchestra, military bands and chorus. It comprised a Prelude, the 'Marseillaise', 'California, Land of Fruit and Flowers' and, as recognition of Hispanic associations, themes such as La Jota and Sevillana. When he had completed this epic he went to Monte Carlo to supervise a revival of *L'Ancêtre*. At Marseilles he set another patriotic poem, 'La Française', for unaccompanied choir, which was featured at the Opéra Comique. An offspring of *Le Petit Parisien*, a popular daily paper, it contained a curious reference to 'traitors', probably signifying those on the Left whose international socialist sympathies were thought to have weakened France in the pre-war years. He expressed his annoyance to Renaud that he had had no time to take English lessons before leaving for America. 'I will not understand a word of what is being said.' Gabriel was still very ill. *L'Ancêtre* had been a success in Monte Carlo, but the pleasure ground of the rich was a 'desert' because of the war.

At the end of April he embarked on the *Rochambeau* for a crossing of the Atlantic, a brave journey at a time of naval warfare. His title was that of First Delegate to a Franco-American Commission on Political and Cultural Relations, and the venture was intended to win American sympathy for the Allied cause, not least because there were many American musicians of German origin. His first comments in New York did nothing to help to win friends, for, asked about American music, he replied that he had never heard of any. Yet, since his life reached back to within a decade of the deaths of Beethoven and Schubert, it was as if some equally legendary figure had emerged from the Pantheon and landed upon American soil. During a performance of his Third Symphony by the Boston Symphony Orchestra, word spread through the house that the composer was present and spontaneous calls for him to appear came first from one group and finally from the whole audience of 4000. Women waved their handkerchiefs and there were cries of '*Vive la France!*' The conductor Karl Muck and the orchestra led a great crescendo of applause, which was remembered as one of the most exciting moments of the Exposition Year. The Festival Hall at San Fransisco seated 3782 persons, although Muck described the acoustics as so bad that all orchestras sounded alike. The stage contained a four-manual Austin organ, seventh largest in the world, and it was reported that in its most spacious wind-chamber there was room for seventy-five diners. The critic of the *San Francisco Examiner* noted the pleasure that Sousa and other musicians took in watching Saint-Saëns conduct. The orchestral players, many of them German, were equally impressed and played with veneration, even when the 'Marseillaise' occurred in the score. The composer would have taken particular pleasure in the compliments paid to his singing voice at eighty. 'Sometimes he would sing, not in the raucous Kapellmeister voice of tradition, but with a good tone.' If there were errors in the parts he would segregate an instrumental choir and make them play until he could determine just what the fault was and remedy it. Among many errors, copyists in transcribing tuba parts for the military bands had transposed them according to French practice so that the players had to read one note and play another. 'For two hours', said the *Examiner*, 'this young man of four score rehearsed and every minute was put to hard work ... Saint-Saëns was all bonhomie and the players all enthusiasm.'

'All Saint-Saëns Concerts' were presented; the Third Symphony, all four symphonic poems, two concertos and numerous miscellaneous works, and at each concert the vast *Hail California* resounded. A celebration of the completion of the Panama Canal, it was performed by the Boston Symphony Orchestra and Sousa's band. Before the third concert on a Sunday afternoon, the mighty organ developed a mighty cipher. The moving of the console to and fro had caused friction in the cables and every pipe suddenly sounded simultaneously. An unearthly roar bellowed forth; in a faltering speech the organist tried to explain to the audience that repairs were being done while his inadequate French and the composer's unwillingness to converse in English added to the disorder. It was decided to abandon the instrument, but just as the stage-hands began to move the console the tumult ceased and the organ became as docile as it should have been at the start.

The Promised Land frayed the nerves of those present even further.

The scores had been delayed in transit and the chorus was suffering from lack of rehearsal. It floundered helplessly and found Saint-Saëns's beat unfamiliar. The sound began to resemble the organ mishap so that he stopped the performance and the Finale was begun again. In the midst of an incessant round of lunches and dinners he found time to deliver a lecture on performances of ancient music and even had the typically American experience of a lawsuit. This was over the payments for *Hail California* and the three concerts, but many famous artists commanded huge fees in the United States for single performances, which bore no comparison with the labours of scoring this huge cantata. The old man added to his work by giving recitals, including one of two hours during which he played his salon waltzes and his own paraphrase on the final quartet from *Henry VIII*, following on pieces by Rameau, Chopin and Liszt. He took the train across America to New York while sketching out his Cavatina for Tenor Trombone, written for the Musical Director of the Exposition and admirably devised to show off the resources of the instrument. For another patron he wrote an Elegy for Violin (Opus 143). He looked forward to his return to French cuisine and, when resting back in France at Bourbon l'Archambault, wrote to Renaud of the 'pretentious horrors of luxury hotels'.

His stay there was a convalescence, for, as soon as he disembarked he had recommenced his round of charity concerts. At Deauville he played his *Rhapsodie d'Auvergne* and accompanied a recital of his songs. On the following days he performed for wounded men from the Western Front, then went on to Dieppe to repeat the gesture. While on his travels he set a Hugo poem, 'S'il est un charmant garçon', of which a light-hearted setting still lay among his juvenilia. Another song, 'Ne l'oubliez pas', set words by the wife of Dr Felix Regnault. His departure for Bourbon was hastened by numbness in his limbs and a fear of paralysis, but the cure was only a brief pause between engagements. The Opéra, after sixteen months of closure, reopened in October and honoured the recent emissary to America with a Festival of selections from several operas and *Javotte*. As an additional item he played his Polonaise for Two Pianos. When he repeated this piece a few weeks later at a concert he told Renaud, 'Astonishingly no one knew this work. Everyone asked if it were a recent composition. It was written in 1886!' His correspondence continued to roam far and wide. Although 'amorous' of Mme de Pompadour, he had no time for Mme de Montespan. This led him on to discuss famous women of Louis XIV's reign and to express his disapproval of the royal bastards occupying the first floor of Versailles, while the Queen was relegated to the second.

He informed Fauré that he had not found the song-cycle *Le Jardin Clos* very easy to comprehend. It seemed to be a garden of thorns and he preferred those of Fauré's earlier songs, which breathed the fragrance of the 'Roses of Isphahan'. He suspected that there were some wrong notes in Fauré's D-flat Valse Caprice. '"Remove my doubts", as they say in *Le Cid*!' He lent Debussy the original MS of Chopin's Second Ballade to help him in his Durand editions of the piano works. There was a return to religious composition: two motets, *Quam Dilecta* dedicated to the organist Jules Meunier and *Laudate Dominum* written for a clerical acquaintance, the Abbé Renoud. He reacted with an indignation, which was indeed righteous, to a lecture by d'Indy which described Franck as 'the leading figure in the founding of the Société Nationale'. 'César Franck, whose works were mostly unheard, seized the propitious moment to emerge from the shadows and hurry off to the proper office to become a naturalised Frenchman in order that he might be eligible to join . . . I often gave him help and co-operation in getting his works performed.' Much of the blame for the nervous tone of controversy at this time must be attributed to rumours and opinions that swept the capital concerning the war. Hyperactivity affected even the most balanced intelligences. Saint-Saëns had taken on the difficult task of translating *The Promised Land* into French for the Paris première scheduled for February. There was a charity gala at the Trocadéro and a concert in aid of poor artists from the Opéra, as many singers and dancers had been hurt financially by its closure. All these activities left him too little time to supervise the rehearsals for *The Promised Land*, which was given at the Théâtre des Champs Elysées. He then set off on a concert tour with his old colleague Joseph Hollmann and a Mlle Marthe de Villers, which began at Bordeaux and included Tours, Nantes, Lyon, Montpellier and Marseilles. The demands of these wartime concerts forced him still to carry out his daily regime of practice. He had also begun to write incidental music for de Musset's *On ne badine pas avec l'amour*.

Monte Carlo revived *Hèléne* in 1916 and he stayed for a further week in March to perform at a charity concert for foreigners. Back in Paris he both played and conducted at rehearsals of *Phryné* at the Opéra Comique. His old collaborator of *Les Barbares*, Gheusi, had become Director in 1913. He had soon been contacted by Saint-Saëns from Algeria urging a return to the commissioning of short one-act pieces, once the hallmark of the theatre, which gave opportunities to young composers. Gheusi received a wistful note from Cairo, which said that the writer longed for the joy of hearing *Etienne Marcel* again, 'before I go off to tune the pianos on the planet Mars'. Sadly he concluded, 'But an opera has only to be mine to make it unwanted.' He had at least the joy of the revival of *Phryné* in the early spring of 1916. 'My warmest thanks for this second birth of *Phryné*, more brilliant still than the first,' he wrote to Gheusi. It was typical that he should have enclosed some rewards for the stage-hands. 'What would one do without these humble and indispensable collaborators?' He was about to make yet another journey across the Atlantic, from Genoa to Brazil, not this time with any diplomatic intent, but in order to see the Southern Cross once again and the night skies of another hemisphere. Had he known the joy which *Phryné* afforded him he would have cancelled the trip and continued to conduct it after the first performances. 'The second act is astonishing,' he concluded. 'I don't understand how it can be mine.'[1] He found that his rereading of Musset made the journey on the *Tomaso de Savoia* relaxing. He disembarked at Buenos Aires in May with his score completed in rough. His first task was to supervise the final rehearsals for *Samson* at the Teatro Colón and, although he had been contracted to conduct just two performances, he did seven. There then took place a series of concerts arranged in his honour by an Argentine chamber-music society. He crossed over to Montevideo, where a single evening included a Mozart concerto, his own Fifth and the *Rhapsodie d'Auvergne*. The Government of the Republic of Uruguay had declared 14 July a national festival. The hymn which Saint-Saëns had written earlier became a kind of national anthem. At railway stations on his route he was invariably welcomed with brass bands and choirs: 'It is flattering but deadly boring.' The strenuous nature of the tour revived disturbing signs of paralysis in his

---

[1] 'If I do not come back from my adventurous voyage I will have had the pleasure of finishing with one of the greatest joys of my interminable existence.'

left hand and he returned sooner than expected via Lisbon, to rest once again at Bourbon l'Archambault.

Fauré, who at this time was making efforts to heal the breach between the Société Nationale and the Société Musicale Indépendante, was the recipient of letters querying the accuracy of certain notes in his barcarolles and nocturnes, and the fingering, in which the ambidextrous Fauré could sometimes err.[1] The affection had not diminished and, in thanking Fauré for including the Prelude from *Le Déluge* in a memorial service for members of the Conservatoire lost in the war, he added: 'Your "Pie Jesus" is the *only* "Pie Jesus", just as the "Ave Verum" of Mozart is the *only* "Ave Verum".' He published a fresh series of his articles under the title *Au Courant de la Vie*, but set himself against writing an autobiography. 'There are too many wicked things in the box, which I shall never open,' he had told Fernand Braun in 1913. 'The public does not like the truth; it likes to see people peacefully installed under the aureole that legend has bestowed upon them, even when the falsity of the legend is well established.' He added that he would 'love to weave lies and cover all the iniquities with flowers'.

Although in correspondence with Dr Regnault Saint-Saëns continued to uphold an unflinching atheism, his Seven Organ Improvisations, begun in December 1916, have strange traces of obedience to the 'Motu Proprio'. This was his first major work for organ since 1899, was dedicated to Eugène Gigout and built around various Gregorian chants. The times dictated a bleak mood. There are in the Improvisations signs of a turning away, even from those earlier German composers whom he loved, to the sounds that had been intoned across French soil through long centuries. The first uses the whole-tone scale, the second a Gregorian hymn, 'Beata Nobis Gaudia'. The fifth, 'Pro Martyribus', employs part of a Gregorian melody taken from the Mass of a non-episcopal martyr; the sixth, 'For the Dead', a phrase from the Offertory on the Day of Death or Burial, while the seventh, the longest, evokes the memory of a real or imagined folk hymn. The homage to old chants is suffused also with various Greek modes as, unconsciously, only the mood of Greek tragedy seemed appropriate to France's war-torn condition. Towards

---

[1] A diminuendo appeared to be missing from a Fauré barcarolle. 'Would the illustrious master be kind enough to consent to give me some light on the subject? I approach Your Highness on my knees.'

the end of the war Gheusi found Saint-Saëns weeping uncontrollably at the story of a rough Parisian with some experience of night flying who had volunteered to pursue a feared Zeppelin bomber over Paris and dispose of it in a suicide mission. He asked for no reward save a street-plaque to which his son might one day point. The combination of war and fatherhood evoked ghosts he could not exorcise.

He set himself to reduce his *On ne badine* music to a piano score undisturbed, by taking a room in a dwelling near his apartment. Only a few months before, he had set down his thoughts on privacy during composition: 'Massenet received only at certain hours in the afternoon, and then at his publishers, Heugel. I have seen Sardou refuse to receive Gailhard and Gheusi who had come from Paris in transport to see him at Marly. When I am writing I hide myself in a hotel nearby and do not go out until five to seven.' In the badly lit corridors of the Odéon, where the Musset play was in rehearsal, a young actress offered to lead him to the conductor's office. 'Lead me, Mademoiselle? I am not senile,' he expostulated, then sent her a signed photograph of himself by way of apology.[1] The première was delayed because of wartime restrictions on the opening of theatres and the music received a muted response from the critics. Pierre Lalo wrote in *Le Temps* of 'the incompatibility of thought and sentiment which separated author and musician. The music ... from the moment it appears, chases from it everything that de Musset had put there.' In the following June Saint-Saëns had further cause to be displeased with Lalo when Fauré's *Prometheus* was criticised for combining music with declamation: 'a combination of bellowings, yellings and bleatings'. Saint-Saëns rushed to reassure his pupil. 'As for the mixture of song and declamation, it goes right back to the Ancient Greeks who have never been accused of lacking artistic taste.' He recalled the great successes of Béziers, 'of which we were the heroes', adding that, for 'certain people *success* never matters'.

Before his Improvisations were heard in public he went with Perilhou to the Temple de l'Etoile to try them out. He arrived punctually and climbed up nimbly to the Tribune, but a coupler proved rather stiff and he found combination pedals in unfamiliar places. He would deprecate himself as an old fool when he found any

[1] In the Paris black-out he bumped into a young woman in the street. She mistook him for a young man and accused him of saucy behaviour. He related the incident to Gheusi with amusement.

of the bars hard to read, but was pleased to find that, played upon the organ, the pieces had a much enhanced effect. When so gratified, the greatest organist of his day would turn to the regular incumbent, Alexander Cellier, and ask him if he did not think organ playing was really great fun. The occasion recalled the happy days spent with Perilhou at St Severin, where, having improvised wonderfully, he would repair during the sermons to an adjacent chamber filled with mournful sarcophagi, often used by the organists for a smoke.

A young organist, Maurice le Boucher, recalled that Perilhou had once asked him to play the Saint-Saëns Prelude and Fugue in E flat. Not having the music, but flushed with pride at having won the organ prize at the Ecole Niedermeyer, he set off, relying on his memory. Perilhou then whispered that Saint-Saëns was listening down below.[1] The confidence of the eighteen-year-old disappeared instantly. His playing and his memory went to pieces and he was forced into the most bizarre improvisations in order to finish in the key of E flat at all. Saint-Saëns understood only too well the reasons for the collapse. He upbraided Perilhou and asked the boy to play again, this time his kindly concern supplying a source of strength. He concluded the session by saying, 'You make me jealous for I have never been able to play that devil of a fugue from memory.'

The old man himself gave the première of the Improvisations in Marseilles, followed by recitals in Nice and Lyon. He introduced the work to Gigout with a letter: 'Since, thanks to you, I have some coal, I am able to give you a dinner. Tomorrow Tuesday. There is a new piece for organ. It is horrible!'[2] At least he was now free from commissioned work. He attended a revival of *Henry VIII* at Monte Carlo, adding a concert for the benefit of army orphans, then travelled on to Rome, which he had long wished to revisit, spending many hours in the museums and among the monuments. He conducted a performance of *Samson* and appeared at a grand concert at the Augusteum. A further cure at Bourbon l'Archambault lightened his spirits and produced a delightful letter to Fauré which ended: 'The

---

[1] Saint-Saëns had once played a similar trick on the young Godowsky. He suggested that his pupil should play some pieces by Tchaikovsky at La Trompette, without telling him that Tchaikovsky would be in the audience. The occasion went off well.

[2] A subsequent note said the coal was used up and the meal would have to be cancelled.

treatment has given me back my fingers. As for the legs, they no longer rival those of the fleet-footed Achilles. Ah! if there is a God of the Left Hand I would really like to get to know him and make offerings unto Him when I feel like playing your music. The Second *Valse Caprice* is terrible from this point of view.'

After a short visit to Dieppe he began Three Choruses for female voices. Like Fauré and Debussy, he heard with alarm of the October revolution in Russia and in France itself there had been strikes and mutinies, which cast shadows upon the likelihood of holding the Western Front. Paul Fournier had been the poet of one of the Choruses, 'Salut au chevalier'. Saint-Saëns had also set a hymn by Fournier, 'Hommage à l'Amérique', for no stone could be left unturned in efforts to persuade America to support the Allies.[1] Inviting a few friends to his eighty-second birthday, *'mon déplorable anniversaire'*, he observed, 'One is only eighty-two once in one's lifetime, but that does not make it more fun. I will have need of consolation.' Soon afterwards came the death of Gabriel from cancer. He had been Saint-Saëns's valet for fifteen years and operations had been carried out by the best surgeons that could be found. His master was distressed that he had been travelling and unable to be present at the final moments.

It is not surprising that at this juncture his polemics against German music should have acquired unpredictability. In *Paris-Midi* a writer, Paul Sonday, defended the French Wagnerians and accused him of writing without knowledge or discrimination on such diverse subjects as Shakespeare and Euripides, motor cars and even football.[2]

For part of this time Saint-Saëns was staying with an old friend, Mme de Chazal, at her château at St Ouen, composing a long and more measured work, *Les Idées de M. Vincent d'Indy*, which was published after the war. Since 1903 d'Indy had been publishing, volume by volume, a *Course on Composition* based on his principles, which were by modern standards stiff and formal. (He had criticised the Organ Symphony because the second subject did not come in the dominant.) In his opera *Fervaal* F sharp major signified 'Divine Love',

---

[1] There were a number of pieces composed at this time that were simply an old man's contribution to the war effort. Works such as *Vers la Victoire* and *Marche Interalliée* for piano duet, etc.

[2] Digression was not necessarily a new activity. In 1912 he contributed an article, 'Blindness in Snails', to a *Revue Scientifique*.

the enharmonic G flat major 'Human Love', A flat major 'False Love', a good example of theorising stifling imagination. Among d'Indy's many commandments he had denounced superfluous modulations as 'indecisive fluctuations between light and shade' and said they produced an impression like that of 'a poor indecisive human being, tossed about between East and West in the course of a lamentable existence, without aim or belief', a description in which Saint-Saëns might be forgiven for divining a reference to himself!

Saint-Saëns's own essay ranged far and wide, emphasising the importance of form and the slow evolution of the arts from a primitive anarchy to which modernists seemed to wish to return. He employed his skill in irony. 'Legends abound regarding the power of expression, the superhuman results obtained by this "primitive" music. Saul's madness soothed . . . by the strains of David's harp . . . the passions of Alexander roused or lulled by the melodies of a lyre, without speaking of walls erected by Amphion's lyre or dashed to the ground by the trumpets of the Hebrews. Wide is our choice among the phenomena of the marvellous, wherein the potency of the results effected contrasts strangely with the poverty of the means employed to bring them about.' He gave a clue to one inspiration for the *Carnival of the Animals* by pointing out how even the 'grave Bach' had used the violins to imitate the braying of an ass to accompany King Midas, foretelling the metamorphosis Apollo has in mind. He allows d'Indy greatness as the founder of a School and a wielder of influence, but cannot agree with the yoking of music to religion. 'We see how careful the author is to look upon art as one of the most serious things in life. He ascends higher and ever higher until we suffer from vertigo as we follow him and find that he places art on a level with religious faith . . . We may remark that Perugino and Berlioz, who were lacking in faith, were none the less admirable artists, even in the religious style, but we need not labour the point. . . . When art was born, religion took possession of it. Religion did not create art.' In one crucial sentence he expressed his belief in form. 'Art came into being on the day that man, instead of being solely concerned with the utility of the object he had made, concerned himself with its form and made up his mind that this form would satisfy a need peculiar to human nature, a mysterious need to which the name "aesthetic sense" has been given.' But by form he did not mean just the familiar patterns of sonata movements, scherzo or rondo etc., but the whole business of fashioning melody, rhythm and

harmony into the communication of charm by design. The most
important designs have come through a long process of evolution,
which it would be rash to ignore. On the necessity of some rules he
was at one with d'Indy. He was correct in prophesying that in a world
where there is no acquired expertise it becomes impossible to
distinguish the genius from the fraud.

Another peroration has a modern resonance. He fears that the
needs of science and production will diminish the areas in which the
imagination can flourish. 'Even the beauties of nature are attacked;
animal species are massacred and disappear for ever; age-long forests
are destroyed, never to be restored. The same thing happens to
cataracts and waterfalls; nowadays we think of them merely as so much
motor-power.' He defended the use of bar-lines, which d'Indy thought
might disappear from musical notation (as in many instances they
have): 'Have they not created syncopation? Have they ever prevented
the emphasis or accent falling where it pleased?' D'Indy had claimed
that harmony was the 'daughter of melody'. He admitted that
harmony had developed later but claimed that it existed from the
beginning in sounds. A bell often gives out a chord; he recalled
detecting a chord in the buzz of a mosquito. He remembered in
Cochin-China hearing a large 'coleopter' (beetle) resounding in rooms
open to the wind.

His valuation of the human voice remained as high as ever. The
great trio – Haydn, Mozart and Beethoven – had elevated the symphony, but in doing so had obscured the long progress of music as
linked to singing. As one fearsomely learned scholar reviewing a
colleague, he could not resist the customary 'I looked in vain for'
method. D'Indy had shown great respect for the fugue and quoted
examples from all nationalities. 'I looked in vain for the names of
Clementi and Cherubini ... And yet Clementi has interspersed his
Gradus with numerous fugues ... and though they may not claim to
rival those of the *Well-Tempered Clavier* they are none the less very
interesting, the canons are of rare merit and some are real masterpieces.' D'Indy had mentioned the decline of the fugue, but praised
Saint-Saëns for keeping the form alive. 'He honours me by including
my name among them, though he finds fault with my fugues for being
somewhat cold and conventional. I cannot well judge what concerns
myself; still, I hardly think this criticism can be brought against the
first movement of my Symphony in A minor, which affects the fugue

form. I remember at the first performance of this movement the adoption of the fugue form appeared scandalous to many listeners.' Above the level plain of good sense and warm reminiscence rose the occasional rough monument to prejudice, especially his scorn for the Wagnerites: 'Nothing could be better than to go to Germany for masterpieces, but do not go for theories';[1] and his objection to placing Franck on some lofty pedestal as 'the greatest creator of musical forms with Beethoven and Wagner. 'To say that his symphony has renewed the form is "to pull the world's leg". He has renewed nothing at all. If one symphony is able to pretend to the honour of renewing the symphonic form it would be my Symphony in C minor by its uncommon design and the use of the organ,[2] but that has taken a place in the musical world which prevents devotees of the Schola Cantorum from sleeping.' Of Franck's use of canon he remarked, 'His canons are always in unison or octaves and thus present no difficulty of any kind.' After praising the 'beautiful soprano air' in Franck's *Rédemption* he describes it as 'illuminating and cheering this austere landscape as does the sun with his genial beams!'

There came a further plea for a reappraisal of Liszt. He could recall the days when certain German orchestras would deliberately play Liszt badly to reduce the effect. He foresaw the appreciation that would in modern times focus upon the Liszt Piano Sonata. 'I congratulate myself on being one of the first to plead his cause against the general hostility.' Opinion is coming round to the view that Richard and Cosima Wagner treated Liszt unfairly and were followed by their enthusiasts. In a letter of 1912, Saint-Saëns says the Wagnerians made 'incessant war upon Liszt'. He had heard the *Faust* and *Dante* Symphonies massacred by German orchestras.

There was remarkable proof of his musical longevity in 1918 in his

---

[1] In anti-German mood he might well have recalled that d'Indy had once thought of Germany as a great defence against democracy. D'Indy shared something of Germany's militarism. At any opportunity he would demonstrate how the Battle of Waterloo might have been won, using crockery and cutlery on the table. Saint-Saëns, though conservative, was a good Republican and more democratic in temperament.

[2] Saint-Saëns could have claimed more credit than this. Although notorious as a champion of classical forms he had, by introducing the symphonic poem, the rhapsody and the suite of linked ideas (e.g. *Algerian Suite*, *Carnival*, etc.), done much to free Debussy, Ravel and others from a slavery to the four-movement symphony, before they could receive recognition.

Morceau de Concert for Harp and Orchestra Opus 154. Nicole Anckier, a prize winner from the Conservatoire, had been persistent in her entreaties for a composition and Saint-Saëns, though fearful of the problems of balance, enjoyed the challenge of pitting the resources of a harpist against an orchestra. The result was a triumph of ingenuity with alternate chords, arabesques and recitatives for the soloist, and the delicate orchestrations in which he excelled. The work is virtually a cyclical concerto with internal movements followed by a return to the sinuous phrases of the opening and a brilliant coda which includes both parties.

Early in 1918 a friendship began with a young poet, Pierre Aguétant, who later published a selection of letters which throw a favourable light on the old gentleman. The affectionate relationship was one of many he conducted with young men of artistic sensibilities. The death of Gabriel had increased his loneliness and emphasised the loss of his sons. Aguétant had sent him some poems with a request that they might be considered for musical settings. Saint-Saëns often sent off brusque replies to such approaches, but Aguétant had the temerity to reply with irritation and drew one of the Master's smiling missives, full of self-deprecation. 'Youth has its faults, which can be adorable. At my age one has no more than faults, which are not adorable at all.' He might be able to set the poem 'Angelus', but hoped 'the pleasure of seeing my name beside yours may not be allowed to go so far as to ensnare you into a catastrophe'. He did in fact set two poems ('a double crime', as he said), 'Angelus' and 'Ou nous avons aimé', both with orchestral accompaniment. A correspondence on literature ensued. He wrote from Cannes to give advice on masculine and feminine endings in poetry and the charms of precision. He condemned exaggeration, citing the descent of architecture from the thirteenth century, 'which ought to remain our national architecture', to the later Gothic excesses, which caused a return to Greek and Roman 'so out of place in northern cities'.

He had left for the South at the end of 1917, after the rehearsals for *Henry VIII* at the Opéra, to remedy bronchial troubles, which were mounting after several cold wartime winters in Paris. He was preparing a fresh edition of *Problèmes et Mystères* under the title *Divagations Sérieuses*. At Nice and Cannes he gave concerts in aid of the Blind and the people of Alsace and Lorraine, and he supervised a revival of *Etienne Marcel* 'shorn of its delicious ballet' at Monte Carlo. He recalled to Fauré hearing the great singer Pol Plançon, as the 'Seneschal of Poitiers' long ago. 'Why isn't the Opéra Comique giving this colourful episode in the history of Paris? . . . The return of cold weather has worsened me a little. Alas what has become of my robust constitution of former days!'

Paris itself continued to come under bombardment and, during the German offensive of May 1918, shrapnel from an exploding shell showered on Widor's table at the Institut. Saint-Saëns meanwhile had been continuing his protests against German music. He had written to Dandelot, 'You have been playing my music in your matinées and I am very grateful, but how can you not understand the anomaly of a Schumann Festival at the moment when the Germans are bombarding Paris and, in a frightful battle, are making superhuman efforts to crush us . . . France first; music afterwards.' Dandelot, who knew that Saint-Saëns's music was impregnated with Schumann's style, wrote sympathetically and reminded him that his own two boys were serving at the front and one had been wounded in action.

Discursive letters to Aguétant described the composer's joy at being once again under the blue skies of the South. The shade of blue 'is marvellous at Cannes, exquisite in Egypt where it is clear and in no way darkened as Gautier says in *La Roman de la Momie*, which he wrote at Alexandria held up by an accident . . . He believed that the sky of Alexandria was that of Egypt, but Alexandria is by the sea and that changes everything . . . it is the single false note.' As a respite from the bad news of war he began a Second String Quartet, which was completed at Bourbon l'Archambault and whose opening bars seemed an appeal for a return to the age of Mozart. A letter of June related: 'Bourbon is a remote place where nothing happens . . . I have played dominoes, I have patted the little dogs, the nightingales sing ravishingly and horrible music is played in the Café du Casino. The preoccupations of the war have blocked the musical spring.' He had remained in Paris in 1914 during the Battle of the Marne and most of the subsequent moments of danger. He returned there in August and began work on the *Morceau de Concert* for Harp, using magnifying glasses to help with the scoring. 'Oh old age! . . . but, as one knows, it is the only means of living a long time.[1] Is it really necessary to live a

---

[1] This remark was originally Auber's.

long life? The Ancients thought the opposite and they were often right about things.' His spirits were much revived by a visit to the Belgian royal family, still exiled from their capital. The Queen had taken him to hear an orchestra she had formed from Belgian soldiers. 'It was well-trained and had, in addition, youth, which nothing can replace. . . . Before dinner I gave the Queen a little concert on a piano which was unfortunately rather "tired" . . . We even played together a Beethoven Adagio [his opposition to German music appears to have melted in the royal presence] . . . the Queen put her bow to the violin, which she had not touched for a long time for obviously her days are passed in ambulances visiting and comforting the sick and the wounded. . . . During the night we were awoken with gunfire and explosions.' When Saint-Saëns left at 8 a.m. the whole royal household, including the young princes on holiday from Eton, turned out to see off his automobile on its way to Boulogne.

As the exhausted combatants fought on, wearisome lists of patriotic songs showed no signs of decline. 'I have just done a song, "Victoire", collaborating with Fournier, who has already worked with me on "Honour to America", another patriotic song. Musically this is a very thankless task. It is necessary that the span should barely exceed an octave, that it can be sung without accompaniment, that it should be easy to remember and – with all these restrictions – it must not resemble anything too well known.' He confessed that he had written the work out of a sense of duty, but such things always resulted in poor music. 'I have done a song of which I don't know the title – for which I was asked by the *Petit Parisien* – which has had no success at all.' When Lecocq died in the autumn he remembered that his friend wrote polished verse and he had even set 'a pretty sonnet'. He also expressed a wish that Lecocq had taken up musical criticism, for, although he had built a career in operetta, the faculty for writing serious music had been found wanting when required. 'In recent times I saw his letters decline in handwriting and style so I knew the end was approaching. Now it is my turn. I await it with indifference . . . I would wish to take leave of life in the same manner as from a banquet – thanking one's host and packing one's bags.'

He would stroll sometimes in the Parc Monceau but his 'paralysed' legs would carry him no further. 'What scholars, thinkers and artists, who would have brightened the future, this horrible war is destroying,' he wrote. He followed its political aspects with interest. In July he had written from Bourbon: 'We are destined to see Germany deflate rapidly like a balloon . . . Its stamina is astonishing, but everything has a limit.' In September, on the news of Bulgaria's collapse, he predicted William II's overthrow. Seeing the Imperial coalition breaking up he said, 'Germany will feel the earth slip from under its feet. One thinks of Nebuchadnezzar – of Sennacharib.'

Early in November he wrote to Hermann Klein. His views on the war may seem self-centred, but he was a musician writing to a colleague. 'I had hoped that, with the Entente, French music would "reign" once more in London, but I perceive that German music still keeps its old place, including Wagner, although the Germans have made the latter their national musician, as we have seen by their giving trenches the names of Hunding, Wotan, Siegfried and Parsifal. It is really incomprehensible. If it were otherwise it seems to me that our *Promised Land* ought to profit by it. I have done nothing better and I am astonished that this work should not take the place that it deserved.' His view then became less parochial. 'But what do such things matter beside the events that are now taking place all over Europe! I dare not yet indulge in feelings of joy. There is still too much mourning in the world. And yet there are some comic features in the awful drama, the thrones of Finland and Albania, Ferdinand and Boris of Bulgaria, William hanging on to his crown, all these ministers handing in their resignations . . . we are about to witness a transformation of Europe, a most curious spectacle, something unique in history! Poor Music in all this chaos cuts a sad figure.' He gave an account of his year at Cannes, Monte Carlo and Bourbon, and added, 'I have written a Quartet,[1] some vocal pieces, and a *March of the Allies* (for four hands) composed for the Cercle Interallié established at the Faubourg St Honoré in the magnificent "Hotel" belonging to Henri de Rothschild, who is building himself another. At the end of this month I am off to Marseilles *en route* for Algiers and Hamman R'Iyah,' he continued, 'where perhaps my legs will be restored to me.'

'My Quartet in G; there is only one sharp in the signature – what originality!' he had told Lecocq. 'The time will come perhaps when composers will write in F double-sharp, but we will not be around to

---

[1] This places the Second String Quartet earlier than 1919. It was Paul Dukas who said that Mozart would always have groups taking refuge in his music in times of chaos. This was true of Richard Strauss in 1945, as of Saint-Saëns in 1918.

see these fine things.' The quartet's mood is initially eighteenth
century, with echoes of Mozart or Haydn and much elaborate
eighteenth-century ornamentation. He described the first movement
as 'Youth'; the second as 'The loss of it'.... 'Consequently it is
perhaps the saddest movement I know.' The second is indeed a
contrast, alternating between an Adagio and Andante, between a
modal theme and Romantic interludes, prefaced by iambic phrases
that link strange changes of key. He described the movement, with its
modernistic touches, as 'deadly dull as befitting an Adagio', but,
though not dull, it has a cold emptiness, as suited the final months of
suffering endured by the exhausted armies. Instead of a cheerful
Scherzo there is an Interlude, plaintively sung by the viola with the
first violin 'tacet'. The ending takes us back to the world of
improvisation. A very eighteenth-century theme is eventually covered
with arabesques and ornamentations, dissonances and an untypically
brief close.

On the day before the Armistice, when Germany was in disarray, he
wrote, 'Ah well! I had predicted William would lose his crown. ...
Every day ministers resign, sovereigns abdicate. But there is one
frightening thing – the mounting tide of socialism.' He was especially
perturbed that trade unionism among technicians was affecting
programmes at the Opéra. On a more general view he thought that
there was a risk of near-anarchy as in Russia. On the following day he
was able to write, 'The War is over! But, as Gambetta said, the era of
difficulties begins. And never were difficulties more difficult. ... I am
not able, as many others, to give myself up to joy ... thinking of a
future so disturbing and of all the bereavements and ruins which
surround us.' 'Let us work. Let us work' were lines in his *Hymn to
Peace*, composed in 1919 on prize-winning words by a surgeon, J.-L.
Faure, which spoke of the cities that had to be rebuilt, and the blood-
drenched fields that had to be cultivated for harvests. Although an
ardent supporter of Clemenceau (he confided that he felt closer to
Clemenceau in character than to Massenet!) he was not prepared to
believe that Alsace was indisputably French. 'For me it is neither
French nor German and its heart is divided between the two – its
heart, no! but its spirit. Its true nature is quite special like that of the
Swiss. ... If reason and not appetites governed the world, Alsace and
Lorraine would be a country apart.'

His longer outlook was even more pessimistic. He had written many works in praise of the March of Science. He now foresaw some of its consequences:

This war, it is said, will be the last. If, in fifty years, another should break out, which would be to it what it was to the preceding. If Science turned from its aim but created some means of destruction so that entire cities disappear as in a dream. If the human species were destined to destroy itself, after having destroyed the others? It will all finish as have finished those of which we rediscover astonishing remains and the Earth, devastated, depopulated, will continue to roll in its orbit having lost its air, its water, extinguished its volcanoes; a dead star, like its companion the moon, awaits only some unknown cause to make it disappear altogether. What does that matter to Nature? Such a small thing as the Earth in the frightening immensity of the Heavens.

14

'I Have Mounted the Acropolis Myself'

By mid-December he was back in Algiers. 'I have the view of the port, the sea, the distant mountains, a view I have known for a long time but which I rediscover with pleasure – in so far as I had thought never to see it again. There are more people here than ordinarily, but not the frightful crowds of Marseilles, which is uninhabitable at the moment.' He must have had an opportunity to play the organ in the cathedral, for he wrote to Gigout to say that he was playing 'as St Orgue himself must play in Paradise'. He was at work on *Cyprès et Lauriers*, to celebrate the Armistice, a work requested by the town of Ostend and dedicated to President Poincaré. The first funereal section was for organ alone (he suggested that it might be suitable for funerals on its own, but he found it difficult himself and, after practising, told Gigout that if he had not worked at it he would never have reached the end). The second triumphant section brought in the orchestra with extended passages for trumpet and horn. In November 1920, after the work had been performed in Paris at the Trocadéro, Saint-Saëns thanked Gigout for a 'perfect performance although warring against a rebellious instrument'. He remembered the effect of the 32 ft pipes in the Adagio of his Organ Symphony on the same instrument, which had been allowed to deteriorate. *Cyprès et Lauriers* shows again Saint-Saëns's desire to experiment, although inevitably the first section, which has two long passages of rising lamentation on solo stops divided by a strident outburst, where harsh Straussian chords depict modern warfare, is overshadowed by anticipation of the still silent orchestra. Strings, first in vibrato and then with a massive uprush, introduce an organ chorale, after which come fugues, fanfares, a section orchestrated with great beauty for harp and strings, which may depict the blessings of peace, where the theme characteristically loses itself before completion. Finally comes a *marche militaire* of great vivacity, with more athletic pedal-work that had given him concern. It is astonishing that at eighty-four he was producing music for orchestra and organ which, for buoyant vigour, no contemporary Frenchman could rival. In July he watched the Victory Procession from a window in the Champs Elysées, where he could not hear the military bands for the cheering.

He maintained a philosophical attitude to his relative immobility. Aguétant was on one occasion trying to hail a lunch-time taxi with Saint-Saëns holding on to him painfully while a fleet went by heedlessly. Aguétant cursed the drivers; Saint-Saëns said, 'You are wrong. They are like us. They are hungry.'

During April and May he was affected by congestion of the lungs, and the artists from the Opéra, who were rehearsing *Hélène*, had to come to his apartment to go through the score. *Hélène* received a better reception than he had feared. The critic of *Le Figaro* understood the whole conception and concluded: 'It is regrettable . . . from a scenic point of view . . . that the curtain does not fall on the exit of the lovers. But of what a sublime page would we then have been deprived. The Master describes there with inexpressible power the rapture, the intoxication and sadness of the two beings whom implacable destiny has just thrown pitilessly into one another's arms.' He prepared for Gheusi a version of Gluck's *Orpheus*, giving the principal role to a tenor as in Gluck's lifetime. This enabled him to show a great display of erudition. 'One must ram home the point that for *Orphée* a tenor who can sing with a "head-voice" is indispensable.' He went on to discuss the tenor roles in Meyerbeer and Rossini: 'The C's of *William Tell* were written for the "mixed voice" of Nourrit, an exceptional voice. Dupuy came on the scene who did them "*en poitrine*", unable to do otherwise, and it appeared fine but was again exceptional. Since then [these high notes] have become war-cries and yells to which the public is so accustomed that it demands them. But for *Orphée* I will not put my name to such horrors. Ah! I would pay a great deal to hear "O Mathilde, idole de mon âme" sung by a fine head voice. But I never shall.' His Fantasy for Organ in C, dedicated to King Manuel of Portugal, was his first piece of this nature for over quarter of a century and followed a production of *Proserpine* in Lisbon. It bore traces of the Franckian 'Prelude, Aria and Finale' with a Prelude that explores the resources of a large organ with special emphasis upon the pedal effects, a melodic solo and then a celebratory burst of sound, which flies all over the keyboard, but the episodes are enclosed in a pastoral theme in thirds, which comes at the beginning and at the close. It was one of the few organ works in which he included directions for fingering. The organ was much in his thoughts as he dedicated to the cellist André Hekking a 'Prayer' for cello and organ.

He had begun to write some articles for a journal, *Annales*, in January. In September he contributed his thoughts on 'Repopulation'. He wrote to Bizet's widow Geneviève to draw her attention to his article that had defended her father, Halévy, 'against that abominable [Pierre] Lalo'. He pressed Geneviève, who had married again, to object formally to the ballet in the last act of *Carmen*. 'A procedure of this kind would be understandable if a work needed support.' Choudens, the publishers, had even used music by Bizet that had no Spanish characteristics. He, Saint-Saëns, would have been very pleased to concoct a ballet with music from the first three acts, if necessary in total secrecy.

During the summer he felt well enough to go to the Jardin des Plantes. Typically, he used his meeting with the hippopotamus to dispute Gautier's poem in which the poet spoke of his own convictions being strong armour with which to go forth into the desert, like the hippo. 'The hippopotamus lives in the water and not in the desert, and it is not its skin but that of the rhinoceros that nothing pierces. Poets sometimes make mistakes.' He visited the reunited provinces and gave concerts in Strasbourg and Mulhouse, and there was a further tour of several French cities from Lille to Arles. In the summons to labour carried by his *Hymn to Peace* he certainly set an example.

He was, however, much concerned with Fauré's health, for his friend had now been for fourteen years in the post of Director, which had exhausted Dubois after ten. Towards the end of the war Fauré had spent much energy in vainly attempting to bring d'Indy and the older generation into a compromise with Ravel and his fellow Independents. Before he left for Algiers, Saint-Saëns arranged for Fauré to have some respite by means of a commission from Monte Carlo, which resulted in the popular *Masques et Bergamasques*. As ever, his own health improved in the North African sun and he gave a concert in Algiers at which he played pieces by Chopin and Rameau, and his own

Caprice on the 'Airs de Ballet' from Alceste. These were followed by the recent *Cyprès et Lauriers* arranged for two pianos, and some fragments of the *Suite Algérienne.* During the interval he gave a totally unexpected lecture on the *Fables* of La Fontaine, their meaning and poetry. One wonders how many modern pianists would break off during a recital and give an illuminating talk on – say – the 'Lyrical Ballads'. The talk was so successful that he repeated the process four days later.

He was trying to follow events at Versailles in the hope that Clemenceau would have his way. He could remember the old Orleanist journals of his childhood and phrases such as 'darkening of the horizon' in the *Constitutionnel.* They matched his mood of the moment: 'Our provinces devastated to a point one cannot imagine if one has not seen them, the general inflation, the growing rise of socialism, the perpetual strikes. . . . The future appears to me as a gigantic question mark.' He admitted that his passion for travel was often the subject of joking: 'There are some people who believe that I still go every year to the Canary Isles and who, when they see me, ask, "When are you setting off?" And I do not always reply as politely as I should.' One more important journey at least remained. 'Where do you think I have been asked to go in April? You will not guess . . . Athens, no less. If my health does not conflict with this plan I will not resist the temptation . . . It is a sorrow to me never to have seen Greece. The imprint of the gods and goddesses is still not effaced there.'

In March he wrote with dismay to say that it had been snowing 'with prodigious abundance' in Hamman R'Iyra.[1] 'What have I done? Some fugues for piano, a half dozen, and as "the dream of compositions" comes to pester me unexpectedly, a piece for flute with orchestra that I have entitled *Odelette,* this word not having been used in music.' He had also completed an Elegy for Violin and Piano. The Six Fugues were composed for his pupil Isidore Philipp. 'The climate, the couscous and perhaps some devil propelling me, I have just written a little collection of six fugues of which I beg you to accept dedication. You will find a distant reflection of the *Well-Tempered Clavier,* in spite of my efforts to distance myself from the idea.' He added that he could have avoided all resemblance to Bach if he had chosen ultra-modern

[1] He was scientifically fascinated by the springs that watered this resort, which were apparently inexhaustible, unaffected by either rain or drought.

themes in no recognisable key, but that would have made the fugue construction pointless. Emile Vuillermoz, although a critic who championed Ravel and the younger composers, was greatly impressed: 'By means exclusively pedagogic and rule-bound tactics these six fugues impose victoriously the rights of clarity, logic and lucidity, our classic inheritance which M. Saint-Saëns means to defend against all the gods of Valhalla.' He described the 'translucence' of writing: 'the parts cross and recross one another, advance and retreat, seek and avoid one another, clasp and unclasp without ever becoming confused or hazy'. The 'devilish promptings' to which he referred are most apparent in the third fugue, which is rapid and ingenious. The sixth in C major, maestoso, is the largest in style with many modulations and a variety of contrapuntal effects.

After a brief return to France during which he played some two-piano works with Jean Nussy-Verdié at Béziers he embarked on 1 May for Greece. The voyage was uncomfortable, for he was again struck by lung congestion, but he was sustained by hopes of climbing up to the Parthenon and embracing the marble under the blue skies. In Athens he gave three recitals and there was a Saint-Saëns Festival held in the ancient theatre of Herod Atticus. The *Hymn to Pallas Athene* was given, the Greek and French national anthems, and the *Jeunesse d'Hercule*, which he himself conducted. There were banquets and receptions, and a chamber-music recital at the Conservatoire, which included both his piano trios. At the close of one performance the students swarmed about his carriage, uncoupled the horses and pulled him like a Byzantine conqueror to his lodgings. He was impressed by a young student, Dimitri Mitropoulos, wrote a glowing article about his work on returning to Paris and helped him towards a scholarship to study with Busoni. Mitropoulos later became a distinguished conductor in America. 'I did it too late,' Saint-Saëns wrote of his journey to Hellas, 'but as the proverb says "Better late than never". I have been fêted there as nowhere else. Sometimes there were great shouts of *"Vive la France"*, which went to my heart. I have seen the King; I have chatted with M. Venizelos . . . I have mounted the Acropolis myself.'

He was not allowed to rest. 'What an existence I have had since I returned from the land of Phidias. Tomorrow I am taken up by a wedding followed by a lunch, which will finish I don't know when. Friday and Saturday I am taken up all day after noon by the competition for the Prix de Rome – great fatigue and great boredom.

For these competition pieces are rarely interesting.' He resigned from the Conseil Supérieur (of the Conservatoire) which he thought contained too few specialist musicians and too many 'journalists, theatre directors and women', and used his time to study the old violin sonatas of Tartini, Corelli 'and a Belgian named Kennis, who is very interesting from the point of view of violin playing'. He reworked his old Cello Suite into a piece for cello and orchestra. His affection for the British royal family was diminished by the apparent support which King George V was giving to Lloyd George, who was thought to be at the heart of every anti-French machination. 'With King Edward [VII] everything would have taken a different turn. And Edward ought to be alive still. He killed himself by a series of imprudences, believing himself invulnerable.' The financial situation was depressing. A financier had advised him he should put everything into precious stones, 'but stones yield no interest and perhaps they will be stolen'. Fortunately he still had his humour intact. 'You can't imagine how much I have studied your Valse Caprice in D flat,' he told Fauré, 'but I have never been able to master it sufficiently to put it into my repertoire . . . When I am ninety I will perhaps be quite sure of it. In October I begin my eighty-five years with a concert tour which without doubt will be the last . . . In Athens I was marvellously finger-free – but I was only eighty-four then!'

The tours he had mentioned covered Switzerland, Belgium and parts of northern France. At his great age he was as much a marvel as he had been when a child. Marguerite Long had her final meeting with him at a concert in his honour at the Ecole Normale where she had participated in his F-major Trio and he had accompanied one of his violin sonatas. Many people came round backstage to congratulate him, but he sat at a little table dipping biscuits into hot chocolate. When Marguerite Long was ready to leave, he rose with his moustache thickly coated with chocolate and kissed her on both cheeks. He was exhausted by his latest tours and set off again for Algiers. He stopped *en route* at Bordeaux, where *Les Barbares* and *Javotte* were being performed, and at Béziers, where the Nussy-Verdié cousins had organised an ambitious concert, which included *La Lyre et la Harpe* and the *Rhapsodie d'Auvergne*. Once back in Algiers, he had a month of treatment when he was not allowed to perform and had no inclination to compose. He relayed a caustic report to Dubois on the standard of the music at the installation of the new Archbishop.

It was on one of these last visits to Algiers that he passed an old beggar with outstretched hand. 'What age are you?' enquired the composer. 'Seventy-five,' croaked the other. 'Ah! Youth is a wonderful thing,' muttered Saint-Saëns, closing the man's hand over a fistful of coins. At the home of a 'rich English lady' he met Princess Beatrice, whom he had accompanied when she sang at Windsor Castle 'before her august mother'. He took a front seat at a concert by a young pianist, Lazare Lévy, who had studied with Diémer, in order to boost the young man's career. He had once written to Lévy to tell him that the Study in the Form of a Waltz could not have been played better. 'I am sure of this, being the composer!' He began to set some poems of Ronsard, which he had selected before his departure. There was no sign of weariness. 'Grasselette and Maigrelette', with its pounding accompaniment to uproarious patter, is a remarkable creation by someone in their ninth decade. He completed some other songs on antique verses. He gave concerts with a violinist, Jean Noceti, and travelled to both Oran and Tunis. 'I have just written a Grand March at the request of the students of Algiers. That is something I would call hard work.' He began to sketch the last Sonatas for Oboe, Clarinet and Bassoon to enlarge the limited repertoire for solo woodwind. A fourth sonata for cor anglais was contemplated but never finished. The Oboe Sonata was given a pastoral quality, as if recalling both the mythical origins of music and fears over the transformation of rural France, which the composer shared with many of his generation. These late works have a curious affinity with the desire for simplicity of line and texture that overtook French composers of the 1920s and share the distaste for pre-war musical opulence. The Clarinet Sonata, with its Adagio, 3:2 in the unusual key of E-flat minor, has the sound of an epitaph. The Bassoon Sonata, with its alternations of lyrical and humorous moods, was dedicated to Léon Letellier.[1] At the same time he was corresponding with Bellaigue, recalling how in Algiers he had written the sea-shore scene from *Phryné* by the sea's edge and speaking of the early productions of *Les Huguenots*, which Meyerbeer had directed.

He finished the three sonatas after his return to Paris in April.[2] He

---

[1] The name of the bassoonist in the Opéra orchestra but also of a Dieppe cousin.

[2] He informed Aguétant that he would be attending the Institut on 21 April after a long absence. '"The immortals" can certainly wait until then!'

was now obliged to take frequent rests, for bronchitis returned and he was suffering from a heart ailment. He fulfilled some engagements, one of which was to support and applaud the dress rehearsal of *The Trojans* at the Opéra. He meditated on the accidents of fame in a letter: 'When Berlioz was alive he was attacked mercilessly and Félicien David was exalted. Now *The Damnation of Faust* is played everywhere and *The Desert* is unknown, 'which is tiresome for it is a charming work which brought orientalism to us'. Franck's *Rédemption*, 'so lacklustre', has driven out Gounod's, 'which is a masterpiece'. He hoped that his own lyric works, so often criticised, would some day be championed. His final comments on 'modern' music were uncompromising: 'We are entering the era of hullabaloo. . . . It is as if we were taking pleasure in eating live crayfish or cacti bristling with spikes, drinking vinegar or munching burning peppers.'

During the war the American General Pershing had enlisted the help of Walter Damrosch, conductor of the New York Philharmonic, to train bandsmen for the American forces in France. After the peace the scheme was perpetuated in a summer school for Americans at Fontainebleau and Saint-Saëns was called upon to make a speech at the opening. He reserved his strength principally for the rehearsals of *Ascanio* at the Opéra, but to distract himself wrote two choruses for Walter Damrosch to take back to America and completed his 'Vieilles Chansons'. On 6 August he gave, at Dieppe, what he truly intended as a 'farewell' to the concert platform. After playing seven pieces he thanked the audience by remarking that his first concert had been given seventy-five years before and he must retire before he became some kind of curiosity. Five days later, at Béziers, he concluded his career as conductor, taking rehearsals for *Antigone* and attending the première.

A September visit to Venice induced a mood swing to melancholy. He understood, he said, the sadness of Mendelssohn's barcarolles: 'I have no project of composition in my head. The harvest is gathered in! At eighty-five one has the right to be silent – and perhaps the duty.'

The rehearsals for *Ascanio* proceeded. He played a lively role, jumping on to the stage and plunging into singing and gestures to indicate his demands. The role of Scozzone was again given to a soprano, and the première on 9 November was conducted by Reynaldo Hahn. Saint-Saëns had his moments of superstition and the revival of the old opera had brought two doleful presages: the baritone singing Charles V died suddenly and some dire domestic drama descended upon the singer playing the Duchess of Etampes. Misfortunes always come in threes, as the saying goes, and Saint-Saëns asked his friend Mme Chazal what she thought would be the third.

A month before his death he played the piano in private for Jacques Durand. The little recital included a piece by Rameau, and Saint-Saëns pointed out the necessity of close-packed and even trills. He added that he had worked hard at these ornamentations and believed that at last he had perfected the technique. Durand marvelled at the artistic conscience of the old man, who had for so long known fame and glory, but still sought to polish aspects of his playing. Not long before, he had played the piano part in his Septet at the Institut at Widor's request. Isidore Philipp, seeing how nervous he was, asked how someone so accustomed to brilliant successes on the platform could have such apprehensions. 'It is not fear,' he replied. 'In the war of '70 I was firing on the battlements of Paris and bullets whistled around me. I was not afraid. But when, after the war, I had to play my Concerto in G minor[1] my heart beat so fast it seemed as if it would burst. Is that fear? Is it vanity? At such moments the virtuoso is a martyr.' On the same occasion Dupré heard him say, while shuffling along with an elderly scientist who lamented that the legs of the academicians were not growing any younger, 'Yes, our legs – but you will soon see how my fingers work.' One of his very last articles, in October 1921, was appropriately on 'Berlioz', expressing a failure to recognise the real Berlioz in the latter's *Mémoires*. When working together on Gluck's *Armide* their emotion had not been as strong as Berlioz suggested and he could not have worked for long periods with Berlioz with 'his continual irritated excitement'.

He still practised daily during his last days in Algiers, to which he travelled after his exertions at the Opéra. Of the pianist's calling he would say, 'One never knows it; one has to learn it every day.' *Ascanio* was well enough received, but did not survive more than half a dozen performances. The Mediterranean crossing was rough and he had some heart trouble. He once more installed himself in the Hôtel de l'Oasis with its views over the port. It was here that he did his final pieces of writing. At the request of Johannes Wolff he orchestrated an old Romance in B flat for Violin. He began, too, the orchestration of his *Valse*

---

[1] At a Conservatoire concert. This must have been in December 1869, before the war.

Nonchalante, which a dancer, Mlle Napierkowska, had requested. 'She is not a Russian dancer,' he told the pianist Henri Etlin. 'She is "Parisienne", with a Polish grandfather. She has great talent and amazing suppleness.' Speaking of his piano studies he said sadly, 'These things are no longer within my powers. I am delighted that you play them. I do play them still, but for myself alone.' He had thoughts of arranging some little-known pieces by Mozart for the piano. On Wednesday 14 December he attended a performance of *Lakmé* at the Grand Theatre. He was an admirer of Delibes and envied his success in the world of ballet. He had spent a lifetime in the theatre and it seems almost as if some film writer had devised a scenario culminating in this last visit, when the programme included 'The Swan' danced by the same Mlle Napierkowska. On the Thursday morning, although he did not feel exceptionally unwell, he saw his doctor and on the Friday he did not leave his room. A piano had been brought up to him and he prepared to restart his finger exercises. He was waiting for the proofs of his *Divagations Sérieuses* and, to while away the time, he read some scores of Verdi, joking that he would like to enjoy a beautiful death like one of Verdi's heroes.

On the Friday evening he played dominoes with Jean Laurendeau, his valet, and enjoyed winning. He retired to read some La Fontaine and Ronsard. The Hôtel de l'Oasis had an orchestra, which, down in the salon, was playing a foxtrot. A little after ten o'clock Saint-Saëns came out of his room, rested his elbows on the balcony rail and waited until the end of the piece to give a little signal of applause. Someone heard him say, 'A foxtrot . . . what a pity.' The strains of modern dance music were the last notes he heard. A few moments later the valet heard a groan. Laurendeau dared not leave the bedside and hotel servants were sent to call the doctor. In a low voice the composer murmured, 'I believe that this is the end.' It was so. At eleven the manager of the hotel indicated to Laurendeau, who was cradling Saint-Saëns in his arms, that all was over. The valet had often been told to do what he thought best in such circumstances. He carefully wrapped up the body and, over the old champion of French music and French musicians, he placed the Tricolore. 'The blood of a People flows through the heart of a single man', ran the line in 'The Ancestor's Song'. To the poet, Victor Hugo, the phrase had been a literary hyperbole; the musician had shaped his career as if it were an injunction.

Bibliography

Abraham, Gerald (ed.)   *New Oxford History of Music*,
'Romanticism', O.U.P., 1990.

Aguétant, Pierre   *Saint-Saëns par lui-même.*

Augé de Lassus, L.   *La Trompette*, Librairie Delagrave, Paris,
1911.
Saint-Saëns, Paris, 1914.

Augé-Laribe   *André Messager, Musicien de Théâtre*, La
Colombe, Paris.

Barrie-Jones, J.   *Gabriel Fauré, A Life in Letters*, Batsford,
London, 1989.

Barzun, J.   *Berlioz and the Romantic Century*, Gollancz,
1951.

Baumann, Emile   *Les Grandes Formes de la Musique*,
Librairie Ollendorff, 1923.

Bernard, Robert   'La Revue Musicale', November 1935.

Bloom, P. (ed.)   *Music in Paris in the 1830s*, Pendragon
Press, New York.

Bondeville, E.   'La Revue Musicale', 1971; *Letters to
Emile Renaud*, 1983; *Hommage à C. Saint-
Saëns, Un grand musicien mal connu.*
Firmin Didot & Cie, 1971.

Bonnerot, Jean   *Camille Saint-Saëns, Sa Vie et son Oeuvre*,
Durand, Paris, 1914.
Un visiteur illustré aux Canaries, Faculte de
Filosophia y Letras Tenerife, 1951.

Bridge, Sir F.   *A Westminster Pilgrim*, Novello, 1919.

Brook, Donald   *Five Great French Composers*, Rockcliffe,
1946.

Bruneau, Alfred   *La Musique Française*, Bibliothèque
Charpentier, Paris, 1901.

Bruyr, José   *Recollections of J. Laurendeau*, 'La Revue
                         Musicale', 1936.

Burnett, James   *Ravel, His Life and Times*, Midas Books,
                         New York 1983.

Cairns, David   *Berlioz, The Making of an Artist*, A.
                         Deutsch, London.

Catalogue   *Une Maître de Musique à Dieppe*, Château-
                         Musée, Dieppe, September 1997.

Cavaillé-Coll, C. & E.   *Aristide Cavaillé-Coll*, Fischbacher, Paris,
                         1929.

Chantavoine, Jean   *Camille Saint-Saëns*, Richard Masse, Paris,
                         1947.

Collet, Henri   *'Samson et Dalila' de C. Saint-Saëns*,
                         Librairie Delegrave, Paris, 1922.

Constant, Pierre   *Le Conservatoire Nat. de Musique et
                         Déclamation*, Imprimerie National, Paris,
                         1900.

Cooper, Martin   *French Music (From the Death of Berlioz to
                         the Death of Fauré)*, O.U.P., 1951.

Cortot, Alfred   *French Piano Music*, Hilda Andrews
                         (trans.), O.U.P., 1932.

Curtiss, Mina   *Bizet and his World*, Secker and Warburg,
                         1959.

Dandelot, Arthur   *La Vie et l'Oeuvre de Saint-Saëns*, Editions
                         Dandelot, Paris, 1930.
                         Petits Memoires Musicaux, Editions 'La
                         Nouvelle Revue', Paris.
                         *Le Centenaire de la Naissance de C. Saint-
                         Saëns*, 'La Nouvelle Revue', 1935.

Davies, Laurence   *César Franck and his Circle*, Barrie &
                         Jenkins, London, 1970.
                         Franck, 'Master Musicians', Dent, 1973.

Dean, Winston   *Georges Bizet, His Life and Work*, J. M.
                         Dent and Sons, 1965.

Debussy, Claude   *Lettres à André Messager*, D. Aime, Paris,
                         1938.
                         Monsieur Croche, Anti-Dilettante, 1921.
                         M. Croche, the Dilettante Hater, Noel
                         Douglas (trans.), 1927.

Delmas, Marc	*Gustave Charpentier et Le Lyrisme Français*, Paris.
D'Indy, V.	*César Franck*, Rosa Newmarch (trans.), John Lane, Bodley Head, 1910.
Dumaine, Robert	*Les Origines Normandes de Camille Saint-Saëns*, Académie de Rouen, 1935.
Dumesnil, René	*Portraits de Musiciens Français*, Librairie Plon, Paris, 1938.
Dunoyer, Cecilia	*Marguerite Long*, Indiana University Press, 1993.
Dupré, Marcel	*Marcel Dupré raconte*, Bornemann, Paris, 1977.
Durand, Auguste	*Correspondence*, Institut Gustave Mahler, unpublished.
Durand, Jacques	*Quelques Souvenirs d'un Editeur de Musique*, Durand, Paris, 1924.
Durand et Cie	*Catalogue of Themes Saint-Saëns*.
Ellis, Katharine	*Music Criticism in Nineteenth-Century France*, Cambridge University Press, 1995.
'Encaenia'	University Records, Bodleian Library, 26 June 1907.
Fallon, D. M.	*The Symphonies and Symphonic Poems of Saint-Saëns*, dissertation, New York University, 1973.
Fauquet, Joël-Marie	*Les Sociétiés de Musique de Chambre*, 'La Musique en France 1830–1870'.
	Eduard Lalo, Correspondence (Ed.), Aux Amateurs de Lívre, 1989.
Fauré, Gabriel	*Camille Saint-Saëns*, 'La Revue Musicale', February 1922.
Faure, Michel	*Musique et Société du Second Empire aux Années Vingt*, Harmoniques Flammarion, Paris, 1985.
Ferrare, Henri	*Lettres de Saint-Saëns à Caroline de Serres*, 'La Revue Musicale', March 1936.
Fevrier, Henri	*André Messager, Mon Maître, Mon Ami*, Amiot-Dumont, Paris.
Fitzlyon, April	*The Price of Genius* (Pauline Viardot), John Calder, London, 1964.

Foster, Myles Birket — *The History of the Philharmonic Society of London*, John Lane, London, 1917.

Gallet, Louis — *Notes d'un Librettist*, Calman Levy, Paris, 1891.

Ganz, Wilhelm — *Memories of a Musician*, John Murray, 1913.

Gavoty, Bernard — *Reynaldo Hahn*, Editions Buchet Chastal, Paris, 1976.

Gefen, Gérard — *Augusta Holmès, L'Outrancière*, Pierre Belfond, Paris, 1987.

Gérard, Yves — *Saint-Saëns, Regards sur mes Contemporains*, Editions, Bernard.

Ginsburg, Lev — *Ysaye*, X. M. Danka (trans.), Paganinnia Publications, New Jersey, 1980.

Gooch, G. P. — *The Second Empire*, Longmans, 1910.

Hahn, Reynaldo — *Thèmes Variés*, 3rd ed., Janin, Paris, 1946.

Harding, James — *Saint-Saëns and his Circle*, Chapman & Hall 1965; *Massenet*, J. M. Dent, 1970.

Harkins, Elizabeth — *The Chamber Music of Saint-Saëns*, dissertion, New York University, 1974.

Hervey, Arthur — *Saint-Saëns*, John Lane, London, 1921.

Howarth, Tom — *The Citizen King*, Eyre and Spottiswoode, 1961.

Johnson, Douglas — *France and the Dreyfus Affair*, London, 1966.

Jordan, Ruth — *Fromental Halévy; His Life and Music*, Kahn and Averill.

Jullian, Philippe — *Robert de Montesquiou*, Paris, 1965.

Jullien, Adolphe — *Musiciens d'Hier et d'Aujourd'hui*, Fischbacher, 1910.

Kern Holoman, D. — *Berlioz*, Harvard University Press, 1989.

Klein, Hermann — *Musicians and Mummers*, Cassell, 1925. *Saint-Saëns as I knew him*, 'Musical Times', February 1922.

Koechlin, Charles — *Article on French Music*, 'La Revue Musicale', April 1935.

Lalo, Pierre — *De Rameau à Ravel*, Albion Michel, Paris, 1947.

	La Musique 1898–1899, Rouart Lerolle, Paris.
Lassabathie, M.	*Histoire du Conservatoire Impérial, 1860*, M. Levy Frères, Paris.
Lavignac, Albert	*Encyclopédie de la Musique*, Paris, 1925.
Lebas, Georges	*Lettres Inédités de Lecocq à Saint-Saëns*, 'La Revue Musicale', January 1924.
Le Boucher, Maurice	*Souvenirs de Saint-Saëns*, 'L'Art Musical', November 1935.
Legrand, Albert	*Conférence de M. Legrand à l'Alliance Francaise*, Imprimerie Dieppoise, 1935.
Locke, Ralph	*Constructing the Oriental*, 'Cambridge Opera Journal', vol. 3, No. 3.
Lockspeiser, Edward	*French Chamber Music*, Pelican Books, London, 1958.
	Debussy, His Life and Mind, London, 1963.
Lyle, Watson	*Camille Saint-Saëns: His Life and Art*, Kegan Paul, 1923.
Malherbe, C.	*Auber. Les Musiciens Célèbres*, Paris, 1912.
Manuel, Roland	*Histoire de la Musique*, 'Encyclopédie de la Pleiade'.
Martinet, André	*Histoire Anecdotique du Conservatoire de Musique*, Ernst Kolb, Paris.
Maurois, André	*Victor Hugo*, Thames and Hudson, 1966.
Melba, Nellie	*Melodies and Memories*, Thornton Butterworth, London, 1925.
Montargis, Jean	*Camille Saint-Saëns, L'Oeuvre et l'artiste*, 'Renaissance du Livre', 1919.
Montesquiou, Robert de	*Les Pas Effacés*, E. Paul, Paris, 1923.
Murphy, Agnes	*Melba. A Biography*, Chatto and Windus, 1909.
Myers, Rollo	*Emmanuel Chabrier and his Circle*, Dent and Sons, 1965.
Nectoux, J.-M.	*Soixante Ans d'Amitié*, Soc. Français de Musicologie, 1973.
Nicholas, Jeremy	*Godowsky. The Pianists' Pianist*, Appian Publications, 1989.
Normington, Susan	*Napoleon's Children*, Sutton Publishers, 1993.
Norris, Gerald	*Stanford. The Cambridge Jubilee and*

Tchaikovsky, David and Charles, 1980.

Orenstein, Arbie — *A Ravel Reader*, Columbia University Press, 1990.

Orledge, Robert — *Gabriel Fauré*, Eulenberg Books, London, 1979.
Charles Koechlin, 1867–1950, Life and Works, 1989.

Poulenc, F. — *Emmanuel Chabrier*, La Palatine, Paris, 1961.

Price, Roger — *The Second French Republic*, Batsford, 1972.

Prodhomme, J. G. — *L'Opéra, 1669–1925*, Librairie Delagrave, 1925.

Proust, Marcel — *Lettres de Marcel Proust à Reynaldo Hahn*, Gallimard, 1958.

Reyer, Ernest — *Quarante Ans de Musique*, Calman Levy, Paris, 1909.

Rich, E. G. — *Saint-Saëns, Musical Memories*, John Murray (trans.), 1921.

Richardson, Joanna — *Victor Hugo*, Weidenfeld and Nicolson, 1967.

Rolland, Romain — *Musiciens d'Aujourd'hui*, Hachette, 1908.

Rollin, Smith — *Saint-Saëns and the Organ*, Pendragon Press, New York.

Rothwell, F. — *Outspoken Essays: Saint-Saëns* (trans.), Kegan Paul, London, 1922; Greenwood Printing, New York, 1970.

Sachs, Leo — *Reminiscences of Saint-Saëns*, 'La Revue Musicale', 1922.

Scherperel, Loretta — *The Solo Organ Works of Saint-Saëns*, dissertation, University of Michigan, 1979.

Séré, Octave — *Musiciens Français d'Aujourd'hui*, Mercure de France, 1911.

Servières, Georges — *Saint-Saëns*, Alcan, Paris, 1923.

Shaw, G. B. — *Music in London*, Constable and Co, London, 1949.

Soubies, A., and Malherbe, C. — *Histoire de l'Opéra-Comique: 1840–1887*, Flammarion, 1892.

Stegemann, Michael — *Camille Saint-Saëns and the Solo French Concerto*, A. Sherwin (trans.), Scolar Press, 1991.

Thiriet, Michel	*The Book of Proust*, J. Dalley (trans.), Chatto and Windus, 1987.
Thomson, Andrew	*Widor: Life and Times of C.-M. Widor*, O.U.P., 1987.
Tiersot, Julian	*Un Demi-Siècle de Musique Française*, Paris, 1918.
	'La Revue Musicale', September 1935.
Vallas, Léon	*Debussy*, Librairie Plon, Paris, 1927.
	The Theories of Claude Debussy, M. O'Brien (trans.), O.U.P., 1929.
	Claude Debussy et Son Temps, Alkan, Paris, 1932.
	Vincent d'Indy, Albion Michel, Paris, 1946.
Walker, Alan	*Liszt*, Faber and Faber, 1989.
Walsh, T. J.	*Monte-Carlo Opéra: 1879–1909*, Gill, McMillan, 1975.
	The Théâtre Lyrique, Paris, 1851–1870, John Calder.
	The History of Opera: Second Empire Opera, London, 1981.
Wolff, S.	*Un Demi-Siècle de L'Opéra-Comique 1900–1950*, Paris, 1853.
	L'Opéra au Palais Garnier, 1875–1962.
Zeldin, Theodore	*Music: France 1848–1945*, 'Oxford History of Modern Europe', Clarendon Press, 1977.

Index